"To Presley, Riley, and Kinley"
—TFO

"To Matt, Caroline, Grace, and Thomas"
—MTM

"To Gail and Sean"
—JMN

"To Kathleen, Eve, and Asher"
—GCD

PREFACE

Most textbooks on abnormal psychology include short descriptions of actual clinical cases. However, those presentations are necessarily brief and too fragmented for students to gain a clear understanding of the unique complexities of a person's troubled life. They cannot describe the client's developmental history, the manner in which a therapist might conceptualize the problem, the formulation and implementation of a treatment plan, or the trajectory of a disorder over a period of many years. In contrast to such brief descriptions, a detailed case study can provide a foundation on which to organize important information about a disorder. This enhances the student's ability to understand and recall abstract theoretical and research issues.

The purpose of *Case Studies in Abnormal Psychology*, 9e is therefore threefold: (a) to provide detailed descriptions of a range of clinical problems, (b) to illustrate some of the ways in which these problems can be viewed and treated, and (c) to discuss some of the evidence that is available concerning the prevalence and causes of the disorders in question. The book is appropriate for both undergraduate and graduate courses in abnormal psychology. It may also be useful in courses in psychiatric social work or nursing and could be helpful to students enrolled in various practicum courses that teach how best to conceptualize mental-health problems and plan treatment. It may be used on its own or as a supplement to a standard textbook in abnormal psychology.

In selecting cases for inclusion in the book, we sampled from a variety of problems, ranging from psychotic disorders (e.g., schizophrenia and bipolar mood disorder) to personality disorders (e.g., paranoid and antisocial) to various disorders of childhood and aging (e.g., attention-deficit/hyperactivity disorder). We focused deliberately on cases that illustrate particular problems that are of interest to students of abnormal psychology. We do not mean to imply, however, that all the cases fit neatly into specific diagnostic molds. In addition to describing "classic" behavioral symptoms (e.g., hallucinations, compulsive rituals, or specific fears), we emphasized the social context in which these disorders appear as well as life problems that are significant in determining the person's overall adjustment, even though they may not be relevant from a diagnostic standpoint. For example, our case on hypertension considers issues in etiology and treatment when the person is African American. Several of the cases include a consideration of marital adjustment and parent–child relationships.

Our coverage extends to examples of eating disorders, dissociative identity disorder, gender identity disorder, borderline personality, and posttraumatic stress disorder (following rape). Each of these disorders represents an area that has received considerable attention in the contemporary literature, and each has been the focus of theoretical controversy.

We have added one new chapter to this ninth edition. It describes a woman who experienced terrifying nightmares and an associated sleep paralysis. The new case provides important coverage of sleep disorders, which affect large numbers of people and have received increased attention in the professional literature.

Our cognitive-behavioral perspective is clearly evident in most of these case discussions. Nevertheless, we also present and discuss alternative conceptual positions. The cases can therefore be used to show students how a given problem can be reasonably viewed and treated from several different perspectives. Although most of the interventions described illustrate a cognitive-behavioral approach to treatment, we have also described biological treatments (e.g., medication, electroconvulsive therapy, and psychosurgery) when they are relevant to the case. In some cases, the outcome was not positive. We have tried to present an honest view of the limitations, as well as the potential benefits, of various treatment programs. Note also that three of the cases were not in treatment. We believe that it is important to point out that many people who have psychological disorders do not see therapists.

Each case study concludes with a discussion of current knowledge about causal factors. Some of these discussions are necessarily briefer than others. More research has been done on schizophrenia, for example, than on gender identity disorder or paranoid personality disorder. We had two goals in mind for these discussions. First, we have tried to use the case material to illustrate the application of research to individual clients' problems. Second, we alert readers to important gaps in our knowledge of abnormal psychology, our abiding belief being that realizing what we do not know is as important as appreciating what we do know. All these discussions have been revised in the ninth edition to include new ideas and empirical evidence that are changing the way that particular disorders are viewed and treated.

We have included discussions of issues associated with gender, culture, and ethnicity in all the previous editions of this book. For example, issues of race and psychotherapy are considered in the case of hypertension. Attention to these issues, particularly those involving gender, have been strengthened in this ninth edition. The case on parasomnia (nightmare disorder) also discusses important issues related to race and gender. Our description of posttraumatic stress disorder following rape trauma includes many issues that are particularly important for women (e.g., helpful and harmful ways in which other people react to the victim; decisions by the victim, her therapist, and her professor about whether to report the rapist; and so on). Our discussion of the causes of major depression includes consideration of possible explanations for gender differences in this disorder. The chapters on dissociative identity disorder and borderline personality disorder both discuss the impact of prior sexual abuse on subsequent development of psychopathology. Both cases of eating disorder involve extended consideration of cultural attitudes that affect women's feelings and beliefs about themselves. These are only a few of the instances in which we have attempted to address gender issues in relation to the etiology and treatment of mental disorders. We are grateful to Patricia Lee Llewellyn (University of Virginia) for many helpful comments on these issues.

All the cases in this book are based on actual clinical experience, primarily our own, but, in some instances, that of our colleagues and students. Various demographic characteristics (names, locations, and occupations) and some concrete clinical details have been changed to protect the anonymity of clients and their families. In some instances, the cases are composites of clinical problems with which we have dealt. Our intent is not to put forth claims of efficacy and utility for any particular conceptualization or intervention but instead to illustrate the ways clinicians think about their work and implement abstract principles to help a client cope with life problems. The names used in the case studies are fictitious; any resemblance to actual persons is purely coincidental.

As in the first eight editions of this book, we have not identified the authors of specific case studies. This procedure has been adopted and maintained to preserve the clients' anonymity. We are grateful to Amy Bertelson, Serrita Jane, Ron Thompson, Kevin Leach, and Kimble Richardson, who provided extensive consultation on five of these cases. We also thank Elana Farace and Sarah Liebman for drafting two others.

We would like to thank the following reviewers for their helpful and constructive comments: Eynav E. Accortt, Wright State University; Dorothy Bianco, Rhode Island College; Mia Smith Bynum, Purdue University; Bernardo Carducci, Indiana University Southeast; Ron Evans, Washburn University; Jan Hastrup, SUNY at Buffalo; Russell Jones, Virginia Polytechnic Institute and State University; Katherine M. Kitzmann, University of Memphis; Patricia Lee Llewellyn, University of Virginia; Richard McNally, Harvard University; Janet Morahan Martin, Bryant College; Linda Musun Miller, University of Arkansas at Little Rock; Mark Pantle, Baylor University; Esther Rothblum, University of Vermont; Gary Sterner, Eastern Washington University; Sondra Solomon, University of Vermont; and John Wixted, University of California–San Diego.

We also want to express our sincere appreciation to the superb staff at Wiley, especially Eileen McKeever, Associate Editor, Psychology; Christopher Johnson, Executive Editor, Psychology; Maura Gilligan, Editorial Assistant; and Yee Lyn Song, Assistant Production Editor. Their conscientious efforts were essential to the successful completion of this revision.

Finally, we remain grateful to our families for their continued love and encouragement. Gail Oltmanns and Matt Martin have both provided invaluable support throughout the preparation of this new edition.

Thomas F. Oltmanns
Michele T. Martin
John M. Neale
Gerald C. Davison

CONTENTS

Preface v
1. Obsessive-Compulsive Disorder 1
2. Panic Disorder with Agoraphobia 17
3. Posttraumatic Stress Disorder: Rape Trauma 35
4. Hypertension in an African American Man 52
5. Dissociative Identity Disorder: Multiple Personality 68
6. Major Depressive Disorder 87
7. Bipolar Disorder 102
8. Somatization Disorder 115
9. Schizophrenia: Paranoid Type 130
10. Psychotic Disorder (NOS), Substance Dependence, and Violence 145
11. Alcohol Dependence 159
12. Sexual Dysfunction: Female Orgasmic Disorder and Premature
    Ejaculation 171
13. Paraphilias: Exhibitionism and Frotteurism 188
14. Gender Identity Disorder: Transsexualism 202
15. Eating Disorder: Anorexia Nervosa 221
16. Eating Disorder: Bulimia Nervosa 234
17. Parasomnia: Nightmare Disorder and Isolated Sleep Paralysis 251
18. Paranoid Personality Disorder 265
19. Borderline Personality Disorder 283
20. Antisocial Personality Disorder: Psychopathy 297
21. Autistic Disorder 309
22. Attention-Deficit/Hyperactivity Disorder 323
23. Oppositional Defiant Disorder 336
References 351
Index 391

CHAPTER 1

Obsessive-Compulsive Disorder

Karen Rusa was a 30-year-old married woman and the mother of four children. Although she had been having anxiety-related problems for a number of years, she had never sought professional help prior to this time. During the preceding 3 months, she had become increasingly depressed; her family physician finally suggested that she seek psychological services.

For the past several months, Karen had been experiencing intrusive, repetitive thoughts that centered on her children's safety. She frequently found herself imagining that a serious accident had occurred, and she was unable to put these thoughts out of her mind. On one such occasion, she imagined that her son, Alan, had broken his leg playing football at school. There was no reason to believe that an accident had occurred, but Karen brooded about the possibility until she finally called the school to see if Alan was all right. Even after receiving reassurance that he had not been hurt, she was somewhat surprised when he later arrived home unharmed.

Karen also noted that her daily routine was seriously hampered by an extensive series of counting rituals that she performed throughout each day. Specific numbers had come to have a special meaning to Karen; she found that her preoccupation with these numbers was interfering with her ability to perform everyday activities. One example was grocery shopping. Karen believed that if she selected the first item (e.g., a box of cereal) on the shelf, something terrible would happen to her oldest child. If she selected the second item, some unknown disaster would befall her second child, and so on for the four children. The children's ages were also important. The sixth item in a row, for example, was associated with her youngest child, who was 6 years old. Thus, specific items had to be avoided to ensure the safety of her children. Obviously, the rituals required continuing attention because the children's ages changed. Karen's preoccupation with numbers extended to other activities, most notably the pattern in which she smoked cigarettes and drank coffee. If she had one cigarette, she believed that she had to smoke at least four in a row or one of the children would be harmed in some way. If she drank one cup of coffee, she felt compelled to drink four.

Karen acknowledged the irrationality of these rituals but, nevertheless, maintained that she felt much more comfortable when she observed them conscientiously. When she was occasionally in too great a hurry to perform the rituals, she experienced considerable anxiety in the form of a subjective feeling of dread and apprehension. She described herself as tense, jumpy, and unable to relax during these periods. Her fears were most often confirmed because something unfortunate invariably happened to one of the children within a few days after each such "failure." The fact that minor accidents are likely to occur at a fairly high rate in any family of four children did not diminish Karen's conviction that she had been directly responsible because of her inability to observe the numerical rules.

In addition to her obsessive ideas and compulsive behaviors, Karen reported dissatisfaction with her marriage and problems in managing her children. Her husband, Tony, had been placed on complete physical disability 11 months prior to her first visit to the mental health center. Although he was only 32 years old, Tony suffered from a serious heart condition that made even the most routine physical exertion potentially dangerous. Since leaving his job as a clerk at a plumbing supply store, he had spent most of his time at home. He enjoyed lying on the couch watching television and did so for most of his waking hours. He had convinced Karen that she should be responsible for all the household chores and family errands. Her days were spent getting the children dressed, fed, and transported to school; cleaning; washing; shopping; and fetching potato chips, dip, and beer whenever Tony needed a snack. The inequity of this situation was apparent to Karen and was extremely frustrating, yet she found herself unable to handle it effectively.

The children were also clearly out of her control. Robert, age 6, and Alan, age 8, were very active and mischievous. Neither responded well to parental discipline, which was inconsistent at best. Both experienced behavioral problems at school, and Alan was being considered for placement in a special classroom for particularly disruptive children. The girls were also difficult to handle. Denise, age 9, and Jennifer, age 11, spent much of their time at home arguing with each other. Jennifer was moderately obese. Denise teased her mercilessly about her weight. After they had quarreled for some time, Jennifer would appeal tearfully to Karen, who would attempt to intervene on her behalf. Karen was becoming increasingly distressed by her inability to handle this confusing situation, and she was getting little, if any, help from Tony. During the past several weeks, she had been spending more and more time crying and hiding alone in her bedroom.

Social History

Karen was raised in New York City by Italian immigrant parents. She was the first of four children. Her family was deeply religious, and she was raised to be a devout Roman Catholic. She attended parochial schools from the first grade through high school and was a reasonably good student. Her memories of the strict practices of the church and school authorities were vivid. The formal rituals of the church played an important role in her life, as they did for the other members of her family. Beginning at an early age, Karen was taught that she had to observe many specific guidelines that governed social behavior within the church (not eating meat on Fridays, going to confession regularly, and so forth). She was told that her strict adherence to these norms would ensure the safety of her immortal soul, and conversely, that transgressions would be severely punished.

The depth of her belief and the severity of its consequences can be seen in the following story, which Karen recalled during an early session. When she was 8 years old, Karen and her classmates at school were to receive their First Communion in the church. This is a particularly important and solemn occasion for Roman Catholics that signifies the child's advancement to adult status in the church community. Before the child is allowed to partake in communion, however, a complete confession must be made of all prior sins. Karen was told that she was to confess all her sins, regardless of their severity or the time of their occurrence, to her priest, who would prescribe an appropriate penance. She remembered her parents' and teachers' warnings that if she failed to mention any of her sins, her soul would be banished to hell for eternity. This threat was still vivid in Karen's mind many years later. Despite the terror aroused by these circumstances, Karen intentionally failed to tell the priest about one of her sins; she had stolen a small picture book from her classroom and was now afraid either to return it or to tell anyone about the crime. She lived with intense guilt about this omission for several years and could remember having occasionally terrifying nightmares that centered on imagined punishments for not providing a complete confession. In subsequent years, Karen intensified her efforts to abide by even the minutest details of church regulations, but she continued to harbor the conviction that she could never atone for this mortal sin.

Karen remembered her parents as having been very strict disciplinarians. Her mother was apparently a rather unemotional and rigid person who had insisted on the maintenance of order and cleanliness in their household. Beyond her unerring adherence to religious rules and regulations, Karen's mother kept the family on a tight schedule with regard to meals and other routine activities. When the children deviated from these guidelines, they were severely punished. Karen's most positive recollections of interaction with her mother centered on their mutual participation in prescribed church functions. She did not remember her parents ever demonstrating affection for each other in front of their children.

Karen married Tony after she graduated from high school, and she became pregnant two months later. During this pregnancy, she witnessed an unfortunate accident at her neighbor's apartment. While Karen was chatting with her friend, the woman's infant daughter crawled off the porch and was run over by another child riding a bicycle. The girl was seriously injured and remained in the hospital for several weeks. Shortly after this accident, Karen began experiencing repetitive, intrusive thoughts about injuring herself. At unpredictable but frequent intervals throughout the day, she would find herself thinking about jumping out of windows, walking in front of cars, and other similar dangerous behaviors. These thoughts were, of course, frightening to her, but she could not prevent their occurrence. When one of the thoughts did come into her mind, she attempted to get rid of it by quickly repeating a short prayer that she had learned as a child and then asking God for forgiveness for having entertained such a sinful impulse. This procedure was moderately successful as a temporary source of distraction, but it did not prevent the reappearance of a similar, intrusive thought several hours later. These thoughts of self-injury occurred less frequently and seemed less troublesome after the birth of her first child, Jennifer, perhaps because Karen was soon preoccupied with all the responsibilities of caring for the baby.

During this same time, Karen began to be disillusioned with the church. Her distress centered on a number of reforms that had been introduced by Pope John XXIII and the ecumenical council. The Mass, for example, was no longer said in Latin, and nonclerical persons were allowed to administer various rites of the church. Similarly, church members were no longer admonished to give up meat on Fridays, and other rituals were modified or completely eliminated. Most people found these changes refreshing, but Karen was horrified. The church's rituals had come to play a central role in her life. In de-emphasizing the importance of traditional rituals, the church was depriving Karen of her principal means of controlling her own destiny. She was extremely uncomfortable with these new practices and eventually stopped going to church altogether.

When Jennifer was 9 months old, Karen once again became pregnant. She and Tony decided to move to the suburbs, where they would be able to afford a house with a yard in which the children could play. Although she was proud of their new home, Karen began to feel depressed during this period because she missed her old friends.

Karen's situation showed little change throughout the next few years. By the time she was 25 years old, she had four children. She found this responsibility overwhelming and was generally unhappy most of the time. Her relationship with Tony had essentially reached a stalemate; they were not satisfied with their marriage, but they agreed to stay together for the children. Although they did not fight with each other openly, a sense of covert tension and estrangement pervaded their relationship. Tony refused to participate in what he considered unnecessarily rigid and complicated household regulations, particularly those dealing with the children's behavior. Karen had established very specific guidelines for meals, bedtime, and so on but found that she was unable to enforce these rules by herself. She remained distant from Tony and resisted most of his attempts to display physical affection. Thus, overall, Karen was chronically unhappy and generally dissatisfied with her life, but she nevertheless clung to her miserable surroundings and established patterns of behavior out of fear that any change would be for the worse.

This unhappy, yet tolerable, equilibrium was disturbed by Tony's deteriorating health. One day, while he was working at the store, he experienced sudden chest pains and numbness in his extremities. Recognizing these symptoms as serious in nature (he had had high blood pressure for years and was therefore well informed in this regard), Tony asked a friend to drive him to the hospital. His experience was diagnosed as a mild heart attack. Further testing revealed serious structural abnormalities in his heart. He was eventually discharged from the hospital, given a complete medical disability, and laid off from his job.

Karen became more and more depressed after Tony began staying home during the day. It was during this time that her fears about the children's safety became clearly unreasonable, and she started performing her counting rituals. Karen realized that her situation was desperate because she felt that she had lost control of her own behavior and experienced considerable anxiety whenever she attempted to resist performing the rituals. At this point, she finally decided to seek professional help.

Conceptualization and Treatment

The therapist saw the ritualistic behavior as one part of Karen's overall difficult situation. Karen's counting compulsion represented her attempt to reintroduce a sense of personal control over her own life. In this sense, the rituals were being performed instead of either the more socially acceptable religious activities that she had employed as a child or the more effective social skills that she had apparently never developed. For example, she was unassertive in her relationship with Tony. Instead of standing up for her rights, she would meekly acquiesce to even his most unreasonable demands. At the same time, she would become extremely frustrated and angry with him and would look for subtle ways to "even the score." She was similarly unable to convey her appreciation to him on those (admittedly rare) occasions when he did please her. Treatment was therefore initially aimed at the development of interpersonal skills that would give Karen more control over her environment. It was hoped that as she was able to create a more satisfactory relationship with her husband and children, her increased competence would eliminate the necessity of turning to admittedly superstitious, ineffective attempts to achieve self-control.

Karen quickly recognized her deficiency in this regard but was unable to change her behavior spontaneously. She and the therapist therefore agreed to pursue a systematic program of assertion training. The initial sessions in this sequence were devoted to a careful assessment of the situations in which Karen was unassertive. She was asked to keep a daily notebook of such situations in which she noted the people involved, the nature of their interaction, and her perception of the situation, including what she thought would happen if she did behave assertively. Having identified typical problem situations, Karen and her therapist role-played several incidents as a way of introducing Karen to more appropriate responses. They also discussed Karen's irrational fears associated with assertion. These thoughts centered on her implicit belief that everyone should love her, and that if she stood up for her own rights, people would reject her. These irrational self-statements were inhibiting the expression of assertive behaviors. After Karen became proficient with such exercises in the therapy sessions, she was asked to start practicing her new skills in real-life situations outside the clinic.

After assertion training had produced some positive results, the therapist began teaching Karen more effective child-management skills. These were based primarily on procedures associated with instrumental learning (also known as operant conditioning). She was taught, for example, to ignore her daughters when they were quarreling and to reinforce them positively for playing together appropriately. Her efforts were initially channeled toward behaviors that could be changed easily. The most difficult problems, such as getting the children to stop fighting at mealtimes, were left until Karen had mastered some of the general principles of child management.

In addition to these skill-training programs, the therapist also discussed Karen's concerns about religion. It was clear that the church was still important to her and that she experienced considerable guilt and anxiety over her failure to attend services regularly. The fact that her children were not involved in church activities was also troubling to Karen. She worried that if any harm came to one of them, God would not protect them. For these reasons, Karen was encouraged to visit several priests at churches in her area in an effort to find one who was more conservative and thus more compatible with her own views. Although most of the local priests had moved toward contemporary practices in their own churches, they did refer her to an older priest at a church somewhat farther from her neighborhood, who still adhered to several of the traditional rituals she had learned as a child. She made an appointment to visit this priest and was both pleased and relieved after their initial meeting. He was able to discuss with her some of the changes that had been made in the church. In some cases, he was able to explain the rationale behind a particular change in a way that was acceptable to her. This process was, no doubt, facilitated by the fact that he shared many of her concerns about abandoning traditional practices. Karen felt much more comfortable with this priest than she did with the liberal priest who was in charge of the church in her immediate neighborhood. Within weeks, she was once again attending church regularly with her four children.

The combination of assertion training, parent education, and a renewed interest in church activities did lead to an important improvement in Karen's mood. After 3 months of treatment, she reported an increased sense of self-confidence and an improvement in her family life. There was also some reduction in her anxiety level. She continued to observe her number rituals, but they were somewhat less frequent, and when she did fail to perform the counting routines, she was not as distraught as she had been at the beginning of treatment.

At this point, Karen's rituals were addressed directly using a behavioral treatment method known as exposure and response prevention (ERP) (Tolin & Steketee, 2007). This procedure involves purposely exposing the person to stimuli that provoke intense anxiety (either in imagination or in reality) for extended periods of time while preventing the person from performing anxiety-reducing rituals. Karen was asked to smoke a single cigarette at the beginning of a therapy session. When she was finished with the cigarette, she began to feel anxious and worry about her oldest daughter. She was then instructed to resist the temptation to smoke another cigarette. Thus, the response that she typically employed to neutralize her anxiety and to control the ruminations was prevented. The therapist believed that this type of prolonged exposure to the anxiety-provoking situation would lead to a reduction in Karen's anxiety. The procedure was carried out during four consecutive 2-hour sessions. Karen was encouraged to practice the same response-prevention procedure on her own between sessions. When she had mastered the cigarette-smoking problem, the procedure was extended progressively to other similar situations in which she had been concerned about numbers.

Treatment was terminated after 20 sessions. Karen was no longer depressed and had not engaged in her compulsive counting rituals for 4 weeks. The children were better behaved at home, and Karen had plans to institute further changes in this regard. Her relationship with Tony was somewhat improved. Although he had become quite upset initially when Karen began to assert herself, he became more cooperative when he saw an improvement in her adjustment.

Discussion

Obsessive-compulsive disorder (OCD) is included in the *Diagnostic and Statistical Manual of Mental Disorders* (*DSM-IV-TR*; APA, 2000, pp. 462–463) under the general heading of Anxiety Disorders. It is defined by the following criteria:

1. Either obsessions or compulsions:
   Obsessions as defined by (a), (b), (c), and (d):
   a. Recurrent and persistent thoughts, impulses, or images that are experienced, at some time during the disturbance, as intrusive and inappropriate, and that cause marked anxiety or distress.
   b. The thoughts, impulses, or images are not simply excessive worries about real-life problems.
   c. The person attempts to ignore or suppress such thoughts, impulses, or images, or to neutralize them with some other thought or action.
   d. The person recognizes that the obsessional thoughts, impulses, or images are a product of his or her own mind.

Compulsions as defined by (a) and (b):

a. The person feels driven to perform repetitive behaviors (e.g., hand washing, ordering, checking) or mental acts (e.g., praying, counting, repeating words silently) in response to an obsession, or according to rules that must be applied rigidly.

b. The behaviors or mental acts are aimed at preventing or reducing distress or preventing some dreaded event or situation; however, these behaviors or mental acts either are not connected in a realistic way with what they are designed to neutralize or prevent, or are clearly excessive.

2. At some point during the course of the disorder, the person has recognized that the obsessions or compulsions are excessive or unreasonable.

3. The obsessions or compulsions cause marked distress, are time consuming (take more than 1 hour a day), or significantly interfere with the person's normal routine, occupational (or academic) functioning, or usual social activities or relationships.

The most common types of obsessions have been described by Rasmussen and Eisen (1992), who recorded the frequency of specific symptoms in a sample of more than 500 patients. The numbers in parentheses indicate the percentage of patients who exhibited each type of obsession. Most of the patients (72%) had multiple obsessions.

Fear of contamination (50%): A fear of exposure to stimuli such as dirt, germs, poison, or radiation. The person's concern may include fear that other people, as well as themselves, will become ill. Fear of contamination is most often coupled with compulsive hand washing.

Pathological doubt (42%): An inclination to worry that something bad is going to happen because a task has not been completed correctly. People with this symptom often develop counting rituals that may include a complex system of good numbers and bad numbers. They may repeat certain actions a particular magical number of times (as in Karen's case).

Somatic obsessions (33%): The irrational, persistent fear of developing a serious life-threatening illness (often indistinguishable from hypochondriasis, i.e., fear of having some disease despite reassurance from a physician that the disease is not present).

Need for symmetry (32%): An extreme need to have objects or events in a certain order or position, to do and undo certain motor actions in an exact fashion, or to have things exactly symmetric or "evened up."

Aggressive obsessions (31%): Recurrent, ghastly thoughts or images that the person has committed a violent or an inappropriately aggressive act.

Sexual obsessions (24%): Repeated, distressing thoughts about, or impulses to perform, inappropriate sexual behaviors.

In addition to provoking anxiety, sexual and aggressive obsessions are associated with exaggerated feelings of shame and guilt. People with this symptom may seek constant reassurance from friends (or therapists) that they are not really capable of performing such actions.

Compulsions represent patterns of ritualistic behavior and thinking that are usually performed in response to an obsession. Whereas obsessions lead to an increase in subjective anxiety, compulsions reduce the person's anxiety or discomfort. Compulsive behavior is designed to neutralize or to prevent discomfort or some dreaded event or situation. Most patients who seek treatment for obsessive symptoms also exhibit compulsive behaviors (Foa & Franklin, 2001; Parmet, Glass, & Glass, 2004). Compulsive patients fall into two primary groups: "cleaners" and "checkers." Cleaning and washing rituals are associated with fear of contact with contaminating objects. For example, a patient who is afraid of contamination by germs or bodily secretions may spend hours each day bathing or disinfecting his or her home. This ritualistic behavior restores the patient's sense of safety. Repetitive checking, on the other hand, is more often motivated by a fear of some catastrophic event. For example, a patient who experiences obsessive thoughts about gas explosions may engage in compulsive checking of the burners on a gas stove.

Some other behaviors that take a repetitive form and are associated with either a decrease or increase in anxiety have also been considered "compulsive" in the popular media. These include problems such as gambling, drug addiction, and exhibitionism. However, some important distinctions can be made between these actions and truly compulsive behaviors. First, addictive behaviors involve a pleasure-seeking component that is absent in compulsive behaviors. Second, the anxiety that is associated with the performance of criminal activities (e.g., stealing) is appropriate in light of social sanctions; obsessive-compulsive patients experience anxiety that is inappropriate to the situation.

Obsessive-compulsive disorder (OCD) should be distinguished from obsessive-compulsive personality disorder (OCPD). The latter does not involve specific ritualistic behaviors; it is intended to refer to a general personality style. People with an obsessive-compulsive personality are preoccupied with orderliness and perfectionism as well as mental and interpersonal control. They are inflexible and overly devoted to work to the point that they avoid leisure activities and ignore friendships.

The phobic disorders (i.e., specific phobia, social phobia, and agoraphobia) are similar to OCD because they involve severe anxiety and are characterized by behaviors that are designed to reduce that anxiety. Some obsessive-compulsive patients also display phobic avoidance of situations associated with anxiety about dirt or contamination. There are, however, some important differences between OCD and the phobic disorders. For example, phobic patients do not show the same tendency toward superstitious or "magical" thinking that is often characteristic of obsessive-compulsive patients, nor do they manifest compulsive symptoms. Also, for the phobic patient, the anxiety-inducing stimulus is unrelated to the content of any obsessions the patient may experience.

Obsessive thoughts should also be distinguished from delusional beliefs. Two criteria are important in this regard. First, patients with OCD try, often desperately, to resist their intrusive ideas, whereas delusional patients do not. Second, most OCD patients are ambivalent about their thoughts; they realize the essential absurdity of their obsessions and compulsions at the same time that they are preoccupied with them. Some OCD patients do have relatively poor insight regarding the senseless nature of their obsessions, but *DSM-IV-TR* requires for a diagnosis of OCD that, at some point during the course of the disorder, the person must recognize that the obsessions or compulsions are excessive or unreasonable (Eisen, Phillips, & Rasmussen, 1999).

Depression is a common complication of OCD. Two out of every three patients with OCD have experienced at least one episode of major depression at some point during their lives. The relationship between these phenomena is unclear. Sometimes compulsive symptoms appear before the onset of depression; in other cases, this relationship is reversed. The successful treatment or alleviation of depressive symptoms does not invariably lead to a reduction in the frequency of compulsive behaviors and vice versa (Abramowitz, Franklin, Street, Kozak, & Foa, 2000).

Although OCD was previously thought to be relatively rare, results from modern epidemiological studies suggest that milder forms of the disorder may affect between 2 and 3% of the general population at some point during their lives (Fullana et al., 2009). Prevalence rates among untreated community residents must be interpreted with caution, however, because there is disagreement about the best assessment procedures to use in collecting information and the most appropriate diagnostic criteria (Fontenelle, Mendlowicz, & Versiani, 2006). Data from England suggest that the true prevalence of OCD in the community may be closer to 1% (Torres et al., 2006).

Relatively little information is available regarding conditions that set the stage for later development of OCD. Nevertheless, some interesting clues were provided in one classic study. Kringlen (1970) reported the results of a 20-year follow-up assessment of 91 patients who had been hospitalized with obsessive-compulsive disorder. More than 80% of these patients had exhibited nervous symptoms as children. They had typically been raised in strict, puritanical homes. The average age of onset for compulsive symptoms in female patients was between 10 and 20 years, although most of the women did not seek professional help until some years later. More than half of the patients showed an acute onset of symptoms following a specific stressful event. Marital problems were common among compulsive patients.

The prognosis for patients with OCD is mixed. Although the disorder can last many years, most patients do improve. One study conducted follow-up assessments with a group of patients 40 years after they had been treated in a hospital in Sweden (Skoog & Skoog, 1999). This was, of course, a group of severely disturbed patients because most people with OCD do not need to be treated in an inpatient setting. Nevertheless, the results suggest that many patients recover from OCD. At the time of the final follow-up, half of the patients had recovered from their disorder (defined as the absence of clinically relevant symptoms for at least 5 years). Another 30% showed some improvement, although they still experienced clinical symptoms. Approximately 20% of OCD patients do not improve following extended treatment (Besiroglu et al., 2007).

Karen was in many ways a typical OCD patient. She had, in fact, been raised in a strict, puritanical family setting. As a child, she was generally anxious and concerned with order and rituals. Since mid-adolescence, Karen had experienced difficulty with intrusive, repetitive ideas that she found distressing. These problems would come and go without apparent reason. She was also prone to serious depression. Karen's family background is also consistent with the literature on OCD (e.g., Pauls et al., 1995). There is a relatively high incidence of psychiatric anomalies—particularly obsessional traits, anxious personalities, and mood disturbances—among the biological relatives of obsessive-compulsive patients.

The similarity in behavior between many obsessive-compulsive patients and their parents probably reflects the influence of both genetic and environmental variables (Grabe et al., 2006; Hudziak et al., 2004). In Karen's case, her mother's rigid, moralistic behavior may have had an important influence on the development of later symptoms. Karen's mother provided a salient model for her daughter's subsequent compulsive behavior. She also reinforced early tendencies toward such response patterns.

Theoretical Perspectives and Treatment Implications

According to traditional psychoanalytic theory, compulsive symptoms are the product of the ego's unconscious attempt to fend off anxiety associated with hostile impulses. Freud (1909, 1925) argued that compulsive patients had experienced overly harsh toilet training and were therefore fixated in the anal-sadistic stage of development. Such individuals presumably suffer serious conflict over the expression of anger. Because these feelings are dangerous, or unacceptable to the ego, the anticipation of their expression is seen as anxiety provoking. This anxiety is dealt with primarily through the defense mechanism known as reaction formation, in which the original impulse (anger) is transformed into its antithesis (love or oversolicitude). This conceptual approach is not incompatible with Karen's situation. Her principal symptoms were compulsive rituals that were intended to protect her children from harm. But her feelings about her children were, in fact, ambivalent. It would not be unreasonable to assume that she was most often very angry with them, perhaps to the point that she might have considered doing them physical harm. Of course, this impulse would be anxiety provoking to the ego, which would convert it to its opposite form. Thus, instead of injuring the children, she would spend a good deal of her time every day performing irrational responses aimed at protecting them.

Most contemporary therapists agree that people with OCD have trouble expressing anger (Moritz, 2011; Osborn, 1998). Some recognition was given to these considerations in the treatment that was employed. Karen's anger and frustration were identified as central features of her adjustment problems, but the therapeutic procedures went beyond the goal of insight-oriented treatment. Karen's recognition of her anger and hostility was not sufficient to effect change; specific training procedures were used to help her develop more adaptive responses.

Learning theorists would view Karen's problems in a distinctly different fashion (Abramowitz, Taylor, & McKay, 2007; Houts, 2005). Within this general model, two factors would be given primary consideration. Both involve the principle of negative reinforcement, which states that the probability of a response is increased if it leads to the termination of an aversive stimulus. Consider, for example, the net effect of Karen's rituals. Their performance ensured that she would be away from her home for extended periods of time. If she went to her neighbor's house for coffee, she would be gone for at least two hours before she could consume enough cups and smoke enough cigarettes to satisfy the rituals. Grocery shopping, which she did by herself, had also turned into a long, complicated process. Given that being at home with her family was mostly an aversive experience for Karen, her rituals might be seen as an operant response that was being maintained by negative reinforcement.

A behavioral clinician would be most likely to point to the anxiety reduction associated with the performance of the rituals. Whenever Karen was engaged in an activity that reminded her of numbers and, consequently, her children, she became anxious. She was able to neutralize this anxiety temporarily by counting the appropriate number of boxes and so on. This ritual was therefore reinforced and maintained by the reduction of anxiety. This notion is similar to the psychoanalytic view in that the symptom is produced as a means of reducing tension. The two theories differ in that the behavioral view does not see her anxiety as being directly attributable to the unconscious urge to harm her children, nor does the behavioral view hold that the anxiety reduction is mediated by an unconsciously activated defense mechanism.

Some elements of the behavioral view were incorporated into the treatment procedure followed with Karen. In particular, by teaching her to be more assertive and to manage her children more effectively, the therapist was able to make her home life less aversive. She now experienced more pleasurable interactions with her children and her husband, and one important source of negative reinforcement for her rituals was removed. Unfortunately, this view of human behavior is fairly limited. In particular, it does not account for the importance of cognitive events. By focusing exclusively on environmental events, behaviorists may ignore important factors associated with the client's perceptions, beliefs, and attitudes. These variables also seemed to play an important role in Karen's problem.

Cognitive theories regarding the etiology of OCD emphasize the importance of excessive feelings of responsibility and guilt (Shapiro & Stewart, 2011).

This viewpoint begins with the recognition that most normal people experience intrusive thoughts from time to time, especially when they have been exposed to stress or negative mood states. Most intrusive thoughts do not become persistent or troublesome because people do not assign special meaning to them. According to the cognitive model, obsessions may develop if people interpret their intrusive thoughts as proof that they will be responsible for harm (to themselves or others) if they do not do something immediately to correct the thought. People most likely to develop OCD may be those who (a) learned a broad sense of responsibility and a high level of conscientiousness at an early age, (b) were exposed to rigid and extreme codes of conduct and duty (e.g., have learned that some thoughts are particularly dangerous or unacceptable), and (c) experienced a critical incident in which their action (or inaction) or their thoughts seemed to be connected to a harmful incident that affected them or someone else. Alarmed by the intrusive appearance of forbidden thoughts, the person may struggle to avoid them, but cognitive events are difficult to control. In fact, active attempts at thought suppression often backfire and increase the severity of the problem (Wegner, 1994). This vicious negative feedback loop magnifies feelings of helplessness and loss of control and also serves to focus attention on the content of unwanted thoughts. The person's anxiety level continues to escalate, and compulsive rituals are employed in an attempt to regain control over mental events as well as life experiences.

The relevance of this perspective to Karen's case is clear. She had experienced frequent intrusive thoughts related to her children's safety, and she did believe that a failure to act in response to these thoughts would result in harm coming to her children. As a child, Karen had been taught that certain thoughts and ideas were bad and that strict observation of the rituals of the church would guarantee her salvation and prevent harm from coming to her. These rituals became the primary means for controlling her fate and ensuring her safety. As an adult, Karen found herself stripped of these control mechanisms. The church now maintained that salvation (or the protection of one's soul) depended more on faith than on the performance of specific overt behaviors. When Karen experienced the critical incident in which her friend's infant daughter was injured, and she began to experience intrusive thoughts about harming herself, she turned to the use of private prayers in an attempt to protect herself. In some ways, Karen's subsequent development of counting rituals represented a substitute for the formal religious practices she had learned as a child. She admitted that they were irrational and probably unnecessary, but they did reduce her immediate anxiety in much the same way that going to church had left her with a comforting feeling as a child.

Karen's treatment addressed various cognitive factors, including efforts to improve her sense of self-control. Treatment was aimed initially at reducing the level of stress, improving Karen's mood, and giving her alternative means of controlling her environment, such as assertion training and instruction in parenting skills. Considering her deeply ingrained religious beliefs, it was also judged necessary to help her reestablish contact with the church. After these procedures had achieved some modest success, it was possible to attack the counting rituals directly through the use of exposure and response prevention. A cognitive therapist would view the process of exposure and response prevention as a kind of "behavioral experiment" in which the person is given an opportunity to disconfirm exaggerated beliefs about responsibility (i.e., "if I do not count the cereal boxes, something bad will happen to my children").

An extensive body of evidence indicates that behavior therapy is effective in treating compulsive disorders (Houghton, Saxon, Bradburn, Ricketts, & Hardy, 2010; Tolin et al., 2007). The most useful procedure seems to be *in vivo* (i.e., in the natural environment) exposure coupled with response prevention (ERP). Studies that have compared ERP with control treatments, such as applied relaxation, have found that patients who receive ERP (typically between 15 and 20 sessions) are more likely to experience substantial improvement. Some patients, of course, refuse to enter or drop out of behavioral treatment, perhaps because it is initially anxiety provoking. Motivational interviewing can be used as an additional procedure to increase adherence to behavioral treatment methods (Riccardi, Timpano, & Schmidt, 2010). Among those who do complete ERP, approximately 80% have been classified as improved, and most OCD patients maintain these improvements several months after the end of treatment.

Cognitive therapy is another psychological approach to the treatment of OCD (Abramowitz, 2010; Salkovskis, 1999). It is concerned primarily with the meanings that a person assigns to intrusive thoughts, images, and impulses. Symptoms of OCD are presumably more likely to occur if the person interprets the thoughts as an unquestionable sign that he or she is responsible for either causing or preventing harm that might come to oneself or other people. Cognitive therapy helps the person develop and use different interpretations of intrusive thoughts that do not require or motivate the person to continue to engage in compulsive rituals that are clearly ineffective and self-defeating. Treatment outcome studies report that this type of cognitive therapy can be an effective form of treatment for people with OCD (McLean et al., 2001).

Medication is also beneficial for many patients. Clomipramine (Anafranil) has relatively specific effects in reducing OCD symptoms; its therapeutic effects cannot be attributed solely to a reduction in comorbid depressive symptoms (Kim, Koo, & Kim, 2010). Sustained improvement depends on continued use of the drug. Most patients experience a return of OCD symptoms within 4 weeks after they stop taking the medication. The newer generation of antidepressant drugs known as selective serotonin reuptake inhibitors (SSRIs), including fluoxetine (Prozac), fluvoxamine (Luvox), and sertraline (Zoloft), has also been used with OCD patients. Controlled studies indicate that these drugs are also effective in the treatment of OCD (Dell'Osso, Nestadt, Allen, & Hollander, 2006). The SSRIs are often preferred to other forms of medication because they have fewer side effects.

Several issues will need to be addressed in future studies of treatment outcome. Relatively few direct comparisons of medication and ERP have been reported. It is not clear whether the combination of pharmacological and behavioral treatments is more effective than either one by itself (Albert & Brunatto, 2009). Perhaps more important, it is not currently possible to predict whether a particular patient will respond better to ERP or to medication. In actual clinical practice, medication is often used in combination with behavioral therapy for the treatment of OCD.

When both psychotherapy and medication fail, one other form of treatment may be considered: neurosurgery, which refers to techniques in which neural pathways in the brain are surgically altered in an effort to change the person's behavior. Although neurosurgery was originally intended to be used with psychotic patients, clinical research indicates that it may be most effective with obsessive-compulsive disorder (Csigó et al., 2010). One longitudinal study described 26 patients who had received neurosurgery after failing to respond to all other forms of treatment. In comparison to similar OCD patients who had not received surgery, 10 of the 26 patients were obviously improved several years after the procedure was performed, 6 others showed mild improvement, 6 were unchanged, and 4 had gotten worse (Hay et al., 1993). Because the duration of illness prior to surgery was several years for all the patients in this study, the reported rates of improvement are probably not due to placebo effects or spontaneous remission.

These results cannot be ignored, but they should also be interpreted with considerable caution. First, it is virtually impossible to conduct a double-blind evaluation of neurosurgery. Second, surgical procedures have varied widely across studies, thus making general statements about neurosurgery questionable. Third, and perhaps most important, neurosurgery may produce general changes in the patient's intellectual and emotional capacities. These changes remain unpredictable and poorly understood. Thus, most investigators agree that such radical procedures should be considered only when the patient's symptoms are chronic and severely disturbing and when other treatment programs have already been unsuccessful.

Discussion Questions

1. What is the difference between an obsession and a delusional belief? In what ways are obsessions different from the everyday worries that all of us experience?
2. Most people experience brief intrusive thoughts, impulses, and images on a regular basis. Could the ability to experience such thoughts be adaptive, from an evolutionary perspective? When does the pattern cross the line to become maladaptive?

3. What impact does obsessive-compulsive disorder have on other members of a patient's family? Should the person's spouse agree to tolerate or participate in compulsive rituals, such as special cleaning or checking procedures?

4. Exposure and response prevention is a challenging treatment procedure that can be anxiety provoking for patients. How hard should therapists push their patients to participate in treatments that will be upsetting in the short run if they know that they will be successful in the long run?

CHAPTER 2

Panic Disorder with Agoraphobia

Dennis Holt was 31 years old, divorced, and a successful insurance salesman. He had experienced panic attacks on several occasions during the past 10 years, but he did not seek psychological treatment until shortly after the last incident. It happened while Dennis and his fiancée, Elaine, were doing their Christmas shopping at a local mall. Their first stop was a large department store, where Elaine hoped to find a present for her mother. Dennis was in a good mood when they arrived at the store. Although he was usually uneasy in large crowds of people, he was also caught up in the holiday spirit and was looking forward to spending the bonus that he had recently received from his company. Ten minutes after they began shopping, Dennis suddenly felt very sick. His hands began to tremble uncontrollably, his vision became blurred, and his body felt weak all over. He experienced a tremendous pressure on his chest and began to gasp for breath, sensing that he was about to smother. These dramatic physical symptoms were accompanied by an overwhelming sensation of apprehension. He was terrified but did not know why. Without saying anything to Elaine, he whirled and dashed from the store, seeking refuge in their car, which was parked outside. Once there, he rolled down the windows to let in more air, lay down on the back seat, and closed his eyes. He continued to feel dizzy and short of breath for about 10 minutes more.

Elaine did not find him for more than an hour because she had been browsing in an adjacent aisle and had not seen him flee from the store. When she noticed that he was gone, she looked for him in other stores before she realized that something was wrong and finally decided to check the car. This was the first panic attack that Dennis had experienced since he and Elaine had begun dating several months previously. After they returned to his apartment, he explained what had happened and his past history of attacks in somewhat greater detail; she persuaded him to seek professional help.

When Dennis arrived at the psychological clinic for his first appointment, he was neatly dressed in an expensive suit. He was five minutes early, so the receptionist asked him if he would like to take a seat in the large, comfortably furnished waiting room where several other clients were sitting. Politely indicating that he would prefer to stand, Dennis leaned casually against the corridor wall. Everything about his physical appearance—his posture, his neatly trimmed hair, his friendly smile—conveyed a sense of confidence and success. Nothing betrayed the real sense of dread he had struggled with since he had promised Elaine that he would consult a psychologist. Was he, in fact, crazy? He wanted help, but he did not want anyone to think that he was emotionally unstable.

The first interview was not very productive. Dennis cracked jokes with the psychologist and attempted to engage in an endless sequence of witty small talk. In response to the psychologist's persistent queries, Dennis explained that he had promised his fiancée that he would seek some advice about his intermittent panic attacks. Nevertheless, he was reluctant to admit that he had any really serious problems, and he evaded many questions pertaining to his current adjustment. Dennis seemed intent on convincing the psychologist that he did not have a serious psychological problem. He continued to chat on a superficial level and, at one point, even began asking the psychologist whether she had adequate life insurance coverage.

In subsequent sessions, it became clear that the panic attacks, which never occurred more than two or three times per year, were simply the most dramatic of Dennis's problems. He was also an extremely tense and anxious person between attacks. He frequently experienced severe headaches that sometimes lasted for several hours. These generally took the form of a steady, diffuse pain across his forehead. Dennis also complained that he could not relax, noting that he suffered from chronic muscle tension and occasional insomnia. His job often required that he work late in the evening, visiting people in their homes after dinner. When he returned to his apartment, he was always "wound up" and on edge, unable to sleep. He had tried various distractions and popular remedies, but nothing had worked.

Dennis was very self-conscious. Although he was an attractive man and one of the most successful salespersons in his firm, he worried constantly about what others thought of him. This concern was obvious in his behavior both before and after sessions at the clinic. At the end of every session, he seemed to make a point of joking loudly so that anyone outside the psychologist's office would hear the laughter. He would then open the door, as he continued to chuckle, and say something like, "Well, Alicia [the therapist's first name], that was a lot of fun. Let's get together again soon!" as he left her office. The most peculiar incident of this sort occurred prior to the fourth treatment session. Dennis had avoided the clinic waiting room on past visits, but this time it happened that he and his therapist met at a location that required them to walk through the waiting room together to reach her office. Thinking nothing of it, the therapist set off across the room in which several other clients were waiting, and Dennis quickly followed. When they reached the middle of the long room, Dennis suddenly clasped his right arm around her shoulders, smiled, and in a voice that was slightly too loud said, "Well, Alicia, what's up? How can I help you today?" The therapist was taken completely by surprise but said nothing until they reached her office. Dennis quickly closed the door and leaned against the wall, holding his hand over his heart as he gulped for air. He was visibly shaken. After he had caught his breath, he apologized profusely and explained that he did not know what had come over him. He said that he had always been afraid that the other people in the clinic, particularly the other clients, would realize that he was a client and therefore think he was crazy. He had become extremely uncomfortable as they walked across the waiting room and had been unable to resist the urge to divert attention from himself by seeming to be a therapist.

This preoccupation with social evaluation was also evident in Dennis's work. He became extremely tense whenever he was about to call on a prospective client. Between the point at which an appointment was arranged and his arrival at the person's home, Dennis worried constantly. Would he or she like him? Could he make the sale? His anxiety became most exaggerated as he drove his car to the person's home. In an effort to cope with this anxiety, Dennis had constructed a 45-minute audio recording that he played for himself in the car. The recording contained a long pep talk, in his own voice, in which he continually reassured and encouraged himself: "Go out there and charm 'em, Dennis. You're the best damn salesman this company's ever had! They're gonna be putty in your hands. Flash that smile, and they'll love you!" and on and on. Unfortunately, the net effect of the recording was probably an increase to his tension. Despite this anxiety, he managed to perform effectively in the selling role, just as he was able to project an air of confidence in the clinic. But, on the inside, he was miserable. Every 2 or 3 months, he would become convinced that he could no longer stand the tension and decide to quit his job. Then he would make a big sale or receive a bonus for exceeding his quota for that period and change his mind.

Social History

Dennis was an only child. His father was an accountant, and his mother was an elementary-school teacher. No one else in his family had been treated for adjustment problems.

Dennis and his mother got along well, but his relationship with his father had always been difficult. His father was a demanding perfectionist who held very high, probably unrealistic, expectations for Dennis. When Dennis was in elementary school, his father always wanted him to be the best athlete and the best student in his class. Although Dennis was adequate in both of these areas, he did not excel in either. His father frequently expressed the hope that Dennis would become an aeronautical engineer when he grew up. Now that Dennis was working as an insurance salesman, his father never missed an opportunity to express his disapproval and disappointment. He was also unhappy about Dennis's previous divorce. When his parents came to visit, Dennis and his father usually ended up in an argument.

Dennis remembered being shy as a child. Nevertheless, he enjoyed the company of other children and always had a number of friends. When he reached adolescence, he was particularly timid around girls. In an effort to overcome his shyness, he joined the high school drama club and played bit parts in several of its productions. This experience provided an easy avenue for meeting other students with whom he became friends. He also learned that he could speak in front of a group of people without making a fool of himself, but he continued to feel uncomfortable in public-speaking and social situations.

After graduating from high school, Dennis attended a private liberal arts college for two years. Although he had been a reasonably good student in high school, he began to experience academic problems in college. He attributed his sporadic performance to test anxiety. In his own words, he "choked" on examinations. Shortly after he entered the classroom, the palms of his hands would begin to perspire profusely. Then his breathing would become more rapid and shallow, and his mouth would become very dry. On the worst occasions, his mind would go blank.

Some of his instructors were sympathetic to the problem and allowed him to take extra time to finish examinations; others permitted him to turn in supplementary papers that were written out of class. Nevertheless, his grades began to suffer, and by the end of his first year, he was placed on academic probation.

During his second year in college, Dennis began to experience gastrointestinal problems. He had always seemed to have a sensitive stomach and avoided rich or fried foods that often led to excessive flatulence or nausea. Now the symptoms were getting worse. He suffered intermittently from constipation, cramping, and diarrhea. He would frequently go for 3 or 4 days without having a bowel movement. During these periods, he experienced considerable discomfort and occasional severe cramps in his lower abdominal tract. These problems persisted for several months until, at the urging of his roommate, Dennis finally made an appointment for a complete gastrointestinal examination at the local hospital. The physicians were unable to find any evidence of structural pathology and diagnosed Dennis's problems as irritable bowel syndrome. They prescribed some medication, but Dennis continued to suffer from intermittent bowel problems.

Dennis had several girlfriends and dated regularly throughout high school and college. During his sophomore year in college, he developed a serious relationship with Mary, who was a freshman at the same school. She and Dennis shared some interests and enjoyed each other's company, so they spent a great deal of time together. At the end of the academic year, Dennis decided that he had had enough of college. He was bored with his classes and tired of the continual pressure from his parents to get better grades. An older friend of his had recently landed a well-paying job with an insurance firm, so Dennis decided that he would complete applications with a number of companies. He was offered a position in sales with a company in a nearby state. Mary decided that she would also drop out of school. She and Dennis began living together, and they were married 2 years later.

Dennis and Mary were reasonably happy for the first 3 years. He was successful at his job, and she eventually became a licensed realtor. As they were both promoted by their respective firms, they found themselves spending more and more time working and less and less time with each other. Their interests also began to diverge. When Mary had some time off or an evening free, she liked to go out to restaurants and parties. Dennis liked to stay home and watch television.

Dennis's first real panic attack occurred when he was 24 years old. He and Mary were at a dinner theater with three other couples, including Mary's boss and his wife. The evening had been planned for several weeks, despite Dennis's repeated objections. He was self-conscious about eating in public and did not care for Mary's colleagues; he had finally agreed to accompany her because it seemed that it would be important for her advancement in the firm. He was also looking forward to seeing the play, which would be performed after the meal was served. As the meal progressed, Dennis began to feel increasingly uncomfortable. He was particularly concerned that he might experience one of his gastrointestinal attacks during dinner and be forced to spend the rest of the evening in the men's restroom. He did not want to have to explain the problem to all of Mary's friends. In an attempt to prevent such an attack, he had taken antispasmodic medication for his stomach and was eating sparingly. Just as everyone else had finished eating dessert, Dennis began to experience a choking sensation in his throat and chest. He could not get his breath, and it seemed certain to him that he was going to faint on the spot. Unable to speak or move, he remained frozen in his seat in utter terror. The others quickly realized that something was wrong, and assuming that he had choked on some food, Mary began to pound on his back between the shoulder blades. There was now a sharp pain in his chest, and he began to experience heart palpitations. Dennis was finally able to wheeze that he thought he was having a heart attack. Two of the other men helped him up, and a waiter directed them to a lounge in the building where he was able to lie down. In less than 30 minutes, all of the symptoms had passed. Dennis and Mary excused themselves from the others and drove home.

Dennis was frightened by this experience, but he did not seek medical advice. He was convinced that he was in good physical condition and attributed the attack to something he had eaten or perhaps to an interaction between the food and medication. He did, however, become even more reluctant to go to restaurants with Mary and her friends. Interestingly, he continued to eat business lunches with his own colleagues without apparent discomfort.

The second panic attack occurred about 6 months later, while Dennis was driving alone in rush-hour traffic. The symptoms were essentially the same: the sudden sensation of smothering, accompanied by an inexplicable, intense fear. Fortunately, Dennis was in the right lane of traffic when the sensation began. He was able to pull his car off the road and lie on the seat until the experience was over.

By this point, Dennis was convinced that he needed medical help. He made an appointment with a specialist in internal medicine who gave him a complete physical examination. There was no evidence of cardiovascular or gastrointesti-nal pathology. The physician told Dennis that the problem seemed to be with his nerves and gave him a prescription for alprazolam (Xanax), a high-potency ben-zodiazepine often used in treating anxiety disorders and insomnia. Dennis took 2 milligrams of Xanax three times per day for 4 months. It did help him relax and, in combination with his other medication, seemed to improve his gastrointestinal dis-tress. However, he did not like the side effects (such as drowsiness and lighthead-edness) or the feeling of being dependent on medication to control his anxiety. He saw the latter as a sign of weakness and eventually discontinued taking the Xanax (decreasing his daily dosage gradually, as recommended by his physician).

Mary asked Dennis for a divorce 3 years after they were married (2 years after his first panic attack). It came as no surprise to Dennis; their relationship had dete-riorated considerably. He had become even more reluctant to go out with her in the evening and on weekends, insisting that he needed to stay home and rest his nerves. He was very apprehensive in crowded public places and also careful about where and when he drove his car. He tried to avoid rush-hour traffic. When he did drive in heavy traffic, he always stayed in the right lane, even if it was much slower, so that he could pull off the road if he had an attack. Long bridges made him extremely uncomfortable because they did not afford an opportunity to pull over; he dreaded the possibility of being trapped on a bridge during one of his "spells."

These fears did not prevent him from doing his work. He continued to force himself to meet new people, and he drove long distances every day. The most drastic impact was on his social life. These increased restrictions led to greater tension between Dennis and Mary. They had both become more and more irrita-ble and seldom enjoyed being with each other. When she decided that she could no longer stand to live with him, he agreed to the divorce.

After Mary left, Dennis moved to an apartment in which he was still living when he entered treatment 5 years later. His chronic anxiety, occasional panic attacks, headaches, and gastrointestinal problems persisted relatively unchanged, although they varied in severity. He had a number of friends and managed to see them fairly frequently. He did, however, avoid situations that involved large crowds. He would not, for example, accompany his friends to a professional foot-ball game, but he did like to play golf, where he could be out in the fresh air with very few people and a lot of open space around him. He met Elaine 4 years after the divorce. She was slightly older than he and much less active socially than Mary had been. They enjoyed spending quiet evenings watching television and occa-sionally got together with one or two other couples to play cards. Although they planned to get married, neither Dennis nor Elaine wanted to rush into anything.

Conceptualization and Treatment

When Dennis entered treatment, he expressed a desire to learn how to control his anxiety, particularly when it reached its most excessive proportions in the form of panic attacks. He did not feel comfortable taking medication because he considered it to be an artificial "crutch." He had read about cognitive-behavioral approaches to the treatment of anxiety and was looking for a psychologist with whom he could follow such an approach. He had, in fact, found such a person.

The difficulties that Dennis had experienced over the past several years included a complex blend of generalized anxiety and occasional panic attacks. His therapist viewed Dennis's problems as being the result of an interaction between vulnerability to stress and various cognitive and behavioral responses that exacerbate and maintain high levels of anxiety. Like many other patients with panic disorder, Dennis had experienced his first panic attack during an event that he perceived to be very stressful (the dinner with his wife's boss). After that traumatic experience, he became increasingly afraid of (and tried to avoid) situations in which he might have another attack. This avoidance was maintained, in part, by distorted and unrealistic things that he said to himself about future events and his interactions with other people. For example, Dennis believed that it would be a catastrophe if someone did not like him. He also insisted to himself that he had to be the best salesperson in this firm, and, if he was not, then he would be a failure. These maladaptive attitudes had most likely been instilled in Dennis by his father, who had continually emphasized his demand for perfection and whose affection seemed to hinge on its attainment. More useful self-statements would have to be substituted for these maladaptive demands before Dennis would feel more comfortable in social situations, particularly those that involved his work.

The therapist agreed to help Dennis reduce his generalized anxiety as well as to help him eliminate panic attacks. In Dennis's case, this was particularly important because his panic attacks were relatively infrequent. The reduction in generalized anxiety would be accomplished by teaching him more appropriate ways of coping with, and thinking about, his environment. Treatment would include applied relaxation training and cognitive restructuring. After these skills were learned, therapy sessions would turn to situational exposure aimed at decreasing Dennis's avoidance of situations in which he feared having another panic attack. The process of discussing this conception of the problem and arriving at a treatment plan was accompanied by an obvious change in Dennis's behavior toward the therapist. He became much less defensive and dropped his annoying, superficial displays of bravado when he realized that the psychologist intended to function as a teacher, not as a judge who would rule on his sanity.

The therapist decided to begin treatment with training in relaxation. Her purpose at the outset was not to eliminate the occurrence of any more panic attacks. They were, of course, the most dramatic and perhaps the most difficult of Dennis's problems. But their infrequency also meant that even if Dennis learned to control them, he would not be able to notice any improvement in his adjustment for a long time. Therefore, the therapist's first goal was to select a simpler problem and an area in which Dennis could see rapid improvement, thus enhancing his motivation for further change efforts. The most suitable place to begin, therefore, was his inability to relax when he returned to his apartment after work.

Relaxation training was introduced to Dennis as an active coping skill that he could use to control muscular tension. The therapist explained that she would begin by teaching Dennis how to use the procedure in the clinic setting. Dennis would be expected to practice relaxation at home on a daily basis for several weeks. He was cautioned against expecting a sudden change in his anxiety level and was told that, for most people, the development of relaxation skills takes considerable effort.

Relaxation training began during the sixth treatment session. The therapist asked Dennis to stretch out in a comfortable reclining chair and then demonstrated the procedure, which involved the alternate tensing and relaxing of a sequence of muscle groups. The therapist drew Dennis's attention to his pattern of breathing and asked him to take deep, slow breaths. When Dennis was comfortable, the therapist asked him to lift his forearms off the arms of the chair and tighten his hands into fists. He was instructed to hold that position for five seconds, noting the muscle tension, and then let go. This cycle was repeated through a sequence of several other groups of muscles. Throughout this process, the therapist reminded Dennis to breathe slowly and deeply.

Dennis responded positively to relaxation training. He felt awkward and self-conscious at the beginning of the procedure but quickly overcame his apprehension. Although he did not think that he had reached a state of complete relaxation, he did feel much more relaxed than he had when he arrived for the session; he indicated that he was looking forward to practicing the procedure during the coming week. The therapist explained a subjective rating scale that he could use to keep track of his progress. Using a 10-point scale, with 1 being *complete relaxation* ("similar to the quiet, drifting feeling that you have before you go to sleep") and 10 being *maximum tension* ("like you feel when you've already had a tough day and a potential client has just decided against buying a policy"), Dennis was asked to keep a record of his subjective level of tension before and after each practice session.

Dennis was faithful in completing his homework assignment. His average self-rating of tension was about 6 or 7 before practice and 3 or 4 at the end of each session. He enjoyed the exercise and was pleased finally to be learning a skill to help him cope with his tension. His outlook was clearly hopeful.

By the end of the first month of training, Dennis was consistently able to reduce his subjective tension to a level of 1 or 2 at the end of each practice session. His only problem arose in trying to use the procedure during periods of very high tension. For example, during the second week of practice, he had tried unsuccessfully to use the exercise to eliminate a severe headache that had developed in the afternoon and persisted throughout the evening. The therapist pointed out that Dennis should not be discouraged because he had not reached a stage of proficiency that would allow him to deal with the most serious levels of stress. She also noted that the object of relaxation was primarily to teach Dennis to be aware of muscular tension before it had progressed to such an advanced level. Relaxation could therefore be seen as a kind of preventive procedure, not as a way of coping with problems such as headaches after they became severe.

After Dennis was making satisfactory progress with relaxation, the therapist shifted the focus of their discussions to introduce a process known as cognitive restructuring. She began with the observation that emotions, or feelings, are influenced by what people say to themselves. In other words, it is not necessarily the objective situation with which we are confronted, but rather what we tell ourselves about the situation that determines our emotional response. For example, a woman who is fearful when speaking in front of a large group of people is not in physical danger. It is probably what that woman is telling herself about the audience ("They'll all think I'm stupid," or "I'm sure none of them will like me") that leads to undue levels of anxiety. The therapist explained the general principles behind cognitive restructuring while carefully avoiding specific reference to Dennis's own experience.

After Dennis understood the assumptions behind cognitive restructuring, the therapist outlined several cognitive distortions that are associated with severe anxiety. One example, called *probability overestimation,* refers to the tendency to overestimate the probability that a negative event will occur. Another form of cognitive distortion, called *catastrophic thinking,* refers to the tendency to exaggerate the consequences of negative events. People who engage in this type of thinking act as though an imagined event would be completely devastating when, in fact, it would be more accurate to say it would be unpleasant but tolerable.

Dennis was intrigued by these notions and, throughout the discussion, often thought of examples of situations in which other people (such as his former wife, Mary) seemed to be making themselves unhappy by engaging in cognitive distortion. As they talked further, the therapist asked Dennis if he could think of examples in which he engaged in this kind of thinking. Initially, this was difficult. The therapist noted that we are often unaware of the distorted thoughts; they have been so deeply instilled and overlearned that they become automatic. Confronted with an audience, the person with public-speaking anxiety does not actually whisper, "I have to be perfect in everything I do, including public speaking, and it is imperative that they all think that I am witty and clever. If they don't, I'm a miserable failure." The only subjective experience may be an immediate sensation of overwhelming fear. Nevertheless, that emotional response may be mediated by these self-statements. Furthermore, if that person could learn to think in a less distorted fashion (e.g., "I hope that I will do well and that many of the people will enjoy my talk, but if they don't, it's not the end of the world"), anxiety could be controlled.

These discussions filled the next several sessions. Much of the time was spent taking specific experiences that had been anxiety provoking for Dennis and analyzing the self-statements that might have accompanied his response. Many centered on contacts with clients. The applicability of the cognitive-restructuring approach to these situations was particularly evident given the audio recording that he had made to coach himself before appointments. The therapist pointed out that Dennis had been on the right track in this attempt to cope with his anxiety, but many of the statements created unrealistic expectations that probably exacerbated his problem. Instead of assuring himself that the client would like him because he was the best salesperson in the company, Dennis would have been better able to control his anxiety if he had reduced the demands that he placed on himself and recognized that the success or failure of his career did not depend on the outcome of a single client contact.

Dennis gradually became proficient in noticing the distorted thoughts that led to his anxiety in various situations. At first, he could only dissect these situations in discussions with his therapist. Together, they challenged his catastrophic thoughts and substituted more realistic, evidence-based reasoning. Dennis found it helpful to recognize that the impact of negative events (such as being turned down by a client) would be manageable and short-lived. The goal, of course, was to help him practice this skill until he could employ adaptive self-statements as a coping response before and during stressful experiences. To facilitate this process and provide for generalization of these new cognitive responses outside of the therapy sessions, the therapist asked Dennis to begin a diary. Each night, he was to take a few minutes to describe any situation in which he had become particularly anxious during the day. He was instructed to note distorted thoughts that might have been associated with his anxiety as well as complementary self-statements that would have been more appropriate. After keeping this record for 4 weeks, Dennis noted that he was beginning to feel less anxious in social situations and during sales visits.

The final step in treatment was concerned with Dennis's avoidance of situations that had been previously associated with panic attacks. He had not experienced an attack in the 3 months since his first visit to the psychologist, probably because he had refused to accompany Elaine to any movies, restaurants, or department stores. He was now able to achieve a state of relaxation quickly and without the aid of the formal tension-relaxation procedure. The therapist therefore decided to begin a program of exposure to feared and avoided situations. This would be accomplished *in vivo* (i.e., in the natural environment) by having Dennis purposefully enter situations that had previously led to feelings of apprehension and dread and then remain there until he had successfully demonstrated to himself that he would not have a panic attack. At the beginning of treatment, this procedure would have been likely to fail because Dennis did not believe that he could handle such situations. The therapist noted that he had now acquired new skills with which he would be able to cope with whatever anxiety, if any, he might experience.

They intentionally began with a fairly easy situation and arranged for Elaine to accompany Dennis. He indicated that her presence would make him feel less vulnerable. His assignment for the week was to go to a specific department store, during the morning on a weekday when there would not be a large crowd present, and spend 15 minutes browsing in the men's department, which was located just inside the front entrance. When this task had been successfully accomplished, Dennis and the therapist designed a hierarchy of stressful situations to which he would expose himself in sequence and for increasing amounts of time. These began with further simple situations, such as the first one at the men's department, and continued on to those that had previously been most difficult for him. The latter included activities such as attending a play with Elaine and sitting in the middle of a center row (where he did not have easy access to an aisle or exit).

The treatment sessions were terminated after 6 months. Dennis had made considerable progress during that time. He had successfully mastered all the situations in the exposure hierarchy and had not experienced a panic attack since the one that provoked his entry into treatment. His general anxiety level was also considerably reduced. He continued to experience occasional tension headaches, particularly after especially busy days, but they were less frequent (perhaps two or three each month) and less severe than they had been in the past. His insomnia had disappeared completely. Whenever he did have trouble sleeping, he would use the formal tension-relaxation procedure. In this way, he was able to eliminate muscular tension and simultaneously distract himself from whatever problems he was worrying about. Unfortunately, his gastrointestinal problems remained. He still suffered from intermittent constipation and diarrhea and continued to use medication to relieve these discomforts on an ad hoc basis.

Discussion

Disorders in which anxiety is the most prominent symptom are quite common. During any given year, 17% of the people in the United States may suffer from at least one form of anxiety disorder, although only one out of four of these people receive treatment for the problem (Young, Klap, Shoai, & Wells, 2008). The *Diagnostic and Statistical Manual of Mental Disorders* (*DSM-IV-TR;* APA, 2000) recognizes eight disorders that involve anxiety and avoidance:

1. Panic disorder (with or without agoraphobia)
2. Agoraphobia without history of panic disorder
3. Specific phobia
4. Social phobia
5. Obsessive-compulsive disorder (OCD)
6. Posttraumatic stress disorder (PTSD)
7. Acute stress disorder
8. Generalized anxiety disorder (GAD)

Many people exhibit a mixture of symptoms and meet the criteria for more than one disorder (panic disorder and GAD, in Dennis's case). Most individuals who meet the diagnostic criteria for GAD also qualify for a diagnosis of at least one other type of anxiety disorder or major depression (Moffitt et al., 2007;

Turk & Mennin, 2011). The *DSM-IV-TR* (APA, 2000) description and organization of anxiety disorders pay special attention to the presence or absence of panic attacks. These extraordinarily frightening experiences, which seldom last more than a few minutes, are discrete periods of apprehension or fear, accompanied by sensations such as shortness of breath, palpitations, chest pains, choking or smothering sensations, dizziness, perspiring, and trembling or shaking. Some patients, like Dennis, experience only one or two attacks a year, whereas others may have them on a daily basis.

The *DSM-IV-TR* definition of a panic attack includes the following criteria: a discrete period of intense fear or discomfort, in which four (or more) of the following symptoms develop abruptly and reach a peak within 10 minutes:

1. Palpitations, pounding heart, or accelerated heart rate
2. Sweating
3. Trembling or shaking
4. Sensations of shortness of breath or smothering
5. Feeling of choking
6. Chest pain or discomfort
7. Nausea or abdominal distress
8. Feeling dizzy, unsteady, lightheaded, or faint
9. Derealization (feeling of unreality) or depersonalization (being detached from oneself)
10. Fear of losing control or going crazy
11. Fear of dying
12. Paresthesias (numbness or tingling sensations)
13. Chills or hot flushes

The *DSM-IV-TR* criteria for panic disorder require that the person experience recurrent, unexpected panic attacks. At least one of these attacks must be followed by a period of at least 1 month in which the person has worried about having further attacks or else changes his or her behavior as a result of the attacks.

In phobic disorders, the most important element is a persistent, irrational fear of a specific object or situation that the person goes out of his or her way to avoid. *Agoraphobia* is defined as an exaggerated fear of being in situations or places from which escape might be difficult, or in which help, if needed, might be unavailable. In severe cases of agoraphobia, the person becomes entirely housebound—unable to venture outside for fear of experiencing intense anxiety. Agoraphobics frequently report fear of becoming physically ill, fainting, having a heart attack, or dying, particularly during a panic attack. These fears increase if the person's access to support (e.g., a companion) or an avenue of escape is blocked or impaired. Most cases of agoraphobia begin with the experience of panic attacks.

In contrast to the circumscribed fears seen in phobic disorders, generalized anxiety disorder (GAD) is characterized by unrealistic and excessive worry and anxiety occurring more days than not for at least 6 months. The person must exhibit three or more of the following symptoms in association with these worries: restlessness or feeling keyed up or on edge, being easily fatigued, having difficulty concentrating, irritability, muscle tension, and sleep disturbance.

Dennis met the criteria for both panic disorder with agoraphobia and GAD. Although his panic attacks were not especially frequent, he was persistently afraid of having another. His behavior met the criteria for agoraphobia in that he was apprehensive about being in public places from which escape might be difficult. He had occasionally forced himself to enter such situations, but the constriction of his social activities had a very negative impact on his life. Dennis's fear was not so severe that he was entirely housebound, but he did avoid public places from which he was afraid he might not be able to escape.

Dennis also met *DSM-IV-TR* criteria for GAD (APA, 2000). His muscle tension was clearly evidenced by his inability to relax, his frequent tension headaches, and the constant fatigue from which he suffered. His irregular bowel movements and diarrhea were further signs of autonomic difficulties. He experienced continual apprehension and frequently had difficulty sleeping.

Data regarding the frequency of specific anxiety disorders in the community have been reported by investigators involved in a large-scale epidemiological study, known as the ECA study, concerned with the distribution of mental disorders in five American cities (Robins & Regier, 1991). Approximately 6 out of every 100 people interviewed in a 12-month period reported some form of phobic disorder; some people fit more than one subcategory. Specific phobias were the most common (about 5%), followed by agoraphobia (about 3%), and social phobias (about 2%). Specific phobias and agoraphobia were more common among women than men; gender differences are less pronounced for social phobias. GAD was also relatively common among people in this study, with a 12-month prevalence rate of 4%. Panic disorder, on the other hand, was the least common form of anxiety disorder. Slightly more than 1% of the subjects in the ECA study qualified for a diagnosis of panic disorder during the 12-month period immediately prior to their interview.

Depression and drug abuse are often associated with anxiety disorders (Conway, Compton, Stinson, & Grant, 2006). At least half of all patients with an anxiety disorder have also experienced an episode of major depression at some point. Alcoholism and barbiturate abuse are common results of attempts to use drugs to cope with chronic tension and generalized anxiety. In fact, some patients become addicted to minor tranquilizers that have been prescribed by physicians. Fortunately, Dennis did not become dependent on the use of medication. Although Xanax did make him feel more relaxed, he resisted its use because it made him feel even less in control of his own emotions.

When people with panic disorder decide to seek treatment, most begin by going to a general medical clinic rather than a mental health facility (Craske et al., 2009). They are among the heaviest users of medical care. Dennis became convinced that he needed help after having a panic attack while driving in rush-hour traffic. Rather than consulting a psychologist or a psychiatrist, he visited a specialist in internal medicine. This pattern is important for a number of reasons. To avoid the use of inappropriate and expensive medical tests and treatments, primary care physicians must be alert to the possibility that many of their patients are suffering from mental disorders, especially anxiety and depression. Identification and effective treatment of problems such as panic disorder can simultaneously minimize the distress experienced by patients and reduce the overall cost of medical services.

Unfortunately, it is sometimes difficult to make the distinction between anxiety disorders and other medical disorders. Patients with panic disorder experience a broad range of medical symptoms, including headaches, cardiovascular problems, and gastrointestinal difficulties (Eaton et al., 1998). Again, Dennis's experience is consistent with the literature on these points, including his chronic gastrointestinal problems. There is a strong connection between panic disorder and irritable bowel syndrome, which is the most common type of functional gastrointestinal disorder.

Etiological Considerations

Several twin studies have found that genetic factors are influential in the transmission of anxiety disorders, especially those that involve the experience of panic attacks (e.g., Hettema, Prescott, Myers, Neale, & Kendler, 2005). The data indicate that GAD is somewhat less heritable than other forms of anxiety disorder. Studies of the distribution of various psychological disorders in families also suggest that the etiology of some forms of anxiety and depression may be related. First-degree relatives of patients diagnosed as having both major depression and panic disorder show markedly increased rates of depression, anxiety disorders, and alcoholism in comparison to relatives of normals and those of depressed patients without anxiety disorder. Thus, biological factors appear to be important in the etiology of anxiety disorders, but environmental events are also influential.

Traditional psychological views of anxiety have been based on psychoanalytic and learning theories. Although there are obvious differences between these points of view, both theories treat anxiety as a signal of some expected negative event. Neither draws an important distinction between chronic anxiety and panic attacks. A psychoanalytically oriented therapist would have viewed Dennis's chronic anxiety as a symptom of unconscious conflict between the ego and previously punished id impulses (Compton, 1992). These impulses are usually presumed to be sexual or aggressive in nature and traceable to early childhood experiences. It might have been argued, for example, that Dennis secretly harbored violent impulses toward his father, who criticized and belittled him. Because he was also afraid of his father (a classic assumption of psychoanalytic theory) and because he would be punished if he harmed his father, these impulses were anxiety provoking and therefore repressed. But when he entered situations in which he might be evaluated by other people, he was reminded of his father's criticism. The hostile impulses then became more intense, and his anxiety would increase proportionately.

There was, however, no clear evidence to support this notion. Dennis did not hide his resentment of his father. They argued openly and frequently about every imaginable topic.

The conditioning model would view Dennis's problem as a fear response that had been learned through the association of previously neutral stimuli (e.g., a crowded theater) with a painful or frightening stimulus. After Dennis had learned to fear particular situations, his avoidance of them would presumably be reinforced by the reduction in anxiety that he experienced after he fled. There are a number of problems with this model (see Mineka & Zinbarg, 1995). One is that very few patients with anxiety disorders can remember having experienced a traumatic event. In Dennis's case, his first panic attack was certainly a terrifying experience, and the fear that he experienced may have become paired with the stimuli that were present when it occurred. This process might explain the main-tenance of his desire to avoid crowded public places, but it does not explain the original onset of his intense fear.

Cognitive perspectives on anxiety disorders emphasize the way in which people interpret information from their environment (Roth, Wilhelm, & Pettit, 2005). Maladaptive emotions such as chronic, generalized anxiety are presuma-bly products of self-defeating cognitive schemas. Some people make themselves unnecessarily anxious by interpreting events in a negative fashion. They view the world in a distorted manner that is biased against themselves. The negative thoughts and images that are triggered by environmental events lead to persistent feelings of threat and insecurity.

One cognitive theory of panic disorder was proposed by Clark et al. (1997), who argued that panic disorder is caused by catastrophic misinterpretation of bodily sensations. An anxious mood presumably leads to a variety of bodily sen-sations that accompany negative emotional reactions (changes in heart and respi-ration rates, dizziness, and so on). This process is accompanied by a narrowing of the person's attention focus and increased awareness of bodily sensations. Next, the person misinterprets the bodily sensation as a catastrophic event.

Consider how this approach might explain one of Dennis's panic attacks. After he had his first attack, Dennis became highly vigilant, watching for the slightest indication that he was having another one. If he became short of breath, for whatever reason, he would interpret the experience as being a sign that he was about to have another attack. This reaction ensured continued operation of the feedback loop, with the misinterpretation enhancing Dennis's sense of threat and so on until the process would spiral out of control. Thus, according to the model by Clark et al., (1997) cognitive misinterpretation and biological reactions associ-ated with the perception of threat are both necessary for a panic attack to occur.

Treatment

The therapist who treated Dennis combined the use of relaxation with a cogni-tive approach to his problems (e.g., Craske et al., 2009; Rodebaugh, Holaway, &

Heimberg, 2004). She hypothesized that Dennis's perceptions of social events and the things that he said to himself about these events played an important role in the maintenance of his anxiety. The therapist helped Dennis recognize the general kinds of self-statements that were associated with his anxiety and then modeled more appropriate statements that he would be able to use to cope more effectively with stressful situations. The latter component of the process is particularly important. In addition to helping Dennis gain insight into his problem, the therapist taught him specific cognitive skills (adaptive self-statements) that had previously been absent from his repertoire of coping responses. If insight had been sufficient, Dennis would have experienced a decline in his anxiety level as soon as he recognized that he engaged in distorted thinking, but he did not. Positive change was evident only after a prolonged period of practice employing more realistic self-statements, both in and out of therapy sessions.

It should also be noted that the therapist did not rely solely on the cognitive form of intervention. In addition to talking with Dennis about his problem, the therapist helped him learn specific behavioral responses (e.g., applied relaxation) and insisted that he confront various situations in the natural environment. This approach was founded on the realization that although cognitive variables may play an important role in the change process, the most effective treatment programs are performance based. This was clear in Dennis's case. His apprehension in crowded public places was not significantly reduced until he had actually mastered a series of such situations following the exposure procedure.

One version of cognitive-behavioral treatment for panic disorder includes some additional procedures that were not employed in Dennis's case. *Panic control treatment* typically follows a 12-session sequence and incorporates three specific methods (Barlow, 1997). First, cognitive restructuring is used to correct the person's erroneous appraisals of physical sensations and to reduce the frequency of catastrophic thinking. Second, breathing retraining is used to help the person avoid hyperventilation (a common trigger for panic). Third, structured exposure to bodily sensations is employed to reduce the person's sensitivity to cues that have come to be associated with panic attacks (e.g., increased heart and respiration rates). This is accomplished by having the person participate in a series of exercises such as running in place or breathing through a narrow straw. If the person has also developed agoraphobic avoidance, *in vivo* exposure is also incorporated into the treatment program.

Panic disorder can also be treated with various forms of medication. Selective serotonin reuptake inhibitors (SSRIs), which are widely employed in the treatment of depression, are also used for the treatment of panic disorder (Simon & Pollack, 2000). These drugs include fluoxetine (Prozac) and fluvoxamine (Luvox). In comparison to high-potency benzodiazepines such as alprazolam (Xanax), patients are less likely to become addicted to an SSRI, and they experience fewer problems when the medication is withdrawn. Tricyclic antidepressants, such as imipramine (Tofranil), are also effective in the treatment of panic disorder. Patients often prefer the SSRIs because they produce fewer side effects than tricyclic antidepressants.

Anxiety disorders are also treated with minor tranquilizers from the class of drugs known as benzodiazepines, which includes alprazolam (Xanax) and diazepam (Valium). Dennis had taken Xanax for a few months after his second panic attack. The benzodiazepines reduce many symptoms of anxiety, especially vigilance and subjective somatic sensations, such as increased muscle tension, palpitations, increased perspiration, and gastrointestinal distress. They have relatively less effect on the tendency to worry and ruminate. Some psychiatrists consider alprazolam to be the drug of choice for patients with panic disorder because it leads to more rapid clinical improvement than antidepressant medication, and it has fewer side effects. Several placebo-controlled outcome studies indicate that alprazolam is an effective form of treatment for patients with panic disorders (Verster & Volkerts, 2004).

Of course, some side effects are associated with the use of benzodiazepines. These include sedation accompanied by mild psychomotor impairment as well as problems in attention and memory. Dennis discontinued taking Xanax because he was bothered by these side effects. The most serious adverse effect of benzodiazepines is their potential for addiction. Approximately 40% of people who use benzodiazepines for 6 months or more will exhibit symptoms of withdrawal if the medication is discontinued (Shaner, 2000).

Controlled-outcome studies indicate that cognitive-behavioral procedures and medication are effective forms of treatment for the anxiety disorders (Roy-Byrne et al., 2005). One report compared several forms of intervention for panic-disorder patients (Barlow, Gorman, Shear, & Woods, 2000). More than 300 clients were randomly assigned to one of five forms of treatment: cognitive-behavior therapy (CBT); antidepressant medication (imipramine); CBT plus medication; placebo medication; or CBT plus placebo. Clients were treated weekly for 3 months. Those who improved during this period were then treated once a month for 6 more months and followed up 6 months after treatment had been terminated. Medication and CBT were both found to be superior to placebo by the end of treatment. Panic attacks were significantly reduced in both groups. There were no significant differences between CBT alone and medication alone, although more patients dropped out of the medication group because of unpleasant side effects. Overall, the results of this study suggest that cognitive-behavioral procedures and antidepressant medication are effective forms of intervention for patients with panic disorders.

Discussion Questions

1. Dennis met the diagnostic criteria for both panic disorder and GAD. Did he, in fact, suffer from two separate disorders? What does your answer say about the issue of comorbidity in the current classification system?

2. What is the difference between the anxiety experienced by a person who is having a panic attack and the anxiety of a person who engages in excessive worrying? Consider the intensity of the anxiety, its duration, and its focus.

3. During his first few meetings with his therapist, Dennis was self-conscious and defensive. How could his behavior have interfered with the development of the therapeutic relationship and with the initial assessment of his problems? What skills did the therapist need to use to avoid potential problems?

4. Should a therapist actively encourage a patient to take medication that has been shown to be effective, even if the patient has strong objections to the use of a pharmacological approach to treatment?

CHAPTER 3

Posttraumatic Stress Disorder: Rape Trauma

Jocelyn Rowley, a 20-year-old single woman, was a sophomore at a midwestern university. She had always been a good student, but her grades had fallen recently, and she was having trouble studying. Her academic difficulties, coupled with some problems with relationships and with sleeping, had finally led Jocelyn to see a therapist for the first time. Although she was afraid of being alone, she had no interest in her current friends or boyfriend. She told the therapist that when she was doing everyday things like reading a book, she sometimes was overcome by vivid images of violent events in which she was the victim of a mugging or an assault. These symptoms had begun rather suddenly, and together they made her afraid that she was losing her mind.

Most of Jocelyn's symptoms had begun about two months before she visited the university's counseling service. Since then, she had been having nightmares almost every night about unfamiliar men in dark clothing trying to harm her. She was not having trouble falling asleep, but she was trying to stay awake to avoid the nightmares. During the day, if someone walked up behind her and tapped her unexpectedly on the shoulder, she would be extremely startled, to the point that her friends became offended by her reactions. When she was studying, especially if she was reading her English textbook, images of physical brutality would intrude on her thoughts and distract her. She had a great deal of difficulty concentrating on her schoolwork.

Jocelyn also reported problems with interpersonal relationships. She and her boyfriend had argued frequently in recent weeks, even though she could not identify any specific problems in their relationship. "I just get so angry at him," she told the therapist. Her boyfriend had complained that she was not emotionally invested in the relationship. He had also accused her of cheating on him, which she denied. These problems were understandably causing her boyfriend to distance himself from her. Unfortunately, his reaction made Jocelyn feel abandoned.

Jocelyn was afraid to walk alone to the library at night. She could not bring herself to ask anyone to walk with her because she didn't know if she could feel safe with anyone. Her inability to study in the library intensified her academic problems. Jocelyn's roommates had begun to complain that she was unusually sensitive to their teasing. They noticed that she cried frequently and at unexpected times.

In the course of the first few therapy sessions, the psychologist asked a number of questions about Jocelyn's life just prior to entering therapy. Because the symptoms had such a rapid onset, the therapist was looking for a specific stressful event that might have caused her symptoms. During these first few sessions, Jocelyn reported that she had begun to feel more and more dissociated from herself. She would catch a glimpse of herself in the mirror and think, "Is that me?" She would walk around in the winter weather with no gloves on and be relieved when her hands hurt from the cold, because "at least it's an indication that I'm alive."

After several sessions, Jocelyn mentioned to her therapist that she had been raped by the teaching assistant in her English literature course. The rape occurred 2 months before she entered therapy. Jocelyn seemed surprised when the therapist was interested in the event, saying "Oh, well, that's already taken care of. It didn't really affect me much at all." The therapist explained that serious trauma such as rape is rarely resolved by itself, and especially not quickly. When it became apparent that Jocelyn had not previously reported the rape to anyone else, her therapist strongly advised her to contact the police. She refused, citing a number of reasons, ranging from her conviction that no one would believe her (especially 2 months after the incident) to the fear of facing cross-examination and further humiliation. Without Jocelyn's consent, the therapist could not report the rape because the information she had obtained from Jocelyn was protected by confidentiality (the ethical obligation not to reveal private communications, in this case, between psychologist and client). There are some rare exceptions to this ethical principle. State laws require mental-health professionals to break confidentiality and report cases of child abuse. Psychologists are also required to report clients who are imminently dangerous to themselves or others. These exceptions did not apply to Jocelyn's situation.

Jocelyn gradually revealed the story of the rape over the next few sessions. She had needed help writing an English paper, and her T.A. had invited her to his house one night so that he could tutor her. When she arrived at the house, which he shared with several male graduate students, he was busy working. He left her alone in his room to study her English textbook. When he returned, he approached her from behind while she was reading and grabbed her. The T.A. forced her onto his bed and raped her. Jocelyn said that she had not struggled or fought physically because she was terrified and stunned at what was happening to her. She had protested verbally, saying, "No!" and, "Don't do this to me!" several times, but he ignored her earnest objections. She had been afraid to yell loudly because there were only other men in the house, and she was not sure whether or not they would help her.

After the rape, the T.A. walked Jocelyn back to her dorm and warned her not to tell anyone. She agreed at the time, thinking that if she never told anyone what had happened, she could effectively erase the event and prevent it from having a negative effect on her life. She went up to her dorm room and took an hour-long hot shower, trying to scrub away the effects of the rape. While describing these events to the therapist, Jocelyn shook and her voice was breathy. She kept saying, "You believe me, don't you?"

For several days after the rape occurred, Jocelyn believed that she had been able to keep it from affecting her everyday life. The more she tried not to think about it, however, the more times it came to mind. She began to feel stupid and guilty for having gone to a T.A.'s house in the first place, and because she had not been able to anticipate the rape, Jocelyn wondered whether her own behavior had contributed to the rape: Had she dressed in some way or said something that indicated a sexual invitation to him? She was ashamed that she was not strong enough to have prevented the rape or its negative consequences.

Jocelyn had initially believed that only one aspect of her life changed after the rape; she no longer attended discussion sections for her English course. Unfortunately, several other problems soon became evident. Her exaggerated startle response became more and more of a problem because her friends were puzzled by her intense reactions to their casual, friendly gestures. Frequent nightmares prevented her from getting any real sleep, and she was having trouble functioning academically. She had no further contact with her T.A. unless she saw him while walking across campus. When that happened, she would duck into a doorway to avoid him. She also began to withdraw from relationships with other people, especially her boyfriend. He responded to this retreat by pressuring her sexually. She no longer had any interest in sex and repeatedly rejected his physical advances. All these problems finally made Jocelyn believe that she was losing control of her feelings, and she decided to seek professional help.

Social History

Jocelyn had grown up in a small midwestern town 100 miles away from the university. She was the oldest of three children. Both of her parents were successful in their professional occupations, and they were involved in the community and their children's schools. Jocelyn had attended public schools and was mostly an A student. She was involved in several extracurricular activities. In high school, she had some trouble making friends, both because she was shy and because it was considered "nerdy" to be an A student. It wasn't until she enrolled at the university that she was able to form a relatively large peer group.

Jocelyn's parents were strict about dating and curfews. She had not been interested in attending large parties or drinking when she was in high school. She did have a boyfriend during her junior and senior years. They began dating when they were both 16 years old and became sexually involved a year later. That relationship had ended when they left their hometown to attend different colleges.

Jocelyn recalled that her high school boyfriend had occasionally pressured her into having sex when she thought it was too risky or when she was not interested. She denied having previously been a victim of sexual assault, although one incident she described did sound abusive to the therapist. When she was about 13 years old, Jocelyn went to a summer music camp to play the trombone, an instrument not usually played by a female. One day after rehearsal, the boys in her section ganged up on her, teasing her that "girls can't play trombones!" One boy began to wrestle with her and, in the melee, placed a finger inside her shorts into her vagina. Jocelyn remembered yelling at him. The boy let her go, and then all the boys ran away. Jocelyn had never viewed that event as being assaultive until she thought about it in reference to being raped.

Jocelyn's adjustment to college had been good; she made several friends, and most of her grades were good. She had never before sought psychological help. Jocelyn felt as if she had the world under control until she was raped by someone she knew.

Conceptualization and Treatment

As Jocelyn began to address her anxiety symptoms, additional problems were caused by other people's reactions to the account of her rape. These difficulties kept the focus of treatment away from her primary anxiety symptoms. After telling her psychologist that she had been raped, Jocelyn began to tell other people in her life, including her boyfriend and her roommates. Her roommates were understandably frightened by what had happened to her, and they tried to divorce themselves from the possibility that it might happen to them. They did this by either accusing her of lying or pointing out differences between them: "I never would have gone to a T.A.'s house," or, "You've slept with more people than me; he must have sensed that," or, "You didn't look beat up; you must not have fought back hard enough." The absence of meaningful support from her friends fueled Jocelyn's progressive withdrawal. Her anxiety symptoms became more pronounced, and she also became depressed.

Her boyfriend's unfortunate and self-centered reaction to the description of her rape quickly led to the end of their relationship. He sought help to cope with his own feelings about her rape by talking to some mutual friends. Jocelyn had specifically asked him not to discuss the attack with other people she knew. Jocelyn's general feelings of being out of control of her life were exacerbated by her apparent inability to contain the spread of gossip about her assault. One specific event, which would have been trivial under ordinary circumstances, led to a series of heated exchanges between Jocelyn and her boyfriend. He approached her from behind and playfully put his arms around her. When she jumped and screamed in fright, he tightened his grip, preventing her escape.

After arguing about this incident a number of times, they decided not to see each other anymore.

Jocelyn finally approached her English professor and told her that she had been sexually assaulted by the T.A. The professor's reaction progressed from shock to outrage. She recommended that Jocelyn report the attack to the appropriate campus office. Unfortunately, Jocelyn still refused. She was not ready to report her attacker to the university or to press legal charges, in part because she felt that she could not bear being in the same room with him for any reason. The professor did assign Jocelyn to a different T.A. so that she could continue to go to discussions for the class. She also told Jocelyn that she was uncomfortable letting the matter drop. She asked whether Jocelyn would mind if she discussed the situation with the dean and with campus police. Jocelyn agreed reluctantly, only after the professor promised not to use Jocelyn's name in any of these conversations.

Treatment during this time focused primarily on giving Jocelyn an opportunity to express her considerable anger and frustration about her situation. Jocelyn frequently railed to her therapist against the unfairness of the situation. For example, to deal with her fear of walking alone after dark, she was trying to find someone to walk with her. It seemed bitterly ironic, however, that she wanted a friend to protect her from violence from strangers. It was, after all, someone she knew rather well who had raped her.

Jocelyn also felt a great deal of guilt over not having been able to prevent her assault. Perhaps she hadn't fought hard enough. Maybe she had unknowingly flirted with him. Did he assume that she knew he was inviting her to his house for sex? Was she a fool for not having recognized that implicit invitation? She also felt guilty about the effect of her situation on her boyfriend and roommates. Was she responsible for the fact that she had made them fearful and resentful?

In one session, the therapist pointed out that the intrusive images that Jocelyn now experienced while reading her English textbook might result from the fact that she had been reading that textbook when her attacker grabbed her from behind. Jocelyn was relieved to hear this explanation because she had worried that she really was going crazy. This insight did not immediately diminish the frequency of her intrusive images, however, and she remained frustrated and depressed.

By this time, Jocelyn's nightmares had become increasingly severe. The content of her dreams was more and more obviously rape related. The dream would begin with Jocelyn in a crowded parking lot. Then a shadowy male in dark clothing would approach her, tell her he wanted to rape her, and proceed to attack her. She remembered trying to fight off the attack in her dream, but her limbs felt as if they were in thick glue and her struggles were ineffective. The other people in the parking lot stood watching, clapping and cheering for her assailant. Jocelyn would wake up in the middle of the room, crouched as if awaiting attack. These experiences terrified Jocelyn, and they also frightened her roommates.

The therapist's treatment strategy moved to a focused, cognitive-behavioral intervention that had two main parts. The first part was to address the cognitive processes that prolong a maladaptive view of traumatic events. Specific procedures included self-monitoring of activities, graded task assignments (such as going out alone), and modification of maladaptive thoughts regarding the event (such as guilt and self-blame) (Yadin & Foa, 2007). This part of the treatment procedure had actually begun as soon as Jocelyn entered therapy. It was continued in parallel with the second part of the therapy, which is based on prolonged exposure.

In prolonged exposure, the victim reexperiences the original trauma in a safe situation to decrease slowly the emotional intensity associated with memory of the event. This step is based on the notion that repeated presentation of an aversive stimulus will lead to habituation (defined as the process by which a person's response to the same stimulus lessens with repeated presentations). Jocelyn had, of course, experienced many fleeting and terrifying images of the rape during the weeks after it happened. This form of "reliving" the traumatic experience is symptomatic of the disorder. It presumably does not lead to improvement in the person's condition because the experiences are too intensely frightening and too short-lived to allow negative emotions to be processed completely. In the therapy, Jocelyn was asked to relive the rape scene in her imagination. She described it aloud to the therapist in the present tense. The therapist helped Jocelyn repeat this sequence many times during each session. The sessions were recorded on audiotape, and Jocelyn was required to listen to the tape at least once every day.

As the end of the semester approached, Jocelyn was able to resume her studies. This was an important sign of improvement. Flunking out of school would have been the ultimate proof that the rape had permanently affected her life, and she struggled not to let that happen. She ended the semester by passing three of her four classes, including English. Therapy was terminated somewhat prematurely after 16 sessions (twice weekly for 8 weeks) because the semester was ending, and Jocelyn was going home for the summer. The psychologist could not convince her to continue therapy during the summer, although she still suffered from occasional nightmares and other symptoms. Jocelyn refused to see a therapist in the summer because she would have to tell her parents, and she was not ready to do that.

A follow-up call to Jocelyn when she returned the following spring, after having taken a semester off, revealed that Jocelyn had finally told her parents about the rape. They were much more supportive than Jocelyn had anticipated. She had continued treatment with another therapist, and her symptoms had diminished slowly over time. She now had nightmares only on rare occasions, and they were usually triggered by a specific event, such as viewing a sexually violent movie or when someone physically restrained her in a joking manner. Jocelyn decided not to return to therapy at the university's counseling service, saying that she was tired of being preoccupied by the rape. She believed that it was time for her to concentrate on her studies.

Ten-Year Follow-Up

Jocelyn performed well in school and on the job in the years following her rape. She completed college and then earned her master's degree in library science. She enjoyed her work as a librarian at a small college in her hometown. Her social life recovered more slowly. Jocelyn experienced residual symptoms of posttraumatic stress disorder (PTSD) intermittently for several years. She no longer met the formal diagnostic criteria for PTSD, however, because her symptoms were not sufficiently frequent or severe. In the following pages, we describe her experiences during this time.

Jocelyn still suffered from occasional nightmares if she watched a movie or a TV show with a scene containing sexual violence. Rape scenes did not have to be overtly graphic to cause a nightmare. In fact, scenes in which a rape was alluded to rather than depicted on screen were just as disturbing to Jocelyn. She tried to avoid movies or TV shows with sexual violence. This decision might be interpreted as avoiding stimuli associated with her rape trauma (a symptom of PTSD). Her avoidance was also the product of Jocelyn's conscious decision not to support the segment of the entertainment industry that profits from depicting such scenes.

Other examples of lingering mild PTSD symptoms included hypervigilance and increased startle response. Jocelyn was hypervigilant in situations that might present a threat to her own safety. For example, when speaking with a male colleague in his office, she was often concerned about the distance to the door and the proximity of assistance if she called for it. Of course, we all protect ourselves by being cautious and alert. But Jocelyn found herself worrying too much about potential threats when none existed. This hypervigilance occasionally intruded on Jocelyn's professional career. It could make her appear unnecessarily suspicious and aloof to her coworkers, especially the men. Jocelyn also continued to be jumpy if someone touched her from behind, though the degree of her startle response had diminished greatly since college.

The residual effects of the rape trauma could also be seen in the way that Jocelyn struggled to control her temper, which had become volatile. When provoked, the intensity of her subjective response was often out of proportion to the situation. Events that would annoy or irritate most people (such as being treated rudely by a boss) would cause her to become enraged. Because she knew that the intensity of her anger was often inappropriate, she almost always suppressed it. Jocelyn was afraid of what might happen if she acted on her feelings. Suppressing her anger interfered with her ability to have discussions or arguments with other people. If Jocelyn was involved in a discussion, she would often concede a point with which she disagreed to avoid "blowing up." She became unnecessarily timid about stating her opinions.

Jocelyn's relationships with men were also affected by the lingering impact of her rape. For a period of time in her early 20s (immediately following the rape), Jocelyn avoided intimate contact with men entirely. She referred to this time as her "celibacy" years. Jocelyn avoided intimacy with men to sort through her own feelings about herself, her remaining guilt surrounding her rape, and her feelings about men. Several young men found her attractive during this time (perhaps because she was uninterested in them), but she rejected their overtures. Jocelyn's parents and friends were afraid that surviving the rape had "turned her into a lesbian" because she was not interested in dating men. Perhaps in rebellion against her parents' concerns, Jocelyn joined a women's poetry cooperative and a women's music group that included women of all sexual orientations. She found this community to be warm and supportive. She made several close female friends, but she never felt any sexual attraction to them. This was a difficult time in which Jocelyn forged new friendships and also reestablished relationships with her previous social support network whenever possible.

When Jocelyn eventually began dating again, she seemed to choose relationships that allowed her to avoid emotional intimacy. She pursued men who were inappropriate for her (such as someone who lived a thousand miles away, or someone who was already married). Her affairs were brief and even exciting, but they did not result in significant, long-term relationships. At times, she could not imagine having a meaningful emotional relationship with a partner. Establishing clear consent to have intercourse prior to engaging in any type of sexual foreplay was of ultimate importance to her. Therefore, her sexual relationships tended to be "all or nothing"; she either had intercourse with the man she was dating or did not share any physical intimacy at all. Jocelyn realized later that she probably conducted her relationships in this fashion so that decisions of consent were as unambiguous and unemotional as possible.

Recognition of these ongoing difficulties led Jocelyn to decide to go back into therapy with a local psychologist. She had just met a new boyfriend and seemed to sense something special about this relationship from the beginning. Jocelyn wanted to work on issues involving intimacy, trust, and sexuality, in the hope that progress in these areas would help her forge a better relationship with her new boyfriend (who did eventually become her husband).

During this therapy, Jocelyn acknowledged that she felt very close to her boyfriend, but she had a great deal of difficulty learning to trust him. She found it hard to believe him when he said that he loved her. They were also having some trouble in their sexual relationship. Many forms of touching, if the touch was not gentle enough, were upsetting to Jocelyn. If her partner accidentally did anything that caused her discomfort during physical intimacy, Jocelyn would think to herself: "This is it. He's been good until now, but now he's going to hurt me." Because of these irrational thoughts, Jocelyn frequently interrupted sexual contact with her boyfriend abruptly. He found these reactions confusing, and their relationship was becoming strained.

Jocelyn's therapist used cognitive therapy to address these problems. Her goal was to eliminate the systematic biases in thinking that were responsible for Jocelyn's maladaptive feelings and behavior. She treated Jocelyn's distorted patterns of thinking and her biased conclusions as being testable hypotheses. She used their therapy sessions as an opportunity to identify, test, and challenge these hypotheses. Several strategies were employed. Her distorted thoughts were either *decatastrophized* (developing what-if strategies to deal with feared consequences), *reattributed* (considering alternative causes of events), or *redefined* (changing the perspective of the problem so that the person feels some control over it). For example, Jocelyn's reactions to painful stimuli during physical intimacy with her boyfriend were reattributed (Could your discomfort be the result of something other than his desire to hurt you?). Her fears during normal verbal arguments with men were decatastrophized (What is the worst thing that could really happen?).

Therapy also included some elements of anger-management training (Novaco & Taylor, 2006). In the initial phase of this process, Jocelyn learned to monitor her own anger and the situations that triggered it. Applied relaxation was employed to help her learn to regulate arousal in situations that were potentially provocative. The same cognitive-restructuring procedures that had been used to address her anxiety and fear were now used to help her modify distorted thoughts and misinterpretations of events that sometimes led to inappropriate anger. Finally, the therapist helped her to rehearse assertive communication skills that would allow Jocelyn to express herself clearly in situations that had previously led to withdrawal or the suppression of her true feelings.

Cognitive therapy and anger-management training helped Jocelyn improve her communication skills with others, including her boyfriend, as well as people at work. Her mood was more stable, and she felt better about herself. She also developed a deeper, more meaningful relationship with her boyfriend. They were married soon after the therapy was completed.

The fact that Jocelyn's PTSD symptoms persisted for several years after the rape may seem discouraging. Nevertheless, beyond her subtle relationship problems, the long-term impact of the rape was not devastating. Jocelyn was able to complete school, have a successful career, regain closeness with family and friends, and (with a little additional help in therapy) form an intimate and lasting relationship with a loving partner. She occasionally mourns the loss of her 20s because her relationships were so chaotic, but she also has many important plans and hopes for the future.

Discussion

Rape is an alarmingly frequent problem on college campuses and in other areas of our society (Elliott, Mok, & Briere, 2004). Consider, for example, the results of the National Health and Social Life Survey, the first large-scale examination of sexual behavior in the United States since the Kinsey reports (Laumann, Gagnon, Michael, & Michaels, 1994). In this national probability sample of women between the ages of 18 and 59, 22% reported that they had been forced by a man to do something sexually that they did not want to do. Only 4% of these coercive sexual acts were committed by a stranger.

Unfortunately, most rapes are never reported. On college campuses, less than 5% of rapes are reported to police (Cole, 2006). Victims like Jocelyn, whose immediate reactions to the rape included intense fear, helplessness, avoidance, and emotional detachment, may be particularly unlikely to contact legal authorities.

Should other people have reported Jocelyn's rape when they heard about it? Her therapist was clearly prevented from filing a complaint by the ethical principle of confidentiality. If her therapist had reported the rape against Jocelyn's objections, the therapist would have violated her trust and seriously damaged their therapeutic relationship. Her English professor, on the other hand, was not strictly bound by this professional obligation. Policies guiding the behavior of faculty members in this circumstance currently vary from one university to the next and are the topic of heated debate. Some might argue that Jocelyn's professor should have reported the rapist to police or campus administrators, even if it meant acting against Jocelyn's wishes. One justification would be to protect other students. Other people might believe that Jocelyn's decision not to report the rape should be respected so that she would not feel even more helpless or out of control. Would she be exposed to further danger if charges were filed without her knowledge? What would happen if the rapist tried to retaliate, and Jocelyn did not know that he had been confronted by authorities? What action could be taken against him without Jocelyn's direct testimony, and how would his right to due process be protected? These are all difficult questions. We encourage people to seek advice on these matters from local police officials and from sexual assault resource agencies. Just as many state laws now require therapists to break confidentiality to warn potential victims of violence, new regulations may be passed to deal with the plight of rape victims and the need to report this heinous crime.

One frequent outcome of rape is posttraumatic stress disorder (PTSD). PTSD is included in the *Diagnostic and Statistical Manual of Mental Disorders* (*DSM-IV-TR*; APA, 2000, pp. 467–468) under the general heading of Anxiety Disorders. PTSD is defined by the following criteria:

1. The person has been exposed to a traumatic event in which both of the following were present:
    a. The person experienced, witnessed, or was confronted with an event or events that involved actual or threatened death or serious injury, or a threat to the physical integrity of self or others.
    b. The person's response involved intense fear, helplessness, or horror.

2. The traumatic event is persistently reexperienced in one (or more) of the following ways:
   a. Recurrent and intrusive distressing recollections of the event, including images, thoughts, or perceptions
   b. Recurrent distressing dreams of the event
   c. Acting or feeling as if the traumatic event were recurring
   d. Intense psychological distress at exposure to cues that symbolize or resemble an aspect of the traumatic event
   e. Physiological reactivity on exposure to cues that symbolize or resemble an aspect of the traumatic event
3. Persistent avoidance of stimuli associated with the trauma and numbing of general responsiveness (not present before the trauma), as indicated by three (or more) of the following:
   a. Efforts to avoid thoughts, feelings, or conversation associated with the trauma
   b. Efforts to avoid activities, places, or people that arouse recollections of the trauma
   c. Inability to recall an important aspect of the trauma
   d. Markedly diminished interest or participation in significant activities
   e. Feeling of detachment or estrangement from others
   f. Restricted range of affect (such as being unable to have loving feelings)
   g. Sense of a foreshortened future (e.g., does not expect to have a career, marriage, children, or a normal life span)
4. Persistent symptoms of increased arousal (not present before the trauma), as indicated by two (or more) of the following:
   a. Difficulty falling asleep or staying asleep
   b. Irritability or outbursts of anger
   c. Difficulty concentrating
   d. Hypervigilance
   e. Exaggerated startle response
5. Duration of the disturbance is more than 1 month.
6. The disturbance causes clinically significant distress or impairment in social, occupational, or other important areas of functioning.

The rape and the fear surrounding it were clearly responsible for provoking the symptoms that Jocelyn experienced. One of the key elements of PTSD is the recurrence or reexperience of stimuli associated with the event. Jocelyn initially experienced this symptom in the form of intrusive, violent images that came to mind whenever she opened her English textbook. Her recurrent nightmares were another symptom linked to reexperiencing the event. Whenever one of these images or dreams occurred, Jocelyn would become extremely fearful and distract herself (escape) as quickly as possible. This type of reexperiencing of the trauma should be distinguished from the procedures used in cognitive-behavioral treatment. The latter is designed to ensure prolonged exposure in the context of a safe and supportive environment, which allows the person's intense emotional response to diminish gradually.

Avoidance of rape-related stimuli has been shown to differentiate rape victims with PTSD from those rape victims who did not develop PTSD. Jocelyn's avoidance was manifested by withdrawal from her friends, her decision not to report the rape, and perhaps her reluctance to return to therapy for several years. Her feelings of dissociation, such as asking, "Is that me?" when looking in the mirror, were another sign of Jocelyn's avoidance.

Jocelyn's increased arousal was consistent with the *DSM-IV-TR* (APA, 2000) description of PTSD. Her exaggerated startle response, irritability in interpersonal relationships, difficulty studying, and sleep disturbance are all signs of the heightened arousal that is associated with this disorder. The length of time that had elapsed since the initial appearance of her symptoms and the obvious impact that these symptoms had on her adjustment also indicate that Jocelyn met the formal diagnostic criteria for PTSD.

The term posttraumatic stress disorder was introduced to the formal diagnostic manual with the publication of *DSM-III* in 1980 (APA, 1980). The concept of a severe and maladaptive reaction to a traumatic event was recognized many years earlier, but it was described in different terms. The disorder had been observed among soldiers returning from World War II and was known as Traumatic Neurosis of War in *DSM-I* (APA, 1952). The category was dropped in the next edition of the diagnostic manual, *DSM-II* (APA, 1968), even though the phenomenon had been well documented in combat veterans. *DSM-III* (APA, 1980) returned the concept to the manual and listed it with other types of anxiety disorders. This version of the manual expanded the range of possible stressors from a limited focus on combat experiences to the consideration of any traumatic event that was "outside the range of usual human experience" (APA, 1980, p. 247). In other words, people who had been victims of a crime or survivors of a natural disaster might also develop the symptoms of PTSD.

Following the publication of *DSM-III*, clinicians reported that many victims of rape suffered from the symptoms of PTSD. There were problems, however, with the way in which the disorder was described in the diagnostic manual. For example, epidemiological studies indicated that rape was not "outside the range of usual human experience." Rape is not an uncommon event. The *DSM-III* (APA, 1980) criteria also put the therapist in the difficult position of having to make a judgment about the expected or usual impact of an environmental event. The authors of *DSM-IV* (APA, 1994) corrected some of these problems when they revised the criteria for PTSD. The traumatic event is now described as one in which the person experienced a threat of death or serious injury and responded with intense fear. This description clearly includes rape as a traumatic event.

The classification of PTSD has been criticized on a number of grounds (McNally, 2003). Some scientists suggest that PTSD may not be a mental disorder because it is a reaction to an event that would be distressing for almost anyone. Thus, perhaps PTSD should be separated from anxiety disorders and placed in an etiologically based category along with other disorders that follow traumatic events. This grouping would include adjustment disorders and enduring personality changes that may follow trauma. This approach is currently used in the *International Classification of Diseases* (*ICD*; World Health Organization, 1990).

Further questions about the classification of PTSD as an anxiety disorder involve the nature of its core symptoms (Friedman, 2009; Zohar, Juven-Wetzler, Myers, & Fostick, 2008). Some symptoms in PTSD do involve anxiety, such as recurrent, intrusive images; avoidance; hypervigilance; and startle responses. These are similar to the symptoms of obsessive-compulsive disorder (OCD), phobic disorder, and generalized anxiety disorder (GAD). But PTSD also shares many symptoms with dissociative disorders such as amnesia, fugue, and multiple personality. These include flashbacks, memory impairment, and body dissociation. These classification issues will need to be addressed in future versions of the DSM.

It is difficult to estimate the true prevalence of PTSD from epidemiological studies because the disorder is precipitated by traumatic events (Keane, Marshall, & Taft, 2006). These events may be personal, affecting one person at a time, as in the case of rape, but they may also be events that affect a large number of people simultaneously, as in the case of a hurricane. How many people in the general population are exposed to traumatic events that might trigger PTSD? The National Comorbidity Study (NCS) found that 60% of men and 51% of women reported at least one such traumatic event at some time during their lives (Kessler et al., 1999). Many of these people had been exposed to more than one traumatic event. The most frequently reported traumatic events were witnessing someone being badly injured or killed, being involved in a natural disaster, being involved in a life-threatening accident, and being the victim of an assault or robbery. These alarming numbers indicate that traumatic events are unfortunately a relatively common experience in our society.

The overall rate of PTSD in the general population is higher for women (10%) than for men (5%) (Kilpatrick & Acierno, 2003). This pattern may be surprising in light of the fact that men are somewhat more likely to be exposed to traumatic events. How can it be explained? The NCS investigators suggest that, in comparison to men, women may be more likely to be exposed to traumatic events that are psychologically catastrophic. Rape is one example. Women are much more likely to be raped than men, and the rate of PTSD (for both male and female victims) is much higher following rape than following any other type of traumatic event. What are the distinguishing features of rape that account for its devastating impact? In comparison to many other traumatic events, rape involves directed, focused, intentional harm that is associated with the most intimate interpersonal act (Calhoun & Wilson, 2000).

The prevalence rate for symptoms of PTSD is highest immediately after the traumatic event. Most rape victims (95%) show symptoms of PTSD within 1 or

2 weeks of the crime (although the person cannot technically meet the *DSM-IV-TR* criteria until after the symptoms have been present for at least 1 month). The rate tapers off over time, with 48% of the victims meeting the criteria for PTSD 3 months after the rape. For many people, PTSD can become a chronic condition (Kuwert et al., 2010). Jocelyn certainly experienced some symptoms of PTSD for many years, even though her overall condition had improved, and she no longer met the formal criteria for the disorder.

Etiological Considerations

Not all victims of trauma develop PTSD. What determines whether or not a victim will develop PTSD following a traumatic event? There do not appear to be systematic differences between crime victims who develop PTSD and those who do not in terms of demographic characteristics such as race, employment, education, and income. One common line of investigation is whether or not rape victims who developed PTSD had different premorbid personality characteristics or a different pattern of adjustment that may have contributed to developing PTSD. Some evidence suggests a relationship between depression prior to the crime, the level of stress associated with the crime (e.g., an attack with life threat, actual injury, or completed rape), and the probability of developing PTSD. If the victim is depressed before the assault, and if the victim is assaulted in a particularly severe manner, then she is more likely to suffer from PTSD following the crime in comparison to victims of lower stress crimes (Bonanno, Galea, Bucciarelli, & Vlahov, 2007; Ozer & Weiss, 2004).

Cognitive factors may also influence whether a rape victim will develop PTSD. A perceived life threat may be present even in situations that are not overtly violent. In fact, the severity of perceived life threat, rather than actual life threat, may be the best predictor of whether a person will develop PTSD (Basoglu & Paker, 1995). The person's beliefs about whether she or he can control future events are also important. Victims who perceive (perhaps with justification) that future negative events are uncontrollable are much more likely to have severe PTSD symptoms than those victims who perceive some future control (Basoglu & Mineka, 1992). This indication is particularly important when viewed in light of the fact that many women who have been raped report that they expect to be raped again.

Risk for persistent problems following a traumatic event is also increased by avoidance of emotional feelings and rumination about the traumatic event. Victims who suppress their feelings of anger may have an increased risk of developing PTSD after a rape (Foa & Riggs, 1995). Intense anger may interfere with the modification of the traumatic memory (to make it more congruent with previous feelings of safety). Anger also inhibits fear, so the victim cannot habituate to the fear response. Jocelyn's ongoing problems with the experience of anger may have helped to prolong her other symptoms of PTSD, such as nightmares and hyperarousal.

Protective factors such as the person's level of social support may help to prevent or limit the development of PTSD and other psychological consequences of rape (Andrews, Brewin, & Rose, 2003; Keane, Fisher, Krinsley, & Niles, 1994). Unfortunately, simply having a social support network may not be enough. The tendency of the victim to withdraw and avoid situations is an inherent part of the disorder. This avoidance may mean that victims do not take advantage of social support, even if it is available to them. In Jocelyn's case, the reactions of her friends often led to further problems and made her feel less in control and more alienated from other people. This kind of problem may help to explain why some studies do not find that social support serves as a protective factor.

The moderating effects of social support may also be complex. Consider, for example, the evidence regarding traumatic stress responses among survivors of torture (Başoğlu et al., 1994). Those victims with extensive social support networks were less likely to be anxious or depressed, but social support did not specifically reduce the frequency or severity of PTSD symptoms. This pattern suggests that the needs of trauma survivors must be addressed broadly. In other words, factors that alleviate some of the more general consequences of exposure to trauma may not have a direct impact on the more focal symptoms of PTSD, such as avoidance and numbing, reexperiencing, and increased arousal.

Attitudes that society holds toward victims of sexual assault are also important in relation to social support (Ullman & Filipas, 2001). Some people apparently believe that certain women somehow deserved to be raped. These women undoubtedly receive less social support than other victims. People may also be more supportive after hearing the details of an assault that was clearly non-consensual—one in which the victim violently fought back when attacked by a stranger—than when the circumstances surrounding the assault were more ambiguous (the woman's protests were verbal and not physical). Myths about rape, especially about acquaintance rape, may decrease the amount of social support received by victims of these crimes.

Jocelyn's case also highlights another frequent consequence of rape trauma. Many victims develop sexual dysfunctions. These problems include decreased motivation for sexual activity, arousal difficulties, and inhibited orgasm (Gillock, Zayfert, Hegel, & Ferguson, 2005). Their onset is undoubtedly mediated by a complex interaction of emotional responses to the rape, including anxiety, depression, and guilt. They can be exacerbated by interpersonal difficulties with, and lack of support from, sexual partners, as illustrated by Jocelyn's boyfriend at the time of her rape. Sexual difficulties may be an important consideration in planning treatment for some victims of sexual trauma.

Treatment

The most effective forms of treatment for PTSD involve the use of either cognitive-behavior therapy or antidepressant medication, alone or in combination (Foa, Keane, Friedman, & Cohen, 2009; Forbes et al., 2010). The psychological intervention that has been used and tested most extensively is prolonged exposure. This procedure starts with initial sessions of information gathering. These are followed by several sessions devoted to reliving the rape scene in the client's imagination. Clients are instructed to relive the assault by imagining it and describing it to the therapist, as many times as possible, during the 60-minute sessions. Sessions are recorded, and patients are instructed to listen to the tape at least once a day. Patients are also required to participate in situations outside the therapy sessions that are deemed to be safe but also elicit fear or avoidance responses. An adapted form of this treatment was used in Jocelyn's therapy.

Cognitive therapy is another effective psychological approach to the treatment of PTSD. It can be used on its own or in combination with prolonged exposure. Perceived threat, more than actual threat, is a better predictor of many of the symptoms of PTSD. Cognitive therapy can address maladaptive ways of perceiving events in the person's environment. It can also be used to change unrealistic assumptions and beliefs that lead to negative emotions such as guilt. For example, in Jocelyn's case, her therapist might have used cognitive-therapy procedures to reduce her feelings of guilt about the assault and its consequences (i.e., blaming herself for the rape). Cognitive therapy and prolonged exposure are both effective and approximately equal in their effects on reducing symptoms of PTSD (Bradley, Greene, Russ, Dutra, & Westen, 2005).

Various types of antidepressant medication are also effective forms of treatment for PTSD (Osterman, Erdos, Oldham, & Ivkovic, 2011). Carefully controlled outcome studies indicate that selective serotonin reuptake inhibitors, such as sertraline (Zoloft) and paroxetine (Paxil), lead to a reduction in PTSD symptoms for many patients within a period of 6 weeks. In actual practice, cognitive-behavior therapy is often combined with the use of medication.

Final Comments

We have used the term *victim* rather than *survivor* to describe a person who experienced a traumatic event. This choice was made primarily because *victim* is the term used in the scientific literature on PTSD. We also want to point out, however, that many rape victims prefer to think of themselves as survivors to enhance their sense of control over events in their environments. Further information and resources are also available in Robin Warshaw's book, *I Never Called It Rape* (1994). Her descriptions are less technical than this case, and they may provide additional sources of support.

Discussion Questions

1. Discuss the issues surrounding Jocelyn's reluctance to report her rape. Should her therapist have reported it to the police without her patient's consent? Was there a better way for the English professor to handle the situation?

2. How did Jocelyn's friends respond to her problems? Did they help the situation or make it worse? Is there anything that they could have done that would have been more beneficial to her?

3. Do you think that a person can develop PTSD after witnessing an assault, a bad accident, or some other kind of traumatic event (that happened to someone else)? Or does PTSD only occur in people who are directly the victims of trauma? What kind of evidence would be needed to answer this question empirically?

4. Do you think that PTSD should be classified as a form of anxiety disorder? Should it be included with the dissociative disorders? Why?

CHAPTER 4

Hypertension in an African American Man

John Williams had been complaining to his wife of dizziness, fatigue, and occasional light-headedness that almost caused him to faint one day at the water cooler in the law office where he worked downtown. His boss had been after him for weeks to see a physician, but John had stubbornly refused and felt angry that his boss was being condescending. He was frightened, though, because he felt something must be wrong.

His first clear knowledge of having hypertension, or high blood pressure, came during a visit to his dentist. Before taking X-rays, the dental assistant wound a blood pressure cuff around John's right arm, pumped it full of air until the blood stopped flowing, and then slowly released the valve, noting when the first and the last sounds of the pulse could be heard through the stethoscope pressed to the vein in his arm beneath the cuff. Alarmed at the reading—165/110—she took the pressure reading again after doing the X-rays and found it to be almost exactly the same. She tried to smile pleasantly and reassuringly, but found this difficult, especially when she noticed John's worried expression.

He did not ask about the blood pressure reading until he was sitting across from the dentist in the consulting room to discuss treatment plans. His dentist asked how he had been feeling lately, whether he had been feeling tired, irritable, or under pressure. John searched his dentist's face for some hint of what was going on, but he already knew that his blood pressure must be much too high. Finally, he just asked for the numbers, thanked the dentist, and went home.

It took him 30 minutes to reach his condominium in the suburbs. As he unlocked the door, he wondered how, or whether, he would raise the issue with his wife. Although he wasn't a physician himself, he knew what high blood pressure might mean to a 40-year-old like himself, especially someone who was so driven to succeed professionally and financially. Certainly he would have to slow down and perhaps also take some medication. But what else, he wondered.

Social History

John Williams was the only child of an upper-middle-class African American family in Atlanta. His father was a successful attorney, and his mother was a high school music teacher. Life was sweet in his childhood, and he had many friends. Although he was raised in a segregated city, he seldom felt excluded from anything important. John was taught during countless dinnertime conversations that there were plenty of opportunities for success; he had superior intelligence, an engaging wit, and a degree of ambition that matched that of his hardworking father.

In high school, John excelled at everything he attempted. A straight-A student, he was also a varsity athlete in three sports, dated the most popular girls, and was senior class president. He graduated from high school during the middle 1950s, well before the Civil Rights Movement. John wanted to leave Georgia for college, and this created anxiety in John's mother and anticipatory pride in his father. Mr. Williams wanted his son to have a college education with "class," as he put it. With the encouragement of his guidance counselor and the urging of his father, John applied to several Ivy League schools. He was accepted at Harvard University.

Years later, John's college roommate, Bill, confided to him that a month before school started their freshman year, he had received a letter from the housing office indicating that he had been assigned to room with a Negro student, but only if he had no objection. Bill, a Jew from Brooklyn, New York, was outraged at the discrimination and prejudice of this inquiry. They had many discussions about the pressures on members of ethnic minority groups who tried to succeed in society, especially in the elite circles of a private, selective college.

One night, a handwritten invitation to join a fraternity was slipped under John's door. Fraternities at Harvard differed from their Greek-letter counterparts on other campuses in that they were not residential. All undergraduates were affiliated with a house, modeled after the "colleges" of Oxford and Cambridge, in which they lived and took all their meals. The fraternities operated outside the house system and were by invitation only. Some of them bore names of winged and sharp-toothed animals such as bats and wolves, others the more familiar Greek initials. John had felt sure that he would be excluded from these clubs, although he hated even thinking about it. Thinking implied that he cared, and to care about the clubs was to accord them a legitimacy and importance he desperately resisted. As he picked up the engraved envelope, he could feel the blood pound in his ears.

When he looked back on things, this single moment crystallized much of the conflict he felt about his blackness in a White world. John knew he and his race had come far from the days when a fair-skinned youngster might hope to "pass" for White. He had grown up proud of the fact that he was African American and felt that whatever barriers there might be in succeeding in a White society could not outweigh his self-respect. But as he lingered over breakfast coffee with Bill the morning the invitation arrived, he felt it was strange that one of the prestigious clubs wanted him as a member. Bill had an uneasy feeling about it all, but he kept it to himself, wondering whether he was just jealous that he had not been invited.

John agonized all day over whether to attend the reception for newly solicited members. He was tempted to call his parents, but what would he tell them, and how? Was there something to celebrate? Would his father smile quietly to himself as he heard the news, confirming his own good judgment in sending his son to one of the bastions of eastern elitism? In the end, John did not call. He feared that his father would either congratulate him on the invitation or chide him for even considering it. No way to win, he told himself. At some level he knew that it was his own conflict he was wrestling with, not his father's reaction.

The day of his initiation, John awoke with a screaming headache. He took three aspirins—a habit he had gotten into since coming to college—and told himself to stop worrying about the party that evening. Perhaps he need not have worried. The welcome he received seemed genuine. And yet he could not shake the feeling that his new "brothers" were being nicer to him than they were to the other initiates, too nice somehow. His wineglass was never empty, always filled by a brother who, it struck John, smiled a bit too ingratiatingly. In fact, it seemed to him that his new friends must have suffered from aching mouths from the broad smiles they wore whenever they talked to him. He tried to reassure himself that the cordiality was real, and maybe it was. The problem, he knew, was that he did not really know, nor could he devise a practical way to find out.

His membership in the club turned out to be a boon to his social standing but an emotional disaster. Headaches and feelings of pressure in the brain were more regularly part of his existence than ever before. He hated himself for even being in the club, yet he prided himself on being the only African American member. He was furious at the fact that so few Jews were members and was also suspicious that there were no other African Americans, but he found the young men in the club congenial and enjoyable to spend time with, and he did experience a thrill whenever he donned the club necktie. His friends from the club were certainly no less bright than his other classmates, no less interested in abstract ideas and "deep" conversations over sherry after dinner. But the clubs were by nature exclusionary, and John was coming to realize that he might be seen as the quintessential Uncle Tom. He began to think of himself as the "club nigger."

His anger at himself and at his brothers grew to an intensity that was frightening. To Bill, in whom he confided his doubts, fears, guilt, and rage, there seemed to be no way for John to win. To express his concerns to his club brothers seemed out of the question. But not to do so, at least to one of them, had begun to make the thought of going to the handsome Georgian building for the evening a challenge, almost a dare. He dreaded the possibility of someone making a racist remark. How should he react? He had learned to let it pass, but the muscle tension that mounted in his body told him this was not the best thing for him to do. Once a club member used the word *niggardly*, and he felt himself blush. How infantile to react that way, he told himself. And yet, maybe the word was used to taunt him. But how inane to think that. Sure, Uncle Tom, he concluded.

The 4 years of college passed quickly. As his family and friends expected, John did very well academically and also earned a varsity letter in baseball. He was admitted to a first-rate law school, although John's problem by this time was his uncertainty as to whether he had been admitted solely on his academic merits, or whether the several prestigious schools, like the club, wanted him primarily for his color. And so his internal conflicts continued through law school. By this time, they took the form of John's having to excel to what even his ambitious father regarded to be an unreasonable degree. John just had to prove he was good enough, indeed, that he was the best.

John became engaged to an African American woman from a prominent family, but the joys of the relationship were dulled by his relentless drive for excellence and perfection. One major change was that his problems with hypertension were now impossible to hide. She insisted that he have a complete physical examination, something he had consciously avoided since entering college. The reading was 130/85, something the doctor called "high normal," but high enough to cause concern because he was a young man and in very good physical condition. His fiancée was convinced that John's grim pursuit of straight A's, law review, and all the rest were the cause. But she did not know the reasons behind his near-obsessive push.

John graduated at the top of his law school class. It was now the middle 1960s, and the developing social turmoil surrounding Vietnam and the Civil Rights Movement affected him deeply. On one hand, he felt that he should be out protesting, but his studies and his new job at a top law firm took precedence. He tried to assuage his guilt by donating money to civil rights groups, but it did not seem to help. He had cast his lot with the White world, he told himself, and his wife and his own family back in Atlanta supported that decision. Middle- and upper-middle-class professional African Americans had their role to play, his father continually reminded him, and who could better play that role than him? The sense he had that it was, indeed, a role turned out to be important in the psychotherapy he began after the alarmingly high blood pressure reading in the dentist's office.

Conceptualization and Treatment

Choosing a therapist is never easy. For John, it presented special difficulties. Though he lived near a large city, there were few African American psychiatrists or psychologists. As he had grown accustomed to doing in most other areas of his life, John decided to work with a White person, but was uncertain whether he could relate openly to a European American. His only really close White friend was his old college roommate, Bill, and even then he sometimes held back his thoughts and feelings about race. Would this same problem arise in a therapeutic relationship? In fact, was race even an issue?

"Well, what do you really want out of life?" asked Dr. Shaw, a distinguished and experienced clinical psychologist. "The same thing everyone else is after," was his reply. "But what is that?" questioned the psychologist.

The first couple of sessions were like this: Dr. Shaw trying to get John to examine what he really wanted, and John sparring with him, fending off the probes with generalities about "all other people." In Shaw's mind, John Williams did not want to confront the conflicts of playing a role in the White professional world. He identified with being African American, Shaw believed, but he sensed a falseness about his life. Racial slurs went by without comment. He took pride in the fact that his wife wore her hair straight but at the same time castigated himself for feeling this way. He hid from his colleagues the fact that he was a member of several civil rights groups and that he considered Martin Luther King, Jr. to have been too moderate. But what was he doing about it? King and others had risked personal safety in freedom marches, but John was terrified of being seen in one. What would the people in the firm think of him? Would they want a "radical" in the office?

Dr. Shaw thought to himself during these early sessions that he should pressure his client more and realized he was holding back in a way he would not with a White client. Was it his right to suggest to John that he was at the same time proud and ashamed of his racial heritage, and that he despised himself for hiding his feelings? Indeed, was it his duty? But how could Shaw be certain, and wouldn't it be terrible if he suggested something to John that was off base? But that, too, was something he worried far less about with his White clients. No therapist is infallible, but somehow he believed that with John, he had to be more certain about his interpretations.

Dr. Shaw routinely referred clients with medical or psychophysiological problems to an internist. This doctor prescribed some antihypertensive medication for John to take daily. But the physician also hoped that this relatively young patient would not come to rely on the drug. In an extended consultation, Shaw and his medical colleague agreed that John's high-pressure lifestyle was a major factor in his hypertension. What they could not agree on was what role the man's race played. There was no family history of hypertension; they agreed that, for whatever reason, John's particular response to stress was hypertension, more specifically essential hypertension, because a medical evaluation had ruled out physical causes.

A crisis took place in the fifth and final session. For months afterward, Dr. Shaw wondered whether he had blundered so badly that his client was driven from therapy.

| Dr. Shaw: | John, I've been wondering about what you've told me about your college days. |
| John (a bit suspiciously): | What aspect of them? |

Dr. Shaw:	Well, I guess I was thinking about the club. (Shaw noted to himself that he seldom said "I guess" in such circumstances. Stop pussyfooting, he told himself.)
John (feeling his ears becoming warm):	Well, what about the club?
Dr. Shaw:	Your feelings of being the only Black.
John:	Well, I felt really good about it. I used to daydream about what my high school friends would think.
Dr. Shaw:	And what would they have thought?
John:	They'd have envied me to the utmost. I mean, I must be doing something right to get into one of the Greeks.
Dr. Shaw:	Yes, I know you were quite proud about it.... But I wonder if you had any other feelings about it.
John (definitely on edge, wary):	What do you mean?
Dr. Shaw:	Well, lots of times people are conflicted about things that are important to them. Like the nervous bridegroom on the wedding day. He's eager for the honeymoon, but he knows he's giving up something.
John:	What do you think I was giving up?
Dr. Shaw:	You feel you were giving up something by being in the club?
John:	Come on, Doc, don't play games. You know damn well that you think I gave up something. What did I give up?
Dr. Shaw:	John, if anything was given up, it was you who gave it up, not I. (That sounded too harsh, he told himself immediately, but maybe it was time to apply more pressure on him. Otherwise, he might never move.)
John:	I resent what you're implying.
Dr. Shaw:	Okay, but can you explore it, just hypothetically?
John (suspicion mounting, almost a feeling of panic setting in):	Okay, Shaw, let me think of what I gave up.

At this point there was a lengthy silence. John stared at his feet, Dr. Shaw at his notes, occasionally glancing up at John but not wanting to look at him too much. John began to dwell on the thoughts he had never shared with anyone, not even with his roommate, Bill. Oreo cookie, he called himself, black on the outside and white on the inside. Who needs the damned club? If they were serious about being democratic, I would not be the only African American. Just me, and oh, that Chinese kid, whose family just happened to own half of Hong Kong. Yeah, David and me, the two typical minority members. And they can congratulate themselves for being so damned liberal. And I can congratulate myself for making it in the door. But how would they have reacted if I had dated a White woman? Or worn my hair in an Afro? Or put on a dashiki? Ha! How do you wear a club tie with a dashiki? Even the one overt sign of club membership conflicts with a dashiki! What am I doing with them? How hypocritical can I be?[1]

Dr. Shaw:	John, can you share some of your thoughts with me?
John:	Doc, I can't do it. You're one of them.
Dr. Shaw:	One of whom?
John:	Doc, I can't talk to a White man about this. I can't talk to a Black man about this. I'm too ashamed, too mixed up (beginning to sob). I can't handle this.
Dr. Shaw:	This is hard for you, I know, John. But this is a place you can use to look at those feelings. Try to sort them out. Try to figure out what you really want—
John (interrupting the psychologist):	No! It's not for you to tell me what I should be doing. I'm the one who has to decide. (long silence again)
Dr. Shaw:	John?
	John just stares at his feet, jaws clenched, that familiar tightness in his head. My blood pressure must be soaring, he told himself. I can't handle this. If I'm not careful, I'll be a psychological success, but I'll die from a stroke. No, that's an exaggeration. Or is it? I'm bullshitting myself so much that I don't even know what I want, or think, or feel . . .
Dr. Shaw:	John, perhaps that's enough for today.
John (relieved):	Yes, that's right. That's enough . . . for today.
Dr. Shaw:	See you next week, same time.
John (knowing he would break the appointment):	Yeah. Thanks. I'll see you next week.

---

[1]Dr. Shaw learned later on something of what was going through John's mind during these lengthy silences.

Discussion

It has been known for thousands of years that mental and emotional states can affect the functioning of the body. When a person is under emotional stress, there are numerous physiological changes, such as increases in heart rate and in blood pressure; these changes are usually temporary, diminishing when the stressor is removed. But in some individuals, the changes persist; when this happens over a long period of time, a disorder can result. Many medical illnesses are caused in part, or are markedly affected by, psychological factors. A disease such as hypertension can be life threatening even when it appears to be arising primarily from a person's emotions. Both biological and psychological theories have been proposed to explain why certain people who are exposed to stress will develop a disorder.

Biological Theories

The somatic-weakness theory states that a particular organ—for genetic reasons or because of poor diet or earlier illnesses—can be weak and thus vulnerable to stress. Thus, the connection between stress and a particular medical disorder is a weakness in a specific bodily organ.

According to the specific-reaction theory, individuals respond to stress in their own idiosyncratic ways, and the bodily system that is the most responsive becomes a likely candidate for the locus of a subsequent disorder. For example, someone reacting to stress with elevated blood pressure may be more susceptible to essential hypertension.

A third biological theory asserts that the biological changes that stress produces are adaptive in the short run, for example, mobilizing energy resources in preparation for physical activity, but that the body pays a price if it must constantly adapt to stress (McEwen, 1998). This can take the form of difficulties "shutting down" the biological stress response, for example, by exhibiting an unusually high level of cortisol secretion even after the stress has abated.

A fourth theory focuses on the body's immune system, which is involved in fighting off infections. Stress can weaken the functioning of the immune system and thereby play a role in such diseases as cancer and allergies as well as autoimmune diseases such as rheumatoid arthritis, in which people's immune systems actually attack their own bodies. Chronic psychological stress, such as long-term work-related difficulties, is particularly strongly associated with immune system dysregulation (Graham, Christian, & Kiecolt-Glaser, 2006). Many stressors produce negative effects on the immune system—exams in school, bereavement, divorce, looking after a relative with Alzheimer's disease, and natural disasters (Howell, Kern, & Lyubomirsky, 2007).

Psychological Theories

Our autonomic nervous systems are equipped to respond to danger with either fight or flight, and the healthy body prepares itself by increasing the rate of breathing, diverting blood into the muscles, and releasing sugar into the blood-stream. When danger has passed, this burst of sympathetic nervous system activity subsides. People respond in this way to psychological dangers as well. Thoughts can activate our autonomic nervous systems, thereby maintaining our bodies in a state of hyperarousal, as if we were runners in a 100-yard dash crouched at the starting line and tensely ready for the race, expectant and highly aroused.

People can become distressed and emotionally aroused by thinking about regrets from the past and worries about the future. Appraisal, one characteristic of our cognitive activity, is important: One person can judge a particular situation as dangerous, whereas another may view it as challenging and interesting; these different cognitions lead to different reactions in the body.

Investigators have to consider both physical diatheses, or predispositions, and highly specific psychological ways of reacting to stress. One person might have a genetically determined tendency to react to emotional situations with elevated blood pressure, and thus be at risk for hypertension, but will not develop it without a stressful life. Another person might have a constitution that is not disposed to react in an abnormal way to stress and have blood pressure that declines rapidly after a stressor is removed.

Essential Hypertension

High blood pressure, or hypertension, is involved in many deaths each year and is occurring at younger and younger ages. Despite better treatments, there has recently been a 3% increase in Americans' hypertension-related deaths (Farag & Mills, 2004). If blood pressure remains elevated—above 140/90 is regarded as high—a strain is placed on the cardiovascular system, and over time, there is an increased risk of stroke or heart attack. Only about 10 to 15% of all cases of hypertension in the United States are due to an identifiable physical cause; the other 85 to 90% are essential or primary hypertension. Hypertension is more likely in developed, industrialized societies than in traditional, less-developed societies (Dressler, 2004). In industrialized countries, the lifetime risk of hypertension is more than 90% (Messerli, Williams, & Ritz, 2007).

According to recent estimates, 20% of adults in the United States have varying degrees of hypertension; it is twice as frequent in African Americans as in European Americans. Obesity, especially fat stored in the abdomen, is linked to hypertension, and adolescent boys with higher waist circumference show more increases in blood pressure in response to physical and mental stress (Goldbacher, Matthews, & Salomon, 2005). As many as 10% of college students are hypertensive; most are unaware of their illness. Unless people have their blood pressure checked, they may go for years without realizing it. This disease is referred to as the "silent killer" because, over time, it is dangerous to a person's physical health, and it can be present for years without the person knowing it. Sometimes symptoms do develop, as they did for John: fatigue, nervousness, dizziness, heart palpitations, headaches, and sometimes even a feeling of pressure in the head. In addition to stroke and heart attack, uncontrolled hypertension can eventually lead to renal failure and dementia (Messerli et al., 2007).

A number of psychosocial factors are related to hypertension: mental stress, anger and hostility, depression, social isolation, and effects of racism. These factors tend to cluster in low socioeconomic groups and compound the risk for cardiovascular disease (Williams, Barefoot, & Schneiderman, 2003). Research on each will be examined.

The first factor is stress, which increases blood pressure in the short term. Jobs that have high levels of strain and stress have been linked to higher levels of blood pressure, especially when high levels of psychological demands (quantity of work, intellectual effort, and time pressure) are paired with low ability to control one's decisions (Guimont et al., 2006). Cumulative job strain over time leads to increased blood pressure for men working in white-collar jobs, especially when levels of social support in the workplace are low. People who report low levels of control in their jobs, such as not being able to control when they take breaks, have higher blood pressure (Steptoe & Willemsen, 2004). People who work in active jobs that combine high levels of control with high levels of challenge were found to have lower blood pressure and less hypertension (Stephan & Roesler, 2010). In a study of a manufacturing plant in Norway undergoing two rounds of layoffs, there was a significant increase in blood pressure in both groups, those laid off and those continuously employed, during the first round, in which orders were coming from a central office, and the local management and unions were powerless (Kjeldsen et al., 2006). During the second round, there was no increase, perhaps because decision-making control was retained at the plant. However, people differ in their reactivity to stress. Research has shown that people who show more cardiovascular reactivity to stress (greater changes in heart rate and blood pressure) and longer periods of time after the end of the stress to return to baseline levels, are more likely to later become hypertensive (Stewart, Janicki, & Kamarck, 2006).

The next psychosocial factor to be considered is anger. Of various negative emotions, anger is most strongly linked to elevated blood pressure (Faber & Burns, 1996). People with Type A behavior patterns (competitive, achievement oriented, and hostile) are more likely to have hypertension, and anger and hostility are the key elements. People who are impatient and hostile and who feel high levels of time urgency are more likely to develop hypertension, even many years later (Yan et al., 2003). Experiencing anger has been conclusively linked to higher blood pressure, but expressing anger is linked to lower blood pressure (Schum, Jorgensen, Verhaeghen, Sauro, & Thibodeau, 2003). People with essential hypertension may have a social skills deficit, that is, an inability to be assertive when angry (Larkin & Zayfert, 2004). Assertive, constructive responses to anger are linked to lower blood pressure (Hogan & Linden, 2004).

One relevant study examined hostility (cynicism, distrust, resentment, and anger) and suppression (tendency to not disclose negative psychological symptoms, along with trying to conform to society). Researchers found that people who are high on suppressed hostility (trying to avoid reporting their angry feelings) were significantly more likely to have hypertension 3 years later (Zhang et al., 2005). Either intentionally or unconsciously suppressing hostile, angry feelings was thought to lead to chronic physiological arousal for fear of losing control of the anger, and therefore raising blood pressure. John's habit of inhibiting anger and avoiding thinking about it, and his resentment of racial discrimination, likely played a role in his high blood pressure.

Depression has also been examined for its contributions to hypertension. Negative mood states have been linked to hypertension (Pollard & Schwartz, 2003). People who are depressed are more likely to have hypertension (Bosworth, Bartash, Olsen, & Steffens, 2003). Negative emotions (depression, anxiety, hostility, and emotional suppression) were found to be more likely in people who grew up in families that lived in poverty or were characterized by harshness, and these negative emotions were linked to higher blood pressure in adulthood (Lehman, Taylor, Kiefe, & Seeman, 2009). In a study of African American men with hypertension, depression was linked to poorer adherence to treatment and to alcohol and tobacco use (Kim, Han, Hill, Rose, & Roary, 2003). Depression and social isolation may interact in contributing to hypertension. Social support may serve as a protective factor. People in cohesive, supportive marriages had lower levels of hypertension (Baker, Szalai, Paquette, & Tobe, 2003). In addition, depression likely directly impacts hypertension through sympathetic nervous system activity and cortisol levels (Scherrer et al., 2003).

There is a higher incidence of hypertension among African Americans. One reason for this might be their experience of racism and discrimination (Clark, Anderson, Clark, & Williams, 1999). Exposure to racism has been repeatedly shown to elevate blood pressure among African American participants in research experiments. The blood pressure increase depends on the type of racism expressed, the perception of the racism by the research participant, and the person's psychological and situational characteristics. Subtle forms of racism, when perceived, led to a greater increase in blood pressure among college student participants than blatant racism (Merritt, Bennett, Williams, Edwards, & Sollers, 2006). Moreover, significant physical reactions to racist images occurred in some people even though they had no subjective awareness of distress (Peters, Butler, Gjini, Yeragani, & Boutros, 2011). African American female college students showed more cardiovascular reactivity to stress when they had higher levels of perceived racism but only for women who had low levels of seeking social support (Clark, 2006). The type of coping mechanism the person uses may make a difference (Brondolo, Rieppi, Kelly, & Gerin, 2003). One hypothesis to explain the higher risk for hypertension among African Americans is the John

Henryism hypothesis, based on a legend about a man of that name. It suggests that people who face socioeconomic adversity and inequity with active coping strategies of commitment to hard work and a strong determination to succeed are actually at higher risk for high blood pressure (Fernander, Durán, Saab, & Schneiderman, 2004). This coping strategy was linked with higher blood pressure among African American men with high education and African American women with low education. John Williams fits this hypothesis particularly well. His constant striving for perfection exacerbated his level of stress, over and above the pressure probably created by the prejudice he sometimes encountered. He was also affected by worrying about whether or not subtle forms of racism were occurring in his club. His blood pressure was apparently increased as well by the tremendous conflicts he experienced as an African American man who felt he was being false to himself, who compromised his beliefs and ideals to succeed in White society. A core issue in the identity of African American men is the tension between African cultural values of communalism, interdependence, and emotional expression, and European American cultural values of independence, competitiveness, and suppression of emotions (Bridges, 2010). The value systems of family, church, community, and place of employment sometimes clash, causing stress.

Much of the research has been a search for risk factors for hypertension. A newer research focus is a search for protective factors, traits, or experiences that prevent hypertension. There is evidence that having high levels of positive emotions reduces the chance of developing hypertension. These effects are more than the absence of negative emotions; a person with positive emotions has lower blood pressure than a person with neither positive nor negative emotions. Two positive emotions that are particularly linked are hope and curiosity (Richman et al., 2005). Hope is a sense of optimism about the future and a feeling of competence to meet future demands, and curiosity is how much a person is engaged by the social environment and will explore new things. People with the highest levels of either of these positive emotions had about a 48% reduction in their risk of developing hypertension during the following year as compared to the people with the lowest levels of either of these emotions.

Psychological Treatment of Hypertension

Medications to lower blood pressure are effective. But the undesirable side effects of these medications—drowsiness, light-headedness, and, in men, erectile difficulties—as well as the growth of behavioral approaches to treatment, have led many investigators to explore nonpharmacological treatments for borderline essential hypertension. Those with more severe hypertension usually take drugs to control its deleterious long-term effects. However, studies looking at large numbers of patients in the community who have taken medication for many years found increased rather than decreased mortality, and there is increasing interest in nonpharmacological treatments (Linden, 2003).

Healthy weight loss, improved diet, and increased exercise are effective at reducing high blood pressure (Elmer et al., 2006). But these medical measures also involve psychological change components (Dubbert, 1995). Many therapists agree that anxiety, and sometimes anger, must be reduced to lessen the sympathetic nervous system arousal that plays a role in maintaining blood pressure at abnormally high levels. Therapy can help the client cope better with pressures and anxiety and thereby reduce blood pressure.

Client-centered therapists would focus on John's denial of his inner self, that is, not marching to the beat of his own drum and compromising his ideas and deeply felt beliefs to meet with favor and acceptance from others (especially his father), or "conditions of worth" (Rogers, 1951). Dr. Shaw was operating in this framework, but we have seen that he did not get further than suggesting to John that he might be acting against his own self. The transcript provided earlier shows the kind of empathic listening and reflection common in client-centered therapy. Note, however, that Dr. Shaw did not merely reflect back to John what he had just said, but empathizes:

John: Doc, I can't talk to a White man about this. I can't talk to a Black man about this. I'm too ashamed, too mixed up (beginning to sob). I can't handle this.
Dr. Shaw: This is hard for you, I know, John....

Dr. Shaw acknowledges that he appreciates how difficult it is for John to talk about his private thoughts. The hope is that the relationship will be strengthened and that John will be encouraged to continue exploring his feelings. In another part of the session, however, Dr. Shaw goes beyond what John has expressed, restating to him what he believes is going on with John. He makes an inference, an interpretation about what is troubling the client in the hope of helping John view himself in a new, better perspective, one that will generate movement and greater self-honesty (Dr. Shaw has asked John how he felt about being the only African American in his club at college).

Dr. Shaw: [I'd like to know about] your feelings of being the only Black.
John: Well, I felt really good about it.... My high school friends would've envied me to the utmost....
Dr. Shaw: Yes, I know you were quite proud about it.... But I wonder if you had any other feelings about it.

This statement was too confrontational. Dr. Shaw was on target, but John was too frightened, too angry to consider the interpretation. This error in pushing too quickly for movement may have been because of Dr. Shaw's impatience with himself for dancing too gingerly around John's problems for fear of sounding bigoted.

Relaxation training and meditation have also been used with some success in efforts to control hypertension (Yung & Keltner, 1996). When relaxation was compared with an information-only treatment, anger and hostility were reduced more by the relaxation, and this was accompanied by a reduction in blood pressure (Davison, Williams, Nezami, Bice, & DeQuattro, 1991). Teaching clients coping skills for handling stress and encouraging meditation have been effective treatments (Williams et al., 2003). Some clinicians target Type A behavior directly, to reduce hostility and time urgency. Others advocate the treatment of depression to improve hypertension.

African American urban residents have particularly low levels of adherence with medication therapy and are sometimes suspicious and distrustful of their physicians (Lukoschek, 2003). For urban African American men who are at high risk for hypertension but are often underserved by the health-care system, an intensive team approach that incorporated education, home visits, and telephone checks produced more reductions in hypertension than a traditional medical approach (Hill et al, 2003). In one study, some African American patients expressed concern that they would become addicted to their medication and would only take them if they felt symptoms (Ogedegbe, Harrison, Robbins, Mancuso, & Allegrante, 2004).

Issues of Race and Psychotherapy

When clients and therapists are similar in ethnicity, it is easier to establish and maintain a therapeutic alliance and obtain a positive therapeutic outcome (Farsimadan, Draghi-Lorenz, & Ellis, 2007). At the same time, studies suggest that racial differences are not insurmountable barriers to understanding between counselor and client (Beutler, Machado, & Neufeldt, 1994). Therapists with high levels of empathy are perceived as more helpful by clients, regardless of ethnic background. Therapists report that when they address race with their clients who are a different race, it has positive effects on the therapy (Knox, Burkard, Johnson, Suzuki, & Ponterotto, 2003). Talking openly about these issues improves rapport.

Therapists need to understand that virtually all African Americans have encountered prejudice and racism, and many must often wrestle with their anger at a majority culture that is sometimes insensitive to and unappreciative of the emotional consequences of growing up as a feared, resented, and sometimes hated minority (Hardy & Laszloffy, 1995). They have to be aware of the subtle forms of aggression, exclusion, and invalidation that can occur during interactions between White Americans and members of racial and ethnic minority groups (Sue et al., 2007). It takes extra effort on the part of therapists to be aware of their own subtle prejudices, and managing this aspect of the therapeutic relationship is an important part of the therapy. Often, White therapists become anxious and defensive when openly discussing race, and this damages the therapist–client rapport. These difficulties may lead clients who are members of racial or ethnic minority groups to leave therapy prematurely. African Americans who are more acculturated to the dominant culture may have a greater expectation that therapy would work but also may have mixed feelings about being in therapy because they have had more experiences of being discriminated against by members of the dominant culture (Obasi & Leong, 2009). These issues are vividly illustrated in the case of John Williams, both throughout his life and in his brief dealings with his therapist.

Mention has already been made of how being African American might contribute to high blood pressure. John Williams's race also played a role in his therapy.

Therapists have to get past any prejudices they may have to relate to clients of different racial and ethnic backgrounds and to place race in a context that will promote a fruitful assessment and intervention instead of impeding them.

These issues are seen in the case of John Williams. Should the therapist have encouraged a more assertive stance toward the prejudices that seemed to be oppressing him? Or should he have promoted an adjustment to the situation, an attitude that John really had things good, that life is imperfect, and perhaps he should just find a way to make the best of it? Did John Williams wish that he were White? Should John have declined the invitation to the club at Harvard? Was his wish to be accepted by his White classmates an unhealthy one, or could it be seen as no less healthy than the wish a White initiate would have? Was John really "Uncle-Tomming" by joining the exclusive group while fearing that true acceptance would ultimately be denied him? Was he not "truly" accepted by his club members? If people were being nice to him, was it because he was African American and they were trying to demonstrate their liberalism and open-mindedness? How was he to know if they really liked him?

Dr. Shaw was reluctant to push John more than he would have a White client. There is a general issue in psychotherapy about how much pressure a therapist should place on a client. Clients can be hurt if their therapists demand more of them than they are capable of giving. On the other hand, the art of therapy requires that therapists encourage movement on the part of their clients that might not occur otherwise. After some hesitation, Dr. Shaw did apply such pressure, but he seemed to misread his client's readiness to explore his conflicts and lost the opportunity to work further with him. By most standards, Dr. Shaw failed with John Williams.

Dr. Shaw should have anticipated the difficulties in establishing rapport. John was suspicious and hostile, wondering whether Dr. Shaw would be able to empathize with his suffering: Will he truly be able to appreciate the tensions I am under? How will he judge my desires to be accepted by Whites for what I am, my fierce pride in being African American, especially as I succeed in a White world? Will he see me as copping out or decide that my inhibition of resentment is adaptive and healthy? Indeed, will and can the therapist help me explore within myself what I really want? Must I want only what other African Americans want to be a whole person?

Discussion Questions

1. If you were a psychotherapist treating a person of a different racial or ethnic background, do you think there would be any issues for you to consider? Do you agree with those who recommend discussing these issues in the therapy, or do you think that would be counterproductive?
2. Were you surprised at the letter Bill received from the university about rooming with John? Are subtle forms of racism continuing today, or have things really changed?
3. What did you think about John's thoughts and feelings about the club? How did his cognitions and coping style about this and about his ambivalence about his career success help him? How did it hurt him?
4. Which personality traits increase a person's risk for hypertension? Which protect them from hypertension?

CHAPTER 5

Dissociative Identity Disorder: Multiple Personality

The instructor in Paula's human sexuality course suggested that she talk to a psychologist. Several factors contributed to his concern: Although Paula was a good student, her behavior in class had been rather odd on occasion. Every now and then, it seemed as though she came to class "high." She participated actively in the discussions, but she did not seem to be familiar with the readings or previous lecture material. Her scores on the first two exams had been A's, but she failed to appear for the third. When he asked her where she had been, Paula maintained with apparent sincerity that she couldn't remember. Finally, she had handed in an essay assignment that described in rather vague, but sufficiently believable, terms the abusive, incestuous relationship that her father had forced upon her from the age of 5 until well after she was married and had had her first child. All of this led her professor to believe that Paula needed help. Fortunately, she was inclined to agree with him because several things were bothering her. She made an appointment to talk to Dr. Harpin, a clinical psychologist at the student health center.

Paula Stewart was 38 years old, divorced, and the mother of a son who was 18 and a daughter who was 15. She was about 90 pounds overweight, but in other ways, her appearance was unremarkable. For the past 5 years, Paula had been taking courses at the university and working part time at a variety of secretarial positions on campus. She and her daughter lived together in a small, rural community located about 20 miles from the university—the same town in which Paula had been born. Her son had moved away from home after dropping out of high school. Paula's mother and father still lived in their home just down the street from Paula's.

Over a series of sessions, Dr. Harpin noticed that Paula's behavior was often erratic. Her moods vacillated frequently and quickly from anger and irritability to severe depression. When she was depressed, her movements became agitated, and she mentioned that she experienced sleep difficulties. She threatened suicide frequently and had, on several occasions, made some attempts to harm herself. In addition to these emotional difficulties, Paula frequently complained of severe headaches, dizziness, and breathing problems.

It also seemed that Paula abused alcohol, although the circumstances were not clear. This situation was a source of distress and considerable confusion for Paula. She had found empty beer cans and whiskey bottles in the back seat of her car, but she denied drinking alcoholic beverages of any kind. Once every 2 or 3 weeks, she would wake up in the morning with terrible headaches as though she were hungover. Dr. Harpin believed that her confusion and other memory problems could be explained by her alcohol consumption.

Paula's relationships with other people were unpredictable. She would explode with little provocation and often argued that no one understood how serious her problems were. On occasion, she threatened to kill other people, particularly an older man, Cal, who lived nearby. Paula's relationship with Cal was puzzling to both of them. They had known each other since she was an adolescent. Although he was 15 years older than she and had been married to another woman for more than 20 years, Cal had persistently shown a romantic interest in Paula. He would frequently come to her house saying that she had called. More often than not, this made Paula furious. She maintained that she was not at all interested in him and would never encourage such behavior. At other times, however, she insisted that he was the only person who understood and cared for her.

Paula's father was still alive, but she did not spend any time with him. In fact, he behaved as though she didn't exist. She was able to recall and discuss some aspects of the incestuous relationship her father had forced upon her in previous years, but her memory was sketchy, and she preferred not to discuss him.

Throughout the first year of treatment, Paula's memory problems became increasingly severe. The notes she wrote during classes were often incomplete, as though she had suddenly stopped listening in the middle of a number of lectures. She sometimes complained that she lost parts of days. On one occasion, for example, she told Dr. Harpin that she had gone home with a severe headache in the middle of the afternoon and then couldn't remember anything until she awakened the following morning. Another time she was eating lunch, only to find herself hours later driving her car. Her daughter asked her about a loud argument Paula had had with her mother on the phone, and she couldn't remember even talking to her mother that day. These unexplained experiences were extremely frustrating to Paula, but the therapist continued to believe that they were induced by alcohol.

One day, Dr. Harpin received a message from his secretary saying that a woman named Sherry had called. She had identified herself as a friend of Paula's and had said that she would like to discuss the case. Before responding directly to this request, Dr. Harpin decided to check with Paula to find out more about this friend and determine whether she would give her consent for this consultation. Paula denied knowing anyone named Sherry, so Dr. Harpin did not return the call. It did strike him as odd, however, that someone knew that he was Paula's therapist.

Two weeks after receiving this call, Dr. Harpin decided to use hypnosis in an attempt to explore the frequent gaps in Paula's memory. They had used hypnosis on one previous occasion as an aid to the process of applied relaxation, and it was clear that Paula was easily hypnotized. Unfortunately, it didn't help with the memory problem; Paula couldn't remember anything else about the time she had lost.

Upon waking out of a trance, Paula complained of a splitting headache. She gazed slowly about the room as though she were lost. Dr. Harpin was puzzled. "Do you know where you are?" he asked. She said she didn't know, so he asked if she knew who he was. Rather than providing a quick answer, she glanced around the room. She noticed his professional license hanging on the wall, read his name, and finally replied, "Yes. You're Dr. Harpin, the one who's working with Paula." This switch to her use of the third person struck Dr. Harpin as being odd and roused further curiosity about her state of mind.

"How do you feel?"
"Okay."
"Do you still have a headache?"
"No. I don't have a headache."

The way she emphasized the word "I" was unusual, so Dr. Harpin said, "You make it sound like somebody else has a headache." He was completely unprepared for her response:

"Yes. Paula does."

Pausing for a moment to collect his wits, Dr. Harpin—who was simultaneously confused and fascinated by this startling exchange—decided to pursue the identity issue further.

"If Paula has a headache, but you don't, what's your name?"
"Why should I tell you? I don't think I can trust you."
"Why not? Don't you want to talk to me?"
"Why should I? You wouldn't talk to me when I called last week!"

Dr. Harpin finally remembered the call from Sherry, who had wanted to talk to him about Paula's case. He asked the woman, once again, what her name was, and she said, "Sherry." After they talked for a couple of minutes, Dr. Harpin said, "I'd like to talk to Paula now."

"Oh, she's boring."
"That doesn't matter. She's my client, and I want to talk to her to see how she feels."

"Will you talk to me again?"

"Yes."

"Why should I believe you? You wouldn't talk to me before."

"Now I know who you are. Please let me talk to Paula."

At that point, she closed her eyes and waited quietly for a few moments. When her eyes opened, Paula was back and her headache was gone, but she could not remember anything about the past half hour. Dr. Harpin was stunned and incredulous. Although he was aware of the literature on dissociative identity disorder (DID) and a few well-known cases, he could not believe what Paula had said.

When Paula appeared for their next appointment, she still could not remember anything that had happened and seemed just as she had before this remarkable incident. Dr. Harpin decided to attempt to discuss with Paula a traumatic incident that had happened a number of years ago. Paula had frequently mentioned a day when she was 15 years old. She couldn't remember the details, but it was clearly a source of considerable distress for her and seemed to involve her father.

Dr. Harpin asked Paula to describe what she could remember about the day: where they were living at the time, what time of year it was, who was home, and so on. Paula filled in the details slowly and as best she could. Her father had grabbed her, hit her across the face, and dragged her toward the bedroom. No matter how hard she tried, she couldn't remember anything else. Paula said that she was getting a headache. Dr. Harpin suggested that she lean back in the chair and breathe slowly. She paused for a moment and closed her eyes. In a few moments, she opened her eyes and said, "She can't remember. She wasn't there. I was!" Sherry was back.

Paula's appearance had changed suddenly. She had been very tense, clutching the arms of the chair and sitting upright. She also had had an annoying, hacking cough. Now she eased down in the chair, folded her arms, and crossed her legs in front of her. The cough was completely gone. Sherry explained why Paula couldn't remember the incident with her father. As Sherry put it, when Paula was dragged into the bedroom, she "decided to take off," leaving Sherry to experience the pain and humiliation of the ensuing rape. Dr. Harpin translated this to mean that Paula had experienced a dissociative episode. The incident was so extremely traumatic that she had completely separated the experience and its memory from the rest of her consciousness.

After discussing the rape in some detail, Dr. Harpin decided to find out as much as he could about Sherry. She provided only sketchy information, admitting that she was in her thirties but denying that she had a last name. Sherry's attitude toward Paula was contemptuous. She was angry because Paula had so frequently left Sherry to experience painful sexual encounters. They discussed numerous incidents dating from Paula's adolescence to the present, but none of Sherry's memories traced back prior to the incident with Paula's father. Since that time, Sherry was apparently aware of everything that Paula had done. Paula, on the other hand, was completely oblivious to Sherry's existence.

Toward the end of this conversation, Dr. Harpin asked whether it was Sherry or Paula who had been responsible for the beer bottles Paula found in her car. Sherry said, "Oh, we did that." Intrigued by the plural pronoun, Dr. Harpin asked whom she meant to describe, and the patient said, "Oh, Janet and I."

"Who's Janet?"

"You don't want to talk to her. She's always angry. You know how adolescents are."

By this point, Dr. Harpin knew that Sherry found it easier than Paula to switch back and forth among these personalities, so he encouraged her to try. Sherry agreed, somewhat reluctantly, and soon there was another dramatic change in Paula's appearance. She fidgeted in her chair, pulled at her hair, and began to bounce her leg continuously. She was reluctant to talk, but adopted a coy, somewhat flirtatious manner. She claimed to be 15 years old.

Several sessions later, Sherry presented Dr. Harpin with a request. She said that she and Janet were extremely concerned about Caroline, who was presumably only 5 years old and had been crying a lot lately. Sherry and Janet wanted Dr. Harpin to talk to Caroline. He agreed to try. Sherry closed her eyes and effortlessly transformed her posture and mannerisms to those of a little girl. She pulled her legs up onto the chair and folded them under her body. Holding her hand in a fist clenched close to the side of her mouth almost as if she were sucking her thumb, she turned sideways in the chair and peered at Dr. Harpin bashfully out of the corner of her eye. She seemed to be rather frightened.

"Will you talk to me, Caroline?" Dr. Harpin began.

After an extended pause, Caroline asked, "What's your name? I don't know you." Her voice seemed higher and weaker than it had been moments before.

"I'm Dr. Harpin."

"Do you know my mommy and daddy?"

"No. But I'm a friend of Sherry's. She asked me to talk to you. Do you know Sherry?"

"Yes. She watches me. She takes care of me."

"Do you know Janet?"

"She's big. She has fun!"

"Do you know her very well?"

"Not really. She gets mad easy."

"Sherry told me that you've been feeling sad. Why is that?"

"I'm a bad girl."

"Why do you think you're bad?"

"Mommy told me I'm bad. That's why she has to punish me."
"I don't think you're a bad girl."
"Yes I am. If I'm not bad, why would they punish me?"
"What do they punish you for?"
"I don't know. They just do. They hurt me. Once I pinched my brother when he took my toy puppy. Then they took my puppy away, and they won't give it back! Grandpa gave it to me. He's good to me."

At their next session, Dr. Harpin asked Paula if she remembered ever having a stuffed puppy when she was a child. A fond smile of recognition followed several moments' reflection. She had indeed had such a toy. He asked if she knew what had happened to it. She insisted that she had no idea. It had been almost 30 years since she remembered seeing it, but she agreed to look around in the attic of her mother's house.

Much to everyone's surprise, Paula was able to find the puppy, which was known as Jingles because of the sound made by a small bell sewn into its tail. Unfortunately, it became the source of considerable aggravation for Paula. The first day she found it, she left it in the living room before she went to bed. When she woke up in the morning, Jingles was in bed with her. This happened two nights in a row. On the third night, she locked the puppy in her car, which was kept in the garage, and went to bed. Once again, the puppy was in bed with her when she woke up in the morning. She was annoyed and also a bit frightened by this strange turn of events. In subsequent sessions, Sherry provided the following explanation for what had happened. Caroline would wake up in the middle of the night crying, wanting to hold her stuffed animal. In an effort to console her, Sherry would then retrieve Jingles from the living room or garage. Of course, Paula would not remember what had happened.

Thus far there were four names: Paula, Sherry, Janet, and Caroline. The clinical picture was as fascinating as it was unbelievable. Dr. Harpin felt that he needed help as much as his client. In his 15 years of clinical experience, he had never seen a case that resembled Paula's in any way. It fit closely with some of the published cases of DID, but he had never really believed that this sort of thing happened, except in fiction. Surely it was the product of the therapist's imagination, or the client's manipulative strategy, he had believed. He sought advice from colleagues about a plan for the treatment of this complex set of problems. His contacts with Paula continued to deal largely with day-to-day crises.

He asked Paula if she had read any of the well-known books or watched any of the popular films dealing with DID (which was formerly called multiple personality). She had not. Because she was not familiar with other examples of this phenomenon, it seemed unlikely that she had simply invented the alter personalities as a way of attracting attention or convincing others of the severity of her problems. In an attempt to help Paula—who was not aware of the alters—understand the problems that she faced, Dr. Harpin asked her to read *The Three Faces of Eve*, the book upon which the famous film was based. She reacted with interest and disbelief. What did it have to do with her situation? She was still completely unable to remember those times when she spoke as if she were Sherry, Janet, or Caroline. Later, however, there were times when Sherry discussed the book with Dr. Harpin, and Janet was also reading it. To make matters more confusing, they all seemed to be reading at a different pace. Paula might be two thirds of the way through the book, but Janet—an adolescent who did not read as quickly—was aware of only the first part of the book.

Dr. Harpin also used videotape to help Paula understand the problem. With her consent, he recorded her behavior during a sequence of three therapy sessions. She alternated among the various personalities several times during the course of these tapes. Paula was then asked to view the tapes and discuss her reactions to her own behavior. Again, she was surprised, interested, and puzzled, showing no signs of previous awareness of this behavior. She would often ask, "Did I say that?" or "Who am I? What am I?"

Another unusual set of circumstances led to the identification of still another personality, Heather. Paula had complained on numerous occasions that a loaded shotgun, which belonged to her father, kept appearing at her house. She had no use for guns, and their presence upset her, so she would take the gun back to her father's house. Several days later, she would find it again at her house. Her parents and daughter adamantly denied knowing anything about the gun. Recognizing that Paula was frequently unaware of things that she did as the other personalities, Dr. Harpin discussed the gun with Sherry and Janet. Both denied any knowledge of these incidents. Janet said, "I know you think it's me, but it's not!" Finally, Sherry suggested that it might be someone else. "You mean there might be others?" Dr. Harpin asked. Sherry acknowledged the possibility, but said that she was not aware of any others.

At the beginning of the next session, Dr. Harpin decided to use hypnosis in an effort to see if he could identify more alters. While Paula was in the trance, he asked if anyone else, with whom he had not yet spoken, was able to hear what he was saying. This was when Heather emerged. She was presumably 23. It was she who had been bringing the gun to Paula's house, and it was she who had been calling Cal. Heather told Dr. Harpin that she was in love with Cal. If she couldn't marry him, she wanted to kill herself. This was the first alter with whom Sherry did not have co-consciousness, and her existence explained several important inconsistencies in Paula's behavior and gaps in her memory.

Heather's affection for Cal illustrates another important characteristic of the dissociative identity phenomenon. There were important, and occasionally radical, differences among Paula, Sherry, and the other alters in terms of tastes and preferences as well as mannerisms and abilities. Heather loved Cal (she couldn't live without him), but the others hated him. In fact, Paula's most remarkable reaction to videotapes of her own behavior centered around one conversation with Heather. Paula insisted that it was not she. "I would never say those things!" she said. Paula's attitude toward her parents was also at odds with those of some of the alters, and this inconsistency undoubtedly explained some of the erratic shifts in her behavior and relationship with other people. Sherry didn't like Paula's children and was inconsiderate in her behavior toward them. She frequently promised them things to keep them quiet and then failed to honor her commitments.

Social History

Paula grew up in a small rural community. She had one older brother. Her mother was an outspoken, dominant woman who maintained firm control of the family. Both parents were strict disciplinarians. The parents of Paula's mother lived nearby. This grandfather was the only sympathetic adult figure throughout Paula's childhood. It was he who gave her the stuffed puppy, Jingles, which became such an important source of comfort to her until her parents took it away. When Paula was upset, her grandfather was the only person who was able to console her and stop her crying (although she never dared to tell him about the things that her father forced her to do).

Paula's father was a shy, withdrawn, unaffectionate man who did not have many friends. For the first few years of her life, he ignored her completely. Then, when she was 5 years old, he began to demonstrate physical affection. He would hug and kiss her roughly, and when no one else was around, he would fondle her genitals. Paula didn't know how to respond. His touches weren't pleasant or enjoyable, but she would accept whatever affection he was willing to provide.

When she was 15, their sexual encounters started to become violent. The pretense of affection and love was obviously dissolved; he wanted to hurt her. In one incident, which Paula and Dr. Harpin had discussed repeatedly, her father dragged her into his bedroom by her hair and tied her to the bed. After slapping her repeatedly, he forced her to have intercourse with him. The incest and physical abuse continued until she was 20 years old.

Paula's mother was a strict disciplinarian who often punished Paula by putting her hands in scalding hot water or locking her in a dark closet for hours on end. Mrs. Stewart did not realize—or seem to care—that her husband was abusing Paula sexually. If she did know, she may have been afraid to intervene. Mr. Stewart may also have abused his wife as well as his daughter, but Paula could not remember witnessing any violence between her parents.

Perhaps in an effort to tear herself away from this abusive family, Paula pursued relationships with other men at an early age. Many of these men were older than she, including teachers and neighbors. The longest relationship of this sort was with Cal, the owner of a small construction business. Paula was 16 and Cal was 31 when they started seeing each other. Although he took advantage of Paula sexually, Cal was a more sympathetic person than her father. He did listen to her, and he seemed to care for her. On numerous occasions, Cal promised that he would marry her. For Paula, he was a "rescuer," someone who offered a way out of her pathological family situation. Unfortunately, he didn't come through. He married another woman but continued to pursue Paula's affection and sexual favors. She continued to oblige, despite the strong feelings of anger and betrayal that she harbored.

A few incidents that occurred while Paula was in high school were probably precursors of the memory problems and dissociative experiences that she later encountered as an adult. They suggest that the problem of alter personalities began during adolescence, although it was not discovered until many years later. People sometimes told Paula about things that she had done, things that she could not remember doing. Most of these involved promiscuous behavior. Paula was particularly upset by a rumor that went around the school when she was a sophomore. Several other girls claimed that Paula had been seen in a car with three men. They were parked in a remote picnic area outside town, and Paula presumably had intercourse with all of them. She couldn't remember a thing, but she also didn't know where she had been that night.

After graduating from high school, Paula enrolled in the university's school of education, but she dropped out after 1 year. For the next few years, she worked at various clerical jobs, while living either at home with her parents or in apartments that she rented nearby. She was married briefly, gave birth to her children, and was then divorced. Paula decided to return to the university many years later, after her son left home.

Conceptualization and Treatment

Dr. Harpin's initial diagnostic impression, before the emergence of the alter personalities, was that Paula fit the *Diagnostic and Statistical Manual of Mental Disorders* (*DSM-IV-TR*; APA, 2000) criteria for both dysthymia (a long-lasting form of depression that is not sufficiently severe to meet the criteria for major depressive disorder) and borderline personality disorder. Throughout the first year of treatment, his approach to the problem was focused primarily on the management of frequent, specific crises. These included numerous transient suicidal threats, fights with her mother and daughter, confusion and anger over her relationship—or lack of a relationship—with Cal, difficulties in her schoolwork and with professors teaching her classes, and a variety of incidents involving her employers. When immediate problems of this sort were not pressing, Paula usually wanted to talk about the way her father had abused her. Her focus was on both the anger and the guilt that she felt about these incidents. She wondered whether in some way she hadn't encouraged his sexual advances.

After the appearance of the alter personalities, Dr. Harpin's initial hypothesis was that Paula was malingering, that is, feigning a dramatic set of symptoms in an effort to gain some benefit from him or her family. This explanation was attractive for several reasons, including his skepticism regarding the existence of a phenomenon such as DID. Nevertheless, he eventually abandoned this view. One problem was the apparent absence of information that would have been necessary for Paula to fake this disorder. She had not read or seen any of the popular descriptions of the disorder, and it was therefore unlikely that she would be able to create or imitate the problem in such a believable, detailed fashion. The other problem was the lack of a clear motive. She was not, for example, facing criminal charges that might be avoided by the existence of a severe form of mental illness. Nor was she able to avoid personal or family responsibilities by the onset of these conditions because she continued to go to school, perform her work, and take care of her daughter after the emergence of the alters. The only thing she might stand to gain was increased attention from Dr. Harpin. It seemed unlikely that this would explain the problem because he had already been spending an inordinate amount of time and energy on the case as a result of the previous suicidal gestures, and he had repeatedly conveyed to Paula his concern for her problems.

It eventually became clear that Paula was experiencing a genuine disruption of consciousness that was usually precipitated by stressful experiences. Faced with an extremely threatening or unpleasant circumstance, Paula would often dissociate—entirely blot out (or repress) her awareness of that event. This pattern of cognitive activity could apparently be traced to the violent abuse that she received from her father during adolescence. By her own description, when these events began, Paula would usually "leave" the situation, and Sherry would be left to face her father. The turbulent nature of these years and the concentration of abuse during this time might account for the fact that the ages of most of the alters seemed to cluster between 15 and 23. Over time, the extent of this fragmentation of conscious experience became more severe, and her control over changes in her patterns of awareness eroded progressively.

One approach to the resolution of these dissociative episodes might involve the recall and exploration of previous traumatic experiences that seemed to be responsible for particular splits in Paula's consciousness. Perhaps the most salient of these episodes was the rape scene involving Paula's father. The existence of Sherry suggested that the split could be traced to about this period of time, and it was an incident that Sherry mentioned repeatedly. Previous accounts of DID suggest that the patient's disturbance in consciousness might improve if the repression of such memories can be lifted. Unfortunately, this approach did not seem to be useful in Paula's case. She and Dr. Harpin spent many hours discussing this incident—from the perspectives of both Paula and Sherry—but it only seemed to make things worse.

A different approach was needed. Dr. Harpin had two principal goals in mind during the next several months of treatment: to discourage further fragmentation of Paula's conscious experience and to facilitate the integration of information across the divisions of conscious experience. In other words, without encouraging or crystallizing the existence of separate personalities,

Dr. Harpin wanted to help Paula recognize the nature of the problem and the way her behavior patterns changed in association with loss of memory for these incidents. This was done, in part, by having her read and discuss *The Three Faces of Eve* and allowing her to view videotapes of her own behavior. Dr. Harpin's hope was that the videotapes might jog Paula's memory and begin to break down the barriers that had been erected to prevent the exchange of information between the subdivisions of her conscious working memory.

Ten-Year Follow-Up

Paula remained in treatment with Dr. Harpin for several years during which they were able to establish a strong working relationship. Paula trusted Dr. Harpin, and based on their extended discussions, she eventually accepted his diagnosis of her problem. Treatment continued to follow an interpersonal, problem-solving approach, in which Paula was encouraged to learn and use new, nondissociative coping skills to deal with stressful events. Emphasis was placed on the identification of strong feelings and the recognition of logical connections between these feelings and specific life events.

Paula's relationship with Cal, the older businessman, illustrates the utility of this approach. Their disagreements, and the confusion associated with their on-and-off affair, had been a source of considerable anxiety and anger for many years. Although it had originally seemed that Cal might rescue Paula from her terrible family situation, he had betrayed her by marrying another woman. Many people experience this type of bitter disappointment; most find a way to resolve their strong, ambivalent feelings and move on to other relationships. Unfortunately, for more than 20 years, Paula had responded to her encounters with Cal using dissociative responses. She continued the romance through one of her alters, Heather. Switching between Paula and Heather, she would alternately threaten to kill Cal and then herself. After many extended discussions of this situation with Dr. Harpin, Paula was finally able to recognize that Cal provided one of the consistent triggers for her dissociative episodes. She confronted Cal and ended their relationship. Shortly after this success, Heather stopped appearing. That particular alter had apparently been integrated with Paula, the host personality.

Paula's relationship with her children had been another source of considerable stress over the years. Arguments with them, and with her mother over her role as a parent, may also have served as a stimulus for dissociative responses. Her son and daughter, now young adults, remained angry for many legitimate reasons. They had been left alone frequently and inconsistently while they were growing up. They had also been bitterly disappointed on numerous occasions when Paula had failed to honor promises that she made to them. Previous attempts to discuss these feelings had been fruitless, in large part because Paula did not recognize her dissociative disorder as the root of the problem with these relationships. Paula had to accept responsibility for her own inconsistent and occasionally harmful parenting behaviors. The children also had to understand her disorder. Many sessions were devoted to discussions of these issues and to face-to-face meetings between Paula and her daughter (her son lived too far away to be included in this process). This aspect of Paula's family situation improved a great deal.

As treatment progressed, Dr. Harpin made an effort to avoid, whenever possible, speaking directly to the alters. For example, he sometimes received phone calls from Sherry, usually to report something inappropriate that Paula had done. Whenever the caller identified herself as one of the alters, Dr. Harpin would ask to speak to Paula. He also began to discourage their appearance in sessions. Over a period of several months, some of the alters stopped making appearances and seemed no longer to influence Paula's behavior. When asked about them, Paula and Sherry (the alter who had been most aware of the others) would reply, "Oh, she's not around anymore."

As the number of alters decreased, Dr. Harpin also noticed a shift in Sherry's attitude toward Paula. She had originally been contemptuous and hostile, but she gradually became compassionate and protective. Dr. Harpin sometimes felt that Sherry had become something like a surrogate therapist. Paula became increasingly aware of Sherry's attitudes and feelings, which were sometimes more adaptive or appropriate than Paula's because they were informed by a more complete understanding of her experience (Janet's being more fragmented by dissociative experiences). Some of the tangible distinctions between these personalities also seemed to fade. For example, the voices in which Paula and Sherry spoke had always been easy to distinguish. Paula was usually distressed when she called, and her voice was often agitated and shrill. Over time, it became softer and more stable in tone. Their accents and vocabularies had also been different (with Sherry using a more prominent rural dialect).

Discussion

The complex and puzzling nature of dissociative identity disorder (DID) is illustrated in the controversy surrounding its name. It was formerly known as multiple personality disorder because most descriptions of the syndrome have emphasized the diagnostic importance of several alter personalities. One unfortunate consequence of this approach has been a tendency toward public sensationalism and a preoccupation with counting the exact number of alters exhibited by any patient. These estimates have occasionally reached preposterous numbers, with some clinicians claiming to see patients who have hundreds of personalities. The dissociative disorders committee for *DSM-IV* (APA, 1994) felt strongly that a different approach should be encouraged. The chairperson of that committee, David Spiegel, explained that "there is a widespread misunderstanding of the essential psychopathology in this dissociative disorder, which is failure of integration of various aspects of identity, memory, and consciousness. The problem is not having more than one personality; it is having less than one personality" (cited in Hacking, 1995, p. 18). For this reason, the name was changed, and it is called dissociative identity disorder (DID) in *DSM-IV-TR* (APA, 2000).

Dissociative identity disorder is a rare phenomenon. Prior to 1980, fewer than 200 or 300 cases had been reported in the professional literature (Pope, Barry, Bodkin, & Hudson, 2006). This number is incredibly small compared to the millions of patients who suffer from disorders such as schizophrenia and depression at any point in time. Some investigators have suggested that DID appears more frequently than previously assumed (e.g., Ross, 1997; Sar, 2006), but these claims have been disputed (e.g., Lynn, Fassler, Knox, & Lilienfeld, 2006; Piper & Merskey, 2004). The prevalence of DID in the general population is almost certainly much less than 1%.

DID has attracted considerable attention, partly because a few dramatic cases have received widespread publicity through popular books and films. These include *The Three Faces of Eve* (Thigpen & Cleckley, 1957) and *Sybil* (Schreiber, 1973). Sybil was one of the most famous cases in psychiatry during the 20th century; interest surrounding the book and the film fueled an enormous increase in interest in this fascinating phenomenon throughout the 1970s and 1980s. The authenticity of the Sybil case has been seriously questioned, however. Some critics contend that the therapist influenced this patient to adopt alternate personalities by employing different names to identify her varying mood states (Rieber, 2006). Unfortunately, for many years, case studies such as these were our best source of information about the disorder. A few investigators have managed to identify samples of patients with DID for the purpose of research. Their descriptions have made significant contributions to the base of knowledge that is now available regarding this enigmatic disorder.

Among the cases of DID that have been reported, a few patterns stand out. First, most cases of DID are women, with the ratio of women to men being at least five to one. Most DID patients are first assigned that diagnosis in their late twenties or early thirties. Many of these people have already received mental health services while receiving a different diagnosis, often some type of mood disorder, substance-use disorder, schizophrenia, or borderline personality disorder (Dorahy, Mills, Taggart, O'Kane, & Mulholland, 2006; Sar, Akyuz, & Dogan, 2007).

DSM-IV-TR (APA, 2000) lists the following diagnostic criteria for DID:

1. The subject exhibits two or more distinct identities or personality states (each with its own relatively enduring pattern of perceiving, relating to, and thinking about the environment and self).
2. At least two of these identities or personality states recurrently take control of the person's behavior.

3. The subject is unable to recall important personal information that is too extensive to be explained by ordinary forgetfulness.
4. The disorder is not due to the direct physiological effects of a substance (such as blackouts or chaotic behavior during alcohol intoxication).

The manual also notes that the transition between different personalities is usually sudden and often beyond voluntary control.

Memory disturbances are perhaps the most important feature of this disorder (Kihlstrom, 2005). Most people behave differently, or may seem to be somewhat different people, as a function of the environmental stimuli with which they are confronted, but the changes are seldom as dramatic or complete as those seen in cases of DID. Furthermore, very few people forget what they have done or who they are whenever they alter their pattern of behavior. In DID, the original personality is presumably unaware of the existence of the alters. It is not unusual for the person to express concern about large chunks of time that seem to be missing or unaccounted for. The alter personalities may, or may not, be aware of one another or co-conscious. At any given moment only one personality is controlling the person's behavior and interacting with the environment, but other personalities may simultaneously perceive, and subsequently remember, events that are taking place. Of course, the inability to recall personal information is based almost exclusively on self-report. There is a serious need for the development of more objective measures of memory impairment in DID (Allen & Iacono, 2001; Kong, Allen, & Glisky, 2008).

The boundaries of this diagnostic category are difficult to define (Gillig, 2009; Spiegel, 2001). Some clinicians have argued that it should be considered broadly, whereas others would prefer that the term be applied only to severe or classic cases. Putnam (2006), author of the most authoritative book on DID (Putnam, 1989), has recommended that clinicians make a diagnosis of DID only after they have (a) witnessed a switch between two alter personality states, (b) met a given alter personality on at least three separate occasions so that they can evaluate the degree of uniqueness and stability of the alter personality state, and (c) established that the patient has amnesias, either by witnessing amnesic behavior or by the patient's report.

Because the disorder is rare and clinicians are not routinely familiar with its manifestations, some patients have probably been misdiagnosed as suffering from other disorders, most notably schizophrenia and borderline personality disorder. Several diagnostic signs might alert a clinician to suspect that a patient may be experiencing DID (Greaves, 1980):

1. Reports of time distortions or time lapses
2. Reports of being told of behavioral episodes by others that are not remembered by the patient
3. Reports of notable changes in the patient's behavior by a reliable observer, during which time the patient may call himself or herself by different names or refer to himself or herself in the third person
4. Elicitability of other personalities through hypnosis

5. The use of the word "we" in the course of an interview in which the word seems to take on a collective meaning rather than an editorial "we"
6. The discovery of writing, drawings, or other productions or objects among the patient's personal belongings that the patient does not recognize and cannot account for
7. A history of severe headaches, particularly when accompanied by blackouts, seizures, dreams, visions, or deep sleep

Paula exhibited almost all the signs included on this list. Time lapses and headaches were a frequent source of concern when she began treatment at the student health center. She had been told about incidents that she could not remember as far back as high school. Her children and at least one professor had noticed marked changes in her behavior that were not easily explained by environmental circumstances. It should be emphasized, of course, that none of these problems, alone or in combination, can be considered sufficient evidence to diagnose DID if the patient does not also meet other specific diagnostic criteria such as those listed in *DSM-IV-TR* (APA, 2000).

Etiological Considerations

A variety of hypotheses have been proposed to account for the development of DID. One simple explanation is that the patient produces the symptoms voluntarily, or plays the role of having several different personalities, in an effort to attract attention or avoid responsibility. The intentional production of false symptoms is called *malingering*. A few widely publicized criminal trials in which the defendant claimed innocence by reason of insanity have indicated that the syndrome can be faked rather convincingly (James, 1998).

The best-known example of malingering involves the case of Kenneth Bianchi, also known as the Hillside Strangler. Several experienced clinicians interviewed Bianchi after he was arrested. With the aid of hypnosis, they discovered an alter personality, Steve, who proudly claimed responsibility for several brutal rape-murders. The prosecution called Martin Orne, a psychiatrist at the University of Pennsylvania, as an expert witness to examine Bianchi. Orne raised serious questions about the case by indicating that the defendant was probably faking hypnosis during the interviews and by demonstrating that Bianchi's symptoms changed dramatically as a result of subtle suggestions (Orne, Dinges, & Orne, 1984). He proposed that the defendant was faking symptoms of DID in an attempt to avoid the death penalty. The court found Orne's skepticism persuasive, and Bianchi was eventually convicted of murder. These circumstances are clearly rather extreme; very few patients have such an obvious motive for feigning a psychological disorder. Although the Bianchi case should not be taken to mean that all patients who exhibit signs of DID are malingering or faking, it does indicate that therapists should be cautious in evaluating the evidence for any diagnostic decision, particularly when the disorder is as difficult to define and evaluate as DID (Thomas, 2001).

The sociocognitive model holds that DID is a product of the therapist's influence on the client (Lilienfeld et al., 1999; Loewenstein, 2006). This is not to say that the patient is faking the disorder, but rather that DID patients respond to cues that are provided during the course of assessment and treatment. Clinicians have frequently noted, for example, that patients with DID are easily hypnotized and that the alter personalities are often "discovered" during hypnosis, a process that is capable of inducing phenomena such as amnesia, one important symptom of dissociative disorders. According to this view, some therapists may provide their patients with information and suggestions about DID, subtly and unconsciously encouraging them to behave in ways that are consistent with these expectations and rewarding them with extra attention and care when they adopt the role. In this regard, it is interesting to note that although the vast majority of clinicians work an entire career without seeing a single case of DID, a small handful of therapists claim to have treated large numbers of these patients (Modestin, 1992). This radically disproportionate distribution of cases is consistent with the hypothesis that some clinicians find (and perhaps encourage the development of) symptoms in which they are particularly interested.

Are all patients with DID simply trying to please their therapists or responding to subtle suggestions? The sociocognitive model may explain some cases, but it does not provide a convincing explanation for many others. The model has a number of serious limitations (Gleaves, May, & Cardena, 2001). In many cases, important symptoms have been observed before the patient enters treatment. In Paula's case, the phone call from Sherry (which was the first clear-cut evidence of an independent alter personality) occurred before the use of hypnosis. Furthermore, most therapists are not looking for DID. Dr. Harpin, for example, had never seen a case of this sort before treating Paula. He went out of his way to consider other explanations of her behavior before considering the diagnosis of DID.

If DID is, in fact, a genuine psychological phenomenon involving a disturbance in consciousness and loss of volitional control, how can we account for its development? Current etiological hypotheses focus on two primary considerations: (a) the impact of repeated, overwhelming trauma during childhood—especially sexual abuse, and (b) individual differences in the ability to enter trancelike states (Forrest, 2001).

One influential model, proposed by Putnam (1989), starts with the proposition that the behavior of all human infants (less than 12 months old) is organized in a series of discrete behavioral states, which are characterized by marked contrasts in emotion and behavior. As the child matures, these states become more integrated. Transitions among them become less abrupt and increasingly subject to voluntary control. Failure to accomplish this integration can set the stage for DID. Putnam also assumes that children are able to enter dissociative states spontaneously. Some children may find this process easier than others. Those who are adept at it can presumably escape into trances as a way of protecting themselves from the psychological impact of intense trauma. This mechanism allows the child to contain painful memories and emotions outside normal conscious awareness. Alter personalities become stronger, more elaborate, and solidified as the child repeatedly enters particular dissociative states. The child eventually loses control of the process and is unable to stop it or recognize that it is happening. DID is the final product of these tragic events.

The credibility of Putnam's developmental model rests on a number of assumptions. Perhaps most important is the presumed connection between repeated traumatic events during childhood, particularly sexual abuse, and the subsequent onset of dissociative symptoms. Does the repetition of severe trauma lead inevitably to dissociative disorders? Are patients with DID always victims of prior sexual abuse? Are patients' memories always authentic? The answers to these questions are open to question (Hacking, 1995; Hornstein & Putnam, 1996). Evidence regarding DID is particularly difficult to evaluate because it is based largely on individual cases. Since the 1970s, most published cases have involved patients who reported being sexually abused as children. Paula is one example. The frequency of such reports has persuaded many clinicians that repeated sexual abuse is a necessary and sufficient condition in the etiology of DID. But how do we know that the patients' memories are accurate? This is an extremely controversial issue. Efforts to confirm patients' memories of prior abuse meet with mixed results; some can be confirmed whereas others cannot (Kluft, 1995; Yeager & Lewis, 1997). Cautious skepticism seems to be warranted with regard to the etiological link between abuse and DID.

Treatment

Most efforts to treat patients with DID have focused on two principal strategies: Stabilize the most functional or competent personality, or integrate the disparate personalities into one. The former approach was employed initially by Thigpen and Cleckley (1957) in treating the patient described in *The Three Faces of Eve*. Follow-up reports on this case, which described the subsequent emergence of numerous additional personalities, illustrate the difficulties and possible futility of this method.

Most experts agree that integration is presently the treatment of choice (Loewenstein, 2006). Dr. Harpin employed a number of techniques in trying to help Paula fuse the various alters. The first step involves facilitating recognition by the patient of the existence of alter personalities. One approach might be to use videotapes of the alter behavior in an effort to help the patient recognize radical changes that are otherwise unknown. It may also be important to help patients understand the general nature of the problem as it has appeared in others' lives so that they can gain perspective on their own dilemma. This was the goal that Dr. Harpin had in mind when he asked Paula to read *The Three Faces of Eve*. Fusion may eventually be accomplished if the main personality comes to share the memories and emotions of the alters. Finally, the most important step involves learning to react to conflict and stress in an adaptive fashion rather than engaging in the avoidance behaviors associated with dissociative states (Lynn et al., 2006).

While working toward the process of integration, it is also important that the therapist avoid further fragmentation of the patient's behavior or personality. Unfortunately, this is a difficult caveat to heed. The existence of independent personalities of such different tastes and styles is fascinating, and the therapist is easily tempted to explore and discuss every exotic detail of the patient's experience. Extended and persistent questioning of this sort may encourage additional dissociative experiences and impede integration. The use of separate names to describe and address alter personalities may also serve to stabilize and condone their existence. Finally, although hypnosis can be a useful tool in attempting to facilitate the patient's recall of forgotten events, it can also lead to the emergence of additional personalities. None of these problems is easy to avoid. They all suggest that therapists who are confronted with patients exhibiting symptoms of DID must be extremely cautious in planning their interventions. They must attend to the unique features of the patient's dissociative experience without ignoring other potentially crucial aspects of the person's problem.

The outcome of treatment for DID is sometimes very positive. Many patients respond well to extensive and prolonged psychological treatment (Brand et al., 2009; Maldonado, Butler, & Spiegel, 2002). In that respect, Paula may also be a typical case. Optimistic impressions about the prognosis for this disorder are based largely on clinical impressions because we do not have data from long-term outcome studies with this disorder. One 2-year follow-up study of 54 patients found that many were substantially improved (Ellason & Ross, 1997). Unfortunately, randomized clinical trials comparing the efficacy of treatments and placebo programs have not been conducted. The effective ingredients of therapy have not been identified. Treatment research in this area is well behind that in most other areas of mental-health services.

Discussion Questions

1. The initial presentation of DID can be very confusing, both for the patient and the therapist. What were the various diagnostic options that Dr. Harpin originally considered when he began working with Paula? Why was DID a more appropriate diagnosis?

2. After he had been working with Paula for several years, Dr. Harpin stopped asking to talk to her alter personalities by name, preferring instead to address only Paula. Should he have adopted that strategy from the beginning of the

case? Do you think his willingness to talk to her using different names could have contributed to the problem? Or did it help him sort out the problem and establish a strong working relationship with his client?

3. Have you seen reports or discussions of DID in the popular media? Why do you think some therapists say they have treated dozens of patients with DID while the vast majority of mental-health professionals have never seen a single case?

4. Like patients with PTSD, people with DID have often been the victims of serious sexual abuse. How are the symptoms of the two disorders similar? In what ways are they different?

CHAPTER 6

Major Depressive Disorder

Janet called the mental-health center to ask if someone could help her 5-year-old son, Adam. He had been having trouble sleeping for the past several weeks, and Janet was becoming concerned about his health. Adam refused to go to sleep at his regular bedtime and also woke up at irregular intervals throughout the night. Whenever he woke up, Adam would come downstairs to be with Janet. Her initial reaction had been sympathetic, but as the cycle came to repeat itself night after night, Janet's tolerance grew thin, and she became more argumentative. She found herself engaged in repeated battles that usually ended when she agreed to let him sleep in her room. Janet felt guilty about giving in to a 5-year-old's demands, but it seemed like the only way they would ever get any sleep. The family physician was unable to identify a physical explanation for Adam's problem; he suggested that Janet contact a psychologist. This advice led Janet to inquire about the mental-health center's series of parent-training groups.

Applicants for the groups were routinely screened during an individual intake interview. The therapist began by asking several questions about Janet and her family. Janet was 30 years old and had been divorced from her husband, David, for a little more than a year. Adam was the youngest of Janet's three children; Jennifer was 10, and Claire was 8. Janet had resumed her college education on a part-time basis when Adam was 2 years old. She had hoped to finish her bachelor's degree at the end of the next semester and enter law school in the fall. Unfortunately, she had withdrawn from classes 1 month prior to her appointment at the mental-health center. Her current plans were indefinite. She spent almost all of her time at home with Adam.

Janet and the children lived in a large, comfortable house that she had received as part of her divorce settlement. Finances were a major concern to Janet, but she managed to make ends meet through the combination of student loans, a grant-in-aid from the university, and child-support payments from David. David lived in a nearby town with a younger woman whom he had married shortly after the divorce. He visited Janet and the children once or twice every month and took the children to spend weekends with him once a month.

Having collected the necessary background information, the therapist asked for a description of Adam's sleep difficulties. This discussion covered the sequence of a typical evening's events. It was clear during this discussion that Janet felt completely overwhelmed. At several points during the interview, Janet was on the verge of tears. Her eyes were watery, and her voice broke as they discussed her response to David's occasional visits. The therapist, therefore, suggested that they put off a further analysis of Adam's problems and spend some time discussing Janet's situation in a broader perspective.

Janet's mood had been depressed since her husband had asked for a divorce. She felt sad, discouraged, and lonely. This feeling had become even more severe just prior to her withdrawal from classes at the university (1 year after David's departure). When David left, she remembered feeling "down in the dumps," but she could usually cheer herself up by playing with the children or going for a walk. Now she was nearing desperation. She cried frequently and for long periods of time. Nothing seemed to cheer her up. She had lost interest in her friends, and the children seemed to be more of a burden than ever. Her depression was somewhat worse in the morning, when it seemed that she would never be able to make it through the day.

Janet was preoccupied with her divorce from David and spent hours each day brooding about the events that led to their separation. These worries interfered considerably with her ability to concentrate and seemed directly related to her withdrawal from the university. She had been totally unable to study assigned readings or concentrate on lectures. Withdrawing from school precipitated further problems. She was no longer eligible for student aid and would have to begin paying back her loans within a few months. In short, one problem led to another, and her attitude became increasingly pessimistic.

Janet blamed herself for the divorce, although she also harbored considerable resentment toward David and his new wife. She believed that her return to school had placed additional strain on an already problematic relationship, and she wondered whether she had acted selfishly. The therapist noted that Janet's reasoning about her marriage often seemed vague and illogical. She argued that she had been a poor marital partner and cited several examples of her own misconduct. These included events and circumstances that struck the therapist as being very common and perhaps expected differences between men and women. For example, Janet spent more money than he did on clothes, did not share his enthusiasm for sports, and frequently tried to engage David in discussions about his personal habits that annoyed her and the imperfections of their relationship. Of course, one could easily argue that David had not been sufficiently concerned about his own appearance (spending too little effort on his own wardrobe), that he had been too preoccupied with sports, and that he had avoided her sincere efforts to work on their marital difficulties. But Janet blamed herself. Rather than viewing these things as simple differences in their interests and personalities, Janet saw them as evidence of her own failures. She blew these matters totally out of proportion until they appeared to her to be terrible sins. Janet also generalized from her marriage to other relationships in her life. If her first marriage had failed, how could she ever expect to develop a satisfactory relationship with another man? Furthermore, Janet had begun to question her value as a friend and parent. The collapse of her marriage seemed to affect the manner in which she viewed all of her social relationships.

The future looked bleak from her current perspective, but she had not given up all hope. Her interest in solving Adam's problem, for example, was an encouraging sign. Although she was not optimistic about the chances of success, she was willing to try to become a more effective parent.

Social History

Janet was reserved socially when she was a child. She tended to have one or two special friends with whom she spent much of her time outside of school, but she felt awkward and self-conscious in larger groups of children. This friendship pattern persisted throughout high school. She was interested in boys and dated intermittently until her junior year in high school, when she began to date one boy on a regular basis. She and her boyfriend spent all of their time together. Janet remembered that the other kids teased them about acting as if they were married. Unfortunately, she and her boyfriend broke up during Janet's first year in college.

Janet met David a few weeks afterward, and they were married the following summer. Janet later wondered whether she had rushed into her relationship with David primarily to avoid the vacuum created by her previous boyfriend's sudden exit. Whatever her motivation might have been, her marriage was followed shortly by her first pregnancy, which precipitated her withdrawal from the university. For the next seven years, Janet was occupied as a full-time mother and homemaker.

When Adam was 2 years old and able to attend a day-care center, Janet decided to resume her college education. Her relationship with David became increasingly strained. They had even less time than usual to spend with each other. David resented his increased household responsibilities. Janet was no longer able to prepare meals for the family every night of the week, so David had to learn to cook. He also had to share the cleaning and drive the children to many of their lessons and social activities. A more balanced and stable relationship would have been able to withstand the stress associated with these changes, but Janet and David were unable to adjust. Instead of working to improve their communications, they bickered continuously. The final blow came when David met another woman to whom he was attracted and who offered him an alternative to the escalating hostility with Janet. He asked for a divorce and moved to an apartment.

Janet was shaken by David's departure, despite the fact that they had not been happy together. Fortunately, she did have a few friends to whom she could turn for support. The most important one was a neighbor who had children of approximately the same ages as Janet's daughters. There were also two couples with whom she and David had socialized. They were all helpful for the first few weeks, but she quickly lost contact with the couples. It was awkward to get together as a threesome, and Janet had never been close enough with the women to preserve their relationships on an individual basis. That left the neighbor as her sole adviser and confidante, the only person with whom Janet felt she could discuss her feelings openly.

For the next few months, Janet was able to continue her studies. With the children's help, she managed the household chores and kept up with her work. She even found time for some brief social activities. She agreed to go out on two blind dates arranged by people with whom she and David had been friends. These were generally unpleasant encounters; one of her dates was boring and unattractive, and the other was obnoxiously aggressive. After the latter experience, she discontinued the minimal efforts she had made to develop new friendships.

As time wore on, Janet found herself brooding more and more about the divorce. She was gaining weight, and the children began to comment on her appearance. To make matters worse, Claire became sick just prior to Janet's midterm exams. The added worry of Claire's health and her concern about missed classes and lost studying time contributed substantially to a decline in Janet's mood. She finally realized that she would have to withdraw from her classes to avoid receiving failing grades.

By this point, 1 month prior to her appointment at the mental-health center, she had lost interest in most of her previous activities. Even casual reading had come to be a tedious chore. She did not have any hobbies because she never had enough time. She also found that her best friend, the neighbor, was becoming markedly aloof. When Janet called, she seldom talked for more than a few minutes before finding an excuse to hang up. Their contacts gradually diminished to an occasional wave across the street or a quick, polite conversation when they picked up their children from school. It seemed that her friend had grown tired of Janet's company.

This was Janet's situation when she contacted the mental-health center. Her mood was depressed and anxious. She was preoccupied with financial concerns and her lack of social relationships. Adam's sleeping problem, which had begun about a week after she withdrew from her classes, was the last straw. She felt that she could no longer control her difficult situation and recognized that she needed help.

Conceptualization and Treatment

The therapist and Janet discussed her overall situation and agreed that Adam was only a small part of the problem. They decided to work together on an individual basis instead of having Janet join the parent-training group.

Janet's depression was clearly precipitated by her divorce, which had a drastic impact on many areas of her life. Increased financial burdens were clearly part of this picture, but interpersonal relationships were even more meaningful. Although the marriage had been far from ideal in terms of meeting Janet's needs, her relationship with David had been one important part of the way in which Janet thought about herself. She had lost one of her most important roles (as a wife). The therapist believed that an enduring improvement in her mood would depend on her success in developing new relationships and expanded roles for herself. And she would eventually need to learn parenting skills that would allow her to perform her maternal role more successfully. In other words, the therapist adopted a problem-solving approach to Janet's situation. He was particularly concerned about the passive and ruminative way in which she had begun to respond to the circumstances in her life. The therapist decided to encourage her to engage more actively with her environment while also teaching her to perform specific behaviors more effectively.

As an initial step, the therapist asked Janet to list all the activities that she enjoyed. He wanted to shift attention away from the unpleasant factors with which Janet was currently preoccupied. Most of the activities Janet mentioned were things that she had not done for several months or years. For example, prior to her return to school, her favorite pastime had been riding horses. She said that she would like to begin riding again, but she felt that it was prohibitively expensive and time consuming. With considerable prodding from the therapist, Janet also listed a few other activities. These included talking with a friend over a cup of coffee, listening to music late at night after the children were asleep, and going for walks in the woods behind her home. In some cases, Janet indicated that these activities used to be pleasant, but she did not think that they would be enjoyable at the present time.

Despite Janet's ambivalence, the therapist encouraged her to pick one activity that she would try at least twice before their next meeting. A short walk in the woods seemed like the most practical alternative, considering that Adam might interrupt listening to music and she did not want to call Susan. The therapist also asked Janet to call the campus riding club to inquire about their activities.

At the same time that the therapist encouraged Janet to increase her activity level, he also began to concentrate on an assessment of her interactions with other people. For several sessions, they covered topics such as selecting situations in which Janet might be likely to meet people with whom she would be interested in developing a friendship, initiating a conversation, maintaining a conversation by asking the other person a series of consecutive questions, and other elementary issues. Having identified areas that were problematic for Janet, they discussed solutions and actually practiced, or role-played, various social interactions.

During the first few weeks of treatment, Janet's mood seemed to be improving. Perhaps most important was her luck in finding a part-time job at a local riding stable. She learned of the opening when she called to ask about the campus riding club. They were looking for someone who would feed and exercise the horses every morning. The wages were low, but she was allowed to ride as long as she wanted each day without charge. Furthermore, the schedule allowed her to finish before the girls returned from school. The money also helped her return Adam to the day-care center on a part-time basis. Janet still felt depressed when she was at home, but she loved to ride, and it helped to know that she would go to work in the morning.

An unfortunate sequence of events led to a serious setback shortly after it seemed that Janet's mood was beginning to improve. Her financial aid had been discontinued, and she could no longer cover her monthly mortgage payments. Within several weeks, she received a notice from the bank threatening to fore-close her mortgage and sell her house. Her appearance was noticeably changed when she arrived for her next appointment. She was apathetic and lethargic. She cried through most of the session, and her outlook had grown distinctly more pessimistic. The therapist was particularly alarmed by an incident that Janet described as happening the previous day. She had been filling her car with gas when a mechanic at the service station mentioned that her muffler sounded like it was cracked. He told her that she should get it fixed right away because of the dangerous exhaust fumes. In his words, "that's a good way to kill yourself." The thought of suicide had not occurred to Janet prior to this comment, but she found that she could not get it out of her mind. She was frightened by the idea and tried to distract herself by watching television. The thoughts continued to intrude despite these efforts.

The therapist immediately discussed several changes in the treatment plan with Janet. He arranged for her to consult a psychiatrist, who prescribed fluox-etine (Prozac), an antidepressant drug. She also agreed to increase the frequency of her appointments at the clinic to three times a week. These changes were primarily motivated by the onset of suicidal ideation. More drastic action, such as hospitalization or calling relatives for additional support, did not seem to be necessary because her thoughts were not particularly lethal. For example, she said that she did not want to die, even though she was thinking quite a lot about death. The idea frightened her, and she did not have a specific plan arranged by which she would accomplish her own death. Nevertheless, the obvious deteriora-tion in her condition warranted a more intense treatment program.

The next month proved to be a difficult one for Janet, but she was able to persevere. Three weeks after she began taking the medication, her mood seemed to brighten. The suicidal ideation disappeared, she became more talkative, and she resumed most of her normal activities. The people who owned the riding stable were understanding and held Janet's new job for her until she was able to return. The financial crisis was solved, at least temporarily, when her father agreed to provide her with substantial assistance. In fact, he expressed surprise and some dismay that she had never asked him for help in the past or even told him that she was in financial trouble. The problem-solving and social skills pro-gram progressed well after Janet began taking medication. Within several weeks, she was able to reestablish her friendship with Susan. She was able to meet a few people at the riding stable, and her social network seemed to be widening.

After Janet's mood had improved, the issue of Adam's sleeping problem was addressed. The therapist explained that Janet needed to set firm limits on Adam's manipulative behavior. Her inconsistency in dealing with his demands, coupled with the attention that he received during the bedtime scene, could be thought of as leading to intermittent reinforcement of his inappropriate behavior. Janet and the therapist worked out a simple set of responses that she would follow whenever he got up and came downstairs. She would offer him a drink, take him back to his room, tuck him in bed, and leave immediately. Ten days after the procedure was implemented, Adam began sleeping through the night without interruption. This rapid success enhanced Janet's sense of control over her situation. Her enthusiasm led her to enroll in the parent-training program for which she had originally applied. She continued to improve her relationship with her children.

Janet's individual therapy sessions were discontinued 9 months after her first appointment. At that point, she was planning to return to school, was still working part time at the riding stable, and had started to date one of the men she met at work. Her children were all healthy, and she had managed to keep their house. She continued to take antidepressant medication.

Discussion

A sad or dysphoric mood is obviously the most prominent feature of clinical depression. Depressed patients describe themselves as feeling discouraged, hopeless, and apathetic. This dejected emotional state is usually accompanied by a variety of unpleasant thoughts that may include suicidal ideation These cognitive features of depression are sometimes called *the depressive triad*: a negative view of the self, the world, and the future. Depressed people see themselves as inadequate and unworthy. They are often filled with guilt and remorse over apparently ordinary and trivial events. These patients hold a similarly dim view of their environment. Everyday experiences and social interactions are interpreted in the most critical fashion. The future seems bleak and empty. In fact, some extremely depressed patients find it impossible to imagine any future at all.

Clinical depression is identified by changes in several important areas in the person's life. In addition to a prominent and relatively persistent dysphoric mood, *DSM-IV-TR* (APA, 2000, p. 356) lists several features for major depressive episodes. Specifically, at least five of the following symptoms must have been present nearly every day for at least 2 weeks if the patient is to meet the criteria for this diagnostic category:

1. Depressed mood most of the day
2. Markedly diminished interest or pleasure in all, or almost all, activities most of the day
3. Significant weight loss (when not dieting) or weight gain, or decrease or increase in appetite

4. Insomnia or hypersomnia (prolonged sleep)
5. Psychomotor agitation or retardation
6. Fatigue or loss of energy
7. Feelings of worthlessness or excessive or inappropriate guilt (not merely self-reproach or guilt about being sick)
8. Diminished ability to think or concentrate, or indecisiveness
9. Recurrent thoughts of death (not just fear of dying), recurrent suicidal ideation without a specific plan, or a suicide attempt or a specific plan for committing suicide

Janet clearly fit these criteria. Her mood had been markedly depressed since her separation from David. She had gained considerable weight—25 pounds in 9 months. Her concentration was severely impaired, as evidenced by her inability to study and her loss of interest in almost everything. Excessive and inappropriate guilt was clearly a prominent feature of her constant brooding about the divorce. Although she did not actually attempt to harm herself, she experienced a distressing period of ruminative suicidal ideation. Sleep impairment may also have been a problem, but it was difficult to evaluate in the context of Adam's behavior. Prior to her first visit at the clinic, Janet had been sleeping less than her usual number of hours per night, and she reported considerable fatigue. It was difficult to know whether she would have been able to sleep if Adam had not been so demanding of her attention throughout the night.

Most therapists agree that it is important to recognize the difference between clinical depression and other states of unhappiness and disappointment. Consider, for example, people who are mourning the loss of a friend or relative. *DSM-IV-TR* (APA, 2000) suggests that a diagnosis of a major depressive episode should be made only if bereavement persists for more than 2 months (assuming that the person meets the diagnostic criteria for this condition). Is this a qualitative or a quantitative distinction? Are patients who might be considered clinically depressed simply more unhappy than their peers, or are these phenomena completely distinct? This is one of the most interesting and difficult questions facing investigators in the field of mood disorders. The present diagnostic system handles the problem by including an intermediate category, dysthymia, which lies between major depressive disorder and normal mood. This category includes patients who exhibit chronic depressed symptoms that are not of sufficient severity to meet the criteria for major mood disorder.

Etiological Considerations

Several psychological models have been proposed to account for the development of major depression. Each model focuses on somewhat different features of depressive disorders (e.g., interpersonal relations, inactivity, or self-deprecating thoughts), but most share an interest in the role of negative or stressful events in the precipitation of major depression.

Freud's explanation for the development of depression began with a comparison between depression and bereavement (Freud, 1917, 1925). The two conditions are similar. Both involve a dejected mood, a loss of interest in the outside world, and an inhibition of activity. One principal feature distinguishes between the person who is depressed and the person who is mourning: a disturbance of self-regard. Depressed people chastise themselves, saying that they are worthless, morally depraved, and worthy of punishment. Freud noted the disparity between such extreme negative views and the more benign opinions of other people who do not hold the depressed person in such contempt. In other words, the depressed person's view does not seem to be an accurate self-perception. Freud went on to argue that depressed people are not really complaining about themselves but are, in fact, expressing hostile feelings that pertain to someone else. Depression is therefore the manifestation of a process in which anger is turned inward and directed against the self instead of against its original object.

Why would some people direct hostility against themselves? Freud argued that the foundation for this problem is laid in early childhood. For various reasons, people who are prone to depression have formed dependent interpersonal relationships. This dependency fosters frustration and hostility. Because these negative feelings might threaten the relationship if they are expressed openly, they are denied awareness. Problems then arise when the relationship is ended, for whatever reason. The depressed person's ego presumably identifies with the lost loved one. The intense hostility that had been felt for that person is now turned against the self, or introjected. Following this model, treatment would consist of an attempt to make the client aware of these unconscious, hostile impulses. Their more direct expression would presumably eliminate the depression.

At least one aspect of this model seems consistent with Janet's situation. She had, in fact, formed a series of intense, dependent relationships with men, beginning in high school. One might argue that her depression was precipitated by the loss incurred during her separation and divorce from David. She resented the separation deeply. Her guilt might be seen as a criticism of David's behavior. Other aspects of Janet's behavior, however, are inconsistent with Freud's model. Although Janet was critical of herself, she was also quite vocal in David's presence. They fought openly several times, both before and after the divorce, and he was fully aware of Janet's anger and resentment. It therefore seems unlikely that Janet's depression was a simple manifestation of misdirected hostility. It is also unlikely that her depression would be relieved by simply encouraging her to express her feelings more openly.

More recent attempts to explain the development of depression in psychological terms have borrowed and extended various aspects of Freud's psychoanalytic model. One important consideration involves his observation that the onset of depression is often preceded by a dependent personality style and then precipitated by the loss of an important relationship. Personality factors and relational distress may help to explain the fact that women are twice as likely as men to develop major depression. Dependent people base their self-esteem on acceptance and approval by others. Some authors have suggested that, throughout their social development, women are frequently taught to think this way about themselves (Crick & Zahn-Waxler, 2003; Gilligan, 1982). Stereotypes of female roles include descriptions of personality traits such as being passive, dependent, and emotional (whereas men are presumably more often encouraged to be aggressive, autonomous, and rational). An extension of this hypothesis holds that women are more likely than men to define themselves in terms of their relationships with other people. Women would then presumably be more distressed by marital difficulties and divorce. In Janet's case, the loss of her relationship with David was certainly an important consideration in the onset of her depression. Her sense of self-worth was severely threatened by the divorce, despite the fact that her marriage had been far from ideal.

Stressful life events play a causal role in the etiology of depression (Harkness et al., 2010; Monroe & Harkness, 2005). One classic study has received considerable attention because it led to the development of a model that begins to explain the relationship between environmental conditions and the onset of depression. Brown and Harris (1978) found an increased incidence of stressful events in the lives of depressed women but only with regard to a particular subset of such events—those that were severe and involved long-term consequences for the woman's well-being. Divorce and marital separation were prominent among these events, which also included events such as illness, loss of a job, and many other types of personal adversity. The impact of a stressful event apparently depends on the meaning that the event has for the person. Severe events that occur in the context of ongoing difficulties (such as a chronically distressed marriage) and events that occur in areas of a woman's life to which she is particularly committed (such as a child's health or the development of a career) are most likely to lead to the onset of depression (Brown, 2002).

The association between stressful life events and depression is apparently bidirectional. Stress may cause depression, but depression also causes stress. In comparison to women who are not depressed and women with medical disorders, depressed women generate higher levels of stress, especially in interpersonal relationships such as marriage (Hammen, 2005). This result indicates the operation of a dynamic process. Stressors that are not related to the person's own behavior may precipitate the onset of a depressed mood. The depressed person may then engage in maladaptive ways of coping with the immediate situation, and these dysfunctional behaviors may lead to even higher levels of stress.

Several of these concepts are consistent with Janet's situation. She had clearly experienced a high level of stress in the months before she entered therapy. The divorce from David is one obvious example. Her difficulties with the children may be another instance. When Claire's illness eventually forced her to withdraw from the university, there were important long-term consequences for her graduation and subsequent plans to enter law school.

Stressful life events are likely to precipitate depression, particularly in the absence of adequate social support. The manner in which these experiences combine to take their effect, however, is currently a matter of dispute and speculation. It is important to remember that most people experience stressful events at one time or another, but most people do not become seriously depressed. What factors make some people more psychologically vulnerable? Do people who are prone to depression respond differently than others to the problems of everyday life? Are they less likely than other people to establish or maintain a protective social support network? These questions have been addressed by other etiological models.

Social-learning theorists (Joiner, Coyne, & Blalock, 1999) also emphasize the importance of interpersonal relationships and social skills (cf. narcissism and dependence) in the onset and maintenance of depression. This model provides an interesting account of the way in which depressed people respond to stressful life events and the effect that these responses have on other people. Others respond empathically and are initially attentive when the depressed person talks about depressing experiences, yet, the long-range result of this process is usually negative. The depressed person's few remaining friends eventually become tired of this behavior and begin to avoid further interactions. Whatever sources of social support may have been available are eventually driven away. One important factor in this regard is a deficit in social skills. Depressed people may be ineffective in their interactions with other people. An important aspect of treatment would therefore be to identify specific skills in which the person is deficient and to teach the person more effective ways of interacting with others.

Several aspects of this model are consistent with the present case. After her separation from David, Janet had become isolated. Her long discussions with her neighbor had eventually soured their relationship and eliminated one of her last sources of social support. When Janet and her therapist discussed things that she might do to meet new friends, she seemed lost. The few attempts that she had made, such as her blind dates, had gone badly, and she did not know where else to begin.

Another consideration in social-learning views of depression involves the way in which people respond to the onset of a depressed mood. Some people try to distract themselves from negative emotions by becoming involved in some activity. Others respond in a more passive fashion and tend to ruminate about the sources of their distress. Nolen-Hoeksema (2002) proposed that people who respond in a passive, ruminative way experience longer and more severe periods of depression. She also suggested that this factor may account for gender differences in the prevalence of depression because women are more likely than men to employ this response style. Janet's behavior following her divorce fits nicely with Nolen-Hoeksema's conceptual framework. Although Janet initially tried to cope actively with her various problems, she soon relinquished most of her efforts to find new friends or to keep up with her studies. She frequently found herself brooding about the divorce and the hopeless nature of her circumstances. Her therapist encouraged Janet to engage more frequently in pleasant activities in an effort to break this cycle of passive, ruminative behavior.

In addition to the social and behavioral aspects of depression, it is also important to consider the way in which depressed people perceive or interpret events in their environment. What do they think about themselves and things that happen in their world? More specifically, how do they explain the experience of negative events? Cognitive perspectives suggest that patterns of thinking and perception play a prominent role in the development of depression (Gotlib & Joormann, 2010; Mathews & MacLeod, 2005). According to one influential theory, the occurrence of negative life events may lead to the development of hopelessness, which in turn causes the onset of symptoms of depression (Alloy, Abramson, Walshaw, & Neeren, 2006). Two cognitive elements define the state of hopelessness: (a) the expectation that highly desired outcomes will not occur or that highly aversive outcomes will occur, and (b) the belief that the person cannot do anything (is helpless) to change the likelihood that these events will occur.

Why do some people become hopeless after negative experiences whereas others do not? The theory holds that the likelihood of developing hopelessness will depend on the person's inferences regarding three factors: the cause of the event, the consequences of the event, and the implications of the event with regard to the self. For example, hopeless depression is likely to occur if the person views a negative event as being important and also attributes the event to factors that are enduring (stable) and likely to affect many outcomes (global). The theory also recognizes that the perceived consequences of the negative event may be as important as inferred causes. If the person views the negative consequences of the event as important, persistent, and wide ranging, depression will be more likely to develop than if the consequences are viewed as unimportant, short lived, or limited in scope. The third and final consideration involves negative inferences about the self. Depression is a more likely outcome if the person interprets a negative event to mean that she or he is a less able, worthy, or desirable person.

Depressed people do express an inordinately high proportion of negative statements about themselves and how they relate to the world. Janet's interpretation of the events leading up to and surrounding her divorce fit with the hopelessness theory. She believed that the disintegration of her marriage was her own fault rather than David's; she argued that her failure in that relationship was characteristic of her interactions with all other men rather than specific to one person; and she maintained that she would never be able to change this pattern of behavior.

Treatment

Janet's treatment involved a combination of psychotherapy and antidepressant medication. Following the social learning/interpersonal model, her therapist focused on increasing Janet's activity level and helping her learn new social skills. By encouraging activities such as riding, the therapist hoped to interrupt and reverse the ongoing, interactive process in which social isolation, rumination, and inactivity led to increased depression, depression led to further withdrawal, and so on. Through the development of new response patterns, particularly those involving interpersonal communication and parenting skills, he hoped to enable Janet to deal more effectively with future stressful events. Increased social activity and more effective communication would also lead to a more supportive social network that might help reduce the impact of stressful events. Recent evidence suggests that behavioral activation—increasing pleasant activities and positive interactions with others—is one effective approach to the treatment of depression (Lejuez, Hopko, Acierno, Daughters, & Pagoto, 2011; Mazzuccelli, Kane, & Rees, 2009).

The therapy that Janet received was, in many respects, similar to another psychological approach to treating depression that is known as *interpersonal psychotherapy*, or IPT (Mufson et al., 2004; Weissman, 2007). The focus of IPT is the connection between depressive symptoms and current interpersonal problems. Relatively little attention is paid to long-standing personality problems or developmental issues. The treatment takes a practical, problem-solving approach to resolving the sorts of daily conflicts in close relationships that can exacerbate and maintain depression. Deficits in social skills are addressed in an active and supportive fashion. The depressed person is also encouraged to pursue new activities that might take the place of relationships or occupational roles that have been lost. Therapy sessions often include nondirective discussions of social difficulties and unexpressed or unacknowledged negative emotions as well as role-playing to practice specific social skills.

Antidepressant medication was introduced when the risk of suicide became apparent. Janet's suicidal ideation was not extremely lethal. She had not planned a particular method by which she might end her life, and she reported that the idea of harming herself was frightening. The risk would have been much greater if she did have more specific plans and if she had really wanted to die. Nevertheless, her morbid ruminations marked a clear deterioration in her condition that called for more intensive treatment. Three general classes of drugs are useful in the treatment of depression: selective serotonin reuptake inhibitors (SSRIs), tricyclics (TCAs), and monoamine oxidase (MAO) inhibitors. Improvements in the patient's mood and other specific affective symptoms are typically evident after 2 to 4 weeks of drug treatment. Their continued administration also reduces the probability of symptomatic relapse.

Janet was given fluoxetine (Prozac), which is an SSRI. Selective serotonin reuptake inhibitors were developed in the 1980s and now account for most prescriptions written for antidepressant medication (Hameed, Schwartz, Malhotra, West, & Bertone, 2005; Hirschfeld, 2001). Additional examples of SSRIs include fluvoxamine (Luvox), sertraline (Zoloft), and paroxetine (Paxil). The SSRIs inhibit the reuptake of serotonin into the presynaptic nerve ending and therefore increase the amount of serotonin available in the synaptic cleft. SSRIs have fewer side effects (such as weight gain, constipation, and drowsiness) than

TCAs or MAO inhibitors; they are easier to take (one pill a day instead of experimenting for weeks to find the proper dosage); and they are less dangerous if the patient takes an overdose. This does not mean that they are without side effects of their own. Some patients experience nausea, headaches, fatigue, restlessness, and sexual side effects such as difficulty in reaching orgasm. Controlled outcome studies indicate that Prozac and other SSRIs are at least as effective as traditional forms of antidepressant medication (Kroenke et al., 2001). Medication and psychotherapy are both effective forms of treatment for people who suffer from major depression (Hollon, Thase, & Markowitz, 2002).

One obvious disadvantage associated with both medication and psychotherapy is the extended delay involved in achieving therapeutic effects. In the face of a serious suicidal threat, for example, the therapist may not be able to wait several weeks for a change in the patient's adjustment. Also, many patients do not respond positively to medication or psychosocial treatment approaches. Another form of intervention that may be tried with depressed patients, particularly if they exhibit profound motor retardation and have failed to respond positively to antidepressant medication, is electroconvulsive therapy (ECT). In the standard ECT procedure, a brief seizure is induced by passing an electrical current between two electrodes that have been placed over the patient's temples. A full course of treatment generally involves the induction of six to eight seizures spaced at 48-hour intervals. The procedure was first introduced as a treatment for schizophrenia, but it soon became apparent that it was most effective with depressed patients. Many studies have supported this conclusion (Husain, Kevan, Linnell, & Scott, 2004).

Much of the controversy surrounding ECT is based on misconceptions concerning the procedure and its effects. Although it is often referred to as "shock therapy," ECT does not involve the perception of an electrical current. In fact, a short-acting anesthetic is administered prior to the seizure so that the patient is not conscious when the current is applied. Many of the deleterious side effects of ECT have been eliminated by modifications in the treatment procedure, such as the use of muscle relaxants to avoid bone fractures during the seizure (Abrams, 2002). The extent and severity of memory loss can be greatly reduced by the use of unilateral electrode placement. If both electrodes are placed over the nondominant hemisphere of the patient's brain, the patient can experience less verbal memory impairment, but the treatment may be less effective in terms of its antidepressant results. There is, of course, the serious question of permanent changes in brain structure and function. Some critics of ECT have argued that it produces irreversible neurological impairment. Proponents of ECT maintain that the evidence for this conclusion is inadequate (Abrams, 2002). Most of the objections to the use of ECT are based on misconceptions. The evidence supporting its therapeutic efficacy seems to justify the continued use of ECT with some severely depressed patients who have not responded to less-intrusive forms of treatment.

Discussion Questions

1. Patients who are experiencing serious suicidal thoughts are frequently hospitalized involuntarily. What are the advantages and disadvantages of forcing people to be hospitalized against their will?

2. Janet had experienced a series of stressful events and circumstances. Would anyone have become depressed if they were in the same situation? If not, what other factors might have combined with these stressful events to lead to her depression?

3. From the beginning of therapy, the psychologist encouraged Janet to become more actively involved in various pleasant activities. Do you think treatment would have been even more effective if they had initially spent more time discussing at length the sources of her distress (such as her feelings about her divorce)?

4. Imagine that one of your close relatives has been depressed for several years. The person has not responded to previous forms of treatment (both medication and psychotherapy) and is now talking about committing suicide. Would you be willing to authorize a series of ECT for your relative? Why or why not?

CHAPTER 7

Bipolar Disorder

By the time he was admitted to the hospital, George Lawler was talking a mile a minute. He harangued the other patients and ward staff, declaring that he was the coach of the U.S. Olympic track team and offering to hold tryouts for the other patients in the hospital. His movements were rapid and somewhat erratic as he paced the halls of the ward and explored every room. At the slightest provocation, he flew into a rage. When an attendant blocked his entrance to the nursing station, he threatened to report her to the president of the Olympic committee. He had not slept for 3 nights. His face was covered with a stubbly growth of beard, and his hair was scattered in various directions. His eyes were sunken and bloodshot, but they still gleamed with an intense excitement.

His life had taken a drastic change over the past 2 weeks. George was 35 years old, married, and the father of two young children. He worked at a small junior college where he taught physical education and coached both the men's and women's track teams. Until his breakdown, the teams had been having an outstanding season. They were undefeated in dual competition and heavy favorites to win the conference championship. The campus was following their accomplishments closely because it had been many years since one of the school teams had won a championship. In fact, track was the only sport in which the school had a winning record that season.

This was not the first time that George had experienced psychological problems. His first serious episode had occurred during his junior year in college. It did not seem to be triggered by any particular incident; in fact, things had been going well. George was playing defensive back on the university football team. He was in good academic standing and fairly popular with the other students. Nevertheless, during the spring semester, George found that he was losing interest in everything. It was not surprising that he did not look forward to classes or studying. He had never been an outstanding student. But he noticed that he no longer enjoyed going out with his friends. They said he seemed depressed all the time. George said he just did not care anymore. He began avoiding his girlfriend, and when they were together, he found fault with almost everything she did. Most of his time was spent in his apartment in front of the television. It did not seem to matter what program he watched because his concentration was seriously impaired. He kept the TV on as a kind of distraction, not as entertainment. When he did not show up for spring football practice, the coach called him to his office for a long talk. George told his coach that he did not have the energy to play football. In fact, he did not feel he could make it through the easiest set of drills. He did not care about the team or about his future in sports. Recognizing that George's problem was more than a simple lack of motivation, the coach persuaded him to visit a friend of his—a psychiatrist at the student health clinic. George began taking antidepressant medication and attending individual counseling sessions. Within several weeks, he was back to his normal level of functioning, and treatment was discontinued.

George had also experienced periods of unusual ambition and energy. As a student, he had frequently spent several days cramming for exams at the end of a semester. Many of his friends took amphetamines to stay awake, but George seemed able to summon endless, internal reserves of energy. In retrospect, these periods seemed to be hypomanic episodes (i.e., periods of increased energy that are not sufficiently severe to qualify as full-blown mania). At the time, these episodes went relatively unnoticed. George's temporary tendency toward excess verbosity, his lack of need for sleep, and his ambitious goals did not seem pathological. In fact, his energetic intervals were productive, and his behavioral excesses were probably adaptive in the competitive university environment.

There had been two subsequent episodes of depression with symptoms that were similar to those of the first episode. The most recent incident had occurred 8 months prior to his current hospitalization. It was September, 2 weeks after the start of the fall semester. George had been worried about his job and the team all summer. Who would replace his star sprinter who had transferred to the state university? Would his high jumper get hurt during the football season? Could they improve on last year's winning record? Over the past month, these concerns had become constant and consuming. George was having trouble getting to sleep; he was also waking up in the middle of the night for no apparent reason. He felt tired all the time. His wife and children noticed that he was always brooding and seemed preoccupied. Then came the bad news. First, the athletic department told him that he would not get an increase in travel funds, which he had expected. Then he learned that one of his assistant coaches was taking a leave of absence to finish working on her degree. Neither of these events would have a drastic effect on the upcoming season, but George took them to be disasters. His mood changed from one of tension and anxiety to severe depression. Over several days, George became more and more lethargic until he was almost completely unresponsive. His speech was slow and, when he did say more than a word or two, he spoke in a dull monotone. Refusing to get out of bed, he alternated between long hours of sleep and staring vacuously at the ceiling. He called the athletic director and quit his job, pointing to minor incidents as evidence of his own incompetence. He believed, for example, that the assistant coach had quit because of a brief argument that he had had with her 6 months earlier. In fact, they had a positive relationship, and she had always planned to return to school at one time or another. She was leaving earlier than she had expected for personal reasons. George seemed to be blaming himself for everything. He apologized profusely to his wife and children for failing them as a husband and father. His despair seemed genuine. Suicide appeared to be the only reasonable solution. He threatened to end it all if his family would only leave him alone.

George's wife, Cheryl, called the psychiatrist who had treated him during his last episode (2 years earlier) and arranged a special appointment. The psychiatrist decided to prescribe lithium carbonate, a drug that is used to treat manic episodes but that is also an effective antidepressant with bipolar patients (those who show both manic and depressed phases of disturbance). Although George had never been hospitalized for a manic episode, the psychiatrist suggested that his past history of "maniclike" behavior (increased energy, sleeplessness, inflated self-esteem, and so on) and his positive family history for bipolar disorder (his uncle Ralph) were both consistent with the diagnosis of bipolar disorder. The lithium seemed to be effective. Three weeks later, George was back at work. Maintenance doses of lithium were prescribed in an attempt to reduce the frequency and severity of future mood swings.

His first fully developed manic period began suddenly near the end of the next spring track season. The team was having a good year, and a few team members had turned in remarkable individual performances. Two days before the conference meet, Cheryl noticed that George was behaving strangely. There was a driven quality about his preparation for the meet. He was working much longer hours and demanding more from the athletes. When he was home, he talked endlessly about the team, bragging about its chances for national recognition and planning intricate strategies for particularly important events. Cheryl was worried about this change in George's behavior, but she attributed it to the pressures of his job and assured herself that he would return to normal when the season was over.

George was clearly losing control over his own behavior. The following incident, which occurred on the day of the conference meet, illustrates the dramatic quality of his disturbance. While the men's team was dressing in the locker room prior to taking the field, George paced rapidly up and down the aisles, gesturing emphatically and talking at length about specific events and the virtues of winning. When the men were all in uniform, George gathered them around his own locker. Without Cheryl's knowledge, he had removed a ceremonial sword from their fireplace mantel and brought it with him that morning. He drew the sword from his locker and leaped up on a bench in the midst of the men. Swinging the sword above his head, he began chanting the school's fight song. The athletes joined in, and he led them out onto the field screaming and shaking their fists in the air. A reporter for the school newspaper later described the incident as the most inspirational pregame performance he had ever seen in a locker room. Without question, the team was driven to an exceptional emotional peak, and it did go on to win the meet by a huge margin. In fact, George was later given the school's annual coaching award. His behavior prior to the meet was specifically cited as an example of his outstanding leadership qualities. Unfortunately, the action was also another manifestation of psychopathology and a signal of further problems that would soon follow.

George did not return home after the meet. He stayed in his office, working straight through the night in preparation for the regional meet. Cheryl was finally able to locate him by phoning his friend who worked in the office next door. She and his colleagues tried to persuade him to slow down, but he would not listen. The next morning George was approached by a reporter from the school newspaper. Here, George thought, was the perfect opportunity to expound on his ability as a coach and to publicize his exciting plans for future competition. The interview turned into a grandiose tirade, with George rambling uninterrupted for 3 hours. The reporter could neither interrupt nor extract himself from this unexpected and embarrassing situation.

The interview turned into a professional disaster for George. Among other things, George boasted that he was going to send the star high jumper from the women's team to the NCAA national meet in Oregon. He planned to go along as her chaperone and said that he would pay for their trip out of the proceeds of a recent community fund-raising drive. This announcement was startling in two regards. First, the money in question had been raised with the athletic department's assurance that it would be used to improve the college's track facilities and to sponsor running clinics for local children. George did not have the authority to redirect the funds. His announcement was certain to anger the business leaders who had organized the drive. Second, the prospect of a married male coach chaperoning a female athlete, who also happened to be quite attractive, promised to raise a minor scandal in their small, conservative community. Recognizing the sensitive nature of these plans, the reporter asked George if he might want to reconsider his brash announcement. George replied—asking the reporter to quote him—that it was not every year that he had the opportunity to take a free trip with a pretty girl, and he was not about to pass it up. He added that this might blossom into a genuine romance.

The article appeared, along with a picture of George, on the front page of the school paper the next morning. His disheveled appearance and outrageous remarks raised an instant furor in the athletic department and the school administration. The head of the department finally located George in his office making a series of long-distance calls. The director demanded an explanation and immediately found himself in the midst of an ear-shattering shouting match. George claimed that he had just been named head coach of the Olympic track team. He was now calling potential assistant coaches and athletes around the country to organize tryouts for the following month. Any interference, he claimed, would be attributed to foreign countries that were reluctant to compete against a team led by a coach with such a distinguished record.

The department head realized that George was not kidding and that he could not reason with him. He returned to his own office and phoned Cheryl. When she arrived, they were unable to convince George that he needed help. They eventually realized that their only option was to call the police, who then took George to a psychiatric hospital. Following an intake evaluation, George was committed for 3 days of observation. Because he did not recognize the severity of his problems and refused to cooperate with his family and the hospital staff, it was necessary to follow an involuntary commitment procedure. The commitment order was signed by a judge on the following day, after a hospital psychiatrist testified in court that George might be dangerous to himself or others.

Social History

In most respects, George's childhood was unremarkable. He grew up in a small, midwestern town where his father taught history and coached the high school football team. He had one older brother and two younger sisters. All of the children were fair-to-average students and very athletic. George loved all sports and excelled at most. When he accepted a football scholarship to the state university, everyone expected him to go on to play professional ball.

He was always popular with his peers. They looked to him for leadership, and he seemed to enjoy the role. He and his friends were mischievous but were never serious discipline problems. Although some of his friends began drinking alcohol during high school, George always refused to join them. His father had been a heavy drinker, and he did not want to follow the same path. After several years of problem drinking, George's father had joined Alcoholics Anonymous and remained sober. Everyone agreed that the change in his behavior was remarkable.

George's uncle (his mother's brother) had also experienced serious adjustment problems. This uncle was several years older than George's mother, and the principal incidents occurred before George was born. George was therefore uncertain of the details, but he had been told that his uncle was hospitalized twice following periods of rather wild behavior. A later search of hospital records confirmed that these had, in fact, been maniclike episodes. Although the uncle had been assigned a diagnosis of "acute schizophrenic reaction," contemporary diagnostic criteria would certainly have required a diagnosis of bipolar disorder.

Conceptualization and Treatment

When George was admitted to the hospital, he was clearly out of control. He was racing in high gear despite the fact that he had not slept for several days. He was nearing a state of physical exhaustion. The psychiatrist immediately prescribed a moderate dosage of haloperidol (Haldol), an antipsychotic drug that is also used to treat schizophrenia. George was supposed to have been taking lithium carbonate prior to the onset of the episode, but a check of his blood-lithium level indicated that he had not been following the prescribed procedure. He was therefore started on a dose of 900 mg of lithium on the first day. This was increased to 1,800 mg per day over the next 2 weeks. The hospital nursing staff took blood tests every third day to ensure that the blood lithium level did not exceed 1.4 milliequivalents per liter—the point at which toxic effects might be expected. After 3 weeks, the Haldol was discontinued, and George continued to receive maintenance doses of lithium (2,100 mg per day).

George and Cheryl were, once again, given specific instructions pertaining to the potential hazards of taking lithium. The importance of a proper diet, and particularly a normal level of salt intake, was stressed. They were also told about the early warning signs of lithium intoxication (e.g., nausea, gastrointestinal distress, muscular weakness), so that they could warn George's psychiatrist if the dosage needed to be reduced.

In addition, George was involved in a number of other therapeutic activities. He and the other patients on the ward met daily for sessions of group psychotherapy. There were also several recreational and occupational activities that the patients could choose according to their own interests. Visits by family members and close friends were encouraged during the evening hours. When George's behavior improved, he was taken off restricted status and allowed to leave the ward for short periods of time.

George was discharged from the hospital after 3 weeks. His behavior had improved dramatically. The first few days in the hospital had been difficult for everyone concerned. He had been so excited that the entire ward routine had been disrupted. Mealtimes were utterly chaotic, and when the patients were supposed to go to sleep for the night, George shouted and ran around like a child going to his first slumber party. The physical exertion finally took its toll. He fell into a state of nearly complete exhaustion. After sleeping for the better part of 3 days, George's demeanor was somewhat more subdued. He had given up the grandiose notion about Olympic fame and seemed to be in better control of his speech and motor behavior. But he had not returned to normal. He was still given to rambling speeches and continued to flirt with the female staff members. His mood was unstable, fluctuating between comical amusement and quick irritation. In contrast to most of the other patients, George was gregarious and energetic. He organized group activities and saw himself as a hospital aide, not as a patient.

These residual symptoms dissipated gradually over the next 2 weeks. He was switched to voluntary status and now recognized the severity of his previous condition. In retrospect, the events that had struck him as exhilarating and amusing seemed like a nightmare. He said that his thoughts had been racing a mile a minute. He had been totally preoccupied with the conference meet and upcoming events. The locker room incident caused him considerable concern as he admitted the possibility that he could have seriously injured someone with the sword.

Following discharge from the hospital, George was kept on a maintenance dosage of lithium. He attended an outpatient clinic regularly for individual psychotherapy, and his blood levels of lithium were carefully monitored. George and Cheryl also began conjoint therapy sessions with a dual purpose in mind. They needed to work on improving their own relationship, and they also wanted to acquire more effective means of interacting with and controlling their children. This aspect of the treatment program was unsuccessful. Cheryl had been seriously embarrassed by George's behavior during the manic episode. The cruelest blow came with the newspaper article in which George had announced his affection for another woman. That incident seemed to leave an insurmountable wall of tension between George and Cheryl, even though they both made a serious effort to improve their relationship. The therapist noticed an improvement in their interactions during therapy sessions, but they continued to have periodic, heated fights at home. Cheryl finally decided that the situation was hopeless, and 6 months after George was discharged from the hospital, she filed for a divorce.

George was, of course, shaken by this development, but he managed to avoid becoming seriously depressed. His friends from work were an important source of social support, particularly during the first weeks after Cheryl and the children moved to another apartment. He also met more frequently with his therapist during this period and continued to take lithium carbonate.

Discussion

Mood disorders are characterized by a serious, prolonged disturbance of the person's emotional state. These disturbances may take the form of depression or elation. They are accompanied by a host of other problems, including changes in sleep patterns, appetite, and activity level.

Several classification systems have been used to subdivide this broad category into more homogeneous groups. The classification system that currently seems most useful and that is represented in *DSM-IV-TR* (APA, 2000) draws a distinction between bipolar and unipolar mood disorders. In bipolar disorders, the patient experiences periods of extreme elation (and/or irritability) known as manic episodes. These periods usually alternate with periods of normal mood and periods of severe depression to form a kind of unpredictable emotional cycle that some patients liken to a roller-coaster ride. Unipolar patients, on the other hand, experience serious depression without ever swinging to the opposite extreme. George had exhibited manic as well as depressive symptoms, so his problem would be diagnosed as a bipolar disorder.

DSM-IV-TR (APA, 2000, p. 362) lists the following criteria for a manic episode:

1. A distinct period of abnormally and persistently elevated, expansive, or irritable mood lasting at least one week (or any duration if hospitalization is necessary).

2. During the period of mood disturbance, three (or more) of the following symptoms have persisted (four if the mood is only irritable) and have been present to a significant degree:
   a. Inflated self-esteem or grandiosity
   b. Decreased need for sleep, for example, feeling rested after only 3 hours of sleep
   c. More talkative than usual or pressure to keep talking
   d. Flight of ideas or subjective experience that thoughts are racing
   e. Distractibility, for example, attention too easily drawn to unimportant or irrelevant external stimuli
   f. Increase in goal-directed activity (either socially, at work or school, or sexually) or psychomotor agitation
   g. Excessive involvement in pleasurable activities that have a high potential for painful consequences; for example, the person engages in unrestrained buying sprees, sexual indiscretions, or foolish business investments
3. The mood disturbance is sufficiently severe to cause marked impairment in occupational functioning or in usual social activities or relationships with others, or to necessitate hospitalization to prevent harm to self or others.

Bipolar disorders should be distinguished from schizophrenia as well as from unipolar mood disorders. Kraepelin (1919, 1971) recognized that manic and schizophrenic (dementia praecox) patients often exhibit similar symptoms. These include disorganized speech, flight of ideas, and delusional thinking. He argued that the difference between the two disorders became apparent on examination of their long-term course. Most patients who fit Kraepelin's definition of schizophrenia showed a progressive deterioration without periods of recovery. Manic-depressive patients, on the other hand, frequently followed a remitting course. Although they might have repeated episodes of psychotic behavior, their adjustment between episodes was relatively unimpaired. This distinction has continued to be one of the most important considerations in the classification of serious mental disorders (Miklowitz & Johnson, 2006).

A less severe form of bipolar disorder is experienced by people who go through episodes of expansive mood and increased energy that are not sufficiently severe to be considered manic episodes. These are called *hypomanic episodes*. According to *DSM-IV-TR* (APA, 2000), a person who has experienced at least one major depressive episode, at least one hypomanic episode, and no full-blown manic episodes, would be assigned a diagnosis of bipolar II disorder. A hypomanic episode is defined in terms of the same symptoms as those that describe a manic episode. The distinction between manic and hypomanic episodes is based on duration and severity. The minimum duration of symptoms for a hypomanic episode is 4 days, as opposed to 1 week for a manic episode. In a hypomanic episode, the mood change must be noticeable to others, but it must not lead to impairment in social or occupational functioning or require hospitalization. If the mood change becomes that severe, it is considered a manic episode.

Another type of mood disorder is known as *cyclothymia*, which is a chronic but less severe form of bipolar disorder. People who meet the criteria for cyclothymia experience several hypomanic episodes and several periods of minor depression during a period of 2 years. They do not, however, experience periods of disturbance that are sufficiently severe to meet the criteria for major depressive episode or manic episode during the first 2 years of their disturbance. After the initial 2 years of cyclothymia, full-blown episodes of mania or major depression will require that an additional diagnosis, such as bipolar I disorder or bipolar II disorder, be superimposed on the cyclothymic disorder.

Estimates of the prevalence of mood disorders in the general population indicate some fairly consistent patterns (Waraich, Goldner, Somers, & Hsu, 2004). In the National Comorbidity Survey Replication (NCS-R) study, lifetime prevalence was 1.0% for bipolar I disorder and 1.1% for bipolar II disorder. In addition to those people who meet definite criteria for a bipolar disorder, many people are affected by recurrent episodes of hypomania but do not fully qualify for a formal diagnosis according to *DSM-IV-TR*. The lifetime prevalence of subthreshold bipolar disorder was 2.4% in the NCS-R. The lifetime prevalence for major depression was much higher—16.2% overall—than the combined rate for various forms of bipolar disorder (Kessler, Merikangas, & Wang, 2007). Gender differences are not found in the risk for bipolar disorders, but there are important gender differences in the rates of major depression for men and women. Women are roughly twice as likely as men to experience major depression at some point during their lives.

There are also important differences between unipolar and bipolar disorders in terms of both the age of onset and the course of the disorder (Johnson & Kizer, 2002). Bipolar patients tend to be younger than unipolar patients at the time of their first episode of disturbance, usually between the ages of 20 and 30. Bipolar patients also tend to experience a greater number of psychotic episodes during subsequent years. Both unipolar and bipolar mood disorders are associated with substantial impairment in social and occupational functioning. In fact, subthreshold bipolar disorders were associated with as much, if not more, role impairment than was found for major depression in the NCS-R (Kessler et al., 2007).

George's case was typical of the classic picture of manic-depressive illness. He showed an early onset of symptoms and a relatively complete remission between episodes. His behavior was so disruptive during each manic episode that it had long-term, negative consequences for his social and occupational adjustment. He had serious problems with his job, and his marriage ended in divorce.

Etiological Considerations

The fact that George's maternal uncle had also experienced manic episodes is consistent with the literature concerning genetic factors in mood disorders. Several family studies have found that the biological relatives of patients with mood disorders are more likely to develop mood disorders than are people in the general population. These data are usually reported in terms of "morbid risk," or the probability that given individuals will develop the disorder during their life-time. Several studies have now reported that the relatives of unipolar depressives are at increased risk for unipolar depression but that they are unlikely to exhibit bipolar disorder (McGuffin et al., 2003). The relatives of bipolar patients, on the other hand, typically demonstrate an increased risk for both unipolar and bipolar disorders. These data have generally been taken to indicate that the bipolar and unipolar subgroups are genetically distinct. George's positive family history for bipolar disorder thus may be taken as further validation of his bipolar diagnosis and was, in fact, helpful in the decision to try lithium carbonate prior to his first full manic episode.

The role of genetic factors in the etiology of mood disorders would be clearer if a specific model of genetic action could be identified. Molecular genetic studies have identified linkage to several potential chromosome regions that may contain genes that contribute to the development of bipolar disorder (Farmer, Elkin, & McGuffin, 2007). Unfortunately, other laboratories have failed to replicate many of the preliminary findings that have been reported over the past few years. What should we make of these inconsistencies? The likely explanation is that mood disorders are genetically heterogeneous (i.e., they are produced by different genes in different people with similar disorders). Further evidence is needed from additional linkage studies, and the next few years will undoubtedly witness exciting reports in this area of research (Lau & Eley, 2010).

Although genetic factors play some role in the development of bipolar dis-order, they cannot account for it completely. Various experiences throughout the person's life must also influence the onset or expression of psychotic symptoms as well as the course of the disorder (Miklowitz & Johnson, 2009). The gener-ally accepted diathesis-stress model would suggest that bipolar patients inherited some unidentified form of predisposition to the disorder and that the expres-sion of this predisposition then depends on subsequent environmental events. Stressful life events frequently play an important role in the course of the disor-der, particularly in triggering relapse (Cohen, Hammen, Henry, & Daley, 2004).

In George's case, it would be reasonable to wonder whether the highly competitive atmosphere associated with college coaching might have triggered the onset of his manic symptoms or his depressive episodes. The weeks pre-ceding his manic episode were busier than usual. His teams had been winning, and the athletic department's administration seemed to be putting considerable emphasis on the final meets of the season. Viewed from George's perspective, this amounted to enormous pressure. The job situation was also compounded by his family responsibilities. As he began to spend more and more time with his team, his wife became increasingly discontent and irritable. Her demands, coupled with his coaching responsibilities, placed George in a difficult position; he could reduce the amount of time spent planning and supervising workouts, thus increasing the probability that the team would lose, or he could reduce the amount of time spent with his wife and children, thus increasing the probability that she would ask for a divorce.

George's relationship with his family illustrates the complex interactive nature of mood disorders. Although his marital problems may not have been caused by his mood-disorder symptoms, they certainly made an already difficult situation virtually impossible. The marital adjustment of bipolar patients has received considerable attention in the research literature, which indicates that bipolar patients are much more likely than unipolar patients or people in the general population to be divorced (van der Voort, Gossens, & van der Bijl, 2007). The emotional atmosphere within a family is also related to the patient's social functioning and the course of the disorder. Patients who live in a stressful family environment are much more likely to relapse than patients from families that are characterized by lower levels of interpersonal stress (Miklowitz, 2007).

George's situation was probably typical of the problems experienced by manic patients. Cheryl was forced by his erratic behavior to act as a buffer between George and the community. When he acted strangely at work, his colleagues called her to see if she could explain his behavior. She often found herself making up excuses for him to avoid the unpleasant necessity of disclosing the personal details of his problems. Her efforts were then "rewarded" by his continued excesses. Cheryl gradually came to see herself as a victim. The incident with the undergraduate student was the last straw. George's behavior was even more difficult for Cheryl to understand and accept because of his inconsistency. She argued that if he were always irrational or out of control, she could easily attribute these problems to a psychiatric disorder. However, between episodes, and most of the time, George was a very reasonable, considerate person. Cheryl found it difficult to believe that he could change so drastically over such a short period of time. Her first inclination was always to attribute his wild, manic behavior to some malicious intent on his part. When he became depressed, she often blamed herself. Eventually, the problem was simply more than she could handle.

Treatment

Lithium is the treatment of choice for bipolar disorders. The therapeutic effects of lithium salts were first reported in 1949 by John Cade, an Australian psychiatrist. Cade had been studying the toxic effects of uric acid in guinea pigs and the possibility that the lithium ion might reduce this toxicity. He was not initially interested in behavioral effects, but he happened to notice that guinea pigs that had been injected with lithium carbonate became lethargic and unresponsive to stimuli despite remaining fully conscious. This unexpected finding led Cade to wonder whether lithium carbonate might have beneficial effects for psychotic patients who were extremely excited. He used the drug with a sequence of 10 manic patients and obtained remarkable results. Even chronic patients who had been considered untreatable responded favorably within a period of several days. Furthermore, several patients with schizophrenia who had previously been markedly restless and excited became quiet and amenable. When lithium was discontinued, the patients generally returned to their previous patterns of wild behavior.

Other clinicians soon began to experiment with the use of lithium and met with similar results. Their favorable impression of lithium's effects were later confirmed by a number of controlled double-blind studies (Young & Newham, 2006). In fact, lithium can be beneficial for patients who are depressed as well as for those who are manic. This is particularly true for bipolar patients. Several studies that used double-blind procedures and placebo control groups have concluded that lithium is effective in preventing the recurrence of manic episodes and probably effective in preventing recurrent depression in bipolar patients (Smith, Cornelius, Warnock, Bell, & Young, 2007).

Other forms of medication can also be useful in treating bipolar disorders. For example, certain anticonvulsant drugs such as carbamazepine (Tegretol) and valproic acid (Depakote) often lead to improvement in patients who have not responded to lithium. This is an important consideration because about 40% of bipolar patients do not show an adequate clinical response to lithium alone. These are often patients whose moods cycle rapidly (defined in *DSM-IV-TR* as bipolar patients with four or more separate episodes of depression, mania, or hypomania within 12 months). The anticonvulsants may be used either on their own or in combination with lithium (Nasrallah, Ketter, & Kalali, 2006).

George responded favorably to lithium during his brief stay in the hospital, and he returned to his job soon after discharge. It is possible that the episode might have been partially caused by his failure to take the medication regularly. This is a serious problem with all forms of psychopharmacological treatment. It is particularly severe with psychotic patients who characteristically lack insight into the severity of their problem. Every effort is usually made to educate the patient in this regard. The cooperation of family members is often enlisted to assist in the regulation of daily doses. The dangers of lithium also require that patients being treated on an outpatient basis be seen regularly to monitor levels of lithium in the blood. Despite these precautions, many patients fail to follow medication schedules designed to prevent relapse.

Psychotherapy is also an important part of treatment for many patients with bipolar disorder (Benyon, Soares-Weiser, Wollacott, Duffy, & Geddes, 2008; Geller & Goldberg, 2007). Used in combination with lithium or other types of medication, psychotherapy can help patients cope with social circumstances that may trigger further episodes. These include family conflict and stressful life events. Treatment may be aimed at improving the person's communication skills and problem-solving abilities to strengthen interpersonal relationships (Frank, 2005). Psychological interventions can also be used to increase medication compliance by identifying and addressing patients' reservations about taking lithium and other drugs.

Discussion Questions

1. Patients with bipolar disorder are often reluctant to take their medication because they don't want to give up periods of hypomania, when they feel exceptionally upbeat and productive. What would you say to a close friend with bipolar disorder who did not want to take medication?

2. Bipolar disorder can have a devastating impact on family relationships. Is there anything about the behavior of bipolar patients (especially during a manic episode) that might make it particularly difficult for a spouse to understand and accept the person's behavior as being part of a psychological disorder (rather than simply bad judgment)?

3. What evidence supports the decision to separate unipolar and bipolar mood disorders in the official classification system? In what ways are they different? In what ways are they similar? Can you think of other ways in which the mood disorders might be subdivided into more homogeneous subtypes?

4. Do you think that people who suffer from bipolar disorder are more likely than other people to seek out and participate in activities and occupations that are particularly stressful?

CHAPTER 8

Somatization Disorder

Meredith Coleman opened her eyes, groggy from the anesthesia, and blinked several times. She began to moan softly. The nurse turned toward her and asked how she was feeling. She felt queasy and cold, so the nurse gently pulled the blanket up to her chin. She was 25 years old and had just had a hysterectomy because she had suffered from heavy menstrual bleeding and constant uterine pain for the past year. Her physician was very reluctant to do the operation because Meredith was young and had never had any children, but her frequent visits to his office and complaints of pain and heavy flow had finally convinced him to go ahead. He was optimistic that the procedure would improve her condition, and she was eager for relief from the bleeding and repeatedly expressed her desire to have the surgery.

Meredith spent a restless night in the uncomfortable hospital bed, her pain from the surgery only partly eased by pain medication. The next morning her gynecologist came in to check on her. Meredith was worried about the pain she still felt in her abdomen, but her doctor assured her it was normal and that she should expect the pain to continue until she had healed fully which would take weeks. At her checkup 6 months after the surgery, she had experienced no improvement at all in the uterine pain, despite the fact that her uterus had been removed. If anything, the pain was a little worse. The doctor assured her that it could not be uterine pain and that nothing was wrong with her. Meredith was unsatisfied after this checkup and scheduled an appointment with her regular doctor, Dr. Griffin.

Meredith, in fact, had a number of physicians treating her for many different physical problems. She had been in poor health since she was a teenager. She had severe, stabbing pain that radiated down both of her legs nearly every day. The pain seemed to originate in her lower back and was somewhat unpredictable. It would seem to "burst" in her toes. Sometimes it would occur only once a day and last just a few minutes, and other times it would last for hours and bring her to tears. The pain was ruining her life.

She vaguely remembered sharp pains in her calf muscles when she was in high school, but her legs really started bothering her when she was a sophomore in college. In the beginning, the pain only occurred occasionally, but now it was a constant problem. Over the past 3 years, her legs had also become progressively weaker. The muscles in her legs would at times be so weak she could barely stand. She could not walk any distance at all due to this weakness. She had begun using her grandmother's old wheelchair that had been stored in the family's attic since her grandmother died. It was especially helpful when she was going to the mall where she would have to walk long distances. On certain days, her legs would completely give out, and she would fall to the ground. She had been to many specialists to try to find the cause of the problem with her legs, but no one had been able to figure it out. She had been evaluated by neurologists and had MRIs, but there was no evidence of any condition that could be responsible for her symptoms. She was frequently tearful and despairing about her health, and her emotional outbursts worried her parents.

She had a number of other physical problems. Since puberty, she had suffered from frequent headaches that were characterized by sharp pain. They did not fit the typical symptom pattern of migraine headaches. She also had chest pains and often thought she was going to have a heart attack. The chest pains were her most recent symptom, only occurring over the past 6 months. One day, she went to the emergency room because of the chest pain and had a full workup to rule out a heart attack. The emergency physician told her anxiety was causing her chest pains and that her heart was normal and healthy. She was surprised and insulted by these comments because it was clear to her that she wasn't going crazy and that her chest pains were not in her head.

After meals, she frequently experienced abdominal distention and uncomfortable bloating. She ate infrequently because of the bloating and because she often had nausea that made food very unappetizing. When she did eat, she would often have to lie down because of the bloating and stomachaches so severe she doubled over in pain. She had been tested extensively to rule out an ulcer or food allergy, but no cause had been discovered. Her gallbladder had been removed two years ago, but that did not relieve her symptoms.

Meredith met her husband, Steve, in college. He was a year older, and they married when he graduated from college and started his job as an insurance agent. At the time, Meredith was 21 years old. After the wedding, she never finished her degree, and her grades were suffering when she left college because her headaches made it difficult to study. Steve left her 2 years later, and she worked as a secretary to support herself. She lost her job after about a year when her health problems had caused her to miss too much work. So at 24 years old, she moved back in with her parents.

She did not go out very often anymore because she had trouble walking any distance and was afraid her legs would give out. She accompanied her parents to church but always wanted to hold onto her father's arm to steady herself. Her mother did all her laundry and prepared the meals. Her parents were both very concerned about their daughter's well-being. They were frustrated that no doctor could solve her problems.

When she went in for the appointment with Dr. Griffin that she made after her gynecologist told her nothing was wrong with her, she discussed her continuing uterine pain, her headaches, and her leg pains. The doctor listened sympathetically, but eventually interrupted Meredith and told her that she didn't understand what was going on. She said she could try another medication to help manage Meredith's digestive problems, to see if that would work. When Dr. Griffin handed her the prescription and opened the door of the examining room to leave, Meredith became very upset with her for giving her 12 months' worth of refills. To her, that made it clear that Dr. Griffin did not want to see her back for another 12 months. When she began to cry about that, Dr. Griffin suggested that she see a psychologist for an evaluation. Meredith became indignant and angry at the suggestion of a psychologist, accusing Dr. Griffin of suggesting that she was insane. The doctor explained to Meredith that sometimes emotions complicate medical problems and suggested that a psychological evaluation would help her determine the best course of medical treatment. Meredith finally agreed to be seen by a psychologist.

Social History

Meredith grew up in a small town where her father was a bank president, and her mother was a homemaker. She was the youngest of three children. Her brother Wallace was 5 years older. Wallace was a natural athlete, popular, and a good student. He played baseball throughout his childhood and in college. He had attended law school and was now married and busy working to establish his law practice. Her sister Claire was 2 years older and had been a cheerful, calm-natured girl who loved to ride horses. During high school, she had spent all her free time at the stables. Claire was now married to her high school sweetheart and busy with 5-year-old twins.

During Meredith's childhood, her father's mother lived with the family. She had survived a stroke that had left her very debilitated, and she had trouble walking. Meredith's mother, Evelyn, spent a lot of time caring for her. Evelyn would prepare special meals for her and would feed her because the stroke affected the use of her hands, which she could not hold steady. Evelyn was quite devoted to her mother-in-law and made sure she had everything she needed. Unfortunately, Meredith's grandmother died when Meredith was 12 years old. Meredith later told all her friends in college about her grandmother and how traumatic it had been when she died. She described her feelings of grief and the funeral in a dramatic fashion.

Evelyn was outgoing like Wallace, and she had a lot of friends. She had a busy social life and was active in church groups and in civic organizations. As early as she could remember, Meredith never felt like she fit in. She was large-framed and tall for her age, not pretty or petite like her mother or sister. Meredith was somewhat outspoken and bossy with the other children and did not have many friends. Her mother always seemed a little embarrassed by her.

However, her mother clearly was very proud of Wallace. She went to every one of his Little League games and was always bragging about his accomplishments to her friends. Meredith always felt "insignificant" and ignored, and it seemed to her that her mother had time for everyone else but her. When Meredith would try to talk to her mother about feeling left out at school with the other girls, her mother would tell her to pray about it and not to feel sorry for herself.

When Meredith began having headaches shortly after her grandmother died, her mother was very sympathetic. She would tell her to lie down and would bring her a cool compress for her head. That seemed to ease the pain some. When Meredith complained of bloating and nausea, her mother recommended that she eat blander foods that might be easier on her stomach. She began to prepare special foods for Meredith when the family meal might be too spicy or hard to digest.

In high school, Meredith became active in chorus. She was very talented and had a beautiful voice. Through her singing, she began to find a measure of acceptance with other students. The chorus members hung out together, and Meredith was included in their activities. She continued to sing in college and decided to become a music major. She hoped for a career as an opera singer, and her professors encouraged her to develop her voice, which showed a great deal of promise. She met Steve when he asked her out after he saw her perform in a college production. He was enthralled by her voice and her stage presence. They quickly fell in love and were engaged 3 months later.

After they married, he was protective and tender toward her when she would take to bed with a headache or other ailment. She adored him and tried to be the perfect wife. She spent a lot of time decorating their first apartment, and she fixed him gourmet meals. He threw himself into work, trying to establish his clientele. Meredith found it somewhat difficult to adjust to his long hours at work and his preoccupation with success. Increasingly during the day when he was gone, she would have problems with her legs. Eventually she brought her grandmother's wheelchair from home to their apartment to help her cope with getting around and to keep from falling when she felt weak. This bothered Steve. He began to criticize her and started to complain about the cost of medical bills from her frequent doctor's appointments. They continued this way for the rest of their marriage, with increasingly frequent arguments. One day, Steve announced that he wanted a divorce and that he had fallen in love with someone else. Meredith was completely devastated, but she could not convince him to stay. When he moved out and filed for divorce, she stayed in their apartment, got a job, and tried to cope until eventually she moved back with her parents.

Treatment

Meredith reluctantly made an appointment with the clinical psychologist recommended by Dr. Griffin. The psychologist, Dr. Edwards, conducted an extensive interview and tried to construct a medical history. It was difficult to get clear dates from Meredith about when her various symptoms had begun. With her written consent, Dr. Edwards obtained Meredith's medical records from Dr. Griffin and all the other physicians who had treated her. He needed to use these records to construct the chronology. They would also allow him to evaluate whether there was any medical basis to explain her numerous physical complaints. He was struck by Meredith's distress over her divorce and her despair and sadness over her physical problems. He scheduled a follow-up appointment with her so he could propose a plan of treatment after he had reviewed all the medical records.

When reviewing the reams of medical records from all her treatments and evaluations, Dr. Edwards discovered that physician after physician had been unable to establish any physical basis for her numerous symptoms. Meredith's symptoms met criteria for *somatization disorder*. A person with this disorder has numerous physical symptoms that are not due to medical problems but have a psychological origin.

At their next session, he proposed a course of treatment to address her depressed mood and her somatic symptoms. Unfortunately, Meredith refused to agree to treatment. She became tearful again and told him that the only reason she agreed to see him was to help Dr. Griffin in planning her medical treatment. She didn't believe she needed a psychologist because she wasn't crazy. None of Dr. Edwards' rationales for entering psychological treatment could convince her. He eventually agreed to call Dr. Griffin with his findings to help with her medical treatment.

He described the findings of his evaluation to Dr. Griffin and suggested that she attempt to manage Meredith's problems by providing counseling in her medical practice. They discussed a general treatment plan in which Dr. Griffin would schedule regular appointments with Meredith. Meredith would also meet biweekly with Dr. Griffin's nurse. The nurse would record her symptoms, check her vital signs, and provide support and encouragement (especially for spending fewer days in bed and decreasing her wheelchair use). Dr. Griffin would meet every other month with Meredith and would review the nurse's notes on their sessions. Meredith seemed relieved by this plan and readily agreed. Dr. Griffin also prescribed an antidepressant, which she convinced Meredith to take by discussing the role of emotional upset in exacerbating pain. Dr. Edwards also encouraged Dr. Griffin to stop sending Meredith to specialists, and Meredith agreed not to contact any other physicians. After a few months, they were to decrease the frequency of these regularly scheduled sessions.

Meredith responded well to this treatment strategy. She continued to have problems with her symptoms, but with the predictable contact with her physician and the increased support and reassurance, she was somewhat less distressed by them. She kept her word about not going to other physicians. Her depressed mood improved, and she did not have any more emergency room visits. The frequency of her contact with physicians decreased, and the weakness in her legs subsided. She eventually began another job, and she made plans to find a new apartment of her own.

Discussion

Somatization disorder is one of the somatoform disorders, a category that also includes conversion disorder, hypochondriasis, pain disorder, and body dysmorphic disorder. Somatoform disorders are characterized by physical symptoms that appear to be due to a somatic (bodily) disease or disorder that cannot be medically explained and that frequently lead to visits to physicians for diagnosis and treatment. Many researchers believe that the physical symptoms originate in psychological distress and that somatization is a psychological mechanism in which physical symptoms express this distress (Hurwitz, 2004). People with a somatoform disorder do not intentionally or consciously produce the symptoms, as in malingering, which is pretending to have symptoms to avoid military service or legal responsibility for a crime, or for financial gain in a lawsuit or for disability benefits. People with a somatoform disorder also differ from those with factitious disorder, which is pretending to have symptoms to assume the sick role. Instead, they actually experience the symptoms, such as feeling pain, experiencing weakness or seizures, or feeling bloated or nauseous, and fully believe they have a bodily medical condition. They typically seek treatment from physicians rather than psychologists or psychiatrists (Hurwitz, 2004).

Somatization disorder is defined in the *Diagnostic and Statistical Manual of Mental Disorders* (*DSM-IV-TR*, APA, 2000, pp. 486–490) by the following criteria:

1. The person has a history of many physical complaints beginning before age 30 that occur over a period of several years and result in treatment being sought or significant impairment in social, occupational, or other important areas of functioning.

2. Each of the following criteria must have been met, with individual symptoms occurring at any time during the course of the disturbance:

    a. Four pain symptoms: a history of pain related to at least four different sites or functions (e.g., head, abdomen, back, joints, extremities, chest, rectum, during menstruation, during sexual intercourse,[1] or during urination)

    b. Two gastrointestinal symptoms: a history of at least two gastrointestinal symptoms other than pain (e.g., nausea, bloating, vomiting other than during pregnancy, diarrhea, or intolerance of several different foods)

    c. One sexual symptom: a history of at least one sexual or reproductive symptom other than pain (e.g., sexual indifference, erectile or ejaculatory dysfunction, irregular menses, excessive menstrual bleeding, vomiting throughout pregnancy)

---

[1] Some experts on sexual disorders propose that vaginismus and dyspareunia be classified as pain disorders rather than as sexual disorders (e.g., Binik, 2005; Binik et al., 2002).

    d. One pseudoneurological symptom: a history of at least one symptom or deficit suggesting a neurological condition not limited to pain (conversion symptoms such as impaired coordination or balance, paralysis or localized weakness, difficulty swallowing or lump in throat, aphonia [inability to speak], urinary retention, blindness, deafness, seizures; dissociative symptoms such as amnesia; or loss of consciousness other than fainting)

3. Each of the symptoms in Criteria 2 cannot be fully explained by a known general medical condition or the direct effects of a substance, or when there is a related general medical condition, the physical complaints are in excess of what would be expected from the history, physical examination, or laboratory findings.

People with somatization disorder often have histrionic, excessively emotional, dramatic, vague, or attention-seeking ways of describing their physical symptoms. They are hopeful about receiving a diagnosis that will give meaning to their symptoms. The symptoms they experience fit the patient's beliefs about disease rather than actual disease process and characteristics of physiology, so they appear unusual or bizarre to the physician (Hurwitz, 2004). For example, a person with a somatoform disorder might experience loss of touch in a hand that affects the area covered by a glove rather than the areas of the hand and arm actually controlled by individual nerves.

When the concept of somatizing was originally developed, symptoms were thought to symbolize the patient's emotional problem (Merskey, 2004), such as a patient's aphonia (inability to speak) symbolically enacting their feeling of stifling their emotions to avoid interpersonal conflict. This speculation, rooted in psychoanalytic theories of repression, was not supported by empirical data. Current theories of pain downplay dualism, or mind-body separation, and argue that the mind and body are the same. Research indicates that the experience of pain is always the result of input both from the site of the pain and from the central nervous system, which is affected by emotions and interpersonal conflicts. It is therefore difficult to untangle the physical and psychological contributions to the experience of pain (Kirmayer, Groleau, Looper, & Dao, 2004). Emotional stress may affect a person's physical health in subtle ways through chronic activation of the hypothalamic-pituitary-adrenocortical axis or by interfering with normal sleep, which can produce physical symptoms. Immune function is also compromised by stress.

Often people with somatoform disorders are not identified as having a psychological disorder. One study conducted a follow-up of patients with somatic symptoms. Years later, they continued to have somatic symptoms and continued to have frequent visits to physicians. Their general-practice physician would not find any medical cause for their symptoms. After running some of their own diagnostic tests, they would refer them to specialists, who also found no cause. Eventually, the patient switched to a new general practitioner and began the course of diagnostic tests and referrals anew (Crimlisk et al., 2000). Even after many unproductive medical visits, few patients believed that psychological factors caused their symptoms. If they had depression or anxiety, they typically viewed it as a reaction to their symptoms. Some continued to believe they had a diagnosis that physicians had definitively ruled out. Few patients ever received a referral for mental-health treatment or evaluation. In another national sample, about 20% of people with severe somatoform disorders had received mental-health treatment for comorbid anxiety or depression (Leiknes, Finset, Mourn, & Sandanger, 2007).

The underdiagnosing of somatization disorder is very costly to both the patient and to society. The patient is at real risk for iatrogenic harm (illnesses or damage caused by medical treatment). For example, a patient who undergoes a spinal tap could be harmed by the procedure. Being hospitalized to run a battery of tests could expose the patient to infectious diseases that patients sometimes contract in hospitals, such as staph infections. Social costs include the significant burden to the health-care system of repeated, unnecessary diagnostic procedures and emergency room visits in addition to loss of productivity at work.

The extent of unnecessary medical procedures that were conducted on patients with somatization disorder was examined in an important study by Fink (1992). He identified people between the ages of 17 and 49 years who had been hospitalized at least 10 times during an 8-year period. Somatizers were identified as those for whom no clear diagnosis had been established. The somatizers were compared to the rest of the patients in the sample for whom a clear diagnosis, such as diabetes mellitus or cancer, had been found. The somatizers actually had received more surgeries than the medically ill control group. Of the somatizers, 9% had more than 20 unnecessary surgeries. The most frequently performed types of surgery for the somatizers were gynecological procedures such as uterine curettage and hysterectomy, gastrointestinal surgeries, appendectomies, and laparoscopies. Almost none of the hysterectomies resulted in the patient's symptoms being resolved. In terms of providing symptom improvement, the success rate for all the surgical procedures performed on the somatizers was about 25%, about the same as the placebo effect. This study clearly documents the risks and costs of failing to recognize a patient's somatoform disorder. These costs were evident for Meredith. She had gallbladder surgery and a hysterectomy by the age of 25. Both were medically unnecessary and occurred because different physicians were only aware of some of her difficulties. If her gynecologist had been aware of all her other medical history, he may have decided against surgery.

Physicians and mental-health professionals must be equally cautious about overdiagnosing somatoform disorders. Medically unexplained symptoms are common and account for up to 30% of all primary-care visits (Kirmayer et al., 2004). Medical knowledge is certainly far from perfect and complete. Nevertheless, physicians may be reluctant to admit they do not know the cause of a symptom, and they may shift the blame for the symptom to the patient's emotional state by invoking a somatoform diagnosis.

Researchers have found that five times as many women as men meet the criteria for somatization disorder (Karvonen et al., 2004). From 0.2% to 2% of women and fewer than 0.2% of men qualify for a diagnosis of somatization disorder at some point in their lives (Mai, 2004). Many experts advocate changing the criteria, which are very specific and involve many symptoms in particular combinations, to make them more inclusive because many more patients that don't meet these criteria have medically unexplained symptoms and are seeking help from physicians (Kroenke, Sharpe, & Sykes, 2007). The age of onset of the disorder is most commonly in adolescence (Noyes, Stuart, Watson, & Langbehn, 2006). Somatization disorder is more common among people with lower income and lower social status (Ladwig, Marten-Mittag, Erazo, & Gündel, 2001). It is also more common among people with high emotional distress. People with the disorder often have a history of marriages that ended in divorce (Tomasson, Kent, & Coryell, 1991).

A number of people with somatization disorders also meet diagnostic criteria for a personality disorder. In one study, 72% had a personality disorder, most commonly dependent and histrionic types (Stern, Murphy, & Bass, 1993). This was a higher rate of coexisting personality disorders than for any other mental illness. A number of people with somatization disorder also meet the criteria for an anxiety or depressive disorder (Leibbrand, Hiller, & Fichter, 2000). People with somatization disorder are significantly more likely to make a suicide attempt, even when comorbid depression and anxiety are controlled (Chioqueta & Stiles, 2004). This may be due to the greater likelihood that they have poor social functioning, marital instability, emotional distress, and impulsive, histrionic personality traits. For some people, diagnosing and providing appropriate treatment for somatization disorder is a matter of life or death.

Although patients with somatization disorder experience chronic somatic symptoms over many years, the specific symptoms they experience frequently shift. At one point in time, the patient will experience one type of problem, but a year later that symptom may have disappeared while another has developed (Simon & Gureje, 1999). In one 2-year follow-up of individuals with somatization, only one-third continued to have the same symptoms (Craig, Boardman, Mills, Daly-Jones, & Drake, 1993).

People with somatization disorder have many impairments in their ability to function; in fact, the rates of impairment rival that of people with schizophrenia (Bass, Peveler, & House, 2001). Up to 10% in one sample were confined to a wheelchair. Overall, people with somatization disorder spend an average of 7 days a month in bed. Often they are unable to hold a job. Impairments are typically worse than those associated with medically explained symptoms because the somatization was more likely to be chronic and persistent (Harris, Orav, Bates, & Barksy, 2008). In addition to health-care costs to society associated with somatization, loss of work productivity is a significant social burden (Bermingham, Cohen, Hague, & Parsonage, 2010). Some of these impairments were evident in Meredith's life, although she was not as disabled as others with the disorder.

Etiological Considerations

Psychodynamic theorists have suggested that somatization disorder is related to the use of the psychological defense mechanism of denial. People with the disorder presumably substitute somatic symptoms for the direct expression of psychological distress. Some early reports indicated that people from non-Western cultures found it more acceptable to express their feelings in somatic rather than psychological terms. Less-sophisticated people who were not particularly psychologically minded, or people from cultures that did not promote a psychological focus, were thought to be more likely to somatize (Gureje, Simon, Ustun, & Goldberg, 1997). Children brought to a mental-health clinic for treatment were more likely to present with somatic complaints if they were in Thailand and with depressive symptoms if they were in the United States; however, there were no differences in rates of depressive symptoms and somatic complaints among Thai and U.S. children in the community (Weiss, Tram, Weisz, Rescorla, & Achenbach, 2009). This suggests that cultural factors may affect how people describe their problems when seeking help but not necessarily their experiencing of the symptoms. Investigators who conducted a study of more than 25,000 patients in 14 countries on 5 continents found that there were no differences among the different countries in the relationship between psychological and physical symptoms (Simon, VonKorff, Piccinelli, Fullerton, & Ormel, 1999). Many patients with depression who reported a lot of somatic symptoms were also able to acknowledge and describe their psychological phenomena, so they did not seem to manifest somatization as denial of psychological distress. Denial may play a role for some, but not all, people with somatic complaints.

Even though somatization disorder occurs in cultures all around the world, cultural factors must still be considered in the development of these symptoms. Certain cultural groups have specific syndromes consisting of somatic, and sometimes emotional, symptoms (Kirmayer & Young, 1998). Among people of Korean descent, *hwa-byung* consists of feelings of heaviness or burning in the throat, headaches, muscle aches, dry mouth, insomnia, indigestion, and heart palpitations. Koreans view this syndrome as being caused by suppressed rage, particularly at interpersonal or social injustice. In Nigeria, *brain fag* consists of heat or heaviness in the head associated with studying, typically among students with high levels of pressure for success. The *DSM-IV-TR* (APA, 2000) requires careful consideration of any cultural factors that may explain symptom presentation.

The personality style of alexithymia is a concept first described by psychodynamically oriented clinicians but is now receiving acceptance by a broader group of researchers as a predisposing factor for somatization disorder. *Alexithymia* is a difficulty in identifying and describing one's emotions. This difficulty could lead people to focus on and misinterpret the bodily states associated with emotional arousal, therefore heightening them and leading to somatization. A review of the research literature concluded that there is a moderate relationship between alexithymia and somatization (De Gucht & Heiser, 2003). Meredith had some trouble being aware of and expressing her emotions. Her family did not allow her to talk about feelings, and she was not encouraged to think about or discuss her emotions.

Another psychodynamic concept that has been tested empirically is *secondary gain*, the idea that symptoms provide situational benefits that reward their expression.[2] Some examples of secondary gain are sympathy from family members, relief from chores or work, or attention from physicians. In an in-depth study comparing somatizers with physically ill, psychologically distressed, and healthy controls, Craig, Drake, Mills, and Boardman (1994) evaluated the role of stressful life events in somatic symptoms and their potential for secondary gain if the person developed illness symptoms. Situations with high potential for secondary gain involved rejection by another person, personal failures, and situations with obligations or commitments. For example, if a spouse threatens to terminate the marriage, symptoms of physical illness might elicit guilt, sympathy, caregiving behavior, and a renewed commitment to the relationship, which all constitute secondary gain. Both the somatizers and the psychologically distressed group had significantly higher levels of stressful life events directly preceding the onset of symptoms than the physically ill or healthy controls. This supports the idea that emotional distress and other psychiatric symptoms are related to somatizing. The somatizers were also more likely to have experienced a life crisis with the potential for secondary gain and were much less likely to make attempts to solve the conflict directly. Active problem solving would publicize their emotional distress to others and eliminate the effectiveness of somatic complaints in obtaining secondary gain. For Meredith, stress in her marriage when she felt neglected by her husband's commitment to his work can be seen as increasing her somatizing in an attempt to regain his attention; if she had directly communicated her feelings of being neglected by him, her physical symptoms would have been less effective in eliciting his care.

Somatization disorder may be viewed as learned illness behavior based on observing a sick parent or other family member (Mai, 2004). The child may identify with the ill person, who then models the behavior. The child's behavior is, in turn, reinforced by parents, teachers, or health-care professionals who give the child more attention or sympathy. The child may subsequently attempt to meet emotional or social needs through behaviors such as taking medicine, going to the doctor, going to bed, and acting as a patient. Children and adolescents with a number of somatic complaints are more likely to have a family member with a chronic physical illness (Fritz, Fritsch, & Hagino, 1997). They also are more likely to have family members who use illness for stress reduction. Meredith clearly had this risk factor. Her grandmother was disabled after

---

[2] In psychodynamic theory, primary gain refers to the main function of a symptom of protecting the ego from anxiety-provoking thoughts or feelings by disguising them as symptoms.

her stroke, and Meredith grew up observing the special treatment and attention she received from Meredith's mother. Meredith probably longed for this special attention.

Childhood adversity may also play a role in the development of somatization disorder. A history of childhood sexual abuse has been implicated in adult somatization disorder (Spitzer, Barnow, Gau, Freyberger, & Grabe, 2008). In general, people with medically unexplained symptoms are more likely to report a history of traumatization, such as child sexual, physical, or psychological abuse (Roelofs & Spinhoven, 2007). The relationship between childhood sexual abuse and adult somatization may be due to dissociation (a disintegration of consciousness with experiences of amnesia, depersonalization, and derealization). People who were sexually abused as children are more likely to somatize, but this association is only found among those who also dissociate (Salmon, Skaife, & Rhodes, 2003).

People with somatization are more likely to have a history of childhood illness requiring surgery or hospitalization (Craig et al., 1993). However, this history of childhood illness was only related to adult somatizing when it was combined with parental neglect, or with parental illness that interfered with the parent's availability for caregiving. More often than not, the parental neglect came before the childhood illness. This suggests that for some people, the childhood illness may have resulted in the attention the child wanted desperately from an unresponsive or withdrawn parent. This experience may teach the child that the only way to have emotional needs met is through being nursed and cared for when sick. A striking example of this is the experience of one of the women with a somatoform disorder who participated in the study by Craig and his colleagues (1993). When she was 12 years old, she had been institutionalized and did not see her mother even for visits. The only contact she ever had again with her mother was when she was hospitalized with kidney disease at the age of 15 and her mother visited her. Although Meredith was not neglected, she always felt excluded from the family and unimportant to her mother. She received the most loving attention from her mother when she complained of physical symptoms. This pattern clearly contributed to the development of her somatization.

Some studies have examined specific somatic symptoms. Harris (1989) interviewed women seeking medical treatment for menorrhagia (abnormally excessive menstrual bleeding) to evaluate how life events might relate to this symptom. The 98 women with menorrhagia were compared with 224 control women. Over half of the women with menorrhagia experienced a severe life event in the 12 months preceding the onset of their menstrual disorder, such as a divorce or the loss of a relationship with a boyfriend, compared to 30% of the other group. The menorrhagic women focused on their pain and devastation in describing their responses to the loss. They reported that they became depressed after the loss and before the onset of the menorrhagia. A hysterectomy was conducted on 58% of the women with heavy bleeding. Of the women who had hysterectomies, 40% had completely normal uteruses with no sign of any organic pathology. An additional 32% had conditions that were not known to cause excessive bleeding. It is unclear whether women seeking treatment for menorrhagia actually have more menstrual flow or just perceive that they do. Some researchers have speculated that autonomic nervous system arousal associated with emotional distress could induce dilation of the blood vessels, which could increase the blood flow. Meredith's menorrhagia began after her husband divorced her. She reacted to this loss with depression and acute distress, and there was no evidence of any pathology in her hysterectomy. It is likely that the loss of her marriage and her subsequent depression were related to her heavy menstrual bleeding.

Genetic factors may also play a role in somatization disorder. Women whose biological parents had criminal or psychotic behavior and who were adopted by nonrelatives had higher rates of somatizing (Mai, 2004). Fathers of women with somatization disorder are more likely to have antisocial personality disorder. However, results from twin studies have been mixed. Preliminary investigations indicate that people who somatize have abnormalities in tryptophan levels in their bloodstream (Rief et al., 2004). Tryptophan is an amino acid that is used in the brain to manufacture serotonin. Serotonin is involved with mood and with inhibitory processes from the central nervous system to the peripheral nervous system. The exact relationship between tryptophan levels and somatizing is not yet clear, and more research is needed. Another study found abnormally low glucose metabolism in certain regions of the brain among women with a severe somatoform diagnosis, suggesting that these areas were underactive (Hakala, Vahlberg, Niemi, & Karlsson, 2006).

Treatment

Research on psychopharmacological treatments for somatization disorder suggests that antidepressants are useful in reducing pain and other somatic symptoms and associated disability (Mai, 2004; Menza et al., 2001). Antidepressants appear to be effective, even with patients who do not have a depressed mood. Some patients are resistant to taking an antidepressant, though, because of the implication that their somatic symptoms are psychiatric. When the patient with somatization disorder has coexisting depression or anxiety, those conditions can also be treated, either with medication or psychotherapy.

Like Meredith, patients with somatization disorder are often reluctant to follow recommendations by their physicians to seek psychiatric treatment. The patient's attitude toward psychotherapy when entering treatment affects the long-term effectiveness of that treatment; patients who were more accepting of psychotherapy had better symptom ratings at the 1-year follow-up after treatment (Timmer, Bleichhardt, & Rief, 2006). When the psychiatrist and the physician work together, patient compliance and satisfaction are more likely. Successful medical management involves one (and no more) thorough medical evaluation to rule out organic conditions; the use of treatments that are not dangerous, such as vitamins, lotions, and slings, to allow the patient to "save face"; and moving the patient away from focusing on obtaining a diagnosis (Fritz et al., 1997). The physician can legitimize the patient's somatic complaints by describing them in medical language while refraining from providing a diagnosis (Fishbain, Lewis, Gao, Cole, & Rosomoff, 2009). The physician should schedule regular visits to evaluate any new symptoms and physically examine the patient while refraining from using testing and medical treatments (Looper & Kirmayer, 2002). This strategy reduces doctor shopping and health-care expenditures, as well as the patient's risk of injury or complications due to testing or treatment. Dr. Griffin used this strategy effectively with Meredith. A schedule of regular appointments gave Meredith a chance to have new symptoms evaluated without resorting to seeing specialists and being subjected to unnecessary and potentially dangerous medical procedures.

Often patients feel that their physician is denying the reality of their symptoms (Salmon, Peters, & Stanley, 1999). This occurs when their doctor says she does not know what is causing the symptoms or that everything is fine. Patients are also unsatisfied when their physician simply agrees with their proposed explanation for the symptoms' cause, which undermines their trust in their physician's competence and openness. The most successful patient–physician interactions occur when the physician legitimizes the patient's suffering and provides an explanation that allows the patient to escape blame for the condition (but which also allows them a way to manage it).

Group cognitive-behavioral therapy (CBT) is also effective in treating somatization disorder (Lidbeck, 2003; Looper & Kirmayer, 2002). Treatment typically focuses on relaxation training, problem solving, coping with stress, health education, assertiveness training, and encouraging emotional expression. Individual affective CBT has been shown in a controlled study to effectively improve symptoms and reduce health-care costs, with improvements lasting at least 1 year after treatment completion (Woolfolk, Allen, & Tiu, 2007). First, relaxation training to cope with physical discomfort is taught, then patients learn to differentiate their thoughts and feelings and regulate their emotions effectively. Identifying feelings can be very difficult at first, so it is useful to begin by focusing on feelings related to physical symptoms (Woolfolk & Allen, 2010). Cognitive restructuring and distraction from physical symptoms is also employed. Finally, the costs and benefits of playing the sick role are explored, and alternative strategies are developed. This treatment in conjunction with medical management by the primary-care physician appears to be an effective approach to treating somatization disorder.

Discussion Questions

1. What experiences from Meredith's childhood were important in leading to her somatization disorder?

2. Dr. Edwards was not able to convince Meredith to enter psychological treatment. Do you think he did enough to try? Do you think she would have benefited from therapy, or was the medical management enough?
3. In what way does *not* identifying somatization disorder when it is there harm patients? In what way does identifying it when it *is not* there harm patients?
4. How do patients with somatization disorder cause special difficulty for primary-care physicians? What makes them especially hard to treat?

CHAPTER 9

Schizophrenia: Paranoid Type

Bill McClary made his first appointment at the mental-health center reluctantly. He was 25 years old, single, and unemployed. His sister, Colleen, with whom he had been living for 18 months, had repeatedly encouraged him to seek professional help. She was concerned about his peculiar behavior and social isolation. He spent most of his time daydreaming, often talked to himself, and occasionally said things that made little sense. Bill acknowledged that he ought to keep more regular hours and assume more responsibility, but he insisted that he did not need psychological treatment. The appointment was finally made in an effort to please his sister and mollify her husband, who was worried about Bill's influence on their three young children.

During the first interview, Bill spoke quietly and frequently hesitated. The therapist noted that Bill occasionally blinked and shook his head as though he was trying to clear his thoughts or return his concentration to the topic at hand. When the therapist commented on this unusual twitch, Bill apologized politely but denied that it held any significance. He was friendly yet shy and clearly ill at ease. The discussion centered on Bill's daily activities and his rather unsuccessful efforts to fit into the routine of Colleen's family. Bill assured the therapist that his problems would be solved if he could stop daydreaming. He also expressed a desire to become better organized.

Bill continued to be guarded throughout the early therapy sessions. After several weeks, he began to discuss his social contacts and mentioned a concern about sexual orientation. Despite his lack of close friends, Bill had had some limited and fleeting sexual experiences. These had been both heterosexual and homosexual in nature. He was worried about the possible meaning and consequences of his encounters with other males. This topic occupied the next several weeks of therapy.

Bill's "daydreaming" was also pursued in greater detail. It was a source of considerable concern to him, and it interfered significantly with his daily activities. This experience was difficult to define. At frequent, though irregular, intervals throughout the day, Bill found himself distracted by intrusive and repetitive thoughts. The thoughts were simple and most often alien to his own value system. For example, he might suddenly think to himself, "Damn God." Recognizing the unacceptable nature of the thought, Bill then felt compelled to repeat a sequence of self-statements that he had designed to correct the initial intrusive thought. He called these thoughts and his corrective incantations "scruples." These self-statements accounted for the observation that Bill frequently mumbled to himself. He also admitted that his unusual blinking and head shaking were associated with the experience of intrusive thoughts.

Six months after Bill began attending the clinic regularly, the therapist received a call from Bill's brother-in-law, Roger. Roger said that he and Bill had recently talked extensively about some of Bill's unusual ideas, and Roger wanted to know how he should respond. The therapist was, in fact, unaware of any such ideas. Instead of asking Roger to betray Bill's confidence any further, the therapist decided to ask Bill about these ideas at their next therapy session. It was only at this point that the therapist finally became aware of Bill's extensive delusional belief system.

For reasons that will become obvious, Bill was initially reluctant to talk about the ideas to which his brother-in-law had referred. Nevertheless, he provided the following account of his beliefs and their development. Shortly after moving to his sister's home, Bill realized that something strange was happening. He noticed that people were taking special interest in him and often felt that they were talking about him behind his back. These puzzling circumstances persisted for several weeks during which Bill became increasingly anxious and suspicious. The pieces of the puzzle finally fell in place late one night as Bill sat in front of the television. In a flash of insight, Bill suddenly came to believe that a group of conspirators had secretly produced and distributed a documentary film about his homosexual experiences. Several of his high school friends and a few distant relatives had presumably used hidden cameras and microphones to record each of his sexual encounters with other men. Bill believed that the film had grossed over $50 million at the box office and that this money had been sent to the Irish Republican Army to buy arms and ammunition. He therefore held himself responsible for the deaths of dozens of people who had died as the result of several recent bombings in Ireland. This notion struck the therapist and Bill's brother-in-law as being quite preposterous, but Bill's conviction was genuine. He was visibly moved as he described his guilt concerning the bombings. He was also afraid that serious consequences would follow his confession. Bill believed that the conspirators had agreed to kill him if he ever found out about the movie. This imagined threat had prevented Bill from confiding in anyone prior to this time. It was clear that he now feared for his life.

Bill's fear was exacerbated by the voices that he had been hearing for the past several weeks. He frequently heard male voices discussing his sexual behavior and arguing about what action should be taken to punish him. They were not voices of people with whom Bill was personally familiar, but they were always males and they were always talking about Bill. For example, one night when Bill was sitting alone in his bedroom at Colleen's home, he thought he overheard a conversation in the next room. It was a heated argument in which one voice kept repeating "He's a goddamned faggot, and we've got to kill him!" Two other voices seemed to be asking questions about what he had done and were arguing against the use of such violence. Bill was, of course, terrified by this experience and sat motionless in his room as the debate continued. When Roger tapped on his door to ask if he was all right, Bill was certain that they were coming to take him away. Realizing that it was Roger and that he had not been part of the conversation, Bill asked him who was in the next room. Roger pointed out that two of the children were sleeping in the next room. When Bill went to check, he found the children asleep in their beds. These voices appeared at frequent but unpredictable intervals almost every day. It was not clear whether or not they had first appeared before the development of Bill's delusional beliefs.

The details of the delusional system were elaborate and represented a complex web of imaginary events and reality. For example, the title of the secret film was supposedly *Honor Thy Father*, and Bill said his name in the film was Gay Talese. *Honor Thy Father* was, in fact, a popular novel that was written by Gay Talese and published several years prior to the development of Bill's delusion. The actual novel was about organized crime, but Bill denied any knowledge of this "other book with the same title." According to Bill's belief system, the film's title alluded to Bill's disrespect for his own father, and his own name in the film was a reference to his reputation as a "gay tease." He also maintained that his own picture had been on the cover of *Time* magazine within the past year with the name Gay Talese printed at the bottom.

An interesting array of evidence was marshaled in support of this delusion. For example, Bill pointed to the fact that he had happened to meet his cousin accidentally on a subway in Brooklyn 2 years earlier. Why, Bill asked, would his cousin have been on the same train if he were not making a secret film about Bill's private life? In Bill's mind, the cousin was clearly part of a continuous surveillance that had been carefully arranged by the conspirators. The fact that Bill came from a very large family and that such coincidences were bound to happen did not impress him as a counterargument. Bill also pointed to an incident involving the elevator operator at his mother's apartment building as further evidence for the existence of the film. He remembered stepping onto the elevator one morning and having the operator give him a puzzled, prolonged glance. The man asked him if they knew each other. Bill replied that they did not. Bill's explanation for this mundane occurrence was that the man recognized Bill because he had obviously seen the film recently; he insisted that no other explanation made sense. Once again, coincidence was absolutely impossible. His delusional system had become so pervasive and intricately woven that it was no longer open to logical refutation. He was totally preoccupied with the plot and simultaneously so frightened that he did not want to discuss it with anyone. Thus, he had lived in private fear, brooding about the conspiracy and helpless to prevent the conspirators from spreading knowledge of his shameful sexual behavior.

Social History

Bill was the youngest of four children. He grew up in New York City where his father worked as a firefighter. Both of his parents were first-generation Irish Americans. Many of their relatives were still living in Ireland. Both parents came from large families. Bill's childhood memories were filled with stories about the family's Irish heritage.

Bill was always much closer to his mother than to his father, whom he remembered as being harsh and distant. When his parents fought, which they did frequently, Bill often found himself caught in the middle. Neither parent seemed to make a serious effort to improve their relationship. Bill later learned that his father had carried on an extended affair with another woman. His mother depended on her own mother, who lived in the same neighborhood, for advice and support and would frequently take Bill with her to stay at her parents' apartment after particularly heated arguments. Bill grew to hate his father, but his enmity was tempered by guilt. He had learned that children were supposed to respect their parents and that, in particular, a son should emulate and revere his father. Mr. McClary became gravely ill when Bill was 12 years old, and Bill remembered wishing that his father would die. His wish came true. Years later, Bill looked back on this sequence of events with considerable ambivalence and regret.

Bill could not remember having any close friends as a child. Most of his social contacts were with cousins, nephews, and nieces. He did not enjoy their company or the games that other children played. He remembered himself as a clumsy, effeminate child who preferred to be alone or with his mother instead of with other boys.

He was a good student and finished near the top of his class in high school. His mother and the rest of the family seemed certain that he would go on to college, but Bill could not decide on a course of study. The prospect of selecting a profession struck Bill as an ominous task. How could he be sure that he wanted to do the same thing for the rest of his life? He decided that he needed more time to ponder the matter and took a job as a bank clerk after graduating from high school.

Bill moved to a small efficiency apartment and seemed to perform adequately at the bank. His superiors noted that he was reliable, though somewhat eccentric. He was described as quiet and polite; his reserved manner bordered on being socially withdrawn. He did not associate with any of the other employees and rarely spoke to them beyond the usual exchange of social pleasantries. Although he was not in danger of losing his job, Bill's chances for advancement were remote. This realization did not perturb Bill because he did not aspire to promotion in the banking profession. It was only a way of forestalling a serious career decision. After 2 years at the bank, Bill resigned. He had decided that the job did not afford him enough time to think about his future.

He was soon able to find a position as an elevator operator. Here, he reasoned, was a job that provided time for thought. Over the next several months, he gradually became more aloof and disorganized. He was frequently late to work and seemed unconcerned about the reprimands that he began receiving. Residents at the apartment house described him as peculiar. His appearance was always neat and clean, but he seemed preoccupied most of the time. On occasion he seemed to mumble to himself, and he often forgot floor numbers to which he had been directed. These problems continued to mount until he was fired after working for 1 year at this job.

During the first year after finishing high school, while working at the bank, Bill had his first sexual experience. A man in his middle forties who often did business at the bank invited Bill to his apartment for a drink, and they became intimate. The experience was moderately enjoyable but primarily anxiety provoking. Bill decided not to see this man again. Over the next 2 years, Bill experienced sexual relationships with a small number of other men as well as with a few women. In each case, it was Bill's partner who took the initiative. Only one relationship lasted more than a few days. He became friends with a woman named Patty who was about his own age, divorced, and the mother of a 3-year-old daughter. Bill enjoyed being with Patty and her daughter and occasionally spent evenings at their apartment watching television and drinking wine. Despite their occasional sexual encounters, this relationship never developed beyond the casual stage at which it began.

After he was fired from the job as an elevator operator, Bill moved back into his mother's apartment. He later recalled that they made each other anxious. Rarely leaving the apartment, Bill sat around the apartment daydreaming in front of the television. When his mother returned from work, she would clean, cook, and coax him unsuccessfully to enroll in various kinds of job-training programs. His social isolation was a constant cause of concern for her. She was not aware of his bisexual interests and encouraged him to call women that she met at work and through friends. The tension eventually became too great for both of them, and Bill decided to move in with Colleen, her husband, and their three young children.

Conceptualization and Treatment

Bill's adjustment problems were obviously extensive. He had experienced serious difficulties in the development of social and occupational roles. From a diagnostic viewpoint, Bill's initial symptoms pointed to schizotypal personality disorder. In other words, before his delusional beliefs and hallucinations became manifest, he exhibited a series of peculiar characteristics in the absence of floridly psychotic symptoms. These included several of the classic signs outlined by Meehl (1964): anhedonia (the inability to experience pleasure), interpersonal aversiveness, and ambivalence. Bill seldom, if ever, had any fun. Even his sexual experiences were described in a detached, intellectual manner. He might indicate, for example, that he had performed well or that his partner seemed satisfied, but he never said things like, "It was terrific," or "I was really excited!" He strongly preferred to be alone. When Colleen and Roger had parties, Bill became anxious and withdrew to his room, explaining that he felt ill.

Bill's ambivalence toward other people was evident in his relationship with his therapist. He never missed an appointment; in fact, he was always early and seemed to look forward to the visits. Despite this apparent dependence, he seemed to distrust the therapist and was often guarded in his response to questions. He seemed to want to confide in the therapist and was simultaneously fearful of the imagined consequences. Bill's pattern of cognitive distraction was somewhat difficult to interpret. His "scruples" were, in some ways, similar to obsessive thoughts, but they also bore a resemblance to one of Schneider's (1959) first-rank symptoms of schizophrenia—thought insertion. Considering this constellation of problems, it was clear that Bill was in need of treatment, but it was not immediately obvious that he was psychotic. The therapist decided to address Bill's problems from a cognitive-behavioral perspective. The ambiguity surrounding his cognitive impairment seemed to warrant a delay regarding biological interventions such as medication.

The beginning therapy sessions were among the most difficult. Bill was tense, reserved, and more than a bit suspicious. Therapy had been his sister's idea, not his own. The therapist adopted a passive, nondirective manner and concentrated on the difficult goal of establishing a trusting relationship with Bill. In the absence of such an atmosphere, it would be impossible to work toward more specific behavioral changes.

Many of the early sessions were spent discussing Bill's concerns about homosexuality. The therapist listened to Bill's thoughts and concerns and shared various bits of information about sexuality and homosexual behavior in particular. As might be expected, Bill was afraid that homosexual behavior per se was a direct manifestation of psychological disturbance. He also wondered about his motivation to perform sexual acts with other men and expressed some vague hypotheses about this being a reflection of his desire to have a closer relationship with his father. The therapist assured Bill that the gender of one's sexual partner was less important than the quality of the sexual relationship. In fact, the therapist was most concerned about Bill's apparent failure to enjoy sexual activity and his inability to establish lasting relationships. Instead of trying to eliminate the possibility of future homosexual encounters or to impose an arbitrary decision based on prevailing sexual norms, the therapist tried to (a) help Bill explore his own concerns about the topic, (b) provide him with information that he did not have, and (c) help him develop skills that would improve his social and sexual relationships, whether they involved men or women.

As their relationship became more secure, the therapist adopted a more active, directive role. Specific problems were identified, and an attempt was made to deal with each sequentially. The first area of concern was Bill's daily schedule. The therapist enlisted Colleen's support. Together with Bill, they instituted a sequence of contingencies designed to integrate his activities with those of the family. For example, Colleen called Bill once for breakfast at 7:30 a.m. If he missed eating with everyone else, Colleen went on with other activities and did not make him a late brunch as she had done prior to this arrangement. In general, the therapist taught Colleen to reinforce appropriate behavior and to ignore inappropriate behavior as much as possible. Over the initial weeks, Bill did begin to keep more regular hours.

After several weeks of work, this home-based program began to produce positive changes. Bill was following a schedule closer to that of the rest of the family and was more helpful around the house. At this point, the therapist decided to address two problems that were somewhat more difficult: Bill's annoying habit of mumbling to himself and his lack of social contacts with peers. Careful interviews with Bill and his sister served as a base for a functional assessment of the self-talk. This behavior seemed to occur most frequently when Bill was alone or thought he was alone. He was usually able to control his scruples in the presence of others; if he was particularly disturbed by a distracting thought, he most often excused himself and retired to his room. Colleen's response was usually to remind Bill that he was mumbling and occasionally to scold him if he was talking loudly. Given the functional value of Bill's scruples in reducing his anxiety about irreverent thoughts, it seemed unlikely that the self-talk was being maintained by this social reinforcement.

The therapist decided to try a stimulus-control procedure. Bill was instructed to select one place in the house in which he could daydream and talk to himself. Whenever he felt the urge to daydream or repeat his scruples, he was to go to this specific spot before engaging in these behaviors. It was hoped that this procedure would severely restrict the environmental stimuli that were associated with these asocial behaviors and thereby reduce their frequency. Bill and the therapist selected the laundry room as his daydreaming room because it was relatively secluded from the rest of the house. His bedroom was ruled out because the therapist did not want it to become a stimulus for behaviors that would interfere with sleeping. Colleen was encouraged to prompt Bill whenever she noticed him engaging in self-talk outside of the laundry room. The program seemed to have modest, positive results, but it did not eliminate self-talk entirely.

Interpersonal behaviors were also addressed from a behavioral perspective. Since moving to his sister's home, Bill had not met any people his own age and had discontinued seeing his friends in New York City. Several avenues were pursued. He was encouraged to call his old friends and, in particular, to renew his friendship with Patty. The therapist spent several sessions with Bill rehearsing telephone calls and practicing conversations that might take place. Although Bill was generally aware of what things he should say, he was anxious about social contacts. This form of behavioral rehearsal was seen as a way of exposing him gradually to the anxiety-provoking stimuli. He was also given weekly homework assignments involving social contacts at home. The therapist discussed possible sources of friends, including a tavern not far from Colleen's home and occasional parties that Colleen and Roger had for their friends. This aspect of the treatment program was modestly effective. Bill called Patty several times and arranged to stay with his mother for a weekend so that he could visit with Patty and her daughter. Although he was somewhat anxious at first, the visit was successful and seemed to lift Bill's spirits. He was more animated during the following therapy session and seemed almost optimistic about changing his current situation.

It was during one of their visits to the neighborhood tavern that Bill first mentioned the imagined movie to Roger. When the therapist learned of these ideas, and the auditory hallucinations, he modified the treatment plan. He had initially rejected the idea of antipsychotic medication because there was no clear-cut evidence of schizophrenia. Now that psychotic symptoms had appeared, an appointment was arranged with a psychiatrist who agreed with the diagnosis and prescribed risperidone (Risperdal), one of the atypical (or "second-generation") antipsychotic drugs. Because Bill's behavior was not considered dangerous and his sister was able to supervise his activities closely, hospitalization was not necessary. All other aspects of the program were continued.

Bill's response to the medication was positive but not dramatic. The most obvious effect was on his self-talk, which was reduced considerably over a 4-week period. Bill attributed this change to the virtual disappearance of the annoying, intrusive thoughts. His delusions remained intact, however, despite the therapist's attempt to encourage a rational consideration of the evidence. The following example illustrates the impregnable quality of delusional thinking as well as the naiveté of the therapist.

One of Bill's ideas was that his picture had been on the cover of *Time* magazine. This seemed like a simple idea to test, and Bill expressed a willingness to try. Together they narrowed the range of dates to the last 8 months. The therapist then asked Bill to visit the public library before their next session and check all issues of *Time* during this period. Of course, Bill did not find his picture. Nevertheless, his conviction was even stronger than before. He had convinced himself that the conspirators had seen him on his way to the library, beaten him there, and switched magazine covers before he could discover the original. Undaunted, the therapist recommended two more public libraries for the next week. As might have been expected, Bill did not find his picture at either library but remained convinced that the cover had appeared. Every effort to introduce contradictory evidence was met by this same stubborn resistance.

Over the next several weeks, Bill became somewhat less adamant about his beliefs. He conceded that there was a chance that he had imagined the whole thing. It seemed to him that the plot probably did exist and that the movie was, in all likelihood, still playing around the country, but he was willing to admit that the evidence for this belief was less than overwhelming. Although his suspicions remained, the fear of observation and the threat of death were less immediate, and he was able to concentrate more fully on the other aspects of the treatment program. Hospitalization did not become necessary, and he was able to continue living with Colleen's family. Despite important improvements, it was clear that Bill would continue to need a special, supportive environment, and it seemed unlikely that he would assume normal occupational and social roles, at least not in the near future.

Discussion

The diagnostic hallmarks of schizophrenia are hallucinations, delusions, and disturbances in affect and thought. *DSM-IV-TR* (APA, 2000, p. 312) requires the following to support a diagnosis of schizophrenia:

1. **Characteristic symptoms:** Two (or more) of the following, each present for a significant portion of time during a 1-month period (or less if successfully treated):
   a. Delusions
   b. Hallucinations
   c. Disorganized speech
   d. Grossly disorganized or catatonic behavior
   e. Negative symptoms, such as affective flattening, alogia, or avolition
      Note: Only one of these symptoms is required if delusions are bizarre, hallucinations consist of a voice keeping up a running commentary on the person's behavior or thoughts, or two or more voices are conversing with each other.
2. **Social/occupational dysfunction:** For a significant portion of the time since the onset of the disturbance, one or more major areas of functioning, such as work, interpersonal relations, or self-care, are markedly below the level achieved prior to the onset.
3. **Duration:** Continuous signs of the disturbance persist for at least 6 months. This 6-month period must include at least 1 month of symptoms that meet Criterion 1 (active phase symptoms) and may include periods of prodromal or residual symptoms. During these prodromal or residual periods, the signs of the disturbance may be manifested by only negative symptoms, or two or more symptoms listed in Criterion 1 present in an attenuated form (such as odd beliefs, unusual perceptual experiences).

Bill clearly fit the diagnostic criteria for schizophrenia. Prior to the expression of his complex, delusional belief system, he exhibited several of the characteristics of a *prodromal phase*. He had been socially isolated since moving to his sister's home. Although he did interact with his sister and her family, he made no effort to stay in touch with the few friends he had known in New York City, nor did he attempt to meet new friends in the neighborhood. In fact, he had never been particularly active socially, even during his childhood. His occupational performance had deteriorated long before he was fired from his job as an elevator operator. Several neighbors had complained about his peculiar behavior. For example, one of Colleen's friends once called to tell her that she had been watching Bill as he walked home from the grocery store. He was carrying a bag of groceries, clearly mumbling to himself, and moving in a strange pattern. He would take two or three steps forward, then one to the side onto the grass next to the sidewalk. At this point, Bill would hop once on his left foot, take one step forward, and then step back onto the sidewalk and continue the sequence. Thinking that this behavior seemed similar to games that children commonly play, Colleen asked Bill about his walk home. He told her that each of these movements possessed a particular meaning and that he followed this pattern to correct scruples that were being placed in his head as he returned from the store. This explanation, and his other comments about his scruples, would be considered an example of magical thinking. Overall, Bill's delusional beliefs and auditory hallucinations can be seen as an extension of the deterioration that began much earlier.

Schizophrenia is a relatively common disorder, affecting approximately 1 to 2% of the population (Messias, Chen, & Eaton, 2007; Wu, Birnbaum, Hudson, & Kessler, 2006). Although gender differences in prevalence are not large, the disorder may affect more men than women. Onset usually occurs during adolescence or early adulthood, but somewhat later for women than for men. The prognosis is mixed. When Emil Kraepelin first defined the disorder (originally known as *dementia praecox*), he emphasized its chronic deteriorating course. Many patients do, in fact, show a gradual decline in social and occupational functioning and continue to exhibit psychotic symptoms either continuously or intermittently throughout their lives. However, a substantial number of patients seem to recover without signs of residual impairment. Much of the most informative data pertaining to prognosis have come from the World Health Organization's International Study of Schizophrenia (Hopper, Harrison, Janca, & Sartorius, 2007). Compared to people with other mental disorders, such as mood disorders, schizophrenics tended to have a worse outcome 20 years after their initial treatment for the disorder. There was substantial overlap between the groups, however, and considerable variability within the schizophrenic patients. The results of this study and several others indicate that roughly 60% of schizophrenic patients follow a chronic pattern, and approximately 25% recover within several years after the onset of the disorder (Heiden & Häfner, 2000).

Although people with schizophrenia share some important common characteristics, they are also an extremely heterogeneous group. This feature was emphasized in the title of Eugen Bleuler's classic monograph, *Dementia Praecox or the Group of Schizophrenias* (1911/1950). Kraepelin and Bleuler both outlined subtypes of schizophrenia, including catatonic, paranoid, hebephrenic, and simple types. Each of these subtypes was defined in terms of a few characteristic symptoms. *Catatonic* patients were identified by their bizarre motor movements and the unusual postures they would assume. Their motor behavior might include either a rigid posture with total immobility or undirected, maniclike excitement. *Paranoid* patients were those who expressed delusions of persecution and reference. The primary features of *hebephrenia* were taken to be inappropriate affect and florid symptomatology (e.g., bizarre delusions and hallucinations). Bill would clearly be included in the paranoid subcategory of schizophrenic disorders.

Symptomatically defined subgroups possess a certain intuitive appeal, but they have not proved to be particularly useful in other respects (Helmes & Landmark, 2003). One major problem has been a lack of reliability in assigning patients to subcategories. Because of problems in identifying the general category of schizophrenia, it is not surprising that the subtypes present further difficulties. Inconsistency is another drawback; patients who exhibit a particular set of prominent symptoms at one point in time may exhibit another set of features during a later episode. The symptomatically defined subgroups have also not been shown to possess either etiological or predictive validity. For example, a specific treatment that is more or less effective with catatonic patients in comparison with hebephrenics has not been found.

Another system for subdividing schizophrenic patients is based on the use of three symptom dimensions: psychotic symptoms, negative symptoms, and disorganization (Andreasen, Arndt, Alliger, Miller, & Flaum, 1995; O'Leary et al., 2000). Psychotic symptoms include hallucinations and delusions. Negative symptoms include blunted or restricted affect, social withdrawal, and poverty of speech. Verbal communication problems, such as disorganized speech and bizarre behavior, are included in the third symptom dimension, which is called disorganization. The distinctions among psychotic, negative, and disorganized symptom dimensions have generated a considerable amount of interest and research.

Etiological Considerations

Genetic factors are clearly involved in the transmission of schizophrenia (Mitchell & Porteous, 2010). The most persuasive data supporting this conclusion come from twin studies and investigations following various adoption methods. Twin studies depend on the following reasoning: Monozygotic (MZ) twins develop from a single zygote, which separates during an early stage of growth and forms two distinct but genetically identical embryos. In the case of dizygotic (DZ) twins, two separate eggs are fertilized by two sperm cells, and both develop simultaneously. Thus, DZ twins share only, on average, 50% of their genes, the same as siblings who do not share the same prenatal period. Based on the assumption that both forms of twins share similar environments, MZ twins should manifest a higher concordance rate (i.e., more often resemble each other) for traits that are genetically determined. This is, in fact, the pattern that has now been reported for schizophrenia over a large number of studies (Pogue-Geile & Gottesman, 2007). For example, one study conducted in Finland reported a concordance rate of 46% for MZ twins and only 9% among DZ twins (Cannon, Kaprio, Loennqvist, Huttunen, & Koskenvuo, 1998). This substantial difference between MZ and DZ concordance indicates the influence of genetic factors. On the other hand, the absence of 100% concordance among the MZ twins also indicates that genetic factors do not account for all of the variance. The development of the disorder must therefore depend on a dynamic interaction between a genetically determined predisposition and various environmental events (Gottesman & Hanson, 2005).

We do not know how genetic factors interact with environmental events to produce schizophrenia. This problem is enormously complex because the environmental events in question might take any of several different forms (Walker, Kestler, Bollini, & Hochman, 2004). Some investigators have focused on factors such as nutritional deficiencies or viral infections. One hypothesis suggests that prenatal infections increase vulnerability to schizophrenia by disrupting brain development in the fetus (e.g., Brown & Derkits, 2010). Another approach to environmental events and vulnerability to schizophrenia has focused on interpersonal relations within the family. Adverse family circumstances during child hood may increase the probability of subsequently developing schizophrenia among people who are genetically predisposed toward the disorder (Schiffman et al., 2001).

In addition to questions about the causes of the disorder, a considerable amount of research has also stressed the family's influence on the course of the disorder. These studies follow the progress of patients who have already been treated for schizophrenia, and they are concerned with expressed emotion (EE), or the extent to which at least one family member is extremely critical of the patient and his or her behavior. The patients are typically followed for several months after discharge from the hospital, and the outcome variable is the percentage of patients who return to the hospital for further treatment. Relapse rates are much higher for patients who returned to high EE homes (Aguilera, Lopez, Breitborde, Kopelowicz, & Zarate, 2010; Hooley, 2007).

The data regarding EE are consistent with Bill's experience. Bill remembered that when he and his mother were living together, they made each other anxious. His descriptions of her behavior indicate that her emotional involvement was excessive, given that he was an adult and capable of greater independence; she was always worried about his job, his friends, or what he was doing with his time. Her constant intrusions and coaxing finally led him to seek refuge with his sister's family.

The supportive environment provided by Colleen and her family and their willingness to tolerate many of Bill's idiosyncrasies were undoubtedly helpful in allowing Bill to remain outside a hospital during his psychotic episodes.

Treatment

There are several important variables to consider in selecting a treatment for acute schizophrenic disturbance. Antipsychotic drugs have become the principal form of intervention since their introduction in the 1950s (Haddad, Taylor, & Niaz, 2009). A large number of carefully controlled studies have demonstrated that these drugs have a beneficial effect for many patients with schizophrenia. They lead to an improvement in symptoms during acute psychotic episodes. Antipsychotic medications also reduce the probability of symptom relapse if they are taken on a maintenance basis after the patient has recovered from an episode. Unfortunately, some patients, perhaps as many as 25%, do not respond positively to antipsychotic medication.

Antipsychotic medication seems to have a specific effect on many psychotic symptoms, such as hallucinations and disorganized speech. In Bill's case, medication did have a positive effect. The administration of antipsychotic medication was associated with an improvement in his most dramatic symptoms.

Despite these positive effects, several limitations and some problems are also associated with the use of antipsychotic drugs. One problem, which was evident in Bill's case, is that medication is only a partial solution. After the most dramatic symptoms have improved, most patients continue to suffer from role impairments that are not the direct product of hallucinations and delusions. In short, medication can sometimes relieve perceptual aberrations, but it does not remove deficiencies in social and occupational skills.

Another problem arises with treatment-refractory patients. Approximately 10 to 20% of schizophrenic patients do not benefit from traditional forms of antipsychotic medication (Kane, 1996). Others who respond initially will relapse repeatedly during maintenance drug treatment. Therefore, pharmaceutical companies continue to develop new forms of medication. Clozapine (Clozaril) and risperidone (Risperdal) are examples of the so-called second generation of antipsychotic drugs. They are also known as *atypical antipsychotic* drugs because they produce fewer adverse side effects and seem to have a different pharmacological mode of action than more traditional antipsychotic drugs. Controlled studies of clozapine and risperidone have found significant improvement in approximately 30% of patients who were previously considered "treatment resistant" (Turner & Stewart, 2006). The availability of these new forms of medication offers new hope for many patients and their families.

A final problem has been the development of long-term side effects, most notably a serious, involuntary movement disorder known as *tardive dyskinesia*. The most obvious signs of tardive dyskinesia include trembling of the extremities, lip smacking, and protrusions of the tongue. These symptoms can be disconcerting to both patients and those with whom they interact. Fortunately, atypical antipsychotic drugs are less likely to lead to the development of motor side effects such as tardive dyskinesia (Kane, 2004).

Psychosocial treatment programs are also beneficial for patients with schizophrenia (Bustillo, Lauriello, Horan, & Keith, 2001). Perhaps most important is the use of family-based programs in conjunction with maintenance medication. Several studies have evaluated treatment programs designed to help patients with families that are rated high in EE (Girón et al., 2010). In addition to antipsychotic medication, treatment typically includes two principal components. First, the therapist provides family members with information about schizophrenia, on the assumption that some hostility and criticism result from failure to understand the nature of the patient's problems. Second, the therapist focuses on enhancing the family's ability to cope with stressful experiences by working on problem-solving and communication skills. Results with this type of family intervention have been very encouraging.

In Bill's case, his sister's family was not high in EE. Direct treatment focused on family patterns of communication was therefore unnecessary. The therapist did, however, spend time talking with Colleen and Roger about Bill's situation in an effort to help them cope with his idiosyncratic behavior. Bill's therapist also directed his attention to the development of social skills. These efforts met with mixed success. Social skills programs are often useful with schizophrenics who are being treated on an outpatient basis (Pilling et al., 2002).

There is also some reason to be cautious about the use of active psychological approaches to the treatment of patients who are socially withdrawn and exhibiting other negative symptoms (e.g., Kopelowicz, Liberman, Mintz, & Zarate, 1997). Programs that increase the level of social interaction among chronic schizophrenic patients may have adverse effects on other areas of the person's adjustment. Patients with severe, persistent negative symptoms and those who are not on medication may not be able to cope with the increase in stress that is associated with an active, directive form of social intervention. This effect may have been evident in Bill's case. He was not receiving medication until after the therapist became aware of his extensive delusional system. His response to the behavioral program seemed to be more positive after the introduction of antipsychotic medication. Prior to that point, the role-playing that was attempted during sessions and the homework assignments during the week actually seemed to increase his level of anxiety.

Discussion Questions

1. One simple way to define a delusion is to say that it is false belief. But there is more to it than that. How would you describe Bill's delusional belief about the film that had presumably been made about him? What characteristics of his belief system were important, beyond the fact that it was not based on evidence that could be shared with other people?
2. What were the earliest symptoms that Bill was beginning to develop a psychotic disorder? Were there any meaningful signs of his disorder prior to the onset of hallucinations and delusions? If medication is effective for most people who have psychotic symptoms, should it also be prescribed

for people who seem to be vulnerable to schizophrenia? What are the possible advantages and disadvantages of this approach to treatment? How could it be evaluated?

3. Given the broad range of symptoms and social deficits that are often associated with schizophrenia, these patients often need a broad array of services and support systems. Other than antipsychotic medication, what are the most important forms of mental-health service that would be helpful, both to the patients and to their families?

4. Who should pay for mental-health services to patients with serious mental disorders such as schizophrenia? Should they be included in standard health-insurance programs? Should they receive a priority that is comparable to other medical disorders, such as cancer and heart disease?

CHAPTER 10

Psychotic Disorder (NOS), Substance Dependence, and Violence

This case illustrates several difficult and confusing issues that are faced by mental-health professionals working in community mental-health settings. The woman in this case had been homeless for many months, perhaps several years. Many details of her life history were missing because of her chaotic lifestyle. Her own descriptions of herself and the events in her life were inconsistent and unreliable. She was often psychotic, and she apparently used drugs on a fairly regular basis. Because contact with clients who are homeless and seriously mentally ill is often sporadic and unpredictable, cases such as this one are hard to describe and even more difficult to manage. The information presented in this chapter is based on intermittent therapeutic contacts with the woman as well as one meeting with her brother, one phone conversation with her daughter, and one discussion with a woman who let her stay with her on occasion.

Angela was 36 years old and had apparently experienced nearly constant auditory hallucinations for the past 20 years. It was difficult to know very much about the nature of these experiences because she did not like to talk about the topic. Angela said that she heard several different voices, mostly males, talking about her. The volume, clarity, and emotional tone of the voices varied tremendously. Sometimes they were distinct, loud, and angry. Most of the time, they seemed almost like a dull, rumbling noise, running day and night in the background of her mind. At times, it seemed like listening to a radio talk show with the volume turned down.

Angela also had a long-standing problem with substance dependence, especially crack cocaine and heroin. Her heavy use of drugs started a few years after she had been experiencing hallucinations, and she sometimes used the drugs to try to drown out the voices. Angela's pattern of drug use escalated when her living circumstances were most chaotic, when she was least stable emotionally, and when her voices were most intrusive. Of course, it is impossible to untangle the direction of these effects; increased stress might have caused Angela to increase her consumption of drugs, but she also might have become more disorganized because she was using more drugs.

Many of the people with whom Angela spent her time were people who used drugs frequently. She had been drawn into (and also sought out) a social world that was dangerous, threatening, and hostile. She frequently spent periods of several days at a time hanging out in dirty, abandoned buildings with groups of other people who were also taking drugs. Her descriptions of these experiences were both confusing and frightening. Angela claimed that she had witnessed many assaults and more than one murder in such circumstances. Many of the other people also engaged in sexual activities, often as a way of earning money to purchase drugs or in exchange for drugs. According to Angela's description of her own behavior, she was able to obtain heroin and crack by conning other people. She denied being a prostitute and said that she did not exchange sex for drugs.

She had been in and out of drug rehabilitation programs many times. She had also been arrested once for possession of a small amount of cocaine and another time for stabbing a man in the stomach (see below). She had spent 18 months in prison for the assault before being released on parole and finding her way back onto the streets.

Her typical pattern in rehabilitation was to find a way—usually a desperate suicidal threat or gesture—to enter a program, go through detoxification quickly, and then leave after a few days (without completing the therapeutic program). These experiences usually allowed her to escape an unpleasant circumstance, such as living temporarily with a friend who had grown tired of her company. They also allowed her to get some relatively undisturbed sleep and to eat a few nourishing meals.

Angela was the mother of three children, two daughters and a son, who ranged in age from 20 to 15. They were all raised by Angela's mother—who lived in a neighboring state—because of Angela's long-standing problems with mental illness as well as her legal difficulties. Angela had been unable to visit them for many years because one of the conditions of her parole was that she could not travel to another state. The oldest child, a daughter, was an honors student at an elite, private college. Although Angela had not been able to spend much time with her children, she was very proud of them and kept track of their lives through intermittent conversations with her mother and one of her brothers.

Social History

Angela was born in Philadelphia, the second of four children in a lower-middle-class, single-parent family. Her mother had been addicted to heroin as a young adult, but she had been free of drugs for many years, certainly since Angela and her siblings were small children. The family lived on disability payments that her mother collected as the result of a chronic problem with back pain. Angela's mother was a strong, dependable, and conscientious parent. Her children all attended public schools, and they all graduated from high school, even though the family endured many difficult financial times.

Like many of the other students in her high school, Angela drank alcohol and smoked marijuana as a teenager. She gave up drinking early because she said it "didn't do anything for her." She had hoped that it would make the voices go away, but it didn't. She did continue to smoke pot.

Angela graduated from high school, 1 year after the birth of her first child. Although her behavior was often impulsive and unpredictable, she was considered to be a very bright student. She was talkative in class and made intelligent, though occasionally obscure, comments in discussions with other students. Angela also liked to write. Teachers in her English classes said that she wrote interesting poetry; it was often ethereal and concerned with depressing themes.

Following graduation, she worked for short periods of time but never at the same job for more than 6 months. One of her first jobs was as a clerk for a drugstore. She was fired for stealing money that she used to buy marijuana. She also held several lower-level secretarial positions. Her second and third children were born within 3 years after she graduated. Her relationships with the men who were the fathers were not stable, and both of these men disappeared from her life soon after she learned that she was pregnant.

Angela's use of drugs escalated dramatically after the birth of her third child, when she was 22. She began smoking crack and heroin. At first, she used these drugs separately. Later she began to combine cocaine and heroin into a mixture known as a speedball that could be injected. This process seemed to enhance the positive subjective feelings. Two motives seemed responsible for this change in her use of drugs. One was that her hallucinations had become more prominent and distressing. Angela took more drugs to try to quiet the voices. The other reason involved a process that she called "chasing the first high." None of her drug experiences ever seemed quite as wonderful as the feeling that she had had the first time she smoked crack. In an effort to be able to feel that way again, she kept taking increased doses and different combinations of drugs.

Her behavior became increasingly erratic. She would sometimes show up, unannounced, at her mother's house, asking to spend a few days with the children. Then she would disappear again. Her mother and her brothers and sister were extremely upset as they watched her health deteriorate, but they were unable to persuade her to change.

When she was 24 years old, Angela's mother finally persuaded her to make a serious attempt to stop using heroin. She had tried before unsuccessfully, both on her own and with friends. She always went back to using within a couple of days, unable to bear the symptoms of drug withdrawal. This time, she was accepted into a community treatment program. She went to meetings (Narcotics

Anonymous) as well as a day treatment program, which included group therapy specifically directed at substance abuse and dependence. While she was participating in these meetings, she met a man who was also in the program. They became romantically involved, and after a few months, Angela began living with him at his apartment. She had been off drugs for 4 months at that point. Unfortunately, he was a difficult person with many demons of his own, including a violent temper. He began to abuse her physically.

An Episode of Violence

Angela lived with this man and endured his beatings for a few months. She was constantly afraid and physically exhausted. Her voices were becoming more prominent once again, as the level of stress increased. At times, they warned her about things that her boyfriend was planning to do to her. The voices also urged her to protect herself and to get even with him. Frightened and confused, Angela left the apartment and began wandering the streets, looking for a way to get money so that she could buy heroin and drown out the voices.

She found herself in a busy area of the city, late at night. The street was lined with bars, tourist shops, and all-night markets. Cars were jammed at the intersection while many pedestrians were crowded onto the sidewalk. It was very noisy—horns honking, people shouting, and music blaring from car stereos and the bars. Angela was becoming increasingly agitated, while also feeling frustrated and angry about the way she was being treated. Her boyfriend was beating her. Now the people on the street were bumping and pushing and jumping in front of her. Everyone seemed to be taking advantage of her in one way or another. As her desperate search for money and drugs wore on, she was feeling more irritated, vigilant, and on edge.

A middle-aged man, who had clearly consumed a lot of alcohol, suddenly walked out of a bar and stumbled toward Angela. His speech was slurred, and his balance and vision seemed impaired. He mumbled that he would give Angela $20 if she hailed a cab for him. She did that. The man moved toward the cab and started to get in without giving Angela the money that he had promised. Feeling angry because she had been manipulated by him, Angela grabbed his arm and demanded her money. He laughed, called her a name, and started to pull away, falling backward toward the door of the cab. She became enraged, pulled a small knife out of her jacket, and stabbed him in the stomach. As the man screamed and collapsed onto the sidewalk, several other people grabbed Angela and pulled her to the ground.

The police arrived within seconds. Angela was handcuffed and driven to the nearest police station. Her behavior was wild and erratic. Her mood was unstable, vacillating quickly among anger, fear, and sadness. Many of the things that Angela said were incoherent. She was interviewed by a court-appointed psychiatrist who met with her once and prescribed antipsychotic medication that could be administered by injection (so that they would be certain that she took it). Her mood and behavior improved after she had been in jail for about 10 days.

Several days later, the judge ordered a competence evaluation. She had been charged with aggravated assault, and conviction would carry a sentence of up to 5 years in prison (depending on any prior convictions). Before she could stand trial, the court had to determine whether Angela was able to understand the charges against her and participate in her own defense. The central question in this decision was whether or not she was still actively psychotic. By the time this interview was conducted, her speech was coherent and her mood was stable. She denied hearing voices because she did not want to be sent, on an involuntary basis, to a state facility for criminal defendants with mental disorders. The psychiatrist who conducted the evaluation recommended that she was competent to stand trial.

With consultation from the public defender who had been assigned to her case, Angela decided to plead guilty to a reduced charge. By this point, her victim had recovered from his painful wound. She was sentenced to 18 months in jail, with the possibility of release on parole for good behavior. Angela was very upset during her first few days at the women's prison. According to the guards, she "went crazy." She had to be put in solitary confinement after she attacked another prisoner in her cell. She was not allowed to leave her cell to eat meals because she threw food and trays of dishes and could not be restrained. On the third day, she set fire to her own cell. Because of her wild, uncontrolled behavior, she was transferred to another institution with a psychiatric ward for people convicted of violent crimes.

The psychiatrist at the prison prescribed antipsychotic medication. Angela's behavior was extremely agitated for the first few days that she was living on the ward. She was belligerent and argumentative, frequently picking fights with staff members and other patients. Some of her time was spent in physical restraints because there was no other way to control her behavior. The medication eventually helped her calm down.

Because of her violent and disruptive behavior, Angela served the full 18-month sentence, some of it in the psychiatric unit and other times in the regular prison population. When she was finally discharged, she was 26 years old and homeless.

She was released from jail on probation and was required to check with her parole officer once a week. Another condition of her parole was that she had to remain in treatment for her mental-health problems.

Angela went to live with her brother for a while, but her behavior was too disruptive. She argued with him and his wife several times a day. Her schedule was completely unpredictable. Some days, she would leave home in the late afternoon and not return for 2 or 3 days. Other times, she would stay in her room for several days, refusing to talk to anyone else. Her brother eventually asked her to leave because the stress associated with Angela's presence was causing too much conflict in his family. He and his wife were also extremely worried about the possible negative impact that Angela might have on their young children.

Community Treatment

For the next 10 years, Angela moved from place to place. She lived with friends at times, and sometimes she stayed on the streets or in community shelters. Now and then, she would find a way to gain entrance to another rehabilitation program. Access to treatment was not easy. For a person without health insurance or any other way to pay for services, Angela had to rely on public programs, and these often have extremely long waiting lists and strict criteria for admission. Very few beds are available in the detoxification programs run by most large cities. Angela found two methods that would usually result in immediate admission. One was to appear at a public mental-health clinic and make a serious suicide threat. Once she told the counselor that she was going to jump off a bridge. She was admitted later that day.

Angela continued working on her poetry when she wasn't too high and could find a quiet place to write. She showed some of these poems to her counselor, who was impressed with the quality of her writing. Most of them were concerned with the use of drugs, especially how she felt when she stopped taking them (loneliness, emptiness, darkness, and so on).

After her release from prison, Angela began to experience occasional periods of severe depression. These episodes would last anywhere from 2 weeks to a month or more. Feelings of hopelessness and guilt would overwhelm her, and she would retreat from interactions with other people. Her inability to care for her children became a major preoccupation for her during these times. Although she was usually a prolific writer, she lost all interest in her journals during these episodes. Her appetite was also very poor when she was depressed, but it was difficult to know whether that was a symptom of depression or the result of the fact that she usually stopped taking drugs when she was severely depressed (perhaps because she didn't have the energy to go out and hustle the money she would need to buy the drugs).

Angela may have also experienced episodes of mania or hypomania. This is another issue that was difficult to understand, based on her own description of events. There were definitely periods of several days in a row when she would sleep very little and become extremely active. However, these were also times when she increased her use of illegal drugs, and it is difficult to know whether her maniclike behavior was the simple product of cocaine and other stimulants.

When she was admitted to the community treatment program, Angela was assigned two diagnoses on Axis I of the *Diagnostic and Statistical Manual of Mental Disorders* (*DSM-IV-TR*; APA, 2000): psychotic disorder not otherwise specified (NOS) and substance dependence (opioids). The diagnosis of psychotic disorder NOS is used to describe psychotic symptoms when there is not enough information to make a specific diagnosis, such as schizophrenia, or when there is contradictory information. For example, the clinician may not be able to determine whether the person's psychotic symptoms are caused by the ingestion of psychoactive substances. It is difficult for clinicians to draw the distinction between different diagnostic categories, such as schizophrenia and major depressive disorder with psychotic features, when the person's self-report is unreliable and when it is not clear what the person is like when not taking drugs.

Angela's behavior also raised a number of questions about the possible diagnosis of one or more personality disorders. Paranoid, antisocial, and narcissistic personality disorders all seemed to be possible diagnoses. She did not trust anyone, including members of her own family. Of course, the hostile and threatening world in which she had lived for most of her adult life made it difficult to determine whether her vigilance and suspicions were justified. Is this pattern entirely irrational for a person who had lived in such difficult circumstances? She had undoubtedly been abused and been taken advantage of for many years. Unfortunately, her pervasive mistrust also made it difficult to establish a relationship with her in therapy. Her speech was guarded, and she did not confide easily in her therapist.

Because there was no evidence that Angela showed signs of conduct disorder as a child, she would not meet the formal diagnostic criteria for antisocial personality disorder. Nevertheless, she did exhibit several other features of the disorder, such as a failure to conform to social norms with respect to lawful behavior. She lied frequently to her therapist, to her family, and to the people with whom she spent time on the streets. She was often irritable, aggressive, and irresponsible.

Angela took great pride in her ability to con and manipulate others. For example, she once told her therapist that she was terribly afraid of dying. She said she was feeling that her physical health was even worse than usual, and she cried at great length about this concern. Her specific concern was pancreatic cancer, which she claimed to be the cause of death for two close relatives. Preliminary tests indicated that she did have a very low glucose level. Upon further testing, however, physicians at the clinic were able to determine that Angela was intentionally taking too much insulin and thereby inducing these symptoms in an effort to gain admission to the hospital. As with many of her other problems, it was impossible to know whether these characteristics played an active role in the original onset of her mental disorder or whether they were the consequences of living in a dangerous and chaotic environment.

Impulsive and hostile behaviors were also serious problems for Angela. Her inability to maintain regular clinic appointments provided only one example. She would come to appointments whenever she wanted to be there, and she would storm out if the therapist asked her to wait until she was finished with her current appointment. Then she would disappear for a few weeks. Her impulsivity was also evident in decisions about housing. She would leave where she had been living without giving any thought to where she would go next. Her therapist once spent weeks finding a new home for Angela, and she immediately provoked a fight with another woman who lived there. She was thrown out within a week because she wouldn't follow any of the rules (not coming in at the right time; refusing to help with cleaning and cooking).

Discussion

Many people who are seriously mentally ill qualify for more than one specific diagnosis. The term *dual diagnosis* has often been used to describe people who would meet the diagnostic criteria for both schizophrenia and substance-use disorder (Staiger et al., 2011). Some estimates indicate that 50% of patients with schizophrenia also have a substance-use disorder of some kind (Lewis, 2002). The concept of dual diagnosis has drawn needed attention to these issues, but it may fail to reflect the overwhelming range of problems that people like Angela face. In addition to her problems with psychosis and drug dependence, Angela experienced difficulties involving legal issues, physical illness (including increased risk of exposure to HIV), and homelessness. The combination of psychosis and substance dependence decreases the probability that a person will respond positively to treatment and amplifies the severity of social and occupational impairment associated with either type of disorder on its own. Substance-use disorders are often associated with schizophrenia and depression, especially among people who are homeless (North et al., 1997).

Homelessness is an important and difficult problem that is often associated with mental disorders. Substance abuse and medication noncompliance (failure to take prescribed drugs) are both associated with an increased risk for homelessness among patients with schizophrenia. Being homeless leaves the person more vulnerable to many other negative environmental events. Women like Angela who are seriously mentally ill and homeless are often victims of sexual assault and physical violence (Friedman & Loue, 2007; Gearson, Kaltman, Brown, & Bellack, 2003).

According to *DSM-IV-TR* (APA, 2000), people who exhibit psychotic symptoms but do not meet the specific criteria for a disorder, such as schizophrenia, may be given a diagnosis of psychotic disorder not otherwise specified (NOS). One example is the presence of persistent auditory hallucinations in the absence of other features of schizophrenia. Angela admitted hearing voices on a continuous basis for several years, but she did not like to talk about them, and her descriptions of these experiences were rather vague. Criterion 1 for schizophrenia requires that the person exhibit two or more types of psychotic symptoms, such as hallucinations, delusional beliefs, disorganized speech, catatonic behavior, or negative symptoms (such as affective flattening). Angela did not exhibit any of these other symptoms of schizophrenia. According to *DSM-IV-TR* (APA, 2000), only one symptom is required in Criterion 1 if the hallucinations conform to a certain description, such as a voice keeping up a running commentary on the person's behavior. This might have been true in Angela's case, but it was difficult to be certain of their character. Therefore, the diagnosis remained ambiguous, and psychotic disorder NOS provided the most accurate description of her condition.

Similar NOS options are available for mood disorders, eating disorders, personality disorders, and most of the other general headings in the diagnostic manual. The NOS categories are used to describe people who experience significant distress or social impairment but whose symptoms fall outside the official diagnostic boundaries. These options indicate that the categories defined in the manual do not provide an exhaustive description of all forms of mental disorder.

Another possible diagnosis for Angela's condition would have been schizoaffective disorder. This concept is used to describe patients who present a mixture of symptoms that fall on the boundary between schizophrenia and mood disorder with psychotic features (Cheniaux et al., 2008). In *DSM-IV-TR* (APA, 2000), the diagnosis of schizoaffective disorder is restricted to the description of a single episode rather than a lifetime diagnosis. Therefore, when her condition was viewed from a broad perspective over a period of several years, Angela's diagnosis would be psychotic disorder NOS or perhaps schizophrenia. If a clinician looked only at a specific episode, however, she might have been assigned a diagnosis of schizoaffective disorder. The *DSM-IV-TR* criteria for schizoaffective disorder (APA, 2000, p. 323) include the following:

1. An uninterrupted period of illness during which, at some time, there is either a major depressive episode, a manic episode, or a mixed episode concurrent with symptoms that meet Criterion 1 for schizophrenia.
2. During the same period of illness, there have been delusions or hallucinations for at least 2 weeks in the absence of prominent mood symptoms.
3. Symptoms that meet criteria for a mood episode are present for a substantial portion of the total duration of the active and residual periods of the illness.
4. The disturbance is not due to the direct physiological effects of a substance (e.g., a drug of abuse, a medication) or a general medical condition.

Angela would have fit this description during some of her episodes of depression, when she also experienced auditory hallucinations. Note that this diagnosis would require the inference that she met Criterion 1 for the definition of schizophrenia (which was uncertain because of the ambiguous nature of her auditory hallucinations).

Etiological Considerations

Research studies indicate that schizoaffective disorder is a heterogeneous category (Cheniaux et al., 2008). Most of the evidence suggests that genetic factors play a role in its development. Family history studies suggest that schizoaffective disorder does, in fact, represent a form of psychosis that is intermediate between schizophrenia and mood disorders. The first-degree relatives of people with schizoaffective disorder show an increased risk for schizophrenia, compared to the relatives of people with mood disorders. They also show an increased risk for mood disorder, compared to relatives of people with schizophrenia (Bertelsen & Gottesman, 1995).

Angela's case also raises interesting questions about the analysis of specific symptoms rather than global diagnosis categories. Her most long-standing symptoms were auditory hallucinations; she had been hearing voices that were not really there for many years. Hallucinations, or perceptual experiences in the absence of external stimulation, are associated with many kinds of disorders, including some that are mental disorders and many that are not. They are also found in some people without mental disorders. One study of people in the general population (i.e., people who are not patients) found that 39% reported some type of hallucinatory experience, when that category was defined broadly to include hallucinations in any sensory modality (hearing, vision, taste, and smell) as well as "out-of-body experiences." Most people who reported hallucinations said that they had this type of experience less than once a month. Only 2% experienced hallucinations more than once a week (Ohayon, 2000).

The mechanisms that are responsible for auditory hallucinations are not entirely clear. Clinical scientists who study hallucinations have focused on two complementary views of these phenomena. Each view is focused on a different level of analysis. One focuses at the level of neurochemical events in the brain. Brain-imaging studies indicate that auditory hallucinations are associated with abnormal patterns of neural activation in extended auditory pathways of the brain (Allen, Lorai, McGuire, & Aleman, 2008). These include areas of the temporal lobes and the prefrontal cortex. Another approach to studying hallucinations has focused on psychological factors or the mental mechanisms that are associated with neural activities. Cognitive studies suggest that patients who experience hallucinations make errors in attributing internal sensations to external events (Laroi & Woodward, 2007). In other words, these people may have trouble distinguishing between their own thoughts and voices coming from other people (Johns et al., 2001).

Violence and Mental Disorders

The connection between mental disorders and violence has been a controversial topic for many years. Unfortunately, many laypeople hold the mistaken belief that most people with disorders such as schizophrenia are more likely to commit crimes of violence, such as murder and assault (Harris & Lurigio, 2007; Pescosolida, Monahan, Link, Stueve, & Kikuzawa, 1999). This belief may be partially responsible for the stigma—a sign of shame or discredit leading to social rejection—associated with mental disorders. Of course, most people with schizophrenia and other major forms of mental disorder are not violent or unusually aggressive, and most violent crimes are committed by people who do not have a mental disorder (Stuart & Arboleda-Florez, 2001).

It is not accurate to say, however, that mental disorders are not associated with an increased risk for violence. People who have been treated for mental disorders represent an extremely heterogeneous group. Some specific combinations of symptoms are associated with greater risk for violence. For example, patients with diagnoses of schizophrenia and mood disorders are not more violent than others living in the same community, unless they also have substance-use disorders. Problems with substance dependence and abuse increase the rate of violence in both groups, especially people with mental disorders (Steadman et al., 1998). People who have co-occurring problems with major mental disorders and drugs or alcohol are much more likely to engage in aggressive or violent behavior. Therefore, the combination of these problems, rather than schizophrenia or depression alone, leads to a serious increase in dangerousness (Walsh et al., 2004).

Personality disorders are also related to the risk for violent behavior. Patients with a major mental disorder, such as schizophrenia, who also exhibit features of antisocial personality disorder are more likely to be violent toward other people (Monahan, 2001; Nestor, 2002). In addition to antisocial traits, people who meet the diagnostic criteria for paranoid and borderline personality disorder may also be more aggressive and dangerous than others, particularly in the presence of problems with alcohol and drug use (Tardiff, 2001). Angela had exhibited features of antisocial personality, especially aggression and impulsiveness, for many years. Her impulsiveness seemed to contribute to her substance dependence. It also exacerbated problems encountered by her therapist in attempting to maintain consistent contact with Angela and trying to arrange for stable housing and employment.

Men are much more likely to be aggressive and violent than women. Nevertheless, research studies indicate that the association among mental illness, drugs, and violence applies to both men and women (Thomson, Bogue, Humphreys, & Johnstone, 2001). For example, one study conducted in Finland (a country with a low crime rate compared to the United States) examined rates of mental disorder among women who had been convicted of murder. These women were more likely than women in the community to meet the criteria for schizophrenia. Problems with substance dependence and antisocial personality disorder were also common in this group of women (Eronen, 1995).

Specific types of psychotic symptoms also seem to be associated with violent behavior. Prominent among these are command hallucinations—in which the person hears a voice telling him or her to perform a particular action. Patients who hear a voice telling them to harm someone else may follow that instruction (Braham, Trower, & Birchwood, 2004). Violent behavior is particularly likely when a patient is agitated, actively psychotic, and is using drugs and not receiving treatment for his or her condition (Swanson et al., 1997). Some experts also believe that patients with paranoid delusions are more dangerous than other patients. Delusions can influence a person's propensity toward violence because they shape his or her interpretation of situations. People who feel threatened by others may believe that a violent response is justified. Although

Angela did not report paranoid delusions, it seems likely that she did feel threat-ened by the man she stabbed. It is, of course, impossible to know what her voices might have seemed to be saying to her in that moment.

The victims of acts of violence committed by people with mental disor-ders are most often family members and friends. Angela's assault was there-fore somewhat unusual. It is also understandable, however, in the sense that the man she stabbed had provoked her. This is not to say the assault was justified, but rather that he had, in fact, taken advantage of her. When she protested, he responded in a hostile and disrespectful manner. She was in a desperate emo-tional state. She was not high on drugs at the time, but she was going through withdrawal and actively seeking the drug. This was a particularly unfortunate time for him to take advantage of her and then insult her.

Treatment

Many men and women who are seriously mentally ill are often confined to jails rather than treated in hospitals. Fazel and Danesh (2002) reviewed a large number of studies that examined the prevalence of psychopathology among prison inmates in 12 different countries (more than 22,000 prisoners) and found that 3 to 7% of male prisoners and 4% of female prisoners had psychotic dis-orders. Ten percent of men and 12% of women in prison suffered from major depressive disorder. In another study in the United States of more than 1,200 incarcerated women who were awaiting trial, more than 80% met the criteria for at least one type of mental disorder, with the most common diagnosis being sub-stance abuse or dependence (Teplin, Abram, & McClelland, 1996). These data indicate the dramatic need to identify people with mental disorders in jails and prisons and to provide them with treatment for their disorders.

Patients such as Angela require a broad array of treatment services. Because most patients continue to experience occasional episodes of acute psychosis, hospital beds are necessary. The typical duration of a hospital admission is less than 2 weeks, so mental-health services must also be available in the community following discharge. Many states have closed public psychiatric hospitals. One paradoxical effect of these closings is that the cost of care for patients who are seriously mentally ill has increased because they must be admitted to emergency facilities at other hospitals (Rothbard, Schinnar, Hadley, Foley, & Kuno, 1998).

Treatment guidelines for patients with schizoaffective disorder indicate that symptoms of psychosis, such as hallucinations, and symptoms of mood disorder should be given equal emphasis in planning the patient's treatment (Levinson, Umapathy, & Musthaq, 1999). Antipsychotic medication is obviously one important consideration in this regard. Atypical antipsychotic drugs, such as clozapine, olanzapine, and risperidone, have been shown to be effective for patients with schizoaffective disorder (Baethge, 2003; Janicak et al., 2001). The newer, atypical forms of antipsychotics are beneficial in treating both psychotic symptoms and mood-disorder symptoms. Nevertheless, many patients receive more than one type of medication, and combination treatments have increased in recent years. Patients with schizophrenia are often prescribed antidepressants and mood stabilizers in addition to antipsychotic drugs. As many as 25% may also receive more than one type of antipsychotic medication at the same time (Clark, Bartels, Mellman, & Peacock, 2002).

Failure to take antipsychotic drugs as prescribed (medication noncompliance) is often associated with repeated episodes of psychosis and the need for readmission to the hospital (Perkins, 2002). Many of these patients are admitted after they have engaged in highly disruptive or dangerous behaviors (such as exhibiting extremely bizarre behavior, attempting suicide, or threatening other people). The use of atypical antipsychotic medication may help to reduce noncompliance because the side effects associated with these drugs are much less troublesome than those associated with traditional or classic forms of antipsychotic medication.

Violent patients present an important risk to mental-health workers while the patients are in treatment. They are also more likely than other patients to be aggressive and violent after they return to the community. Those who remain involved in outpatient treatment are less likely to engage in further violent behavior than those who drop out of treatment (Elbogen, Van Dorn, Swanson, Swartz, & Monahan, 2006). The most direct approach to treating violent patients with mental disorders is to address their psychotic symptoms. This is often done through the use of medication. Outcome studies indicate that atypical antipsychotic drugs, especially clozapine, produce a reduction in violent behavior at the same time that patients show an improvement in their clinical condition (Citrome & Volavka, 2000).

The management of substance dependence among psychotic patients is an extremely difficult problem that has received increased attention in recent years (Tiet & Mausbach, 2007). Unfortunately, treatment services for these two domains—psychosis and substance-use disorders—are often not integrated. Too often, patients must work within two separate systems, with different goals and different staff members. They may attend an outpatient mental-health clinic to receive antipsychotic medication and psychosocial rehabilitation aimed at symptoms associated with schizophrenia. And they may be expected to participate in self-help or 12-step programs, such as Narcotics Anonymous or Alcoholics Anonymous, for their problems with drugs or alcohol. The latter type of program may present special problems for people with a psychotic disorder because they have an inflexible goal (total abstinence from drugs and alcohol) and because they are sometimes opposed to the use of medication. Important efforts are underway to develop special, integrated treatment programs that can simultaneously address the many complex needs of patients such as Angela.

Discussion Questions

1.   Angela clearly suffered from a wide variety of problems that involved symptoms associated with many different diagnostic categories in *DSM IV-TR*. If

you were in charge of her treatment, which do you think were most important or central? Where would you start in terms of trying to begin to help her?

2. Patients who qualify for more than one diagnosis represent the most severely disturbed and least-understood people being treated by mental-health service providers. What do you think are the most important barriers to understanding and serving the needs of these people?

3. Auditory hallucinations were a prominent part of Angela's symptom profile. Should research on the causes and treatment of mental disorders focus on specific symptoms, such as hallucinations, rather than diagnostic categories (such as schizoaffective disorder)? Or would that effort be similar to trying to study the origins of fever, which is symptomatic of many different kinds of medical illness?

4. Some psychotic patients do not want to take medication because they do not have insight into the nature of their disorder. Others find that it does not improve their symptoms, and many find the side effects troublesome. Should psychotic patients be forced to take medication, even if they do not want to take it, especially if there is some reason to believe that they may become violent?

CHAPTER 11

Alcohol Dependence

Grace Patterson decided to call a psychologist, Dr. Lawton, about her husband, Michael. She was worried about his history of heavy drinking, which had escalated recently. Dr. Lawton suggested that she talk to Michael about her concerns. He recommended that she pick a time when Michael had not been drinking. She should tell him that she had spoken to a psychologist who agreed to see Michael for an evaluation and make recommendations.

Grace called again several weeks later. Michael had refused to consider the possibility of seeing a psychologist. Grace had no idea what to do next, so Dr. Lawton scheduled an appointment to meet with her alone. They discussed ways Grace could change her interactions with Michael to motivate him to enter treatment. She was instructed to describe calmly to him the negative consequences of his drinking and to express how concerned she was about it. Grace and Dr. Lawton identified several recent incidents and rehearsed how she could respond. For example, several weeks ago Michael and Grace had dinner plans with another couple, but by late afternoon Michael was too drunk to go out. Grace had to call the other couple and make an excuse about canceling the dinner. That evening they had a huge argument about his drinking. Whenever Michael was really drunk, it was impossible to have a reasoned conversation with him, especially about his drinking. In the future, Grace was to wait until the next morning and then express her concerns about the drinking and how this pattern might cause them to lose good friends. The problem was ruining their marriage.

A month later, Grace called Dr. Lawton to say that there had been no change in Michael's drinking. She described several occasions in which she had talked with him about the destructive effects his drinking was having on their lives. Although Grace was discouraged, Dr. Lawton persuaded her to continue the plan. Three weeks later, Grace called to make an appointment for both her and Michael to come in for the evaluation. They had a terrible fight the night before; Michael had raised his hand to hit her but held back at the last second. This incident apparently alarmed Michael as much as it frightened Grace, and so he finally agreed to come in.

Dr. Lawton greeted Michael and Grace in the waiting room and invited them into his office. One primary goal of the initial session was to avoid scaring Michael out of therapy. Dr. Lawton explained that he understood his reluctance to come for the appointment. He told him that the purpose of this session was to gather information about his drinking habits and any problems that alcohol might be causing. Toward the end of the session, if Michael wanted to, they could discuss treatment options.

Michael was drinking heavily on a daily basis, beginning after work and continuing into the evening. On weekends, he typically started to drink around noon and was intoxicated by dinner. He recognized that his drinking was out of control and that it was having adverse effects on both him and his wife. They had begun arguing frequently. On several occasions, Michael had broken dishes and punched holes in walls. The couple now saw friends infrequently. Michael's high blood pressure had been worsened by the alcohol. Toward the end of the session, when the issue of treatment was raised, Michael said that he knew he should cut back on his drinking but that he did not really want to stop entirely. He knew that abstinence was the goal of alcohol treatment programs like Alcoholics Anonymous (AA), and he did not want to become totally abstinent. At this point, Dr. Lawton explained that some treatments are focused on making changes that lead to moderate drinking. Michael seemed interested in this possibility. The session ended with Michael agreeing to consider entering treatment. A week later, he called and scheduled another appointment.

Social History

Michael's childhood was rather uneventful. His father was an electrical engineer, and his mother worked part time in a local library when Michael and his older brother, James, were in school. Michael's mother and father were very light drinkers—an occasional beer or glass of wine. Michael recalled that his older brother was closer to their father than Michael. James shared his father's interest in electronic projects, and the two of them often worked together. Michael, in contrast, had little interest and even less aptitude for electronics. He was more interested in reading, particularly about history.

Michael made excellent grades in elementary, middle, and high school. In high school, he was also on the wrestling team. He began drinking then, usually at parties on the weekends. He recalled that he found drinking relaxing and that it reduced his anxiety in social situations. He remembered that he was most nervous around women; he often felt tongue-tied and felt unable to talk with them.

He graduated from high school and went to a small college, where he majored in history and education. His goal was to become a high school history teacher. His drinking increased somewhat in college, both in amount and frequency. It was no longer confined to weekends, and he typically drank six or more beers at a sitting. As he had said about his drinking in high school, he reported that he drank mostly to relax. He maintained a decent GPA but recalled that his anxieties around women persisted. He met Grace at college in an art history class. They were immediately attracted to each other. Grace's social and conversational skills put Michael at ease, and they began seeing each other regularly. They married at the end of college.

Michael took a job teaching high school history, and Grace found work at a jewelry store. They lived in an apartment for two years, saving money for the down payment on a house. Because he aspired to become head of the history department or perhaps get into school administration, Michael enrolled in an evening graduate program at a local university to work on his master's degree. Michael recalled this as a very happy time. He and Grace were deeply in love.

He was drinking regularly now, a couple of scotches before dinner on weekdays and the usual scotches plus wine with dinner on the weekends. Grace joined her husband in a scotch before dinner, but only one. Michael remembered that when he and Grace went out for dinner with friends, he would wolf down two drinks before dinner while everyone else had only one. And when they were at a party, Michael would generally drink considerably more than anyone else. He claimed he needed the alcohol to feel at ease in social situations.

This drinking pattern continued for several years. During this time, Michael finished his master's degree, and he and Grace had a child, Ethan. The couple bought a small house, and life continued smoothly for the most part. Four years later, the position of head of the history department opened, and Michael applied for the job. When he didn't get it, he was both crushed and very angry. His drinking began to increase. He would secretly freshen up his scotch when Grace was out of the room, so he was probably having three or four instead of his usual two. After a while, Grace noticed that they were buying liquor more often and began to suspect that Michael was drinking heavily. When she confronted him, he angrily denied it and changed his drinking pattern.

Now he began drinking on the way home from work. He would stop at a liquor store, buy a half pint of brandy, and drink it on the way home. He was careful to vary the liquor stores he stopped at and took back routes home to reduce the chance of being stopped by a police officer. Before getting home, he put the empty bottle in the trunk of his car, ate a breath mint, and was ready to greet Grace and start in on the scotch. He began to fall asleep, possibly passing out, regularly after dinner. His after-work drinking led him to give up his afternoon racquetball games, and he no longer was able to do anything after dinner. He started forgetting appointments he had made. For example, friends might call to invite Michael and Grace to a movie or dinner, but the next day Michael had no memory of the call. Friends stopped calling as often. During this period, Grace was becoming increasingly upset. She was interacting less and less with Michael, and she was coming to believe that he must be drinking secretly. After several months, Grace became fairly certain that Michael must be drinking outside the home. One day, she checked his trunk and found a dozen empty brandy bottles. Beside herself with anger and anxiety, she confronted him, and an ugly argument ensued—the first of many. Michael became even more secretive about his drinking, now throwing the empties away before arriving home, but his drinking did not decrease. He realized his drinking was out of control and tried several times to cut back. Unfortunately, his resolve lasted only a day or two.

Treatment

During the first session, Dr. Lawton and Michael discussed treatment options in more detail. Michael was adamant that he wanted to cut down rather than quit completely. Dr. Lawton told him that while he thought abstinence was a better goal, he was willing to help Michael reduce his consumption. To help Michael regain control of drinking, Dr. Lawton insisted on a month of abstinence first. While Michael showed signs of increased tolerance for alcohol, he had not experienced withdrawal symptoms; therefore, quitting "cold turkey" appeared to be a safe procedure. Michael reluctantly agreed to this period of abstinence. They also discussed the positive and negative consequences of his drinking. Somewhat surprisingly, Michael was hard pressed to come up with much in the way of positives. He said that alcohol had allowed him to cope with stress in the past, but now it had just become a habit, a way of filling time. Their discussion of negative consequences produced a long list—marital problems, loss of friends, giving up hobbies and interests, and the fact that his high blood pressure was undoubtedly worsened by alcohol. Dr. Lawton also provided normative information about the amounts people typically drank. Michael was surprised at how much he deviated from the average.

Both Grace and Michael were present for the next session. They discussed ways for Michael to cope with abstinence. Dr. Lawton pointed out that urges to drink would pass with time, especially if Michael could engage in some alternative activities. Michael was taught to think past the urge and to focus on the longer-term consequences of heavy drinking. In therapy sessions, he practiced how to imagine longer-term consequences of getting drunk, such as being arrested for drunk driving, ruining his marriage, and losing friends. Together they planned a number of strategies to keep Michael busy after work. He decided to help out with the wrestling team at school and also return to playing racquetball. If neither of these activities was possible on a given day, Michael was to stay later at work and grade papers or revise lectures. If he was having difficulty controlling his urges, he was to call Grace. Michael agreed to have Grace remove all alcohol from their home, and the couple came up with a list of things they could do to fill the time that he would have previously spent drunk or "asleep." These involved social activities such as going to the movies with friends, renting a film to watch at home, playing bridge, and going out for dinner.

Over the next several weeks, Michael met with Dr. Lawton twice a week, with Grace present at some of the sessions. Michael was able to maintain abstinence and followed through on the plan to become involved in alternative activities. He had experienced cravings, mostly after work and in the evening, but they were not too severe. The cravings were nothing like those he had experienced when he had quit smoking. He described them as rather vague hungers, "like when you're sort of hungry but don't know what you really want." During these sessions, Michael was also taught deep muscle relaxation as a way to cope with the negative emotions that he experienced with the urge to drink.

After the abstinence period was over, alcohol was reintroduced. Michael agreed to have no more than two drinks per day, which had to be carefully measured in contrast to his earlier practice of just filling a highball glass with scotch. He also agreed to drink only in Grace's company. Drinks were now to be sipped, and a 20-minute waiting period had to elapse between drinks. Michael reported that he was enjoying his new activities, especially the racquetball and renewing old friendships.

The moderate drinking pattern seemed well established in about a month, so the frequency of sessions was reduced. Over the next months, Michael and Dr. Lawton continued to discuss Michael's efforts to cope with urges. They also began to discuss the possibility of relapse. Dr. Lawton distinguished between a lapse—drinking too much on a single day—and relapse—returning completely to his old pattern. Dr. Lawton pointed out that while lapses would likely occur, a lapse would not mean that all of Michael's progress had been lost. They also discussed the need for continuing treatment and attending meetings of a local group of recovering alcohol abusers. The group was similar to AA but with less discussion of religion and less emphasis on abstinence as the only solution to alcohol abuse. Michael agreed to attend meetings and treatment was ended.

Follow-Up

Three years later, Dr. Lawton received another call from Grace, who told him that Michael had returned to heavy drinking. She and Michael had discussed returning to treatment, but he was reluctant, saying that it clearly hadn't worked the first time. Dr. Lawton suggested that she try to get Michael to call him. Michael called several days later and reiterated his belief that treatment had failed. He said that he had started drinking heavily when he had again been passed over for a promotion and then had just slipped back into his old pattern. Dr. Lawton pointed out that maintaining moderate drinking for several years was not really a failure. He told Michael that he believed treatment could again help but that they would need to attend more carefully to maintaining treatment gains this time. Sensing his continuing reluctance to return to treatment, Dr. Lawton told him that because his drinking had only been out of control for a short time, a period of abstinence would not be necessary this time. Michael agreed to come for a session with Grace.

Grace was the first to speak. Tearfully, she explained that Michael was drinking heavily again. Michael sat quietly, head down, as Grace related recent events. She indicated that she wasn't sure she could get through another prolonged episode of the problems that always occurred when Michael was drinking. She was considering divorce. Michael didn't disagree with anything Grace said. He wanted to try treatment again, and would make an effort to stay sober.

Treatment was similar to before, but there was no period of abstinence. Michael was quickly able to reestablish a pattern of moderate drinking. In addition, a lot of time was spent discussing Michael's reaction about being passed over for promotion. Michael's view of this event was that it was a catastrophe and proved how worthless he was. Dr. Lawton worked with Michael to help him see it as unfortunate but not a complete disaster. Michael admitted that after therapy had concluded before, he had not followed through with the suggestion to attend group meetings. As with the first therapy, the last sessions were spent discussing maintenance of the gains that had been achieved. Michael insisted that he would attend group meetings this time, and Dr. Lawton agreed to continue to see him once a month. Michael was also told to call Dr. Lawton and schedule a meeting if he drank heavily for more than two days in a row.

Michael continued to see Dr. Lawton for the next 6 months. Although he had a couple of lapses, for the most part, he maintained moderate drinking and attended group meetings regularly. But then he began to cancel appointments and missed several without calling. At the end of a year, Dr. Lawton closed the case.

Two years later, Grace called to say the old pattern had returned. This time Michael was unwilling even to call Dr. Lawton. She was filing for divorce. She felt depressed and wanted to schedule some therapy sessions. These sessions dealt mostly with her feelings about Michael. Grace was not clinically depressed, but she was indeed experiencing considerable distress. Michael continued to drink heavily, and Grace finally ordered him out of the house. Shortly thereafter, Michael had a major heart attack and died. Therapy with Grace continued for several months, focusing on her distress and guilt over his death.

Discussion

According to *Diagnostic and Statistical Manual of Mental Disorders* (*DSM-IV-TR*; APA, 2000), the maladaptive use of various substances falls into two categories: substance dependence and substance abuse. Alcohol dependence is diagnosed if the person meets three of the following criteria:

- Withdrawal symptoms (negative psychological and physical effects) appear if the person stops drinking.

- Tolerance develops. The person needs to drink more and more alcohol to produce the desired effect.
- The person uses more alcohol than intended or uses it for a longer time than intended.
- The person wants to reduce alcohol consumption and may have unsuccessfully tried to cut down or stop.
- Much time is spent trying to obtain alcohol or recover from its effects.
- Alcohol use continues despite psychological or physical problems caused by it.
- Participation in many activities (work, recreation, social) is reduced because of the drug.

Alcohol dependence can be diagnosed as being accompanied with physiological dependence if either tolerance or withdrawal is present. Physiological dependence is what many people mean when they use the term *addiction*.

Alcohol abuse, a less serious disorder, is diagnosed if one of the following is present:

- Failure to fulfill major obligations due to recurrent drinking, for example, absences from work
- Repeated exposure to physical dangers while drinking, such as driving while intoxicated (DWI)
- Legal problems due to drinking, such as disorderly conduct or DWI
- Continued drinking despite persistent social problems, such as arguments with spouse

Michael clearly met the criteria for alcohol dependence. He had developed tolerance, recognized that he was drinking too much, had unsuccessfully tried to cut back, given up activities that he had previously enjoyed, and continued to drink despite knowing that it was creating serious marital problems and contributing to his high blood pressure.

Lifetime prevalence rates for alcohol dependence are 17.4% for men and 8.0% for women (Hasin, Stinson, Ogburn, & Grant, 2007), making it one of the most prevalent mental disorders. In the United States, alcohol abuse and dependence is more prevalent among Whites than among African Americans (Breslau et al., 2006). Alcohol dependence is less common than alcohol abuse (Somers, Goldner, Waraich, & Hsu, 2004). The path to the development of alcohol problems is somewhat variable. Some people, like Michael, progress steadily from moderate use to heavy use and then to abuse and dependence. But for many others, the pattern is less regular. For example, some people abuse alcohol during a time of stress and then return to light drinking when the stress has resolved (Vaillant, 1996). After a person becomes dependent, however, the disorder is often chronic. For example, in one study, two-thirds of men with alcohol dependence were still dependent 5 years later (Schuckit et al., 2001). Some people who are dependent are able to stop drinking without treatment (Bischof, Rumpf, Hapke, Meyer, & John, 2003). Those who maintain abstinence from alcohol for 3 years are very likely to remain abstinent for the rest of their lives (Vaillant, 2003). Heavy drinkers were more likely to report that negative consequences from their drinking led them to stop, whereas those with less severe alcohol use reported that they stopped drinking due to changes in their living situations, such as a move, getting older, or having children (Cunningham, Blomqvist, Koski-Jännes, & Cordingley, 2005). This was the case with Michael—his motivation to stop his heavy drinking came from the negative consequences it was causing in his relationship with Grace, rather than a situational change.

Many people with alcohol dependence have comorbid major depression (Wang & El-Guebaly, 2004), especially those who are divorced, separated, or widowed, and those with lower incomes. The more alcohol one consumes, the higher the risk for a number of health problems, including cancer (of the mouth, esophagus, liver, and breast), stroke, heart disease, and diabetes (Room, Babor, & Rehm, 2005). This is reflected in Michael's fatal heart attack. Many people who are dependent on alcohol have malnutrition and vitamin deficiencies because the alcohol's calories replace calories from food (Manari, Preedy & Peters, 2003). Chronic alcohol dependence can result in shrinking of the brain, particularly in frontal lobe areas contributing to problem solving, judgment, and reasoning (Rosenbloom, Sullivan, & Pfefferbaum, 2003).

Etiological Considerations

Alcohol dependence is a complex disorder with multiple causes. These causes include multiple genes that interact with each other and with environmental factors (Edenberg & Foroud, 2006). About half of the causal influences for alcohol dependence are thought to be genetic, and half environmental (Sartor et al., 2009). Genes regulating different functions, such as the neurotransmitter GABA, and the rate of metabolism of alcohol, may be linked to different forms of alcohol dependence. Also, the neurotransmitter dopamine is linked to reward and alcohol craving, and genetic factors affecting dopamine's actions may be important. People who carried a specific form of a gene regulating dopamine were only found to develop alcohol dependence if they were also exposed to a risky environment, such as being raised in an abusive or neglectful family or being active in a college fraternity or sorority, while people without the form of the gene did not develop alcohol dependence even if exposed to those risky environments (Park, Sher, Torodov, & Heath, 2011).

Relatives of people with alcohol dependence were found to have found higher rates of drug abuse, antisocial personality disorder, anxiety disorder, and depression (Nurnberger et al., 2004). One study examined the effects of being raised with a parent with alcohol dependence among biological and adoptive children and found that genetic but not environmental factors played a role in transmitting drinking (King et al., 2009). The inheritance of problem drinking may be due to a genetically determined behavioral disinhibition that includes delinquent behavior, a deviant peer group, antisocial attitudes, aggression, and impulsivity. Luczak, Wall, Cook, Shea, and Carr (2004) argued that the different rates of alcohol dependence found in different ethnic groups, such as European Americans and Chinese Americans, are due to the protective presence of a specific gene found much more often in Chinese Americans. However, the protective effect of this gene is also significantly affected by environmental factors, such as the social acceptability of drinking (Luczak, Glatt, & Wall, 2006). Michael did not have a clear family history of problem drinking. Neither his parents nor his brother drank heavily, but he had an uncle who always seemed to be drunk at family parties.

Other evidence suggests that prenatal exposure to alcohol is an additional risk factor for drinking in young adulthood, separate from the contribution of family history of alcohol use (Baer, Sampson, Barr, Connor, & Streissguth, 2003). The chance of a 21-year-old offspring reporting alcohol dependence was tripled by maternal heavy drinking during that pregnancy.

Personality traits may affect a person's risk for alcohol dependence. Alcohol use has been linked to negative moods such as sadness and hostility (Hussong, Hicks, Levy, & Curran, 2001). Researchers have found that people with high levels of negative emotions, such as sadness, anger, and anxiety, are more likely to later develop a drinking problem (Elkins, King, McCue, & Iacono, 2006). They also found that people who had high levels of constraint, which includes having traditional values, avoiding thrill-seeking, and acting cautiously and in a restrained manner, were significantly less likely to later develop a drinking problem. Although Michael did not have low levels of constraint, he did report high levels of negative emotions, consistent with an increased risk for alcohol dependence predicted by this research. Alcohol has been shown to significantly reduce people's stress response (Sher, Bartholow, Peuser, Erickson, & Wood, 2007). It may do this in two ways. The first is by directly muting anxiety, which could occur either because of alcohol's actions on the body or by alcohol's stimulation of the reward pathways in the brain, resulting in positive reinforcement that competes with anxiety. The second is by altering people's ability to pay attention to stressful stimuli. Alcohol use might therefore be reinforcing, either by reducing negative emotions or by enhancing positive ones. Heavy alcohol use may be a way to regulate mood and may reflect a failure of other means of coping with emotional states. Research in which people recorded their moods and drinking on a daily basis has shown that nervousness predicted increased use of alcohol (Swendsen et al., 2000). And people seeking treatment for alcohol dependence who have difficulty managing a variety of negative emotions, such as anger, depression, boredom, and loneliness, were found to be more likely to drink during treatment and to experience relapse (Berking et al., 2011). This tension-reduction model fits the clinical information on Michael. He initially related urges to drink to reduce his anxiety in social situations and began heavy drinking when faced with major disappointments in life.

Alcohol's effects on mood depend on the situation in which it is consumed. Alcohol impairs effortful cognitive processing and narrows attention to immediately available cues, called alcohol myopia (nearsightedness); intoxicated people have less cognitive processing capacity for both ongoing activity and worry (Moss & Albery, 2009). If a distracting activity is available, intoxicated people focus on it instead of worrying about their stress. But alcohol can increase negative moods if there are no distractors; in this case, intoxicated people focus their limited cognitive capacity only on the unpleasant source of worry and feel even worse. What a person expects the effects of drinking alcohol to be also plays a role. The tension-reducing effects of alcohol may only be found among some people. The relationship between alcohol use and negative moods has been found to be stronger among males, people who lack alternative ways of coping with stress, and those who expect alcohol to alleviate their negative moods (Kushner, Abrams, & Borchardt, 2000). Similarly, the relationship is stronger among people with less intimate and supportive social relationships (Hussong et al., 2001).

One other way people may become alcohol dependent is by consuming alcohol more frequently and in greater amounts. A large population was studied over a period of 26 years, and it was found that men who drank more than 21 drinks per week, or who drank on a daily basis, had an increased risk of later developing alcohol dependence, whereas the risk was increased for women by drinking at all. The more a woman drank, even from one to seven drinks per week, the more she increased her risk for later becoming alcohol dependent (Flensborg-Madsen, Knop, Mortensen, Beeker, & Grønbæk, 2007). At least within that generation, alcohol exposure at even relatively modest doses involved greater risk for women. These findings may seem obvious but may also provide a warning to social groups that encourage a lot of drinking.

Treatment

Many people with drinking problems do not believe they have a problem and, therefore, are unwilling to enter treatment. Only one in seven people with an alcohol-related disorder ever receive any treatment (Cohen, Feinn, Arias, & Kranzler, 2007). When people resist treatment, as Michael did, initial treatment efforts are focused on convincing them to change their drinking. This is what Dr. Lawton tried to accomplish by having Grace describe the negative consequences of Michael's drinking and later listing these negative consequences during treatment. Providing Michael with feedback about how far his drinking departed from national norms was also part of this process (as recommended by Sobell & Sobell, 1976).

After the person agrees to treatment, many options are available. Hospitals provide detoxification, supervised withdrawal from alcohol, and a variety of group and individual therapies. Benzodiazepines are used to manage alcohol withdrawal (Myrick & Anton, 2004). However, hospital treatment does not appear to be superior to outpatient therapy, except for people with few sources of social support and other psychological problems (Finney & Moos, 1998).

Two medications, disulfiram and naltrexone, are used to prevent relapse (Myrick & Anton, 2004). Disulfiram interacts with alcohol to produce unpleasant side effects, so the person feels sick if they drink. However, patients often will not take the disulfiram as prescribed to avoid this effect. Naltrexone may reduce cravings but is only modestly effective in preventing relapse. Researchers are experimenting with repetitive transcranial magnetic stimulation (rTMS), a non-invasive treatment that is effective in treating depression, to control cravings. One study comparing rTMS to a placebo sham treatment found that it resulted in moderate reductions in craving (Mishra, Nizamie, Das, & Praharaj, 2009). Psychopharmacological treatment of anxiety and depression in people with alcohol dependence is also important to consider because it improves the success of treating the drinking (Mann, 2004). However, treatment of depression alone does not improve the person's drinking (Nunes & Levin, 2004). Relapse after treatment is the most common outcome, so helping people predict and manage their vulnerability to relapses is critically important (Witkiewitz & Marlatt, 2007). Although people who never receive treatment sometimes recover on their own, those who do receive treatment do significantly better (Cohen et al., 2007).

The most common type of treatment is AA (Cohen et al., 2007). In its regular meetings, new members announce that they are alcoholics, and older members relate stories about their problem drinking and how their lives have improved since giving up alcohol. The group provides emotional support, understanding, and a social life to relieve isolation. There is a religious emphasis; one of the 12 steps is "Make a decision to turn our will and our lives over to the care of God." Members are encouraged to call on one another for companionship or encouragement not to relapse. AA views alcoholism as a disease that can never be cured. Complete abstinence is necessary because it is believed that a single drink can trigger a complete relapse. Evidence shows that AA is an effective treatment (Gossop et al., 2003; Kahler et al., 2004). In addition, it is free of charge and widely available, even on the weekends and evenings (Kelly, Magill, & Stout, 2009). In a longitudinal study of men, Vaillant (2003) found that AA attendance predicted sustained abstinence.

After his treatment with Dr. Lawton, Michael was encouraged to join a local group that had many features of AA but without the religious components or the emphasis on abstinence. Many similar groups (such as Rational Recovery) now exist throughout the country. Outpatient group therapy is also effective in reducing drinking. Litt, Kadden, Cooney, and Kabela (2003) found that cognitive-behavioral group therapy and interactional group therapy, which focuses on the patient's relationship patterns, produced significant gains even 18 months later. Both of these treatments were more effective than AA.

The treatment Michael received drew on the work of the Sobells (1976), who initiated moderate drinking as a treatment goal and demonstrated the effectiveness of such an approach. Patients are taught to respond adaptively to situations in which they might otherwise drink excessively. Social skills, relaxation, and assertiveness training (especially regarding how to refuse a drink) can be part of the treatment. Other strategies include increasing exercise, reducing the presence of cues for drinking (e.g., taking a new route home that does not go by a bar), sipping rather than gulping drinks, and imposing a delay between drinks. Relapse prevention, pioneered by Marlatt (1985), is also a component. As was done with Michael, a distinction is drawn between a lapse and a relapse. Patients are taught that a lapse does not signal a total relapse. A lapse should be regarded as a learning experience, not as a sign that the battle has been lost. There has often been strong disagreement between those who advocate abstinence-only focused treatment, the mainstream view of treatment providers, and those who also consider controlled or moderate drinking as a legitimate goal. Complete abstinence as the only accepted goal may alienate some prospective patients and may be difficult for others to achieve, resulting in them being viewed as treatment failures, even if they have reduced the amount of alcohol they consume (Gastfriend, Garbutt, Pettinati, & Forman, 2007). Reduction in quantity of alcohol consumed reduces the risk of negative health and social outcomes, such as suicide and domestic violence. Although abstinence from alcohol is the best outcome, it may not always be possible for a given client.

This case did not have a happy ending. Michael's fatal heart attack was probably related to his high blood pressure, which was worsened by his chronic alcohol abuse. Stress also plays a role in raising blood pressure, and Michael certainly experienced a lot of it, related both to his job and his marriage.

Discussion Questions

1. What do you think about therapists advocating controlled or moderate drinking instead of abstinence? Do you think Michael might have been more successful in stopping his drinking if Dr. Lawton encouraged him to be abstinent?
2. What are some of the social or cultural groups that encourage excessive alcohol consumption? What are the risks of doing this? What groups discourage alcohol consumption?
3. What are the health and social risks and costs of alcohol dependence? What do you think about how our society handles this problem? Is there more we should be doing, or is society too involved in this issue?
4. What does it mean to say that alcoholism is a complex disorder with multiple causes that interact with each other? What are examples of ways this could occur?

CHAPTER 12

Sexual Dysfunction: Female Orgasmic Disorder and Premature Ejaculation

Barbara Garrison was concerned about a number of problems when she arrived for her first appointment at the mental-health center. Her principal complaint was an inability to achieve orgasm during sexual intercourse with her husband, Frank. They were both 33 years old and had been married for 15 years. Frank was a police detective, and Barbara had recently resumed her college education. Their children, a daughter and a son, were 15 and 12, respectively.

Barbara's orgasmic problem was situational in nature. She had experienced orgasms through masturbation, and she masturbated an average of once or twice a week; however, she had never reached orgasm during sexual activity with Frank. The problem did not involve sexual desire or arousal. She found Frank sexually attractive, wanted to enjoy a more satisfying sexual relationship with him, and did become aroused during their sexual encounters. They had intercourse two or three times each month, usually late at night after the children had gone to sleep and always at Frank's initiative. Their foreplay was primarily limited to genital manipulation and seldom lasted more than 5 minutes. Frank always reached orgasm within a minute or two after penetration and often fell asleep shortly thereafter, leaving Barbara in a frustrating state of unfulfilled sexual arousal. On many occasions, she resolved this dilemma by slipping quietly out of the bedroom to the TV room, where she would secretly masturbate to orgasm. Frank realized that Barbara did not experience orgasms during intercourse but chose not to discuss the problem. He did not know that she masturbated.

This situation was distressing to Barbara. She felt considerable guilt over her frequent masturbation, particularly after sexual intercourse, because she believed that masturbation was a deviant practice. She was also concerned about the sexual fantasies she had during masturbation. She often imagined herself in a luxurious hotel room having sexual intercourse with a sequence of 8 or 10 men. They were usually men she did not know, but she would sometimes include men to whom she had been attracted, such as classmates from the university and friends of her husband. Barbara believed that these promiscuous fantasies proved that she was a latent nymphomaniac. She feared that she could easily lose control of her own desires and worried that she might someday get on a train, leave her family, and become a prostitute in a large city.

Her anxiety regarding sexual interests and arousal was also a problem during intercourse with Frank. He had, in fact, made numerous efforts to find out what she found arousing, but she remained uncommunicative. She was afraid to tell him what she liked because she thought that he would then realize that she was "oversexed." She was self-conscious during sexual activity with Frank. She worried about what he would think of her and whether she was performing adequately. Questions were continually running through her mind, such as "Am I paying attention to the right sensations?" or, "Will it happen this time?" The combination of fear of loss of control of her sexual impulses and continual worry about her inadequacy as a sexual partner finally persuaded Barbara to seek professional help.

In addition to Barbara's inability to reach orgasm during intercourse, Barbara and Frank were not getting along as well as they had in the past. Several factors were contributing to the increased strain in their relationship. One involved Barbara's decision to resume her education. Frank had not completed his college education, and the possibility that Barbara might finish her degree was threatening to him. He was also uncomfortable around the friends Barbara had met at the university. His job as a detective seemed to increase this tension because relations between students and the police had been strained by campus arrests for use of drugs and alcohol. Frank believed that Barbara's younger classmates saw him as an unwelcome authority figure who could present a threat to their independence. He resented changes in the way she dressed and also attributed their increasingly frequent disagreements to the influence of the university environment.

They also had more financial concerns than in previous years. Barbara's tuition and other fees amounted to a considerable amount of money each semester, and within 3 years, their daughter would be old enough to go to college. They had also taken out a substantial loan to build an addition onto their home. To make more money, Frank had been working many more overtime hours. Considering that he was away from home so often, Barbara resented the fact that he spent most of his spare time working on the new rooms in their house.

Despite their frequent arguments and differences of opinion, Barbara and Frank were both seriously committed to their marriage. Neither of them was particularly happy, but they were not considering a divorce. Barbara believed that their relationship would be markedly improved if she could overcome her orgasmic dysfunction. Frank was less concerned about that particular issue but agreed that Barbara might feel better if a therapist could "help her understand her problem."

Social History

Barbara's parents were both in their middle forties when she was born. They had one other child, a boy, who was 5 years older than Barbara. Her father was a police officer, and her mother was a homemaker. Barbara's parents clearly cared for each other and for the children, but they were not openly affectionate. She could not remember seeing them embrace or kiss each other except for occasional pecks on the cheek or top of the head; nor, on the other hand, could she remember hearing them argue. It was a quiet, peaceful household in which emotional displays of any kind were generally discouraged.

Barbara's parents and her older brother were unusually protective of her. She was "the baby of the family" and was always closely supervised. It seemed to Barbara that she was not allowed to do many of the things that her friends' parents permitted. When she was young, she was not allowed to leave their yard. When she was older and in high school, she was not allowed to go out on school nights and had to be home by 10 p.m. on weekends. Her parents insisted on meeting all of her friends and, in some cases, forbade her to associate with certain other children. Until she was 16 years old, Barbara was not allowed to go to parties if boys were also invited.

She remembered her first date as an awkward experience that occurred during her junior year in high school. A boy whom she had admired for several months had finally asked her to go to a movie. Her parents agreed to allow her to go after her father asked several of his friends about the boy and his parents. When he picked her up before the movie, Barbara's parents asked so many questions that they were finally late for the show. Later, as they were leaving the theater, Barbara realized that her brother and his girlfriend, who both attended a local junior college, had been sitting several rows behind them. Their parents had called him and asked if he would keep an eye on her "to be sure everything was okay." He did not intend to be secretive and, in fact, asked Barbara if she and her friend would like to go out for hamburgers and Cokes after the show. This carefully arranged supervision did not ruin the experience. Everyone had a good time, and Barbara went out with this same boy several times in the next year. Nevertheless, the protective manner in which Barbara's family treated her prevented her from developing close relationships with boys her own age and later left her feeling uncomfortable when she was alone with men.

Barbara's knowledge about and experiences with sexual activity were extremely limited during childhood and adolescence. Neither of her parents made an effort to provide her with information about her own body or reproductive functions. Her mother did discuss general issues such as romance and marriage with Barbara, but only at the most abstract level. All of the books and magazines in their home were carefully screened to avoid exposing the children to suggestive literature or photographs. Barbara was not able to learn much about these matters from her friends because she was so closely supervised. After she began menstruating at the age of 11, her mother gave her a book that explained the basic organs and physiology associated with the human reproductive system and, once again, avoided any personal discussion of Barbara's concerns about sexuality. The implicit message conveyed by her parents' behavior and attitudes was that sex was a mysterious, shameful, and potentially dangerous phenomenon.

After she graduated from high school, Barbara began taking classes at the local junior college. She continued to live at home with her parents and maintained several of the same friends she had had in high school. During her first semester, Barbara met Frank, who was then a student at the police academy. After several weeks, they began to see each other regularly. Her parents liked Frank, perhaps because her father was also a policeman, and they gradually began to allow her greater freedom than they had when she dated in high school. Frank and Barbara were both 18 years old, but he was much more mature and experienced. He had been dating regularly since he was 15 and had had sexual intercourse for the first time when he was 17.

Their sexual relationship progressed rapidly. Although she was initially apprehensive and shy, Barbara found that she enjoyed heavy petting. She refused to have intercourse with Frank for several months; finally she gave in one evening after they had both been drinking at a party. She later remembered being disappointed by the experience. Frank had climaxed almost immediately after penetration, but she had not reached orgasm. Her guilt was replaced by utter shock when she realized several weeks later that she was pregnant. They did not discuss the pregnancy with her parents and agreed they should be married as soon as possible. Their daughter was born less than 6 months after their marriage. Despite the obvious "prematurity" of the birth, Barbara's parents never mentioned the issue of premarital intercourse or pregnancy. Barbara dropped out of college and did not return to school for many years.

Barbara and Frank's sexual relationship did not change much over the next few years, although their frequency of intercourse declined markedly during their second year of marriage. Intercourse continued to be a pleasurable experience for both of them, even though Barbara was not able to experience orgasm. Her first orgasm occurred after they had been married for more than three years and both of their children had been born. Following their typical pattern, Frank had fallen asleep after intercourse and Barbara was lying in bed, half awake and very much aroused. She was lying on her stomach, and some of the blankets happened to be bunched up under her pelvis and between her legs. Without recognizing what she was doing, Barbara began rocking rhythmically from side to side. She was relaxed and noticed that this motion created a pleasurable sensation. Several minutes after she began rocking, she experienced an intense, unmistakable orgasm. It was an extremely pleasurable phenomenon restrained only by her fear of waking Frank. After her accidental discovery of masturbation, Barbara experimented further with various styles of self-manipulation and was soon masturbating regularly. She was afraid to describe these experiences to Frank, however, because she believed that masturbation was an immoral and selfish act, and her ability to reach orgasm by self-stimulation did not generalize to intercourse with Frank. Barbara also avoided conversations about sex when she was talking to other women. She believed that masturbation and sexual fantasies were immoral, and she was convinced that none of her friends had ever had such experiences.

Conceptualization and Treatment

In approaching the sexual problem described by Barbara, the therapist focused on Barbara and Frank as a couple, not on Barbara as an individual. She was principally concerned with the things Barbara and Frank did and said when they were together. It was clear from Barbara's description of the problem that she knew very little about sexual behavior. Her reports also indicated that she and Frank were not communicating effectively during sexual activity and were not engaging in effective sexual behaviors. To focus on the relationship, the therapist asked Barbara to bring Frank with her to the second treatment session.

Frank was initially reluctant to join Barbara in treatment because he had always believed that the problem was primarily hers. Nevertheless, he agreed to talk to the therapist at least once, and, during this interview, he indicated that he was also dissatisfied with their sexual relationship. On further questioning, he even admitted that he had secretly worried that he was to blame for Barbara's orgasmic difficulty. This thought had caused him considerable anxiety from time to time, particularly when he was also worried about his performance in other roles such as work and his relationship with the children.

The therapist asked Frank to describe their sexual activity from his perspective and noted, as Barbara had previously indicated, that little emphasis was placed on foreplay. Two considerations seemed to be particularly important in this regard. First, Frank said that he did not know what sorts of activity might be more pleasurable for Barbara because she had never expressed any feelings in this regard. Second, Frank indicated that he generally felt unsure of his own ability to delay ejaculation and therefore preferred to insert his penis in Barbara's vagina before he "lost control." This concern was related to his belief that intercourse was the most mature form of sexual activity and his fear that Barbara would begin to question his virility if he were unable to accomplish intercourse. Although he realized that Barbara was not entirely happy with their sexual relationship, Frank privately conceded that he would rather not draw attention to his own difficulty. The therapist responded in a reassuring manner, emphasizing that she did not want to ascribe responsibility to either partner. The primary concern of treatment, she said, would be to increase both partners' satisfaction with their sexual relationship. She also noted that most forms of sexual dysfunction, particularly premature ejaculation, are amenable to brief, behavioral forms of therapy. Given this explanation of the problem and considering the optimistic prognosis, Frank agreed to work together with Barbara toward a solution to their problems.

During her initial interviews with both Barbara and Frank, the therapist made an effort to consider various factors that might contribute to sexual dysfunction, such as depression, fatigue, and marital distress. None of these seemed to account for the problem. Both partners were somewhat unhappy, but neither was clinically depressed. Although their relationship had been strained by the sexual problem, they were both committed to the marriage. Neither was involved in an extramarital relationship, which might detract from their involvement in treatment or their interest in change, and both Barbara and Frank expressed affection for each other. It was interesting to note that they were more willing to express their positive feelings for the other person when they were talking with the therapist than when they were interacting directly. Overall, the sexual dysfunction did not seem to be secondary to other adjustment problems.

Before beginning a psychological approach to their sexual problem, Barbara and Frank were also asked to obtain complete physical examinations. This assessment was recommended in an effort to rule out the possibility that their difficulty could be traced to a physical disorder. Various diseases that affect the central nervous system, hormone levels, and vascular functions can influence sexual arousal and performance. Abnormalities in the musculature and tissue structure of the genital area can also be problematic. None of these factors was evident in this particular case.

During the third session, the therapist explored many of Barbara's and Frank's attitudes and beliefs about sexual behavior. Her purpose was to improve their communication with each other about sexual matters and to open a discussion in which they could acquire additional knowledge and correct mistaken beliefs. Several issues were particularly important and seemed to be related to their failure to engage in more satisfying sexual behavior. For example, both Barbara and Frank believed that vaginal stimulation should be the principal source of sexual pleasure for women and that orgasm during coitus is dependent solely on such stimulation. The therapist explained that the clitoris is, in fact, more sensitive than the vagina. Female orgasm depends on both direct and indirect stimulation of the clitoris during both masturbation and intercourse.

Considerable time was also spent discussing the Garrisons' attitudes toward and use of sexual fantasies. The topic was broached cautiously by the therapist. She commented in a matter-of-fact tone that most normal adults engage in sexual fantasies; she then asked Frank to describe one of his favorite fantasies. Despite some initial embarrassment, and much to Barbara's surprise, Frank told Barbara and the therapist that he often pictured himself working late at night and being seduced in the detectives' lounge by an attractive female colleague. This was the first time that Barbara and Frank had discussed sexual fantasies. While Barbara expressed some mild jealousy that Frank would think about another woman, she was relieved to learn that he also used sexual fantasies. His self-disclosure lowered her anxiety on the topic. She then shared a description of one of her own fantasies—admittedly one that was less provocative than her thoughts of having intercourse with several men in a row. Having explored these and other issues at length, the therapist recommended a few books that the Garrisons should read to learn more about human sexuality. One of the books was *Because It Feels Good: A Woman's Guide to Sexual Pleasure and Satisfaction* (Herbenick, 2009). It was hoped that this information would reduce their anxiety about their own interests and practices and, at the same time, suggest new activities that they had not yet tried.

The next step in treatment was to eliminate some of the obstacles that were interfering with Barbara's ability to become totally aroused and to teach her and Frank to engage in more enjoyable sexual behavior. This could be accomplished only in a totally nondemanding atmosphere. Because of their history of sexual difficulty and dissatisfaction, Barbara and Frank had become self-conscious about their sexual behavior. Barbara felt considerable pressure, which was mostly self-imposed, to reach orgasm; Frank was secretly concerned about whether he could delay ejaculation long enough for Barbara to become more aroused. From the point at which Frank initiated sexual activity, both of them tended to assume a detached perspective as they observed what they were doing and how they were feeling. The therapist attempted to eliminate pressure to perform by telling Barbara and Frank that they were not to attempt sexual intercourse under any circumstances during the next few weeks. She told them that she was going to ask them to practice an exercise known as *sensate focus* in which their only goal would be to practice giving and receiving pleasurable sensations.

Sensate focus is a touching exercise in which the partners simply take turns gently massaging each other's body. The therapist instructed them to begin by finding a quiet time when they would not be disturbed or distracted and they were not overtired. Having removed their clothes, Barbara was to lie on her stomach across the bed while Frank massaged her back and legs. She was encouraged to abandon herself to whatever pleasures she experienced. Barbara's instructions were to concentrate on the simplest sensations—warm and cold, smooth and rough, hard and soft—and to let Frank know what she enjoyed and what she wanted to change. Stimulation of Barbara's breasts and genital area was expressly prohibited to avoid demand for increased sexual arousal. They were asked to practice sensate focus at least four times before their next session.

Barbara and Frank both responded positively to this initial exercise. They described these extended periods of touching and caressing as relaxing and pleasurable; they both said that they had felt a sense of warmth and closeness that had disappeared from their relationship years ago. Barbara also expressed relief that she was able to focus on the pleasure of Frank's touch without worrying about whether she would have an orgasm or whether he would ejaculate quickly and leave her stranded in a state of unfulfilled arousal. With this positive beginning, the therapist suggested that they move on to the next step. They were to change positions for the next week. Frank would sit on the bed with his back against the headboard and his legs spread apart. Barbara would sit in front of him, facing in the same direction, with her back resting against his chest and her legs resting over his. In this position, Frank would be able to touch and massage the front of her body; the restrictions against touching her breasts and genitals were removed. He was told, however, to avoid direct stimulation of the clitoris because it can be irritating and in some cases painful. Barbara was instructed to rest her hand gently on his and to guide his touch to convey the sensations that were most pleasurable to her, including location, pressure, and rhythm of movement. The therapist emphasized that Barbara was to control the interaction. As before, they were asked to practice at least four times in the following week.

At the beginning of the next session, minor problems were noted in the progress of treatment. Barbara reported that she had become somewhat self-conscious with the new exercise. She found the experience pleasant and arousing, but her mind wandered and she was unable to achieve a state of total abandon. Frank had also encountered difficulty with ejaculatory control. On the third evening of practice, he had become totally absorbed in the process and, without completely realizing what he was doing, he had rubbed his erect penis against Barbara's back and reached orgasm. The therapist reassured Frank that this experience was not unexpected and could, in fact, be seen as the predictable outcome of his immersion in the sensate focus exercise. It was also clear, however, that additional changes should be made in the process to help Frank gain more control and to reduce Barbara's tendency toward detachment.

The therapist addressed the issue of ejaculatory control by recommending that Barbara and Frank practice the "start-stop" procedure. Frank was instructed to lie on his back so that Barbara could stimulate his erect penis manually. His task would be to concentrate on his own level of arousal and signal Barbara when he experienced the sensation that immediately precedes ejaculation. At this point, Barbara would discontinue stimulation. When Frank no longer felt that ejaculation was imminent, she would resume stimulation until he again signaled that he was experiencing the urge to ejaculate. They were asked to repeat this cycle four or five times initially and to work toward achieving 15 to 20 minutes of continuous repetitions.

The sensate focus exercise was also continued with additional instruction. Barbara was encouraged to engage in her favorite sexual fantasies while guiding Frank's hands over her body. Frank's acceptance and support were particularly helpful in this regard because of Barbara's guilt about the use of sexual fantasies. By concentrating on these images, she would be able to avoid other mental distractions that had impaired her ability to become completely involved in the exercise.

The next 2 weeks of practice were very successful. Frank was able to control his ejaculatory urges within 4 or 5 days; Barbara found that the start-stop exercise was also quite pleasurable for her. In the past, Frank had always discouraged her from stroking or playing with his erect penis because he was afraid that he would ejaculate prematurely. It was becoming clear that their improved communication about what they enjoyed and when to start and stop various activities resulted in considerably greater freedom and pleasure than their previously constricted interactions had allowed. Barbara was now able to reach orgasm through Frank's manual stimulation of her breasts and clitoris. She was much less inhibited about directing his touch, and he noted he had learned a lot about Barbara's erotic zones. Much of the tension and inhibition had been reduced.

The final step was to help Barbara experience orgasm during intercourse. The prohibition against intercourse was lifted, and a new procedure was introduced. As before, they were instructed to begin their exercises by alternating in sensate focus. When they were both moderately aroused, Frank would lie on his back and Barbara would sit on top of him with her knees drawn toward his chest and insert his penis into her vagina. She would then control the speed and rhythm of their movements. Emphasis was placed on moving slowly and concentrating on the pleasurable sensations associated with vaginal containment. If Frank experienced the urge to ejaculate, Barbara was instructed to withdraw his penis until the sensation had passed. If she became less aroused during intercourse, they would also separate, and Frank would once again employ clitoral stimulation until Barbara reached a stage of more intense arousal, at which point they would resume coitus.

Barbara and Frank practiced this procedure many times over the next few weeks. It was an extremely pleasurable experience, and they noticed that they had made considerable progress, most notably Frank's ability to delay ejaculation throughout 20 to 30 minutes of intercourse with Barbara in the superior position. Nevertheless, Barbara was not able to reach orgasm through penile stimulation alone. They continued to alternate periods of insertion with manual stimulation of the clitoris, but Barbara's orgasms were limited to the latter intervals. The therapist noted that this was not uncommon and encouraged them to begin experimenting with other positions for intercourse that would also allow manual stimulation of her clitoris during coitus. The Garrisons were perfectly satisfied with this solution.

Fifteen weeks after their initial visit, Barbara and Frank had made significant changes in their sexual adjustment. Both of them were pleased with these developments, which included Frank's confidence in his ability to control ejaculation and Barbara's ability to reach orgasm during intercourse. Perhaps most important, these changes were not specifically limited to their sexual interactions. They reported that they also talked more frequently and openly about other areas of their lives and felt closer to each other than they had at the beginning of treatment. Thus, the new lines of communication that had been developed in sexual activities did generalize, or transfer, to other situations.

Discussion

Sexual dysfunctions are defined by interference with any phase of the sexual-response cycle. This cycle may be thought of as a continuous sequence of events or sensations, beginning with sexual excitement and ending with the decrease in tension following orgasm. This cycle can be roughly divided into three phases that are characteristic of both men and women. During the excitement phase, the person begins to respond to sexual stimulation with increased flow of blood to the genital area. This engorgement leads to erection in the male and vaginal lubrication in the female. Various physiological changes, including more rapid breathing and an increase in heart rate and blood pressure, occur throughout the excitement phase. These changes reach their maximum intensity during the orgasmic phase, a brief period of involuntary response. In males, the orgasmic phase occurs in two stages, beginning with the collection of sperm and seminal fluid in the urethra (creating a sensation of inevitability, or "point of no return") and ending with ejaculation. In females, the orgasmic phase involves rhythmic contractions in the outer third of the vagina. From a subjective point of view, the orgasmic phase is the point of peak physical pleasure. It is followed by a rapid dissipation of tension. The period following orgasm, known as the resolution phase, encompasses the return of bodily functions to a normal resting state (LeVay & Valente, 2003).

Interference with sexual response may occur at any point and may take the form of subjective distress (such as the fear of losing ejaculatory control) or disrupted performance (such as the inability to maintain an erection sufficient for intercourse).The *Diagnostic and Statistical Manual of Mental Disorders* (*DSM-IV-TR*; APA, 2000, pp. 535–558) provides the following definitions of problems experienced by men and women:

Hypoactive sexual desire disorder: Persistently or recurrently deficient (or absent) sexual fantasies and desire for sexual activity.

Sexual aversion disorder: Persistent or recurrent extreme aversion to, and avoidance of, all (or almost all) genital sexual contact with a sexual partner.

Female sexual arousal disorder: Persistent or recurrent inability to attain, or to maintain until completion of the sexual activity, an adequate lubrication-swelling response of sexual excitement.

Male erectile disorder: Persistent or recurrent inability to attain or maintain, until completion of the sexual activity, an adequate erection.

Female orgasmic disorder (inhibited female orgasm): Persistent or recurrent delay in, or absence of, orgasm following a normal sexual excitement phase.

Male orgasmic disorder: Persistent or recurrent delay in, or absence of, orgasm following a normal sexual excitement phase during sexual activity.

Premature ejaculation: Persistent or recurrent ejaculation with minimal sexual stimulation before, on, or shortly after penetration and before the person wishes it.

Dyspareunia: Recurrent or persistent genital pain in either a male or a female before, during, or after sexual intercourse.

Vaginismus: Recurrent or persistent involuntary spasm of the musculature of the outer third of the vagina that interferes with sexual intercourse.

All these problems may be general or situational in nature. In the case of male erectile disorder, for example, the person may never have been able to attain or maintain an erection until completion of the sex act. On the other hand, he may have been able to do so in the past, or with a different partner, but cannot do so presently.

Most people with hypoactive sexual desire retain the capacity for physical sexual response, but they are generally unwilling to participate and are unreceptive to their partner's attempts to initiate sexual relations. Lack of interest in sexual activity may be an important source of distress, particularly for the spouse or partner of such an individual, but it is also a difficult problem to define. What is a normal sexual appetite? Instead of establishing an arbitrary standard, *DSM-IV-TR* (APA, 2000) has opted for a flexible judgment in this area that depends on a consideration of factors that affect sexual desire such as age, sex, health, intensity and frequency of sexual desire, and the context of the individual's life.

Diagnostic judgments in the area of sexual dysfunction often depend on subtle considerations. Is the problem sufficiently persistent and pervasive to warrant treatment? And, if it is, does the problem center on one partner or the other? These may be difficult questions. In the Garrisons' case, for example, it was not clear whether Barbara's inability to reach orgasm during intercourse could be attributed to Frank's difficulty in delaying or controlling his ejaculatory response. On the other hand, if she had been able to reach orgasm quickly, he might not have worried about the question of control. Two conclusions can be drawn from these considerations. First, sexual dysfunction is most easily defined in the context of a particular interpersonal relationship. The couple, not either individual, is the focus for assessment and treatment. Second, the identification of sexual dysfunction rests largely with the couple's subjective satisfaction with their sexual relationship and not with absolute judgments about typical, or normal, levels of performance.

Various forms of sexual dysfunction are common (Christensen et al., 2011). The best information on the epidemiology of sexual dysfunction comes from the National Health and Social Life Survey (NHSLS) (Laumann, Gagnon, Michael, & Michaels, 1994). These investigators used probability sampling to select people for their study. They interviewed nearly 3,500 men and women between the ages of 18 and 59 throughout the United States. Each person was asked whether, during the past 12 months, he or she had experienced "a period of several months or more when you lacked interest in having sex; had trouble achieving or maintaining an erection or (for women) had trouble lubricating; were unable to come to a climax; came to a climax too quickly; or experienced physical pain during intercourse." For men, the most frequent form of sexual dysfunction was premature ejaculation, affecting 29% of the men in the study. Arousal problems were reported by 10% of the men overall (and 20% of those over the age of 50). For women, the most frequently reported difficulties were low sexual desire (33%), lack of orgasm (24%), and arousal problems (19%). Fourteen percent of the women (and 3% of the men) indicated that they had recently experienced a period of several months during which intercourse was painful.

The NHSLS data regarding the prevalence of sexual dysfunction should be interpreted with caution because they are not based on diagnostic judgments made by experienced clinicians. Participants' responses may overestimate the prevalence of sexual dysfunction. Consider, for example, the frequency of female orgasmic disorder. One fact is relatively clear: Approximately 10% of adult women report a total lack of previous orgasmic response (Clayton, 2007). Does this failure to experience orgasm automatically indicate a dysfunction or the absence of the capacity to reach orgasm? Some women voluntarily refrain from sexual activity. Others may not have engaged in activities, such as masturbation, that are likely to result in orgasmic response. The *DSM-IV-TR* (APA, 2000) definition of female orgasmic disorder stipulates that the delay or absence of orgasm must follow a normal sexual excitement phase. The diagnosis is to be made only if the clinician decides that the woman's orgasmic capacity is "less than would be reasonable for her age, sexual experience, and the adequacy of sexual stimulation she receives" (*DSM-IV-TR*, APA, 2000, p. 547). Based on this more restrictive definition, fewer women would meet the criteria for this disorder.

Another important diagnostic consideration involves the issue of personal distress. Is the person upset about diminished sexual responsiveness? The NHSLS investigators asked people whether they had experienced a period of time in which they had lost interest in sexual behavior or had trouble becoming aroused or reaching orgasm. The *DSM-IV-TR* (APA, 2000) definition considers whether the person experienced subjective distress or interpersonal difficulty as a result of the lack of sexual response. Recommendations regarding further refinements in the classification of female sexual dysfunction have placed increased emphasis on personal distress as a necessary feature in the definition (Both, Laan, & Schultz, 2010).

Etiological Considerations

Some cases of sexual dysfunction may be the result of other forms of physical or mental disturbance. Human sexual response involves a complicated and delicate system that may be disrupted by many factors. Several physical conditions and medical disorders, including diseases of the central nervous system, head and spinal cord injuries, drug ingestion, and fatigue, can impair the person's interest in sexual activity or the ability to perform sexual responses (Burns, Rivas, & Ditunno, 2001). Other psychological adjustment problems can also lead to disturbances in sexual activity. Depression, for example, is commonly associated with a drastic decline in a person's interest in sex. People who are taking antidepressant medication, including selective serotonin reuptake inhibitors (SSRIs), may also experience sexual dysfunctions as a side effect (Clayton & West, 2003). These factors should be considered before a psychological treatment approach is attempted.

Many different psychological explanations have been proposed to account for the development and maintenance of sexual dysfunction (McConaghy, 2005).

Psychoanalytic theory traces sexual problems to an inadequate resolution of the Oedipal conflict. In Barbara's case, for example, a psychoanalyst might have argued that her inability to reach orgasm during intercourse was associated with fear of success in the sense that being successful in her adult sexual relationship might be analogous to succeeding in the Oedipal situation. According to this notion, Barbara wanted to have intercourse with her father and was thus in competition with her mother. But she was also afraid that if she succeeded, her mother would punish her severely. To the extent that her husband was symbolic of her father and reaching orgasm during intercourse with him was equivalent to "winning" the struggle with her mother, Barbara's orgasmic inhibition could be determined by this unconscious mental conflict. The treatment approach that follows from this theoretical position would involve long-term, individual psychotherapy with Barbara in which the goal would be to help her achieve insight into her frustrated sexual desire for her father, her consequent fear of her mother, and the relationship between this conflict and her current relationship with her husband.

Certain aspects of this theory are consistent with the present case. Most notable might be the resemblance between her father and her husband, Frank. They were both police officers and shared various interpersonal characteristics, such as conservative social and political beliefs. Barbara's current relationship with her mother might also be raised as evidence in support of a psychoanalytic approach to the case. Her father had died shortly after Barbara and Frank were married. Barbara and her mother continued to see each other often. Barbara admitted privately that her mother was usually more of an annoyance than a help, meddling in their daily activities and criticizing the manner in which Barbara and Frank handled the children. Barbara was markedly unassertive with her mother and usually acquiesced to her demands. A psychoanalyst might have argued that this close, ongoing interaction exacerbated and maintained Barbara's rivalry with her mother.

Learning theorists have also stressed the importance of past events in determining present sexual adjustment, but they have emphasized the importance of conditioning procedures, not unconscious mental conflict and sexual desire for one's parents. From a behavioral perspective, many forms of sexual dysfunction can be seen as the product of learned inhibitions that are acquired as a result of unsuccessful, early sexual experiences. In some cases, these may have been traumatic events such as being raped or molested (Leonard & Follette, 2002).

Behavioral models of sexual dysfunction emphasize the importance of learned, anticipatory anxiety that is associated with sexual stimulation and the development of avoidance responses that serve to reduce this anxiety. This aspect of the model is weak; there is little scientific evidence indicating that either classical or operant conditioning plays an important role in learning sexual responses (Letourneau & O'Donohue, 1997). On the other hand, behavioral models also stress the importance of social skills, in this case knowing how to engage in effective sexual behaviors. They focus on what the people do during sexual activity instead of on the symbolic meaning of the act. This aspect of the behavioral approach has had important implications for the development of psychological treatments for sexual dysfunctions.

Several elements of Barbara's case are compatible with a social skills approach to sexual dysfunction. Her parents' inability to display physical affection (at least in front of the children), their failure to provide her with any information about sexual behavior, and the implicit message that sexual activity was somehow shameful or disgusting, were all important factors that contributed to both her anxiety regarding sexual activity and her lack of appropriate heterosexual social skills. Prior to her relationship with Frank, Barbara had no sexual experience other than brief kisses and hugs after dates. She and Frank, at his insistence, progressed rapidly in their own sexual relationship without giving Barbara sufficient time to extinguish gradually her fear of physical intimacy. Furthermore, their first experience with intercourse was generally unpleasant. This unfortunate event, coupled with their subsequent realization that Barbara had become pregnant, added to her discomfort in sexual activity. Instead of addressing the problem directly and learning more enjoyable ways of interacting sexually, Barbara and Frank tried to ignore the problem. They had intercourse infrequently and shortened the occasions when they did have sex to the briefest possible intervals.

Response patterns that provoke and exacerbate sexual problems tend to fall into four general categories. The first is failure to engage in effective sexual behavior. This category includes practices such as rushing to the point of penetration before the woman is sufficiently aroused, as was the Garrisons' habit. This sort of error is almost always the result of ignorance about human sexual responses and not the product of deeply ingrained neuroses or personality disorders. Frank and Barbara did not know that most women take longer than men to reach an advanced stage of sexual arousal, and, as a result, neither of them had made a serious effort to improve or prolong their activity during foreplay.

The second type of maladaptive response is sexual anxiety, which includes subjective factors such as the pressure to perform adequately and fear of failure. This type of interference was clearly present in the Garrisons' case. Frank had been concerned for a number of years about losing control of his ejaculatory response. Because of this fear, he continued to rush through the initial stages of sexual activity and resisted any subtle efforts that Barbara made to slow things down. She, on the other hand, was troubled by a double-edged concern. Although she always tried very hard to have an orgasm (and was, in fact, self-conscious about her failure to reach a climax), she was simultaneously worried about getting carried away. Barbara was convinced that if she really abandoned herself completely and followed her "raw sexual instinct," she would lose control of herself. In so doing, she feared that she would risk losing Frank completely because he would be repulsed by her behavior. This was truly a vicious dilemma. If she did not relax and let herself go, she would not have an orgasm, thus perpetuating her own unhappiness as well as Frank's conviction (as she imagined it) that she was an inadequate lover. On the other hand, if she did relax and let herself go, she would lose control and run the risk of alienating him completely.

The third set of factors that maintain sexual dysfunctions include perceptual and intellectual defenses against erotic feelings. Sexual responses are not under voluntary control. The surest way to lose an erection, for example, is to think about the erection instead of the erotic stimuli. Nevertheless, some people engage in a kind of obsessive self-observation during sexual activity and, as a result, become spectators, not participants, in their own lovemaking. Laboratory studies have provided further insight regarding this phenomenon, and they have suggested a few interesting distinctions between sexually functional and dysfunctional people (Wiegel, Wincze, & Barlow, 2002). The arousal levels of sexually functional subjects are typically enhanced by performance-related erotic cues, such as the presence of a highly aroused partner. The same kind of stimulation can distract people who are sexually dysfunctional. The cognitive interference that they experience in response to these stimuli leads to a decrease in their sexual arousal. This problem was particularly characteristic of Barbara's behavior. She often found herself ruminating during sexual activity and asking herself questions about her own performance and desires (Will I come this time? What would happen if Frank knew what I have been thinking about?).

Failure to communicate is the final category of immediate causes of sexual dysfunction. Women suffering from orgasmic disorder report that, in addition to holding negative attitudes toward masturbation and feeling guilty about sex, they are uncomfortable talking to their partner about sexual activities, especially those involving direct clitoral stimulation (Kelly, Strassberg, & Turner, 2004). The Garrisons' failure in this regard was painfully obvious. Both were unwilling to talk to the other person about their desires and pleasures. In Barbara's case, her inhibitions could be traced to the environment in which she was raised. Her parents explicitly conveyed the message that decent people did not talk about sex. If she could not talk to her own mother about basic matters such as menstruation and pregnancy, how could she expect to discuss erotic fantasies with her husband? Consequently, Barbara and Frank knew little about the kinds of stimulation and fantasies that were most pleasing to their partner.

Treatment

The widely publicized work of Masters and Johnson (1970) had an important impact on the development and use of direct psychological approaches to the treatment of sexual dysfunction. Although questions have been raised about the way in which they evaluated and reported the results of their treatment program, their apparent success created an optimistic and enthusiastic environment in which further research and training could be accomplished. Instead of treating the problem as a symbol of unconscious turmoil, sex therapists are primarily concerned with the problem itself and the current, situational determinants that serve to maintain it. This is clearly a cognitive-behavioral approach. Therapists seek to eliminate sexual anxiety by temporarily removing distracting expectations (intercourse is typically forbidden during the first several days of treatment) and substituting competing responses. The sensate focus exercise, for example, is employed to create an erotic atmosphere, devoid of performance demands, in which couples can learn to communicate more freely. In later sessions, couples are instructed in the use of specific exercises designed to foster skills related to their specific sexual problem (Bach, Wincze, & Barlow, 2001; McCarthy, 2004).

The start-stop procedure for treating premature ejaculation is a good example of this approach. The male partner is taught to attend to important sensations that signal the imminence of ejaculation and to interrupt further stimulation until the urge passes. Frank's experience indicates that important cognitive changes accompany the physiological and behavioral components of this technique. As he became more successful in controlling his ejaculatory responses, Frank experienced less apprehension during extended periods of foreplay. His increased confidence and willingness to communicate were, in turn, important assets in addressing Barbara's orgasmic difficulty. Considerable success has been achieved with this approach (Grenier & Byers, 1995).

Antidepressant medication provides another useful approach to the treatment of premature ejaculation. Double-blind, placebo-controlled studies have shown that SSRIs, such as paroxetine (Paxil), can lead to a significant delay in ejaculation after 3 or 4 weeks of treatment (Waldinger, Zwinderman, & Olivier, 2001).

The prognosis for orgasmic dysfunction in women is also quite good (McCabe, 2001). For example, one study reported a 95% rate of success for directed masturbation training with 150 women who had never had an orgasm prior to treatment (LoPiccolo & Stock, 1986). Approximately 85% of the women were also able to reach orgasm if they were stimulated directly by their partners. It is also important to note, however, that only 40% of these women were able to reach orgasm during intercourse. With few exceptions, all women can learn to experience orgasm, but a substantial percentage cannot reach climax through the stimulation afforded by intercourse alone. As in Barbara's case, many women require additional stimulation beyond that associated with the motion of the erect penis in the vagina. These women should not be considered treatment failures. Orgasm during intercourse does not have to be the ultimate measure of treatment success (Stock, 1993).

Research studies have tended to focus on certain aspects of sexual performance, such as the ability to delay ejaculation and orgasmic responsiveness. It must be remembered, however, that performance variables represent only one aspect of sexual adjustment. Factors such as subjective arousal, personal satisfaction, and feelings of intimacy and closeness with one's partner are also important considerations. Barbara and Frank were happy with their sexual relationship despite the fact that she could not achieve orgasm through intercourse alone. They had made remarkable changes in their ability to communicate and share sexual pleasure and were content to use positions that allowed either Frank or Barbara to stimulate Barbara's clitoral area manually while they were having intercourse. With this limitation in mind, direct approaches to orgasmic dysfunction have been successful (Heiman, 2002).

Discussion Questions

1. Barbara and Frank were both experiencing difficulties with their sexual relationship. She could be assigned a diagnosis of female orgasmic disorder. But was the problem hers? Or was it his or theirs? Could sexual dysfunction be treated in an individual who came to therapy without a partner?
2. What impact does culture have on the development and maintenance of sexual dysfunctions? Do you think the popular media have a positive or negative impact on attitudes regarding sexual behavior?
3. Did Barbara's parents play an influential role in the development of her sexual problems? Many children grow up in similar homes without experiencing orgasmic difficulties as adults. Why did Barbara develop a problem while other people do not?
4. Viagra is now one of the most widely promoted and prescribed forms of medication in our society. If a female version of Viagra had been available when Barbara was being treated, do you think it would have solved her problem?

CHAPTER 13

Paraphilias: Exhibitionism and Frotteurism

Pete began court-ordered therapy in November with a clinical psychologist. During the initial interview, Pete, a 34-year-old married man, explained that he was coming for therapy concerning a sexual problem that he had had for years. He was seeking treatment now because he had been arrested in September for a sexual assault. He had been driving home, taking a shortcut along some back roads, when he saw a car with its hood up and a woman looking at the engine. He stopped to offer assistance. The woman had pulled over because her alternator light had come on, and Pete was able to correct the problem by adjusting the fan belt. When the woman thanked him, he pulled her close to him, trying to fondle her buttocks. As she pushed him away, he exposed himself and started masturbating. The woman ran to her car and drove off. Pete made no attempt to follow. Later that night the police came to his home and arrested him. An initial hearing was held the next day, and bail was set. Pete's wife attended the hearing and paid the bail. At his subsequent trial, Pete was allowed to plead guilty to a reduced charge of attempted assault and was put on probation for 2 years. Part of the probation agreement was that he seek treatment.

This was not the first time that Pete's sexual behaviors got him into trouble. He had a long history of sexual deviance since early adolescence. His deviant sexual practices took two forms. One was going into crowded places—shopping centers or subway trains—moving up close behind a woman, and rubbing his pelvis against her buttocks. This type of activity is called *frottage*; the disorder is called *frotteurism*. Pete's other deviant sexual practice was exhibitionism. Sometimes he would park his car in a place where many women were walking, remain seated behind the wheel, and masturbate as he watched them. He did not expose himself directly but hoped that the passing women would look into his car and see him. Other times he would masturbate under a raincoat in a place frequented by women. Teenagers with "cute little behinds" were his preferred target for both activities.

Pete had engaged in frottage and exhibitionism since adolescence. The first time he clearly remembered doing either was as a 16-year-old high school student. He was at a football game on a drizzly Saturday afternoon and had on a raincoat, one in which the pockets allow a hand to go from the outside all the way through the coat to the body. Sitting next to a female acquaintance, he found himself sexually aroused and masturbated to orgasm, his actions apparently undetected by anyone.

When he got his driver's license later that year, he began to openly masturbate in his car. Since then, he had engaged in either frottage or exhibitionism fairly regularly—an average of 15 to 20 times per year. Pete reported that the urge to do so usually increased when he was under stress, such as during exams in high school and college or while under work pressures in adulthood. His sexual behavior had worried him for some time. He had been in therapy for brief periods on three previous occasions. Each time he dropped out after several sessions because it seemed to him that little progress was being made. This time Pete could not drop out of therapy because doing so would violate the terms of his probation.

Other important facets of his problem were explored over several sessions, including his sexual fantasies, which were a mirror of his deviant sexual practices. During the day, he often imagined rubbing against or masturbating in front of young women. His masturbatory fantasies also had the same content. He reported that the frequency of his sexual fantasies had been increasing lately. But there was an important difference between his fantasies and his actual sexual experiences. In real life, he had never succeeded in arousing a woman by rubbing against her or publicly masturbating. Women he rubbed against moved away from him or, less frequently, threatened to call for help if he persisted. When women saw him masturbating in his car, their reaction was shock or disgust. In his fantasies, however, Pete's frottage or masturbation usually served as a prelude to intercourse. The young women of his dreams became aroused as he rubbed against them or when they saw his erect penis. His fantasy would then expand to include a more conventional sexual encounter. Fantasies limited only to vaginal intercourse, however, were not stimulating to Pete.

Pete also had problems in other areas of his life. Although he was a college graduate, he had never been able to find a job that he found satisfying. His interests in painting and music had never been profitable. He had held a long series of jobs he regarded as dull. His longest period of employment in the same job was 18 months. He was currently working as a bartender in a topless bar, which was not a good choice for someone with paraphilias.

Pete and Helen married when he was 24 and she was 22 after dating for 6 months. They had a 5-year-old son. Helen was a high school graduate and worked as an executive secretary for the vice president of an engineering firm. She had held this relatively high-paying and responsible job for 4 years. Pete reported that their marriage had gradually gone downhill. They did not fight or argue much, but he felt that Helen had become less affectionate, less interested in sex, and did not seem to care as much for him as she once had. Currently, he said, she found excuses to avoid most of his sexual advances. The frequency of intercourse had dropped to less than once per month. He reported that he did enjoy sex with his wife. Foreplay usually involved rubbing his penis on her bare buttocks, and intercourse was in the rear entry position. As with his fantasies, however, frottage was a necessary prelude to arousal and subsequent intercourse. According to Pete, the birth of their son seemed to coincide with the beginning of Helen's decline in interest in him. Pete was initially uninvolved and refused to help with feedings and diaper changes. More recently, he was beginning to feel and act more like a father.

Social History

The origins of Pete's current problems seemed to lie in his childhood. He reported he had been "emotionally deprived" as a child. His father never held jobs for very long; consequently, the family moved a great deal. For this reason, Pete felt that he never had a chance to develop close childhood friendships. Furthermore, he felt rejected by his father. He reported that they never played or went on outings together and that his father always seemed cold and distant. Pete's father died when he was 12 years old.

Pete felt that his relationship with his mother was warm, but he thought that she was overprotective and somewhat smothering. After the death of Pete's father, his mother never dated and seemed to invest all her emotional needs in her children, especially Pete. She crossed appropriate boundaries that regulate interactions between family members in ways that were sexually abusive. For example, she continued to bathe him until he was 15 years old. During these baths in Pete's early adolescence, she took great care in cleaning his penis, stroking it with the wet bar of soap and seeming to enjoy the erections that were often produced.

When Pete was 13 years old, he and his family were living in an apartment complex. His principal playmates were three slightly older female teenagers. The four often engaged in rough-and-tumble play like wrestling. During one of these play sessions, Pete had his first orgasm. He was wrestling with one of the girls and was on top of her, his genitals against her buttocks. While moving, he became erect and continued thrusting until he climaxed. He was able to keep his orgasm secret from his friends and went home quickly to clean up.

After this initial pleasurable experience, Pete began sexually abusing his 8-year-old sister. At night whenever he had the opportunity, he would go to her bed, take off her pajama bottoms, and rub his penis against her bare buttocks until he reached orgasm. He continued this practice regularly for the next couple years and stopped only after his sister threatened to tell their mother. When he stopped the frottage with his sister, he turned to regular masturbation with fantasies of both rubbing and sexual intercourse during his self-stimulation. When he was 15 years old, he had his first consensual sexual experience. Pete had heard stories for some time about the sexual activities of a 17-year-old girl who lived in the same apartment building as he did. He went out of his way to get to know her, did errands and favors for her, and finally was invited to have sex with her one night in a nearby park. Although he became aroused as they kissed and petted, he lost his erection when he attempted intercourse. Thereafter, Pete reported that he became afraid to approach women. His first instance of public masturbation occurred the next year.

On a social level, adolescence was not much better for Pete than childhood had been. He did hang around with a group, but he did not develop any really close relationships. He did not date much and reported that being around popular and attractive women made him anxious. He also indicated that it was difficult for him to participate in conversations. He felt that most often people talked only about trivialities and that he was just not interested in that.

After graduating from high school, Pete attended a local community college and then a university and graduated with a bachelor's degree in psychology. He then drifted through a series of jobs and casual affairs until meeting his wife. She was the first woman with whom he had ever had a lasting relationship.

Another perspective on Pete, and particularly on his marriage, was gained through a marital assessment conducted in separate sessions with Pete and Helen. Pete's main complaints about Helen centered on her lack of affection and their poor sexual relationship. He also reported that they argued about how to spend their leisure time. Helen liked to socialize with friends, but Pete found most of them boring. Helen did not know about Pete's long history of sexual problems. She thought that Pete's trouble with the law was the only time he had ever engaged in such activity and could not understand why he had done it. She was extremely upset and repulsed by the entire incident but stood by him. However, she made it clear that another such incident would end their marriage.

Helen's description of the problems in their marriage was similar to Pete's. She recognized that infrequent sex, absence of affection, and disagreements about socializing with friends were serious problems. She had tolerated Pete's frottage before intercourse but did not find it appealing. Helen also complained about Pete as a father and husband. She resented the fact that he was less than a full partner in the marriage, sharing only minimally in parenting and other household duties. Her resentment was increased because she worked all day and then had to come home to cook, clean, and take care of their son while Pete did little but watch television. Even when Pete was not working, which was frequently, he made little attempt to help out. She had lost respect for him because of his failure to share in the marriage and because of his job history and consequent inability to make much of a financial contribution. She was currently somewhat ashamed of Pete's job as a bartender in a topless bar and suspected that he might be having an affair. Indeed, she attributed most of her inability to be affectionate and her declining interest in sex to this loss of respect. She added that she wished Pete would not always follow the same routine in their sexual encounters.

Conceptualization and Treatment

Initially, Pete's therapist needed to implement some procedures to increase the likelihood that Pete would be able to stop both the public masturbation and the frottage and thus avoid being jailed. He had not engaged in either for almost 2 months, the longest period for which he had refrained since adolescence. But Pete reported that the urges were still there and that they would appear unexpectedly. Because the frottage and public masturbation were linked to particular situations—parking lots, shopping centers, and subways—Pete was told to avoid these situations as much as possible. In addition, Pete was taught how to handle an urge if it arose. Because his urges were linked to heightened arousal, he was instructed about how to relax himself by imagining that he was on a beach, feeling drowsy, and enjoying the warm sun. In this and subsequent therapy sessions, Pete practiced imagining typical situations that would generally elicit the urge to exhibit or engage in frottage, but instead of acting on his urges, he relaxed and imagined that he overcame the urge.

Over subsequent sessions, several other components were added to the therapy. First, an attempt was made to try to change Pete's sexual fantasies, both when masturbating and when he felt attracted to or aroused by any woman. Second, marital therapy seemed necessary, both for the marriage itself and, more specifically, for the sexual relationship between Pete and Helen. Both aspects of the therapy were directed toward increasing the frequency and attractiveness of intercourse.

The first step in trying to make consensual intercourse more attractive to Pete was to have him masturbate while fantasizing only about intercourse. Initially, Pete reported that he was unable to develop a full erection unless he imagined frottage or public masturbation. He was first instructed to arouse himself with any fantasy (for him this was most often frottage or public masturbation), to begin masturbating, and, when he was close to orgasm, to switch to an intercourse scene. He was able to do this easily. After a week of practice, he was told to switch to the intercourse fantasy closer to the start of masturbation. He was able to do so with no loss of arousal. By the fourth week, he was able to initiate and complete masturbation with no fantasies of frottage or public masturbation.

As this part of the therapy was progressing, Pete also began to work on altering fantasies elicited by women. His usual response to seeing a young woman, particularly one in tight jeans or slacks, was to begin imagining rubbing against her buttocks. A treatment was devised to help Pete change these fantasies. Initially during a therapy session, Pete was shown a series of pictures of young women in tight jeans. For each stimulus he was asked to generate a nonsexual fantasy, such as trying to guess the woman's occupation. He was encouraged to focus on the woman's face instead of her buttocks as he thought about the picture. Over a series of trials in which Pete verbalized his thoughts, a repertoire of distracting thoughts and fantasies were developed, with the therapist guiding Pete and providing feedback. This repertoire would help him have non-sexual thoughts when he encountered an attractive woman. Over the next several weeks, Pete continued to practice his new fantasies, both in session and at home. As this skill became better established, Pete was also encouraged to use it in his day-to-day life. He soon reported that he was beginning to have fewer and fewer thoughts of frottage when he encountered attractive young women.

Pete's fantasies regarding women responding positively to his sexual advances were also addressed. Although he had never succeeded in arousing a woman by exhibiting or rubbing, in his fantasy life, he had continually imagined that his advances led to sexual contact. The therapist pointed out the striking inconsistency between his fantasies and real life. With this point beginning to sink in, Pete was also encouraged to reflect on how these incidents actually affected his victims. Pete was guided to have a more empathic sense of the upsetting emotions his advances actually created.

Marital therapy was then initiated. At first, the focus was on the nonsexual problems in the marriage. With the therapist functioning as a mediator and facilitator, the couple was instructed to talk about the various difficulties they were experiencing. The first problem they discussed was Pete's failure to help out with household chores. He acknowledged that he had not helped out very much but added also that when he did try to do something, Helen usually found fault with his efforts.

Helen agreed in part with Pete's analysis. For example, when Pete did the laundry, he would leave the clothes in the dryer, and they became wrinkled and would need ironing. From Helen's perspective, she was therefore not really saved from any work; if she had done the laundry herself, she would have quickly folded the clothes and not had to iron them. From Pete's viewpoint, his efforts had gone unappreciated. With the therapist's guidance, Helen and Pete were able to realize the aspects of the situation that were creating the problem. Neither was feeling good about what the other had done. To solve the problem, Pete agreed to do the laundry and fold it immediately, and Helen agreed to be sure to let Pete know that she appreciated his efforts. A similar system was instituted for several other household chores (cooking, vacuuming, general cleaning) in which Pete had previously tried to be helpful, but his efforts had not elicited Helen's approval.

Next, the therapist directed the couple to consider Pete's belief that Helen was not affectionate toward him. But the therapist was not able to limit the discussion to this problem; Helen was soon talking about her general lack of respect for Pete. The session became highly emotional. Pete, understandably somewhat defensive, argued that he had always done the best he could to be a provider for the family. This issue was not even close to resolution by the end of the session; the therapist instructed Pete and Helen not to talk about it further over the coming week but to think about it and be ready to discuss it the next week.

Two days later, Pete called the therapist to request an extra session. Pete was visibly tense when they met the next day. He said that he had really been shaken by the last session, that he had no idea that Helen had come to view him so negatively. This realization, he said, had a profound effect on him, and he felt compelled to let the therapist know something that he had previously not told anyone. Over the past several years, he had engaged in a series of casual sexual experiences with young women, principally dancers at the bar. During most of them, he had not been able to complete intercourse satisfactorily. The pattern was similar to his initial attempt at intercourse. He would first become aroused and fully erect but later would lose his erection. He said that he wanted to start over now, to stop the affairs and do more to please Helen.

At the next session with Pete and Helen, Pete quickly announced that he had decided to change jobs, was job hunting, and had several promising leads. Seeing that Pete was serious about improving the marriage, Helen was obviously delighted. She also reported that he was helping out more around the house. She was beginning to believe that he was serious about improving their marriage, and she felt good about expressing her appreciation toward him. The next week, Pete landed a job as a camera salesperson in a department store. Helen was very pleased. The two of them stated that they were ready to deal with sex.

Before beginning this phase of therapy, the therapist met individually with Pete to check on his progress in dealing with the urge to masturbate publicly or engage in frottage. Pete had continued to masturbate successfully to fantasies of consensual intercourse. Furthermore, he reported that seeing an attractive young woman no longer led automatically to thoughts of frottage and that he had not really experienced any of his old urges.

From this point on, the therapy progressed quickly. Because Helen was beginning to feel better about Pete, she said that she would not resist his sexual advances. They discussed with the therapist their sexual likes and dislikes and agreed to plan several sexual experiences over the next week. Pete was told to refrain from his usual foreplay (rubbing his penis against Helen's buttocks). The couple agreed on manual and oral stimulation to take its place. They had intercourse four times the next week. Over the next few sessions, the couple continued working on their marital problems. Progress was excellent. They reported that their sexual interactions were both frequent and pleasurable. Occasional sessions with Pete alone revealed that he no longer felt the urge to masturbate publicly or engage in frottage.

Discussion

Pete's problems fall within the *Diagnostic and Statistical Manual of Mental Disorders* (*DSM-IV-TR*; APA, 2000) category of *paraphilias*—frequently occurring sexual urges, fantasies, or behaviors that involve unusual objects and activities. The diagnosis is made only if the person is distressed by the urges or behavior or if social or occupational functioning is impaired. *DSM-IV-TR* lists nine paraphilias, as follows:

Fetishism: The repeated use of nonliving objects to produce sexual excitement.

Transvestic fetishism: Recurrent cross-dressing to produce sexual arousal.

Pedophilia: Sexual activity with prepubescent children.

Voyeurism: Repetitive looking at unsuspecting people, either while they are undressing or engaging in sexual activity.

Sexual masochism: The production of sexual arousal by being made to suffer.

Sexual sadism: The production of sexual arousal by inflicting physical or psychological suffering on someone else.

Paraphilia not otherwise specified: A heterogeneous group of unconventional activities (e.g., coprophilia—obtaining sexual gratification from handling feces; and necrophilia—being sexually intimate with a corpse).

The remaining two paraphilias, exhibitionism and frotteurism, were Pete's specific problems. In *exhibitionism*, the person repeatedly exposes his genitals to a stranger for the purpose of achieving sexual excitement. *Frotteurism* involves intense sexual urges and sexually arousing fantasies involving touching and rubbing against a nonconsenting person. It is the touching, not the coercive nature of the act, that is sexually exciting. Little is known about frotteurism, although clinical reports indicate that it does not often occur in isolation and commonly appears in conjunction with other paraphilias such as exhibitionism (Krueger & Kaplan, 1997). Often victims are unaware of what has happened and typically do not report incidents even if they are; prosecuting acts of frotteurism is difficult because perpetrators usually deny their criminal act (Guterman, Martin, & Rudes, 2011). In addition to his frotteurism and exhibitionism, Pete also had an incestuous relationship with his sister, in which he repeatedly sexually abused her. *Incest* is sexual relations between close family members and is listed in the *DSM-IV-TR* (APA, 2000) as a form of pedophilia. As with Pete, incest is most common between brother and sister.

Like the other paraphilias, exhibitionism is practiced almost exclusively by men. It is the most common sexual offense for which people are arrested, accounting for about one-third of all such arrests. Exhibitionism can involve either the exposure of a flaccid or an erect penis, accompanied by masturbation, as in Pete's case. The motivation for exhibiting seems to vary as the disorder progresses. When it begins in adolescence, it is sexually exciting, but in adulthood, exhibiting is accompanied by general arousal rather than by sexual excitement (McConaghy, 1994). At the time of the act, the adult exhibitionist typically feels both cognitive and physiological signs of arousal—nervousness, palpitations, perspiring, and trembling. Many report that the urge becomes so powerful that they lose control and even some awareness of what they are doing. The most common triggers to the urge to expose themselves that men with exhibitionism reported were boredom and stress (Grant, 2005). Most wanted the target of their exposure to notice and respond with interest and excitement, whereas only a few reported that they wanted to elicit shock or disgust in their target. Exhibitionists prefer to exhibit to people they do not know (Freund & Watson, 1990).

Although clinical lore suggests that exhibitionists typically do not seek further sexual contact with their victims, research evidence indicates that, like Pete, some do get arrested for crimes involving actual sexual contact. For example, Sugarman, Dumughn, Saad, Hinder, and Bluglass (1994) followed a large sample of exhibitionists and found that 26% subsequently were convicted for sexual crimes, including rape. Others have found about half of exhibitionists that were caught reoffended over the 5 years following their initial arrests, and a significant number of them go on to commit violent sexual offenses (Rabinowitz-Greenberg, Firestone, Bradford, & Greenberg, 2002). Some report that exhibitionism often co-occurs with frotteurism (Tan & Zhong, 2001).

People with paraphilias often have other psychological disorders. Kafka and Hennen (2002) evaluated 88 men who voluntarily sought outpatient treatment for paraphilias and found that 17% reported a childhood history of physical abuse, and 18% reported a history of childhood sexual abuse; 61% had been arrested (not always related to the paraphilia); and 25% had been hospitalized for psychiatric problems. Exhibitionism was the most common paraphilia in the sample, followed by pedophilia and voyeurism. Many had a history of other psychiatric diagnoses, especially mood disorders: 69% met criteria for dysthymic disorder, 39% for major depression, and 7% for bipolar disorder; 42% had substance abuse, 42% had attention-deficit/hyperactivity disorder, 39% had an anxiety disorder, and 22% had a conduct disorder. Others have also found that people with a paraphilia were very likely to also have a substance-abuse disorder, a mood disorder, or an antisocial personality disorder (Dunsieth et al., 2004).

There may be differences, though, between people with paraphilia who seek treatment voluntarily and those who do not seek treatment but are identified because they are arrested. The rates of comorbid psychological disorders among 30 men with a paraphilia arrested for hands-on sexual offenses (pedophilia and sexual sadism) were examined by Leue, Borchard, and Hoyer (2004). Seventy-three percent met criteria at some point in their lives for an anxiety disorder, 57% for a substance-abuse disorder, 30% for a mood disorder, and 74% for a personality disorder (most commonly antisocial personality disorder or avoidant personality disorder). Men with exhibitionism who go on to be arrested for committing additional sexual offenses were more likely to report problems with drinking (Firestone, Kingston, Wekler, & Bradford, 2006).

In their review of paraphilias, Saleh and Berlin (2003) noted that the disorder typically emerges in adolescence and, once established, is usually stable and long-lasting. Men with exhibitionism typically expose themselves fairly frequently, at least once a month, and for many, weekly (Grant, 2005). Most people with paraphilias do not voluntarily seek treatment but are court mandated to attend or receive treatment while incarcerated. Often people with paraphilias do not freely admit to the extent of their deviant sexual behavior. Up to 90% of adult sex offenders commit their first sex offense in early adolescence

(Shi & Nicol, 2007). When questioned during polygraph (lie detector) testing, sexual offenders admitted to greater numbers of episodes of paraphilic behavior and significantly earlier ages of onset than was known from probation records (Wilcox & Sosnowski, 2005). They admitted to twice as many episodes of exhibitionism and public masturbation. Moreover, none of the probation records contained references to frottage, but half of the men admitted under polygraph examination that they had committed frottage. This suggests that the frequency and scope of deviant sexual behavior of sexual offenders is much larger than might be suspected. In addition, the men admitted that they began their sexual offending an average of 14 years before they were arrested for it. According to data from court referrals, exhibitionism usually begins in adolescence, continues into the twenties, and declines thereafter. Whether the frequency truly declines or whether older exhibitionists are arrested less frequently is unknown.

Etiological Considerations

Biological theories of the origin of the paraphilias suggest that the behavior originates in problems in the structure or functioning of the brain or endocrine system. Perhaps abnormalities in some area of the brain could lead to paraphilia. About 8% of men who experience a traumatic brain injury show some sort of sexually aberrant behavior after the injury, such as exhibitionism or inappropriate touching (Simpson, Tate, Ferry, Hodgkinson, & Blaszczynski, 2001). However, neuropsychological evaluations of people incarcerated for sexual offenses have not been able to consistently document any brain dysfunction. Nor has research been able to identify any specific site in the brain consistently involved in the sexually aberrant behavior. Overall, though, evidence that brain injury can lead to behaviors such as inappropriate touching and exhibitionism suggest that more research is needed in this area. Abnormalities in the excitatory and inhibitory functions of the brain as they relate to sexuality may be involved in the paraphilias (Toates, 2009). Stress and substance use undermine a person's ability to engage in self-restraint, and people with paraphilia sometimes intentionally avoid thinking about negative outcomes for their actions; all of these result in reduced inhibitory function.

A link has been found between a person having a paraphilia and reporting high rates of sexual behavior, including use of pornography, frequency of masturbation, and numbers of sexual partners (Långström & Seto, 2006). Researchers are exploring how this heightened focus on sexuality might be related to paraphilias. Some have speculated that hormonal abnormalities might be related, but findings have not consistently supported this theory.

People incarcerated for paraphilias were more likely to have been emotionally, physically, and sexually abused as children; were more likely to have had behavior problems as children; and were more likely to have come from dysfunctional families than people incarcerated for nonviolent and nonsexual crimes (Lee, Jackson, Pattison, & Ward, 2002). Some researchers argue that this history of trauma and family dysfunction is an important etiological factor for the paraphilias. Exhibitionism has been linked to childhood emotional abuse, family dysfunction, and childhood behavior problems. Men with exhibitionism were more likely to report that their parents were less caring (Bogaerts, Vanheule, Leeuw, & DeSmet, 2006). Some features of Pete's background, however, are similar to characteristics of exhibitionists in general. Many exhibitionists grow up in families in which there is a considerable amount of disturbance (Murphy, 1997). Furthermore, their marriages tend to be dysfunctional, with special difficulties in sexual adjustment. Interpersonally, exhibitionists tend to be socially isolated, with few close friends.

Some researchers propose that paraphilias may be understood as a disorder of courtship behaviors and skills in men. They hypothesize that men who have difficulty understanding interpersonal cues or who lack the social skills to follow societally accepted patterns of expressing sexual interest may develop a paraphilia. The penile plethysmograph, a device that measures the circumference of the penis, was used in a study of male exhibitionists to determine whether they are sexually aroused by stimuli that do not arouse nonexhibitionists (Fedora, Reddon, & Yeudall, 1986). Compared with normal men and with sex offenders who had committed violent assaults, the exhibitionists showed significantly greater arousal to slides of fully clothed women in nonsexual situations, such as riding on an escalator or sitting in a park; they showed similar levels of sexual interest in erotic and sexually explicit slides. These results suggest that exhibitionists misread cues in the courtship phase of sexual contact, in the sense that they construe certain situations to be sexual that are judged to be unerotic by people without exhibitionism. In a more recent study using similar methods, it was found that exhibitionists also showed relatively more sexual arousal to scenes of violence, consistent with the fact that some of them do commit violent offenses (Seto & Kuban, 1996). Sexual arousal to violence was the best predictor of sexual reoffending in a longitudinal study of sex offenders over a 20-year period (Kingston, Seto, Firestone, & Bradford, 2010).

Others have speculated that sexual offenders have a deficit in social skills, which makes it difficult for them to form intimate romantic relationships. Emmers-Sommer et al. (2004) examined 10 studies of sex offenders to evaluate their social skills. They found that sex offenders have poorer social skills. In Pete's case, this is consistent with his difficulties in forming peer relationships and his difficulties relating in his marriage.

A learning-based conceptualization of Pete's case, which in part guided his therapy, involves the following considerations. First, during early adolescence, Pete experienced a chance conditioning trial in which orgasm was linked to rubbing. Although a single experience like this one would not likely produce a durable effect, the link between rubbing and orgasm may have been strengthened through the many similar experiences he arranged between himself and his sister and the repetition of these encounters in his masturbation fantasies. His initial failure in conventional intercourse, coupled with his lack of social skills and infrequent dates, maintained his interest in frottage and set the stage for the development of exhibitionism. Finally, his unsatisfactory sexual relationship with his wife did not provide him with an opportunity to give up his old behavior patterns.

This account is still incomplete in many respects. Why did Pete reinforce his habit of frottage with his younger sister? What led him to exhibit instead of trying to develop skills that might have enabled him to date and to enjoy more conventional sexual pleasures? Why did his sexual fantasies involve the idea that exhibiting or rubbing would sexually arouse women? The theory also implies that early sexual experiences have very durable effects, but it appears that early sexual experiences need not have lifelong effects. The point has been clearly made in a study of the Sambia tribe in New Guinea (Bhugra, Popelyuk, & McMullen, 2010). All male members of the tribe are exclusively homosexual from age 7 to marriage. During a first stage from 7 years old to puberty, the boys perform fellatio on older boys as often as possible because it is their belief that they have to drink a lifetime's supply of semen. From puberty to marriage, women are taboo, and the young men are fellated often by the younger boys. After marriage, the tribesmen become completely heterosexual. Their early homosexual experiences apparently have had little effect on their capacity for and interest in heterosexual arousal.

Treatment

Treatment of the paraphilias has often been complicated by the involvement of the criminal justice system and its goal of punishing crime and preventing reoffending. Interventions have included involuntary surgical castration (Gordon, 2008). There are very few controlled studies of the effectiveness of particular therapies in treating exhibitionism, frotteurism, and the other paraphilias. A major reason for the lack of controlled studies is the ethical problem that would be created by withholding treatment from the control group and then releasing them into the community untreated. Results from the studies that do exist are highly variable, with success rates from about 30 to 90% (Marshall, Jones, Ward, Johnston, & Barabee, 1991). The warmth, empathy, and encouragement of the therapist are especially strongly related to the effectiveness of the treatment for men with paraphilias (Marshall, Marshall, & Serran, 2006). These therapist traits help to overcome the client's defensiveness and resistance to treatment because motivation for change is characteristically low, and research suggests that they may even be more powerful than the specific type of treatment used in determining who does and does not reoffend.

Cognitive-behavioral interventions have evolved from focusing on the application of single techniques to more multidimensional treatments. An example of the former is aversion therapy to reduce the attractiveness of exhibiting (Marshall, Eccles, & Barbaree, 1991). Contemporary treatments include overcoming denial of responsibility, improving the capacity to form interpersonal relationships by strengthening social skills and addressing thoughts about the self, and directly modifying deviant sexual arousal patterns, as well as relapse prevention and aftercare (Marshall et al., 2006).

Pete's therapy illustrates the use of multiple procedures. One component of the therapy was similar to a procedure originally developed by Davison (1968) in treating a case of a young man who required sadistic fantasies to produce sexual arousal. As in the present case, Davison had the client initiate sexual arousal with a sadistic fantasy and then masturbate while looking at a picture of a nude woman. If arousal began to wane, he could return to his sadistic images, but he was told to ensure that orgasm was associated only with the picture. As therapy progressed, the sadistic fantasies were relied on less and less until the client could masturbate to orgasm relying only on the stimulation produced by the nudes. Like Davison's client, Pete learned to become fully aroused and reach orgasm by changing his masturbatory fantasies from exhibiting and frottage to conventional intercourse.

Changing the masturbation fantasies of the person with a paraphilia is a common type of treatment. Dandescu and Wolfe (2003) examined the use of fantasy among people with exhibitionism and pedophilia who were in mostly court-ordered treatment. Of the 82 participants in their sample, 25 were exhibitionists. The majority of both participant types experienced deviant masturbatory fantasies prior to engaging in their first sexual experience related to the paraphilia. For the exhibitionists, 76% had deviant masturbatory fantasies before their first offense, and 88% did after their first offense. The average number of deviant fantasies increased after the first offense. This suggests that deviant masturbatory fantasies are a critical part of the etiology and maintenance of paraphilias for most but not all men with paraphilias.

Another procedure used with Pete is called alternative behavioral completion (Maletzky, 1997). It involves imagining a scene in which the urge to exhibit appears but is overcome by relaxation. In addition, Pete came to change the fantasies that attractive women elicited by practicing new ones, first with pictures and then with women he encountered in the natural environment. Attempts were also made to alter his distorted cognitions and increase his empathy toward his victims. Finally, a reduction in marital conflict and an improved sexual relationship between him and his wife likely contributed to the overall success of the therapy.

Biological interventions have also been employed. Case studies suggesting positive outcomes have been reported for antidepressants and antianxiety drugs (Abouesh & Clayton, 1999; Terao & Nakamura, 2000). Researchers have evaluated an antiandrogen cyproterone acetate for treatment of paraphilia, which decreases all sexual behavior. In studies with exhibitionists, it was found to be effective in completely eliminating deviant behavior for some even after its discontinuation, but it does have side effects (Bradford, 2001). Several studies have also been conducted with medroxyprogesterone acetate, a drug that reduces testosterone levels and thereby lowers sexual arousal. Although effective in reducing recidivism when taken regularly, the disorders recur when the treatment is discontinued (Meyer, Cole, & Emory, 1992). This is problematic because the drug produces a number of unpleasant side effects that are likely to lead to discontinuation. A newer testosterone-lowering medication, leuprolide acetate, has shown promise in the treatment of paraphilia and has fewer side effects (Saleh, Niel, & Fishman, 2004).

Discussion Questions

1. What childhood experiences do you think were particularly important in the development of Pete's paraphilias? How do you think they relate to his later symptoms?

2. One common characteristic among men with paraphilias is a lack of consideration of the effects of one's sexual behaviors on others. How did Pete manifest this? Did it also extend to other areas of his life?

3. What are some of the particular challenges and difficulties in conducting research on people with paraphilias? How could this affect what we know about paraphilias?

4. Pete disclosed to his therapist that he had been having affairs. Do you think the therapist should have encouraged him to confess this to Helen? Why? Would it help or hurt?

CHAPTER 14

Gender Identity Disorder: Transsexualism

Chris Morton was a 21-year-old senior in college. In most respects, she was an exceptionally well-adjusted student, successful academically and active socially. Her problem involved a conflict in gender identity—a problem so fundamental that it is difficult to decide whether to refer to Chris as he or she, although Chris used the masculine pronoun. We have somewhat arbitrarily decided to use the feminine pronoun in relating this case because it may be less confusing to the reader. And in many respects this is a confusing case. It calls into question one of the most fundamental, and seemingly irrefutable, distinctions that most of us make—the distinction between men and women.

Chris's physical anatomy was that of a woman. But this distinction was not made easily on the basis of overt, physical appearance. She was tall and slender: 5'8" and about 130 pounds. Her hips were narrow and her breasts, which she wrapped with an Ace bandage under her clothes, were small. Chris's face was similarly androgynous; her skin had a soft, smooth appearance, but her features were not particularly delicate or feminine. Her hair was cut short, and she wore men's clothes. A typical outfit included Levi's and a man's shirt with a knit tie and a sweater vest. She wore men's underwear and men's shoes, often Oxfords or penny loafers. She also wore a man's ring on her right hand and a man's wristwatch. Her appearance was generally neat and preppy. At first glance, it was not clear whether Chris was a man or a woman. Listening to Chris's voice did not provide any more useful clues because it was neither deep nor high pitched. Many people assumed that she was a man; others were left wondering.

On the basis of her own attitudes and behaviors, Chris considered herself to be like men. Like other transsexuals, she described herself as being a man trapped in a woman's body. She did not consider herself to be confused about her gender identity. From a biological point of view, Chris recognized that she was not a man. She knew that she had breasts and a vagina. She menstruated. But there was more to it than physical anatomy. In every other way possible, and for as long as she could remember, Chris had always felt more male than female. When she tried to explain this feeling to others, she would say, "You can think what you want—and I know that most people don't want to believe this—but if you spend time with me, talk to me, you will see what I mean. You'll know that I am not a woman." The details of this subjective perception, the experiences that served as support for Chris's belief, lie at the core of our notions of what is feminine and what is masculine.

Chris felt a sense of camaraderie in the presence of men. She wasn't sexually attracted to them, and it never would have occurred to her to flirt with them. She wanted to be buddies with them—to swap stories about adventures and compare notes on sexual exploits with women. They were her friends. In her behavior toward women, Chris was often characteristically masculine and excessively polite; she liked to hold doors for women, to pull out their chairs when they sat down to eat, to stand up when they entered a room. This is, of course, not to say that these behaviors are innately masculine, for they are learned as part of our upbringing. Chris felt more comfortable behaving this way because it made her feel masculine, and she said it seemed natural.

People responded in a variety of ways when meeting Chris for the first time. Most assumed that she was a man, but others took her to be a woman. Chris usually corrected people if they happened to address her as a woman. For example, if an instructor used a feminine pronoun when addressing or describing Chris during an initial meeting, she would quickly say "he" or "his." In situations that might arouse curiosity or attract attention, Chris tried to adopt exaggerated male postures or vocal patterns to overcome the observer's sense of ambiguity. One example occurred when she walked into a small seminar for the first time. Chris sauntered across the room, sat down so her legs crossed with one heel on the other knee, and then slouched down in the chair, adopting a characteristically masculine posture. When answering the phone, she usually tried to lower the pitch of her voice.

Chris was sexually attracted to women, and consistent with her male gender identity (her conviction that she was more like men than women), she considered herself to be heterosexual. In fact, she had had two long-term, intimate relationships, and both were with other women. Her present lover, Lynn, was a 26-year-old bisexual who treated Chris as a man and considered their relationship to be heterosexual. Lynn said that when they first met, she thought that Chris was a woman and she was attracted to her as a woman. But as their relationship developed, Lynn came to think of Chris as a man. Part of this impression could be traced to physical behaviors. Lynn agreed that making love with Chris was more like making love with a man than a woman. Although this impression was difficult to describe in words, it seemed to revolve around the way Chris held her and touched her. Perhaps more important were the emotional and intellectual qualities that Lynn noticed. Chris cried about different things than Lynn cried about and seemed unable to empathize with many of Lynn's experiences—experiences that seemed characteristically feminine. She was surprised, for example, at Chris's apparent inability to empathize with her discomfort during menstruation. And Lynn was often surprised by Chris's questions. Once when they were making love, Chris asked Lynn what it felt like to have something inside her vagina. It was a sensation Chris had never experienced (and never wanted to experience).

Chris's parents had known about her gender identity conflict since her senior year in high school. This was a difficult issue for them to address, but they both assured Chris that their love for her was more important than their concern about the problems she would face as a transsexual. Their reactions were also very different. Chris's mother accepted the problem and made every effort to provide emotional support for Chris. Her father, on the other hand, seemed to deal with the issue at a more intellectual level and continued to believe that it was merely a phase that she was going through. Both were opposed to her interest in physical treatment procedures that might permanently alter her appearance.

Although Chris's life was going well in most respects, she wanted to do something about her body to make it more compatible with her masculine gender identity. Several options seemed reasonable. First, she wanted to have her breasts removed. She also wanted to begin taking male hormones so that her voice would deepen and she would grow facial hair. Finally, she wanted to have surgery to remove her uterus and ovaries, primarily because their continued presence might conflict with the consumption of testosterone. Although she would also have preferred to have a penis, she did not want to go through genital surgery because it would not leave her with a functional male organ. Furthermore, the possibility of "mutilating" her existing organs and losing her capacity for orgasm through clitoral stimulation frightened her.

One interesting feature of Chris's masculine identity was revealed in her discussion of the advantages and disadvantages of the physical procedures involved in changing her body. Lynn mentioned, for example, the possible traumatic consequences of losing the capacity to bear children. What if Chris decided in a few years that she had been mistaken and now wanted to raise a family? The idea was totally foreign to Chris! It was a concern that never would have occurred to her. For Chris, the justification for the change was primarily cosmetic. Her concern involved plans for the future. "Right now I can pass for a young man. That's okay when I'm 21, but what happens when I'm 40 and still look like I'm 20 because I don't have facial hair? I can't date 20-year-old women all my life. I wouldn't be happy."

During her senior year in college, Chris made an appointment to see a psychologist at the student health center on campus. She wanted to talk about her desire to take male hormones and alter her body surgically. Although she had thought about the decision for a long time and discussed it with several other people, she wanted to get the opinion of a mental-health professional.

Social History

Chris was the oldest of four children. She had one brother, who was 1 year younger than she, and two younger sisters.

Chris said that she had always felt like a boy. Other people viewed her as a typical "tomboy," but Chris recognized the difference. When she was very young, she and her brother and their father played together all the time. Sports were a central activity in the family, especially basketball. Mr. Morton spent numerous hours teaching Chris and her brother Rick to dribble and shoot baskets on their driveway. These were pleasant memories for Chris, but she also remembered feeling excluded from this group as she and her brother grew older. For example, at that time, Little League rules prohibited girls from participating, and Chris found that she was generally discouraged from playing with boys in the organized games that became more common when they were 9 or 10 years old. She and her brother both played on organized youth teams, and their father served as a coach for both of them. But Chris had to play on girls' teams, and she didn't think that was fair, either for her or to the other girls. She remembered thinking to herself that, although she was always the best player on the girls' team, she would have been only an average player on a boys' team, and that was where she felt she belonged. When she got to high school, she finally quit the team, despite the fact that she was one of the best players, because she didn't want her name or picture to appear in the paper as being part of a girls' team.

Although Chris spent a great deal of time with her father and brother, she also had a good relationship with her mother, whom she remembers as being a source of emotional support and sympathy in difficult times. Her mother was not athletically inclined, so she didn't participate in the activities of Mr. Morton and the children, but she and Chris did spend time talking and shopping together. On the other hand, Chris was never interested in many of the other activities that some girls share with their mothers, such as cooking.

She also wasn't interested in playing with toys that many other girls preferred. She and Rick shared most of their favorite toys, including slot cars, toy soldiers, and baseball cards. She and a friend did play with Barbie dolls for a while, but they only did so when combining them with G.I. Joes and weaving them into mock wars and sexual adventures.

When she started school and began meeting other children in public situations, Chris began to confront and think about issues that are taken for granted by virtually everyone else. How many children, for example, ever think twice about which bathroom to use? As early as first- and second grade, Chris could remember feeling uncomfortable about using the girls' room. In the first grade, she attended a parochial school in which the girls were required to wear uniforms. She wore the dress and had her hair long and in a ponytail but that changed as soon as she reached the second grade. After their parents arranged for Chris and Rick to transfer to a public school, Chris cut her hair very short and began wearing slacks and shirts that made her indistinguishable from the boys.

Similar issues centered on locker rooms. When Chris was 9 years old, her mother arranged for her and Rick to take swimming lessons at a public pool. Chris developed a crush on a cute girl in her class. She remembered feeling ashamed and embarrassed at being in the same locker room with the other girls and being seen in a girl's swimming suit.

Chris's sex play as a child involved little girls rather than little boys. When she was 9 years old, Chris spent long hours "making out" with an 11-year-old neighbor girl, who also experimented sexually with many of the young boys in their neighborhood. Thus, even at this fairly young age, Chris was sexually attracted to girls rather than boys. She had numerous opportunities to play sex games with young boys, who occasionally asked Chris to "mess around," but she wasn't interested. Girls were more attractive and interesting.

By the time she reached junior high school, Chris had begun systematically to avoid using her given name, Christine. She also came to dislike Chris, because although it is a name that is used by both men and women, she thought of it as being more feminine. She came instead to be known by her nickname, "Morty," which sounded more masculine to her.

Adolescence presented a difficult turning point for Chris. The separation of the sexes became more obvious. All of the girls wanted to wear dresses and date boys. Chris wanted to wear pants and date girls. The situation became even more frustrating in high school as her body began to change in obvious ways. The onset of menstruation was awkward, and the development of her breasts presented an even more difficult situation because their presence could be noticed by other people. As soon as her breasts began to enlarge, Chris began binding them tightly with a skin-colored belt that would not show through her shirt. The belt often left bruises on her chest. When she had to change clothes for gym class, she always had to find an isolated locker, away from the other girls, so that no one would see her taking off the belt. Nevertheless, the discomfort and pain associated with this procedure were preferable to the embarrassment of having other people realize that she was developing a woman's body.

Chris continued to have a lot of friends and to be active in academic and extracurricular activities despite her discomfort with gender-specific roles and behaviors. In fact, she was so popular and well respected by the other students that she was elected president of her freshman class in high school. Although she dressed in masculine clothes, everyone knew that she was a girl because she was forced to take the girls' gym class at school. Many of the social activities in which Chris and her friends engaged centered on roller-skating in the evening and on weekends. Large numbers of teenagers from their own school and several others in the city gathered at the roller-skating rink to skate to rock music, eat pizza, and have a good time. Because she was a good athlete and enjoyed physical activity, these were pleasant times for Chris. There were awkward moments, however, such as when the disc jockey would announce "girls only" or "boys only." In either case, Chris would leave the rink; she didn't want to be seen with the girls and wasn't allowed to be with the boys.

Chris's parents separated and were eventually divorced when she was a sophomore in high school. Because their parents had concealed the fact that they were not getting along, the news came as a shock to all of the children. In retrospect, Chris said that she should have known that something was going on because her parents had been spending so much time together talking quietly in their room; her parents had usually been content to go their separate ways. There were, of course, hard feelings on both sides, but the arrangements for the separation were made to minimize the children's involvement in the dispute. They continued to live with their mother and visited their father on weekends.

When Chris was 17, she finally decided to have a talk with her mother about her discomfort with femininity. She told her mother that she wanted to be a boy. Her mother's reply was, "I know you do. I was also a tomboy when I was your age, but you'll grow out of it." Her mother tolerated her masculine dress but didn't seem to comprehend the depth of Chris's feelings.

Chris's best friends in high school were three boys who spent most of their time together. They were the liberal intellectuals of the class. These boys accepted Chris as one of their group without being concerned about her gender. One of her friends later told her, "I never really thought of you as a girl. I guess it wasn't important. You were just Morty." She did attract some attention, however, from other children and teachers. She wore men's pants and shirts, and sometimes ties and sport coats. Chris and her friends were also good dancers and spent a lot of time on weekends at a local club. They were the life of the party. When they arrived, everyone else started dancing and having fun.

Sex presented an extremely frustrating dilemma for Chris. She was attracted to girls, as were all of her male friends. When the boys talked—in the usual crude adolescent way—about girls they knew, Chris wanted to join in. But all of her friends knew that she was a girl. She was particularly attracted to one girl, Jennifer, who had moved to their school the previous year. Jennifer was bright, attractive, and engaging. Her appearance and manners were quite feminine. She spent a lot of time with Chris and her friends, but she was going with a boy who was the captain of the basketball team. Chris and Jennifer began to spend more and more time together as the school year wore on. They talked on the phone every night for at least an hour and were virtually inseparable on weekends.

During their junior year, Jennifer's boyfriend moved away to go to college. The relationship began to deteriorate, but Jennifer didn't know how to break things off. Chris became her principal source of emotional support during these difficult months. Chris became very fond of Jennifer and recognized that she was sexually attracted to her but feared that she might destroy their relationship if she mentioned these feelings to Jennifer.

This all changed rather abruptly one Saturday evening. They went to see a movie together, and as they were sitting next to each other in the darkened theater, Jennifer became conscious of the strong emotional attraction that she felt toward Chris. She sat wishing that Chris would put her hand on her leg or put her arm around her. Jennifer explained these feelings to Chris as they drove home after the film was over, and Chris, in turn, made an effort to explain her feelings for Jennifer. They continued the discussion inside Jennifer's house and eventually retired to Jennifer's bedroom, where they spent the rest of the night talking and making love.

Their physical relationship—which both Chris and Jennifer considered to be heterosexual in nature—was an exceptionally pleasant experience for both of them. It was not without its awkward moments, however. For example, Chris would not let Jennifer touch her breasts or genitals for the first 6 months after they began having sex. She touched Jennifer with her mouth and hands, but did not let Jennifer reciprocate beyond holding and kissing. In fact, Chris always kept her pants on throughout their lovemaking. This hesitation or resistance was primarily due to Chris's sense that she was in the wrong body. If she allowed Jennifer to touch her, they would both be reminded that she had a woman's body. This was frustrating for both of them, but especially for Jennifer, who by this point was not concerned about whether Chris was a man or a woman. She was simply in love with Chris as a person and wanted a complete, reciprocal relationship. Chris was also frustrated because she continued to feel—despite Jennifer's frequent protests to the contrary—that she could not satisfy Jennifer in the way that Jennifer most wanted because she did not have a penis. Their relationship gradually extended to allow more open physical reciprocity, primarily as a result of Jennifer's gentle insistence. Chris found that she enjoyed being stimulated manually and orally by Jennifer and had no trouble reaching orgasm.

Chris and Jennifer were able to continue their intimate relationship without interference from their parents because their parents viewed Chris as a girl and never considered the possibility that she and Jennifer were lovers. They frequently spent nights together at Jennifer's house without arousing any serious suspicion. Jennifer's mother occasionally made comments and asked questions about Chris's masculine wardrobe and manners, but she was totally oblivious to the complexities of Chris's behavior and to the nature of her daughter's involvement.

Despite Jennifer's obvious affection for Chris, their relationship created problems as Jennifer became increasingly sensitive to the reactions of other people. Part of the problem centered on gossip that spread quickly through their school, despite attempts by Chris and Jennifer to conceal the fact that they were dating. Other students had always been reasonably tolerant of Chris's masculine behavior, but their criticism became more overt when a close friend, in whom they had confided, let it become known that Chris and Jennifer were dating each other. That seemed to step beyond most other students' limit for acceptable behavior.

Their sexual relationship ended during Chris's freshman year at college. Jennifer's mother discovered some intimate love letters that Chris had written to Jennifer, who was also in college. She was furious! She threatened to discontinue financial support for Jennifer's education and refused to let her be in their home as long as Jennifer continued to see Chris. The pressure was simply too much. Chris and Jennifer continued to be good friends, but the romantic side of their relationship had to be abandoned. Jennifer dated two or three men afterward and was eventually married.

After breaking up with Jennifer, Chris met and dated a few other women before starting her relationship with Lynn. One of these encounters is particularly interesting because it also provides some insight into Chris's sexual orientation and gender identity. One of her male friends from high school, Robert, was also a freshman at the university. They continued to spend a lot of time together and eventually talked openly about Chris's "story" and the fact that Robert was gay. Both admitted considerable interest regarding sexual response in bodies of the opposite sex—responses that neither had had the opportunity to observe. To satisfy their curiosity, they decided to have sex with each other. Chris later described it as a pleasant experience, but one that felt uncomfortable. They engaged in mutual masturbation, but Chris did not allow him to penetrate her vagina with his penis. Chris had never experienced a sexual encounter with a male before, and her principal interest was in observing Robert's behavior. She wanted to watch him become aroused and reach orgasm. She had always sensed that her own sexual behavior was more like that of a man than a woman, and this would give her a chance to decide. She ended the evening convinced more than ever that her own behavior was masculine and that she was not sexually attracted to men.

Chris strongly preferred monogamous relationships. This was in part a matter of convenience because it was obviously very difficult for her to get to know someone with sufficient intimacy to begin a sexual relationship. It was also a matter of choice. She did not understand, for example, how some people— particularly males—could be so promiscuous.

During her sophomore year in college, Chris stumbled across some literature on transsexualism. This was the first time that she realized that other people experienced the same feelings that she had and that the condition had a formal label. In addition to the comfort that she was not alone in this dilemma, she also obtained some useful information. For example, she learned that many transsexual females use Ace bandages, rather than belts, to bind their breasts. She felt much more comfortable after the change. She also learned about the possibilities of hormonal treatments and various surgical procedures that might be used to alter the appearance of her body. Recognition of these alternatives led Chris to pursue extensive reading at the university library. Having decided that she would like to change the appearance of her body, she made an appointment at the student health center.

Conceptualization and Treatment

When Chris came to see a psychologist at the student health center, she did not indicate that she wanted to change her behavior. Extended consultation with a mental-health professional is generally considered to be a prerequisite for the other procedures that might be used to alter her appearance. Chris sincerely wanted to learn as much as possible about her feelings and motivations for change before embarking on a difficult set of procedures that carried some possibility for health hazards. She knew, for example, that the hormone treatments might lead to the development of acne and that the hair on the top of her head might begin to thin out. Although she felt strongly about her masculine gender identity, she was willing to consider the possibility that she needed psychological treatment rather than the sex-change procedure.

Chris's exceptional social adjustment was an important consideration in the evaluation of her condition. She was clearly functioning at a high level; her grades were good, and she had lots of friends—many of whom knew her only as a man—and she was satisfied with her current sexual relationship, which was based on her masculine identity. Even if procedures were available to alter her gender identity and convince Chris to act and feel like a woman, it did not seem likely that she could be any better adjusted. And, in all probability, she would have been miserable. Therefore, the psychologist decided that she would not try to persuade her that her problem regarding gender identity was the manifestation of more deeply ingrained psychopathology. She played a supportive role as Chris made her own decision about the pending medical procedures.

Fifteen-Year Follow-Up

In the following pages, we describe many important experiences that Chris has had since this case was originally written. Chris is now living as a man. This successful transition leads us to use the masculine pronoun, "he," when referring to Chris in this update.

Chris attended psychotherapy on a regular basis for approximately 2 years. As Chris had hoped, the psychologist referred him to an endocrinologist (a physician who specializes in disorders of the hormonal system) after the first year of psychotherapy. The doctor asked Chris to complete a battery of psychological tests and a psychiatric evaluation prior to beginning hormone therapy. The doctor wanted this information so that he could be certain that transsexualism was the correct diagnosis.

The psychological test profile and psychiatrist's report indicated that Chris was an intelligent person who was able to evaluate the external world objectively. There was no evidence of psychotic thinking. The endocrinologist therefore granted Chris's request for hormone therapy. Chris was 22 years old and in his first year of graduate school. He can recall with vivid detail the first injection of a synthetic male hormone he received at the medical center. The prescription was depo-testosterone 300 mg (1-1/2 cc) every 3 weeks. He looked at his face in the mirror and wondered how he might change physically and emotionally. Would he be satisfied with the results? What if he didn't feel "like himself"?

The first major physical change came 2 months later with the cessation of the menstrual period. There would be no more obvious monthly reminders that he was physically female. The other changes were more gradual. His voice deepened and cracked just like the voices of pubescent boys. His fat distribution changed, especially around the hips and thighs. He became more muscular and his breast tissue shrank so he no longer had to wear the Ace bandage to conceal his breasts. It would take at least 5 years for the torso bruising (from the bandaging) to disappear completely. Chris grew more hair on his arms, legs, stomach, and chest. The hair on his face took longer to grow. In the beginning, he shaved every 4 to 5 days. He now shaves every other day and sports a handsome mustache and goatee.

Chris had not anticipated a change in his feelings about sex. He had always seemed to have a normal sex drive. Nevertheless, his sex drive skyrocketed during the first 2 years of hormone therapy. He felt as though he was experiencing puberty all over again. His "first puberty" was spent daydreaming of kissing girls and holding hands. Now he could understand the urges adolescent boys feel for sex. It was often difficult to think of anything other than sex and how to get it. Fortunately, his age and maturity afforded him some control over such impulses. Chris developed sexual relationships with three women during graduate school. He noticed his orgasms were more intense. He was becoming much more comfortable with his own body and could even enjoy masturbating.

Chris could no longer hide the physical changes from his family. People were asking questions about his voice, and the hair on his legs was quite noticeable. Chris enlisted the help of his father and stepmother, who agreed to explain his transsexualism to most of his relatives. But he wanted personally to discuss the situation with his brother and sisters. To Chris's surprise and great relief, not one family member rejected or ridiculed him. Some did not understand his psychosexual disorder, but all professed their love as well as admiration for his courage in pursuing his dream. He had always enjoyed a great deal of support from his friends. Now, with his family's blessing, he no longer had to pretend to be a woman in any aspect of his life. He would now be known as a man.

Chris received a master's degree and landed his first professional job in the crisis department of a major metropolitan hospital. He was initially anxious about being discovered as a transsexual because he was living near the area where he grew up. Fortunately, this never happened. Over the next 2 years, he grew to trust several colleagues and eventually told them his story. His colleagues readily accepted his situation.

Many transsexuals resort to creative means to pass for the gender they want to be. Chris frequently had to think fast on his feet to escape awkward situations. He demonstrated considerable ingenuity when he decided it was time to have the gender changed on his driver's license. This is normally a formal process that requires a court order and official documents, which he did not possess. He devised another approach. He began by renewing his current license, allowing his old information to be transferred to the new one. His gender was listed as "F" for female. A few days later, he returned to the same license branch and nonchalantly explained that someone must have made an honest error in recording his gender. He noted that it was a common mistake. Sometimes people would just look at the name "Chris," assume the person was female, and record it as such. The clerk apologized profusely and immediately issued a new license. He said it was obvious "just by looking" that Chris was male.

Chris was functioning as a male at work and with his friends. At 25 years of age, it was time to consider officially changing his name and gender. Chris hired an attorney to help guide him through the legal system. Chris asked his psychologist, physician, employer, and friends to write letters of endorsement to the court attesting to his stature as an upstanding citizen in the community who was living and functioning as a man. Several months later, after a 5-minute hearing, the judge lowered his gavel and declared Christine to be now Christopher and legally male. This was done without any surgeries to remove organs (uterus, ovaries, breasts) or to add them (creation of a penis and scrotum).

To date, Chris has opted to forgo surgical interventions. He accepts his body, even though he is not entirely satisfied with it. He wishes that he had been born with a penis, but he does not need one to live, function, and be accepted as male. He will need medication for the rest of his life, although he now requires less testosterone to maintain his outward appearance. He does acknowledge some concern about the medication because the long-term effects of hormone use for female-to-male transsexuals have not been studied extensively. If Chris were to stop the injections for several months, the menstrual cycle would resume, body fat would redistribute, and his facial hair would be lost. His voice would retain its low pitch. Once the vocal cords thicken as the result of male hormones, they will remain so unless surgically altered. Chris has no plans to stop the medication.

Important developments have also taken place in Chris's social life. He had always loved Jennifer, his high school sweetheart, despite his involvement in other romantic relationships. Jennifer was married, but Chris never lost hope of renewing his relationship with her. As luck would have it, they became reacquainted while working on their high school 5-year reunion committee. Their friendship picked up where it left off. Jennifer confided to Chris that she was unhappy in her marriage and was contemplating divorce. Chris hoped that their renewed friendship would evolve into something more intimate, but he did not want to be the cause of Jennifer's divorce. Jennifer believed that she would have been divorced eventually regardless of her relationship with Chris.

Jennifer was introduced to Chris's circle of friends and was invited to their social events. Jennifer began to spend occasional nights at Chris's apartment, although they slept separately. After a few months, their relationship became sexual. Sex was now more satisfying to them than it had been before, perhaps because Chris was more comfortable with his own body. Despite the excitement and happiness that they found in their new romance, Chris and Jennifer felt uneasy having an illicit affair. One year after they became reacquainted, Jennifer filed for divorce and moved into an apartment near Chris. Soon, they moved in together. Chris's dream of marrying his high school sweetheart was going to come true. They had been living together for 4 years when he proposed to Jennifer.

Now they had lots of planning to do. Could they apply for a marriage license? Who would marry them? Would they need to disclose the fact that Chris was transsexual? They struggled with these and many other issues. Their relationship had faced many obstacles over the years, but could it survive planning a wedding? They were confronted with even more stressful situations during that year. Jennifer graduated from nursing school and took her licensing board examination. Some of Chris's extended family members refused to attend the wedding because of their religious beliefs. Despite these hurdles, they obtained a wedding license, found a judge, and had a beautiful ceremony.

Chris's life was normal in most ways. He and Jennifer both had successful careers. They bought a house. However, Jennifer felt something was missing. She wanted children. Despite a few reservations about parenthood, they forged ahead with the process of artificial insemination. They chose an anonymous donor who matched Chris's physical characteristics and personality type. Two years later, Jennifer was pregnant . . . with twins!

Chris and Jennifer faced some unique circumstances, above and beyond all the normal anxieties that come with first-time parenthood. Preparing for the births of their son and daughter made them wonder how they would handle Chris's transsexuality. How would they deal with their own nudity? How would they respond to the children's normal curiosity about sex? As it turned out, the most pressing issues during the first year of parenthood were finding time for sleep and keeping enough diapers on hand.

It would have been impractical to expect that the children would never see Chris's body, though he tried his best to be discreet. Jennifer and Chris decided to respond to the children's questions about sexuality with honest, age-appropriate explanations. They learned quickly that all their rehearsed responses could be easily thwarted by their children's brutal honesty. For example, Chris recalled a dinner table conversation in which his 3-year-old son announced that "when I grow up, I want to be a man without a penis, like Daddy." Perhaps the most interesting implication of this bold declaration is the fact that Chris's son viewed him as a man, despite his physical anatomy. In fact, neither child ever confused Chris with a woman. Their daughter sometimes announced proudly to her brother, "Mommy and I are girls, and you and Daddy are boys." To date, Chris only once has explained his genitalia to the children. He said, "Daddy's penis didn't get made all the way. But your penis and vagina were made just fine." Chris knows that the issue will come up again; simple explanations will not always be sufficient.

Chris's transsexuality is with him every day, but it is no longer the focal point in his life. The issues arise infrequently now. Although the old anxieties of rejection and ridicule can still be evoked from time to time, he accepts himself and lives a full and happy life. Chris does not think of his transsexualism as a disorder from which he can be cured. He views it as a condition that he has learned to integrate and manage.

Discussion

Because the discussion of this case involves a number of subtle and frequently controversial issues, it may be helpful to begin with the definition of some elementary terms. *Gender identity* involves a person's belief or conviction that he or she is a male or a female. The public expression of this belief involves role-specific behaviors associated with masculinity and femininity. *Sexual orientation*, on the other hand, represents the person's preference for male or female sexual partners. In the infinite variety of human behavior, there can be endless combinations of gender identity, gender-role behaviors, and sexual orientations (Clemans, DeRose, Graber, & Brooks-Gunn, 2010; Kessler & McKenna, 2000).

People with gender identity disorders vary considerably with regard to the severity and persistence of their problems. Relatively few children who exhibit gender identity problems continue to experience similar problems as adults (Zucker, 2005). In the *Diagnostic and Statistical Manual of Mental Disorders* (*DSM-IV-TR*; APA, 2000), the term *transsexualism* is used to describe severe gender identity disorder in adults.

Why is gender identity disorder a controversial topic? Perhaps because it raises such difficult questions about the way in which we view ourselves and our world. Perhaps because the attitudes of many transsexuals, as well as the surgical procedures that have been used to help them attain their goals, are inconsistent with popularly held notions about men and women (Lev, 2005). The following discussion focuses on clinical and scientific issues involved in the study of transsexualism rather than its political and social implications.

In *DSM-IV-TR* (APA, 2000), gender identity disorder is listed in a general section with sexual dysfunctions and paraphilias. There is, of course, an important difference between gender identity disorders and sexual disorders. The latter are defined primarily in terms of problems that interfere with the capacity for reciprocal, affectionate sexual activity. Chris's situation illustrates why gender identity disorders are not considered sexual disorders. Although she was uncomfortable with her anatomic sex and wanted to live as a man, she was sexually functional and actively involved in a mutually satisfying relationship.

The *DSM-IV-TR* (APA, 2000, pp. 581–582) description of gender identity disorder can apply to children, adolescents, or adults. In fact, most transsexuals report that their discomfort with their anatomic sex began during childhood. The disorder is defined by the following criteria:

1. A strong and persistent cross-gender identification (not merely a desire for any perceived cultural advantages of being the other sex).
   In children, the disturbance is manifested by four (or more) of the following:
   a. Repeatedly stated desire to be, or insistence that he or she is, the other sex

    b.   In boys, preference for cross-dressing or simulating female attire; in girls, insistence on wearing only stereotypical masculine clothing

    c.   Strong and persistent preferences for cross-sex roles in make-believe play or persistent fantasies of being the other sex

    d.   Intense desire to participate in the stereotypical games and pastimes of the other sex

    e.   Strong preference for playmates of the other sex

    In adolescents and adults, the disturbance is manifested by symptoms such as a stated desire to be the other sex, frequent passing as the other sex, desire to live or be treated as the other sex, or the conviction that he or she has the typical feelings and reactions of the other sex.

2. Persistent discomfort with his or her sex or sense of inappropriateness in the gender role of that sex.

3. The disturbance is not concurrent with a physical intersex condition.

4. The disturbance causes clinically significant distress or impairment in social, occupational, or other important areas of functioning.

Because discomfort with one's anatomic sex and the desire to be rid of one's own genitals form a central part of this definition, it is important to point out that transsexuals are not the only people who seek sex-reassignment surgery. People who seek sex-change surgery occasionally include self-stigmatized homosexuals who believe that they should be punished, schizoid and psychotic individuals, and sadomasochists who derive sexual pleasure from inflicting and experiencing physical pain (Sohn & Bosinski, 2007).

Disturbances in gender identity should also be distinguished from two related but generally distinct conditions. First, it would be misleading to say that transsexuals are, by definition, delusional. There are, of course, some transsexuals who are psychotic, but the vast majority are not. They acknowledge the inconsistency between their anatomy and their gender identity. A delusional man might argue, for example, that he is a woman; a transsexual would be more likely to say, "I am not a woman *anatomically*, but I am a woman in almost every other way." Furthermore, unlike delusional patients, whose beliefs are completely idiosyncratic, transsexuals are frequently able to convince other people that they are right. In Chris's case, for example, Jennifer and Lynn concurred with the belief that Chris was more like a man than a woman.

Second, there is an important difference between transsexualism and transvestic fetishism, but the two conditions are not mutually exclusive (Zucker & Bradley, 2000). Transvestic fetishism is a disorder in which heterosexual (or bisexual) men dress in women's clothing for the purpose of sexual excitement. The gender identity of transvestic fetishists is typically not inconsistent with their anatomic sex, and many transsexuals do not become sexually excited by cross-dressing. Nevertheless, a substantial proportion of male-to-female transsexuals do become sexually aroused at least occasionally when they dress in women's clothing (Blanchard & Clemmensen, 1988), and some transvestic fetishists do seek sex-reassignment surgery. According to the *DSM-IV-TR* (APA, 2000), males who meet the criteria for both gender identity disorder and transvestic fetishism should be assigned both diagnoses.

Precise epidemiological data regarding transsexualism are difficult to obtain. Estimates of the prevalence of the disorder are based on the number of people who apply for treatment rather than comprehensive surveys of the general population. We do know that transsexualism is a relatively infrequent problem and that it may be more common among men than women. Early studies reported a male-to-female ratio of approximately 3:1, but the proportion of females may be increasing. One study computed prevalence based on the number of patients who sought sex-reassignment surgery in Belgium. The investigators reported a prevalence of 1 transsexual in every 12,900 males and 1 in 33,800 females (De Cuypere et al., 2007). Data from other studies suggest that, when narrow diagnostic criteria are employed, the incidence of new cases may be roughly equivalent in men and women (Zucker & Lawrence, 2009).

Some fairly consistent differences exist between male and female transsexuals in terms of psychological characteristics. For example, female transsexuals tend to report better relationships with their parents, more stable relationships with sexual partners, and greater satisfaction with their sexual experiences prior to treatment (e.g., Lewins, 2002).

Many male transsexuals, perhaps as many as half of those seeking treatment, experience additional psychological problems. The most common symptoms are depression, anxiety, and social alienation (Bower, 2001; Campo, Nijman, Merckelbach, & Evers, 2003). Some exhibit severe personality disorders, but very few are considered psychotic. The level of psychopathology observed in female transsexuals, on the other hand, does not seem to be different from that seen in the general population. Chris may therefore be similar to other female transsexuals. Aside from the issue of gender identity, he was well-adjusted in terms of his mood as well as his social and occupational functioning.

The relationship between transsexualism and homosexuality has been the source of some controversy (Chivers & Bailey, 2000). Some people have argued that transsexuals are simply homosexuals who use their cross-gender identity as a convenient way of escaping cultural and moral sanctions against engaging in sexual behavior with members of their own sex. There are a number of problems with this hypothesis. First, unlike transsexuals, homosexual men and women are not uncomfortable with their own gender identities. Lesbians, for example, are typically proud of their status as women and would be horrified at the suggestion that they want to be men. Second, many transsexuals, like Chris, are not obviously uncomfortable with homosexuals. The suggestion that transsexuals are denying their homosexual inclinations is sometimes supported by the observation that some transsexuals go out of their way to avoid any contact or association with homosexual men or women. However, some of Chris's friends were homosexual men and women. One of his previous lovers, Lynn, was bisexual and had been living with another woman when they met.

Etiological Considerations

It is not clear why some people develop gender identity disorders. In fact, the process by which anyone develops a sense of masculine or feminine identity is a matter of considerable interest and dispute (Gangestad, Bailey, & Martin, 2000; Herman-Jeglinska, Grabowska, & Dulko, 2002). As in other areas of human behavior, alternative explanations invoke the ubiquitous nature/nurture controversy. Is gender identity determined genetically prior to the infant's birth, or is it largely determined by biological or social factors that the individual encounters in his or her environment? Explanations for the development of transsexualism have taken both sides of this argument.

Some investigators and clinicians have emphasized the importance of the parents and family in the etiology of the disorder. Stoller (1985), for example, placed principal emphasis in male transsexualism on the absence (either physical or psychological) of the father and the presence of a close-binding, dominant mother. A different family pattern was identified in cases of female transsexualism. In these families, according to Stoller, the mothers are prone to depression. Rather than providing support and care for their spouses, the fathers are presumably aloof and uninvolved. Thus, the daughter is forced to fill the supportive, masculine role vacated by her father. Other masculine behaviors are also reinforced by the father, but femininity is discouraged.

Chris's experience was not consistent with Stoller's hypothesis. His mother was not depressed while Chris was a child, and he was not expected to take the place of his father. Chris's parents were not close to each other, but they did not involve the children in their disagreements. His masculine gender identity was clearly fixed several years before his parents' conflict became known to the children. Although he did not spend a great deal of time with his mother, they did have a good relationship; they spoke to each other openly—including several talks about the fact that Chris felt more like a boy than a girl—and cared very much for each other.

Green (1987) proposed a multifaceted model for the development of feminine behavior in boys and masculine behavior in girls. His view places considerable emphasis on learning principles such as modeling and social reinforcement. According to Green, gender identity disturbances are likely to develop when the parent of the opposite sex is dominant and provides the most salient model for the child's social behavior. The same-sexed parent is presumably retiring or unavailable. When the child begins to imitate cross-role behaviors, rather than objecting, the parents provide attention and praise. Peer relations also play a role in Green's model; feminine boys prefer and spend more time with girls while masculine girls spend more time with boys. This combination of parental and peer support enhances the process of identification with the opposite sex. Eventually, this process of socialization becomes an obstacle to any attempt to change the pattern and integrate the child with members of his or her own sex.

In Chris's case, his father certainly provided reinforcement for playing masculine games. Chris spent a great deal of time in rough, competitive play with boys. His father also discouraged open displays of emotion, such as crying. It is difficult to say, however, that the social reinforcement he provided was definitely responsible for Chris's gender identity disorder, particularly because so many other girls are treated in similar ways without becoming transsexual.

Relatively little empirical evidence is available regarding the influence of environmental events in the development of transsexualism. A few research studies have compared people with gender identity disorders and control subjects in terms of their recollections of their parents' behavior. One study found that male-to-female transsexuals remembered their fathers as having been less warm and more rejecting in comparison to the way in which control subjects remembered their fathers (Cohen-Kettenis, & Arrindell, 1990). It is important to note, however, that these data were collected after the people with gender identity disorder were adults and had sought treatment for their condition. It is not clear that the styles of interaction that were reported by these people preceded or contributed to the original development of their problems in gender identity. Interactions between the parents and their transsexual sons and daughters may have been determined, at least in part, by a reaction to the gender identity problems of the children. Prospective data, collected prior to the onset of gender identity problems, have not been reported on this issue. Analyses based on comparisons of concordance rates in monozygotic (MZ) and dizygotic (DZ) twin pairs suggest that genetic factors make a larger contribution than environmental factors in the development of gender identity disorder (Coolidge, Thede, & Young, 2002).

Case studies provide the basis for much speculation regarding the possible influence of environmental and biological factors in the etiology of transsexualism. For example, Segal (2006) described two pairs of female MZ twins who were discordant for gender identity disorder. The author noted that in each pair, differences in the twin's gender identity emerged at a young age. Unusual life experiences did not seem to play a causal role in this process. The fact that these genetically identical individuals were discordant for the condition indicates that genetic factors do not account for all the variance in its etiology. That is, of course, not a particularly surprising result because concordance rates in MZ twins do not approach 100% for any form of mental disorder.

Biologically minded investigators (e.g., Diamond, 2009; Hines, 2004) have argued that gender identity may be shaped very early, during the development of the human embryo, by exposure to male hormones. This possibility suggests that Chris's masculine gender identity is, at least in part, the product of a fundamental, biological process. Viewed from a subtle neurological perspective, and regardless of the shape of his external sexual characteristics, this argument would hold that Chris's brain is essentially masculine. Unfortunately, although there is considerable reason to believe that reliable group differences exist between men and women in terms of brain structure and function, there are no valid tests that would be useful in this regard at an individual level. The issue is, therefore, unresolved.

Treatment

There are two obvious solutions to problems that involve gender identity conflict: Change the person's gender identity to match his or her anatomy, or change the anatomy to match the person's gender identity. Various forms of psychotherapy have been used in an attempt to alter the gender identity of transsexual patients, but the success of these interventions has been limited.

As an alternative to trying to change the transsexual's gender identity, some physicians have used surgical procedures to transform transsexuals' bodies so that they will match their gender identities. Surgical procedures can be used to alter and construct both male and female genitalia. Some of these methods were initially developed for the treatment of problems such as traumatic loss or congenital abnormalities. An artificial penis can be constructed from abdominal tissue that is transplanted and formed into a tube. The goals of such surgery may include cosmetic considerations (i.e., the construction of an organ that resembles a penis) as well as physiological criteria (e.g., passing urine in a standing position, accomplishing intercourse, and sensing stimulation). Although it is not possible to construct a completely functional penis that will become erect in response to sexual stimulation, erection can be achieved through the use of removable implants made of bone, cartilage, or silicone. In the case of female-to-male transsexuals, the labia are fused, but the clitoris is left intact and remains the primary receptor for sexual stimulation. Prostheses can be inserted to resemble testicles in a scrotum.

Surgical procedures for transsexuals can become complex and involve several areas of the body in addition to the genitals. Surgery for male-to-female transsexuals may include breast augmentation as well as changing the size of the nose and shaving the larynx. Surgery for female-to-male transsexuals can involve a series of steps, including removal of the ovaries, fallopian tubes, uterus, and breast tissue.

Clinical impressions regarding the success of these procedures have been positive. Case studies suggest that most patients are pleased with the results of the surgery and relieved finally to have the body they desire. Many are able to adjust to life as a member of the opposite sex, and some report adequate sexual functioning and marriage (Smith, van Goozen, Kuiper, & Cohen-Kettenis, 2005). Almost no one reports postsurgical grief over the loss of his sexual organ, although isolated cases have occurred. The most frequent complaints center on requests for further medical and surgical procedures. In the case of male-to-female transsexuals, these requests include improvements in genital appearance and functioning, increased breast size, and inhibition of beard growth.

Although these results seem encouraging, some limitations are associated with the data used to evaluate the outcome of sex-reassignment surgery. Postsurgical adjustment is often assessed in terms of the surgeon's global, subjective impression of the patient's adjustment rather than specific measures of occupational and social functioning made by people who do not know that the patient had received surgery. Appropriate control groups are seldom employed, and follow-up periods are often rather short. Some reports provide a more pessimistic picture of surgical outcome (Lindemam, Korlin, & Uddenberg, 1986; Meyer & Reter, 1979).

Surgery and psychotherapy are not the only options available to people with gender identity disorders. Chris was already well adjusted in his personal and professional roles without surgery. It seems unlikely that the surgical alteration of his body would lead to an even better adjustment. Like Chris, many transsexuals forgo surgery but still cross-dress and live full time as a member of the opposite gender with the help of hormone therapy. This alternative has become a more reasonable and appealing option as the law and popular opinion have become somewhat more tolerant of people with gender identity disorders (Green, 1994; Michel, Ansseau, Legras, Pitchot, & Mormont, 2002). People who are considering treatment for gender identity disorders and the mental-health professionals who want to help them should consider carefully the many thoughtful recommendations that are included in a set of standards of care for gender identity disorders, written by an international committee of experts on these problems (Levine, 1999).

Discussion Questions

1. What are the most important considerations in determining whether a person is a man or a woman? Are there things that matter *other than* genital characteristics?
2. Jennifer believed that her relationship with Chris was heterosexual in nature. On what basis was that argument made?
3. Chris decided against having sex-reassignment surgery. What would be the potential advantages and disadvantages of making that change? What do you think you would do if you were in the same situation?
4. How would you react if a member of your own family experienced gender identity disorder? Imagine that a sister or a brother told you that they were trapped in the wrong body. What would you advise your sibling to do?

CHAPTER 15

Eating Disorder: Anorexia Nervosa

Joan was a 38-year-old woman with a good job and family life. She lived with her second husband, Mitch; her 16-year-old son, Charlie, from her first marriage; and her husband's 18-year-old daughter from a previous marriage. Joan was employed as a secretary at a university, and Mitch was a temporary federal employee. Joan was 5'3" and weighed approximately 125 pounds. Although she was concerned about her weight, her current attitudes and behaviors were much more reasonable than they had been a few years earlier, when she had been diagnosed with anorexia nervosa.

Joan had struggled with a serious eating disorder from the ages of 29 to 34. She was eventually hospitalized for 30 days. The treatment she received during that hospital stay had finally helped her overcome her eating problems. Four years later, her condition continued to be much improved.

Social History

Joan was born in a suburb on the outskirts of a large northeastern city. Her one brother was 2 years younger. Her father worked as a supervisor for an aircraft subcontractor. Joan's mother stayed at home while the children were young and then worked part time for a number of years as a waitress and bookkeeper. Both parents were of average weight.

Joan's early childhood was ordinary. She was an above-average student and enjoyed school. She and her brother bickered, but their disagreements did not extend beyond the usual sibling rivalry. Her family lived in a large neighborhood filled with lots of children. Joan was somewhat overweight during elementary school. She had high personal standards and strove to be a perfect child. She always did what was right and conformed completely to the wishes of her parents.

When Joan was 14 and entering the ninth grade, tragedy struck her family and forever changed her home life. She and her 12-year-old brother were home while her parents were at work. Although her brother was too old to require babysitting, she was supposed to keep an eye on him. Joan had a friend over, and the two girls were upstairs in her room. Joan heard some loud noise outside and looked out the window. She saw her brother lying dead in the road. He had been run over by a car. Although the feeling became less intense as years passed, Joan continued to feel guilty about her brother's death well into adulthood.

After the accident, Joan's parents changed. They became extremely overprotective, and Joan felt as if she "had a leash on all of the time." From age 14 on, she no longer had a normal childhood. She could not hang out with friends, be away from the house for long periods of time, or go out in cars. Her parents wanted to know where she was and what she was doing, and they set a strict curfew. Joan knew that if she were late, her parents would worry, so she always tried to be home early. She made a special effort to do exactly as she was told. Joan did not go out much because she felt the need to stay near her parents so that they would know that she was alive and well.

The rest of high school was unremarkable. Joan earned reasonably good grades and got along well with the other students. During the summer after her brother's death, when Joan was 15, she met and began to date a boy who was 2 years older than she. Joan's parents were initially unhappy with this relationship, in part because Randy owned a car, and they didn't want her to ride around with him. Joan had to meet Randy secretly for the first few months. As her parents got to know him better, they grew to like him, and the young couple no longer had to sneak around. During this time, Joan continued to feel guilty when she was in cars because she was reminded of her brother's death. She frequently stayed home because she knew that her parents would suffer horribly if anything happened to her.

After high school, Joan attended a two-year business school and became engaged to Randy. The couple was married after Joan graduated. She was 19 years old as she began her marriage and her first full-time job as a secretary in a medical office. Prior to this time, Joan's father had never allowed her to hold even a part-time job. He insisted on providing for all of her needs.

Although this marriage lasted legally for 6 years, it became clear within 9 months that the relationship was in trouble. Joan cared for her husband, but she did not love him. She soon realized that she had used Randy as an escape route from her parents' home. She felt as if she had simply jumped from one dependent relationship into another. When she had been at home, her parents provided everything. Now Randy was taking care of her. Joan worried that she did not know how to take care of herself. Despite these negative feelings, Joan and Randy tried to make the marriage work. They bought a home 1 year after their wedding. Two years later, Joan accidentally became pregnant.

Joan gained 80 pounds during the course of her pregnancy. When Charlie was born, she weighed 200 pounds. Over the next few months, Joan found it difficult to lose weight but eventually got down to 140 pounds. Although it was hard for her to adjust to this weight gain, she did not try to change her weight because it felt "safe" to her. Joan and Randy were legally separated 2 years after Charlie was born. They continued to see each other occasionally and sought marital counseling at various times during the next couple of years. They could not reconcile their differences, however, and Randy eventually moved to another state. The divorce was finalized when Joan was 25 years old.

Shortly after she and Randy were separated, Joan stopped working and went on welfare. With financial help from her father, she managed to keep up the mortgage payments on her house for several months. She and Charlie continued to live on their own, but Joan fell further into debt while she and Randy tried to work things out. She was forced to sell her home when the divorce became final. Although she came to regret the decision, she moved back into her parents' home. Living there was stressful for Joan. Although she was 25 years old, she felt like a child. Her parents once again took care of Joan, and now they also provided for her son. In this submissive role, Joan started to feel more like Charlie's older sister than his mother.

Joan lost some weight after she and Charlie were involved in a serious car accident, 6 months after moving back to live with her parents. Charlie was not hurt, but Joan's left hip and leg were broken. She spent a month in the hospital. She was immobile when she came home, and her mother had to take even greater care of her and Charlie. Joan needed repeated surgery on her knee, as well as extensive physical therapy, and she had to relearn how to walk. During her recovery, she had little appetite, was nauseated, and did not eat much, but she was not consciously dieting. Joan's weight went down to about 110 pounds, which she considered to be a reasonable weight.

While she was recovering from her injuries, Joan became involved with a man named Jack, whom she met in one of the hospital's rehabilitation programs. She was now 27 years old. To escape her parents' overly protective home, she decided to take Charlie and move in with Jack. This move actually created more problems than it solved, in large part because Jack had a serious problem with alcohol. Joan had never been a heavy drinker. In the beginning of their relationship, she drank only during the weekend. After she started living with Jack, drinking became a daily activity. Much of their relationship and socializing revolved around alcohol. On the average weekday, Joan consumed a couple of beers and some wine, or perhaps a glass or two of bourbon. On weekends, she drank considerably more. Charlie was increasingly left at day-care centers and with babysitters. Joan eventually recognized the destructive nature of this relationship and ended it after a few months. She reluctantly moved back into her parents' home. After leaving Jack, Joan stopped drinking, except occasionally when she was out socializing.

Onset of the Eating Disorder

After breaking up with Jack, Joan lived with her parents for 2 more years. When she was 29 years old, almost 3 years after her accident, Joan returned to the hospital for more surgery on her leg. After being discharged, she began the diet that set the stage for 5 years of serious eating problems and nearly destroyed her life. Joan had gained a few pounds while she was drinking heavily and now weighed 125 pounds. She was concerned that she would start to gain more weight while she was inactive, recovering from surgery.

Joan's diet was strict from the beginning: She measured and weighed all her food. Within a year, she weighed less than 100 pounds. Her food intake was severely restricted. During the day, she consumed only coffee with skim milk and an artificial sweetener. Occasionally, she ate a piece of fruit or a bran muffin. When she and Charlie ate dinner with her parents, Joan took a normal amount of food on her plate but played with it rather than eating it. After dinner, she usually excused herself to go to the bathroom where she took laxatives in an effort to get rid of what little food she had eaten. Joan hardly ate any meats, breads, or starches. She preferred fruits and vegetables because they consist mainly of water and fiber. Although she did not allow herself to eat, Joan still felt hungry; in fact, she was starving most of the time. She thought about food constantly, spent all her time reading recipe and health books, and cooked elaborate meals for the family.

Although she weighed less than 100 pounds, Joan still felt overweight and believed that she would look better if she lost more weight. She had an overwhelming fear of getting fat because she believed that gaining weight would mean that she was not perfect. She tried to be a model young adult and struggled to be what she imagined everybody else wanted. She gave little thought to what she would want for herself. She felt like everything in her life was out of her control except for her weight and body. The demonstration of strict self-control over eating was a source of pride and accomplishment to Joan.

As she lost weight, Joan experienced several of the physical effects that accompany starvation. Her periods stopped; she had problems with her liver; her skin became dry and lost its elasticity; her hair was no longer healthy; and she would often get dizzy when she stood up. At this time, Joan was working as a secretary in a university medical school. Some of her coworkers noticed the drastic change in her appearance and became concerned. An internist in her department recognized her symptoms as those of anorexia nervosa and tried to get Joan to seek help. Joan agreed to attend an eating disorders support group and even went to some outpatient therapy sessions, mostly in an attempt to appease her friends. She also consulted a dietician at the university hospital and worked on an eating plan. There were moments when Joan considered the possibility that her behavior was not normal, but most of the time, she viewed her ability to control her weight and appetite as a sign of strength. When she was transferred to a different department within the university, she left therapy and returned to her restrictive dieting.

Joan's parents were also acutely aware of their daughter's abnormal patterns of eating and her excessive weight loss. They were extremely worried about her health. The more they tried to talk to her about this issue, the more resistant she became to their pleadings. Arguments about eating became frequent, and the level of tension in the home escalated dramatically.

A year and a half after the onset of her eating disorder, Joan moved with Charlie into her own apartment. Her decision was prompted in large part by the aversive nature of her interactions with her parents. She continued to diet and now weighed about 90 pounds. Charlie's diet had also become restricted, in part because there was very little food in the house. Joan could hardly bring herself to go to the grocery store. Once there, she made an effort to behave normally and went through the store putting food into her shopping cart. When it came time to pay, however, she would not actually buy anything. She believed that food was bad and that it was a waste of money. Instead of purchasing anything, she would wander up and down the aisles, eating much of what was in her shopping cart. Her reasoning was that it made no sense to pay for food that could be eaten while you were in the store.

This type of binge eating also happened whenever she did manage to buy something. In one afternoon, she would occasionally eat two dozen donuts, a five-pound box of candy, and some ice cream. After this, Joan took 20 to 30 laxatives to rid herself of the food. At times she made herself vomit by sticking a toothbrush down her throat, but she preferred to take laxatives. Some weeks she did not binge at all, others once or twice. On the days in between binges, she ate only a little fruit and drank some liquids.

Joan's eating problems persisted for the next 5 years. Her weight fluctuated between 90 and 105 pounds during this period. At times she ate more normally, but then she would eat practically nothing for months. She tried therapy, though she was not seriously or consistently committed to changing her behavior. Her life seemed like a roller coaster, as she cycled back and forth between relatively healthy patterns of eating, severe restricting, and bingeing and purging. Most of her diet consisted of liquids such as diet soda, water, and coffee. Occasionally she drank beer, seeking the numbing effect it had on her appetite. She was pleased with her weight when it was very low, but she felt horrible physically. She was weak most of the time, and other people constantly told her that she was too thin. In Joan's mind, however, she was still too heavy.

When she was 32 years old, almost 3 years after the onset of her eating problems, Joan met Mitch at a church group she was attending. They began to date on a regular basis. Mitch was different from all of the other men in Joan's past. He genuinely cared about her, and he also liked her son. Her weight was at one of its peaks when they met, somewhere between 100 and 105 pounds, so her eating problems were not immediately obvious to him.

Unfortunately, soon after they began dating, Joan once again began to restrict her eating, and her weight quickly dropped to another low point. Mitch noticed the obvious change in her behavior and appearance. His reaction was sympathetic. As their relationship grew stronger, Mitch seemed to help Joan feel differently about herself. They talked frequently about her weight and how little she ate. Mitch expressed great concern about her health, pleading gently with her to gain weight, but her restrictive patterns of eating persisted despite the other psychological benefits that accompanied the development of this relationship. One year after she started dating Mitch, Joan needed major abdominal surgery to remove two cysts from her small intestine. During the operation, the surgeon saw that she had other problems and reconstructed her entire bowel system. When she left the hospital, Joan's weight had fallen to 85 pounds. She ate reasonably well at first, trying to regain her strength. After 2 months, she was feeling better, returned to work, and went back on a restrictive diet. This time, however, Mitch and her friends would not let her continue this prolonged pattern of self-imposed starvation.

Treatment

Mitch and one of Joan's friends from the medical school sought help for her. Realizing that she would never be free of her problems unless she faced them, Joan agreed to contact an eating-disorder specialist. Though it was one of the hardest decisions she ever made, Joan had herself committed to a 30-day stay in a psychiatric ward. She was now 34 years old.

Joan's diet was completely controlled in the hospital. She was started on a 1,500-calorie-per-day diet and was required to eat three meals a day in the presence of a staff member. Privileges such as use of the phone, visitors, and outings were made contingent on eating. Specific goals were set for weight gain, and caloric intake was increased gradually. There were also daily individual therapy sessions in which a staff psychologist explored with Joan how she felt about herself.

At first, hospitalization was difficult for Joan. The amount of food that she was required to eat for breakfast (two pancakes, a bowl of cereal, a glass of milk, one piece of fruit, and a piece of toast) would previously have lasted her for several days. She was initially rebellious, refusing to eat or giving her food away to other patients. She didn't earn any privileges in the first 10 days of her hospital stay. Unaccustomed to eating, she experienced severe constipation, bloating, and indigestion. At times she tried to vomit to get rid of the food, but she was not successful. She eventually accepted the fact that she had no choice and allowed herself to gain 15 pounds. She felt stronger physically but was still troubled. Joan convinced herself that she would lose that weight as soon as she was released from the hospital.

An important turning point in her attitude came during the third week of treatment when Joan received a pass to go home. Outside the hospital, she felt out of control, as if she were too weak to take care of herself. She asked Mitch to take her back to the hospital immediately. Safely back in her hospital room, she cried and felt as though she would never get better. This wrenching experience helped Joan recognize that she would, indeed, need to change her eating behavior as well as her attitudes regarding weight control and physical appearance. Somehow at the end of 30 days, Joan found the strength to leave the hospital. She was frightened at first, but with support from Mitch and her family, she was able to maintain a normal pattern of eating. She remained in therapy for 6 more months and was able to gain another 15 pounds.

While she was in the hospital, Joan learned that her own attitudes about eating and her body were the principal problem, and she had become her own worst enemy. She learned that she could control her weight without becoming extremely restrictive in her eating. She began to feel differently about herself and food. Joan could not pinpoint exactly what had happened, but she had become a different person who was no longer preoccupied with dieting and weight control.

Discussion

Anorexia nervosa and bulimia nervosa (discussed in the next chapter) are the two principal eating disorders described in the *Diagnostic and Statistical Manual of Mental Disorders* (*DSM-IV-TR*; APA, 2000). Anorexia nervosa is a condition characterized by extreme weight loss. Ninety to ninety-five percent of anorexics are female. Lifetime prevalence rates for white women range from 1.4 to 2% (Wade, Bergin, Tiggemann, Bulik, & Fairburn, 2006). Over time, about half of people with anorexia stop having any symptoms, and another 25% are improved. However, the course of the disorder can be chronic, and 5% of patients with anorexia starve to death (Steinhausen, 2002). Deaths also occur from physical complications of the illness and from suicide. Careful medical supervision of weight gain for severely malnourished patients is necessary to prevent refeeding syndrome, another cause of death and other serious complications, caused by too-rapid changes in phosphorus and electrolyte levels when food is reintroduced (Katzman, 2005). Complications such as osteoporosis, anemia, and compromised immune function are common (Misra et al., 2004). The *DSM-IV-TR* (APA, 2000, p. 589) diagnostic criteria are as follows:

1. Refusal to maintain body weight at or above a minimally normal weight for age and height (e.g., weight loss leading to maintenance of body weight less than 85% of that expected; or failure to make expected weight gain during a period of growth, leading to body weight less than 85% of that expected).
2. Intense fear of gaining weight or becoming fat, even though underweight.
3. Disturbance in the way in which one's body weight or shape is experienced, undue influence of body weight or shape on self-evaluation, or denial of the seriousness of the current low body weight.
4. In postmenarcheal females, amenorrhea, that is, the absence of at least three consecutive menstrual cycles.

The *DSM-IV-TR* (APA, 2000) specifies two types of anorexia nervosa. Individuals are considered to be the *restricting type* if during the episode of anorexia nervosa, they do not regularly engage in eating binges or purge themselves of the food they have eaten during a binge (whether through vomiting or laxative misuse). The *binge-eating/purging type*, which is consistent with Joan's behavior, involves the regular occurrence of binge eating or purging behavior during the episode of anorexia. This approach to subclassification of eating disorders recognizes the frequent appearance of overlapping symptoms. Approximately one-half of patients with anorexia also have bulimic symptoms, and roughly one-third of patients with bulimia have a history of anorexia. When patients are followed over a period of several years, many people who originally fit the description for restricting type have changed over to the binge-eating/purging type (Eddy et al., 2002). About half of those with an eating disorder do not clearly fit into one or the other category, and are given a diagnosis of eating disorder, not otherwise specified (Thomas, Vartanian, & Brownell, 2009), leading some to recommend the relaxing of diagnostic criteria to include those who do not have the symptoms of amenorrhea or fear of fat.

Research has revealed some important differences between the two subtypes of anorexia nervosa. Anorexics who also binge and purge tend to have weighed more before their illness, are more sexually experienced, are more outgoing, tend to have less impulse control, are more likely to abuse drugs or steal, and have more variable moods than restrictors (Casper & Troiani, 2001). The presence of bingeing and purging is also thought to be a sign of greater psychological disturbance and an indication of a poorer prognosis (Van der Ham, 1997).

Anorexia nervosa is often comorbid with several other disorders, including substance abuse, obsessive-compulsive disorder (OCD), several personality disorders, and especially with major depression (O'Brien & Vincent, 2003). Relatives of patients with anorexia are more likely to have mood disorders. People with the bingeing-purging subtype of anorexia nervosa are more likely to have personality disorders, especially borderline personality disorder (Jordan et al., 2008). Comorbid disorders may not be as common among anorexics who do not seek treatment, so studies may have overestimated comorbidity because they have often relied on clinical samples (Perkins, Klump, Iacono, & McGue, 2005).

Patients with anorexia are often characterized as being obsessional, conforming, and emotionally reserved. The research evidence supports this impression but also indicates that many different personality styles are found (Thornton & Russell, 1997). Many researchers and clinicians have described perfectionism as common among people with anorexia (Franco-Paredes, Mancilla-Díaz, Vázquez-Arévalo, López-Aguilar, & Álvarez-Rayón, 2005). A frequent feature of anorexia is overactivity. Patients are often restless, fidgety, and engage in excessive exercise (Klein & Walsh, 2004).

Joan met the diagnostic criteria for anorexia nervosa, binge-eating/purging type. She experienced a drastic, self-induced loss of weight; was intensely afraid of becoming fat; could not recognize the true size of her body or the seriousness of her condition; and was no longer menstruating. In addition to her severe restriction of food intake, Joan would also periodically eat large amounts of food and then try to rid herself of the unwanted calories through vomiting and laxatives. She also experienced many of the physical and psychological side effects that accompany starvation, such as constipation, hypotension, skin changes, bloating, abdominal pains, dehydration, and lanugo (downy hair growth).

It is important to recognize that some of the psychological symptoms of anorexia nervosa are produced by the lack of food and are not necessarily inherent aspects of the anorexic's personality. For example, people who are starving become preoccupied with food and eating. Like Joan, they will often cook for others, read recipe books, and may even develop peculiar food rituals. While people with anorexia nervosa may become preoccupied with interacting with food, they lose their motivational orientation toward eating it (Veenstra & de Jong, 2011). This lack of desire to approach and consume food is what enables them to so severely restrict their food intake. Obsessive behaviors, such as hoarding, may also appear. There is often an exaggeration of previous personality traits, such as increased irritability, avoidance and social withdrawal, and a narrowing of interests (Kaye, Strober, & Rhodes, 2002).

Etiological Considerations

Biological factors have been considered in the search for the causes of anorexia nervosa. It seems likely that biological factors—including hormones and neurotransmitters that regulate metabolism and mediate perceptions of satiety—are involved in the etiology of anorexia nervosa. The exact factors and their role in the disorder have not been determined (Ferguson & Pigott, 2000). But there is compelling evidence that genetic factors are implicated in disordered eating. Both evidence from twin studies and an adoption study consistently show moderate rates of heritability for disordered eating, with genetic factors explaining 59 to 82% of the variance (Klump, Suisman, Burt, McGue, & Iacono, 2009). Environmental influences may lead to eating disorders by interacting with the genetic risk. Having a family member with anorexia increases one's risk of having the disorder tenfold; genes regulating the serotonergic systems have been implicated (Treasure, 2007). More work needs to be done to describe how the gene differences translate into the disorder.

Because anorexia nervosa typically begins during adolescence, some theories frame it as maturational problems that are sparked by the physical, emotional, and cognitive changes that occur at this time. Some clinicians view anorexia as the product of resistance to sexual and psychological maturity, or more broadly as trouble with individuation and separation from the family (Shoebridge & Gowers, 2000). Noting differences in interactions in families with an anorexic child, many have speculated that family factors cause the eating disorder, but these characteristics may be a response to having a child with a severe eating disorder rather than a reason for the original onset of the child's disorder. Decades of research have failed to show family factors playing a primary causal role, but these speculations still have influence, prompting the Academy for Eating Disorders to issue a position paper stating that family factors play no or a small causal role (Le Grange, Lock, Loeb, & Nicholls, 2010), and cautioning against blaming the family for the disorder. Joan's case was atypical, in the sense that her eating problems appeared when she was 29 years old. After her brother's death, her parents became overly protective. When she moved home after her divorce, she felt as if she were a child again. Joan's parents conscientiously provided for her needs, but by not allowing her to work, they may have contributed to her feelings of ineffectiveness and inadequacy.

People with anorexia nervosa have often had childhoods characterized by social discomfort, anxiety, and insecure attachments to others (Zucker et al., 2007). As adults, they are more likely to report no significant attachments to others, and as mothers, they are more likely to have difficulty reading the interpersonal cues of their infants. When in treatment, they have more difficulty developing relationships with the treating clinicians. These problems all may stem from a subtype of the disorder that includes deficits in social cognition, which may also lead to risk for suicide, as people with the disorder have a 57-fold increase in suicide rate, which is more common among people who feel isolated. These deficits in social cognition may predispose the person to developing the eating disorder.

Cultural attitudes and standards are also thought to play an important role in the development of anorexia nervosa (Bordo, 1997; Simpson, 2002). Culture has a strong influence on standards for what is considered to be the ideal female shape. In Western society, for example, the feminine ideal has shifted from the buxom figure of the early 1900s, to the thin flapper of the 1920s, to the hourglass shape of the 1950s, and more recently, back to a thin body shape. In this culture, thinness is perceived as the standard of beauty as well as an indicator of success and self-control.

At the same time that contemporary cultural standards have emphasized thinness, women's body weight has been increasing as a result of improved health and nutrition. These circumstances have created a conflict between the ideal shape and many women's actual shape. The conflict often leads to prolonged or obsessive dieting, which can be a prelude to the development of anorexia nervosa (Hsu, 1996). About 12% of adolescent girls have some form of eating pathology (Stice, Marti, Shaw, & Jaconis, 2009). As predicted by this line of reasoning, the prevalence of anorexia nervosa has increased as the thin feminine ideal took hold, and the prevalence of anorexia nervosa is especially high among women who are under intense pressure to be thin, such as dancers and models.

Of course, not all dieting develops into an eating disorder. The evidence specifically linking media exposure to body dissatisfaction is contradictory and at best shows modest effects; there is more evidence that peer pressure impacts body dissatisfaction, perhaps due to female competition for potential mates (Ferguson, Winegard, & Winegard, 2011). It is hypothesized that sociocultural pressures are part of a larger model of development, which includes other predisposing factors such as problems with autonomy, rapid physical change at puberty, premorbid obesity, personality traits, cognitive style, perceptual disturbances, and interpersonal and familial difficulties (Polivy & Herman, 2002).

The role of sexuality in the development of anorexia is not clear (Ghizzani & Montomoli, 2000). Although some experienced clinicians have described the disorder as a retreat from maturity, sexual issues are not necessarily the central problem. Rather, the patient with anorexia may be focused more specifically on achieving control of her body and diet. Attempts to examine a possible causal connection between sexual behavior and eating disorders is also made more complicated by the need to consider additional variables, such as personality traits and negative body image. For some women, sexual abuse is an important factor in the development of an eating disorder. Nevertheless, there does not appear to be a specific relation between eating disorders and exposure to sexual trauma (Wonderlich, Brewerton, Jocic, & Dunsky, 1997). It has been estimated that 30% of women with eating disorders were sexually abused as children, but it seems to be a more important risk factor for bulimia nervosa than for anorexia nervosa (Jacobi, Hayward, de Zwaan, Kraemer, & Agras, 2004). Sexual abuse does not explain the development of most cases of anorexia nervosa, but it is one important risk factor for eating disorders and other forms of psychological disturbance.

The *adapted to flee famine hypothesis* proposes that anorexia nervosa symptoms are an adaptive mechanism that evolved to protect our ancestors from starvation in famine conditions (Guisinger, 2003). This mechanism would occur when body weight became too low (which now would be due to a diet rather than famine) and only among certain individuals with the genes for it, and would then trigger restlessness, energy, and cognitive distortions about the emaciated state of one's body to enable the starving individual to have both the courage and energy to travel to new locations where food might be more plentiful. This hypothesis could explain the persistent denial of the eating disorder that is a common feature of anorexic patients, a phenomenon that can be hard for clinicians to understand and to overcome (Gatward, 2007). More research is needed to evaluate this interesting hypothesis.

Treatment

Treating anorexia nervosa is extremely difficult. Research has not identified one form of treatment that is consistently more effective than others for all ages. Much more research is needed. Various forms of psychotherapy are employed by clinicians, with most using cognitive-behavioral therapy (CBT) or a combination of cognitive-behavioral and psychodynamic techniques (Peterson & Mitchell, 1999). However, none of these treatments has been conclusively shown to be effective in treating anorexia nervosa (Fairburn, 2005). The most effective form of treatment is family therapy for adolescents with a short history of the disorder (Wilson, Grilo, & Vitousek, 2007).

A number of steps are typically followed in the treatment of anorexia nervosa. The first step is often hospitalization. This may be necessary in cases in which weight loss is extreme, suicidal thoughts are present, the patient is still denying her illness, or previous outpatient therapy has been ineffective (Andersen, 1997). Weight restoration is necessary, both to alleviate the symptoms of starvation and to confront the patient with the body size that she fears. Although there is no single best way to restore weight, the key is to elicit as much cooperation as possible and to be sensitive to the patient's concerns. It is important to work with the patient to set a target weight, usually 90% of the average weight for a particular age and height. Behavioral techniques, such as those used with Joan, are often used to facilitate immediate weight gain. Although inpatient hospitalization seems warranted, there is no research evidence to show that it is more effective than outpatient treatment (Fairburn, 2005).

Various medications are used to treat patients with eating disorders, especially antidepressants, because anorexic and bulimic patients are often depressed. However, studies have not shown them to be any more effective than placebo for anorexia nervosa (Wilson et al., 2007).

Dysfunctional attitudes toward food and body shape are addressed in psychotherapy. This aspect of treatment can be especially challenging because patients with anorexia are usually not self-referred, and most are resistant to treatment. Establishing a connection with the patient and building a therapeutic relationship are particularly important in working with severe cases of anorexia nervosa (Strober, 1997). The therapist's goal is to build a trusting relationship within which other interventions can be employed. Cognitive distortions, superstitious thinking, trouble with expressing emotion, body-image misperceptions, self-esteem, and autonomy are some of the issues that need to be addressed (Cooper, Todd, & Wells, 2002).

Joan's treatment followed parts of this approach. During her hospitalization, various behavioral techniques were used to restore her weight to a healthy level. Because Joan was older and living on her own, she was treated individually, rather than in family therapy. Consistent with a cognitive approach, Joan's ways of viewing the world and herself were challenged directly. Cognitive therapy involves several steps: (a) learning to be more aware of thoughts and beliefs; (b) exploring and clarifying the connection between the dysfunctional beliefs and maladaptive behaviors; (c) examining the truth of those beliefs; (d) learning to replace the dysfunctional beliefs with more realistic ones; and (e) eventually changing the underlying assumptions that are creating the dysfunctional beliefs (Kleifield, Wagner, & Halmi, 1996).

The prognosis for patients with anorexia nervosa is mixed. Approximately 50% relapse after hospitalization. Five percent die as a direct result of the biological effects of self-imposed starvation. Those who have a relatively good outcome often continue to have difficulties with attitudes toward weight and eating (Eckert, Halmi, Marchi, Grove, & Crosby, 1995). Some people are able to recover without professional intervention, but usually this involves the support, encouragement, empathy, and practical help of a parent or close friend (Woods, 2004). One long-term follow-up study of women who had recovered from anorexia investigated the subjective experience of this process. The women were interviewed 20 years after the onset of their disorder. They reported that "personality strength," "self-confidence," and "being understood" were the most important factors in their sustained health (Hsu, Crisp, & Callender, 1992). Joan had some of these factors working in her favor. She was fortunate to have Mitch and close friends as sources of support. She may have also had the advantage of psychological maturity because she was already an adult when she developed her eating disorder. Although she was initially resistant to treatment, she decided to admit herself to the hospital and was determined to change her behavior. These factors may have played an important role in her eventual recovery.

Discussion Questions

1. What special challenges does anorexia nervosa pose for family relationships? How does it affect patients in their roles as children, spouses, and parents?
2. What does anorexia nervosa have in common with substance-abuse disorders?
3. A lot of research has focused on the role of the media and standards of beauty and the thin ideal in the etiology of anorexia nervosa. Do you think these factors are improving or worsening? Is there more or less pressure on adolescent girls and young adult women today to be thin? What about pressures for attractiveness on adolescent boys and young men?
4. No treatments have consistently been shown effective with adults with anorexia nervosa. If you were a psychologist treating a college student with the disorder, what treatment approach would you use? Why?

CHAPTER 16

Eating Disorder: Bulimia Nervosa

Tracy was a 22-year-old junior in college when she was referred to the group therapy program for people with eating disorders. She had entered individual psychotherapy at the student health center 3 months earlier, hoping that her therapist could help her deal more successfully with the stress of university life. Their sessions had focused on the development of better study skills and on issues surrounding Tracy's low self-esteem. Although she was very bright and had managed to earn a 3.2 grade point average, Tracy's academic perform- ance was slipping. Planning and organization were not among her strengths. She attended classes only sporadically and regularly found herself staying up all night to finish writing papers or to prepare for tests.

Her depressed mood and pattern of increasing social isolation were also a source of some concern, perhaps more to her therapist than to Tracy. She lived by herself in an apartment near the campus. Relatively few activities gave her any pleasure. She had developed a small circle of both male and female friends during her 2 years at the university. She had gone out with several different men but had not been involved in a serious romantic relationship for almost 3 years. Her feelings about these dating experiences were largely ambivalent. Occasional casual sexual encounters were more a source of puzzlement than pleasure for her. She couldn't understand why these men found her attractive. Further discus- sion of this issue revealed Tracy's pervasive concerns about her appearance and her strong, negative feelings about her body. She told the therapist that she had tried to lose weight for several years. It eventually became apparent that Tracy had a serious eating disorder. After several extended conversations with her ther- apist, she finally agreed to join an eating disorders group while she continued her individual psychotherapy sessions.

During her first meeting with the woman who ran the therapy group, Tracy was obviously self-conscious and embarrassed while describing the nature of her eating problems. She was a reserved, attractive young woman, dressed neatly in casual clothes. Her graceful, athletic build (5'6" tall and 135 pounds) gave the impression of a person who might be more comfortable with her body than she actually was. Her muscular hips and thighs were especially upsetting to her. She thought they were ugly and said that she very much wanted to lose 15 pounds. Tracy reluctantly provided more complete descriptions of her problems with food as the conversation continued. For the past 2 years, she had been going on private eating binges in which she consumed very large quantities of food and then forced herself to throw up. These episodes currently happened three to four times per week. At its worst, this binge/purge cycle had occurred 8 to 10 times per week.

Tracy took four to six diet pills each day in a largely unsuccessful effort to control her appetite. She hoped that the pills would prevent her binge eating, but they did not. She also took laxatives on a regular basis, usually once a day. This practice was based on her erroneous assumption that the laxatives would decrease her body's absorption of food. Taking the laxatives made Tracy feel that she was somehow losing most of the food that she consumed.

Tracy's notion of an appropriate diet bordered on the concept of starvation. She tried not to eat all day long. After skipping breakfast and lunch, she would invariably experience intense hunger pains during the afternoon. Not trusting these signals from her body, she would manage to fight them throughout the rest of the day. Tracy usually returned to her apartment around 7 or 8 o'clock at night after a hectic day of classes, meetings, and work. By that point, she would be starving. That was the point at which her binges were most likely to occur.

A typical binge would begin with a trip to the nearby grocery store. Tracy would buy a whole chicken and take it home to prepare. The process usually began with a glass of wine, which made her feel more relaxed (particularly on an empty stomach). As she sipped her wine, Tracy would bake the chicken and prepare a large batch of stuffing and mashed potatoes—almost like a Thanksgiving dinner. Then she would order two large sausage pizzas to be delivered from a local restaurant. While she was waiting for the chicken to bake and the pizzas to be delivered, she would eat cookies and potato chips while finishing her bottle of wine. Whenever she started to feel full, she would go in the bathroom and make herself throw up. This lengthy process of eating and regurgitation would continue until all the food was consumed.

Tracy felt helpless and out of control during these binges, which often lasted 2 and sometimes as much as 3 hours. After the process started, it seemed to demand completion. Tracy seldom ate sitting at a table. She ate quickly, pacing about her apartment. At times she felt as if she were outside her body, watching the process unfold. She usually took the phone off the hook so that she wouldn't be interrupted by calls from any of the few friends she still had.

After purging, her mood would go from bad to worse. Tracy felt awful about herself, particularly at these moments. Her stomach hurt, but physical pain was not as debilitating as the psychological consequences of the episode. She invariably felt disgusted by her own behavior and deeply ashamed of her

236 Case Studies in Abnormal Psychology

complete inability to control her binge eating. She felt guilty both because she had eaten so much and also because she didn't have the control that others had. Tracy had read extensively about anorexia nervosa and now told her therapist that she envied the control that those women had over their appetites. If only she could do that!

She began to experience several harmful physical effects from the repeated vomiting. Her dentist noticed that the enamel had begun to erode on the inner surface of her front teeth. He had asked Tracy about the pattern at her last checkup. She denied any eating problems, but the concern that she detected in his voice left her feeling even more unsettled about her problem. The skin over the knuckles on her right hand was now scarred; she put those fingers down her throat to stimulate the gag reflex when she wanted to throw up. She knew that her throat was beginning to suffer, as indicated by recurrent hoarseness and sore throats. Perhaps most alarming was the fact that she had begun throwing up blood on occasion, a sign that the walls of her esophagus were tearing.

The wine that Tracy consumed at the outset of her binges was also a source of some considerable concern and reflected a drinking problem that intensified and complicated her eating disorder. Tracy found it annoying that some of her friends had begun to criticize her drinking, but she privately shared the feeling that she ought to cut back. She often drank heavily when she went out socially with other people, and she sometimes engaged in casual sexual relations that contributed to her already ample feelings of guilt, confusion, and lack of control. This aspect of her interpersonal relationships seemed particularly self-destructive.

Social History

Tracy's parents were divorced when she was 2 years old. Their separation was messy and painful for everyone. Her father had been awarded custody of Tracy because of her mother's substance-use problems and because she had abandoned the family to live with her boyfriend. That relationship didn't last much longer than the divorce proceedings, but her mother did eventually remarry and had two additional children, a girl and a boy.

Tracy grew up living with her father, who provided her with a comfortable home. Unfortunately, he was so preoccupied with his job that he spent little time with her. While she was in elementary school, she was supervised by a housekeeper who lived with Tracy and her father. This woman was fond of Tracy but was also rather rigid and aloof. Tracy spent most of her time alone when she returned home after school. She watched TV and played games until her father got home from work at 8 or 9 o'clock. She looked forward to his arrival because that was when he would spend time with her. Unfortunately, he didn't show much interest in her life. They would fix a meal of frozen dinners, snacks, and desserts, and then sit down and watch TV together.

When Tracy was 13 years old, her mother—who was now 36—suddenly reappeared. She and her second family had moved back to the city in which Tracy lived. She wanted to spend time with Tracy and become friends with her. Tracy's father was understandably opposed to this idea, but the original divorce agreement had stipulated that Tracy could see her mother on week-ends. That agreement was still in effect, even though her mother had never before followed through on the plan. In fact, Tracy had always been curious about her mom and was now anxious to meet her. They agreed to meet for lunch on a couple of occasions.

Tracy was initially struck by her mother's stunning appearance. She was beautiful—still very thin and exquisitely dressed. Tracy was charmed by her mother's warm and friendly manner as well as her physical appearance. Her mother was intrigued by Tracy's interests, her accomplishments, and her friends. This concern was a welcome change from the indifference that her father had always shown her. Tracy and her mother began to spend more time together on weekends and holidays. She admired her mother. It was fun to have a mom who would take her out to lunch and dote on her. As they got to know each other better, however, Tracy's mother became more intrusive and critical of Tracy's behavior and appearance. She began to tell Tracy that it wouldn't hurt for her to lose a few pounds. Tracy's younger half-sister was also very thin, like their mother. She and Tracy soon found themselves competing for their mother's attention.

Like most other teenagers, Tracy was self-conscious about her body and the changes that she was going through at this time. Whatever doubts she already had about her own figure and appearance were seriously exacerbated by these competitive interactions with her mother and half-sister. Tracy was built more like her father—muscular and stocky. At her mother's suggestion, Tracy started to experiment with various kinds of diets. Her mother recommended a sequence of diets that had worked for her. Unfortunately, nothing worked for very long when Tracy tried it. If she did manage to lose 10 pounds, she would gain it back within 3 months. Her weight fluctuated for the next few years between 120 and 145 pounds.

Tracy eventually found herself spending time moving back and forth between her mother's and father's homes. Her patterns of eating became even more inconsistent, perhaps largely because there were different ways to eat in these different places. Her dad lived on packaged cereal, snack food, and late, precooked dinners. Her mom's family ate carefully prepared, nutritious meals that emphasized low-fat foods, including lots of fruits and vegetables. The lat-ter pattern was obviously more healthy, but the atmosphere at these meals fre-quently made Tracy uncomfortable. Her half-sister seemed to be able to eat more than Tracy without gaining weight. Her half-sister and stepfather were always given bigger servings than Tracy, as her mother reminded her to watch what she ate. Whenever Tracy expressed an interest in having a light dessert, her mother would smile at her and ask, "Do you really think you should do that?" For obvious reasons, Tracy experienced a lot of negative emotional responses—guilt, shame, and anger—when she ate with her mother's family.

Like many of her peers, Tracy was rebellious as a teenager. Her father was lenient with her as she entered adolescence, allowing her to run with a crowd of wild boys and girls. Her friends were unconventional and viewed themselves as outsiders in their high school. Their group drank alcohol and smoked marijuana regularly, beginning in their early teens. Her father's house was occasionally the site for these gatherings because he was seldom around to supervise. After smoking marijuana, Tracy and her friends would get "the munchies" and consume large quantities of snacks and desserts (such as chips and cookies, which were in abundant supply at her father's house). This pattern of sporadic binge eating subverted more than one of her diet plans. Her weight increased noticeably.

Although some of her friends skipped classes and used drugs at school, Tracy did not. She didn't study very much, but she was smart enough to be a good student. She did feel that she was subjected to unfair criticism and scrutiny from teachers and administrators because of her friends. Her academic talents were underdeveloped as she became more alienated from the school.

Tracy found her first serious boyfriend at age 16. She fell head-over-heels in love with Jerome, who was 21 years old and working as a clerk at the video store where Tracy and her friends rented movies and games. Their relationship quickly became sexual, which was both exciting and anxiety provoking for Tracy, who had not had any previous sexual experience. When Tracy's father found out that she was dating Jerome, he became angry. He told her mother, and soon everyone was embroiled in the conflict over this new romance. Tracy felt increasingly alienated from both of her parents and from her friends, who somewhat paradoxically shared her parents' concern about her choice of boyfriends.

When Tracy was 17 years old, she dropped out of high school in her senior year and moved to southern California to be with Jerome. He had moved there 3 months before she decided to go. Their romance had actually faded in recent months. Her decision to leave was perhaps more motivated by the desire to avoid high school and her family than by her feelings for Jerome. After she arrived in California, Tracy realized that he no longer cared for her. She started to feel depressed when it became apparent that Jerome did not want to spend much time with her. She realized that she now had no family, no friends, and no job. One night, after she had spent an entire day sitting alone in their small apartment, Tracy told Jerome that she felt like she might be better off dead. His only response was to say, "If that's how you feel, go ahead and kill yourself."

Tracy's binge eating and purging evolved gradually while she was living with Jerome in California. As she became more seriously depressed, she often ate snack foods to make herself feel better. Within 2 months, she had gained eight more pounds. Renewed concern about her appearance and guilt about her inability to control her snacking caused a further decline in her mood. In an attempt to lose the new weight, Tracy went back to some of her earlier diets.

Nothing seemed to work. Increased efforts to control what she ate seemed to produce a paradoxical increase in her consumption of food. One day, after eating two large bags of pretzels, Tracy began to feel nauseated. Rather than waiting to find out whether she would vomit spontaneously, she decided to go to the bathroom and stick her fingers down her throat. The process itself was upsetting, but she felt much better after it was over. Then it dawned on her: Maybe self-induced vomiting was a way to avoid gaining weight. It was easy to do. Because she didn't have a job, she was usually alone with plenty of time and privacy. She couldn't control what she ate, but she could be sure that it didn't sit on her stomach. At first, she only threw up once or twice a week. The frequency progressed slowly over the next year.

Three months after she had moved to California, Tracy returned to live with her father. It was difficult to admit that she had made a mistake, but she was shocked by Jerome's lack of concern for her feelings and disgusted by the dismal quality of their relationship. She returned in a better mood than when she left. Her decision to leave Jerome had given her new energy and confidence. She got a part-time job and went back to high school classes at night. She was able to earn her high school equivalency degree and went on to school at a local community college. From there, she transferred to the university.

Unfortunately, Tracy also returned home in the early stages of an expanding eating disorder. She was already starting to experience some physical consequences from throwing up repeatedly. She had severe stomach pains. One of her friends commented on the fact that she frequently had very bad breath. As her secret problem escalated, she became more embarrassed and ashamed.

Although she had managed to pass all her classes since entering the university, Tracy knew that she was falling behind. She was taking courses in the School of Commerce, which was a very demanding curriculum. Pressure from assignments was becoming overwhelming. Her feelings of depression were beginning to return. Tracy's father suggested to her that she might find it useful to see a psychologist at the student health center, in the hope that psychotherapy would help her cope with stress. She was not enthusiastic about going to see a psychologist, and she wasn't willing to acknowledge the severity of her eating problems. When Tracy did finally make an appointment with a psychologist, she said that she wanted to develop her study skills. Her goal was presumably to become a more effective student. She spent several weeks in treatment before she and her therapist eventually recognized the nature of her eating disorder.

Conceptualization and Treatment

Tracy's individual therapist referred her to a group for people suffering from bulimia nervosa. The group was based on a cognitive-behavioral approach to treatment outlined by Fairburn (1995) in his book, *Overcoming Binge Eating*.

The book provides a useful summary of information about the disorder and can also serve as a self-help manual for those people who are able to change without entering professional treatment. This is an important option because the secretive nature of this problem causes many people to be reluctant to seek help. The short-term approach represents a blend of cognitive procedures that were originally used to treat depression and behavioral approaches for the treatment of obesity. The cognitive elements of the program are aimed at factors such as low self-esteem and extreme concern about body size and shape. The behavioral elements are designed to alter maladaptive patterns of eating.

The group included Tracy and four other women who also suffered from bulimia. Led by a clinical psychologist who specialized in the treatment of eating disorders, they met once a week for 10 weeks and followed a prearranged sequence of topics.

Week 1: Self-Monitoring

The psychologist began their first session by acknowledging the difficulty that they all must have had in deciding to participate in this process. Up to this point, the most common reaction that they had all had from friends and family members involved accusations of weakness and provocation of guilt. Most had been asked over and over again, "Why can't you just stop?" as if it were actually that simple. This group would be a place where they could all share their feelings with people who understood clearly why they couldn't stop.

The first step of the program involved self-monitoring. Participants were asked to keep a careful, daily record of everything they ate or drank. The record included information about binge eating and purging. This information would be used as a baseline against which subsequent progress could be measured. The instructions were to keep a careful record but not to change anything about her eating. The psychologist also asked each woman to begin weighing herself once a week (and no more than once a week).

Tracy was more reserved than the other group members during this first session. She had trouble connecting to the other women. The others felt good about being in the group, but Tracy did not. She said that she did want to stop binge eating and purging, but she also insisted that she still needed to lose 5 pounds before she would be happy with her body.

Week 2: Cues and Consequences

During the second session, group members discussed their self-monitoring records from the preceding week. Did they notice any situations or foods that regularly triggered their binges? Most found it relatively easy and helpful to share their experiences with the group. One woman said that, if she ate one french fry, she would say to herself, "Now it's over." Another said that her binges were set off by fights with her boyfriend. Still another said that her first binge of the week happened immediately after she got off the phone with her mother, who said something critical to her about her attempt to change her eating problems (when she really needed reassurance and support).

Unfortunately, Tracy reported that she had experienced trouble with the assignment. She claimed that she was too busy to keep detailed records of her eating. In fact, the biggest problem was that she was not comfortable sharing descriptions of her binges with the group. She had been struck by the intensity of her negative feelings around binge eating. She was also beginning to understand how negatively she thought about herself.

The psychologist also asked the women to generate a list of other activities that could be used to replace binges. They generated many options, including calling friends on the phone, going for a walk, reading a book, and doing a relaxation exercise. Passive activities would clearly be less effective. For example, watching television did not seem like a useful option because many said that they usually ate while watching TV. The therapist explained that by doing something active in response to an urge to binge, the person is also likely to reduce the duration of any strong, negative feelings that are associated.

For the next week, each woman was encouraged to begin replacing binges with a pattern of regular eating throughout each day. This pattern would include breakfast, lunch, and dinner as well as a planned snack within 2 or 3 hours after each meal. The women were urged not to skip any planned meals or snacks, and also not to eat any unplanned foods. This step was discussed at great length because it is the most important element in the treatment program.

Eating on a schedule struck some as being a bad idea. Tracy expressed concern that she should only eat when her body told her that she was hungry. The problem with this argument is that hunger signals are often disrupted in people who have been involved in binge eating and purging. The therapist explained that until they had returned to normal patterns of eating for a substantial period of time, it would be better to eat at prearranged times. They were encouraged to weigh themselves only once each week. And they were asked to take a leap of faith—to let their weight fluctuate to wherever it was supposed to be, given a regular pattern of eating. This could mean that their weight would go up or down a little bit, even in the first week or two.

Week 3: Thoughts, Feelings, and Behaviors

Tracy called the group's leader before this session to say that she would have to miss the meeting because she had a lot of work to do. She apologized and explained that school had been especially stressful this week. In truth, she had not been doing her self-monitoring and had not been able to begin a regular pattern of eating—even at breakfast. She was too embarrassed to tell the other group members that her binge eating and purging had continued unabated. Tracy was not yet committed to the treatment program.

Everyone else spent the session talking about distorted patterns of thinking. Cognitive therapists assume that if a person is extremely upset, she may not be aware that certain thoughts could have produced her negative emotional state. For example, the women were asked to suppose that they had just eaten a piece of cake that was not on their meal plan. What do you think to yourself? Some volunteered that they would say, "Now I just ruined everything. One piece of cake is as good as a binge. I hate myself! I screwed up, and now I should just finish the binge. I'll start being 'good' again tomorrow." The goal of this session was to help them learn to interrupt the chain that leads from distorted, self-deprecating thoughts to negative feelings and then to bingeing and purging behavior.

Week 4: Perfectionism and All-or-Nothing Thinking

At the beginning of the fourth session, the other members of the group asked Tracy about her absence from the previous meeting. She tried to tell them that she was too busy to attend, but they didn't buy her excuse. She finally confided tearfully, and with great difficulty, that she had become increasingly depressed over the past 2 weeks. Frustrated and disappointed with her inability to engage with the program, she wondered openly whether she would ever be able to eat normally. Tracy confessed that she had stopped monitoring completely and had not been able to follow even the simplest elements of regular eating. She was engaging in binge eating and purging at least as often as before she entered the group. Having disclosed these secrets to the rest of the group, Tracy was overwhelmed with feelings of shame and guilt. She got up and quietly walked out of the room, halfway through the session. She went home to her apartment and immediately ordered food to be delivered. While she was waiting for it to arrive, she had a glass of wine and wrote in her previously empty self-monitoring journal about feelings of giving up.

The other members of the group had mixed reactions to Tracy's message and her early departure. They were all sympathetic, but some also expressed disappointment at her lack of commitment to the therapy process. There was also a feeling of failure and rejection associated with their own apparent inability to make Tracy feel that they could help her succeed in the treatment program. These issues were discussed at length before the therapist continued with their planned agenda for the week.

The remaining portion of this session was devoted to a further discussion of personality traits and distorted thinking patterns that are often associated with binge eating. Examples were, "I need to be thin in order to be liked and successful" and "If I eat regular meals, I will turn into a blimp." Another example followed from Tracy's current distress: "If I don't succeed in the first 2 weeks of treatment, it means that I will never be able to change." Group members were asked to discuss a series of questions: Are these thoughts really accurate? Do you have to be perfect in everything that you do? And do you plan to make yourself miserable unless every aspect of your appearance is perfect?

Week 5: Assertive Behavior

To some people's surprise, Tracy appeared on time for the group's next meeting. She was composed and cheerful, in stark contrast to the state in which she had fled their last session. Tracy explained that, 2 days after their last session, she had an experience that promised to change her entire outlook on her eating disorder.

The fateful event took place while she was babysitting for a neighbor's little girl. The next day was the girl's fifth birthday. A party was planned, with 20 of the little girl's best friends scheduled to attend. Her mother had ordered a special birthday cake and left it in the refrigerator. Tracy hadn't eaten all day when she arrived to babysit. She was starving. As soon as she saw the cake, she knew it was going to be a serious problem. The girl talked about the cake all night, telling Tracy how beautiful it was and what a nice party she was going to have the next day. She repeatedly took Tracy to the refrigerator to look at the cake and talk about its decorations. Tracy resisted the temptation to eat a piece of the cake for 2 hours after the little girl went to sleep. Then she completely lost control. Before she realized what she was doing, Tracy had eaten the whole cake. Horrified and ashamed by what she had done, she quickly found herself in the bathroom. She sobbed uncontrollably as she threw up in the toilet. When she finally stood up, she was staring directly at her face in the mirror. Tears were streaming down her face. Tracy told the group that at that moment she finally acknowledged the reality and the severity of her eating problems. Her eating was so far out of control that she could devour a child's birthday cake the day before her party. Tracy knew then that she would have to take responsibility for changing her own feelings and behavior.

Tracy had not binged or purged since that night. She started monitoring what she ate the next morning and had not missed a day. Although she had not previously kept written records, the discussions in weeks 1 and 2 had been enough to help her recognize that, in her own case, she would have to start eating regularly throughout the day if she wanted to control her late-night binges. She forced herself to eat at least a small breakfast on each of the remaining days. She still skipped lunch on most days, but she did eat a regular evening meal without escalating into a binge. Her decision to avoid having a glass of wine when she arrived home was undoubtedly one important part of that success.

The group listened to her story with rapt attention. Some cried, knowing that they could easily have done the same thing if they found themselves in the same situation. They praised her lavishly for the positive changes that she had already accomplished. Their sympathetic responses helped Tracy to feel that she had finally become part of the group.

For the remaining time in the session, the group returned to a discussion of the topics that had originally been planned: assertive behavior. This issue represents a logical extension of the preceding discussions of negative emotional triggers for binge eating. For some people, anger can be a stimulus for uncontrolled eating. By training the women to behave more assertively, the psychologist hoped that they would be able to solve interpersonal problems more effectively and minimize emotional distress.

For the first time, Tracy participated actively and constructively in this discussion. The relevance to her own situation was apparent. Throughout adolescence, she had been afraid to stand up for herself. She received frequent critical messages from her parents, teachers, and peers. For example, her mother's criticism of her appearance and weight had been a common source of irritation and embarrassment. She role-played with the group ways in which she could tell her mother that these critical remarks made her feel bad, without becoming rude or hostile.

Week 6: Body Image

This session was devoted to a discussion of the women's images of their own bodies. The women had already made it clear to one another that their lives were, in many ways, dominated by concerns about their appearance and their weight. Some said they believed that unless they found a way to keep themselves thin, they would be depressed and lonely for the rest of their lives.

In an effort to help group members identify and challenge their own negative feelings about their bodies, the therapist reviewed a number of facts about physiology. For example, women need a certain amount of body fat to enable reproduction. Their bodies need more fat than men's bodies. Women also have a lower resting metabolism rate than men. Dieting suppresses metabolism even further.

Each member of the group was asked to write down five things about her body that she liked. These were not to be aspects of her appearance. Rather, they were to list things that their bodies did for them. This became a very challenging exercise. Tracy was unable to think of a single thing. Others were able to generate a few items, such as "My body allows me to run for 30 minutes every day. It makes me feel strong." The difficulty that the women had in constructing this particular list helped them realize the extent of the distorted and imbalanced views that they had come to hold about their own bodies.

The session ended with each person reporting her own progress toward the introduction of regular patterns of eating. Tracy noted that she was now eating three regular meals and two scheduled snacks each day. She had completely eliminated her late-night binges. When she experienced an urge to have a glass of wine or bake a batch of cookies, she would record the urge in her journal and then distract herself by doing "stomach crunches." The exercise made her feel better about herself, and she found that the urge to binge usually passed by the time she was finished.

Week 7: Dieting and Other Causal Factors

In the first portion of this session, the group discussed the relation between different types of dieting and the onset of binge eating. Dieting plays a crucial role in most cases of bulimia. People who set dietary restraints make themselves feel food deprived. When they do eat, they are more likely to binge.

There are many forms of dieting. The women were instructed to identify any food groups that they had been trying to avoid. All said that they avoided sweet desserts. Others stayed away from dairy foods, fatty meats, and simple carbohydrates. The psychologist told them that they should gradually introduce small amounts of each type of food into their planned meals and snacks. This process was designed to diminish the probability of further binges by eliminating extreme forms of dietary restraint.

The remainder of this session was devoted to a review of information about causes of bulimia. Emphasis was placed on the notion that no single factor is responsible for all cases of eating disorder. The pathways to bulimia are complex, and the symptoms of the disorder can vary over time. Several family issues were discussed, including traumatic events such as deaths, divorce, parental conflict, and childhood sexual abuse.

Week 8: Problem Solving and Stress Reduction

The women's self-monitoring records indicated clearly that their binge episodes did not occur at random. Rather, their binges were much more likely to occur during moments of increased stress. Their next discussion focused on the development of problem-solving skills that might then serve to decrease the frequency of future binge eating. They began by talking about ways of spotting problems before they became unmanageable. Warning signals would include the onset of negative mood states (particularly sadness or anger) as well as particular situations, such as being alone with nothing to do. After recognizing the presence of a problem situation, the psychologist worked with them on ways to generate a large number of potential solutions to the problem.

Week 9: Healthy Exercise and Relapse Prevention

In their next-to-last session, the women worked on two topics that would help them maintain progress after the group treatment was completed. First, they talked about the benefits of *healthy* exercise. The women listed several considerations, including stress reduction, mood elevation, social interaction with friends, and the regulation of metabolism. The damaging effects of compulsive exercise were also discussed. Exercise should be pleasurable, not a punishment for overeating.

The second half of this session was devoted to the prevention of relapse. Minor setbacks are virtually inevitable in this type of program. It may be unrealistic to assume that, after a person has recovered from binge eating, she will never overeat again. The women acknowledged that eating problems might be their Achilles' heel for the rest of their lives. Particularly during stressful times, they would still be tempted to binge. How would they react when that happened?

They were encouraged to distinguish between temporary lapses and full-blown relapses. If they did slip up, it would not mean that they were back where they had started before the group. It would simply mean that they should address the problem right away and reinstate those aspects of the program that had been most successful initially.

Week 10: Coping with Future Events

The final session was devoted to a review of earlier steps and a discussion of ways that they could reduce their vulnerability to future binge eating. What kinds of situations might contribute to their own relapse? One crucial consideration was obviously the continuation of eating regular meals and avoiding all forms of dieting. They also discussed methods that they had learned to use when coping with stressful events, negative emotions, and self-defeating thoughts.

By the time the group ended, Tracy had made significant improvements with regard to her eating problems. She had eaten regular meals on a daily basis for 5 weeks. She had not binged or purged since the traumatic night when she ate the birthday cake, and she had stopped taking diet pills and laxatives. Somewhat to her surprise, her weight had remained fairly steady for the first couple of weeks and then leveled off at 5 pounds less than it had been when she entered the group. Her mood was much improved, but she still experienced periods of marked sadness and loneliness. Her concerns about drinking as well as difficulties in relationships with boyfriends and her parents had not been resolved. She continued to discuss these issues with her individual therapist.

Discussion

Tracy's disorder, bulimia nervosa, is one of two eating disorders described in *Diagnostic and Statistical Manual of Mental Disorders* (*DSM-IV-TR*; APA, 2000). The other eating disorder is anorexia nervosa: an intense fear of becoming obese resulting in reduced intake of food and severe weight loss. The key to the diagnosis of bulimia nervosa is recurrent episodes of binge eating coupled with compensatory behavior, such as vomiting, to prevent weight gain (Fairburn & Cooper, 2007). Literally, bulimia means "ox hunger," or voracious appetite, but it now refers to binge eating and purging. Although many people report occasional binges, the *DSM-IV-TR* (APA, 2000) diagnosis requires at least two binges per week for at least 3 months. The binges, which are often triggered by stress, typically involve eating high-calorie, easily ingested food in a short period of time (e.g., 2 hours) and in secret. During the binges, the person feels out of control and may consume 2,000 to 4,000 calories, more than someone would usually eat in an entire day. The binges end when the person becomes uncomfortably full or when the person is interrupted or falls asleep. Vomiting frequently follows the binge, either terminating it or allowing further eating to take place. Heavy laxative use and excessive exercise are other ways of trying to compensate for the large number of calories consumed.

People suffering from bulimia are usually intensely concerned about their weight and fear becoming fat. They realize that their eating is abnormal but report that they cannot control themselves. Their inability to control their eating often leads to feelings of depression, guilt, and low self-esteem (Garner & Magana, 2002).

The exact prevalence of bulimia is not known, principally because it is a secretive problem. Approximately 2 to 3% of women and much less than 1% of men will qualify for a diagnosis of bulimia nervosa at some point in their lives (Hudson, Hiripi, Pope, & Kessler, 2007). The disorder typically begins during late adolescence. Evidence regarding the long-term course of bulimia suggests that many people eventually have a good outcome, even though they continue to experience some symptoms of the disorder (Wade, Bergin, Tiggemann, Bulik, & Fairburn, 2006).

Bulimia can occur either by itself, as in Tracy's case, or as an accompanying symptom of anorexia nervosa. About 50% of patients with anorexia also have episodes of binge eating. The frequency of binges and vomiting in these patients, however, is less than was true for Tracy. Bulimia also is comorbid with several other diagnoses, including depression, personality disorders (especially borderline personality disorder), anxiety disorders, and substance-use disorders (Baker, Mazzeo, & Kendler, 2007; O'Brien & Vincent, 2003; van Hanswijck, van Furth, Lacey, & Waller, 2003).

Several serious physical complications may result from bulimia (Mehler, 2011). Tracy experienced several of these problems, including sore throat, swollen salivary glands, and destruction of dental enamel, which occur as a result of the frequent presence of stomach acid in these areas. Repeated vomiting can also lead to potassium depletion, which, in turn, can produce seizures. Urinary infections and kidney failure also occur in some patients. Menstrual irregularity is also common.

Etiological Considerations

Bulimia nervosa is undoubtedly the product of a complex interaction among biological, psychological, and social factors. These include various sorts of antecedent conditions and predispositions to the disorder, such as negative self-evaluations and fear of gaining weight. In the presence of these vulnerability factors, the stress of dieting often triggers the full-blown symptoms of the disorder and sets off a cascade of related biological reactions (Halmi, 2011; Polivy & Herman, 2002).

Biological Factors
Supporting the possible importance of genetics, bulimia nervosa clearly runs in families. Data from twin studies also show higher concordance for monozygotic (MZ) than for dizygotic (DZ) twins (Bulik et al., 2010; Mazzeo et al., 2010).

At a neurochemical level, interest has focused on the neurotransmitter serotonin (Kaye, 2008). Several factors make serotonin an appealing variable to play a role in bulimia. First, drugs that block serotonin receptors lead to increased food intake and appear to do so by reducing feelings of being satiated after eating. Patients with bulimia binge, of course, and also report less satiety after eating. Second, low levels of serotonin are associated with both depression and increased impulsivity. Depression is often found in patients with bulimia, and their binge eating could well be regarded as reflecting a high level of impulsivity. Studies of serotonin in patients with bulimia provide more direct support. Research has found a low level of serotonin in patients with bulimia. Furthermore, studies in which patients with bulimia take drugs that affect serotonin have found that patients with bulimia show smaller responses than normal, again demonstrating the importance of this variable (Ferguson & Pigott, 2000).

Psychological Factors

A fear of being fat is a primary feature of the eating disorders, including bulimia. This fear is likely to lead to dieting, which is an important precursor of bulimia (Austin, 2001; Brewerton, Dansky, Kilpatrick, & O'Neil, 2000). Fear of being fat arises from several sources. First, there are sociocultural influences. Over the past several decades, there has been a steady progression toward thinness as the ideal shape, although this trend now seems to have leveled off. We know that this ideal has been internalized by large numbers of women because many normal-weight women perceive themselves to be overweight. At the same time that society was becoming preoccupied with being thin, the prevalence of bulimia increased markedly (Hoek & van Hoeken, 2003). This cultural influence has had a greater impact on women than men and may thus account for the gender difference in the prevalence of bulimia. As would be expected if cultural effects are important, the frequency of eating disorders is particularly high among women, such as gymnasts and dancers, who are under extreme pressure to keep their weight down.

Several other factors also contribute to fear of being fat. For example, being overweight or having overweight parents are risk factors for bulimia. Being teased by peers or criticized by parents about being overweight can also contribute (Cooper, 2005). In Tracy's case, her mother's persistent comments about Tracy's weight undoubtedly contributed to her own exaggerated concerns about being fat, as well as her low self-esteem. A distorted view of the size of one's body is another risk factor. For example, in one study, women with bulimia were shown silhouettes of very thin to very obese women. They were asked to select the one closest to their own body size and the one they would most like to be. The women with bulimia overestimated their current body size and chose thinner ideal body sizes than control women (Williamson, Cubic, & Gleaves, 1993).

One psychological explanation for the development of bulimia nervosa suggests that the disorder is a combination of extreme weight concerns and dieting practices (Byrne & McLean, 2002; Lowe, Thomas, Safer, & Butryn, 2007). Fear of becoming fat leads to restricting food intake, which then sets the stage for the development of the binge-purge cycle. Dietary restraint paradoxically increases the likelihood of binge eating when the person is stressed (Polivy, Herman, & Boivin, 2008). Emotional arousal increases eating among people who are trying to restrict their food intake. The binge-eating pattern for patients with bulimia is similar but more extreme. Dieting frequently precedes the onset of bulimia, and it also appears to be triggered by episodes of stress. After the binge, the patient with bulimia feels anxious, and the purge is then a way of reducing this anxiety.

What function did binge eating serve for Tracy? Several processes could be involved. First, Tracy was afraid of becoming fat and did often restrain her eating, for example, by skipping breakfast and lunch. Second, Tracy's early binges seemed, at least in part, to be stress related. Binge eating could have been established as a way of coping with stress. Her binges may have filled up a life that was devoid of many other pleasurable activities.

Treatment

Many patients with eating disorders do not seek treatment for their disorder because they do not believe that anything is wrong. Others fail to enter therapy because they are ashamed of their condition or feel hopeless about it. When patients with bulimia do enter therapy, they are treated with both biological and psychological treatments.

Because bulimia is often comorbid with depression, it is not surprising that it has been treated with antidepressant medication, especially SSRIs. Medication is beneficial for some patients, but up to one-third of bulimic patients drop out of therapy because of unpleasant drug side effects, and relapse is the rule when medication is discontinued (Sysko, Sha, Wang, Duan, & Walsh, 2010; Narash-Eisikovits, Dierberger, & Westen, 2002).

The major psychological intervention, as was the case with Tracy, is cognitive-behavior therapy (CBT; Cooper & Fairburn, 2010). Patients are encouraged to question society's standards for physical attractiveness and learn that normal weight can be achieved without extreme dieting. Patients must also learn that dieting can trigger a binge and that all is not lost by eating a high-calorie afternoon snack. Another crucial step involves determining the situations that elicit binges and developing alternative ways of coping with them. The goal, then, is to establish a normal pattern of eating three meals a day and even snacks between meals. Regular meals control hunger and thus make it less likely that a person will binge and then become anxious and purge. Results from these cognitive-behavioral interventions are more favorable than those from treatment with antidepressant medication (Shapiro et al., 2007; Wilson & Sysko, 2006). For some patients, the optimal treatment may involve a combination of both drugs and CBT.

Unfortunately, only about half of bulimic patients improve significantly during treatment. One year after the end of treatment, only one-third are maintaining their treatment gains (Anderson & Maloney, 2001). What factors might explain these high rates of treatment failure? Desire to change is obviously one crucial element in any program aimed at the treatment of eating disorders. Relatively little is known about factors that influence these patients' ability to appreciate the severity of their problems. Some people seem to accept their binge eating and adjust their lives around it. They are not motivated to change. Tracy was unable to benefit from her experience in group therapy until the dramatic evening when she devoured the birthday cake and found herself staring in the mirror of her neighbor's bathroom. This event clearly played a crucial role in her subsequent recovery.

The *abstinence violation effect* can also contribute to continued binge eating and relapse in bulimia nervosa (Schlam & Wilson, 2007). This phenomenon was initially observed among people who are recovering from substance dependence. A single violation of abstinence is often sufficient to wipe out totally any treatment gains that had occurred. When a person violates his or her commitment to stop using drugs, a state of dissonance is created between the behavior and the self-image of the person. This dissonance motivates attempts to reduce it, for example, by changing the self-image: "I guess I haven't really recovered." Furthermore, the transgression is attributed to personal weakness, and thus the person is likely to expect future failures.

Recognition of the impact of the abstinence violation effect led to the inclusion of relapse prevention elements in the type of group therapy that Tracy received. Tracy and the other members of her group were trained to recognize situations that could create pressure for them. Furthermore, she was given specific training in coping with stress, including skills to handle problematic life situations and ways to deal with negative emotional states. Finally, she was told that minor lapses were likely and would not indicate that the treatment had failed or that she was a weak person. Within this framework, she was instructed on ways to cope with a single binge to reduce the likelihood that a single abstinence violation would lead to a complete resumption of her old pattern.

Discussion Questions

1.   How would you draw a distinction between Tracy's behavior during an episode of bingeing and purging and the behavior of a person who is suffering from obsessive-compulsive disorder? Could her purging behavior be considered a compulsion? Why not?
2.   Discuss the differences between bulimia and anorexia, especially with regard to issues related to impulse control.
3.   Why was Tracy's emotional experience with the little girl's birthday cake an important turning point in her treatment? What was the most important factor in changing her motivation for treatment?
4.   What are the connections among cognitive factors, emotion regulation, and binge eating? How are these issues related to dieting and restricted intake of food?

CHAPTER 17

Parasomnia: Nightmare Disorder and Isolated Sleep Paralysis

Daisy could not conceal her distress from Anna, her social worker. She swallowed nervously, trying to keep the tears from spilling down her cheeks. Anna handed her the box of tissues and encouraged her to go on. Two nights before, Daisy had experienced a terrifying and disturbing episode: waking up early in the morning with the intense sensation she was being threatened by an evil spirit and being unable to move. She could see and feel the heavy pressure on her chest of a spirit-like figure sitting on top of her and holding her down. She was gripped by the feeling the figure was sinister and threatening. It looked her directly in the face and was "vividly tangible, transparent, smoke-like," with "an opening for a mouth, a head, no eyes, and a long, flowing body." She felt like she could not breathe and heard a strange buzzing sound. Daisy had tried to scream and push the figure off her, but she had been fully immobilized and had felt completely panicked. She felt sensations at her neck, as if the spirit were going to move inside her, cut her neck, or choke her. Finally she came out of it, after what seemed like a half hour but what she later recognized was probably only several frighteningly long minutes. As she became able to move, the odd hallucinations faded away, but she remained shaky, jumpy, and flooded with dread for the rest of the day.

This was the first time Daisy had experienced anything this horrifying. Although she had been struggling with chronic, regular, and upsetting nightmares for several years, this one was something very different. Anna was alarmed by Daisy's description and privately feared that Daisy was losing touch with reality. Immediately after the session, Anna contacted Daisy's psychiatrist, who decided it was time to refer her to a sleep specialist. Clearly her nightmares were getting worse. The psychiatrist set up an appointment for Daisy at a sleep clinic with Dr. Amy Middleton, a clinical psychologist who specialized in sleep disorders.

Social History

Daisy Wu was a 28-year-old graduate student, working on her doctoral degree in East Asian art history. She had always been a creative, artistic person and had once hoped to have a career as an artist before deciding art history was somewhat more practical. She continued to paint almost every day, though, even during her rigorous graduate program. Daisy lived with her boyfriend Andrew, a graduate student in engineering. They had been together for 3 years, got along well, and talked often about getting married. She was hesitant to make such a commitment, however, as she worried her parents would disapprove of him because he was not Chinese. Andrew was supportive of Daisy. When she had the terrifying episode, he was awake in the other room working on a school project. He was reassuring and gentle when she had rushed out of the bedroom, ashen and shaky. He encouraged her to tell the social worker about the episode, even though Daisy was embarrassed about it and extremely reluctant to discuss it further.

Daisy was struggling in her studies. She had finished all her coursework but could not bring herself to work on her dissertation, which was all that remained to finish her Ph.D. Every time she tried to work on it, she would "freeze up." She felt unsupported by her dissertation advisor and felt that she would not be able to complete her degree. She feared she had wasted the years of her life spent in graduate school. She had received a letter from the department giving her a final deadline to complete her work or risk being excluded from the program, and yet she still found herself unable to work productively. She felt tremendous anxiety about her situation, and her mood was often depressed and sad. She often kept most of her distress to herself and was reluctant to burden those in her life with her problems.

Her parents lived in Hong Kong, where Daisy had been born. The family had moved to Boston when Daisy was 4 years old. After Daisy and her younger brother, who was born in Massachusetts, were both in college, her parents had returned to China to care for their elderly parents. Throughout Daisy's childhood, her father was abusive. He would yell at Daisy's mother and sometimes beat her. He often also was verbally and physically abusive to Daisy. Her struggles with sleeping over the past 4 years led her to see the psychiatrist, who started her on the medication and recommended she work with Anna. She really liked Anna and had been in therapy for about 4 years. They were working on issues from her childhood. At the same time, the psychiatrist continued to prescribe Prozac, BuSpar, and Klonopin for her anxiety and depression.

Since the onset of her sleep difficulties, Daisy had experienced regular nightmares, about one or two a week. During the nightmares, she would often scream out and become violent, kicking in the bed and often injuring herself or Andrew. The nightmares varied in topic but often had themes of having to protect herself from others or having experienced some injustice. Her mood was affected the entire day after a nightmare, and sometimes she would find herself reliving the nightmare while walking down the street, having a "flashback" that would cause her to break suddenly into a run. She was miserable because of the nightmares and felt that they were ruining her mood and affecting her studies. They made her afraid to go to sleep.

Treatment

During her first session with Dr. Middleton, the sleep specialist, Daisy was cooperative and talkative, but she was also fairly irritable. She identified the main reason for her inability to sleep as her nightmares, which would awaken her and make her unable to fall back asleep. Dr. Middleton obtained background information and descriptions of her nightmares, as well as a detailed description of the terrifying paralysis experience. Dr. Middleton also ordered a sleep study because Daisy said she was violent during her dreams, a rarity. Typically during rapid eye movement (REM) sleep, the stage when the majority of dreams occur, people experience muscle atonia (paralysis) that keeps them from acting out dreams and harming themselves. During REM sleep, typically only the eyes move. Daisy's violent movements during dreams could have been part of a neurological disorder, such as a degenerative neurological disease, like Parkinson's disease, or from a lesion due to a stroke; these conditions are rare but could have accounted for her symptoms (Wills & Garcia, 2002). A sleep study, overnight polysomnography, is conducted in a sleep clinic. The patient being evaluated spends the night sleeping in the clinic, and the evaluation involves multiple recordings of electrical impulses on the scalp and face, body movements and positions, and breathing. Daisy's sleep study and medical evaluation ruled out a neurological disorder.

Dr. Middleton also had Daisy complete the Minnesota Multiphasic Personality Inventory (MMPI)-2, a questionnaire that would reveal her personality features so Dr. Middleton could understand her functioning better and make sure Daisy could tolerate the treatment she planned. Daisy's MMPI profile indicated she was experiencing significant distress and discomfort, with fears of inadequacy and high levels of free-floating anxiety. Her responses suggested she had trouble being assertive and felt guilty when she experienced anger. People with a similar profile often come from homes characterized by explosive and violent parents. Those people learn to cope by being unobtrusive to avoid angry attacks. Other coping strategies used by those with a similar set of responses are a tendency to deny having psychological problems and to repress their feelings. Her profile indicated that Daisy had enough psychological resilience to cope with the stress of treatment. In addition, Daisy completed questionnaires assessing her nightmares and how they were impacting her life, which would allow a comparison after treatment to see if the treatment led to a reduction in the severity or frequency of the symptoms.

Dr. Middleton diagnosed Daisy with nightmare disorder. She explained that Daisy's one frightening experience of being paralyzed and seeing and feeling the evil spirit was called Isolated Sleep Paralysis (ISP), actually something distinct from her primary problem of nightmare disorder. While very upsetting, ISP is surprisingly common in the general population. It is more likely to occur when sleep is disturbed and when a person is under a lot of stress. Both of these conditions were true for Daisy, who was experiencing chronic insomnia due to the nightmares and stress from her academic struggles. Dr. Middleton reassured Daisy that the ISP would be less likely to recur if they improved her sleep quality and quantity. Because her nightmare disorder was leading to Daisy's poor sleep, Dr. Middleton proposed treating her nightmare disorder to improve the insomnia and reduce the chance of additional episodes of ISP. The treatment she proposed was Imagery Rehearsal Therapy (IRT), a cognitive behavioral treatment that includes education and cognitive restructuring that conceptualizes disturbing dreams as a habit, and uses imagery training to rewrite the script of a nightmare. IRT increases patients' sense of control and helps them master the upsetting dream content.

After the assessment was complete and Daisy agreed to undergo treatment for the nightmare disorder, the first treatment session was scheduled. During the first session, the goal was to educate Daisy about nightmares and teach her imagery techniques. When a person is exposed to uncontrollable or traumatic events, they seem to develop nightmares that might be viewed as one way to help them process the event emotionally. The nightmares can dissipate the intense negative emotion and help the person adapt. In effect, nightmares can serve as outlets for emotion that is too intense to handle while awake. Also, nightmares can help people focus on and form memories about important details from the traumatic event. These details might have survival value if the person faces a similar threat in the future. When the nightmares continue too long, however, they are no longer useful and instead become harmful. Nightmares can become a habit that interferes with sleep. To change a bad habit, it is necessary to practice undoing it. Dr. Middleton also explained that dreams can be affected by daytime behaviors, as when elements from the day are dreamed about later. So, the goal of IRT is to practice behaviors during the day and to change thoughts about nightmares so Daisy can learn to change her nightmares using imagery. Imagery is a structured, intentional daydream. Daisy readily understood Dr. Middleton's rationale and was interested in this new way of understanding the meaning and purpose of her nightmares, and how they can develop into a bad habit.

The rest of the first session was spent teaching Daisy to practice imagery. First, she was taught to lie on a couch in the therapy room and practice relaxation techniques. Next, she was asked to visualize the color red and then watch it fade to blue. When she was able to successfully imagine that, she practiced hearing the screech of chalk on a chalkboard and then visualizing the chalk crumbling to powder. Next, she practiced changing an imagined scent of ammonia to lemon. She practiced changing the imagined sound of a siren in the middle of the night to a softened sound of a flute. She visualized walking inside a dark tunnel and having it open up into a light, airy beach. After she became proficient at the imagery techniques, she was taught cognitive behavioral tools to deal with unpleasant images. For example, while imagining the beach, she was asked to introduce a vivid image of a storm brewing. Then she learned to interrupt thoughts using a mental image of a stop sign, while also using relaxation techniques. She was taught grounding techniques, where she focused her attention on all the places where her body was touching the couch, rather than focusing attention on the negative images. Also, she was taught mindfulness, the ability to be fully aware of the present moment with a focus on her feelings and physical sensations, not to engage in judgment about the experience but rather to let it occur and then recede.

Daisy seemed to enjoy learning these techniques and was cooperative and engaged during the sessions. As she was leaving the first treatment session, she paused and mentioned to Dr. Middleton that after hearing that ISP was common, she had worked up the courage to describe her terrifying episode to her mother while they were talking on Skype. She was shocked and surprised when her mother smiled calmly and told her that such an experience was called "ghost oppression," because in the past everyone in China had believed that it was caused by ghosts haunting a person in the night. The name had stuck, even though few people still believed it was caused by ghosts. Even though her mother had never had an episode, she was familiar with the terror it caused.

One week later, Daisy returned for the second session. She had completed her homework: practicing what they had worked on during the first session. Dr. Middleton asked her to identify a relatively mild nightmare to start working on and told her they would gradually work up to worse nightmares after she mastered the less upsetting ones. Daisy selected a nightmare she had dreamed recently. In it she woke up in a gray house full of cobwebs and thousands of spiders and found her parents immobilized, half dead, and wrapped in a massive cocoon. She thrashed around in the bed until she woke up. Dr. Middleton asked her to rewrite the dream any way she wanted, but in as much detail as possible. Daisy rewrote the dream so that she woke up to a bright, sunny day. She then walked outside and had breakfast with her family at a small table outside on a patio. It was warm outside with a gentle breeze. She described the garden surrounding the patio in detail—the chirping of the birds visiting a hanging bird feeder, the murmur of a fountain against the wall of the house. Daisy struggled during the rewriting of the dream, finding it difficult to create more positive images because she found herself preoccupied by thoughts of the negative images from the nightmare. Dr. Middleton supported her use of relaxation to cope with these intrusions. At one point, Daisy started to cry and said she felt unable to let the bad images go. Dr. Middleton noted it was difficult for her to let her grief over her childhood go and said the images of her parents in a cocoon could symbolize how they were closed off to her, while the spiders symbolized how her home had actually been full of dangers. But Dr. Middleton also pointed out that focusing on the meanings of a dream was not necessary to be able to change it. She reminded Daisy to rehearse her new dream for 10 minutes each day for the next 2 weeks and after 3 days, to select another nightmare to rewrite on her own. She also instructed Daisy to rehearse both newly changed dreams mentally for the remainder of the 2 weeks.

The third session was held 2 weeks later. Dr. Middleton reviewed the idea that nightmares do not have to be linked to past trauma but can be seen as a learned behavior, a bad habit. The best way to change the bad habit is to change the story of the dream instead of rehashing the original nightmare. She assured Daisy that no one ever felt worse by decreasing the number of their disturbing dreams. Daisy had successfully practiced her imagery exercises and had tackled a more disturbing dream the previous week. In the second nightmare, she was at a movie theatre when a man came into the theatre late with a bunch of circus monkeys. She felt angry at him because he was disrupting the movie. Later in the dream, she returned home to find the same man in her kitchen threatening her with a knife. She rewrote the dream so that the man was not threatening but was friendly and used his knife to help her to chop vegetables to make dinner together. She easily visualized the new ending.

A follow-up session was held 1 month later, during which Daisy repeated the earlier questionnaires. Daisy reported a dramatic reduction in the frequency and severity of her nightmares. Although she had experienced a couple of nightmares during that month, she felt that they were no longer interfering with her life. She had not had any more ISP episodes either. She mentioned that now she actually felt glad she had experienced the ISP because it was what had gotten her in to see the sleep specialist. She had not realized that nightmares could be treated directly. Daisy reported that she had begun using the techniques of visualization, grounding, and mindfulness in her studies. She had visualized herself working on her dissertation and being successful at it. She reported feeling more empowered and more in control of her life and her emotions. Therapy was concluded.

Two months later, Daisy sent a postcard to Dr. Middleton telling her that she had successfully defended her dissertation and was graduating in 2 weeks. She had told her parents about her intention to marry Andrew, and they had come to accept and support her decision. She and Andrew had scheduled their wedding for 1 month after graduation. She expressed her appreciation for the successful resolution of nightmares and insomnia.

Discussion

According to the *Diagnostic and Statistical Manual of Mental Disorders* (*DSM-IV-TR*; APA, 2000, pp. 631–634), Daisy met the criteria for nightmare disorder, which is one of the sleep disorders. Sleep disorders are characterized as either dyssomnias, which are abnormalities in the amount or timing of sleep, or parasomnias, which are abnormal behavioral or physiological events related to sleep. Nightmare disorder, a parasomnia, is defined by the following criteria:

1. A person awakens repeatedly from the major sleep period with detailed recall of extended and extremely frightening dreams, usually involving threats to survival, security, or self-esteem.
2. On awakening from the frightening dreams, the person rapidly becomes oriented and alert.
3. The dream experience, or the sleep disturbance resulting from the awakening, causes clinically significant distress or impairment in social, occupational, or other important areas of functioning.
4. The nightmares do not occur exclusively during the course of another mental disorder and are not due to the direct physiological effects of a substance or a general medical condition.

Sleep is critically important for both physical health and people's sense of general well-being. Inadequate levels of sleep have been linked to problems in mood, cognition, and general performance (Bootzin & Epstein, 2011). People who do not get enough sleep have trouble with memory and concentration, and they are at substantially increased risk to become depressed. Inadequate sleep also predicts later difficulty with anxiety and experiencing a negative mood, and sleep deprivation has been directly linked to problems with regulating emotions; insomnia could be a core mechanism in the cause and maintenance of numerous psychiatric difficulties (Harvey, 2008). Sleep loss results in people feeling worse when they cannot achieve a goal and not feeling as good when they do achieve a goal than if they had slept well. It also exacerbates obesity by increasing appetite and interfering with normal metabolism (Harvey, 2011). Daisy's sleep disturbance could well have played a role in initiating her irritability, depressed mood, and anxiety, and certainly helped to maintain her negative mood. Her mood disturbance also likely exacerbated her sleep difficulties.

Despite growing evidence of the important role sleep plays in people's functioning, a significant proportion of American adults report sleep disturbance or inadequate levels of sleep. Only about 30% of adults report that they always had enough sleep, and 10% indicate that they never sleep well (CDC, 2009). College students are at particular risk for sleep problems, both because their daily schedules vary widely depending on class times and staying up late to study, and also because they are more likely to have poor sleep hygiene practices (Brown, Buboltz, & Soper, 2002). For example, caffeine and alcohol use, noise disturbance, worrying while trying to fall asleep, going to bed thirsty, lack of regular exercise, and lack of a regular bedtime are all associated with poorer sleep. Many college students attempt to catch up on sleep over the weekend, which can actually exacerbate sleep disruption (Gaultney, 2010). In the past several decades, college students have been sleeping less than before and reported greater problems with sleep, both in the United States and in Hong Kong and other areas of China (Sing & Wong, 2010). Female college students in Hong Kong were particularly likely to report sleep problems and worry interfering with their sleep (Suen, Hon, & Tam, 2008). So Daisy's cultural background and early life in China was not inconsistent with her experiences as a college student in the United States, which were linked to worsened sleep quality and quantity.

Daisy's key difficulty with sleep was her chronic nightmares. Dreams can have a potentially beneficial function in helping people deal with traumatic episodes or stress. This may especially be the case with nightmares, which are frightening dreams that portray threats to the dreamer such as danger, humiliation, or personal failure (Roberts, Lenning, & Heard, 2009). Research suggests that nightmares are on a continuum of other coping strategies (Picchioni & Hicks, 2009). There are also cultural differences in how people use nightmares to cope: European Americans are more likely to share their dreams with others and seek social support that involves emotional disclosure, whereas for Asian Americans having more frequent and intense nightmares is correlated with using other coping strategies, such as distancing oneself from the stressor, increasing efforts to control one's feelings, or making attempts to solve the problem. Although nightmares may be an individually oriented method of coping with stress, nightmares do not appear to release tension but rather to induce it, so that people who have more negative life events experience more nightmares, feel more distress about their nightmares, and report significantly higher levels of anxiety (Roberts et al., 2009). For Daisy, nightmares definitely represented a source of anxiety because they were so painful and upsetting.

Nightmares are very common: 86% of college students report having had a nightmare in the past year, and a quarter of students report having monthly nightmares (Zadra & Donderi, 2000). Research also suggests that people asked to recall frequencies of dreams are particularly likely to underreport bad dreams. Up to 10% of people report having nightmares every week (Levin & Nielsen, 2007), and 8% of people report having a significant problem with nightmares (Miró & Martínez, 2005). Nightmares occur more commonly in females and are particularly common in childhood and adolescence, with frequencies reducing throughout adulthood into old age (Levin & Nielsen, 2007). Daisy's sleep difficulties revolved around nightmares and her fear of having one.

Even though she had been struggling with nightmares, it was Daisy's episode of ISP that was the most frightening and ultimately led to her seeking treatment with a sleep specialist. Sleep paralysis occurs when people are either falling asleep or waking up. During the episode, they are able to open their eyes but are otherwise unable to move for up to several minutes, during which time they are fully aware of their surroundings (Paradis et al., 2009). Nearly 30% of college students report having at least one such episode, although the majority never told anyone for fear of a negative reaction. Episodes are commonly associated with fear, the sense of a threatening presence, the feeling of pressure on the chest and trouble breathing, and vivid and frightening auditory or visual hallucinations About 5% of students experienced a combination of numerous symptoms in a detailed episode like Daisy described (Cheyne, 2002; Cheyne, Newby-Clark, & Rueffer, 1999). Even though many people have not heard of ISP, a number of cultures have a widely known word or phrase to describe it. In Japan, experiences matching the typical description of ISP are called *kanashibari* (Arikawa, Templer, Brown, Cannon, & Thomas-Dodson, 1999), meaning "to tie with an iron rope" (Davies, 2003). In Mexico, the phenomenon is described by the folk expression, "a dead body climbed on top of me" (Jiménez-Genchi, Ávila-Rodríguez, Sánchez-Rojas, Terrez, & Nenclares-Portocarrero, 2009). In Great Britain, the experience was traditionally called "stand stills" and thought to occur when the spirit left the body during sleep and failed to return upon awakening (Dahlitz & Parkes, 1993). In Indonesia, it is called *tindihan*, being weighed down by spirits. Research on the Salem witch trials and other historical accusations of witchcraft also reveals episodes similar to modern descriptions of ISP (Davies, 2003). In Hong Kong, the Chinese describe these experiences as "ghost oppression," and a description of ISP appears in a book on dreams written in China in 400 B.C. (Wing, Chiu, Leung, & Ng, 1999). In a number of traditional cultures, the phenomenon is discussed more openly.

Typically, ISP occurs as an isolated incident, but some people experience repeated episodes (Dahlitz & Parkes, 1993). Many people who experience ISP also have significant difficulty with anxiety (Paradis et al., 2009) or depression (Szklo-Coxe, Young, Finn, & Mignot, 2007). ISP has been associated with the position of sleeping on one's back and with stressful life events and sleep disturbance (Paradis, Friedman, & Hatch, 1997). Also, Daisy's episode occurred at a time when her life included many stresses, and her sleep was continually disturbed, which probably increased the likelihood of the episode.

Daisy's parasomnias, her nightmares and ISP, were related to her difficulty sleeping. Dr. Middleton did not address Daisy's insomnia directly but indirectly by changing how she viewed her dreams. The central feature for identifying insomnia is the person's subjective feeling of not having enough sleep, rather than the actual amount of time the person sleeps (Dikeos & Soldatos, 2005). Those who report insufficient sleep have higher levels of central nervous system arousal, both during waking and sleep states, and especially around bedtime due to their anxiety about sleeping. Like Daisy, many individuals who experience chronic insomnia tend to avoid or repress their feelings.

Etiological Considerations

People vary in their tendency to remember their dreams and in the vividness of their report of dreams. Those who report particularly vivid dreams have higher levels of imaginativeness and the ability to become intently absorbed in a task. They are also better able to experience states of flow—a reduced sense of self-consciousness when involved in a productive task (Watson, 2001). This ability to become completely absorbed is also associated with hypnotic ability. Interestingly, Daisy showed high levels of artistic creativity, as might be expected. Such individuals are described as having "thin boundaries," where psychological material can easily cross boundaries between different states of consciousness. These thin boundaries may also be more likely among people who experience hypnagogic hallucinations (intense dreamlike images while falling asleep) and hypnopompic hallucinations (while waking up). People with thin boundaries are more likely to report having frequent nightmares and to be affected by their nightmares during the day (Miró & Martínez, 2005). For people with thin boundaries, nightmare reports are associated with both stressful life events such as problems at work and reports of high levels of childhood adversity, such as abuse, neglect, and unreasonable punishment (Blagrove & Fisher, 2009).

Defining what constitutes a nightmare is complicated. Dreams more often have negative content or emotional tone than positive (Zervas & Soldatos, 2005). Nightmare sufferers, though, are more likely to report current stressful life events and a history of childhood trauma. They score higher on measures of psychological distress and report more feelings of guilt, anxiety, and depression (Berquier & Ashton, 1992). People who are distressed by nightmares are more likely to be physiologically and psychologically reactive when awake (Levin & Nielsen, 2007). They are more likely to focus on internal sensations, report somatic complaints, and be emotionally reactive. They are also more likely to experience *affect distress*—high levels of negative affect and extreme behavioral displays of that affect and distress. This pattern of signaling distress is more likely to be found among those raised with abuse, neglect, or insecure attachments and is particularly likely to be triggered when people feel they are losing control when under stress. Daisy had a family history of abuse but rarely produced extreme behavioral displays of her negative affect, possibly because of Chinese cultural values. Nevertheless, her nightmare distress is consistent with this research evidence.

Dreams may serve the purpose of regulating unpleasant emotions. Upsetting dream images are triggered by emotional events during the day, and dream imagery may be the dreamer's attempt to reduce this distress by changing the meanings or contexts of the experiences so they are not as conflictual (Kirmayer, 2009). When this process is effective, the dreams become less upsetting throughout the night, but when ineffective, the dream becomes too negatively intense and awakens the dreamer as a nightmare. Distressing dreams may be understood as a dysfunction of the dreaming function of eliminating fear memories and reducing negative affect (Levin & Nielsen, 2009). Attempts to suppress thoughts about threatening things during waking states can lead to dream rebound, where the threatening themes or elements are more likely to occur in dreams (Wegner, Wenzlaff, & Kozak, 2004). People who have high levels of affect distress may scan their dream content for threatening elements and experience a panic reaction to them as a danger or threat signal, similar to the false alarm that occurs during panic disorder (Levin & Nielsen, 2009), resulting in distressing chronic nightmares. Daisy had a tendency to try to avoid talking about her personal difficulties because she was raised with the cultural value of avoiding being a burden to others. It is possible that her attempts to avoid thinking about her fears were backfiring and making those fears more salient and more likely to emerge as nightmare content. In addition, Daisy had high levels of affect distress which may have made her vulnerable to reacting fearfully to her own dream images.

Sleep paralysis sometimes occurs as part of another sleep disorder, narcolepsy, which is characterized by involuntary and sudden attacks of sleep during waking states. Narcolepsy has a genetic component. ISP, which occurs separately from narcolepsy, may also have a genetic component, although there are also environmental correlates. In general, things that interfere with sleep (including depression and anxiety, as well as life stresses) increase the likelihood of ISP episodes. The experience of sleep paralysis is thought to be due to REM sleep atonia occurring at inappropriate times (Dahlitz & Parkes, 1993). REM sleep atonia is the lack of muscle control during REM sleep.

Treatment

The most strongly supported treatment of nightmare disorder is imagery rehearsal therapy (IRT), which has been shown to reduce both the frequency of nightmares as well as the distress associated with them (Krakow & Zadra, 2006). IRT has two primary components. The first is educational and cognitive restructuring, changing the way the client views nightmares so he or she sees them as learned behaviors that negatively impact sleep. The second is imagery training, teaching the client how to use imagery to reduce nightmares. Dr. Middleton used this treatment approach in her work with Daisy. One of the main reasons IRT works may be that it increases a person's sense of mastery of their dreams, giving them a feeling of control that reduces their negative emotions and distress (Germain et al., 2004).

Nightmares can be conceptualized as a primary disorder worthy of direct treatment rather than as a secondary symptom of an underlying problem. This view is supported by evidence that IRT is effective. If nightmares were only a secondary symptom, IRT should not work because it does not focus on anything but the nightmares themselves (Moore & Krakow, 2010). IRT leads to reductions in patient reports of depression and anxiety, as well as other posttraumatic stress disorder (PTSD) symptoms, in addition to reduction in nightmare severity and frequency. This evidence supports the approach of treating nightmares directly as a sleep disorder without focusing on traumatic precipitants that may have contributed to the development of the nightmare disorder. Dr. Middleton's approach with Daisy was consistent with this evidence.

Asian Americans and Psychological Intervention

Cultural issues are important to consider, particularly in diverse societies, such as the United States and Canada. Despite our increasing understanding of the role of biological factors in mental illness and how to prevent and treat many disorders, social circumstances also cannot be ignored. Because of Daisy's ethnicity, we close this case study with a consideration of some diversity issues in psychotherapy.

It is generally assumed that patients do better with therapists who are similar to them in cultural and ethnic background. Therapists of similar background and the same gender may better understand the patient's life circumstance and will be better able to build rapport with them. Similarity between patient and therapist may strengthen the therapeutic alliance. Yet it has not been demonstrated that better outcomes are achieved when patient and therapist are similar in race or ethnicity (Beutler, Machado, & Neufeldt, 1994). There are certainly many successful cases involving therapists and patients of different ethnic backgrounds and different genders, including Daisy's case. Research in this area involves making generalizations about the reactions of groups of people to psychotherapy, which runs the risk of oversimplifying or stereotyping people. Nonetheless, ethnic and cultural factors are increasingly being recognized as important. When therapists express values that clash with traditional Asian values, they are perceived as more culturally competent when they openly acknowledge racial differences in discussions with the client than when they do not (Li, Kim, & O'Brien, 2007). Openly discussing these issues is beneficial to the therapeutic relationship.

Because Daisy was Chinese American, some general comments on therapy with Asian Americans are offered here. But first, it is important to bear in mind that Asians living in the United States and Canada, as well as other parts of the world, comprise more than 40 distinct groups (e.g., Filipino, Chinese, Japanese, Vietnamese, Cambodian, Hmong) and differ on such dimensions as how well they speak English, whether they immigrated or came as refugees from war or terrorism in their homeland, and how much they identify with their native land (or that of their parents if they were born in the United States) (Nezu, 2010). In general, Asian Americans are more ashamed of emotional suffering, more reluctant to seek professional help, and less assertive than European Americans. Daisy had been in therapy for 4 years and was willing to seek help for her sleep disorder. However, her embarrassment about discussing her nightmares could have stemmed in part from the cultural values espoused during her upbringing.

Asian Americans have been stereotyped as being highly educated, wealthy, and emotionally well adjusted, but actually they have been the target of severe discrimination (Sue & Sue, 1999). For example, more than 100,000 Japanese Americans were imprisoned in concentration camps for several years during World War II without any evidence that they posed a security threat. Recently, discrimination has been more subtle but nonetheless hurtful.

Many suggestions have been made for conducting psychotherapy with Asian Americans. Sue and Sue (1999) advise therapists to be sensitive to the personal losses that many Asian refugees have suffered and, especially in light of the great importance that family connections have for them, to the likelihood that they are very stressed from these losses. Therapists should also be aware that Asian Americans have a tendency to "somaticize"—to experience and to talk about stress in physical terms, such as headaches and fatigue, rather than to view their stress in psychological terms, which they often see as equivalent to being crazy or inferior (Nguyen, 1985). Asian values are also different from the Western values of the majority culture in the United States. For example, Asians are more likely to respect structure and formality in interpersonal relationships, whereas a Western therapist is likely to favor informality and a less authoritarian attitude. Respect for authority may take the form of agreeing readily to what the therapist does and proposes and, perhaps, rather than discussing differences openly, just not showing up for the next session. Psychotherapy carries more stigma among Asian Americans, whose cultural values encourage emotional self-control (Kim, 2007). Asian Americans may also consider some areas off-limits for discussion with a therapist, such as the nature of the marital relationship and especially sex.

Asian Americans born in the United States are often caught between two cultures. One way they resolve this tension is to identify vigorously with majority values and denigrate anything Asian, a kind of racial self-hate. This phenomenon occurs in other ethnic groups that have been discriminated against, such as African Americans and Jews. Others, torn by conflicting loyalties, are angry at discriminatory Western culture, but at the same time question aspects of their Asian background. A meta-analysis of research on acculturation, the extent to which people of Asian descent have come to identify with American mainstream culture, found that those who were more acculturated to American culture were slightly less likely to be psychologically distressed or depressed (Yoon, Langrehr, & Ong, 2011). Finally, therapists may have to be more directive and active than they otherwise might be, given the preference of many Asian Americans for a structured approach over a reflective one (Iwamasa, 1993).

Where does Daisy fit in here? Like many children of immigrants, she had largely acculturated to the dominant U.S. culture. It is not clear whether cultural factors, individual personality traits, or a combination of the two contributed to her symptoms. It could be that, had the therapy not been time-limited and focused on her sleep disturbance, more information would have emerged about the influence of her cultural background on her presenting problems. When therapists remain sensitive to cultural issues, they will be more likely to be effective in treating their patients' problems.

Discussion Questions

1. How could Daisy's ethnic background have affected her disorder? What Asian cultural values are related to her symptoms?

264 Case Studies in Abnormal Psychology

2. Have you ever heard of any cases of Isolated Sleep Paralysis (ISP)? What effect does change of awareness about this phenomenon have on people who experience it today?
3. What special challenges do you think students today face with sleep? What recommendations would you make to students about how to juggle competing demands on their time?
4. Do you think more direct discussion of racial and ethnic issues in Daisy's therapy would have been useful? Was it unnecessary? Would it have helped or hurt?

CHAPTER 18

Paranoid Personality Disorder

This case study is based on personal, rather than clinical, experience. Joe Fuller was in treatment for a brief period of time, but he terminated the relationship well before a therapy plan was formulated. This pattern is, in fact, characteristic of this type of person; people who are paranoid seldom seek professional services and, when they do, are difficult to work with. One of the authors was well acquainted with Joe during high school and college and has stayed in contact with him throughout subsequent years.

Social History

Joe was the third of four children. He had two older brothers and a younger sister. His father was a steamfitter, and his mother was a homemaker. The family lived in a lower-middle-class neighborhood in a large, northeastern city. Joe's grandmother also lived with them, beginning when Joe was 11 years old. She was an invalid and could not care for herself after Joe's grandfather died.

Our first information about Joe comes from his high school years. Unlike his older brothers, Joe was an exceptionally bright student. On the basis of his performance in elementary school and entrance examinations, he was admitted to a prestigious public high school. The school was widely recognized for academic excellence. More than 90% of the graduating seniors went on to college; most went to Ivy League schools. The school was also known as a "pressure cooker." All of the students were expected to meet very high standards; those who failed were denigrated by their peers. Joe thrived in this intellectually competitive environment. He usually received the highest test scores in his classes, particularly in science. These achievements were based on a combination of intelligence and hard work. Joe was clearly very bright, but so were most of the other students in this school. Joe was a serious student who seemed to be driven by a desire to succeed. Although many of the other students worried about examinations and talked to one another about their fear of failure, Joe exuded self-confidence. He knew that the teachers and other students viewed him as one of the best students; he often made jokes about people who "couldn't make the grade." This critical attitude was not reserved for other students alone. Whenever a teacher made a mistake in class, Joe was always the first to laugh and make a snide comment. His classmates usually laughed along with him, but they also noticed a sneering, condescending quality in Joe's humor that set him apart from themselves.

Joe was a classic example of the critic who could "dish it out but couldn't take it." He was extremely sensitive to criticism. It did not seem to matter whether the criticism was accurate or justified; Joe was ready to retaliate at the slightest provocation. He argued endlessly about examinations, particularly in mathematics and science classes. If he lost points on any of his answers, even if he had gotten an "A" on the exam, he would insist that his answer was correct, the question was poorly written, or the teacher had not adequately explained the topic prior to the exam. He never admitted that he was wrong.

His sensitivity was also evident in interpersonal relationships. Most people are able to laugh at themselves, but Joe could not. His family background was a particularly sore spot. Many of the other students in his school were from wealthy homes. Their parents were mostly professionals with advanced degrees. Joe seemed to be self-conscious about his father's lack of formal education and the fact that his family did not live in a large, modern house. He never admitted it openly, but the topic led to frequent arguments. The following example was a typical instance of this sort. Joe had been arguing in class about his grade on a chemistry examination. After class, he overheard another student say to one of his friends, "I don't know why some people have to work so hard for everything." The other boy's father happened to be a successful businessman. Joe took his comment to mean that Joe was trying to compensate for the fact that his family did not have a lot of money. This implied insult, which may or may not have been a simple comment about Joe's aggressive behavior, infuriated him. Two nights later, while everyone else was watching a school basketball game, Joe sneaked out into the parking lot and poured sugar into the gas tank of the other boy's car so that the engine would be ruined.

Joe did not participate in organized sports or student organizations, and he tended to avoid group activities. He did have a small circle of friends and was particularly close to two other boys. They were people whom he had judged to be his intellectual equals, and they were the only people in whom he could confide. He was interested in women, but his attitude toward them and his interactions with them struck his friends as being somewhat odd. The issues of dependence and control seemed to be of central importance to Joe. Whenever one of his friends spent a lot of time with a girlfriend or went out with her instead of a group of guys, Joe accused him of being spineless or "on a tight leash."

Joe seldom dated the same woman twice. He usually insisted that she was weird or boring, but, if the truth were known, most of them would not have gone out on another date with him if he had asked. They found Joe to be rude and arrogant. He was not interested in being friends; his sole purpose was to make a sexual conquest. He often bragged about having sex with many women, but his closest friends suspected that he was still a virgin.

In most respects, Joe's relationship with his family was unremarkable. They were not a tight-knit family, but he respected his parents and got along well with his older brothers and his sister. His principal problem at home centered on his grandmother, whom he hated. He complained about her continuously to his friends, saying that she was old and crippled, and he wished that his parents would ship her off to a nursing home. Her inability to care for herself and her dependence on Joe's parents seemed to be particularly annoying to him. He noted on several occasions that if he was ever in a similar situation, he hoped that someone would put him out of his misery.

After graduating from high school, Joe enrolled at an Ivy League university, where he majored in chemistry and maintained a straight-A average throughout his first 2 years. He seemed to study all the time; his friends described him as a workaholic. Everything he did became a preoccupation. If he was studying for a particular course, he concentrated on that topic day and night, 7 days a week. If he was involved in a laboratory project, he practically lived in the laboratory. Relaxation and recreation were not included in his schedule. Even if he had the time, there were few leisure activities that Joe enjoyed. He had never been particularly athletic and was, in fact, clumsy. He hated to lose at anything and was also afraid of being ridiculed for looking awkward, so he avoided sports altogether.

Joe's first steady relationship with a woman began during his sophomore year. Carla was a student at a small liberal arts college in upstate New York. They happened to meet at a small party while she was visiting friends in New York City. Several weeks later, Joe drove to spend the weekend with her. They continued to see each other once or twice a month throughout the spring semester. From Joe's point of view, this was an ideal relationship. He liked Carla; she shared his sarcastic, almost bitter, sense of humor, and they got along well sexually. Perhaps most important, the fact that she was not in the same city meant that she could not demand a great deal of his time and could not try to control his schedule or activities.

The relationship ended after a few months when Carla told Joe that she had another boyfriend. Although he was shocked and furious, he made every effort to seem calm and rational. He had always taken pride in his ability to avoid emotional reactions, particularly if they were expected. In discussing the situation with friends, Joe maintained that he had never really cared for Carla and said that he was interested only in her body. Nevertheless, he was clearly interested in revenge. His first plan was to win her back so that he could then turn the tables and drop her. Presumably this process would demonstrate to everyone that he, not Carla, had been in control of the relationship. When this effort failed, he settled for spreading rumors about Carla's promiscuous sexual behavior.

After his breakup with Carla, Joe became more deeply involved in his laboratory work. He would disappear for days at a time and seldom saw any of his friends. The experiments he was running were apparently based on his own ideas. His assigned work and routine studying were largely ignored; consequently, his academic performance began to deteriorate.

The experience with Carla also contributed to an increase in Joe's already cynical attitude toward women. He described her behavior as treacherous and deceitful and took the rejection as one more piece of evidence proving that he could not trust anyone, particularly a woman. He continued to go out on dates, but he was extremely suspicious of women's intentions and obviously jealous of their attention to other men. On one occasion, he went to a party with a woman he met in one of his classes. They arrived together, but Joe chose to ignore her while he chatted with some male friends in the kitchen. When he later discovered his date talking with another man in the living room, he became rude and offensive. He insulted the woman, made jokes about her clothes and the makeup she was wearing, and suggested that her friend was gay. As might be expected, they never saw each other again. Another time, after he had dated a woman once, he sat in his parked car outside her apartment and watched the entrance for 2 nights to determine whether one of his friends was also seeing her.

Later Adjustment

After receiving his B.S. degree, Joe stayed on at the same university to do graduate work in biochemistry. He continued to work very hard and was considered one of the most promising students in the department. His best work was done in the laboratory, where he was allowed to pursue independent research. Classroom performance was more of a problem. Joe resented being told what to do and what to read. He believed that most faculty members were envious of his intellect. Highly structured reading lists and laboratory assignments, which were often time consuming, were taken by Joe to be efforts to interfere with his professional advancement.

In his second year of graduate school, Joe began dating an undergraduate woman in one of his study sections. Ruth was unremarkable in every way. His friends described her as plain, bland, and mousy. They were surprised that Joe was even interested in her, but in retrospect, she had one general feature that made her perfect for Joe—she was not at all threatening. He made all the decisions in the relationship, and she acquiesced to his every whim and fancy. Other men were not interested in her. In fact, they seldom noticed her, so Joe did not have to remain constantly alert to the possibility of desertion. They were perfect complements to each other and were married within a year.

Joe's first job after getting his Ph.D. was as a research chemist for a major drug company. At the beginning, it seemed like an ideal position. He was expected to work somewhat independently doing basic biochemical research.

There was no question that he was intellectually capable of the work, and his willingness to work long hours would be beneficial to his advancement, which was closely tied to productivity. Joe expected to be promoted rapidly and was confident that he would be the head of a division within 5 years.

When Joe began working in the company laboratory, he quickly evaluated all the employees and their relationship to his own position. There were several young Ph.D.s like himself, three supervisors, and the head of the laboratory, Dr. Daniels, a distinguished senior investigator. Joe admired Dr. Daniels and wanted to impress him. He did not think much of his young colleagues and particularly resented the supervisors, whom he considered to be his intellectual inferiors. He believed that they had been promoted because they were "yes-men," not because they were competent scientists. He often complained about them to his peers and occasionally laughed openly about their mistakes. When they asked him to perform a specific experiment, particularly if the task was tedious, he was arrogant and resentful, but he usually complied with the request. He hoped that the quality of his work would be noticed by Dr. Daniels, who would then allow him to work more independently. He also worried, however, that the others would notice that he was being subservient in an effort to gain Dr. Daniel's favor. He became more and more self-conscious and was constantly alert to signs of disdain and rejection from the others in the laboratory. The others gradually came to see him as rigid and defensive, and he eventually became isolated from the rest of the group. He interpreted their rejection as evidence of professional jealousy.

Joe's initial work did gain some recognition, and he was given greater independence in his choice of projects. He was interested in the neurochemical basis of depression and spent several months pursuing a series of animal experiments aimed at specific details of his personal theory. Very few people knew what he was doing. He refused to discuss the research with anyone other than Dr. Daniels. Even then, he was careful to avoid the description of procedural details. His principal concern was that other people might get credit for his ideas. He wanted to impress Dr. Daniels, but he also wanted to take over Dr. Daniels's job. The quickest way to do that was to make a major breakthrough in the laboratory, one for which he alone would receive credit.

Dr. Daniels and the other supervisors recognized that Joe was exceptionally bright and a talented, dedicated scientist. They liked his early work at the company but were dissatisfied with the independent work that he was pursuing. There were no immediate, practical implications to this line of research, and it did not promise to lead to any commercial results in the near future. Consequently, Joe was told that his work was not acceptable and that he would have to return to doing work that was more closely supervised.

Joe's response to this criticism was openly hostile. He complained bitterly about the imbeciles in company management and swore that he would no longer tolerate their jealousy and stupidity. He was certain that someone had learned about his ideas and that Dr. Daniels and the others were trying to force him out of the company so that they could then publish the theory without giving him credit. Their insistence that he discontinue his work and return to more menial tasks was clear proof, from Joe's point of view, that they wanted to slow down his progress so that they could complete the most important experiments themselves. His paranoid ideas attracted considerable attention. Other people began to avoid him, and he sometimes noticed that they gave him apprehensive glances. It did not occur to him that these responses were provoked by his own hostile behavior. He took their behavior as further evidence that the whole laboratory was plotting against him. As the tension mounted, Joe began to fear for his life.

The situation soon became intolerable. After 3 years with the firm, Joe was told that he would have to resign. Dr. Daniels agreed to write him a letter of reference so that he could obtain another position as long as he did not contest his termination. Joe considered hiring a lawyer to help him fight for his job, but he became convinced that the plot against him was too pervasive for him to win. He also had serious doubts about being able to find a lawyer he could trust. He therefore decided to apply for other positions and eventually took a job as a research associate working with a faculty member at a large state university.

In many ways, the new position was a serious demotion. His salary was considerably less than it had been at the drug company, and the position carried much less prestige. Someone with Joe's academic credentials and experience should have been able to do better, but he had not published any of his research. He was convinced that this lack of professional success could be attributed to interference from jealous, incompetent administrators at the drug company. A more plausible explanation was that his work had never achieved publishable form. Although the ideas were interesting, and his laboratory techniques were technically skillful, Joe was not able to connect the two facets of his work to produce conclusive results. He was also a perfectionist. Never satisfied with the results of an experiment, he insisted on doing follow-up after follow-up and could not bring himself to consider a piece of work finished. The thought of submitting an article and having it rejected by a professional journal was extremely anxiety provoking. Thus, despite his recognized brilliance and several years of careful research, Joe was not able to land anything better than this job as a research associate.

Joe did not like the new job, partly because he thought it was beneath him and also because his activity was even more highly structured than it had been at the drug company. He was working on a research grant in which all the experiments had been planned in advance. Although he complained a good deal about the people who had ruined his career and expressed a lack of interest in the new line of work, he did high-quality work and was tolerated by the others in the laboratory. The salary was extremely important to Joe and Ruth because they now had a young daughter, who was 2 years old. There were also some other features about the job that were attractive to Joe. Much of his work was planned, but he was allowed to use the laboratory in his spare time to pursue his own ideas.

It was an active research program, and the department included a number of well-known faculty members. Joe believed that these people, particularly his boss, Dr. Willner, would soon recognize his talent and that he would eventually be able to move into a faculty position.

Things did not work out the way Joe had planned. After he had been working at the university for 1 year, Dr. Willner asked him to curtail his independent research. He explained that these outside experiments were becoming too expensive and that the main research funded by the grant would require more of the laboratory's time. Joe did not accept this explanation, which he considered to be an obvious excuse to interfere with his personal work. He believed that Dr. Willner had pretended to be disinterested in Joe's work while he actually kept careful tabs on his progress. In fact, he took this interference to indicate that Dr. Willner believed Joe's research was on the verge of a breakthrough. Joe continued to work independently when he had the opportunity and became even more secretive about his ideas. Several weeks after these developments, Dr. Willner hired another research associate and asked Joe to share his office with the new person. Joe, of course, believed that the new person was hired and placed in his office solely to spy on his research.

As the tension mounted at work, Joe's relationship with Ruth became severely strained. They had never had a close or affectionate relationship and now seemed on the verge of open conflict. Ruth recognized that Joe was overreacting to minor events. She did not want him to lose another job. She often tried to talk rationally with him in an effort to help him view these events from a more objective perspective. These talks led to arguments, and Joe finally accused her of collaborating with his enemies. He suggested that the people from the drug company and from the university had persuaded her to help them steal his ideas and then get rid of him. As Joe became more paranoid and belligerent, Ruth became fearful for her own safety and for that of her daughter. She eventually took their daughter with her to live with Ruth's parents and began divorce proceedings. Her desertion, as Joe viewed it, provided more evidence that she had been part of the plot all along.

Two weeks after Ruth left, Joe began to experience panic attacks. The first one occurred while he was driving home from work. He was alone in the car, the road was familiar, and the traffic pattern was not particularly congested. Although the temperature was cool, Joe noticed that he was perspiring profusely. His hands and feet began to tingle, and his heart seemed to be beating irregularly. When he began to feel dizzy and faint, he had to pull the car off the road and stop. His shirt was now completely soaked with perspiration, and his breathing was rapid and labored. At the time, he thought that he was going to smother. All in all, it was a terrifying experience. The symptoms disappeared as quickly as they had appeared; within 10 minutes, he was able to get back on the road and drive home. He experienced three such incidents within a 2-week period and became so concerned about his health that he overcame his distrust of physicians and made an appointment for a physical examination.

The physician was unable to discover any medical disorder and recommended that Joe consult a psychiatrist about his anxiety. Joe reluctantly agreed that a psychiatrist might be of help and arranged an appointment with Dr. Fein. The issue of Joe's paranoid thinking did not come up during his conversations with Dr. Fein because Joe did not consider it to be a problem. Furthermore, he knew that other people thought that he was overly suspicious and that some people would consider him to be mentally ill. He therefore carefully avoided talking about the efforts to steal his ideas and did not mention the plot involving his wife and former colleagues. He simply wanted to know what was causing the panic attacks and how he could control them. At the end of his second session, Dr. Fein suggested that Joe begin taking imipramine (Tofranil), an antidepressant drug that has also been effective in treating panic anxiety. This suggestion precipitated an extended conversation about the physiological action of mood-stabilizing drugs that escalated into a heated argument.

Joe had been disappointed with Dr. Fein. He did not believe that Dr. Fein understood his problem (i.e., the panic attacks) and resented the many open-ended, probing questions that he asked about Joe's personal life. Dr. Fein believed that he was trying to complete a thorough assessment that would allow him to place this specific problem in an appropriate context, but Joe considered this line of inquiry an invasion of privacy regarding matters for which he had not sought advice. The prospect of taking antidepressant drugs further aroused Joe's suspicions. He began asking Dr. Fein about the neurological mechanisms affected by this drug—a topic with which he was intimately familiar because of his own research at the drug company. He was obviously better versed on this subject than Dr. Fein and concluded that Dr. Fein was therefore incompetent because he recommended a treatment that he could not explain completely. Joe finally ended the conversation by telling Dr. Fein that he thought he was a quack. He stormed out of the office and did not return.

The panic attacks continued at the approximate rate of one a week for the next 3 months. Joe also noticed that he frequently felt physically ill and nauseated, even on days when he did not experience a panic attack. Searching for an explanation for these escalating problems, and considering his conviction that other people were trying to harm him, he finally borrowed some equipment from another department and checked the radiation levels in his laboratory. He claimed that he found an unusually high level of radiation coming from a new balance that Dr. Willner had recently purchased. That was the final piece of evidence he needed. He believed that the people who were conspiring against him, including Dr. Willner, the people from the drug company, and his wife, had planted the radioactive balance in his laboratory so that he would eventually die from radiation poisoning. It struck him as a clever plot. He spent much more time in the laboratory than anyone else and would therefore receive very high doses of radiation. The others were presumably wearing special clothing to screen them from the radiation, thus further reducing their own risk.

Joe confronted Dr. Willner with this discovery. As expected, Dr. Willner denied any knowledge of radioactivity emanating from the balance. He suggested that Joe should take some time away from the laboratory. He had obviously been under a lot of strain lately, considering the divorce proceedings, and could benefit from the rest. Joe was certain that this was a ruse to allow the conspirators to remove the evidence of what he now called the assassination attempt. He refused to take time off and insisted that he would not let the others steal his ideas. The following day, he went to the office of the president of the university to demand a formal investigation. An informal series of meetings was eventually arranged involving various members of the laboratory and representatives of the university administration. Joe also contacted the government agency that funded Dr. Willner's research, which conducted its own investigation. The result of this time-consuming process was that Joe lost his job. No one was able to find any evidence of a conspiracy to harm Joe or steal his ideas. Both investigations concluded that Joe should seek professional help to deal with his unwarranted suspicions.

When he left the university, Joe took a job driving a cab. This final fiasco had ruined his chances of obtaining another research position. No one would write him letters of recommendation. He was, of course, convinced that he had been blacklisted and did not consider the possibility that his problems were created by his own antagonistic behavior. In many ways, the change in occupations led to positive changes in Joe's adjustment. He seemed to love driving a cab. He worked late at night, when most other cabbies were sleeping, and was thus in a noncompetitive situation. The people with whom he interacted were not threatening to his sense of intellectual superiority In fact, he derived considerable enjoyment from telling his friends stories about the derelicts and imbeciles that rode in his cab. Joe was quite content with the situation. He lived by himself in a small apartment, maintained a small circle of friends, and planned to continue working as a cab driver. He was still arrogant and resented his past treatment but seemed resigned to his status as a martyr in the world of chemistry. The need for constant vigilance was greatly reduced because he no longer had access to a laboratory and could not continue to work on his ideas.

Fifteen-Year Follow-Up

Joe had found an occupational and social niche in which he was able to function on a relatively stable basis. He continued to live in the same community, working as a cab driver. Still convinced that Ruth had betrayed him, Joe never tried to contact her again. He had no further contact with his daughter. He remained grandiose, suspicious, and frequently contemptuous of others, but his condition did not deteriorate any further. In fact, he functioned relatively well, given his maladaptive personality traits. His small and rather loose-knit circle of friends afforded him some support and enough companionship to suit his modest needs. Because he did not see himself as having any psychological problems, Joe did not seek additional treatment after his brief encounter with Dr. Fein.

Five years after Ruth left him, Joe developed a relationship with a new girlfriend. Wendy worked as a dispatcher for the cab company. Like his former wife, she was quiet and shy—a perfect complement to his narcissism. Wendy was infatuated with Joe, and he loved to show off for her. He was obviously different in many ways from the other people who worked for the company. Having only a limited education, Wendy was easily impressed by his intelligence and apparent knowledge of the world. She treated him with extreme deference. At work, she helped him to receive special privileges with the hours and routes that he was scheduled to drive (often to the dismay of his fellow drivers). In their blossoming social relationship, Wendy acquiesced to all his interests and demands. They dated for several months, and she eventually moved into his apartment.

Joe hadn't lost his intellectual curiosity or his passion for natural science. He was still fascinated by theoretical issues in chemistry, especially those related to the quality of the environment (our supply of air and water). Wendy encouraged him to pursue these interests and was happy to give him plenty of time on his own to think and write papers. It is not clear whether this activity is best described as an eccentric hobby or the work of a dissident scholar who had been spurned and persecuted by his jealous peers. Joe certainly favored the latter explanation. Because he didn't have access to a lab, his papers were entirely theoretical in nature. The quality of these papers remained unknown because they were never submitted to professional journals.

Joe's grandiosity was still readily apparent to anyone who met him, but his most pronounced paranoid thoughts, such as his concern about the balance in the chemistry lab, were in remission for several years. He privately viewed the grievous end of his professional career as the product of laboratory intrigue and professional jealousies, but he was no longer preoccupied with these thoughts. His competitive instincts were under control because he was not working in an intellectual environment. His self-esteem was no longer threatened on a daily basis by comparisons with other people in his field.

Joe's paranoid thoughts were suddenly rekindled by an unexpected news event. One day, while driving his cab, he heard on the radio that the Nobel Prize in chemistry had been awarded to a professor at the university where he had received his bachelor's and doctoral degrees. The recipient, a faculty member in that department for 35 years, had been a member of Joe's dissertation committee when he was in graduate school. Everyone in his field considered this man to be a genius of enormous achievement. He was also known as a man who did not "suffer fools gladly" and could respond sharply when he disagreed with an idea. He had, in fact, criticized part of Joe's dissertation plan in front of the other members of the committee. Although the man was only trying to be helpful, Joe had felt enormous anger and embarrassment. Since that incident, Joe had always described this professor as "a simple-minded, unimaginative charlatan."

No one else shared this view, but others hadn't been able to change Joe's bizarre opinion. Joe always considered his own mentor, a senior person who was also a Nobel Laureate in chemistry, to be far superior to this other man.

The most shocking aspect of this news story, from Joe's point of view, was the topic of the work for which the prize was awarded: atmospheric chemistry. This subject had been of great interest to Joe for many years. In fact, he had written two lengthy theoretical papers about it while he was still working for the drug company. Joe had presumably developed a revolutionary new theory regarding the ozone layer and the future of the Earth's atmosphere. He believed that, if only anyone would listen, his ideas would dramatically affect the future of the human race. Unfortunately (from his point of view), most other scientists were too stupid to appreciate his ideas. Those who could understand were the people who plotted against him.

Ruminating about the prize, Joe remembered that he had mailed copies of these papers to the chemistry department at his alma mater when he was leaving his job at the drug company and had been desperate for employment. He had applied for a postdoctoral position in another laboratory. Although he was always reluctant to share his ideas with others in the field, he had mailed copies of these papers in the hope of impressing the head of the lab. He hadn't gotten the job. Surely, he reasoned, this other professor (who had now won the Nobel Prize) had obtained the papers, stolen Joe's ideas, and gone on to conduct brilliant research while pretending that the ideas were his own. Once again, Joe believed that he had been cheated—this time out of the world's most prestigious scientific award.

Unfortunately, little could be done. Joe complained bitterly and continuously to his girlfriend, who believed his story and was as sympathetic and supportive as she could be. He knew that he couldn't complain to any of his peers from graduate school or his former colleagues at the university. They hadn't believed him before, and he was certain that they would not support him now. Joe wisely chose not to file any formal complaints with the university. He was quite upset about this story for several weeks, but he also had enough perspective on his own suspicions to know that other people thought he was irrational. He resigned himself once again to living the life of an exile from the scientific community.

Discussion

Personality disorders (PDs) are defined in terms of stable, cross-situational patterns of behavior that lead to impairment in social and occupational functioning or subjective distress. These response patterns are exhibited in a rigid and inflexible manner, despite their maladaptive consequences (Skodol, 2005; South, Oltmanns, & Krueger, 2011). The principal features of a paranoid personality are unwarranted suspicion and mistrust of other people. People with this PD are often seen by others as cold, guarded, and defensive; they refuse to accept blame, even if it is justified, and they tend to retaliate at the slightest provocation. *Diagnostic and Statistical Manual of Mental Disorders* (*DSM-IV-TR*; APA, 2000, p. 694) lists the following criteria for paranoid PD:

1. A pervasive distrust and suspiciousness of others such that their motives are interpreted as malevolent, beginning by early adulthood and present in a variety of contexts, as indicated by four (or more) of the following:
   a. Suspects, without sufficient basis, that others are exploiting, harming, or deceiving him or her
   b. Is preoccupied with unjustified doubts about the loyalty or trustworthiness of friends or associates
   c. Is reluctant to confide in others because of unwarranted fear that the information will be used maliciously against him or her
   d. Reads hidden demeaning or threatening meanings into benign remarks or events
   e. Persistently bears grudges (e.g., is unforgiving of insults, injuries, or slights)
   f. Perceives attacks on his or her character or reputation that are not apparent to others and is quick to react angrily or to counterattack
   g. Has recurrent suspicions, without justification, regarding fidelity of spouse or sexual partner
2. Does not occur exclusively during the course of schizophrenia, a mood disorder with psychotic features, or another psychotic disorder

These characteristics are not limited to periods of acute disturbance; they are typical of the person's behavior over a long period of time.

Personality disorders are among the most controversial categories included in *DSM-IV-TR* (Krueger & Eaton, 2010; Skodol et al., 2011). Part of the controversy derives from a debate regarding personality traits and situational specificity of behavior. Social-learning theorists have argued that human behavior is largely determined by the context in which it occurs and not by internal personality characteristics. It has been demonstrated, however, that ratings of personality traits are useful predictors of behavior, especially when the ratings are made by several observers, the observers are thoroughly familiar with the people who are being rated, observations are made on a number of occasions, and the ratings are made on dimensions that are publicly observable (Funder, 1999).

Two other issues also contribute to the controversial status of the PDs. One involves reliability. For many years, interrater reliability for PDs was considerably lower than it was for many other disorders. This situation has improved, partly because of the introduction of structured interview schedules aimed specifically at PDs. Lowest reliability is often found for paranoid PD, and higher reliability tends to be associated with antisocial PD. The results of several studies indicate that PDs can be diagnosed reliably by trained clinicians (Widiger & Samuel, 2005).

Another issue that must be mentioned with regard to the PDs is the overlap between diagnostic categories (Grant, Stinson, Dawson, Chou, & Ruan, 2005; Khan, Jacobson, Gardner, Prescott, & Kendler, 2005). Many patients meet the criteria for more than one form of PD. Among people who meet the criteria for paranoid PD, the most frequent comorbid conditions are schizotypal, narcissistic, borderline, and avoidant PDs (Bernstein & Useda, 2007). Extensive overlap among Axis II categories indicates that the specific types of PD listed in *DSM-IV-TR* (APA, 2000) may not be the most efficient or meaningful way to describe this particular type of abnormal behavior.

Joe's case illustrates the overlap among different types of PDs. In addition to paranoid PD, Joe also met the *DSM-IV-TR* (APA, 2000, p. 717) criteria for narcissistic PD, which requires that the person exhibit five (or more) of the following features:

1. Has a grandiose sense of self-importance (e.g., exaggerates achievements and talents, expects to be recognized as superior without commensurate achievements)
2. Is preoccupied with fantasies of unlimited success, power, brilliance, beauty, or ideal love
3. Believes that he or she is "special" and unique, and can only be understood by, or should associate with, other special or high-status people (or institutions)
4. Requires excessive admiration
5. Has a sense of entitlement (i.e., unreasonable expectations of especially favorable treatment or automatic compliance with his or her expectations)
6. Is interpersonally exploitative (i.e., takes advantage of others to achieve his or her own ends)
7. Lacks empathy: is unwilling to recognize or identify with the feelings and needs of others
8. Is often envious of others or believes that others are envious of him or her
9. Shows arrogant, haughty behaviors or attitudes

Joe's inflated sense of his own intellectual abilities and scientific accomplishments clearly fits the pattern for narcissistic PD. He also exhibited the lack of empathy and feelings of entitlement that are described in these criteria. In addition to these characteristics, his behavior was arrogant and occasionally exploitative.

The principal issue regarding differential diagnosis and paranoid PD concerns the distinction between this category and delusional disorder, in which the patients exhibit persistent persecutory delusions or delusional jealousy. Delusional disorder is listed on Axis I, whereas paranoid PD is listed on Axis II. The paranoid ideas in paranoid PDs are presumably not of sufficient severity to be considered delusional, but the criteria to be used in making this distinction are not entirely clear. When does pervasive suspicion and mistrust become a paranoid belief? The two categories may be etiologically distinct, but it has not been demonstrated that they carry different treatment implications. *DSM-IV-TR* (APA, 2000) lists the categories separately, but the reliability and validity of the two categories remain open questions (Bernstein & Useda, 2007).

Personality disorders seem to be among the most common forms of abnormal behavior. It is difficult to provide empirical support for that claim, however, because the existing epidemiological data are inconsistent. The overall lifetime prevalence of Axis II disorders (i.e., having at least one type of PD) varies between 10 and 12% in samples of adults who are not in treatment for a mental disorder (Trull, Jahng, Tomko, Wood, & Sher, 2010). Rates for specific disorders vary from one study to the next, depending on the type of assessment procedure that was used and the way in which the sample of subjects was identified. Several studies that used structured interviews with community residents have reported a lifetime prevalence of approximately 1% for paranoid PD (Lenzenweger, 2008).

Follow-up studies indicate that delusional disorder and paranoid personality characteristics are typically long-term problems that change relatively little over time (Seivewright, Tyrer, & Johnson, 2002; Stephens, Richard, & McHugh, 2000). For many patients, their paranoid beliefs become more pronounced over time.

Psychological Theories

Several theories have been proposed that attempt to account for the development of paranoid ideas (Bentall & Taylor, 2006; Miller, Useda, Trull, Burr, & Minks-Brown, 2001). Perhaps the earliest hypothesis regarding paranoia was suggested by Freud (1909, 1925) in his analysis of the memoirs of Daniel Paul Schreber, an accomplished lawyer who had spent close to 14 years of his life in mental hospitals (Gottlieb, 2006). Schreber's problems centered on an elaborate set of persecutory and grandiose delusions, including the notion that he would be transformed into a woman. Following this transformation, Schreber believed that he would become God's mate and that they would produce a better and healthier race of people. Freud argued that the content of Schreber's delusions revealed the presence of an unconscious homosexual wish-fantasy. This hidden desire was taken to be the core of the conflict motivating paranoid ideas. The process presumably begins with the unacceptable thought that "I (a man) love him (a man)." To avoid the anxiety associated with the conscious realization of this idea, the thought is transformed to its opposite: "I do not love him—I hate him because he persecutes me."

At least two aspects of Joe's case might be consistent with this psychodynamic model. He occasionally made comments about other men's sexual orientation, particularly when he was trying to embarrass them. We might infer from these remarks that he was concerned about his own sexual desires, but we do not have any direct evidence to validate this conclusion. His only sexual experiences had been with women, and he did not express ambivalence about his interest in women. Joe's panic attacks might also fit into Freud's model, which suggests that Joe was using the defense mechanism of projection to avoid the anxiety associated with unconscious homosexual impulses. It could be argued that the panic attacks represented a spilling over of excess anxiety that was not being handled efficiently by projection and other secondary defense mechanisms such as repression. Once again, the model seems plausible, but it cannot be tested directly.

An alternative explanation for the development of paranoid delusions was proposed by Cameron (1959). He argued that predelusional patients are anxious, fearful, socially withdrawn, and reluctant to confide in other people. This suggestion is consistent with recent evidence indicating that people with paranoid PD are more likely than other people to have experienced anxiety disorders when they were children (Esterberg, Golding, & Walker, 2010; Kasen et al., 2001). Cameron went on to point out that social isolation leads to a deficiency in social skills. In particular, he argued that predelusional patients are less adept than others in understanding the motivations of other people. They are therefore more likely to misinterpret other people's behavior and, having done so, are also less able to elicit disconfirming evidence from their peers. From time to time, most of us have thought that someone else was angry with us or trying to do us harm when, in fact, they were not. We usually come to realize our mistake by talking to our friends about what happened. Cameron's argument was that predelusional patients are even more likely to misinterpret other people's behavior and, given an instance of misinterpretation, are also less able to correct the mistake through interaction with other people. According to Cameron's hypothesis, this cycle is perpetuated by the paranoid person's subsequent behavior. For example, someone who believes that his relatives are plotting against him is likely to behave in a hostile, defensive manner when his relatives are present. They, in turn, may become angry and irritable in response to his apparently unprovoked hostility, thus confirming the paranoid person's original suspicion that they are out to get him. Thus, Cameron's formulation allows for a complex interaction of personality traits, social skills, and environmental events.

Several elements of Cameron's theory seem applicable in Joe's case. He was not particularly withdrawn and fearful, but he was reluctant to confide in other people. He tended to be a "loner" and felt awkward in social situations such as parties. His habit of laughing at people and provoking arguments would indicate that he was not sensitive to their feelings and point of view, as suggested by Cameron. Perhaps most important is the effect that Joe's behavior had on other people. He was completely unable to consider the possibility that other people talked about him and avoided him because he was initially hostile and belligerent.

Colby (1977) proposed an information-processing view of paranoid thinking in which the principal feature is sensitivity to shame and humiliation. The model focuses exclusively on verbal interactions. In the "paranoid mode" of processing, people presumably scan linguistic input for comments or questions that might lead to the experience of shame (defined as "a rise in the truth value of a belief that the self is inadequate"). Faced with the threat of humiliation, the person in the paranoid mode responds by denying personal inadequacy and blaming others. The theory implies that paranoia is associated with low self-esteem and that episodes of paranoid behavior may be triggered by environmental circumstances that increase the threat of shame (e.g., failure, ridicule). Other negative emotions, most notably fear and anger, are presumably not likely to elicit paranoid responses. Some support for this hypothesis comes from the observation that people who are paranoid produce low scores on standard measures of self-esteem. Furthermore, when they are studied over time, a decrease in self-esteem is typically followed quickly by an increase in paranoia (Thewissen, Bentall, Lecomte, van Os, & Myin-Germeys, 2008).

Colby's model provides a plausible explanation for Joe's problems at the drug company and the university laboratory; his paranoid comments provided a rationale for his own failure to succeed. Joe was a brilliant chemist, but he had not developed a successful, independent line of research. The limitations of his work were particularly evident after he had been allowed some independence at the drug company. Joe's supervisors finally became so disappointed with his progress that he was reassigned to more structured projects. Shortly after this demotion, his suspicions began to reach delusional proportions. Colby would probably argue that Joe chose to blame his colleagues' interference for failures that would otherwise indicate his own professional inadequacy. The shame-humiliation model also accounts for Joe's later improvement following his change of occupations. As a cab driver, Joe was removed from the field of professional competition in which he was continually exposed to threatening messages. He was reasonably successful as a cab driver, and his self-esteem did not suffer in comparison to the people with whom he usually interacted. There was therefore little need for him to behave in a hostile or defensive manner. His paranoid beliefs did emerge again, however, when he heard about the professor who won the Nobel Prize. This man's success may have, once again, reminded him of his own disappointing career.

Treatment

Psychotherapy can be beneficial for patients with various kinds of PD (Beck, Freeman, & Davis, 2004; Zanarini, 2009). Unfortunately, relatively little evidence is available with regard to the effects of treatment for paranoid PD. Clinical experience suggests that therapy is often of limited value with paranoid patients because it is so difficult to establish a trusting therapeutic relationship with them (McMurran, Huband, & Overton, 2010; Williams, 2010). Joe's case is a good example. He expected the therapist to help him cope with his anxiety but was unwilling to discuss his problems at anything other than a superficial level. This defensive attitude would hamper most attempts to engage in traditional, insight-oriented psychotherapy. The client-centered approach developed by Carl Rogers (2007) might be more effective with paranoid clients because it fosters a nonthreatening environment. The therapist must also be careful to avoid the display of excessive friendliness or sympathy, however, because it might be interpreted as an attempt to deceive the patient (Akhtar, 1992). From Colby's point of view, Rogers's emphasis on the provision of accurate empathy and unconditional positive regard would also be likely to bolster the paranoid's fragile self-esteem and thereby reduce his or her sensitivity to potential embarrassment. Unfortunately, there are no data available to support this type of speculation.

Cameron's model might lead to a more directive form of intervention focused on the development of specific social skills. For example, various situations might be constructed to demonstrate to the client the manner in which his or her behavior affects other people. Similarly, the therapist might practice various social interactions with the client in an effort to improve his or her ability to discuss initial social impressions. It might also be possible to improve the client's ability to read social cues. This behavioral approach would be used in an effort to expand the client's repertoire of appropriate social behaviors so that the client could respond more flexibly to specific situational demands.

Cognitive therapy also has interesting applications for the treatment of paranoid patients. The central assumption of this approach is that PDs are associated with deeply ingrained, maladaptive beliefs (Beck et al., 2004). In the case of paranoid PD, these include thoughts such as "people cannot be trusted" and "if I get close to people, they will find out my weaknesses and hurt me." The therapist works with the client to identify and recognize these cognitive distortions and their influence on the person's behavior. The paranoid person is encouraged to test the validity of these maladaptive thoughts. Over time, the goal is to help the person learn to replace them with more adaptive thoughts and more accurate attributions (Kinderman, 2001).

When paranoid ideas reach delusional proportions, the use of antipsychotic medication may also be considered. These drugs are effective in the treatment of schizophrenia, but their effect has usually been measured in terms of global improvement ratings; it is not clear if they have an equally positive effect on all of the symptoms of schizophrenia. In fact, a few studies have examined changes in specific symptoms and concluded that antipsychotic drugs are most likely to have a positive effect on auditory hallucinations and disorganized speech. Paranoid delusions are among the least-responsive symptoms (Manschreck, 1992). Thus, in the absence of other schizophrenic symptoms, patients with paranoid delusions are not likely to benefit from drug treatment.

Discussion Questions

1. Other than being suspicious and sensitive to criticism, what are the most important characteristics of paranoid people?
2. Joe's friends and coworkers would have described him as being paranoid. But he would not describe himself in that way. He would have said that he was angry (because people were making trouble for him). If other people saw him differently than he saw himself, what problems are raised for the use of self-report instruments in the assessment of paranoid PD?
3. What is the difference between paranoid PD and a paranoid delusion? Do you think that, at some point, Joe might have been considered psychotic (i.e., delusional)?
4. If you were Dr. Fein, the psychiatrist with whom Joe consulted briefly, what could you have done (if anything) to persuade Joe to remain in treatment? Would it have made any difference in his long-term outcome if he had stayed in treatment?

CHAPTER 19

Borderline Personality Disorder

Amanda Siegel was 22 years old when she reluctantly agreed to interrupt her college semester and admit herself for the eighth time to a psychiatric hospital. Her psychologist, Dr. Swenson, and her psychiatrist, Dr. Smythe, believed that neither psychotherapy nor medication was controlling her symptoms and that continuing outpatient treatment would be too risky. Amanda was experiencing brief but terrifying episodes in which she felt that her body was not real. She sometimes reacted by cutting herself with a knife to feel pain, so she would feel real. During the first part of the admission interview at the hospital, Amanda angrily denied that she had done anything self-destructive. The anger dissolved, however, and she was soon in tears as she recounted her fears that she would fail her midterm exams and be expelled from college. The admitting psychiatrist noted that at times Amanda behaved in a flirtatious manner, asking inappropriately personal questions such as whether any of the psychiatrist's girlfriends were in the hospital.

When she arrived at the inpatient psychiatric unit, Amanda once again became angry. She protested loudly, using obscene and abusive language when the nurse searched her luggage for illegal drugs and sharp objects, even though Amanda was very familiar with this routine procedure. These impulsive outbursts of anger were characteristic of Amanda. She would often express anger at an intensity level that was out of proportion to the situation. When she became this angry, she would typically do or say something that she later regretted, such as verbally abusing a close friend or breaking a prized possession. Despite the negative consequences of these actions and Amanda's ensuing guilt and regret, she was unable to stop losing control of her anger. That same day, she filed a "3-day notice," a written statement expressing an intention to leave the hospital within 72 hours. Dr. Swenson told Amanda that if she did not agree to stay voluntarily, he would initiate legal proceedings for her involuntary commitment on the grounds that she was a threat to herself. Two days later, she retracted the 3-day notice, and her anger seemed to subside.

Over the next 2 weeks, Amanda appeared to be doing quite well. Despite some complaints of feeling depressed, she was always well dressed and groomed, in contrast to many of the other patients. Except for occasional episodes when she became verbally abusive and slammed doors, Amanda looked and acted like a staff member. She adopted a "therapist" role with the other patients, listening intently to their problems and suggesting solutions. She would often serve as a spokesperson for the more disgruntled patients, expressing their concerns and complaints to the administrators of the treatment unit. With her therapist's help, Amanda wrote a contract stating that she would not hurt herself and that she would notify staff members if she began to have thoughts of doing so. Because her safety was no longer as big of a concern, she was allowed a number of passes off the unit with other patients and friends.

Amanda became particularly attached to several staff members and arranged one-to-one talks with them as often as possible. She used these talks to flatter and compliment the staff members and tell them that they were one of the few who truly understood her and could help her, and she also complained to them about alleged incompetence and lack of professionalism among other staff members. Some of these staff members Amanda was attached to had trouble confronting her when she broke the rules. For example, when she was late returning from a pass off grounds, it was often overlooked. If she was confronted, especially by someone with whom she felt she had a special relationship, she would feel betrayed and, as if an emotional switch had flipped, would lash out angrily and accuse that person of being "just like the rest of them."

By the end of the third week of hospitalization, Amanda no longer appeared to be in acute distress, and the staff began to plan for her discharge. At about this time, Amanda began to drop hints in her therapy sessions with Dr. Swenson that she had been withholding some kind of secret. Dr. Swenson addressed this issue in therapy and encouraged her to be more open and direct if there was something she needed to talk about. She then revealed that since her second day in the hospital, she had been receiving illegal street drugs from two friends who visited her. Besides occasionally using the drugs herself, Amanda had been giving them to other patients on the unit. This situation was quickly brought to the attention of all the other patients on the unit in a meeting called by Dr. Swenson. During the meeting, Amanda protested that the other patients had forced her to bring them drugs and that she actually had no choice in the matter. Dr. Swenson didn't believe Amanda's explanation and instead thought that Amanda had found it intolerable to be denied approval and found it impossible to say no.

Soon after this meeting, Amanda experienced another episode of feeling as if she were unreal and cut herself a number of times across her wrists with a soda can she had broken in half. The cuts were deep enough to draw blood but were not life threatening. In contrast to previous incidents, she did not try to hide her injuries, and several staff members therefore concluded that Amanda was exaggerating the severity of her problems to avoid discharge from the hospital. The members of the treatment team then met to decide the best course of action.

Not everyone agreed about Amanda's motivation for cutting herself. She was undoubtedly self-destructive and possibly suicidal and, therefore, needed further hospitalization. But she had been sabotaging the treatment of other patients and couldn't be trusted to keep from doing so again. With members of her treatment team split on whether or not Amanda should be allowed to remain in the hospital, designing a coherent treatment program would prove difficult at best.

Social History

Amanda was the older of two daughters born to a suburban middle-class family. She was 2 years old when her sister Megan was born. Amanda's mother and father divorced 4 years later, leaving the children in their mother's custody. The family had significant financial difficulties because Amanda's father provided little child support. He remarried soon afterward and was generally unavailable to his original family. He never remembered the children on birthdays or holidays. When Amanda was 7 years old, her mother began working as a waitress. Neighbors would check in on Amanda and Megan after school, but the children were left largely unattended until their mother returned home from work in the evening. So at a very early age, Amanda assumed a caregiver role toward her younger sister. Over the next few years, Amanda took on a number of household responsibilities, such as regular meal preparation and shopping, which were more appropriate for a teenager. She did not complain about the situation and behaved well at home and in school. However, she remained distressed about the absence of her father. Had she somehow had something to do with the divorce? How much better would her life have been if her father were with her?

When Amanda was 13 years old, her mother married a man she had been dating for about 3 months. The man, Arthur Siegel, had a 16-year-old son named Mike, who joined the household on a somewhat sporadic basis. Mike had been moving back and forth between his parents' houses since their divorce 4 years earlier. His mother had legal custody but could not manage his abusive and aggressive behaviors, so she frequently sent him to live with his father for several weeks or months at a time. Because Amanda still secretly hoped that her parents would remarry, she resented the intrusion of her stepfather and stepbrother into the household and was upset when her mother changed their last name to Siegel. She also resented the loss of some of her caregiving responsibilities, which were now shared with her mother and stepfather.

Soon after her mother and stepfather married, Mike began sexually abusing Amanda. Mike told her that it was important for her to learn about sex and, after raping her, threatened that if she ever told anyone, he would tell all her friends that she was a "slut." When this occurred, she had not been sexually active with anyone. This pattern of abuse continued whenever Mike was living with his father. Even though Amanda was traumatized by the abuse, she felt unable to refuse or to tell anyone what was happening.

Amanda's behavior began to deteriorate. She had been doing very well academically in the seventh grade and then began to skip classes. Her grades fell precipitously over the course of a semester, and she began spending time with peers who were experimenting with alcohol and street drugs. Amanda became a frequent user of these drugs, even though she experienced some frightening symptoms after taking them (e.g., vivid visual hallucinations and strong feelings of paranoia). By the end of the eighth grade, Amanda's grades were so poor and her school attendance so erratic that she was recommended for a psychological evaluation to see if she should be held back for a year. Amanda was given a fairly extensive battery of intelligence, achievement, and projective tests. She was found to be extremely intelligent, with an IQ of 130. Projective test results (Rorschach, Thematic Apperception Test) were interpreted as reflecting a significant degree of underlying anger, which was believed to be contributing to Amanda's behavioral problems. Of more concern was that she gave a number of bizarre and confused responses on the projective tests. For example, when people report what they "see" in the famous Rorschach inkblots, it is usually easy for the tester to share the client's perception. Several of Amanda's responses, however, just didn't match any discernible features of the inkblots. The psychologist, although having no knowledge of Amanda's home life, suspected that her problems may have reflected her difficulties at home and recommended family therapy at a local community mental-health center.

Several months later, Amanda and her mother and sister had their first appointment with a social worker at the mental-health center. Mr. Siegel was distrustful of the prospect of therapy and refused to attend, stating, "No shrink is going to mess with my head!" During the therapy, the social worker first took a detailed family history. She noticed that Amanda was very guarded and was reluctant to share any feelings about or perceptions of the events of her life. The next phase of family therapy was more educational in nature, consisting of teaching Mrs. Siegel more effective methods of discipline and helping Amanda to see the importance of attending school on a regular basis.

Family therapy ended after 3 months with only marginal success. Although Mrs. Siegel had been highly motivated and diligently followed the therapist's suggestions, Amanda remained a reluctant participant in the therapy and was unwilling to open up. She never disclosed the sexual abuse she was experiencing. She felt depressed and guilty, with a very low opinion of herself.

When Amanda was 15 years old, her mother and Mr. Siegel divorced, ending the sexual abuse. When Amanda began high school, she continued her association with the same peer group she had known in junior high. They all regularly abused drugs. Amanda had her first experiences of feeling unreal and dissociated from her surroundings while intoxicated. She felt as though she were ghostlike, that she was transparent and could pass through objects or people.

Amanda also began a pattern of promiscuous sexual activity. She felt guilty for engaging in sex, but, as happened when she was being abused by her stepbrother, she was unable to refuse sexual advances, from either men or women.

She was particularly vulnerable when under the influence of drugs and would, under some circumstances, participate in sadomasochistic sexual activities. For example, Amanda was sometimes physically abused, such as being punched in the face, by her sexual partners while having sex. She didn't protest and, after a while, expected such violence. Sometimes Amanda's sexual partners would ask her to inflict some kind of pain on them during sexual activity, for example, biting during fellatio or digging her nails into her partner's buttocks. Even though these activities left Amanda with a sense of shame and guilt, she felt unable either to set limits or break off these relationships.

By the time Amanda was 16 years old, she never wanted to be alone. She was often bored and depressed, particularly if she had no plans for spending time with anyone else. An important incident occurred at about this time. One night while cruising in a car with friends, they were pulled over by the police because the car had been stolen by one of her friends. Street drugs were also found in the car. Amanda claimed that she had not known that the car was stolen. The judge who heard the case was concerned about the progressive deterioration in Amanda's academic performance and social functioning. Because previous outpatient treatment had failed, he recommended inpatient treatment to help her gain some control over her impulses and prevent future legal and psychological problems. Amanda was being offered a choice between being prosecuted as an accessory to car theft and for possession of illegal substances, or signing into a mental hospital. Reluctantly, she chose the hospitalization.

During this first hospitalization, Amanda's mood swings seemed to intensify. She vacillated between outbursts of anger and feelings of emptiness and depression. She showed signs of depression, such as lack of appetite and insomnia. Antidepressant medication was tried for several weeks but was ineffective. She spent most of her time in the hospital with a male patient. To any observer, their relationship would not have seemed to have a romantic component. They watched TV together, ate together, and played various games that were available on the ward. After only a couple of meetings with him, Amanda had revealed the most intimate details of her life. There was no physical contact or romantic talk. Nonetheless, Amanda idealized him and had fantasies of marrying him. When he was discharged from the hospital and broke off the relationship, Amanda had her first nondrug-induced episode of feeling unreal (derealization) and subsequently cut herself with a kitchen knife in order to feel real. She began making suicide threats over the telephone to the former patient, saying that if he did not take her back, she would kill herself. She was given a short trial of an antipsychotic medication, which was also ineffective.

While in the hospital, Amanda started individual psychotherapy, which was continued after her discharge. The therapy was psychodynamically oriented and focused on helping Amanda to establish a trusting relationship with a caring adult (her therapist). The therapist also attempted to help Amanda understand the intrapsychic conflicts that had started very early in her life. For example, the therapist hypothesized that her biological parents' divorce, and Amanda's idea that she was somehow responsible for it, led to her fear of being abandoned by people who were important to her. One of the therapist's goals was to show Amanda that he would still be available and would not leave her regardless of how she behaved. It was hoped that this would help Amanda to feel more secure in her interpersonal relationships.

Despite these therapy sessions, which she thought were helpful, Amanda continued to experience problems with drug abuse, promiscuity, depression, feelings of boredom, episodes of intense anger, suicide threats, derealization, and self-injurious behavior, such as cutting herself. Several hospitalizations were required when Amanda's threats and self-injurious behavior became particularly intense or frequent. These were usually precipitated by stressful interpersonal events, such as breaking up with a boyfriend, or discussing emotionally charged issues, such as the sexual abuse by Mike, in psychotherapy. Most of the hospitalizations were relatively brief, lasting 1 to 2 weeks, and Amanda was discharged after the precipitating crisis had been resolved. She received a number of diagnoses during these hospitalizations, including brief psychotic disorder, major depressive episode, atypical anxiety disorder, adjustment disorder with mixed emotional features, substance-use disorder, adjustment disorder with mixed disturbances of emotion and conduct, and borderline personality disorder.

During one of these hospitalizations, Amanda decided that she wanted to change therapists, and after careful consideration, her treatment team decided to grant her request. When Amanda was 19 years old, she was introduced to Dr. Swenson, a psychologist, and began individual behaviorally oriented psychotherapy.

Conceptualization and Treatment

As opposed to Amanda's previous therapist, Dr. Swenson's approach was more focused and directive, concentrating on helping her solve specific problems and behave in ways that would be more personally rewarding. At the same time, Dr. Swenson did not try to force change on her. He was empathic and accepting and gave her the opportunity to identify areas that she wanted to work on. Over a number of sessions, Amanda and Dr. Swenson identified several problem areas: (a) lack of direction or goals, (b) feelings of depression, (c) poor impulse control, and (d) excessive and poorly controlled anger. Specific interventions were designed for each of these areas. Concerning the first problem, Amanda had done so poorly in her schoolwork and was so far behind that going back to high school to graduate was not realistic. Amanda therefore decided to study to take an examination for a General Equivalency Diploma (GED), which would then allow her to pursue further education or job training. Amanda passed the exam after studying for approximately 4 months. This success enhanced her self-esteem because she had never before maintained the self-discipline necessary to accomplish any but the most short-term goals.

Because antidepressants had not helped in the past, her depression was treated with cognitive therapy based on the assumption that people's thoughts can influence their mood. To help Amanda become more aware of the thoughts that might make her more vulnerable to depression, she was asked to keep a written record of her mood three times daily. Next to her mood, she wrote down what she was thinking, particularly those thoughts that involved predictions about how a given situation might turn out. Through this exercise Amanda came to realize that she often made negative predictions about how events would turn out and subsequently felt sad and depressed.

To learn to restructure or "talk back" to these negative thoughts, Amanda was given another exercise. When faced with an anxiety-provoking situation, Amanda was asked to write three different scenarios for the situation: (a) a worst-case scenario in which everything that could go wrong did go wrong, (b) a best-case scenario in which events turned out just as she wanted, and (c) a scenario that she believed was most likely to occur. The actual outcome was then compared with the three different predicted outcomes. More often than not, the actual events were markedly different from either the best-case or worst-case predictions. With time, this exercise helped Amanda control some of her more negative thoughts and replace them with more adaptive and realistic ways of thinking that were based on her own experiences.

One example of the cognitive therapy had to do with Amanda's difficulties keeping a job. She held numerous part-time jobs that lasted for 1 or 2 months before she quit or was fired for not showing up to work. She typically believed that people at work, especially her supervisors, did not like her to begin with and were looking for excuses to fire her. After the smallest of negative interactions with someone at work, she assumed that she was about to be fired and stopped showing up to work, creating a self-fulfilling prophecy. Through monitoring her mood, she came to see that the predominant emotion she experienced in these situations was fear that she would be rejected by either her coworkers or supervisors. To prevent that, she typically rejected them first. After Amanda obtained a part-time job in a supermarket, her therapist had her write out the three scenarios mentioned, prior to actually starting work. Her scenarios were

> [worst case] I'll show up to work and nobody will like me. Nobody will show me how to do my job, and they will probably make fun of me because I'm new there. I'll probably quit after one day.

> [best case] This will be a job that I can finally do well. It will be the kind of work I have always wanted, and I'll be promoted quickly and earn a high salary. Everyone at work will like me.

> [most likely] I'm new at work, but everyone else was new at one time, too. Some people may like me, and some may not, but that's the way it is with everyone. Some conflict with other people is inevitable. I can

still do my job even if everyone does not like me. One bad day at work does not mean I have to quit.

She was encouraged to rehearse mentally the "most likely" scenario daily, especially when she felt like quitting. This helped her to keep the part-time job in the supermarket for 18 months, substantially longer than she had kept previous jobs.

Amanda had a number of problems with impulsiveness, drug abuse, self-mutilation, promiscuity, and anger. Dr. Swenson convinced her to join Narcotics Anonymous (NA), a nonprofessional self-help group for drug addicts based on the same principles as Alcoholics Anonymous. Whenever she had an impulse to use drugs, she was to use a technique called time delay. This involves a commitment not to use drugs for at least 15 minutes and during that time to engage in an alternative activity. This alternative activity could be telephoning another member of NA for help in controlling the impulse to use drugs. A similar approach was taken with Amanda's self-mutilating behaviors; she was instructed to telephone Dr. Swenson or go to a hospital emergency room if she thought she could not control the impulse on her own. Her anger was problematic because she impulsively acted it out, so this was handled with similar procedures. Dr. Swenson encouraged Amanda to see anger not as a negative emotion but as a positive emotion that becomes destructive only when it is too intense. He then taught her time-delay procedures to help her wait before expressing anger. During the waiting period, the intensity of the emotion declined, and she had an opportunity to think over different ways of dealing with the situation, helping to result in a more appropriate expression of anger.

Amanda made noticeable progress over the first few months of therapy with Dr. Swenson, showing a marked decline in her symptoms. She felt optimistic for the first time in a long while. However, this optimism soon deteriorated in the face of conflicts at home. For example, Amanda did not want to help maintain the household, either financially or by doing work around the house. She insisted that it was her mother's responsibility to take care of her. She also wanted her boyfriends to be able to spend the night with her, which her mother would not allow. Amanda's mother then asked her to move out of the house, but Amanda refused. Instead, she threatened suicide, superficially cut her wrists with a razor blade, and had to be rehospitalized. Amanda followed this same pattern over the next few years, making apparent gains in therapy for a month or so and then falling back in the face of interpersonal conflict. Each time her problems returned, they seemed increasingly stressful for Amanda because she usually came to believe during her periods of relative stability that her problems had been "cured."

When Amanda was 22 years old, she decided to attend college on a full-time basis while living at home. Dr. Swenson was opposed to this because Amanda had not shown enough psychological stability to complete even a semester of college, let alone a degree program. She went to college anyway and soon became sexually involved with another student. As with previous relationships, Amanda idealized this boyfriend and became dependent on him. She had to be the sole focus of his attention and couldn't tolerate the times when they were apart. After an argument in which Amanda smashed plates and glasses on the floor, her boyfriend left her. Amanda once again became suicidal and self-destructive. This episode led to the hospitalization described at the beginning of this chapter.

Amanda's treatment team at the hospital noted that none of the therapeutic interventions attempted with her (e.g., medication, insight-oriented psychotherapy, behavior therapy) had had any lasting impact. She had a poor employment history and showed little evidence that she would be able to support herself independently in the foreseeable future. It was also feared that she might continue to deteriorate, perhaps winding up in a state hospital on a long-term basis. It was decided that Dr. Swenson needed help in working with her, especially because her symptoms tended to worsen after dealing with difficult issues in therapy. She was referred to a day-treatment program at a local hospital, where she would have regular access to staff members who could provide therapy and support, while living outside the hospital and possibly working part time at an entry-level unskilled job. The treatment team realized that it would require a great deal of work to convince Amanda to accept these recommendations because accepting them would be an admission that she was more seriously disturbed than she cared to admit. Even if she did follow the recommendations, Amanda's prognosis was guarded.

Discussion

As an Axis II diagnosis in the *Diagnostic and Statistical Manual of Mental Disorders* (*DSM-IV-TR*; APA, 2000), *borderline personality* describes a set of inflexible and maladaptive traits that characterize a person's long-term functioning. People with borderline personality disorder (BPD) have instability in relationships, behavior, mood, and self-image (Sanislow, Grilo, & McGlashen, 2000). For example, attitudes and feelings toward others may vary considerably and inexplicably over short periods of time. Emotions are also erratic and can shift abruptly, particularly to anger. People with BPD are likely to experience episodes of rage that are triggered by perceptions that important others are being rejecting or withholding (Berenson, Downey, Rafaeli, Coifman, & Paquin, 2011). A key feature of the disorder is emotional dysregulation, including difficulty understanding, being aware of, and accepting one's emotions; poor strategies for managing one's emotions; and avoidance of situations that elicit emotional distress (Gratz, Rosenthal, Tull, Lejuez, & Gunderson, 2006). They are hypersensitive to negative emotion and focus on their bad feelings, and this exacerbates the intensity of the negative experience and puts them at risk for engaging in some extreme behavior, such as substance abuse or self-injury, to distract them from these feelings (Selby, Anestis, Bender, & Joiner, 2009). Amanda certainly had these difficulties and struggled to cope with and tolerate her own feelings. If she suspected that a situation would lead to her emotional distress, such as fearing that people at work did not like her, then she would avoid going back to work.

People with BPD are argumentative and irritable. Their unpredictable and impulsive behavior, such as suicide attempts, gambling, spending, sex, and eating sprees, is potentially self-damaging. They have not developed a clear and coherent sense of self and remain uncertain about their values, loyalties, and choice of career. They cannot bear to be alone and have fears of abandonment. They tend to have a series of intense relationships that are usually stormy and short-lived, alternating between idealization (the other person is perfect and can do no wrong) and devaluation (the other person is horrible, worthless). They tend to alternatively pursue and avoid interpersonal connectedness, both seeking reassurance from others and pulling away to avoid painful abandonment (Russell, Moskowitz, Zuroff, Sookman, & Paris, 2007). Subject to chronic feelings of depression and emptiness, they make manipulative attempts at suicide. Paranoid ideation and dissociative symptoms may appear during periods of high stress. Amanda's interpersonal relationships were both intense and unstable. She was very impulsive, could not control her anger, and had an unstable self-image. She clearly met the diagnostic criteria for BPD.

Originally, the diagnosis implied that the person was on the borderline between neurosis and psychosis, but the term no longer has this connotation. BPD has a lifetime prevalence of 5.9% and is equally common among men and women (Grant et al., 2008). Though the *DSM-IV-TR* (APA, 2000) reported 75% of those diagnosed with the disorder are women, this is likely due to the greater numbers of women seeking treatment (Skodol & Bender, 2003).

BPD often occurs with other disorders, especially major depression, eating disorders, posttraumatic stress disorder, and substance abuse (Lieb, Zanarini, Schmahl, Linehan, & Bohus, 2004). On several occasions, Amanda met the diagnostic criteria for an episode of major depression with depressed mood, suicidal thoughts, insomnia, poor appetite, and feelings of self-reproach and guilt. About 75% of those diagnosed with BPD attempt suicide, and about 10% eventually do commit suicide (Black, Blum, Pfohl, & Hale, 2004). Self-injury may serve as punishment for the patient's perceived flaws or as a way of eliciting help from others (Critchfield, Levy, Clarkin, & Kernberg, 2008). BPD, like the other personality disorders, has high levels of comorbidity with several other personality disorders, including antisocial, histrionic, narcissistic, and schizotypal (Becker, Grilo, Edell, & McGlashen, 2000).

Etiological Considerations

There is very strong evidence that environmental factors, particularly related to childhood family functioning, are related to BPD (Bandelow et al., 2005). Compared with healthy controls, patients with the disorder were much more likely to report histories of childhood physical and sexual abuse, particularly by family members but not strangers. Specifically, trauma that involves betrayal by a trusted person is linked to the development of borderline symptoms (Kaehler & Freyd, 2009). People with BPD describe their childhood family environments as low in support and closeness and high in conflict (Klonsky, Oltmanns, Turkheimer, & Fiedler, 2000). These findings are consistent with Amanda's childhood family experiences. Although it is possible that the symptoms of their disorder affect their perception or recall of their childhood families, the physical and sexual abuse they reported were independently validated in one study (Johnson, Cohen, Brown, Smailes, & Bernstein, 1999). Patients with BPD have often experienced separation from parents or lack of parental support during childhood (Sansone & Levitt, 2005).

The key causal factor may be an invalidating environment, in which a person's needs and feelings are disrespected, and efforts to communicate feelings are ignored or punished (Linehan, 1993). Among children who are sexually abused, it is their perceptions of being invalidated during childhood, including not being believed or being blamed when disclosing the abuse, that predicted BPD rather than the experience of abuse itself (Hong, Ilardi, & Lishner, 2011). Perceptions of being emotionally invalidated in childhood explain part of the link between BPD and conflict and instability in adult romantic relationships, perhaps because the person feels unlovable, and perhaps because they have not learned how to negotiate relationship difficulties (Selby, Braithewaite, & Fincham, 2008).

A number of studies have explored the neurobiology of BPD, especially focusing on emotional instability and impulsivity (Bohus et al., 2004). Abnormalities in serotonin activity have been found in prefrontal and limbic areas of the brain that may be related to these symptom constellations. The hypothalamic-pituitary-adrenal axis being sensitized by childhood trauma, particularly in the form of abuse, may also be important in the neurobiology of this disorder. Neuroimaging studies have found underactivity in the areas of the brain that regulate emotions, overactivity in the limbic areas that involve fear and anger, and abnormalities in areas that relate to negative affect (Lis, Greenfield, Henry, Guilé, & Dougherty, 2007). Although these findings are interesting, they do not necessarily establish that these differences are causally related because they may be a reflection of the symptoms of the disorder.

BPD runs in families, suggesting it may have a genetic component, but studies investigating this have had methodological limitations (White, Gunderson, Zanarini, & Hudson, 2003). One of the characteristics that may be inherited is neuroticism, a tendency to easily become anxious. Borderline patients are high in neuroticism; this trait is a key feature of BPD and is known to be heritable (Morey & Zanarini, 2000). Problems regulating emotions may be another key component that could be genetically transmitted (White et al., 2003).

An integrative model has recently been proposed that explains how risk factors work together (Crowell, Beauchaine, & Linehan, 2009). To develop BPD, a child inherits genes that affect the serotonin system, and possibly the dopamine system, that lead to impulsivity and emotional instability. Then, the child is exposed to abusive or invalidating environments that include insecure attachment to caregivers. These experiences exacerbate the child's emotional dysregulation and leads to extreme behavioral dyscontrol which develops into a personality disorder.

Treatment

A number of drugs have been tried in the pharmacotherapy of BPD, including antidepressants and atypical antipsychotic medications (Zanarini, 2004). Double-blind, placebo-controlled trials have shown that many of the different drugs help in treating problems managing emotions and controlling impulsiveness and aggression. However, the quality of the research establishing the effectiveness of the medications is often low, and many patients drop out of the trials, so it is difficult to make firm conclusions about the long-term effectiveness of medications in treating symptoms of BPD (Bellino, Paradiso, & Bogetto, 2008). Initial investigations also suggest that dietary supplementation with omega-3 fatty acids may reduce depression and aggression in patients with BPD (Raj, 2004).

Object Relations Psychotherapy

Object relations theory, a branch of psychoanalytic theory, deals with the nature and development of mental representations of the self and others. It includes the representations and the fantasies and emotions attached to these representations and explores how these variables mediate interpersonal functioning. The object relations of borderlines are often described as malevolent. Analyses of borderline patients' responses to projective tests indicate that they view other people as capricious and destructive for no reason (Nigg, Lohr, Westen, Gold, & Silk, 1992). This theory has been particularly important in the field of personality disorders. The leading contemporary object relations theorist is Otto Kernberg, who has written extensively about the borderline personality.

Kernberg (1985) operates from the basic assumption that borderline personalities have weak egos and therefore experience inordinate difficulty tolerating the regression (probing of childhood conflicts) that occurs in psychoanalytic treatment. Kernberg's modified analytic treatment has the goal of strengthening the patient's weak ego. Therapy involves analysis of a principal defense of the borderline person, namely, splitting, or dichotomizing into all good or all bad and not integrating positive and negative aspects of a person into a whole. Splitting is the result of an inability to form complex object representations. That is, the person with BPD does not see people as fairly complex and capable of both good and bad behavior. This causes extreme difficulty in regulating emotions because the person sees the world in black-and-white terms. Other people and even the self are either all good or all bad; there is no middle ground. We saw many examples of this in Amanda, as when she idolized her boyfriend but could then shift rapidly to hate. This therapeutic approach was evaluated in a long-term, randomized study in comparison to dialectical behavior therapy (see below) and a supportive therapy control (Clarkin, Levy, Lenzenweger, & Kernberg, 2004; Levy et al., 2006). Both approaches were effective. Kernberg's approach was particularly effective in changing internal representations of relationships with important others. Future research will evaluate whether certain kinds of patients will respond better to one of these effective treatments than to the other.

Dialectical Behavior Therapy

The other primary treatment for BPD combines client-centered empathy with behavioral problem solving and was developed by Marsha Linehan (1993). Dialectical behavior therapy (DBT) centers on therapists' full acceptance of people with borderline personalities with all their contradictions and acting out, empathically validating their (distorted) beliefs with a matter-of-fact attitude toward their suicidal and other dysfunctional behavior. This total acceptance is necessary, argues Linehan, because the patient is extremely sensitive to criticism and rejection and will pull away from therapy if any hint of a possible rejection is perceived. This acceptance of the current state is a dialectical (or polar opposite) of the goal of bringing about change in the patient. Over time, the goal is to synthesize these opposites and move the patient toward change while maintaining empathic validation of them.

The behavioral aspect of the treatment involves helping patients learn to solve problems, that is, to acquire more effective and socially acceptable ways of handling their daily living problems and controlling their emotions. Work is also done on improving their interpersonal skills and in controlling their anxieties. After many months of intensive treatment, limits are set on their behavior. Patients must commit to 1 year of intensive treatment as part of DBT (Smith & Peck, 2004).

A meta-analysis of all treatment outcome studies evaluating DBT indicates that it is a moderately effective treatment for BPD and results in reductions in symptoms, including suicide attempts and self-injurious behaviors (Kliem, Kröger, & Kosfelder, 2010). There has been an increasing amount of interest in and evidence supporting this treatment approach (Feigenbaum, 2007). Workshops and seminars have been offered around the country, and the therapy is becoming rather widely used. It has also been used in inpatient settings—a 3-month inpatient treatment program using DBT was effective in reducing depression, anxiety, and self-injury and in improving interpersonal functioning (Bohus et al., 2004).

Amanda's therapists faced a common dilemma encountered with borderline patients: Should treatment be aimed at structural intrapsychic change or simply better adaptation to the environment? Waldinger and Gunderson (1984) found in a retrospective study that relatively few borderline patients complete the process of intensive psychotherapy, often terminating when an impasse in therapy occurs. When Amanda decided to change therapists, a decision had to be made as to whether or not she was seeking change to avoid working through a difficult impasse in therapy. It was determined that this may have been the case, but that she was unlikely to remain in therapy if her request was not granted.

Although Amanda's treatment seemed largely unsuccessful, all people with BPD are not equally impaired. Many do have significant disability, but there is a decline in the prevalence of BPD among those older than 44 years (Grant et al., 2008). Not all borderline patients are as self-destructive as Amanda, but they are often challenging to treat.

Discussion Questions

1. What is the main causal factor of BPD? Research has also found evidence for genetic factors; how can they both be related?
2. How did Amanda cause difficulty for the patients and staff in the psychiatric hospital? How could the staff handle this better?
3. Why do therapists find it difficult to treat this disorder? What are the specific symptoms and behaviors that can be challenging?
4. Which treatment would you use if you were the therapist of a patient with BPD: Kernberg's object relations therapy or Linehan's DBT? Why?

CHAPTER 20

Antisocial Personality Disorder: Psychopathy

This case differs from most of the others in this book because Bill was never in therapy. One of the authors was acquainted with Bill during his childhood and adolescence. The following case history is based on this personal experience.

Bill was the third child in the Wallace family. His parents, originally from Europe, had immigrated when Bill was 9 years old. They rented an apartment on the upper floor of a house in a middle-class neighborhood, and Bill's father got a job in a local factory. His mother worked part time in a supermarket. No information is available concerning the family's history when they lived in Europe.

Bill and his older brother, Jack, quickly became part of the neighborhood group and participated in all the activities, including baseball, football, and outings to the beach. Jack became a leader in the group, and Bill, although not as well liked as his brother, was always included.

I began to get to know Bill well. We were the same age; most of the other boys were older. Although we became friends, our relationship was also characterized by a good deal of conflict. When things did not go Bill's way, his response was simple and direct—a fight. My first fight with Bill was during a baseball game at a park. We were on opposing teams and were involved in a close play at second base. He slid into the base; I tagged and called "out," and Bill jumped up swinging his fists. Although he lost these fights as often as he won them, fighting became a consistent pattern in his relationships, both with me and with other neighborhood children. Not even an older and obviously stronger opponent could get Bill to back down.

Bill's aggressiveness was not really what made him seem different as we grew up together. His escalating daredevil and antisocial behavior seemed more peculiar. One of the first of these episodes occurred when Bill organized a window-breaking competition. He explained to me and three other boys that he had recently been walking neighborhood streets at night, throwing rocks through windows. With great enthusiasm, he described the excitement this created and how he had easily eluded the few residents who had come out to try to catch him. Bill wanted the four of us to compete in a window-breaking contest. He had worked out a detailed point system—the larger the window, the more points—and wanted to start that night. We all agreed to meet at 7:30 p.m. in front of his house.

We met as planned and first filled our pockets with stones. The competition soon began, with Bill clearly in the role of leader, encouraging the rest of us and pointing out windows that would yield many points. My own reaction as all this began was extreme fear. All I could think of was, "What if we get caught?" Bill, in contrast, showed no signs of apprehension. Indeed, he seemed ecstatic and was virtually bubbling over with enthusiasm. His only negative reaction of the evening was directed toward me when, after "missing" several windows, I emptied my pockets and withdrew from the competition. "You gutless chicken," he called as I went down the street toward home. The other two boys went along with Bill. They also seemed frightened, but they looked up to Bill and may have been more concerned by his disapproval. Although I was excluded from subsequent nights of competition, Bill eagerly kept me informed of the results. After several months, he was declared the winner when he broke all the large windows of the supermarket where his mother worked.

At age 10, petty theft replaced window breaking as Bill's major source of excitement. It seemed to me that he always stole something whenever I was in a store with him. He would steal anything—candy, fruit, clothing, toys—not just things he wanted. In fact, he often threw away the things he had stolen. He seemed more interested in the excitement than in any actual material gain. He had discovered several ways of getting money. The first was a Roman Catholic church that had two easy sources of cash—a poor box and a container for donations left by worshippers who had lit a candle. Bill cleaned out both on a regular basis. His second source was a restaurant that had a wishing well located in a rear garden, whose proceeds went to the Salvation Army. Although the wishing well was covered with a metal grate, Bill found an opening just large enough to get his hand through. Every couple of weeks, armed with a flashlight and a long stick, he would sneak into the garden at night, move the coins to the right spot, and collect them. Because he often had money, he had to lie regularly to his parents about how he got it, inventing a series of odd jobs he held around the neighborhood. Finally, he regularly stole milk money from various neighborhood homes. Bill even stole the milk money from my home. The first time our money was missing, I went directly after him and accused him of the theft. He denied it. The second time, he admitted the theft and offered to cut me in if I would keep quiet!

One other incident, which occurred when Bill and I were both 12, crystallized for me how Bill was somehow different. About a 15-minute walk from our homes was a river that had many expensive houses along its banks. A tremendous rainstorm caused a flood, and tragically, more than 100 people were killed. Early the next morning, with the news of the disaster in the papers and on the radio, Bill set out for the scene. Because the victims were wealthy, Bill reasoned, he might strike it rich if he could be the first one to find some bodies and take their wallets, watches, and jewelry. He went alone and returned later in the day, proudly displaying his loot—six watches and several hundred dollars. He had found several dead bodies and stolen their possessions. He returned to the river several more times over the next few days, and although he came back empty-handed, he would enthusiastically relate his experiences to anyone who would listen. The excitement and danger seemed more important than the valuables he found.

During these 3 years, most of the neighborhood youngsters had also received more than a glimpse of the Wallaces' family life. Bill's father was frequently out of work and seemed to have trouble holding a job for more than several months at a stretch. He drank heavily. While we played street ball, we often saw him returning home, obviously drunk. At the first glimpse of their drunken father, Bill and Jack would get out of his sight as quickly as possible. Both boys reported frequent beatings, particularly when their father had been drinking. At the same time, Bill's father allowed him to get away with things, such as staying out late at night, which none of the other neighborhood children were allowed to do. Bill and Jack both described their father as unpredictable in his punishments. Their father and mother also fought often, and his mother may well have been physically abused. On many occasions, our play was interrupted by yelling and the sound of loud crashes from their apartment.

The Wallaces eventually moved to an apartment in another area of the city, about a 30-minute bus ride from their first home. Bill and I were no longer close friends, but I kept track of him through Jack, his older brother. According to Jack, Bill's pattern of antisocial behavior escalated. He continued to steal regularly, even from members of his family. He frequently skipped school and got into very serious trouble for hitting a teacher who had tried to break up a fight between him and another boy. Jack was very concerned about Bill and attempted to talk to him several times. Jack reported that during these talks, Bill would genuinely seem to agree that he had to change and would express shame and regret about whatever he had done most recently. However, within a few days the old pattern would be back in full force. Jack eventually came to see Bill's contrition as a con.

We were both 15 the next time I met Bill. Through my continued contacts with Jack, I had learned that Bill had been sent to reform school. I did not know any of the details because Jack had been so ashamed of his brother's behavior that he would not talk about it. One evening shortly after dinner, the doorbell rang. I answered, and Bill motioned me outside. He had escaped from reform school and wanted me to buy him a meal and loan him some money. We went to a local restaurant where I bought a hamburger for him and Cokes for both of us. He told me he had been convicted of car theft and rape the previous year. He had been stealing cars regularly and taking them on joyrides. He was caught when he decided to keep a stolen car, one that had particularly caught his fancy. The third day he had the car, he had parked in a deserted place with a 12-year-old girl he knew from school, where he raped her. As Bill related the story, he became visibly disgusted, not at himself, but at the girl. As he explained it, he was only trying to have some fun and had picked this particular girl because she was only 12 years old and not likely to get pregnant. From his perspective, it was an ideal situation. With pregnancy impossible, she should have just lain back and enjoyed it. He obviously had no concern at all for the feelings of his victim.

I never saw Bill again but through Jack learned what happened to him over the next several years. A few weeks after our meeting, he was apprehended by the police. He had again stolen a car; while driving drunk, he had smashed into a telephone pole. After a short stay in a hospital, he was returned to the reform school, where he spent 2 years. When he was released, Bill had changed greatly. It seemed to Jack that he had now become a real criminal. Car thefts were no longer for joyrides but for profit. Bill became involved in selling stolen cars to others who stripped them to sell their parts. He briefly returned to high school but with no friends there and little real interest, he soon dropped out. He became a regular at the racetrack and lost money there and with several book-makers. As had happened before, Jack tried to talk to his younger brother about the trouble for which he seemed headed. But now even the charade of shame and guilt was gone. Bill expressed an "I'll take what I want when I want it" attitude. When Jack tried to point out the likely negative consequences of his behavior, Bill simply shrugged it off, saying that he was too smart to ever end up in jail.

Shortly after his 18th birthday, Bill attempted a bank robbery, armed with a .38-caliber automatic pistol. Bill was driving a stolen car. On seeing what he thought was a bank, he impulsively decided to rob it. In his rush, he had actually undertaken to rob an office of the electric company. Seeing the people lined up at tellers' windows to pay their bills had made him think it was a bank. Once inside, although recognizing his mistake, he decided to go through with the holdup anyway and had several tellers empty their cash drawers into a sack. A patrol car passed by the office as the holdup was in progress, and seeing what was happening, the policemen stopped to investigate. Bill ran out of the office directly into the police and was easily arrested. He was tried, convicted, and sentenced to 10 years in the penitentiary.

Discussion

The terms *antisocial personality disorder* (ASPD) and *psychopathy* (and sometimes *sociopathy* as well) are often used interchangeably, although there are important differences between the two. Antisocial personality disorder is a diagnostic category that is more centered on the person's behaviors, and psychopathy is a constellation of personality traits as well as behaviors. These traits include callousness, manipulativeness, arrogance, superficiality, and short-temperedness; psychopaths do not form strong emotional connections to others, and they lack empathy, guilt, and remorse (Hare, 2006). Although ASPD is a category, psychopathy probably lies along a dimension (Edens, Marcus, Lilienfeld, & Poythress, 2006). The current *Diagnostic and Statistical Manual of Mental Disorders* (*DSM-IV-TR*; APA, 2000) concept of ASPD involves two major components. The first refers to antisocial behavior before the age of 15. Criteria include truancy, running away from home, frequent lying, theft, arson, and deliberate destruction of property. The second refers to the continuation of this pattern of antisocial behavior in adulthood. Adults with ASPD show irresponsible and antisocial behavior by not working consistently, breaking laws, being irritable and physically aggressive, defaulting on debts, and being reckless. They are impulsive and fail to plan ahead. In addition, they show no regard for truth or remorse for their harmful actions.

The concept of psychopathy is closely linked to the writings of Hervey Cleckley in his classic book, *The Mask of Sanity* (1976). On the basis of his vast clinical experience, Cleckley identified a constellation of personality traits that typify the psychopath. One of the key characteristics of psychopathy is poverty of emotions, both positive and negative. People high on psychopathy have no sense of shame, and even their seemingly positive feelings for others are merely an act. They are superficially charming and manipulate others for personal gain. The lack of some negative emotions, especially anxiety, may make it impossible for psychopaths to learn from their mistakes, and the lack of positive emotions leads them to behave irresponsibly toward others. Cleckley describes the antisocial behavior of the psychopath as "inadequately motivated"; it is not due, for example, to a need for something like money but is performed impulsively, as much for thrills as anything else.

Currently, most researchers identify psychopathy using a checklist developed by Hare et al. (1990). The checklist identifies two major clusters of psychopathic behaviors. The first, referred to as emotional detachment, describes a selfish, remorseless individual who exploits others (descriptors of this cluster include lack of remorse or guilt, callous lack of empathy, and manipulativeness). The second characterizes an antisocial lifestyle (parasitic behavior, pathological lying, history of juvenile delinquency). One important characteristic of people with high levels of psychopathy is their use of instrumental aggression, which is planned, purposeful, and goal directed, as well as the more common reactive aggression, which is characterized by anger and is in response to threat or frustration (Blair, Peschardt, Budhani, Mitchell, & Pine, 2006). Psychopathy is associated with both types of aggression, whereas other disorders are associated with reactive aggression but not instrumental aggression. The degree of psychopathy among adolescents who have committed a crime strongly predicts their likelihood to continue involvement in criminal activities into adulthood, particularly violent offenses (Gretton, Hare, & Catchpole, 2004).

There is continuing controversy about the nature of the relationship between ASPD and psychopathy, but a large study of male offenders suggested that ASPD is a heterogeneous category, and identifying subtypes might be useful (Poythress et al., 2010). This confusion complicates integrating the findings of research in this area because the clinical features are defined in different ways. Bill's behavior during childhood and adolescence clearly meets many of Cleckley's criteria. Bill was unreliable, untruthful, lacking in any feelings of shame about his misconduct, and totally without anxiety. His antisocial behavior (such as stealing) was not motivated by any genuine desire to possess the stolen objects but rather to get some sort of thrill. And he often displayed poor judgment, particularly in his escapades of late adolescence. His poverty of emotion was amply demonstrated by his thefts from the homes of his friends and by the attitude he had toward the victim of his rape, which was completely lacking in empathy.

In a large, nationally representative study, 3.63% of adult Americans met the criteria for ASPD (Grant et al., 2004). Three times as many men as women have the disorder. It is more common among Native Americans, less common among Asian Americans, and less common among older rather than younger age groups. Psychopathy is found in about 1% of Americans, but about 25% of prison inmates (Hare, 2006). There is no significant difference between African Americans and European Americans (whites) on the level of psychopathy (Skeem, Edens, Camp, & Colwell, 2004). Pimps, con artists, murderers, and drug dealers are by no means the only antisocial personalities. Business executives, professors, politicians, physicians, plumbers, salespeople, carpenters, and bartenders can have antisocial personality traits as well. Psychopathy may be more common in business settings than in the general population, and the ability to manipulate others and lie about coworkers may lead to success in a competitive corporate environment as well as in "white-collar" crimes (Gao & Raine, 2010). Adult antisocial personalities have a history of behavior problems and conduct disorder in childhood (Paris, 2004). Their symptoms tend to fade some during middle age, and a number of people with antisocial personalities die prematurely.

Etiological Considerations

Much research has been done on the causes of ASPD, especially in light of its costs to our society. Research evidence from many different areas of focus has shown promise. One area of research has focused on identifying abnormalities in the brain that might explain the disorder. Researchers in one study examined brain reactions to certain kinds of auditory stimuli and found significant differences between incarcerated men classified as psychopathic compared to those classified as nonpsychopathic; these differences were suggestive of problems in the paralimbic system, such as temporal lobe dysfunction (Kiehl, Bates, Laurens, Hare, & Liddle, 2006). Neurobiological investigations have also suggested abnormalities in the functioning of the amygdala (a part of the brain involved in aversive conditioning and responses to facial expressions depicting fear and sadness) among people with high psychopathy (Blair, 2003). Some studies have shown that they have smaller amygdalas, and others have shown reduced amygdala response. The reasons for these brain differences, however, are unknown.

Several psychological and cognitive factors provide important clues to the etiology of ASPD. Some key features of psychopathy are impulsivity and difficulty learning from punishment. In one study demonstrating this phenomenon, participants viewed playing cards on a computer screen (Newman, Patterson, & Kosson, 1987). If a face card appeared, the participant won 5 cents; if a card other than a face card appeared, he lost 5 cents. After each trial, the participant could either continue or quit the game. The probability of losing was controlled by the experimenter and started at 10%, but increased by 10% every 10 cards until it reached 100%. The psychopaths continued to play the game much longer than the control participants. Of the psychopaths, 9 out of 12 continued to play the game even after they had lost money on 19 of the last 20 trials. They appeared unable to alter a maladaptive response. When the same game was played with a 5-second waiting period imposed after each trial, the psychopaths markedly reduced the number of trials for which they played the game. Enforcing a delay may force psychopaths to reflect on their behavior and thus be less impulsive. Psychopaths did not pause after either punishment or reward and seemed not to reflect on feedback; in general, they played more quickly (Moltó, Poy, Segarra, Pastor, & Montañés, 2007).

These findings seem particularly applicable to Bill. The fear that might prevent stealing, breaking windows, and looting seemed totally absent in him. From his own statements, we can conclude that he felt little shame or remorse about his transgressions. Indeed, he seemed proud of them. He clearly had little or no empathy for his victims. Finally, Bill also displayed characteristics similar to those revealed in the study by Newman, Patterson, and Kosson (1987), not reflecting on the negative consequences of his antisocial behavior.

Because of the role of the autonomic nervous system in emotion, investigators have examined psychopaths for both their resting levels of autonomic activity and their patterns of autonomic reactivity to various classes of stimuli. Psychopaths have lower than normal levels of skin conductance, are less autonomically reactive when stressful or aversive stimuli are presented, and have lower resting heart rates (Lorber, 2004). These results are consistent with clinical descriptions of psychopaths as being nonanxious and with research using other measures of emotion, showing that people high on psychopathy are generally less emotionally reactive (Herpetz, Werth, & Lukas, 2001; Patrick, Bradley, & Lang, 1993). While some psychopaths have a fearless temperament, others are impulsive and have difficulty controlling their negative emotions (Dindo & Fowles, 2011).

Overall, the research literature is consistent with the idea that it is difficult to arouse negative emotions in psychopaths. This may well be an important determinant of their repetitive antisocial behavior. But arousing negative emotions is not the only component of socialization; empathy—being aware of and in tune with the emotions of others—could be equally important. The idea that people with high levels of psychopathy lack empathy has been tested by examining their skin conductance responses while viewing slides of varying content. Consistent with the idea that psychopathy involves a lack of empathy, they showed smaller responses to slides showing people in distress (Blair, Jones, Clark, & Smith, 1997).

Other researchers have explored genetic factors. Both criminality and antisocial personality have heritable components (Hicks, Krueger, Iacono, McGue, & Patrick, 2004). Studies of twins reared apart show that genes play a role in the likelihood that a person will commit a criminal act (Gottesman & Goldsmith, 1994). For ASPD, twin studies show higher concordance for monozygotic (MZ) than dizygotic (DZ) pairs (Lyons et al., 1995), and adoption studies show higher rates of antisocial behavior in the adopted children of biological parents with ASPD (Cadoret, Yates, Troughton, Woodworth, & Stewart, 1995). A large, longitudinal twin study identified several different types of etiological genetic factors, including one that is associated with life-course persistent antisocial behavior (lasting from childhood through adulthood) and one that is associated with only adult antisocial behavior. Adolescent antisocial behavior appears to be more related to environmental factors (Silberg, Rutter, Tracy, Maes, & Eaves, 2007). The personality traits of callousness and lack of emotion are also strongly heritable (Gunter, Vaughn, & Philibert, 2010).

Although genetic factors are clearly involved, they may interact with environmental factors. A notable example of this interaction is the monoamine oxidase A (MAOA) gene. The level of MAOA enzyme, regulated by this gene, affects the actions of serotonin, norepinephrine, and dopamine in ways related to the risk for antisocial behavior. When there is a low level of the MAOA enzyme, there is increased antisocial behavior when the adolescent is raised in an environment characterized by parental neglect, exposure to violence between parents, and inconsistent parental discipline (Foley et al., 2004). Physical abuse elevates the risk of dysfunction for both groups but especially strongly for those with the gene for low levels of this enzyme (Kim-Cohen et al., 2006). Child maltreatment led to ASPD when combined with this form of the MAOA enzyme even in an adopted sample (Beach et al., 2010). Genes may only be expressed in certain types of environments, and interactions between genes and environments are an important new line of research.

Researchers have also found a link between prenatal exposure to cigarette smoking of the mother and later antisocial behavior. Research has shown this link to be stronger the more cigarettes that were used, even when genetic risks for antisocial behavior were controlled (Maughan, Taylor, Caspi, & Moffitt, 2004). However, investigators cautioned that the effects could be due to some other difference in the environment that has not been controlled. More research is needed to find out whether cigarette smoking during pregnancy increases the child's later antisocial behavior.

Environmental factors are also implicated in the origins of ASPD. Children who grow up in physically abusive or neglectful homes are at increased risk for antisocial behavior in adolescence and adulthood (Cicchetti & Toth, 2004). Authoritarian parenting characterized by a combination of punitiveness and restrictiveness with low warmth has been linked to antisocial behavior in children (Smith & Farrington, 2004). In addition, conflict and violence between parents increases a child's antisociality. The harsh yet inconsistent disciplinary practices of Bill's father, as well as the conflict between his parents, mesh well with these findings. The link between parents with antisocial traits and children with antisocial traits may be partly due to harsh, inconsistent, or rejecting parenting behaviors (Barnow, Lucht, & Freyberger, 2005). In addition to this link through disrupted parenting, mothers' antisocial behavior is linked to adolescents' antisocial behavior through the teens' awareness of their mothers engaging in this behavior by drinking too much, breaking the law, having a lot of conflicts with others, lying, and engaging in reckless actions; thereby, the mothers serve as a model to imitate (Dogan, Conger, Kim, & Masyn, 2007). If a mother is depressed during her pregnancy, her child has twice the risk of antisocial behavior and four times the risk of violent behavior during adolescence, even when taking into account her depression at other times in the child's life and the family's exposure to adversity (Hay, Pawlby, Waters, Perra, & Sharp, 2010). The depression may affect the developing fetus or may alter the quality of the relationship between the mother and the expected child.

Although parents indeed influence their children, children also influence their parents, so considering parenting styles without also examining temperamental or neurological differences in children might miss important information. For example, Moffitt (1993) proposed that persistent antisocial behavior begins with deficits in neurological functions, such as attention and impulsivity. These deficits make the child difficult for the parents to handle and can produce the type of disciplinary practices that were found by the early studies on parenting and psychopathic behavior. Social factors are important as well; school failure, peer rejection, and identification with a deviant peer group are important predictors of adult antisocial behavior (Granic & Patterson, 2006). Growing up in poverty is also a risk factor for the development of antisocial traits in children. Macmillan, McMorris, and Kruttschnitt (2004) found that when families living in poverty were able to escape the poverty, their children's antisocial behavior was reduced. Long-term exposure to poverty was most harmful.

Recently, psychologists have been reexamining various types of mental disorders from an evolutionary perspective. Antisocial personality traits can be conceptualized as a successful strategy for survival that originated in genes that would have been selected for by the social environment, and thus continued in the human genome. There are two different ways this could be seen as an advantage, either at the individual level or at the societal level. At the individual level, antisociality could be a developmental strategy for harsh, difficult environments, which would trigger the genes controlling it so the child growing up in this harsh environment would develop a cheating or free-riding strategy (Smith, 2006). Such a strategy would be more successful in a harsh environment, at least sometimes, than a cooperative, relational strategy. This model is consistent with the evidence that there is a gene-environment interaction for antisociality that is triggered by child physical abuse. At the societal level, humans typically resided in small social groups and would have had one member with high antisociality, estimating from the current rates of the disorder in contemporary populations. This member would have given the social group experience with deception and manipulativeness and given them a chance to develop the ability to detect and cope with this strategy so that when they faced similar challenges from others outside the group, they would not have been as vulnerable (Miric, Hallet-Mathieu, & Amar, 2005). However, to limit the effectiveness of the manipulativeness of the person with antisociality, the trait was countered by impulsiveness to reduce its destructiveness; the social groups carrying genes of just manipulativeness would have died out. These hypotheses provide interesting explanations for why the genes for this disorder were not eliminated through natural selection.

Treatment

There is general agreement that treatment is often unsuccessful for psychopaths. Cleckley (1976, pp. 438–439) summarized his clinical impressions as follows:

> Over a period of many years I have remained discouraged about the effect of treatment on the psychopath. Having regularly failed in my own efforts to help such patients, ...I hoped for a while that treatment by others would be more successful. I have had the opportunity to see patients of this sort who were treated by psychoanalysis, by psychoanalytically oriented psychotherapy, by group and milieu therapy.... None of these measures impressed me as achieving successful results.... I have now, after more than three decades, had the opportunity to observe a considerable number of patients who, through commitment or the threat of losing their probation status or by other means, were kept under treatment...for years. The therapeutic failure in all such patients leads me to feel that we do not at present have any kind of psychotherapy that can be relied on to change the psychopath fundamentally.

There is not much empirical evidence for the effectiveness of treatments for psychopaths (Lynam, Caspi, Moffitt, Loeber, & Stouthamer-Loeber, 2007). Psychopharmacology is not effective (Rodrigo, Rajapakse, & Jayananda, 2010). Some forms of therapy may even have negative effects. Rice, Harris, and Cormier (1992) compared the results of a therapeutic community to standard institutionalization in a sample of prison inmates. Although the special program reduced recidivism in nonpsychopaths, it actually increased it among psychopaths. The inability of psychopaths to form an honest, trusting relationship with a therapist may be a major reason for the ineffectiveness of psychotherapy. A person who lies, cares little for the feelings of others, and has few regrets about personal misconduct is certainly a poor candidate for most forms of psychotherapy. One experienced clinician (Lion, 1978) has suggested the following guidelines:

> First, the therapist must be continually vigilant with regard to manipulation on the part of the patient. Second, he must assume, until proved otherwise, that information given to him by the patient contains distortions and fabrications. Third, he must recognize that a working alliance develops, if ever, exceedingly late in any therapeutic relationship.

Preventing some cases of ASPD may be possible through programs designed to address situations that put individuals at risk for developing the disorder. For example, programs to reduce child abuse might prevent later antisocial behavior among the children at risk for abuse (Harrington & Bailey, 2004). Also, targeting groups of children and adolescents known to be at high risk for antisocial behavior, such as those with attention-deficit/hyperactivity disorder, might be effective. Behavioral parent-training, which teaches parents behavioral techniques to reinforce their children's adaptive behavior and decrease their antisocial behavior, is moderately effective in reducing antisocial behavior in children, and cognitive-behavioral therapy, which teaches problem solving and corrects perceptual distortions, is moderately effective in reducing antisocial behavior in adolescents (McCart, Priester, Davies, & Azen, 2006). Although the evidence for effective treatments for adults is scant, there is more to show that treating antisociality among adolescents and children does work (Salekin, Worley, & Grimes, 2010). Multisystemic treatment, a treatment approach for juvenile offenders that focuses on family and home interventions, shows promise (Curtis, Ronan, & Borduin, 2004). The treatment focuses on making changes in the family, school, and community settings to reduce their contributions to problem behaviors. A recent meta-analysis found that adolescents who received the treatment had better functioning than 70% of those who did not receive the treatment. This raises the hope that specific types of early intervention may reduce the severity and cost of future adult ASPD.

Discussion Questions

1. How could Bill's ASPD have emerged from the combination of genes and environmental experiences? What specific environmental factors were important in Bill's life? In what we know about the case, was there any evidence for his father having antisocial traits?
2. Which symptoms of ASPD did Bill have?

3. Research suggests that the most effective treatment for ASPD is to prevent cases in the first place by focusing on children and adolescents at risk for the disorder. What are the obstacles to doing this?

4. The difficulty in treating people with ASPD poses great challenges for our society, given their higher rates of violence and criminal behavior. Some have advocated keeping such people incarcerated until they are older in an attempt to prevent their future crimes. What do you think about this? What are the pros and cons of such an approach?

CHAPTER 21

Autistic Disorder

Sam Williams was the second child of John and Carol Williams. The couple had been married for 5 years when Sam was born; John was a lawyer and Carol a homemaker. Sam weighed 7 pounds, 11 ounces at birth, which had followed an uncomplicated, full-term pregnancy. Delivered by caesarean section, he came home after 6 days in the hospital.

His parents reported that Sam's early development seemed quite normal. He was not colicky, and he slept and ate well. During his first 2 years, there were no childhood illnesses except some mild colds. By Sam's second birthday, however, his parents began to have concerns. He had been somewhat slower than his older sister in achieving some developmental milestones (such as sitting up alone and crawling). Furthermore, his motor development seemed uneven. He would crawl normally for a few days and then not crawl at all for a while. Although he made babbling sounds, he had not developed any speech and did not even seem to understand anything his parents said to him. Simple requests, such as "Come" or "Do you want a cookie?" elicited no response.

Initially, his parents thought that Sam might be deaf. Later they vacillated between this belief and the idea that Sam was being stubborn. They reported many frustrating experiences in which they tried to force him to obey a command or say "Mama" or "Dada." Sometimes Sam would go into a tantrum during one of these situations, yelling, screaming, and throwing himself to the floor. That same year, their pediatrician told them that Sam might be mentally retarded.

As he neared his third birthday, Sam's parents noticed him engaging in more and more strange and puzzling behavior. Most obvious were his repetitive hand movements. Many times each day, he would suddenly flap his hands rapidly for several minutes (activities like this are called self-stimulatory behaviors). Other times he rolled his eyes around in their sockets. He still did not speak, but he made smacking sounds, and sometimes he would burst out laughing for no apparent reason. He was walking now and often walked on his toes. Sam had not been toilet trained, although his parents had tried.

Sam's social development was also worrying his parents. Although he would let them hug and touch him, he would not look at them and generally seemed indifferent to their attention. He also did not play at all with his older sister, seeming to prefer being left alone. Even his solitary play was strange. He did not engage in make-believe play with his toys—for example, pretending to drive a toy car into a gas station. Instead, he was more likely just to manipulate a toy, such as a car, holding it and repetitively spinning its wheels. The only thing that really seemed to interest him was a ceiling fan in the den. He was content to sit there for as long as permitted, watching intently as the fan spun around and around. He would often have temper tantrums when the fan was turned off.

At the age of 3, the family's pediatrician recommended a complete physical and neurological examination. Sam was found to be in good physical health, and the neurological examination revealed nothing remarkable. A psychiatric evaluation was performed several months later. Sam was brought to a treatment facility specializing in behavior disturbances of childhood and was observed for a day. During that time, the psychiatrist was able to see firsthand most of the behaviors that Sam's parents had described—hand flapping, toe walking, smacking sounds, and preference for being left alone. When the psychiatrist evaluated Sam, she observed that a loud slapping noise did not elicit a startle response as it does in most children. The only vocalization she could elicit that approximated speech was a repetitive "nah, nah." Sam did, however, obey some simple commands such as "Come" and "Go get a potato chip." She diagnosed Sam as having autistic disorder and recommended placement in a day-treatment setting.

Conceptualization and Treatment

Sam was 4 years old by the time there was an opening for him at the treatment center. He attended the special school 5 days a week, spending the remainder of his time at home with his parents and sister. The school provided a comprehensive educational program conducted by specially trained teachers. The program was organized mainly along operant conditioning principles. In addition, Sam's parents attended classes once a week to learn operant conditioning so they could continue the school program at home. The school's personnel conducted another evaluation of Sam, observing him in the school and later at home. Interviews with the parents established that they were both well adjusted and that their marriage was stable. Both parents were, however, experiencing considerable stress from having to cope with Sam on a day-to-day basis and from their fears that his condition might have been caused by something they had done.

One of the first targets of the training program was Sam's eye contact. When working with Sam, his teacher provided small food rewards when Sam spontaneously looked at him. The teacher also began requesting eye contact and again rewarded Sam when he complied. Along with this training, the teacher worked on having Sam obey other simple commands. The teacher would wait for a time when Sam seemed attentive and would then, establishing eye contact, say the command and model the desired behavior by demonstrating it. For example, the teacher would say, "Sam, stretch your arms up like this," lifting Sam's arms up and rewarding him with praise and a small amount of food, such as a grape. This procedure was repeated several times. When Sam began to become more skilled at following the command, the teacher stopped raising Sam's arms for him and had him do it himself. These training trials were conducted daily. As Sam's response to a particular command became well established, the teacher would expand his learning to following commands in other situations and by other people. Sam's progress was slow. It often took weeks of training to establish his response to a simple command. After his first year in the school, he responded reliably to several simple requests such as "Come," "Give it to me," and "Put on your coat." At the same time that Sam was learning to respond to commands, other aspects of the training program were also being implemented. While Sam was in the classroom, his teacher worked with him on trying to develop skills that would be important in learning, for example, sitting in his seat, maintaining eye contact, and listening and working for longer periods of time. His teacher used the same reward strategy to teach Sam each activity.

As these skills became better established, the teacher also began working on expanding Sam's vocabulary by teaching him the words for pictures of common objects. A picture of one object, such as an orange, was placed on a table in front of Sam. After Sam had looked at the object, the teacher said, "This is an orange. Point to the orange." When Sam pointed to the orange, he was rewarded. If necessary, the teacher would move his hand for him at first. Next another picture, such as a cat, was selected and the same procedure followed. Then the two pictures were placed in front of Sam and the teacher asked him to point to one of them: "Point to the orange." If Sam pointed correctly, he was rewarded. If he did not, the teacher moved his hand to the correct object. After Sam had correctly pointed to the orange several times in a row, the teacher asked him to point to the cat. With that response established, the teacher switched the position of the pictures and repeated the process. When Sam had begun to point correctly to the orange and the cat, a third picture was introduced and the training procedure was started anew. During 1 year of training, Sam learned the names of 38 common objects with this procedure.

Sam's speech therapist, whom he saw daily, was also working with him on language skills. Initially, they worked on getting Sam to imitate simple sounds. Sitting across a table from Sam and waiting until Sam was looking (or prompting him to look by holding a piece of food near his mouth), the teacher would say, "Say this, ah," taking care to accentuate the movements required for this sound. At first, Sam was rewarded for making any sound. Subsequently, rewards were given when Sam approximated more and more closely the required sound. As sounds were mastered, Sam was trained to say simple words in a similar fashion. Over the course of a year, Sam learned a few words—"bye-bye," "no more," and "mine," but overall, his verbal imitation remained poor.

Teaching Sam to dress and undress himself was another target during the first year. Initially, his teacher helped him through the entire sequence, describing each step as they did it. Next, they would go through the sequence again, but now Sam had to do the last step himself (taking off his shoes, putting on his shoes). More difficult steps (tying shoes) were worked on individually to give Sam more practice on them. When some progress was being made, this aspect of the treatment was carried out by the parents. They first observed the teacher working with Sam and then discussed the procedure and were shown how to make a chart to record Sam's progress. Over a period of weeks, the number of steps that Sam had to complete by himself was gradually increased, moving from the last toward the first. Sam was rewarded each time he dressed or undressed, usually with a special treat, such as a favorite breakfast food. In this case, the training was successful. By midyear, Sam had mastered dressing and undressing.

Toilet training was another area that Sam's parents and teachers tackled. At home and at school, Sam was rewarded for using the toilet. He was checked every hour to see if his pants were dry. If they were, he was praised and reminded that when he went to the toilet he would get a reward. Shortly thereafter, Sam would be taken to the toilet, where he would remove his pants and sit. If he urinated or defecated, he was given a large reward. If not, he was given a small reward just for sitting. As this training was progressing, Sam was also taught to associate the word "potty" with going to the toilet. Progress was slow at first, and there were many "accidents," which both teachers and parents were instructed to ignore. But Sam soon caught on and began urinating or defecating more and more often when he was taken to the bathroom. Then the parents and teachers began working on having him tell them when he had to go. When they checked to see if his pants were dry, they would tell him to say "potty" when he had to go to the toilet. Although there were many ups and downs in Sam's progress, by the end of the year, he was having an average of fewer than two accidents per week.

Sam's temper tantrums slowed his progress during his first year in the special school. They occurred sometimes when he was given a command or when a teacher interrupted something he was doing. Not getting a reward during a training session also led to tantrums. Sam would scream loudly, throw himself to the ground, and flail away with his arms and legs. Several interventions were tried. Sam's tantrums usually led to getting his own way, particularly at home. For example, a tantrum had often resulted in getting his parents to keep the ceiling fan on, even when they wanted to turn it off. Ignoring the tantrum was the first approach. Sam's teachers and parents simply let the tantrum play itself out, acting as if it had not happened. This did not reduce the number of tantrums, so "time-out" was tried. Every time a tantrum started, Sam was picked up, carried to a special room, and left there for 10 minutes or until the screaming stopped. This procedure also failed to have much of an effect on the tantrums and screaming, even with several modifications such as lengthening the time-out period.

During Sam's second year of treatment, many of the first year's programs were continued. Sam, now 6 years old, was responding to more commands, and his ability to recognize and point to simple objects increased. In speech therapy, he learned to imitate more sounds and some new words ("hello," "cookie," and "book"), but his progress was slow and uneven. He would seem to master some sound or word and then somehow lose it. He was still dressing and undressing himself and using the toilet reliably.

Feeding skills were one of the first targets for the second-year program. Although his parents had tried to get him to use a knife, fork, and spoon, Sam resisted and ate with his fingers or by licking the food from his plate. Drinking from a cup was also a problem. He still used a baby cup with only a small opening at the top. The feeding skills program was implemented by both Sam's teachers and parents and involved a combination of modeling and operant conditioning. Training sessions conducted at mealtime first involved getting Sam to use a spoon. Sam was shown how to hold the spoon; then the teacher picked up the spoon, saying, "Watch me. You push the spoon in like this and then lift it up to your mouth." Sam did not initially imitate, so the teacher had to guide him through the necessary steps: moving his hand and spoon to pick up food, raising his arm until the spoon was at his mouth, telling him to open his mouth, and guiding the spoon in. Praise was provided as each step in the chain was completed. After many repetitions, he was required to do the last step by himself. Gradually, more and more of the steps were done by Sam himself. Successes were followed by praise and failures by saying "no" or removing his meal for a short time. When eating with a spoon was well established, the training was expanded to using a fork and drinking from a cup. In several months, Sam was eating and drinking well.

Sam's failure to play with other children was also a major focus during the second year. The first step was to get him to play near other children. Most of his playtime was spent alone, even when other children were in the playroom with him. His teacher watched Sam carefully and rewarded him with small bits of food whenever he was near another child with autistic disorder. A procedure was also used to force Sam to interact with another child. Sam and another child would be seated next to each other and given the task of stacking some blocks. Each child was, in turn, given a block and prompted to place it on the stack. In addition to praising them individually as they stacked each block, both children were rewarded with praise and food when they had completed their block tower. After repeating this process several times, the program was expanded to include the cooperative completion of simple puzzles. "Sam, put the dog in here. Okay now, Hannah, put the cat here." Gradually the prompts were faded out, and the children were simply rewarded for their cooperative play. Although this aspect of therapy progressed well, transferring these skills to the natural play environment proved difficult. Attempts were made to have Sam and another child play together with toys such as a farm set or a small train. The teacher encouraged them to move the objects around, talking to them about what they were doing and rewarding them for following simple commands. Although Sam would usually follow these commands, his play remained solitary, with little eye contact or cooperation with the other child.

Sam's self-stimulatory behavior was a final target of the second year. Sam's hand flapping and eye rolling had already decreased somewhat over the past year, perhaps because more of his day was being filled with constructive activities. Now a specific intervention, to be used by Sam's teachers and his parents, was planned. Whenever Sam began hand flapping, he was stopped and told to hold his hands still, except when told to move them, for 5 minutes. During the 5-minute period, he was told to hold his hands in several different positions for periods of 30 seconds. If he did not follow the command, the teacher or parent moved his hands into the desired position; if he did not maintain the position for 30 seconds, the teacher or parent held his hands still. Food rewards were provided for successful completion of each 30-second period. Gradually, the teachers and parents were able to get Sam to comply without moving his hands for him or holding him. Then they turned to the eye rolling and implemented a similar program, having Sam fix his gaze on certain objects around his environment whenever he began to roll his eyes. Over a period of several months of training, Sam's self-stimulatory behavior decreased by about 50%.

At the beginning of his third year in school, Sam, now 7 years old, was given an intelligence test and achieved an IQ of 30, a score reflecting severe mental retardation. The language and speech training continued, as did the attempts to reduce the frequency of his self-stimulatory behavior. His tantrums, which had not responded to previous interventions, were becoming worse. In addition to screaming and throwing himself on the floor, he now became violent at times. On several occasions, he had either punched, bitten, or kicked his sister. His parents reported that during these tantrums he became so out of control that they feared he might seriously injure someone. Similar episodes occurred in school, usually when an ongoing activity was interrupted or he failed at some task.

Trouble had also emerged on the school bus. All children were required to wear seat belts, but Sam would not do so and was often out of his seat. Twice in one week, the bus driver stopped the bus and tried to get Sam buckled back into his seat. He bit the bus driver once the first time and twice the second. The bus company acted quickly and suspended service for Sam. In an initial attempt to resolve the problem, Sam was put on haloperidol (Haldol), a drug widely used in the treatment of schizophrenia in adults. But after a month of the drug and no apparent effect, it was stopped. In the meantime, Sam's mother had to drive him to and from school. He was beginning to miss days or be late when his mother had schedule conflicts.

The seriousness of the tantrum problem and the fact that other treatments had not worked led to the implementation of a punishment system. Because Sam's tantrums and violent outbursts were almost always preceded by loud screaming, it was decided to try to break up the usual behavior sequence and punish the screaming. Whenever Sam began to scream, a mixture of water and Tabasco sauce was squirted into his mouth. The effect of this procedure, which was used by both his teachers and parents, was dramatic. The first day of the treatment, Sam began screaming and was squirted six times. His response to the Tabasco mixture was one of shock and some crying, which stopped quickly after he was allowed to rinse out his mouth. The next day, he was squirted with the Tabasco twice. The third and fourth days, he did not scream at all. The fifth day, he had one screaming episode; thereafter, he neither screamed nor had a severe temper tantrum again for the rest of the year.

Sam's progress in other areas was not so dramatic. His vocabulary slowly expanded, as he learned to say more words and recognize more and more objects. But his performance was highly variable from day to day. His self-stimulatory behavior continued, although at a level below that which had been present earlier. He remained isolated, preferring to be alone rather than with other children.

Discussion

Autistic disorder was first described in 1943 by a Harvard psychiatrist, Leo Kanner, who noticed a group of disturbed children that behaved differently than children with mental retardation or with schizophrenia. He named the syndrome early infantile autism because they had an extreme autistic aloneness that shut out anything from the outside. Kanner considered autistic aloneness the most fundamental symptom, but he also found that these children had been unable from the beginning of life to relate to other people, were severely limited in language, and had an obsessive desire that everything about them remain exactly the same. Despite its early description by Kanner and others, the disorder was not accepted into official diagnostic nomenclature until the publication of the *Diagnostic and Statistical Manual of Mental Disorders* (*DSM-III*) in 1980 (APA). In *DSM-IV-TR* (APA, 2000) *autistic disorder* is classified as one of the pervasive developmental disorders.

A major feature of autistic disorder is abnormality in social development (Volkmar, Chawarska, & Klin, 2005). Children with autistic disorder have a lack of interest in or difficulty relating to people, which is found from the very beginning of life. Infants with autistic disorder are often reported to be "good babies" because they do not place any demands on their parents. They do not fret or demand attention, but nor do they reach out or smile or look at their mothers when being fed. When they are picked up or cuddled, they often arch their bodies away from their caretakers instead of molding themselves against the adult as many other babies do. They are content to sit quietly in their playpens for hours, never paying attention to other people. After infancy, they do not form typical attachments with people but may become extremely attached to mechanical objects such as refrigerators or vacuum cleaners. Normally, developing infants show an ability to pay attention to movements by people as early as the second day of life, but this ability is missing in autistic children even by 2 years of age (Klin, Lin, Gorrindo, Ramsay, & Jones, 2009). This inborn ability, also present in newly hatched chicks and a wide range of other species, is the basis for social interaction, and children with autistic disorder instead focus on inanimate and random movements. As children, they often do not initiate interactions with others, use facial expressions to communicate with others, share enjoyment with others, or offer empathy to others (Bishop, Ganahan, & Lord, 2007). They are less able to identify emotional expressions on others' faces, especially when the expressions are subtle (Rump, Giovannelli, Minshew, & Strauss, 2009). They rapidly fall behind their peers in development. Clearly, this feature was very characteristic of Sam. Although he did not actively avoid human contact or develop an attachment with a mechanical object, he was almost totally asocial.

Communication deficits are a second major feature of autism. Mutism—complete absence of speech—is common, as was true with Sam. About 50% of all children with autistic disorder never learn to speak (Paul, 1987). When they do speak, peculiarities are often found, including echolalia, where children echo, usually with remarkable fidelity, what they have heard another person say. In delayed echolalia, the child may not repeat the sentence or phrase until hours or weeks after hearing it. Another abnormality common in the speech of children with autistic disorder is pronoun reversal. They refer to themselves as "he," "you," or by their own proper names; they seldom use the pronouns "I" or "me" and then only when referring to others.

The ability or inability to speak is often an effective means of predicting the later adjustment of children with autistic disorder, an additional indication of the central role of language. Billstedt, Gillberg, and Gillberg (2007) followed up a community sample of 105 people with autistic disorder from early childhood until young adulthood. They found that those who had developed some spoken language by age 5 had a better outcome as adults than those who had not. In fact, language development by age 5 was the best predictor of adult outcome among these individuals with autistic disorders. Based on these findings, we would predict a relatively poor outcome for Sam.

A third major feature of autistic disorder is restricted or stereotyped interests (Volkmar et al., 2005), including compulsive and ritualistic activity, such as a fascination with spinning objects, as shown by Sam. They may have difficulty walking but be proficient at twirling objects and in performing ritualistic hand movements. Other rhythmic movements, such as endless body rocking, seem to please them. They may also become preoccupied with manipulating a mechanical object and be very upset when interrupted. These behaviors may serve the purpose of soothing or occupying them (Leekam, Prior, & Uljarevic, 2011). Almost all children with autism show some type of repetitive sensorimotor behavior (Lord, 2010). Furthermore, children with autistic disorder often become extremely upset over changes in daily routine and their surroundings. An offer of milk in a different drinking cup or a rearrangement of furniture may make them cry or bring on a temper tantrum. Even common greetings must not vary. These symptoms suggest a compulsive need for stability (Smith et al., 2009). In play, they may continually line up toys or construct intricate patterns out of household objects. They engage in much less symbolic or make-believe play than either normal or mentally retarded children of the same mental age, showing impaired imagination (Leekam et al., 2011). They may become preoccupied with train schedules, subway routes, or number sequences, and even if the focus of their preoccupation is an appropriate one for children, such as dinosaurs, the intensity of it is debilitating, and it interferes with their daily lives (Lord, 2010). Clearly, Sam displayed many of these behaviors.

In addition to these three major signs, many children with autistic disorder have problems in eating, often refusing food or eating only one or a few kinds of food. This hyperresponsiveness, an aversion to new stimuli, is also seen in oversensitivity to new sounds or tactile experiences. Hyperresponsiveness was once thought to be unique to children with autistic disorder, but it is actually strongly linked to mental age; it is observed among children who are mentally retarded as well (Baranek, Boyd, Poe, David, & Watson, 2007). Often the children have sensory problems. Like Sam, some children with autistic disorder are first thought to be deaf because they never respond to any sound; some even seem to be insensitive to sound or light. Development is usually delayed, with frequent difficulty in becoming toilet trained; head banging and other self-injurious behaviors are common (Bishop et al., 2007). Children with autistic disorder whose intelligence score is in the normal range are able to describe their simple emotional experiences such as anger or happiness, but when describing complex emotions such as embarrassment or pride, their accounts are very simplified, even impoverished, and do not fit the context in which they were described as having occurred (Losh & Capps, 2006).

Autistic disorder is being diagnosed more frequently (Barbaresi, Katusic, Colligan, Weaver, & Jacobsen, 2005). From 1980 to 1983, the incidence was 5.5 per 100,000 children, but for 1995 to 1997, it was 44.9 per 100,000, an 8.2-fold increase. The increase was most noticeable after the publication of the *DSM-III-R* in 1988 (APA), which broadened the diagnostic criteria and increased awareness of autism. It is probable that the increase in cases is at least in part due to these changes rather than to an actual increase in the disorder. In addition, the fact that autistic disorder is now being diagnosed at a younger age increases the prevalence rate (Wazana, Bresnahan, & Kline, 2007). Special education services are available for children with a diagnosis of autism, so clinicians may be more likely to make that diagnosis so children who are having difficulty would be able to receive services (Barbaresi, Colligan, Weaver, & Katusic, 2009). It is likely that many real cases of autistic disorder used to go undetected, and it is still not clear whether autistic disorder is becoming more common or just being better identified.

Boys have rates of autistic disorder that are three to four times higher than girls (Volkmar et al., 2005). There is a high comorbidity with seizure disorders. There has been a growing interest in autism spectrum disorders, particularly in

Asperger's syndrome. There is controversy about whether the spectrum disorders are really separate disorders, and the diagnostic criteria are not well defined (Volkmar, Lord, Bailey, Schultz, & Klin, 2004). Without clearly defined criteria, such disorders, especially Asperger's syndrome, are likely to be overdiagnosed. Clinicians must be cautious about doing this because labeling a child who may just have poor social skills as having an autistic disorder could have negative implications for the child and family.

About 75 to 80% of people with autistic disorder are mentally retarded (Kabot, Masi, & Segal, 2003). A very small number of individuals with autistic disorder have the rare savant syndrome, a discrete area of outstanding ability such as calendar calculation or art, music, or memory skills in some very specific area (Heaton & Wallace, 2004). Savant syndrome is associated with autistic disorder but is not understood.

What happens to such severely disturbed children when they reach adulthood? Kanner (1973) reported the adult status of some of the children whom he had described in his original paper. Two developed epileptic seizures; by 1966, one of them had died, and the other was in a state mental hospital. Four others had spent most of their lives in institutions. One had remained mute but was working on a farm and as an orderly in a nursing home. The last two made at least somewhat satisfactory recoveries. Although both still lived with their parents and had little social life, they were gainfully employed and had some recreational interests. From his review of early follow-up studies, Lotter (1978) concluded that only 5 to 17% of autistic children had a relatively good outcome in adulthood. Most of the remaining children had a poor outcome, and 50% were institutionalized. Recent studies have reached similar conclusions (Nordin & Gillberg, 1998).

Etiological Considerations

Investigators believe that neurobiological factors are the cause of autistic disorder (Volkmar et al., 2005). A number of neurological abnormalities have been documented. Toddlers with autistic disorder have heads that are 10% larger in volume than those without autistic disorder (Volkmar et al., 2004). This difference is not present at birth, and the overgrowth during toddlerhood and childhood tends to level off so that differences are not so marked during adulthood. The reason for these differences is not yet understood. Abnormalities are also found in the amygdala, hippocampus, and cerebellum; the nature and causes of these abnormalities are being investigated. Furthermore, the prevalence of autism in children whose mothers had rubella during the prenatal period is approximately 10 times higher than in the general population of children.

Genetic factors in the etiology of autistic disorder are well established. Siblings of children with autistic disorder have a 2% chance of also having the disorder (McBride, Anderson, & Shapiro, 1996). Although this is a small percentage, it represents a 50-fold increase in risk as compared to the morbidity risk in the general population. Further evidence of the importance of genetic factors in autistic disorder is provided by twin studies. Monozygotic twins have concordance rates of over 60%, whereas dizygotic twins have concordance rates of 0% (Muhle, Trentacoste, & Rapin, 2004). At least 3 to 4 but maybe as many as 10 different genes are believed to interact to result in the phenotype of autistic disorder (Volkmar et al., 2004). Some argue that there is not a single cause of autistic disorder and that separate genes may be responsible for each of its three core features, social abnormalities, communication deficits, and restricted or stereotyped interests (Happé, Ronald, & Plomin, 2006).

Family studies reveal delayed language acquisition and social deficits in some nonautistic relatives of index cases with autistic disorder (Piren, Palmer, Jacobi, Childress, & Arndt, 1997). Taken together, the evidence from family and twin studies supports a genetic basis for autistic disorder. In Sam's case, there was no evidence of any neurological abnormality, nor was there any family history of autism. However, his older sister did have a learning disability.

A controversial view that is increasingly supported by research evidence— the prenatal androgen theory—proposes that autism is due to excessive exposure to testosterone during the fetal stage of development (Klin, 2009). This exposure creates an "extreme male brain," a way of conceptualizing autistic traits, one that excels in rules and facts of systems rather than empathy and interpersonal relatedness (Auyeung et al., 2009). Levels of testosterone during fetal development are linked to both boys' and girls' autistic symptoms during childhood. More research is needed to evaluate this interesting theory.

Genetic factors alone may not be the only etiological contributor to autistic disorder. It is possible that genes create a susceptibility to environmental factors, such as toxins (Lawler, Croen, Grether, & Van de Water, 2004). There is no definitive evidence at this time that any specific toxin or teratogen is related, but there is some evidence implicating prenatal exposure to valproic acid, a drug used to treat seizures and bipolar disorder, and thalidomide, a drug that has been used in the past to treat morning sickness during pregnancy (Newschaffer et al., 2007). In addition, links to neurotoxins in air pollution, pesticides in food, and insecticides are being researched further. Others have found that prenatal problems, such as maternal viral infections and vaginal bleeding during pregnancy, and birth complications, such as emergency caesarean section, prolonged labor, and multiple births (twins or triplets) are more likely among those with autistic disorder (Brimacombe, Ming, & Lamendola, 2007).

There are also cognitive explanations for autistic disorder. One conceptualizes autistic disorder as stemming from a deficit in social cognition, such as not having a theory of mind, and the other frames it in terms of broader difficulties with information processing, such as problems with executive brain function (Happé et al., 2006). Theory of mind is the ability to understand the mental states of others, including their perspective, feelings, and goals. Autistic individuals have deficits in theory of mind and also in broader social cognition and communicative abilities, such as empathy and imitation (Tager-Flusberg, 2007). Recent research suggests that the mechanism underlying this deficit may lie in problems with the mirror neuron system. The mirror neuron system consists of networks of neurons in the brain that activate in similar patterns whether one is performing an activity or watching someone perform that activity, such as grasping an object (Oberman & Ramachandran, 2007). This mirror neuron system is thought to underlie many cognitive tasks, including motor, perceptual, and verbal functions, and may allow people to run internal simulations of the experiences of others and use these simulations to make predictions about them. Research has shown that people with autistic disorder do not have mirror neuron systems that function like those of others, and problems in this system could explain many different symptoms of autistic disorder, such as pronoun reversal, lack of imitative behavior, and a tendency to respond to the emotions of others in odd ways. These cognitive and neurological theories of the etiology of autistic disorder are not independent from other theories of etiology and may emerge from genetic or environmental sources.

There has been tremendous focus in the popular media on vaccines, specifically on thimerosal, a preservative used in vaccines, as playing a role in autistic disorder, following a research report published in 1998 that speculated about such a link. However, that report was retracted because it was based on insufficient evidence and because one of the authors had a financial incentive in a lawsuit against the vaccine manufacturers (Fleck, 2004). A careful investigation of the original data revealed that the evidence was falsified, and the report was actually a fraud, based on fictitious data (Godlee, Smith, & Marcovitch, 2011). A flurry of research on vaccines followed the initial publication of the fraudulent report, and no link with autistic disorder has been found (Parker, Schwartz, Todd, & Pickering, 2004). Unfortunately, many parents have withheld vaccines for their children out of fear due to the media reports, and as a result, many children are now at risk for those infectious diseases.

Treatment

Numerous medications have been tried with autistic disorder, most commonly antipsychotics (e.g., haloperidol) and antidepressants (Palermo & Curatolo, 2004). These medications can help in managing stereotyped motor behavior, self-injury, aggression, hyperactivity, and sleep problems. However, medication does not improve the core symptoms of autistic disorder (Sung, Fung, Cai, & Ooi, 2010).

The major psychological treatment for autism is behavior therapy. As we saw in Sam's case, it requires a great expenditure of time and effort. Furthermore, autistic children have several problems that make teaching them particularly difficult. They have difficulty adjusting to changes in routine, such as substitute teachers. Their self-stimulatory behavior interferes with effective teaching, and finding reinforcers that motivate autistic children can be challenging. Whereas children without autism are often motivated by praise, this is not the case for many children with autism.

In general, behavior therapists focus on reliably assessed, observable behaviors and manipulate the consequences these behaviors elicit from the environment. As in Sam's case, desirable behaviors (e.g., speech, playing with other children) are rewarded, and undesirable ones (e.g., hand flapping, screaming) are either ignored or punished. The desired behaviors are broken down into smaller elements that are learned first and then assembled into a whole. A good example of this procedure was seen in the procedures used to try to get Sam to speak. Modeling is a frequent adjunct in these operant behavior therapy programs.

Intensive behavioral intervention programs have shown significant improvements in preschool children's cognitive abilities, self-care skills, language, and positive social behavior (Remington et al., 2007). Ivar Lovaas developed the intensive behavior therapy program with very young (under 4 years old) children with autistic disorder (Lovaas, 1987). Therapy encompassed all aspects of the children's lives for more than 40 hours a week for more than 2 years. Parents were trained extensively so that treatment could continue during almost all waking hours of the children's lives. The 19 children receiving this intensive treatment were compared to 40 control children who received a similar treatment for less than 10 hours per week. All children were rewarded for being less aggressive, more compliant, and more socially appropriate, including talking and playing with other children.

The results were dramatic and encouraging for the intensive therapy group. Their measured IQs averaged 83 in first grade (after about 2 years in the intensive therapy) compared to about 55 for the controls; 12 of the 19 reached the normal range as compared to only 2 (of 40) in the control group. Furthermore, 9 out of the 19 intensives were promoted to second grade in a normal public school, whereas only 1 of the much larger control group achieved this level of normal functioning. A 4-year follow-up showed that they had maintained their gains (McEachin, Smith, & Lovaas, 1993). A recent randomized control trial of this treatment approach confirmed that it was more effective than a parent training control group, although the gains were not as impressive as those reported originally (Volkmar et al., 2004). Moreover, other types of treatment have been shown to be effective as well.

This ambitious study confirms the need for heavy involvement of both professionals and parents in dealing with the extreme challenge of autistic disorder. Such intensive treatment is expensive and time consuming, costing on average about $40,000 a year for each child (Shattuck & Grosse, 2007). However, the long-term dependence and loss of productive work in less intensively treated children with autistic disorder may represent a greater cost to society than a treatment that enables some of these children to achieve a normal level of functioning. Even with intensive early intervention, though, most children will not recover or have normal functioning but will continue to have significant symptoms and impairment (Shea, 2004).

Finally, families of children with autism experience a great deal of stress. Extra financial burdens and the strain of the symptoms and intensive nature of treatment can be great. Although the majority of marriages of parents of a child with autism survive, there is a doubling of the risk of divorce (Hartley et al., 2010).

Discussion Questions

1. To intervene in Sam's tantrums and violent outbursts, the therapy involved squirting Tabasco sauce into his mouth when he started a tantrum by screaming. Do you think this form of intervention is ethical? What are the pros and cons of using such a treatment?
2. Had you heard before about the vaccine controversy related to autistic disorder? Despite repeated investigations that have exonerated vaccines, many parents are still refusing to vaccinate their children. What should researchers, physicians, and the media do about this?
3. Why are there increases in the number of diagnosed cases of autistic disorder?
4. The most effective treatment for autistic disorder is early intensive behavior therapy, which is very costly. What ethical dilemmas does this pose for our society? How should we balance the need for autism treatment with the need for preventative health care for other children with our limited health-care dollars?

CHAPTER 22

Attention-Deficit/Hyperactivity Disorder

Ken Wilson's mother contacted the clinic in the middle of November about her 7-year-old son, a first-grader. She explained that Ken was having trouble at school, both academically and socially. The school psychologist had said that he was hyperactive. The clinic scheduled an initial appointment for Ken and both parents.

Social History

The case was assigned to a clinical psychology intern, who met the family in the clinic's waiting room. After a brief chat with all of them, he explained that he would first like to see the parents alone and later spend some time with Ken.

Mr. and Mrs. Wilson had been married for 12 years. He was a business manager, and she was a homemaker. Ken was the middle of three children; his older sister was 9, and his younger brother was 4. Neither sibling was having any apparent problems. Mrs. Wilson had a full-term pregnancy with Ken. The delivery was without complication, although labor was fairly long. The therapist explained that he would like to get an overview of the problem as it existed now.

According to his parents, Ken's current problems began in kindergarten. His teacher frequently sent notes home about his disciplinary problems in the classroom. In fact, there had been concerns about promoting Ken to the first grade. The final result was a "trial promotion." Everyone hoped that Ken would mature and do much better in first grade, but his behavior became even more disruptive. Ken's mother had received negative reports about him from his teacher several times over the first 2 months of school. His teacher reported that he didn't complete his work, was disruptive to the class, and behaved aggressively.

The therapist then asked about the parents' perception of Ken at home and his developmental history. They described him as a difficult infant, much more so than his older sister. He cried frequently and was described as a colicky baby by their pediatrician. He did not eat well, and his sleep was often fitful and restless. As Ken grew, his mother reported even more difficulties with him. He was into everything. Verbal reprimands, which had been effective in controlling his sister's behavior, seemed to have no effect on him. When either parent tried to stop him from doing something dangerous, such as playing with an expensive vase or turning the stove off and on, he would often have a temper tantrum that included throwing things, breaking toys, and screaming. His relationship with his sister was poor. He bit her on several occasions and seemed to take delight in trying to get her into trouble.

His parents described a similar pattern of aggressiveness in Ken's behavior with the neighborhood children. Many of the parents no longer allowed their children to play with Ken. They also reported that he had low frustration tolerance and a short attention span. He could not stay with puzzles and games for more than a few minutes and often reacted angrily when his brief efforts did not produce success. Going out for dinner had become impossible because of his misbehavior in restaurants. Even mealtimes at home had become unpleasant. Ken's parents had begun to argue frequently about how to deal with him.

Toward the end of the first session, the therapist brought Ken to his office while his parents remained in the clinic waiting room. Ken initially maintained that he did not understand why he was at the clinic, but later he admitted that he was getting into a lot of trouble at school. He agreed that it would probably be a good idea to try to do something about his misbehavior.

Ken and his parents were brought together for the final minutes of the first session. The therapist explained that the next several sessions would be devoted to conducting a more thorough assessment, including visits to the Wilson's home and Ken's school. The parents signed release forms so the therapist could obtain information from their pediatrician and the school. The following information was gathered through these sources and from further interviews with the parents.

The Current Problem

School records generally corroborated his parents' description of Ken's behavior in kindergarten. His teacher described him as being "distractible, moody, aggressive," and a "discipline problem." Toward the end of kindergarten, his intelligence and academic achievement were tested. Although his IQ was placed at 120, he did not perform very well on reading and mathematics achievement tests. An interview with Ken's first-grade teacher provided information that agreed with other reports. Ken's teacher complained that he was frequently out of his seat, seldom sat still when he was supposed to, did not complete assignments, and had poor peer relations. Ken seemed indifferent to efforts at disciplining him. Ken's teacher also completed a short form of the Conners Rating Scale

Table 22.1 Teacher's Ratings of Ken's Behavior on the Short Form of the Conners Rating Scale

Observation: Classroom Behavior	Degree of Activity			
	(0) Not at All	(1) Just a Little	(2) Pretty Much	(3) Very Much
Constantly fidgeting			X	
Demands must be met immediately—easily frustrated				X
Restless or overactive				X
Excitable, impulsive			X	
Inattentive, easily distracted				X
Fails to finish things he starts—short attention span				X
Cries often and easily		X		
Disturbs other children		X		
Mood changes quickly and drastically		X		
Temper outbursts, explosive and unpredictable behavior				X

Source: Sprague, Cohen, and Werry (1974)

(Sprague, Cohen, & Werry, 1974) about Ken's behavior. The instrument verified the picture of hyperactive behavior that had already emerged (see Table 22.1).

The therapist arranged to spend a morning in Ken's classroom. During that time, Ken was out of his seat inappropriately six times. On one occasion, he jumped up to look out the window when a noise, probably a car backfiring, was heard. He went to talk to other children three times. Ken got up twice and just began walking quickly around the classroom. Even when he stayed seated, he was often not working and instead was fidgeting or bothering other children. Any noise, even another child coughing or dropping a pencil, distracted him from his work. When his teacher spoke to him, he did not seem to hear; it was not until the teacher had begun yelling at him that he paid any attention.

Subsequent sessions with Ken's parents focused on his current behavior at home. The pattern that had begun earlier in Ken's childhood continued. He still got along poorly with his sister, had difficulty sitting still at mealtimes, and reacted with temper tantrums when demands were made of him. His behavior had also taken on a daredevil quality, as illustrated by his climbing out of his second-story bedroom window and racing his bicycle down the hill of a heavily trafficked local street. Indeed, his daring acts seemed to be the only way he could get any positive attention from his neighborhood peers, who seemed to be mostly afraid of him. He had no really close friends.

Mr. Wilson missed two of these sessions because of his business schedule. Most days he had to commute to work, a two-hour train trip each way. During a session he missed, Mrs. Wilson hinted that they had marital problems. When this was brought up directly, she agreed that their marriage was not as good now as it once had been. Their arguments centered on how to handle Ken. Mrs. Wilson had come to believe that severe physical punishment was the only answer. She described an active, growing dislike of Ken and feared that he might never change.

The next time Mr. Wilson was present, the therapist asked him about his child-rearing philosophy. He admitted that he took more of a "boys will be boys" approach. In fact, he reported that as a child, he was like Ken. He had "grown out of it" and expected Ken would, too. As a result, he let Ken get away with things for which Mrs. Wilson would have punished him. The couple's arguments, which had recently become more heated and frequent, usually occurred after Mr. Wilson had arrived home from work. Mrs. Wilson, after a particularly exasperating day with Ken, would try to get Mr. Wilson to discipline Ken. "Just wait until your father gets home" was a familiar refrain. But Mr. Wilson would refuse and accuse his wife of overreacting; the battle would then begin.

The next week, the therapist visited the Wilson home, arriving just before Ken and his sister got home from school. The first part of the visit was uneventful, but at about 4:30 p.m., Ken and his sister got into a fight over who was winning a game. Ken broke the game, and his sister came crying to her mother, who began shouting at Ken. Ken tried to explain his behavior by saying that his sister had been cheating. His mother ordered him to his room; shortly thereafter, when she heard him crying, she went up and told him he could come out.

The children ate their dinner at 5:30 p.m.; Mrs. Wilson planned to wait until her husband came home later to have hers. The meal began with Ken complaining that he did not like anything on his plate. He picked at his food for a few minutes and then started making faces at his sister. Mrs. Wilson yelled at him to stop making the faces and eat his dinner. When she turned her back, he began shoving food from his plate onto his sister's. As she resisted, Ken knocked over his glass of milk, which broke on the floor. Ken's mother was enraged at this point. She looked as if she was ready to hit Ken, but she calmed herself, perhaps because of the therapist's presence. Although she told Ken that he would be in big trouble when his father got home, nothing happened. When Mr. Wilson came home, he made light of the incident and refused to punish Ken. Even though Mrs. Wilson's exasperation was obvious, she said nothing.

Conceptualization and Treatment

The therapist conceptualized Ken's problem in an operant-conditioning framework. Although open to possible biological causes of Ken's behavior, the therapist believed that a structured program of rewards and punishments— contingency management—would help. Treatment would then involve trying to increase the frequency of positive behaviors (complying with parental requests, interacting positively with his sister, staying in his seat in the classroom) by providing positive consequences for them. Similarly, undesirable behaviors should be followed by negative consequences. It was explained to Ken's parents that many of these undesirable behaviors had actually been producing positive results for him. His tantrums, for example, frequently allowed him to have his own way. The complicating feature was the attitude of Ken's parents. Would either of them be willing to engage in the considerable effort required to make a contingency management system work? To try to counter this potential problem, the therapist, after explaining the results of his overall assessment and the broad outlines of his treatment plan, asked both parents to try to put aside their current attitudes for a brief period while they implemented a simple, scaled-down version of the overall plan. The hope was that a simple intervention, directed at only a couple of problem areas, would produce visible, quick results. This small change might be sufficient to increase the parents' enthusiasm and allow a complete therapeutic package to be instituted later.

Two target behaviors were selected—leaving his seat in the classroom and inappropriate behavior at mealtimes at home. Mealtime behavior problems were defined as complaining about the food served; kicking his sister under the table; not staying in his chair; and laughing, giggling, or making faces. During the next week, the parents were instructed to record the frequency of disruptive behavior at mealtimes as well as several other target behaviors (temper tantrums, fights with siblings, and noncompliance with parental requests) that could be targets for later interventions. The next day, Ken's teacher was contacted. She agreed to keep a record of the number of times Ken was out of his seat each day.

During the next session, an intervention was planned. The records of the past week indicated that every meal had been problematic. Ken had also been out of his seat when he was supposed to be working at his desk for an average of nine times per day. The therapist explained to Ken and his parents that in the next week daily rewards would be made available if Ken was not disruptive at mealtimes and if he reduced the number of times he was out of his seat at school. Everyone agreed that Ken would be allowed to select an extra half hour of television watching, a favorite dessert, or a game to be played with one of his parents if his behavior met an agreed-on criterion. The initial criterion was being out of his seat less than five times per day at school and being nondisruptive for at least one of the two meals eaten at home each day. The therapist showed Ken's parents how to make a chart that was to be posted on the refrigerator. Ken's teacher would send a daily note home indicating how many times he was out of his seat and that number, along with checks for a "good" meal, would be entered on the chart. Ken's teacher was contacted after the session, and the program was explained. She agreed to send home a daily record of the number of times Ken was out of his seat.

At the beginning of the next session, Ken's parents were clearly pleased. They had brought their chart with them; some changes had obviously occurred. Ken had met the criterion on six of the seven days. The average number of times he was out of his seat went from 9 to 3.6, and he had been unpleasant at mealtimes only five times (two of these occurred on Saturday, resulting in his single failure to obtain a reward). During the next several sessions, the parents and the therapist worked on expanding the program. Temper tantrums, fighting with his siblings, and noncompliance with parental requests had all been frequent the previous week. Ken's parents now were eager to attempt to deal with them.

Of the three targets, noncompliance proved to be the most difficult to address. It presented such a large array of possibilities that a specific description of a criterion was problematic. A program was developed that involved the following components: Temper tantrums would lead to a time-out procedure in which Ken would have to go to his room and stay quietly for 10 minutes. Fighting was handled first by a simple request to stop. If that was ineffective, the time-out procedure would be employed. To try to get Ken to comply with parental requests such as going to bed or to stop teasing his sister, his parents were instructed to make the requests calmly and clearly to be sure he heard them. If he did not comply, they were to give him one reminder, again in a calm fashion; if that failed, he would be sent to his room. The therapist stressed to the parents that their requests to stop or do something had to be made calmly and that time-out should also be administered calmly. Finally, the parents were instructed to provide social reinforcement for cooperative play and being pleasant at meals by simply telling Ken how pleased they were when they saw him playing nicely with his siblings.

Based on the records from the previous weeks, it looked as though Ken would have experienced about 20 time-outs if the new system had been in effect. It was therefore decided that if Ken was sent to his room fewer than 10 times, he would receive a special end-of-week reward, a trip to the theater to see a film. The mealtime procedure was kept in effect, and as before, a chart was to be completed showing school behavior, mealtimes, and frequency of time-outs. This time, the parents were also asked to keep a log of the number of times they praised Ken and of the specific details of instances of noncompliance. The latter feature was included to make sure the parents' requests were not unreasonable.

Meanwhile, the therapist contacted Ken's teacher and increased the scope of the school program. The teacher was asked to maintain her recordkeeping of Ken's being out of his seat, but she was also to praise Ken as often as possible when he was working appropriately. The daily report card was expanded to include the number of assignments completed and the number of aggressive interactions with peers, defined broadly to include both physical and verbal aggression. Other instances of disruptive behavior (being noisy, making faces) were also to be recorded. The records from this week were to be used in planning another intervention during the next session with the parents.

At the session following the implementation of the time-out procedure, the parents were decidedly less enthusiastic than they had been the previous week. Although the improvement in mealtime behavior had been maintained, Ken had been sent to his room 17 times over the course of the week and thus did not get his Sunday trip to the movie. It seemed that time-out was not an effective consequence for Ken. The therapist asked the parents for more details on how they were using the procedure. It turned out that Ken had lots of toys in his room, so the therapist decided to change the system. In an effort to increase the effectiveness of time-out, Ken's toys were put away so that time-out consisted of sitting on his bed with no toys to play with or books to look at. Furthermore, all the at-home targets were linked to a daily reward (one of the three described earlier). Specifically, Ken was to get 2 points for each pleasant meal, 2 points if he had only one time-out before dinner, and 2 points for none after dinner.

The expanded school program was also converted to a point system. The teacher's records for the previous week indicated that Ken had been out of his seat an average of three times per day, had completed 55% of his assignments, and was either aggressive or disruptive five times during the average day. A set of new criteria was adopted for school and linked to points: 2 points for being out of his seat less than three times per day, 2 points for completing 70% or more of his assignments, and 2 points for reducing the frequency of aggressive behavior or disruptiveness to less than three times per day. Thus, Ken could earn 12 points on each school day and 6 on weekends. The criterion for one of the daily rewards was set at 8 points on a school day and 4 points on weekends. In addition, a weekly total of 54 points would result in Ken's being taken to see a movie.

The system now appeared to be working well. During one typical week, Ken earned 58 points and thus got his trip to the movies. In addition, he met the criterion for a daily reward each day. At home, he averaged only one time-out per day, and 12 of 14 meals had been without incident. At school, he was out of his seat slightly less than twice per day, completed an average of 70% of his assignments, and was either aggressive or disruptive fewer than three times per day.

For the following week, the criteria for school behavior were increased again. Points could be earned for being out of his seat less than twice per day, completing 80% of his assignments, and being aggressive or disruptive less than twice per day. At home, the point system was left unchanged. The criterion for a daily reward was raised to 10 for school days and 6 on weekends; the criterion for the end-of-week reward was raised to 66. In addition, a new daily reward was added to the program—a bedtime story from Ken's father. The parents were also encouraged to continue providing praise for good behavior. The therapist called Ken's teacher to discuss a similar tactic for the classroom.

The program continued to evolve over the next few weeks, and Ken made steady progress. By the 14th week, it was clear that Ken's behavior had dramatically changed, and his academic performance was improving. At this point, sessions were held only once every 2 weeks, and the family was followed for 3 more months. Increased emphasis was placed on teaching Ken's parents the general principles that they had been following so that when problems arose they would be able to handle them on their own by modifying the system.

Both Ken's parents and his teacher were also reporting changes in Ken that had not been targets of the intervention. He was described as being less moody, more pleasant, and more able to deal with frustration. He had also begun to form some friendships and was being invited to other children's homes to play.

Although Ken was still somewhat difficult to handle, his parents now believed that they had some skills they could use. Ken's mother reported that she now felt much more positive toward him. The couple also indicated that their arguments had become much less frequent. Two steps remained. First, the daily rewards were phased out. Instead, the parents were to provide social reinforcement for good behavior during the day. The rewards were still provided, but in a less formal manner in which they were not linked explicitly to the number of points earned during the day.

Finally, the formal contingency aspect of the weekend reward was dropped. A "good week" still led to a special treat or activity but was not linked specifically to a particular criterion. Ken's behavior remained stable, and treatment was concluded.

Discussion

According to the *Diagnostic and Statistical Manual of Mental Disorders* (*DSM-IV-TR*; APA, 2000), Ken met the criteria for attention-deficit/hyperactivity disorder (ADHD), one of the subcategories in the manual's section headed "Disorders Usually First Diagnosed in Infancy, Childhood, or Adolescence." This large section encompasses disorders of the intellect (e.g., mental retardation), overt behavior (e.g., attention-deficit/hyperactivity disorder, conduct disorder), and pervasive disorders of development (e.g., autistic disorder, discussed in Chapter 21).

The term *attention-deficit/hyperactivity disorder* reflects the prevailing view that problems with attention are the principal aspect of the disorder. These difficulties include failure to finish tasks, not listening, being easily distracted, and having problems concentrating and maintaining attention. This description fit Ken well. Overactivity and restlessness were reflected in his problems staying seated in school, fidgeting when seated, and being described as "always on the go." Hyperactivity is especially evident in any situation that requires controlling an activity level, such as school and mealtimes.

DSM-IV-TR (APA, 2000) lists three types of ADHD: (a) the primarily inattentive type in which poor attention predominates, (b) the predominately hyperactive type in which hyperactivity and impulsivity are primary, and (c) the combined type in which both hyperactivity and inattention are prominent. Overall, the combined type is most common, but among girls, the inattentive type is more frequent (Biederman, Mick, & Faraone, 2002). Ken's formal diagnosis was ADHD, combined type, because he met the criteria for both the inattention and hyperactivity components.

In addition to their core problems, children with ADHD have a number of other difficulties. They often have deficits in cognitive processing speed and poor handwriting and visual-motor coordination, markers of mild neurological impairments (Mayes & Calhoun, 2007). Children with ADHD also have difficulties getting along with peers and making friends (Hinshaw & Melnick, 1995). They are more likely to be injured in accidental falls, to be hit by a car, or to accidentally ingest poison because their symptoms make them more likely to take risks and ignore safety precautions (Daley, 2006). Up to half experience problems with sleep, typically trouble falling and staying asleep, resisting bedtime, and problems waking up in the morning (Weiss & Salpekar, 2010).

As many as 50% also meet the diagnostic criteria for conduct disorder, behavior that violates the rights of others and basic social norms, for example, being aggressive toward people, lying, stealing, and damaging property (Flory & Lynam, 2003). Many of them also have comorbid oppositional-defiant disorder and learning disabilities. Distinguishing between conduct disorder and ADHD can be difficult because of the overlap of the symptoms of each disorder. In conduct disorder, however, it is thought that the antisocial behavior does not arise from attention deficits or impulsiveness. Therefore, although Ken showed some features of conduct disorder, he was diagnosed with ADHD because his antisocial behavior seemed due to impulsivity. People who have both ADHD and conduct disorder appear to be at particularly high risk for substance abuse in adulthood.

Between 3 and 7% of elementary school children have ADHD (APA, 2000), with two to three times as many boys meeting the diagnostic criteria as girls (Willoughby, 2003). It is much more common in boys than girls in samples seeking treatment, but the gender difference in prevalence appears to be much smaller in community samples (McGee & Feehan, 1991).

The first symptoms typically appear early in toddlerhood, and most children with the hyperactive or combined subtypes are considered to be having serious problems by the time they are 7 years old (Voeller, 2004). If diagnostic criteria are carefully followed, ADHD can be reliably diagnosed in children of preschool age, but most preschoolers who meet these criteria are not identified and brought into treatment (Egger, Kondo, & Angold, 2006). Recently, the trend has been to diagnose adolescents and adults with ADHD, even when they had not been identified as having ADHD as children. However, a recent review of the research concluded that ADHD symptoms generally improve with age (Willoughby, 2003), and people with ADHD are typically identified when they are in elementary school because their problems are already evident, so clinicians should be careful not to overdiagnose ADHD among adults. In both males and females, the number of ADHD cases declines with age (Monuteaux, Mick, Faraone, & Biederman, 2010). Although symptoms do seem to improve with age, childhood ADHD constitutes a risk for poor educational, occupational, and psychosocial outcomes. People with ADHD are more likely to be incarcerated, be unemployed or work in lower status jobs, take risks and have accidents, and experience relationship difficulties (Steinhausen, 2009).

Etiological Considerations

Research indicates a strong genetic component in ADHD. Heritability estimates for ADHD are between 60 and 90% (Kent, 2004). Biederman, Faraone, Mick, & Warburton, (1995) have found that when parents have ADHD, 50% of their children also have ADHD. Similarly, Goodman and Stevenson (1989) found concordance for clinically diagnosed hyperactivity in 51% of monozygotic twins (MZ) and 33% of dizygotic (DZ) twins. Adoption studies further support the importance of a genetic predisposition to ADHD (van den Oord, Boomsma, & Verhulst, 1994). Although genetic factors are clearly central, hundreds of studies have been unable to identify the specific loci of the genes involved, so ADHD is probably caused by multiple genes, genes interacting, or gene-environment interactions (Banaschewski, Becker, Scherag, Franke, & Coghill, 2010). Reports from Ken's father mentioned earlier indicate that he may have had ADHD as a child, so genetic inheritance is consistent for this case.

What do children with ADHD inherit? Research into brain structures has been guided by the idea that ADHD reflects impulsivity; children with the disorder are unable to inhibit activity when the environment calls for it and cannot inhibit attention from distracting stimuli (Quay, 1997). Evidence has accumulated that there may be some impairment in the frontal lobes of the brain, which are known to play an important role in allowing people to inhibit behavioral responses. For example, Castellanos et al. (1996) examined the magnetic resonance imaging (MRI) scans of children with ADHD and found that they had smaller frontal lobes than controls. Evidence of their poorer performance on neuropsychological tests of frontal lobe functioning (such as inhibiting behavioral responses) provides further support for the theory that a basic deficit in this part of the brain may be related to the symptoms of the disorder (Nigg, 2001). Some argue that children with ADHD have an aversion to waiting and that this accounts for their impulsive behavior (Taylor, 2009). Moreover, the lower academic achievement usually seen among children with ADHD is substantially due to genetic factors, independent of intelligence (Saudino & Plomin, 2007), rather than one proposed explanation that ADHD arises from frustration children have with their problems learning, or another, that hyperactivity makes it harder for children to learn in the classroom. It seems that to a large degree, children who have inherited ADHD have also inherited poor academic achievement.

Other biological risk factors that may be linked to ADHD include low birth weight and birth complications (Ben Amor et al., 2005). Maternal smoking during pregnancy may also be important. Millberger, Biederman, Faraone, Chen, and Jones (1996) found that 22% of the children of mothers who smoked a pack or more of cigarettes a day could be diagnosed with ADHD as compared to only 8% in a control sample. Animal research has shown that nicotine interferes with brain development during gestation. Exposure to lead, even at very low levels that are common in the United States, is associated with more symptoms of ADHD (Nigg, Nikolas, Knottnerus, Cavanagh, & Friderici, 2010). Brain injury due to trauma, stroke, or encephalitis can sometimes lead to symptoms of ADHD (Voeller, 2004). Environmental factors such as maternal alcohol use during pregnancy or family adversity might interact with genetic predispositions to cause ADHD (Steinhausen, 2009).

A mother's emotional state during her pregnancy also may affect her child's risk for behavior problems. High levels of anxiety during early pregnancy may affect the developing brain through stress hormones. Van den Bergh and Marcoen (2004) found that maternal levels of anxiety early in pregnancy predicted ADHD symptoms in children when they were 8 and 9 years old. The anxiety levels during early pregnancy were more predictive than those after the birth, which is consistent with the pregnancy hormonal environment programming brain development.

Other environmental causes have been investigated as well. In a rigorously controlled study published in a mainstream medical journal, artificial food coloring and sodium benzoate, a widely used food preservative, were found to increase hyperactive behavior among 3-year-olds and 8- and 9-year-olds (McCann et al., 2007). This study replicated previous similar findings and suggests that both children with and without ADHD respond to these chemicals in similar ways.

Watching a lot of television at 1 and 3 years of age has also been linked to later attention problems (Christakis, Zimmerman, DiGiuseppe, & McCarty, 2004). Television's fast-paced events and quickly changing images may affect the developing brain, shortening attention span. This link between television exposure and attention problems is found for television shows with entertainment content but not for shows with educational content, such as *Sesame Street, Blues Clues,* or *Dora the Explorer,* probably because they are more slowly paced. The link with attention problems is especially strong for entertainment shows with violent content, such as *Power Rangers,* and moderately strong for those with nonviolent content, such as *Rugrats* (Zimmerman & Christakis, 2007). To test whether the relationship between television exposure and attention problems is causal, Landhuis, Poulton, Welch, and Hancox (2007) conducted a longitudinal study in a population sample where they followed children from 5 years of age into adolescence until 15 years of age. They found that childhood television exposure, at 2 hours but especially over 3 hours per day, predicted adolescent attention problems. This link remained even after controlling for child attention problems, child cognitive ability, socioeconomic status, gender, and adolescent television exposure. This study strengthens the argument that television exposure causes attention problems, although it is possible that another yet uncontrolled variable is responsible for the relationship.

Being raised in chaotic or impoverished environments may lead to difficulties regulating attention and controlling impulses (Voeller, 2004). The quality of the parent–child relationship may also be important; maternal warmth was found to predict teachers' ratings of ADHD symptoms in a sample of low birth-weight children who were at risk for behavioral problems (Tully, Arseneault, Caspi, Moffitt, & Morgan, 2004). The parent–child relationship, however, is bidirectional; the behavior of each is determined by the actions and reactions of the other. Whereas parents of children with ADHD give them more commands and have negative interactions with them, children with ADHD have also been found to be less compliant and more negative in their interactions with their parents (Barkley, Karlsson, & Pollard, 1985). As indicated later in the section on treatment, stimulant medication has been shown to reduce hyperactivity and increase compliance in ADHD children. Significantly, when such medication is used, the parent's commands and negative behavior also decrease (see Barkley, 1990), suggesting that the child's behavior influenced that of the parents. In Ken's case, it seemed that his mother's negative attitude toward him was principally a response to his disruptive behavior. Nevertheless, her negative attitude, coupled with the inconsistent disciplinary practices of the parents, may have exacerbated Ken's disorder.

Treatment

The most common therapy for children with ADHD is stimulant medication such as methylphenidate (Ritalin) and amphetamine (Adderall). Many placebo-controlled studies have shown that these two medications are effective in reducing symptoms of ADHD while they are being taken (Greydanus, Nazeer, & Patel, 2009). The drugs reduce aggression and hyperactivity and improve concentration, classroom behavior, and social interactions. One ingenious study even demonstrated that Ritalin helped children with ADHD who were playing softball to assume the ready position in the outfield and keep track of the status of the game. Children given placebos, in contrast, frequently threw or kicked their gloves while the pitch was in progress (Pelham et al., 1990). Short-term side effects of stimulant treatment, principally insomnia and loss of appetite, usually disappear quickly.

The benefits of the drugs are lost, however, if they are discontinued. Therefore, long-term treatment is indicated. Because all of the medications are associated with side effects, the decision to use them should be weighed carefully. Furthermore, although the drugs cause improvement, they do not lead to fully normal functioning. For example, Whalen et al. (1989) found significantly better peer appraisals during treatment, but the boys with ADHD were still liked less than average. The effect of drugs on academic performance also remains controversial, with some studies revealing positive changes and others none (Henker & Whalen, 1989). Finally, there have been concerns that stimulants are being overused and given to children who do not have ADHD. Prescriptions for stimulants have certainly increased in the past decade (Zito et al., 2000). Furthermore, in a study conducted in Virginia, 18 to 20% of fifth-grade boys were on stimulants, a figure much higher than the number expected given the prevalence of ADHD (LeFever, Dawson, & Morrow, 1999). Increasing numbers of preschool children have been prescribed stimulant medication, even though there is little data available for this age group (Kratochvil, Greenhill, March, Burke, & Vaughan, 2004). Some professionals have been concerned that using stimulant medication in childhood would increase the risk of substance abuse in adulthood, but research has shown that it actually decreases the risk, possibly by reducing ADHD symptoms (Wilens, Faraone, Biederman, & Gunawardene, 2003).

A variety of psychological therapies have been used for ADHD, but the most thoroughly studied is an operant learning or contingency management approach such as that used in Ken's case. Positive reinforcement is used to increase on-task behavior such as remaining in one's seat and engaging in positive interactions with peers, teachers, and parents. Negative consequences follow undesirable behaviors such as being disruptive in the classroom.

The comparative effectiveness of different treatments for ADHD has been evaluated in a large-scale, carefully conducted study (MTA Cooperative Group, 1999). Children with ADHD were randomly assigned to one of four groups: (a) stimulant medication, (b) behavioral treatment, (c) medication plus behavioral treatment, and (d) standard community care. In terms of reducing symptoms and increasing positive functioning, the combined treatment was best but only slightly better than medication alone. However, children in the combined treatment group needed less medication, a potential advantage given the possible side effects of drugs. Results for the behavioral treatment were not as positive in this study as in prior research. On certain outcomes such as harsh and ineffective disciplines, combined medication and behavioral treatment was superior to medication alone (Chronis, Chacko, Fabiano, Wymbs, & Pelham, 2004). Behavioral treatment alone is recommended as the first treatment approach for preschool children, when the parents are reluctant to use medication, and for milder forms of ADHD (Root & Resnick, 2003). For preschoolers, parent training is the best form of non-pharmacological treatment, in which the therapist teaches the parents effective strategies to manage their child's behavior (Young & Amarasinghe, 2010).

Discussion Questions

1. In what ways was Ken's disorder linked to added stress on his family? Was this cause or effect?
2. Research has linked watching a lot of television during the toddler years with later attention problems. How common is this practice? Has this increased or decreased in recent years? What advice do you have, given these findings, for parents of toddlers?
3. Ken's therapy did not involve medication. If you were his therapist, would you have recommended medication for him? Why do you think his therapist did not?
4. Up to 20% of fifth-grade boys are taking psychostimulant medications, even though ADHD affects many fewer than one in five boys. What forces do you think this have led to this? What are the consequences?

CHAPTER 23

Oppositional Defiant Disorder

As she stood outside her son's bedroom door holding the handle shut, trying to keep him inside for his punishment, Nicole Helms fought back her tears. She felt like such a failure, and she had no idea what to do. Her 4-year-old son's horrible temper tantrums scared her badly, and she felt both helpless and angry. Her mother-in-law, Mrs. Helms, would be home soon, and Nicole wanted her son, Tyler, to calm down before she arrived. He stopped screaming, kicking at the door, and pulling on the door knob, and she breathed a sigh of surprise and relief, hoping maybe he was going to stop. Then she heard a loud crashing noise that made her jump and fling open the door, fearing for Tyler's safety. To her horror, she saw that he had climbed up on the bookshelf and ripped the curtains off the wall, knocking the bookshelf down in the process. She shouted at him, swatted his bottom, and then started to cry. He ran past her into the living room and flipped on the TV while she sat down on the floor in despair. At that point, she decided she had to get help, or her son would surely end up like his father. The next morning she called Tyler's pediatrician, and his nurse arranged an appointment with a child clinical psychologist, Dr. Bell.

Two weeks later, Nicole and Mrs. Helms brought Tyler for his appointment. Dr. Bell met them in the waiting room, calling Tyler's name. She then kneeled down to his height level, smiled at him, and said hello. She introduced herself to Nicole and to Mrs. Helms, shaking their hands. She brought all three into her office, where she invited Tyler to play with the toys while she talked with his mother and grandmother to gather information about the presenting problem, symptoms, and family history.

When he was younger, Tyler's behavior seemed like that of other children his age, but in the past year or so, his first symptoms had appeared, and his behavior had become quite different from that of other children. He had become very mouthy and angry and said mean things to his mother and grandparents. He would call his mother fat and tell his grandparents he hated them. His mother and grandparents found themselves tiptoeing around him, hoping he would stay in a good mood, because when he was mad, nobody around him could be happy.

Tyler's behavior was mostly unmanageable. Nicole could not control it, nor could her husband's parents. They had tried spanking him, reasoning with him, pleading with him, and taking away his toys. They had even tried rewarding him with candy or ice cream if he stopped having a fit. When he didn't get his way, he would have a temper tantrum until he did. During his temper tantrums, his mother and grandmother had the impression that he was trying to get his way manipulatively, rather than really losing control of his emotions. He would start crying, screaming, fall to the ground, kick and hit the floor, and if that didn't work, he would knock things off the coffee table or tip over a kitchen chair. He would also hit or kick an adult if they tried to stop him. When Nicole tried to spank him for misbehaving, he would laugh at her and say it didn't hurt. Then she would hit him harder until she scared herself and stopped, clutching him close and begging his forgiveness.

He wouldn't go to bed when asked to and fell asleep most nights in front of the television. He wouldn't clean up his toys and even argued about brushing his teeth. When his mother was talking on the telephone, even if it was something important, he would come over and start making clicking noises with his tongue at her over and over, louder and louder, to annoy her until she paid attention to him. Basically, if he got his way, he acted happy and could be very sweet, but he didn't act happy that much anymore. Even when they took him somewhere fun, like Chuck E. Cheese, he wanted more game tokens than he was given or didn't like his pizza. He would argue about which booth they chose to sit in or who should sit next to him. When he was arguing, his tone of voice was harsh and bossy.

On occasions that she tried to discipline him, he would do something to get her back. Once when they were eating lunch at home, he said he wanted a cookie. Nicole told him he could have one when he finished half his sandwich. He looked at her defiantly, then picked up his glass of milk and slowly poured it all over his sandwich and the table. When closed in his room, he would throw his toys everywhere, pull the sheets off the bed, and empty all the clothing out of the drawers until she opened the door and relented. She had stopped trying to take him to church or the grocery store because it was so embarrassing when he acted that way. She dreaded what would happen when he started school next fall.

Social and Family History

Tyler was the only child of Billy and Nicole Helms. They were married the summer after they graduated from high school, and a year and a half later, Tyler was born. Tyler was the product of an uncomplicated, full-term pregnancy, and there were no problems during his birth. He met his early developmental milestones—such as crawling, walking, and talking—on time and had no health problems. He was affectionate, talkative, inquisitive, and curious as a toddler. He loved being read to and could sit for long periods of time listening to a book his mother read to him when he was only 2 years old. Nicole and Tyler developed a close, warm relationship.

Nicole was a full-time homemaker, and Billy worked as a welder. They lived in their own apartment in the same part of town as Billy's parents. Nicole's parents were divorced, and her father lived in another state. She hadn't seen him since she was 8 years old. Nicole's mother did not have a very close relationship with Nicole, and they frequently argued over Nicole marrying Billy, over Nicole's disapproval of her mother's boyfriend, and over how she was raising Tyler. Nicole had pretty much stopped spending time with her. Billy was very close with his parents, though, and they got along well with Nicole. Nicole spent a lot of time with his mother when Billy and Mr. Helms, his father, were at work, and Mrs. Helms would often babysit for Tyler.

Nicole and Billy's relationship was mostly loving and positive, but Billy had episodes of "moodiness," which was probably clinically significant depression. This "moody streak" seemed to run in his father's family, striking the men: His father also had bouts of depression from time to time. Neither Billy nor his father had been treated for their depression. Members of Billy's family worried about all their male children being affected with this affliction, and Mrs. Helms was constantly watching Tyler as a young toddler for early signs that he was going to inherit the moody streak, too.

Billy had begun smoking marijuana when he was in middle school. He used it fairly regularly throughout high school and occasionally after he and Nicole married. Nicole occasionally smoked it with him when she was in high school, but after they married, she stopped using it. They sometimes drank alcohol, but Billy drank more than Nicole. After she got pregnant, Nicole didn't like Billy using drugs and pressured him to keep marijuana out of their home. He mostly complied. He would hang out with his friends and sometimes get high, but he didn't bring it into their apartment anymore. He was an involved father and was close to Tyler, who was his pride and joy. He loved "play wrestling" with his son, and Tyler loved watching him play video games. He would give Tyler a set of controls and let him pretend he was playing, too. Tyler seemed to worship his father and followed him around, imitating him.

Just after Tyler turned 3 years old, Billy began sinking into one of his depressions. He spent less and less time with the family and more time away, with friends or off by himself. He started smelling like marijuana smoke all the time again. Nicole was worried but didn't know what she could do beyond begging him to stop smoking. After 2 months of this behavior, one day he took off. While Nicole and Tyler were at Walmart, he packed up all of his clothes, his video games, and music and left in his pickup truck. He didn't write a note of explanation, didn't say goodbye, and didn't say anything to his friends, parents, or coworkers. Nicole and his parents had not heard anything from him since then. For the first several weeks, Nicole was sure he would come back. When their minimal savings ran out, she and Tyler had to move in with Billy's parents and let their apartment go. Mr. and Mrs. Helms were very loyal to Nicole and ashamed that their son had deserted his family. They were determined to take care of her and Tyler. Mrs. Helms, however, harbored secret fears that this abandonment of Tyler by Billy cemented Tyler's fate of having the moody streak, too.

Conceptualization and Treatment

While gathering this background information, Dr. Bell kept a close eye on Tyler's behavior. He played quietly with the toys and seemed a little shy at first. He was listening carefully to every word that was said but didn't participate in the conversation. He readily went to the waiting room with his grandmother when asked so that his mother could speak privately with Dr. Bell about sensitive information. As the session went on, however, he would occasionally leave the toys and stand by his mother while she talked, touching her hair and laughingly, almost embarrassedly, denying her claims. When his grandmother would chime in, agreeing with and supporting Nicole's reports, Tyler would go back to playing. If asked a direct question, such as what his favorite foods were, or what television shows he liked, he readily responded. His play was age appropriate, and there was no evidence of any problems sustaining attention. In fact, Tyler seemed more mature than many 4-year-olds in his ability to follow the conversation. There was clearly warmth and affection between Tyler and his mother during their interactions in this first session. In addition, Mrs. Helms appeared to be very supportive of Nicole. The problems began to be evident, however, when it was time to leave, and Tyler began to misbehave. He wanted to take one of the toys home. As his mother and grandmother began to set limits on his behavior, he became more defiant until he hurled the toy angrily down and stomped away.

Dr. Bell recommended that Nicole and Tyler come alone to the next session so Nicole could learn the tools she would need to discipline Tyler successfully and to set appropriate and effective limits on his behavior. Tyler's oppositional defiant disorder was seen as emerging out of his difficult emotions stemming from the loss of his father. These emotions, combined with his mother's lack of self-confidence after her own loss of her husband (made particularly difficult for her in light of her own lost relationship with her father) undermined her consistency and sense of certainty in disciplining Tyler. It is also often harder for single parents to maintain discipline because they don't have their spouse's help. From a family systems perspective, Nicole was now almost in a child role in relation to Mrs. Helms, and although Mrs. Helms did not actively undermine her, this child role further weakened her authority with Tyler. Finally, all three adults remaining in Tyler's life were afraid that if they disciplined him too severely, it would scar him for life by making him moody and depressed. The intervention, therefore, was to consist of first teaching Nicole how to manage Tyler's behavior, then elevating her status in the family system to being clearly an adult/authority figure, and next reassuring everyone that Tyler actually needed discipline as much as he needed love. Finally, Tyler would be seen individually in play therapy to address his feelings of loss relating to his father's departure.

Time-Out Procedure

At the next session, Nicole and Tyler were seen together. Again, Tyler was allowed to play with the toys in the room while Dr. Bell talked with his mother. Dr. Bell educated Nicole about the importance of clear, realistic expectations about children's behavior and consistent, predictable, and effective discipline. Again, Tyler listened carefully. After a short time, he interrupted the conversation. Nicole gently reminded him to wait until she finished what she was saying. Tyler started poking her and intentionally getting in the way of her line of vision with Dr. Bell. Nicole looked helplessly at Dr. Bell, who asked her if this behavior was acceptable to her. After Nicole said it was not, Dr. Bell encouraged her to communicate this message calmly, clearly, and directly to Tyler, along with a request of what she expected him to do. When she did so, he hit his mother in the arm. Again, Dr. Bell supported her in setting appropriate limits. With the psychologist's support, Nicole told Tyler to sit in a "time-out" chair until he was ready to behave. She gently guided him to a chair where he sat for a moment, before getting up and misbehaving again. Next, Dr. Bell helped Nicole explain that since he would not sit there himself, his mother would have to hold Tyler in the chair until he was ready to behave. When Nicole held him in her lap in the time-out chair, however, Tyler began kicking and hitting his mother angrily. Again, Dr. Bell supported Nicole's efforts to limit his behavior. Nicole explained to Tyler that because one of the basic rules of their family is that no one can be hurt, she would hold him in such a way that he could not hurt her. Dr. Bell taught her a restraint hold that would let her control his behavior in a nonviolent manner, while keeping Tyler safe and not letting him hurt her.

Tyler reacted as Dr. Bell expected to the hold, but his reaction was extremely upsetting for Nicole. He initially laughed challengingly, but soon his laughter and mocking gave way to worry when his mother did not relent. His physical challenges to the hold increased: He fought and twisted, trying to head-butt his mother, then to kick her. He started crying and sobbing, begging to be let go. Dr. Bell encouraged Nicole through each step of this ordeal. She was told to remind Tyler that when he was calm and quiet and ready to behave, he could get out, but that he was not allowed to hurt people. Tyler continued fighting and began screaming and crying, saying he had to go to the bathroom, that he was thirsty. He tried to spit at his mother. Again, she calmly (although through her own tears) reminded him that when he was calm and ready to behave, he could go. After about 50 minutes of fighting, Tyler finally calmed down and gave up. Before releasing him, Nicole checked again with him to get his agreement that he was ready to behave, and he nodded through his sniffles. When she let him go, he immediately curled up in her lap, subdued and exhausted but behaving appropriately.

At this point, Dr. Bell praised Tyler for his good behavior and effusively praised Nicole for her courage facing the difficult episode and her determination to take good care of her son. She was encouraged to repeat the same procedure at home any time he was defiant, disobedient, or argumentative and to begin with the least-restrictive time-out (a time-out chair by himself) and to move up to physical restraint only if necessary. She was encouraged not to avoid time-out but to seek out the very next opportunity to use it. Another session was scheduled for a few days later.

At the next session, Nicole was happy and excited, and Tyler was quiet and subdued. After the last session, Tyler seemed exhausted and had not misbehaved again that evening. He had even gone to bed when she asked him to. But late the next morning she had to hold him in time-out again for about an hour before he relented. A second time, she had had to hold him in time-out for 20 minutes. After that, when he misbehaved, he would sit in the chair by himself with her watching him. The next few sessions involved strengthening the time-out procedure and helping Nicole understand when and how to use it. Dr. Bell also taught Nicole to positively reinforce Tyler by praising him when he behaved appropriately or did what she asked.

Family Sessions

Mrs. Helms joined Nicole and Tyler in the next few sessions. Mr. Helms was also invited, but he did not feel his work schedule allowed it. During these family sessions, a parental alliance was strengthened between Nicole and Mrs. Helms, and clear boundaries were drawn with Tyler to elevate Nicole clearly to a parental level with Mrs. Helms, while keeping Tyler clearly at the child level. During these sessions, Dr. Bell taught more parent management strategies to help Nicole and Mrs. Helms have age-appropriate and reasonable expectations for Tyler's behavior. During this time, Tyler's behavior was "transformed." Nicole and Mrs. Helms were both happy about Tyler's gains and had been able to follow through very successfully with consistent use of time out. During these sessions, the issues of loss and missing Billy were discussed. After Mrs. Helms expressed her fears that her husband's and Billy's "moody genes" would be passed on, Dr. Bell reassured her.

Individual Play Therapy

After the goals of parent management training had been met, Dr. Bell began to meet individually with Tyler in play therapy. Play therapy is used with preschool children because they often use symbolic play to manage their feelings and practice new skills. Children that age have difficulty verbalizing their feelings directly. Initially, Tyler was aloof and angry when he entered the playroom and resisted symbolic play. Dr. Bell said she understood how mad he must be at her for helping his mom change the rules of their family. During the first few sessions, he used large colored blocks to make sidewalks for him and Dr. Bell to walk on. Dr. Bell remained accepting, following his every lead, and after a few sessions, he warmed up and began engaging more readily in symbolic play. Dr. Bell looked for ways to comment on the feelings the themes of his play reflected. For example, Tyler's play repeated over and over again the theme of a "Daddy" figurine getting on the toy plane and flying away from the "child" figurine. Dr. Bell empathized with how sad the child must be that his daddy is going away and how much he must miss him. She then added that the child must also feel angry at his father for leaving. Tyler nodded at these interpretations. Dr. Bell added that Tyler must miss his father, too. Tyler initially did not respond directly to such comments, but after several sessions, a new theme emerged in his play. He chose to play with a toy mailbox, scribbling on a piece of paper then putting it in the mailbox. He said he was sending a letter to his father. Dr. Bell again focused on the feelings behind these actions, saying to Tyler how much he wished he could write his father a letter and get one back, and how sad it was that this could not happen. After these themes began to recede from his play and his feelings seemed to have been fully processed, Dr. Bell and Nicole decided to end the therapy. By the last session, Nicole felt more confident about her ability to provide effective discipline. Her relationship with Tyler was more positive, and his behavior was much improved.

Discussion

According to the *Diagnostic and Statistical Manual of Mental Disorders* (*DSM-IV-TR*; APA, 2000 pp. 99–102), Tyler met the criteria for oppositional defiant disorder (ODD), one of the disruptive behavior disorders (a section that also includes attention-deficit/hyperactivity disorder [see Chapter 22], and conduct disorder). It is one of the "Disorders Usually First Diagnosed in Infancy, Childhood, or Adolescence." ODD is defined by a pattern of negativistic, hostile, and defiant behavior lasting at least 6 months, during which four (or more) of the following are present:

1. Often loses temper
2. Often argues with adults
3. Often actively defies or refuses to comply with adults' requests or rules
4. Often deliberately annoys people
5. Often blames others for his or her mistakes or misbehavior
6. Is often touchy or easily annoyed by others
7. Is often angry and resentful
8. Is often spiteful or vindictive

The behavioral disturbance must cause significant impairment in the child's functioning, and the child must not meet criteria for conduct disorder, which subsumes oppositional defiant disorder (i.e., all children with conduct disorder would meet criteria for ODD, but not vice versa). Importantly, developmental norms must be considered when determining if the criteria are met. In other words, the clinician must compare the child's behavior against what is typical of children of the same age and developmental level, and the child's behavior must be significantly more frequent or severe.

Disruptive behavior is one of the most common reasons why children are brought in for psychological treatment (Nock, Kazdin, Hiripi, & Kessler, 2007), and many of them are diagnosed with ODD. The disorder typically emerges before age 8 and nearly always by early adolescence. Behavioral disturbance preceding the onset of the disorder, however, is often evident during the pre-school years. Because preschoolers are characteristically negativistic (during the "terrible twos" parents note that children's favorite word is often "no") as part of their developing sense of independence, symptoms should be very significant before assigning this diagnosis to preschool children. A substantial majority of children show aggression and temper tantrums as 2-year-olds, but preschoolers' aggression is more likely to be normative if against other children and indicative of pathology if it targets adults; typical temper tantrums last a few minutes, but sustained and destructive temper tantrums are more characteristic of children with a behavior disorder (Wakschlag et al., 2007). The type of aggression is also important to consider; reactive aggression, which occurs when the child is frustrated, is fairly common among preschoolers, but proactive aggression, which has the goal of injuring another and may occur without direct provocation, is quite rare, even among preschoolers, and more indicative of a clinically significant condition (Wakschlag, Tolan, & Leventhal, 2010). There is a balance to be made between the danger of overidentifying and pathologizing a child for behavior that may be temporary and missing a chance to intervene early before a condition worsens (Banaschewski, 2010). Tyler's symptoms were not typical of usual preschool behavior because they included aggression against adults and destructive temper tantrums, such as knocking things off the coffee table.

Since ODD was first formally introduced as a disorder in 1980, there has not been as much research on the disorder as on some of the other childhood disorders. In addition, because there is substantial comorbidity with conduct disorder and because conduct disorder, if it emerges, replaces ODD as a diagnosis, many longitudinal research studies collapse the two diagnoses into one category. Researchers are still working toward definitively establishing its prevalence rates. About 2% of boys and 1.5% of girls met the criteria for ODD in one community sample (Rowe, Maughan, Pickles, Costello, & Angold, 2002). Other studies have found higher prevalence rates. In one large study of a national sample, adults reported on their history of a number of different psychological disorders, and the lifetime prevalence rate of ODD in that sample was 10% (Nock et al., 2007). In a study that examined a large community sample of 4-year-old preschoolers, 8.3% were found to have moderate to severe ODD (Lavigne, LeBailly, Hopkins, Gouze, & Binns, 2009). Children living in families with lower incomes are much more likely to have the disorder (Steiner & Remsing, 2007).

The course of ODD is complicated. Children who are identified by mothers and preschool teachers as having high levels of disruptive behavior at age 3 are likely to persist in having behavioral problems into adolescence (Pierce, Ewing, & Campbell, 1999). Others who display problems in only one context or whose problems are less severe may grow out of the disruptive behavior. As children with ODD mature into adolescents, some of them begin to meet the criteria for conduct disorder; in these children, the level of oppositionality and defiance does not diminish, but more serious lawbreaking or delinquent behavior is added (Maughan, Rowe, Messer, Goodman, & Meltzer, 2004). One of the best predictors of which children will go on to develop conduct disorder is the symptom of being hurtful, spiteful, or vindictive to others; children with ODD who show this symptom are most likely to develop more serious pathology in adolescence (Kolko & Pardini, 2010). Studies using clinical samples have found that the majority of children with ODD develop conduct disorder as teens, but clinical samples are not typical of all individuals with the disorder, and different findings emerge when community samples are used. In one representative community sample, ODD was a risk factor for conduct disorder for boys but not for girls. Almost half the boys who had ODD at age 9 went on to develop conduct disorder as adolescents. Girls with ODD as children were only at risk for continuing to have the disorder as adolescents (Rowe et al., 2002). So although many do, the majority of children with ODD do not go on to develop conduct disorder.

In clinical samples, more boys than girls are in treatment for ODD. In community samples, boys are somewhat more likely than girls to meet the diagnostic criteria (Maughan et al., 2004). However, mothers report more similar rates of symptoms for girls and boys than do teachers, so perhaps boys' behavior problems are more evident in public settings. In a large household survey, it was found that parents' reports of the numbers of oppositional behaviors did not differ between boys and girls (Lahey et al., 2000). More research is needed on girls with ODD. Tyler had not yet started school, but without treatment, it is probable that his symptoms would have been readily evident to his kindergarten teacher.

As noted in Chapter 22, ODD has a high rate of comorbidity with attention-deficit/hyperactivity disorder (ADHD); about one-quarter of people who reported having ODD also had a history of ADHD (Nock et al., 2007). ODD is also comorbid with depression and anxiety. ODD is typically the first disorder that emerges; the other disorders develop later in life. Although Tyler did not have any problems with impulsiveness, hyperactivity, or inattentiveness, his disorder might have put him at risk later in life for conduct disorder, anxiety, and depression if it had gone untreated.

Etiological Considerations

Much of the research on the causes of ODD has looked more broadly at disruptive behavior disorders, considering ODD in the same category as conduct disorder. Recently, however, separate investigations have examined ODD. Most researchers have concluded that there are multiple factors that add together in causing the disorder (Steiner & Remsing, 2007). One of those causal factors is genetic. In a population-based twin study of children and adolescents from Virginia, both monozygotic (MZ) and dizygotic (DZ) twin pairs' symptoms of ODD were found to be correlated, with a stronger correlation for MZ twin pairs. This indicates that both genetic and environmental factors are involved in its etiology (Eaves et al., 1997). These data also suggested that a common environmental causal factor was linked to both ODD and conduct disorder. Further analysis also found a genetic factor that was common to both disorders (Eaves et al., 2000). In another population-based twin study of children and adolescents in Minnesota, these findings were replicated, strengthening confidence in the finding that both genetic and environmental factors cause ODD (Burt, Krueger, McGue, & Iacono, 2001). The Minnesota study found evidence for one strongly predictive environmental factor that is common to ODD, conduct disorder, and ADHD, as well as separate genetic factors that are linked to each disorder. Further research is needed to specify exactly which genes are involved and what environmental experiences are critical in the etiology of ODD.

Personality traits or temperament may also be important. One line of research examines personality traits characteristic of adult antisocial personality disorder to see if these traits are also evident in children with ODD. The developmental pathway that occurs for a subset of children—ODD in childhood and then conduct disorder in adolescence—sometimes continues into antisocial personality disorder in adulthood. In one study that suggested a connection between ODD and later antisocial personality disorder, children with both ODD and ADHD who scored high on the personality traits of callousness (lack of empathy) and unemotionality (shallow or limited emotions) were also likely to show fearlessness and a lack of concern about their own behavior problems (Barry et al., 2000). They also continued to play a game for a long time after the results switched from winning (rewarding) to losing (punishing). These traits are part of psychopathy. Callousness and unemotionality were the key factors in determining which children had this constellation of traits. Tyler did not have ADHD or display callousness or unemotionality and did not act fearlessly or engage in sensation-seeking, reckless behaviors. Nobody in his family displayed personality traits of psychopathy (including his father by the report of other family members). Because he did not have these traits, he may have been less likely to develop antisocial personality disorder.

Autonomic underarousal in response to reward, which has also been linked to antisocial behavior in adults and conduct disorder in children, has been studied in children with ODD. Autonomic underarousal is measured by heart rate and changes in electrical conductivity in the skin during certain situations. Preschool children with comorbid ODD and ADHD show this underarousal in response to reward (Crowell et al., 2006). Although this response is related to biological factors such as serotonin and noradrenaline systems, interestingly, it can also be affected by environmental experiences such as attending special preschools that feature teachers trained in behavior management and counseling for parents.

In another study, school-age boys with ODD who showed autonomic underarousal also showed less physiological reaction to a punishment (measured as losing points in a game). In addition, they kept using their losing strategy in the game even though the strategy was repeatedly punished (Matthys, van Goozen, Snoek, & van Engeland, 2004). This evidence shows that at least some children with ODD relate to rewarding and punishing experiences the same way people with antisocial personality disorder do.

Environmental causal factors, both biological and social, have also been studied. Toxins have been linked to oppositional behavior. Children whose mothers smoke cigarettes during their pregnancies are at increased risk for ODD. Exposure to prenatal smoking doubled the risk of the child later having ODD compared to children whose mothers never smoked, even when controlling for low birth weight, mothers' educational level, and mothers' antisocial behavior (Nigg & Breslau, 2007). The pathway of this effect could be that cigarette exposure causes a child to have an irritable temperament (a link confirmed by research studies), and irritability might in turn increase the chance of developing oppositional behavior. Although this causal pathway may contribute to some cases of ODD, it does not relate to Tyler. His mother did not smoke cigarettes, and he did not have an irritable temperament; his mother reported that his behavior was easy to manage when he was younger.

The main focus of research on the environmental factors that cause ODD has been on parenting. Many different aspects of the parent–child relationship have been explored, but the best researched one is the way that parents use discipline. Parents of children with disruptive behavior often use inconsistent discipline. They may threaten the child with punishment if they don't comply but then do not follow through with punishing the child. Or their reactions to the child's behavior may be unpredictable, varying from day to day. They may also positively reinforce the child's arguing by giving in to their demands (Steiner & Remsing, 2007). These difficult interactions may develop into a coercive cycle, described by Gerald Patterson (1982). In a coercive cycle (often seen at grocery store checkout lanes), a child engages in an escalation of unpleasant behavior when the parent attempts to set limits (begging, whining, and nagging the parent to buy them candy after the parent first said "no") and negatively reinforces the parent's giving in to their demands (when the parent finally relents and buys the candy, the child immediately stops the unpleasant behavior, therefore negatively reinforcing the parent's conceding). At the same time, the parent inadvertently positively reinforces the child's unpleasant, argumentative behavior by buying them candy after they nag, making the nagging more likely to reoccur. This cycle becomes very stable and resistant to extinction. Tyler and his mother interacted with each other in a coercive cycle. For example, Nicole positively reinforced his disobedient, destructive behavior when he pulled the curtains in his room down by opening the door and giving up her discipline so that he was able to go and watch television, and Tyler negatively reinforced his mother giving up on disciplining him by discontinuing his screaming, destructive behavior.

In addition to inconsistent discipline, other types of dysfunctional discipline can lead to oppositionality or defiant behavior in children. The use of punitive discipline tactics such as yelling, nagging, and threatening and the use of physically aggressive tactics such as beating or hitting have been linked to the development of disruptive behavior problems (Stormshak, Bierman, McMahon, & Lengua, 2000). In addition to finding that children who experience inconsistent discipline have more oppositionality, Stormshak et al. found that those who experience punitive and aggressive discipline also have higher levels of oppositional behavior. Some psychologists include spanking as a form of aggressive discipline, conceptualizing it as similar to shaking, shoving, and beating up the child. Even though many parents advocate the use of spanking as a disciplinary technique, research has confirmed that it increases the child's later aggression and behavior problems, at least among European American (white) families (Deater-Deckard, Dodge, Bates, & Pettit, 1996).

Because of these negative consequences and because it models aggression as an appropriate way to solve problems, psychologists usually do not advocate spanking. For some defiant children, like Tyler, spanking can lead to a power struggle, where the child increases the challenging behavior, provoking the parent to increase the violence of the spanking, until there is a risk for physically abusing the child. This risk is also a danger when parents lose control of their anger while spanking. Among African American families, spanking does not appear to have the same deleterious effects; it may be that it is more accepted in black culture or has a different meaning in black families, such as being a sign of concern or involvement. But for Tyler and Nicole, who are white, spanking seemed to emerge when Nicole's resources for discipline had all failed, and she fell back on spanking as a last resort.

Sometimes parents do not use effective parenting techniques because they do not know or understand them. But at times, other complicating factors get in the way. Some children are more difficult to parent than others, and sometimes there is a bad fit between the temperaments of the parent and child; these relationships in the family system are important (Greene & Doyle, 1999). Tyler's emotional upheaval at the sudden and unexplained loss of his father was expressed as irritability and uncooperative behavior, making him difficult to parent at that time. The adults that remained in his life also lost their confidence to use appropriate discipline because of their sense of the familial legacy of depression, especially in the light of this abandonment. They were afraid that discipline would hurt Tyler, so they became hesitant and inconsistent. Another complicating factor occurs when marital conflict interferes with the parents' ability to implement effective discipline. Marital conflict undermines mothers' ability to discipline effectively, which in turn increases the child's oppositional behavior (Mann & MacKenzie, 1996). Marital dissatisfaction leads to fathers having less warm, accepting relationships with their children, which in turn increases the child's oppositional behavior. The parents of 3-year-old hyperactive children who also have oppositional behavior display more open and intense marital conflict than those whose children are not oppositional (Goldstein et al., 2007). Marital conflict may both increase children's oppositionality and also be increased by it.

In addition to finding high levels of marital conflict, especially overt marital hostility between the parents of boys with ODD, Lindahl (1998) found that these families were characterized by disengagement and disconnectedness between members and lax and inconsistent parenting. Children being brought for mental-health treatment who were diagnosed with ODD were more likely to have experienced victimizing trauma (assault, mugging, family or neighborhood violence, molestation) than children without ODD (Ford et al., 1999). Both oppositionality and delinquent behavior in adolescence are linked with depression; physical aggression is not (Rowe, Maughan, & Eley, 2006).

In addition to marital conflict and victimization, another form of adversity, living in poverty, is strongly linked to children's disruptive behavior. One unique study has clarified the reasons for this phenomenon. Costello, Compton, Keeler, & Angold (2003) were in the process of following a representative population sample of 1,420 children in a longitudinal study when a casino opened on the American Indian reservation in North Carolina where some of the sample lived. This change had the effect of lifting some of the Indian children out of poverty because all the families on that reservation received income from the casino. Children who were persistently poor had a 59% greater chance of having any psychological diagnosis than those who had never lived in poverty. Children that moved out of poverty showed a 40% decrease in their symptoms of ODD and conduct disorder after their families received the additional income, making the levels of their symptoms almost the same as those children who had never lived in poverty. The researchers found that this effect occurred because of how much supervision the parents gave the children. When living in poverty, the parents provided much more lax supervision, and after they were lifted out of poverty, they provided better supervision. This study is so interesting methodologically because it is a natural experiment (the families were "randomly" selected to receive more income), being lifted out of poverty could not be attributed to characteristics in their psychological functioning or genetics. This allows the researchers to conclude that the poverty was a causal factor linked to the children's oppositionality, and not an effect of some third variable or a result of their pathology. It is interesting to consider that for Tyler, his oppositional behaviors emerged after his father left and his mother ran out of money and fell below the poverty line, forcing her to move in with her parents-in-law.

Treatment

The best established type of treatment for ODD is parent management training. There is substantial evidence that this treatment is very effective for reducing children's disruptive behaviors and improving family functioning (Farmer, Compton, Burns, & Robertson, 2002). This intervention has many different forms but always focuses on training parents to improve their interactions with their children and respond successfully to problem behaviors. Parents learn to positively reinforce desired behavior and stop reinforcing problem behaviors. They learn to set up systems of consequences for problem behaviors, such as loss of privileges or time-out, and increase the consistency of their parenting. The evidence shows that parent management training results in substantial improvements for children with disruptive behavior. This treatment is especially effective with children who have ODD as well as another comorbid condition or who have more severe dysfunction as the result of their disorder (Kazdin & Whitley, 2006b).

Cognitive behavioral approaches are also effective in treating ODD (Farmer et al., 2002). One such treatment is collaborative problem solving, which focuses on improving the joint problem solving of parents and children (Greene et al., 2004). This treatment showed similar effectiveness to parent management training at the end of treatment, and children's gains in symptom improvement continued after treatment so that by follow-up, it was significantly more effective. Another treatment combines a set of cognitive behavioral strategies, named by the researchers "Dinosaur School," with parent management training that is more effective than either treatment by itself (Webster-Stratton & Hammond, 1997). Dinosaur School uses dinosaur puppets and fantasy play in conjunction with videotape modeling to teach children successful coping strategies for a wide variety of difficult situations they are likely to encounter.

Family therapy approaches have also been shown to be effective in treating ODD (Farmer et al., 2002), and some of these were used with Tyler. Including his grandmother in the treatment, and specifically focusing on strengthening boundaries between subsystems (the parent subsystem of his mother and grandmother, separated from the child subsystem of Tyler) was an example of this family therapeutic approach. For adolescents, multisystemic therapy has been shown to be very effective, but research needs to establish its effectiveness for school-age children (Farmer et al., 2002). Multisystemic therapy involves targeting the entire family system and how it interfaces with the community—integrating social work, community support, and school support—and has often been used with adolescents with severe conduct disorder.

Most children who are treated for ODD are school age or adolescents; Tyler was treated as a preschooler. Treating preschoolers may be a real advantage because their behavior is not as entrenched by habit and may be easier to change (Nixon, Sweeney, Erickson, & Touyz, 2003). Regardless of the type of therapy used, establishing a strong therapeutic alliance is essential. The alliance between the therapist and the parent is linked to how much the parent is able successfully to change their parenting behaviors (Kazdin & Whitley, 2006a). Dr. Bell focused on developing a supportive, accepting relationship with Nicole, empathizing with her struggles and encouraging her progress. This support helped Nicole through the difficult changes required for therapeutic success. After these changes were established, she was able to focus on helping Tyler with his feelings of sadness and anger at his father for leaving.

Medication is not typically used for ODD unless it is comorbid with ADHD, and then drugs for ADHD are often used. To control aggressive behavior, clinicians sometimes use antidepressants or anticonvulsants that are typically used to treat bipolar disorder (Althoff, Rettew, & Hudziak, 2003). More recently, antipsychotics have been used to target aggression, but these medications have a number of side effects that may outweigh their benefits. Nonpharmacological interventions should be used first to see if medication can be avoided.

Discussion Questions

1. Some television shows featuring people helping families cope with their disruptive children have become popular in the United States. Have you ever seen them? Is disruptive behavior in children on the rise? If so, what factors do you think are responsible?
2. Researchers found that spanking causes increases in children's aggression and oppositionality, at least in some families. How did the researchers establish that spanking caused the aggression, and not that aggressive children caused their parents to spank them more?
3. Were you surprised about the evidence that spanking has different effects in families of different ethnic/racial backgrounds? Do you think the evidence supports the conclusions? What implications does that have for the recommendations psychologists make when treating children?
4. How do positive and negative reinforcement work in a coercive cycle? Have you ever seen a parent and a child engaged in such an interaction? If so, identify what was being positively and negatively reinforced, and how.

REFERENCES

Abouesh, A., & Clayton, A. (1999). Compulsive voyeurism and exhibitionism: A clinical response to paroxetine. *Archives of Sexual Behavior, 28*, 23–30.

Abramowitz, J. S. (2010). Psychological treatment for obsessive-compulsive disorder. In D. J. Stein, E. Hollander, & B. O. Rothbaum (Eds.), *Textbook of anxiety disorders* (2nd ed., pp. 339–354). Arlington, VA: American Psychiatric Publishing.

Abramowitz, J. S., Franklin, M. E., Street, G. P., Kozak, J. M., & Foa, E. B. (2000). Effects of comorbid depression on response to treatment for obsessive-compulsive disorder. *Behavior Therapy, 31*, 517–528.

Abramowitz, J. S., Taylor, S., & McKay, D. (2007). Psychological theories of obsessive-compulsive disorder. In E. A. Storch, G. R. Geffken, & T. K. Murphy (Eds.), *Handbook of child and adolescent obsessive-compulsive disorder* (pp. 109–129). Mahwah, NJ: Erlbum.

Abrams, R. (2002). *Electroconvulsive therapy* (4th ed.). New York, NY: Oxford University Press.

Aguilera, A., López, S. R., Breitborde, N. K., Kopelowicz, A., & Zarate, R. (2010). Expressed emotion and sociocultural moderation in the course of schizophrenia. *Journal of Abnormal Psychology, 119*, 875–885.

Akhtar, S. (1992). *Broken structures: Severe personality disorders and their treatment.* Northvale, NJ: Jason Aronson.

Albert, U., & Brunatto, C. (2009). Obsessive-compulsive disorder in adults: Efficacy of combined and sequential treatments. *Clinical Neuropsychiatry: Journal of Treatment Evaluation, 6*, 83–93.

Allen, J. J. B., & Iacono, W. G. (2001). Assessing the validity of amnesia in dissociative identity disorder. *Psychology, Public Policy, and Law, 7*, 311–344.

Allen, P., Laroi, F., McGuire, P. K., & Aleman, A. (2008). The hallucinating brain: A review of structural and functional neuroimaging studies of hallucinations. *Neuroscience & Biobehavioral Reviews, 32*, 175–191.

Alloy, L. B., Abramson, L. Y., Walshaw, P. D., & Neeren, A. (2006). Cognitive vulnerability to unipolar and bipolar mood disorders. *Journal of Social and Clinical Psychology, 25*, 726–754.

Althoff, R. R., Rettew, D. C., & Hudziak, J. J. (2003). Attention-deficit/hyperactivity disorder, oppositional defiant disorder, and conduct disorder. *Psychiatric Annals, 33*, 245–252.

American Psychiatric Association. (1952). *Diagnostic and statistical manual of mental disorders: First edition (DSM-I).* Washington, DC: American Psychiatric Association.

American Psychiatric Association. (1968). *Diagnostic and statistical manual of mental disorders: Second edition (DSM-II).* Washington, DC: American Psychiatric Association.

American Psychiatric Association. (1980). *Diagnostic and statistical manual of mental disorders: Third edition (DSM-III).* Washington, DC: American Psychiatric Association.

American Psychiatric Association. (1994). *Diagnostic and statistical manual of mental disorders: Fourth edition (DSM-IV).* Washington, DC: American Psychiatric Association.

American Psychiatric Association. (2000). *Diagnostic and statistical manual of mental disorders: Fourth edition, Text revision (DSM-IV-TR)*. Washington, DC: American Psychiatric Association.

Andersen, A. E. (1997). Inpatient treatment of anorexia nervosa. In D. M. Garner & P. E. Garfinkel (Eds.), *Handbook of treatment for eating disorders* (2nd ed., pp. 327–353). New York, NY: Guilford.

Anderson, D. A., & Maloney, K. C. (2001). The efficacy of cognitive-behavioral therapy on the core symptoms of bulimia nervosa. *Clinical Psychology Review, 21*, 971–988.

Andreasen, N. C., Arndt, S., Alliger, R., Miller, D., & Flaum, M. (1995). Symptoms of schizophrenia: Methods, meanings, and mechanisms. *Archives of General Psychiatry, 52*, 341–351.

Andrews, B., Brewin, C. R., & Rose, S. (2003). Gender, social support, and PTSD in victims of violent crime. *Journal of Traumatic Stress, 16*, 421–427.

Arikawa, H., Templer, D. I, Brown, R., Cannon, W. G., & Thomas-Dodson, S. (1999). The structure and correlates of kanashibari. *The Journal of Psychology, 133*, 369–375.

Austin, S. B. (2001). Population-based prevention of eating disorders: An application of the Rose prevention model. *Preventive Medicine, 32*, 268–283.

Auyeung, B., Baron-Cohen, S., Ashwin, E., Knickmeyer, R., Taylor, K., & Hackett, G. (2009). Fetal testosterone and autistic traits. *British Journal of Psychology, 100*, 122.

Bach, A. K., Wincze, J. P., & Barlow, D. H. (2001). Sexual dysfunction. In D. H. Barlow (Ed.), *Clinical handbook of psychological disorders: A step-by-step treatment manual* (3rd ed., pp. 562–608). New York, NY: Guilford.

Baer, J. S., Sampson, P. D., Barr, H. M., Connor, P. D., & Streissguth, A. P. (2003). A 21-year longitudinal analysis of the effects of prenatal alcohol exposure on young adult drinking. *Archives of General Psychiatry, 60*, 377–385.

Baethge, C. (2003). Long-term treatment of schizoaffective disorder: Review and recommendations. *Pharmacopsychiatry, 36*, 45–56.

Baker, B., Szalai, J. P., Paquette, M., & Tobe, S. (2003). Marital support, spousal contact, and the course of mild hypertension. *Journal of Psychosomatic Research, 55*, 229–233.

Baker, J. H., Mazzeo, S. E., & Kendler, K. S. (2007). Association between broadly defined bulimia nervosa and drug use disorders: Common genetic and environmental influences. *International Journal of Eating Disorders, 40*, 673–678.

Banaschewski, T. (2010). Preschool behaviour problems–overpathologised or under-identified? A developmental psychopathology perspective is needed. *Journal of Child Psychology and Psychiatry, 51*, 1–2.

Banaschewski, T., Becker, K., Scherag, S., Franke, B., & Coghill, D. (2010). Molecular genetics of attention-deficit/hyperactivity disorder: An overview. *European Child and Adolescent Psychiatry, 19*, 237–257.

Bandelow, B., Krause, J., Wedekind, D., Broocks, A., Hajak, G., & Rüther, E. (2005). Early traumatic life events, parental attitudes, family history, and birth risk factors in patients with borderline personality disorder and healthy controls. *Psychiatry Research, 134*, 169–179.

Baranek, G. T., Boyd, B. A., Poe, M. D., David, F. J., & Watson, L. R. (2007). Hyperresponsive sensory patterns in young children with autism, developmental delay, and typical development. *American Journal on Mental Retardation, 112*, 233–245.

Barbaresi, W. J., Colligan, R. C., Weaver, A. L., & Katusic, S. K. (2009). The incidence of clinically diagnosed versus research-identified autism in Olmsted County, Minnesota, 1976–1997: Results from a retrospective, population-based study. *Journal of Autism and Developmental Disorders, 39*, 464–470.

Barbaresi, W. J., Katusic, S. K., Colligan, R. C., Weaver, A. L., & Jacobsen, S. J. (2005). The incidence of autism in Olmsted County, Minnesota, 1976–1997: Results from a population-based study. *Archives of Pediatrics and Adolescent Medicine, 159*, 37–44.

Barkley, R. A. (1990). *Attention-deficit hyperactivity disorder: A handbook for diagnosis and treatment*. New York, NY: Guilford.

Barkley, R. A., Karlsson, J., & Pollard, S. (1985). Effects of age on the mother–child interactions of hyperactive children. *Journal of Abnormal Child Psychology, 13,* 631–638.

Barlow, D. H. (1997). Cognitive-behavioral therapy for panic disorder: Current status. *Journal of Clinical Psychiatry, 58* (Suppl. 2), 32–35.

Barlow, D. H., Gorman, J. M., Shear, M. K., & Woods, S. W. (2000). Cognitive behavioral therapy, imipramine, or their combination for panic disorder: A randomized controlled trial. *Journal of the American Medical Association, 283,* 2529–2536.

Barnow, S., Lucht, M., & Freyberger, H. J. (2005). Correlates of aggressive and delinquent conduct problems in adolescence. *Aggressive Behavior, 31,* 24–39.

Barry, C. T., Frick, P. J., DeShazo, T. M., McCoy, M. G., Ellis, M., & Loney, B. R. (2000). The importance of callous-unemotional traits for extending the concept of psychopathy to children. *Journal of Abnormal Psychology, 109,* 335–340.

Başoğlu, M., & Mineka, S. (1992). The role of uncontrollable and unpredictable stress in post-traumatic stress responses in torture survivors. In M. Başoğlu (Ed.), *Torture and its consequences: Current treatment approaches* (pp. 182–225). Cambridge, England: Cambridge University Press.

Başoğlu, M., & Paker, M. (1995). Severity of trauma as predictor of long-term psychological status in survivors of torture. *Journal of Anxiety Disorders, 9,* 339–350.

Başoğlu, M., Paker, M., Paker, Ö., Özmen, E., Marks, I., Incesu, C., . . . Sarimurat, N. (1994). Psychological effects of torture: A comparison of tortured with nontortured political activists in Turkey. *American Journal of Psychiatry, 151,* 76–81.

Bass, C., Peveler, R., & House, A. (2001). Somatoform disorders: Severe psychiatric illnesses neglected by psychiatrists. *British Journal of Psychiatry, 179,* 11–14.

Beach, S. R. H., Brody, G. H., Gunter, T. D., Packer, H., Wernett, P., & Philibert, R. A. (2010). Child maltreatment moderates the association of *MAOA* with symptoms of depression and antisocial personality disorder. *Journal of Family Psychology, 24,* 12–20.

Beck, A. T., Freeman, A., & Davis, D. D. (2004). *Cognitive therapy of personality disorders* (2nd ed.). New York, NY: Guilford.

Becker, D. F., Grilo, C. M., Edell, W. S., & McGlashen, T. H. (2000). Comorbidity of borderline personality disorder with other personality disorders in hospitalized adolescents and adults. *American Journal of Psychiatry, 157,* 2011–2016.

Bellino, S., Paradiso, E., & Bogetto, F. (2008). Efficacy and tolerability of pharmacotherapies for borderline personality disorder. *CNS Drugs, 22,* 671–692.

Ben Amor, L., Grizenko, H., Schwartz, G. Lageix, P., Baron, C., Ter-Stepanian, M., . . . Joober, R. (2005). Perinatal complications in children with attention-deficit hyperactivity disorder and their unaffected siblings. *Review of Psychiatry and Neuroscience, 30,* 120–126.

Bentall, R. P., & Taylor, J. L. (2006). Psychological processes and paranoia: Implications for forensic behavioural science. *Behavioral Sciences & the Law, 24,* 277–294.

Benyon, S., Soares-Weiser, K., Woolacott, N., Duffy, S., & Geddes, J. R. (2008). Psychosocial interventions for the prevention of relapse in bipolar disorder: Systematic review of controlled trials. *British Journal of Psychiatry, 192,* 5–11.

Berenson, K. R., Downey, G., Rafaeli, E., Coifman, K. G., & Paquin, N. L. (2011). The rejection-rage contingency in borderline personality disorder. *Journal of Abnormal Psychology.* Advance online publication.

Berking, M., Margraff, M., Ebert, D., Wupperman, P., Hofmann, S. G., & Junghanns, K. (2011). Deficits in emotion-regulation skills predict alcohol use during and after cognitive-behavioral therapy for alcohol dependence. *Journal of Consulting and Clinical Psychology,* Advance online publication.

Bermingham, S. L., Cohen, A., Hague, J., & Parsonage, M. (2010). The cost of somatisation among the working-age population in England for the year 2008–2009. *Mental Health in Family Medicine, 7,* 71–84.

Bernstein, D. P., & Useda, J. D. (2007). Paranoid personality disorder. In W. O'Donohue, K. A. Fowler, & S. O. Lilienfeld (Eds.), *Personality disorders: Toward the DSM-V* (pp. 41–62). Thousand Oaks, CA: Sage.

Berquier, A., & Ashton, R. (1992). Characteristics of the frequent nightmare sufferer. *Journal of Abnormal Psychology, 101*, 246–250.

Bertelsen, A., & Gottesman, I. I. (1995). Schizoaffective psychoses: Genetical clues to classification. *American Journal of Medical Genetics, 60*, 7–11.

Besiroglu, L., Uguz, F., Ozbebit, O., Ozkan, G., Cilli, A. S., & Rustem, A. (2007). Longitudinal assessment of symptom and subtype categories in obsessive-compulsive disorder. *Depression and Anxiety, 24*, 461–466.

Bettelheim, B. (1967). *The empty fortress*. New York, NY: Free Press.

Beutler, L. E., Machado, P. P. P., & Neufeldt, S. A. (1994). Therapist variables. In A. E. Bergin & S. L. Garfield (Eds.), *Handbook of psychotherapy and behavior change* (4th ed., pp. 229–269). New York, NY: Wiley.

Bhugra, D., Popelyuk, D., & McMullen, I. (2010). Paraphilias across cultures: Contexts and controversies. *Journal of Sex Research, 47*, 242–256.

Biederman, J., Faraone, S. V., Mick, E., Spencer, T., Wilens, T., Kiely, K., . . . Warburton, R. (1995). High risk for attention deficit hyperactivity disorder among children of parents with childhood onset of the disorder. *American Journal of Psychiatry, 152*, 431–435.

Biederman, J., Mick, E., Faraone, S. V., Braaten, E., Doyle, A., Spencer, T., . . . Johnson, M. A. (2002). Influence of gender on attention deficit hyperactivity disorder in children referred to a psychiatric clinic. *American Journal of Psychiatry, 159*, 36–42.

Billstedt, E., Gillberg, I. C., & Gillberg, C. (2007). Autism in adults: Symptom patterns and early childhood predictors. Use of the DISCO in a community sample followed from childhood. *Journal of Child Psychology and Psychiatry, 48*, 1102–1110.

Binik, Y. M. (2005). Should dyspareunia be retained as a sexual dysfunction in DSM-V? *Archives of Sexual Behavior, 34*, 11–21.

Binik, Y. M., Reissing, E., Pukall, C., Flory, N., Payne, K. A., & Khalife, S. (2002). The female sexual pain disorders: Genital pain or sexual dysfunction? *Archives of Sexual Behavior, 31*, 425–431.

Bischof, G., Rumpf, H.-J., Hapke, U., Meyer, C., & John, U. (2003). Types of natural recovery from alcohol dependence: A cluster analytic approach. *Addiction, 98*, 1737–1746.

Bishop, S., Gahagan, S., & Lord, C. (2007). Re-examining the core features of autism: A comparison of autism spectrum disorder and fetal alcohol spectrum disorder. *Journal of Child Psychology and Psychiatry, 48*, 1111–1121.

Black, D. W., Blum, N., Pfohl, B., & Hale, N. (2004). Suicidal behavior in borderline personality disorder: Prevalence, risk factors, prediction, and prevention. *Journal of Personality Disorders, 18*, 226–239.

Blagrove, M., & Fisher, S. (2009). Trait-state interactions in the etiology of nightmares. *Dreaming, 19*, 65–74.

Blair, R. J. R. (2003). Neurobiological basis of psychopathy. *British Journal of Psychiatry, 182*, 5–7.

Blair, R. J. R., Jones, L., Clark, F., & Smith, M. (1997). The psychopathic individual: A lack of responsiveness to distress cues. *Psychophysiology, 34*, 192–198.

Blair, R. J. R., Peschardt, K. S., Budhani, S., Mitchell, D. G. V., & Pine, D. S. (2006). The development of psychopathy. *Journal of Child Psychology and Psychiatry, 47*, 262–275.

Blanchard, R., & Clemmensen, L. H. (1988). A test of the DSM-III-R's implicit assumption that fetishistic arousal and gender dysphoria are mutually exclusive. *Journal of Sex Research, 25*, 426–432.

Bleuler, E. (1950). *Dementia praecox or the group of schizophrenias*. New York, NY: International Universities Press. (Originally published 1911.)

Bogaerts, S., Vanheule, S., Leeuw, F., & DeSmet, M. (2006). Recalled parental bonding and personality disorders in a sample of exhibitionists: A comparative study. *The Journal of Forensic Psychiatry and Psychology, 17*, 636–646.

Bohus, M., Haaf, B., Simms, T., Limberger, M. F., Schmahl, C., Unckel, C., . . . Linehan, M. M. (2004). Effectiveness of inpatient dialectical behavioral therapy for borderline personality disorder: A controlled trial. *Behaviour Research and Therapy*, *42*, 487–499.

Bonanno, G. A., Galea, S., Bucciarelli, A., & Vlahov, D. (2007). What predicts psychological resilience after disaster? The role of demographics, resources, and life stress. *Journal of Consulting and Clinical Psychology*, *75*, 671–682.

Bootzin, R. R., & Epstein, D. R. (2011). Understanding and treating insomnia. *Annual Review of Clinical Psychology, 7*, 7.1–7.24.

Bordo, S. (1997). Anorexia nervosa: Psychopathology as the crystallization of culture. In M. M. Gergen & S. N. Davis (Eds.), *Toward a new psychology of gender* (pp. 423–453). New York, NY: Routledge.

Bosworth, H. B., Bartash, R. M., Olsen, M. K., & Steffens, D. C. (2003). The association of psychosocial factors and depression with hypertension among older adults. *International Journal of Geriatric Psychiatry*, *18*, 1142–1148.

Both, S., Laan, E., & Schultz, W. (2010). Disorders in sexual desire and sexual arousal in women, a 2010 state of the art. *Journal of Psychosomatic Obstetrics & Gynecology*, *31*, 207–218.

Bower, H. (2001). The gender identity disorder in the DSM-IV classification: A critical evaluation. *Australian and New Zealand Journal of Psychiatry*, *35*, 1–8.

Bradford, J. M. (2001). The neurobiology, neuropharmacology, and pharmacological treatment of the paraphilias and compulsive sexual behavior. *Canadian Journal of Psychiatry*, *46*, 26–34.

Bradley, R., Greene, J., Russ, E., Dutra, L., & Westen, D. (2005). A multidimensional meta-analysis of psychotherapy for PTSD. *American Journal of Psychiatry*, *162*, 214–227.

Braham, L. G., Trower, P., & Birchwood, M. (2004). Acting on command hallucinations and dangerous behavior: A critique of the major findings in the last decade. *Clinical Psychology Review*, *24*, 513–528.

Brand, B., Classen, C., Lanins, R., Loewenstein, R., McNary, S., Pain, C., & Putnam, F. (2009). A naturalistic study of dissociative identity disorder and dissociative disorder not otherwise specified patients treated by community clinicians. *Psychological Trauma: Theory, Research, Practice, and Policy*, *1*(2), 153–171.

Breslau, J., Aguilar-Gaxiola, S., Kendler, K. S., Su, M., Williams, D., & Kessler, R. C. (2006). Specifying race-ethnic differences in risk for psychiatric disorder in a USA national sample. *Psychological Medicine*, *36*, 57–68.

Brewerton, T. D., Dansky, B. S., Kilpatrick, D. G., & O'Neil, P. M. (2000). Which comes first in the pathogenesis of bulimia nervosa: Dieting or bingeing? *International Journal of Eating Disorders*, *20*, 259–264.

Bridges, E. (2010). Racial identity development and psychological coping strategies of African American males at a predominantly white university. *Annals of the American Psychotherapy Association*, *13*, 14–26.

Brimacombe, M., Ming, X., & Lamendola, M. (2007). Prenatal and birth complications in autism. *Maternal and Child Health Journal*, *11*, 73–79.

Brondolo, E., Rieppi, R., Kelly, K. P., & Gerin, W. (2003). Perceived racism and blood pressure: A review of the literature and conceptual and methodological critique. *Annals of Behavioral Medicine*, *25*, 55–65.

Brown, F. C., Buboltz, W. C., & Soper B. (2002). Relationship of sleep hygiene awareness sleep hygiene practices, and sleep quality in university students. *Behavioral Medicine*, *28*, 33–38.

Brown, G. W. (2002). Social roles, context and evolution in the origins of depression. *Journal of Health and Social Behavior*, *43*, 255–276.

Brown, G. W., & Harris, T. (1978). *Social origins of depression: A study of psychiatric disorder in women*. New York, NY: Free Press.

Bulik, C. M., Thornton, L. M., Root, T. L., Pisetsky, E. M., Lichtenstein, P., & Pedersen, N. L. (2010). Understanding the relation between anorexia nervosa and bulimia nervosa in a Swedish national twin sample. *Biological Psychiatry*, *67*, 71–77.

Burns, A. S., Rivas, D. A., & Ditunno, J. F. (2001). The management of neurogenic bladder and sexual dysfunction after spinal cord injury. *Spine, 26*, S129–S136.

Burt, S. A., Krueger, R. F., McGue, M., & Iacono, W. G. (2001). Sources of covariation among attention-deficit/hyperactivity disorder, oppositional defiant disorder, and conduct disorder: The importance of shared environment. *Journal of Abnormal Psychology, 110*, 516–525.

Bustillo, J. R., Lauriello, J., Horan, W. P., & Keith, S. J. (2001). The psychosocial treatment of schizophrenia: An update. *American Journal of Psychiatry, 158*, 163–175.

Byrne, S. M., & McLean, N. J. (2002). The cognitive-behavioral model of bulimia nervosa: A direct evaluation. *International Journal of Eating Disorders, 31*, 17–31.

Cade, J. F. J. (1949). Lithium salts in the treatment of psychotic excitement. *Medical Journal of Australia, 36*, 349–352.

Cadoret, R. J., Yates, W. R., Troughton, E., Woodworth, G., & Stewart, M. A. (1995b). Genetic-environment interaction in the genesis of aggressivity and conduct disorders. *Archives of General Psychiatry, 52*, 916–924.

Calhoun, K. S., & Wilson, A. E. (2000). Rape and sexual aggression. In L. T. Szuchman & F. Muscarella (Eds.), *Psychological perspectives on human sexuality* (pp. 573–602). New York, NY: Wiley.

Cameron, N. (1959). The paranoid pseudo-community revisited. *American Journal of Sociology, 65*, 52–58.

Campo, J., Nijman, H., Merckelbach, H., Evers, C. (2003). Psychiatric comorbidity of gender identity disorders: A survey among Dutch psychiatrists. *American Journal of Psychiatry, 160*, 1332–1336.

Cannon, T. D., Kaprio, J., Loennqvist, J., Huttunen, M., & Koskenvuo, M. (1998). The genetic epidemiology of schizophrenia in a Finnish twin cohort: A population-based modeling study. *Archives of General Psychiatry, 55*, 67–74.

Casper, R. C., & Troiani, M. (2001). Family functioning in anorexia nervosa differs by subtypes. *International Journal of Eating Disorders, 30*, 338–342.

Castellanos, F. X., Giedd, J. N., Marsh, W. L., Hamburger, S. D., Vaituzis, A. C., Dickstein, D. P., . . . Rapoport, J. L. (1996). Quantitative brain magnetic resonance imaging in attention deficit/hyperactivity disorder. *Archives of General Psychiatry, 53*, 607–616.

Centers for Disease Control and Prevention (CDC). (2009). Perceived insufficient rest or sleep among adults–United States, 2008. *Journal of American Medical Association, 302*, 2532–2539.

Cheniaux, E., Landeira-Fernandez, J., Telles, L. Lessa, J. M., Dias, A., Duncan, T., & Versiani, M. (2008). Does schizoaffective disorder really exist? A systematic review of the studies that compared schizoaffective disorder with schizophrenia or mood. *Journal of Affective Disorders, 106*, 209–217.

Cheyne, J. A. (2002). Situational factors affecting sleep paralysis and associated hallucinations: Position and timing effects. *Journal of Sleep Research, 11*, 169–177.

Cheyne, J. A., Newby-Clark, I. R., & Rueffer, S. D. (1999). Relations among hypnagogic and hypnopompic experiences associated with sleep paralysis. *Journal of Sleep Research, 8*, 313–317.

Chioqueta, A. P., & Stiles, T. C. (2004). Suicide risk in patients with somatization disorder. *Crisis, 25*, 3–7.

Chivers, M. L., & Bailey, J. M. (2000). Sexual orientation of female-to-male transsexuals: A comparison of homosexual and nonhomosexual types. *Archives of Sexual Behavior, 29*, 259–278.

Christakis, D. A., Zimmerman, F. J., DiGiuseppe, D. L., & McCarty, C. A. (2004). Early television exposure and subsequent attentional problems in children. *Pediatrics, 113*, 708–713.

Christensen, B. S., Grønbæk, M., Osler, M., Pedersen, B. V., Graugaard, C., & Frisch, M. (2011). Sexual dysfunctions and difficulties in Denmark: Prevalence and associated sociodemographic factors. *Archives of Sexual Behavior, 40*, 121–132.

Chronis, A. M., Chacko, A., Fabiano, G. A., Wymbs, B. T., & Pelham, W. E. (2004). Enhancements to the behavioral parent training paradigm for families of children with ADHD: Review and future directions. *Clinical Child and Family Psychology Review, 7*, 1–27.

Cicchetti, D., & Toth, S. L. (2004). Child maltreatment. *Annual Reviews in Clinical Psychology, Reviews in Advance, 1*, 1–30.

Citrome, L., & Volavka, J. (2000). Management of violence in schizophrenia. *Psychiatric Annals, 30*, 41–52.

Clark, D. M., Salkovskis, P. M., Ost, L. G., Breitholtz, E., Koehler, K., Westling, B. E., . . . Gelder, M. (1997). Misinterpretation of body sensations in panic disorder. *Journal of Consulting and Clinical Psychology, 65*, 203–213.

Clark, R. (2006). Perceived racism and vascular reactivity in Black college women: Moderating effects of seeking social support. *Health Psychology, 25*, 20–25.

Clark, R., Anderson, N. B., Clark, V. R., & Williams, D. R. (1999). Racism as a stressor for African Americans: A biopsychosocial model. *American Psychologist, 54*, 805–816.

Clark, R. E., Bartels, S. J., Mellman, T. A., & Peacock, W. J. (2002). Recent trends in antipsychotic combination therapy of schizophrenia and schizoaffective disorders: Implications for state mental health policy. *Schizophrenia Bulletin, 28*, 75–84.

Clarkin, J. F., Levy, K. N., Lenzenweger, M. F., & Kernberg, O. F. (2004). The Personality Disorders Institute/Borderline Personality Disorder Research Foundation randomized control trial for borderline personality disorder: Rationale, methods, and patient characteristics. *Journal of Personality Disorders, 18*, 52–72.

Clayton, A. H. (2007). Epidemiology and neurobiology of female sexual dysfunction. *Journal of Sexual Medicine, 4*, 260–268.

Clayton, A. H., & West, S. G. (2003). The effects of antidepressants on human sexuality. *Primary Psychiatry, 10*, 62–70.

Cleckley, H. E. (1976). *The mask of sanity*. St. Louis, MO: Mosby.

Clemans, K. H., DeRose, L. M., Graber, J. A., & Brooks-Gunn, J. (2010). Gender in adolescence: Applying a person-in-context approach to gender identity and roles. In J. C. Chrisler & D. R. McCreary (Eds.), *Handbook of gender research in psychology: Vol 1. Gender research in general and experimental psychology* (pp. 527–557). New York, NY: Springer.

Cohen, A. N., Hammen, C., Henry, R. M., & Daley, S. E. (2004). Effects of stress and social support on recurrence in bipolar disorder. *Journal of Affective Disorders, 82*, 143–147.

Cohen, E., Feinn, R., Arias, A., & Kranzler, H. R. (2007). Alcohol treatment utilization: Findings from the National Epidemiologic Survey on Alcohol and Related Conditions. *Drug and Alcohol Dependence, 86*, 214–221.

Cohen-Kettenis, P. T., & Arrindell, W. A. (1990). Perceived parental rearing style, parental divorce and transsexualism: A controlled study. *Psychological Medicine, 20*, 613–620.

Colby, K. M. (1977). Appraisal of four psychological theories of paranoid phenomena. *Journal of Abnormal Psychology, 86*, 54–59.

Cole, T. B. (2006). Rape at US Colleges often fueled by alcohol. *JAMA: Journal of the American Medical Association, 296*, 504–505.

Compton, A. (1992). The psychoanalytic view of phobias: III. Agoraphobia and other phobias of adults. *Psychoanalytic Quarterly, 61*, 400–425.

Conway, K. P., Compton, W., Stinson, F. S., & Grant, B. F. (2006). Lifetime comorbidity of DSM-IV mood and anxiety disorders and specific drug use disorders. *Journal of Clinical Psychiatry, 67*, 247–257.

Coolidge, F. L., Thede, L. L., & Young, S. E. (2002). The heritability of gender identity disorder in a child and adolescent twin sample. *Behavior Genetics, 32*, 251–257.

Cooper, M. J. (2005). Cognitive theory in anorexia nervosa and bulimia nervosa: Progress, development and future directions. *Clinical Psychology Review, 25*, 511–531.

Cooper, M. J., Todd, G., & Wells, A. (2002). Content, origins, and consequences of dysfunctional beliefs in anorexia nervosa and bulimia nervosa. In R. L. Leahy & E. T. Dowd (Eds.) *Clinical advances in cognitive psychotherapy: Theory and application*. New York, NY: Springer.

Cooper, Z., & Fairburn, C. G. (2010). Cognitive behavior therapy for bulimia nervosa. In C. M. Grilo & J. E. Mitchell (Eds.), *The treatment of eating disorders: A clinical handbook* (pp. 243–270). New York, NY: Guilford Press.

Costello, E. J., Compton, S. N., Keeler, G., & Angold, A. (2003). Relationships between poverty and psychopathology: A natural experiment. *Journal of American Medical Association, 290*, 2023–2029.

Craig, T. K. J., Boardman, A. P., Mills, K., Daly-Jones, O., & Drake, H. (1993). The South London Somatisation Study: I. Longitudinal course and the influence of early life experiences. *British Journal of Psychiatry, 163*, 579–588.

Craig, T. K. J., Drake, H., Mills, K., & Boardman, A. P. (1994). The South London Somatisation Study: II. Influence of stressful life events, and secondary gain. *British Journal of Psychiatry, 165*, 248–258.

Craske, M. G., Roy-Byrne, P. P., Stein, M. B., Sullivan, G., Sherbourne, C., & Bystritsky, A. (2009). Treatment for anxiety disorders: Efficacy to effectiveness to implementation. *Behaviour Research and Therapy, 47*, 931–937.

Crick, N. R., & Zahn-Waxler, C. (2003). The development of psychopathology in females and males: Current progress and future challenges. *Development and psychopathology, 15*, 719–742.

Crimlisk, H. L., Bhatia, K. P., Cope, H., David, A. S., Marsden, D., & Ron, M. A. (2000). Patterns of referral in patients with medically unexplained motor symptoms. *Journal of Psychosomatic Research, 49*, 217–219.

Critchfield, K. L., Levy, K. N., Clarkin, J. F., & Kernberg, O. F. (2008). The relational context of aggression in borderline personality disorder: Using adult attachment style to predict forms of hostility. *Journal of Clinical Psychology, 64*, 67–82.

Crowell, S. E., Beauchaine, T. P., Gatzke-Kopp, L., Sylvers, P., Mead, H., & Chipman-Chacon, J. (2006). Autonomic correlates of attention-deficit/hyperactivity disorder and oppositional defiant disorder in preschool children. *Journal of Abnormal Psychology, 115*, 174–178.

Crowell, S. E., Beauchaine, T. P., & Linehan, M. M. (2009). A biosocial developmental model of borderline personality: Elaborating and extending Linehan's theory. *Psychological Bulletin, 135*, 495–510.

Csigó, K. K., Harsányi, A. A., Demeter, G. Y., Rajkai, C. S., Németh, A. A., & Racsmány, M. M. (2010). Long-term follow-up of patients with obsessive–compulsive disorder treated by anterior capsulotomy: A neuropsychological study. *Journal of Affective Disorders, 126*, 198–205.

Cunningham, J. A., Blomqvist, J., Koski-Jannes, A., & Cordingley, J. (2005). Maturing out of drinking problems: Perceptions of natural history as a function of severity. *Addiction Research and Theory, 13*, 79–84.

Curtis, N. M., Ronan, K. R., & Borduin, C. M. (2004). Multisystemic treatment: A metaanalysis of outcome studies. *Journal of Family Psychology, 18*, 411–419.

Dahlitz, M., & Parkes, J. D. (1993). Sleep paralysis. *Lancet, 341*, 406–408.

Daley, D. (2006). Attention deficit hyperactivity disorder: A review of the essential facts. *Child Care, Health & Development, 32*, 193–204.

Dandescu, A., & Wolfe, R. (2003). Considerations on fantasy use by child molesters and exhibitionists. *Sexual Abuse: A Journal of Research and Treatment, 15*, 297–305.

Davies, O. (2003). The nightmare experience, sleep paralysis, and witch accusations. *Folklore, 114*,181–203.

Davison, G. C. (1968). Elimination of a sadistic fantasy by a client-controlled counterconditioning technique. *Journal of Abnormal Psychology, 73*, 84–90.

Davison, G. C., Williams, M. E., Nezami, E., Bice, T. L., & DeQuattro, V. (1991). Relaxation, reduction in angry articulated thoughts, and improvements in borderline essential hypertension and heart rate. *Journal of Behavioral Medicine, 14*, 453–468.

De Cuypere, G., Van Hemelruck, M., Michel, A., Caael, B., Heylens, G., Rubens, R., . . . Monstrey, S. (2007). Prevalence and demography of transsexualism in Belgium. *European Psychiatry, 22*, 137–141.

De Gucht, V., & Heiser, W. (2003). Alexithymia and somatisation: A quantitative review of the literature. *Journal of Psychosomatic Research, 54*, 425–434.

Deater-Deckard, K., Dodge, K. A., Bates, J. E., & Pettit, G. S. (1996). Physical discipline among African-American and European-American mothers: Links to children's externalizing behaviors. *Developmental Psychology, 32*, 1065–1072.

Dell'Osso, B., Nestadt, G., Allen, A., & Hollander, E. (2006). Serotonin-norepinephrine reuptake inhibitors in the treatment of obsessive-compulsive disorder: A critical review. *Journal of Clinical Psychiatry, 67*, 600–610.

Diamond, M. (2009). Clinical implications of the organizational and activational effects of hormones. *Hormones and Behavior, 55*, 621–632.

Dikeos, D. G., & Soldatos, C. R. (2005). The condition of insomnia: Etiopathogenetic considerations and their impact on treatment practices. *International Review of Psychiatry, 17*, 255–262.

Dindo, L., & Fowles, D. (2011). Dual temperamental risk factors for psychopathic personality: Evidence from self-report and skin conductance. *Journal of Personality and Social Psychology, 100*, 557–566.

Dogan, S. J., Conger, R. D., Kim, K. J., & Masyn, K. E.(2007). Cognitive and parenting pathways in the transmission of antisocial behavior from parents to adolescents. *Child Development, 78*, 335–349.

Dorahy, M. J., Mills, H., Taggart, C., O'Kane, M., & Mulholland, C. (2006). Do dissociative disorders exist in Northern Ireland?: Blind psychiatric—structured interview assessments of 20 complex psychiatric patients. *European Journal of Psychiatry, 20*, 172–182.

Dressler, W. W. (2004). Culture and the risk of disease. *British Medical Bulletin, 69*, 21–31.

Dubbert, P. (1995). Behavioral (life style) modification in the prevention and treatment of hypertension. *Clinical Psychology Review, 15*, 187–216.

Dunsieth, N. W., Nelson, E. B., Brusman-Lovins, L. A., Holcomb, J. L., Beckman, D., Welge, J. A., . . . McElroy, S. L. (2004). Psychiatric and legal features of 113 men convicted of sexual offenses. *Journal of Clinical Psychiatry, 65*, 293–300.

Eaton, W. W., Anthony, J. C., Romanoski, A., Tien, A., Gallo, J., Cai, G., . . . Chen, L. S. (1998). Onset and recovery from panic disorder in the Baltimore Epidemiologic Catchment Area follow-up. *British Journal of Psychiatry, 173*, 501–507.

Eaves, L., Rutter, M., Silberg, J. L., Shillady, L., Maes, H., & Pickles, A. (2000). Genetic and environmental causes of covariation in interview assessments of disruptive behavior in child and adolescent twins. *Behavior Genetics, 30*, 321–334.

Eaves, L. J., Silberg, J. L., Meyer, J. M., Maes, H. H., Simonoff, E., Pickles, A., . . . Hewitt, J. K. (1997). Genetics and developmental psychopathology: 2. The main effects of genes and environment on behavioral problems in the Virginia Twin Study of Adolescent Behavioral Development. *Journal of Child Psychology and Psychiatry, 38*, 965–980.

Eckert, E. D., Halmi, K. A., Marchi, P., Grove, W., & Crosby, R. (1995). Ten-year-follow-up of anorexia nervosa: Clinical course and outcome. *Psychological Medicine, 25*, 143–156.

Eddy, K. T., Keel, P. K., Dorer, D. J., Delinsky, S. S., Franko, D. L., & Herzog, D. B. (2002). Longitudinal comparison of anorexia nervosa subtypes. *International Journal of Eating Disorders, 20*, 191–201.

Edenberg, H. J., & Foroud, T. (2006). The genetics of alcoholism: Identifying specific genes through family studies. *Addiction Biology, 11*, 386–396.

Edens, J. F., Marcus, D. K., Lilienfeld, S. O., & Poythress, N. G. (2006). Psychopathic, not psychopath: Taxometric evidence for the dimensional structure of psychopathy. *Journal of Abnormal Psychology, 115*, 131–144.

Egger, H. L., Kondo, D., & Angold, A. (2006). The epidemiology and diagnostic issues in preschool attention-deficit/hyperactivity disorder: A review. *Infants and Young Children, 19*, 109–122.

Eisen, J. L., Phillips, K. A., & Rasmussen, S. A. (1999). Obsessions and delusions: The relationship between obsessive-compulsive disorder and the psychotic disorders. *Psychiatric Annals, 29*, 515–522.

Elbogen, E. B., Van Dorn, R. A., Swanson, J. W., Swartz, M. S., & Monahan, J. (2006). Treatment engagement and violence risk in mental disorders. *British Journal of Psychiatry, 189*, 354–360.

Elkins, I. J., King, S. M., McGue, M., & Iacono, W. G. (2006). Personality traits and the development of nicotine, alcohol, and illicit drug disorders: Prospective links from adolescence to young adulthood. *Journal of Abnormal Psychology, 115*, 25–39.

Ellason, J. W., & Ross, C. A. (1997). Two-year follow-up of inpatients with dissociative disorder. *American Journal of Psychiatry, 154*, 832–839.

Elliott, D. M., Mok, D. S., & Briere, J. (2004). Adult sexual assault: Prevalence, symptomatology, and sex differences in the general population. *Journal of Traumatic Stress, 17*, 203–211.

Emmers-Sommer, T. M., Allen, M., Bourhis, J., Sahlstein, E., Laskowski, K., Falato, W. L., . . . Cashman, L. (2004). A meta-analysis of the relationship between social skills and sexual offenders. *Communication Reports, 17*, 1–10.

Eronen, M. (1995). Mental disorders and homicidal behavior in female subjects. *American Journal of Psychiatry, 152*, 1216–1218.

Esterberg, M. L., Goulding, S. M., & Walker, E. F. (2010). Cluster A personality disorders: Schizotypal, schizoid and paranoid personality disorders in childhood and adolescence. *Journal of Psychopathology and Behavioral Assessment, 32*, 515–528.

Faber, S. D., & Burns, J. W. (1996). Anger management style, degree of expressed anger, and gender influence cardiovascular recovery from interpersonal harassment. *Journal of Behavioral Medicine, 19*, 31–53.

Fairburn, C. (2005). Evidence-based treatment of anorexia nervosa. *International Journal of Eating Disorders, 37*, S26–S30.

Fairburn, C. G. (1995). *Overcoming binge eating.* New York, NY: Guilford.

Fairburn, C. G., & Cooper, Z. (2007). Thinking afresh about the classification of eating disorders. *International Journal of Eating Disorders, 40*, S107–S110.

Farag, N. H., & Mills, P. J. (2004). What's next in behavioral hypertension research? *Annals of Behavioral Medicine, 27*, 1–2.

Farmer, A., Elkin, A., & McGuffin, P. (2007). The genetics of bipolar affective disorder. *Current Opinion in Psychiatry, 20*, 8–12.

Farmer, E. M. Z., Compton, S. N., Burns, B. J., & Robertson, E. (2002). Review of the evidence base for treatment of childhood psychopathology: Externalizing disorders. *Journal of Consulting and Clinical Psychology, 70*, 1267–1302.

Farsimadan, F., Draghi-Lorenz, R., & Ellis, J. (2007). Process and outcome of therapy in ethnically similar and dissimilar therapeutic dyads. *Psychotherapy Research, 17*, 567–575.

Fazel, S., & Danesh, J. (2002). Serious mental disorder in 23,000 prisoners: A systematic review of 62 surveys. *Lancet, 359*, 545–550.

Fedora, O., Reddon, J. R., & Yeudall, L. T. (1986). Stimuli eliciting sexual arousal in genital exhibitionists: A possible clinical application. *Archives of Sexual Behavior, 15*, 417–427.

Feigenbaum, J. (2007). Dialectical behaviour therapy: An increasing evidence base. *Journal of Mental Health, 16*, 51–68.

Ferguson, C. J., Winegard, B., & Winegard, B. M. (2011). Who is the fairest one of all? How evolution guides peer and media influences on female body dissatisfaction. *Review of General Psychology, 15*, 11–28.

Ferguson, C. P., & Pigott, T. A. (2000). Anorexia and bulimia nervosa: Neurobiology and pharmacotherapy. *Behavior Therapy, 31*, 237–263.

Fernander, A. F., Durán, R. E. F., Saab, P. G., & Schneiderman, N. (2004). John Henry active coping, education, and blood pressure among urban blacks. *Journal of the National Medical Association, 96*, 246–255.

Fink, P. (1992). Surgery and medical treatment in persistent somatizing patients. *Journal of Psychosomatic Research, 36*, 439–447.

Finney, J. W., & Moos, R. H. (1998). Psychosocial treatments for alcohol use disorders. In P. E. Nathan & J. M. Gorman (Eds.), *A guide to treatments that work* (pp. 156–166). New York, NY: Oxford University Press.

Firestone, P., Kingston, D. A., Wexler, A., & Bradford, J. M. (2006). Long-term follow-up of exhibitionists: Psychological, phallometric, and offense characteristics. *Journal of the American Academy of Psychiatry and the Law, 34*, 349–359.

Fishbain, D. A., Lewis, J. E., Gao, J., Cole, B., & Rosomoff, R. S. (2009). Is chronic pain associated with somatization/hypochondriasis? An evidence-based structured review. *Pain Practice, 9*, 449–467.

Fleck, F. (2004). MMR controversy raises questions about publication ethics. *Bulletin of the World Health Organization, 82*, 311–312.

Flensborg-Madsen, T., Knop, J., Mortensen, E. L., Becker, U., & Grønbæk, M. (2007). Amount of alcohol consumption and risk of developing alcoholism in men and women. *Alcohol & Alcoholism, 42*, 442–447.

Flory, K., & Lynam, D. R. (2003). The relation between attention deficit hyperactivity disorder and substance abuse: What role does conduct disorder play? *Clinical Child and Family Psychology Review, 6*, 1–16.

Foa, E. B., & Franklin, M. E. (2001). Obsessive-compulsive disorder. In D. H. Barlow (Ed.), *Clinical handbook of psychological disorders: A step-by-step treatment manual* (3rd ed., pp. 209–263). New York, NY: Guilford.

Foa, E. B., Keane, T., Friedman, M., & Cohen, J. (Eds.). (2009). *Effective treatments for PTSD: Practice guidelines from the International Society for Traumatic Stress Studies* (2nd ed.). New York, NY: Guilford Press.

Foa, E. B., & Riggs, D. S. (1995). Posttraumatic stress disorder following assault: Theoretical considerations and empirical findings. *Current Directions in Psychological Science, 4*, 61–65.

Foley, D. L., Eaves, L. J., Wormley, B., Silberg, J. L., Maes, H. H., Kuhn, J., & Riley, B. (2004). Childhood adversity, monoamine oxidase A genotype, and risk for conduct disorder. *Archives of General Psychiatry, 61*, 738–744.

Fontenelle, L. F., Mendlowicz, M. V., & Versiani, M. (2006). The descriptive epidemiology of obsessive-compulsive disorder. *Progress in Neuro-Psychpharmacology & Biological Psychiatry, 30*, 327–337.

Forbes, D., Creamer, M., Bisson, J. I., Cohen, J. A., Crow, B. E., Foa, E. B., . . . Ursano, R. J. (2010). A guide to guidelines for the treatment of PTSD and related conditions. *Journal of Traumatic Stress, 23*, 537–552.

Ford, J. D., Racusin, R., Daviss, W. B., Ellis, C. G., Thomas, J., Rogers, K., . . . Sengupta, A. (1999). Trauma exposure among children with oppositional defiant disorder and attention deficit-hyperactivity disorder. *Journal of Consulting and Clinical Psychology, 67*, 786–789.

Forrest, K. A. (2001). Toward an etiology of dissociative identity disorder: A neurodevelopmental approach. *Consciousness and Cognition, 10*, 259–293.

Frances, A., First, M. B., & Pincus, H. A. (1995). *DSM-IV guidebook*. Washington, DC: American Psychiatric Press.

Franco-Paredes, K., Mancilla-Díaz, J. M., Vázquez-Arévalo, R., López-Aguilar, X., & Álvarez-Rayón, G. (2005). Perfectionism and eating disorders: A review of the literature. *European Eating Disorders Review, 13*, 61–70.

Frank, E. (2005). *Treating bipolar disorder: A clinician's guide to interpersonal and social rhythm therapy*. New York, NY: Guilford.

Freud, S. (1925). Mourning and melancholia. In *Sigmund Freud, Collected papers, Volume IV* (A. Strachey & J. Strachey, Trans.). London, England: Hogarth Press. (Originally published in *Zeitschrift*, 1917.)

Freud, S. (1925). Psycho-analytic notes upon an autobiographical account of a case of paranoia (dementia Paranoides). In *Sigmund Freud, Collected papers, Volume III* (A. Strachey & J. Strachey, Trans.). London, England: Hogarth Press. (Originally published in *Jahrbuch für psychoanalytische und psychopathologische Forschungen*, 1909.)

Freund, K., & Watson, R. (1990). Mapping the boundaries of courtship disorder. *Journal of Sex Research, 27*, 589–606.

Friedman, M. J. (2009). PTSD and other posttraumatic syndromes. In D. McKay, J. S. Abramowitz, S. Taylor, & G. G. Asmundson (Eds.), *Current perspectives on the anxiety disorders: Implications for DSM-V and beyond* (pp. 377–409). New York, NY: Springer.

Friedman, S. H., & Loue, S. (2007). Incidence and prevalence of intimate partner violence by and against women with severe mental illness. *Journal of Women's Health, 16*, 471–480.

Fritz, G. K., Fritsch, S., & Hagino, O. (1997). Somatoform disorders in children and adolescents: A review of the past 10 years. *Journal of the American Academy of Child and Adolescent Psychiatry, 36*, 1329–1338.

Fullana, M. A., Mataix-cols, D., Caspi, A., Harrington, H., Grisham, J. R., Moffitt, T. E., & Poulton, R. (2009). Obsessions and compulsions in the community: Stability, and co-occurring psychiatric conditions. *Psychiatry: Interpersonal and Biological Processes*, 329–336.

Funder, D. C. (1999). *Personality judgment: A realistic approach to person perception*. San Diego, CA: Academic Press.

Gangestad, S. W., Bailey, J. M., & Martin, N. G. (2000). Taxometric analyses of sexual orientation and gender identity. *Journal of Personality and Social Psychology, 78*, 1109–1121.

Gao, Y., & Raine, A. (2010). Successful and unsuccessful psychopaths: A neurobiological model. *Behavioral Sciences and the Law, 28*, 194–210.

Garner, D. M., & Magana, C. (2002). Bulimia nervosa. In M. Hersen & L. K. Porzelius (Eds.), *Diagnosis, conceptualization, and treatment planning for adults: A step-by-step guide* (pp. 251–269). Mahwah, NJ: Erlbaum.

Gastfriend, D. R., Garbutt, J. C, Pettinati, H. M., & Forman, R. F. (2007). Reduction in heavy drinking as a treatment outcome in alcohol dependence. *Journal of Substance Abuse Treatment, 33*, 71–80.

Gatward, N. (2007). Anorexia nervosa: An evolutionary puzzle. *European Eating Disorders Review, 15*, 1–12.

Gaultney, J. F. (2010). The prevalence of sleep disorders in college students: Impact on academic performance. *Journal of American College Health, 59*, 91–97.

Gearson, J. S., Kaltman, S. I., Brown, C., & Bellack, A. S. (2003). Traumatic life events and PTSD among women with substance use disorders and schizophrenia. *Psychiatric Services, 54*, 523–528.

Geller, R. E., & Goldberg, J. F. (2007). A review of evidence-based psychotherapies for bipolar disorder. *Primary Psychiatry, 14*, 59–69.

Germain, A., Krakow, B., Faucher, B., Zadra, A., Nielsen, T., Hollifield, M., . . . Koss, M. (2004). Increased mastery elements associated with imagery rehearsal treatment for nightmares in sexual assault survivors with PTSD. *Dreaming, 14*, 195–206.

Ghizzani, A., & Montomoli, M. (2000). Anorexia nervosa and sexuality in women: A revew. *Journal of Sex Education and Therapy, 25*, 80–88.

Gillig, P. (2009). Dissociative identity disorder: A controversial diagnosis. *Psychiatry, 6*, 24–29.

Gilligan, C. (1982). *In a different voice: Psychological theory and women's development*. Cambridge, MA: Harvard University Press.

Gillock, K. L., Zayfert, C., Hegel, M. T., & Ferguson, R. J. (2005). Posttraumatic stress disorder in primary care: Prevalence and relationships with physical symptoms and medical utilization. *General Hospital Psychiatry, 27*, 392–399.

Girón, M. M., Fernández-Yañez, A. A., Mañá-Alvarenga, S. S., Molina-Habas, A. A., Nolasco, A. A., & Gómez-Beneyto, M. M. (2010). Efficacy and effectiveness of individual family intervention on social and clinical functioning and family burden in severe schizophrenia: A 2-year randomized controlled study. *Psychological Medicine, 40*, 73–84.

Gleaves, D. H., May, M. C., & Cardena, E. (2001). An examination of the diagnostic validity of dissociative identity disorder. *Clinical Psychology Review, 21*, 577–608.

Godlee, F., Smith, J., & Marcovitch, H. (2011). Wakefield's article linking MMR vaccine and autism was fraudulent. *British Medical Journal*, 342.

Goldbacher, E. M., Matthews, K. A., & Salomon, K. (2005). Central adiposity is associated with cardiovascular reactivity to stress in adolescents. *Health Psychology, 24*, 375–384.

Goldstein, L. H., Harvey, E. A., Friedman-Weieneth, J. l., Pierce, C., Tellert, A., & Sippel, J. C. (2007). Examining subtypes of behavior problems among 3-year-old children, Part II: Investigating differences in parent psychopathology, couple conflict, and other family stressors. *Journal of Abnormal Child Psychology, 35*, 111–123.

Goodman, R., & Stevenson, J. (1989). A twin study of hyperactivity: II. The aetiological role of genes, family relationships, and perinatal adversity. *Journal of Child Psychology and Psychiatry, 30*, 691–709.

Gordon, H. (2008). The treatment of paraphilias: An historical perspective. *Criminal Behaviour and Mental Health, 18*, 79–87.

Gossop, M., Harris, J., Best, D., Man, L. H., Manning, V., Marshall, J., & Strang, J. (2003). Is attendance at Alcoholics Anonymous meetings after inpatient treatment related to improved outcomes? A 6–month follow-up study. *Alcohol and Alcoholism, 38*, 421–426.

Gotlib, I. H., & Joormann, J. (2010). Cognition and depression: Current status and future directions. *Annual Review of Clinical Psychology, 6*, 285–312.

Gottesman, I. I., & Goldsmith, H. H. (1994). Developmental psychopathology of antisocial behavior: Inserting genes into its ontogenesis and epigenesis. In C. A. Nelson (Ed.), *Threats to optimal development*. Hillsdale, NJ: Erlbaum Associates.

Gottesman, I. I., & Hanson, D. R. (2005). Human development: Biological and genetic processes. *Annual Review of Psychology, 56*, 263–286.

Gottlieb, S. (2006). Some thoughts on Schreber (and Freud): Depression, paranoia and a delusional system. *British Journal of Psychotherapy, 22*, 427–447.

Grabe, H. J., Ruhrmann, S., Ettelt, S., Buhtz, F., Hochrein, A., Schulze-Rauschenbach, S., . . . Wagner, M. (2006). Familiality of obsessive-compulsive disorder in nonclinical and clinical subjects. *American Journal of Psychiatry, 163*, 1986–1992.

Graham, J. E., Christian, L. M., & Kiecolt-Glaser, J. K. (2006). Stress, age, and immune function: Toward a lifespan approach. *Journal of Behavioral Medicine, 29*, 389–400.

Granic, I., & Patterson, G. R. (2006). Toward a comprehensive model of antisocial development: A dynamic systems approach. *Psychological Review, 113*, 101–131.

Grant, B. F., Chou, S. P., Goldstein, R. B., Huang, B., Stinson, F. S., Saha, T. D., . . . Ruan, W. J. (2008). Prevalence, correlates, disability, and comorbidity of DSM-IV borderline personality disorder: Results from the Wave 2 National Epidemiologic Survey on Alcohol and Related Conditions. *Journal of Clinical Psychiatry, 69*, 533–545.

Grant, B. F., Hasin, D. S., Stinson, F. S., Dawson, D. A., Chou, S. P., Ruan, W. J., & Pickering, R. P. (2004). Prevalence, correlates, and disability of personality disorders in the United States: Results from the National Epidemiological Survey and Alcohol and Related Conditions. *Journal of Clinical Psychiatry, 65*, 948–958.

Grant, B. F., Stinson, F. S., Dawson, D. A., Chou, S. P., & Ruan, W. J. (2005). Cooccurrence of DSM-IV personality disorders in the United States: Results from the National Epidemiologic Survey on Alcohol and Related Conditions. *Comprehensive Psychiatry, 46*, 1–5.

Grant, J. E. (2005). Clinical characteristics and psychiatric comorbidity in males with exhibitionism. *Journal of Clinical Psychiatry, 66*, 1367–1371.

Gratz, K. L., Rosenthal, M. Z., Tull, M. T., Lejuez, C. W., & Gunderson, J. G. (2006). An experimental investigation of emotional dysregulation in borderline personality disorder. *Journal of Abnormal Psychology, 115*, 850–855.

Greaves, G. B. (1980). Multiple personality: 165 years after Mary Reynolds. *Journal of Nervous and Mental Disease, 168*, 577–596.

Green, R. (1987). *The 'sissy boy syndrome' and the development of homosexuality*. New Haven, CT: Yale University Press.

Green, R. (1994). Transsexualism and the law. *Bulletin of the American Academy of Psychiatry and the Law, 22*, 511–517.

Greene, R. W., Ablon, J. S., Monuteaux, M. C., Goring, J. C., Henin, A., Raezer-Blakely, L., . . . Rabbitb, S. (2004). Effectiveness of collaborative problem solving in affectively dysregulated children with oppositional-defiant disorder: Initial findings. *Journal of Consulting and Clinical Psychology, 72*, 1157–1164.

Greene, R. W., & Doyle, A. E. (1999). Toward a transactional conceptualization of oppositional defiant disorder: Implications for assessment and treatment. *Clinical Child and Family Psychology Review, 2*, 129–148.

Grenier, G., & Byers, E. S. (1995). Rapid ejaculation: A review of conceptual, etiological, and treatment issues. *Archives of Sexual Behavior, 24*, 447–472.

Gretton, H. M., Hare, R. D., & Catchpole, R. E. H. (2004). Psychopathy and offending from adolescence to adulthood: A 10-year follow-up. *Journal of Consulting and Clinical Psychology, 72*, 636–645.

Greydanus, D. E., Nazeer, A., & Patel, D. R. (2009). Psychopharmacology of ADHD in pediatrics: Current advances and issues. *Neuropsychiatric Disease and Treatment, 5*, 171–181.

Guimont, C., Brisson, C., Dagenais, G. R., Milot, A., Vézina, M., Mâsse, B., . . . Blanchette, C. (2006). Effects of job strain on blood pressure: A prospective study of male and female white-collar workers. *American Journal of Public Health, 96*, 1436–1443.

Guisinger, S. (2003). Adapted to flee famine: Adding an evolutionary perspective on anorexia nervosa. *Psychological Review, 110*, 745–761.

Gunter, T. D., Vaughn, M. G., & Philibert, R. A. (2010). Behavioral genetics in antisocial spectrum disorders and psychopathy: A review of the recent literature. *Behavioral Sciences and the Law, 28*, 148–173.

Gureje, O., Simon, G. E., Ustun, T. B., & Goldberg, D. P. (1997). Somatization in crosscultural perspective: A World Health Organization study in primary care. *American Journal of Psychiatry, 154*, 989–995.

Guterman, J. T., Martin, C. V., & Rudes, J. (2011). A solution-focused approach to frotteurism. *Journal of Systemic Therapies, 30*, 59–72.

Hacking, I. (1995). *Rewriting the soul: Multiple personality and the sciences of memory*. Princeton, NJ: Princeton University Press.

Haddad, P. M., Taylor, M., & Niaz, O. S. (2009). First-generation antipsychotic long-acting injections v. oral antipsychotics in schizophrenia: Systematic review of randomised controlled trials and observational studies. *British Journal of Psychiatry, 195*(Suppl 52), s20–s28.

Hakala, M., Vahlberg, T., Niemi, P. M., & Karlsson, H. (2006). Brain glucose metabolism and temperament in relation to severe somatization. *Psychiatry and Clinical Neurosciences, 60*, 669–675.

Halmi, K. A. (2011). Eating disorders: Anorexia nervosa, bulimia nervosa, and obesity. In R. E. Hales, S. C. Yudofsky & G. O. Gabbard (Eds.), *Essentials of psychiatry* (3rd ed., pp. 429–453). Arlington, VA: American Psychiatric Publishing.

Hameed, U., Schwartz, T. L., Malhotra, K., West, R. L., & Bertone, F. (2005). Antidepressant treatment in the primary care office. *Annals of Clinical Psychiatry, 17*, 77–81.

Hammen, C. (2005). Stress and depression. *Annual Review of Clinical Psychology, 55*, 11.1–11.27.

Happé, F., Ronald, A., & Plomin, R. (2006). Time to give up on a single explanation for autism. *Nature Neuroscience, 9*, 1218–1220.

Hardy, K. V., & Laszloffy, T. A. (1995). Therapy with African-Americans and the phenomenon of rage. In *Session: Psychotherapy in Practice, 1*, 57–70.

Hare, R. D. (2006). Psychopathy: A clinical and forensic overview. *Psychiatric Clinics of North America, 29*, 709–724.

Hare, R. D., Harpur, T. J., Hakstian, R. A., Forth, A. E., Hart, S., & Newman, J. P. (1990). The revised Psychopathy Checklist: Reliability and factor structure. *Psychological Assessment, 2*, 338–341.

Harkness, K. L., Alavi, N., Monroe, S. M., Slavich, G. M., Gotlib, I. H., & Bagby, R. M. (2010). Gender differences in life events prior to onset of major depressive disorder: The moderating effect of age. *Journal of Abnormal Psychology, 119*, 791–803.

Harrington, R., & Bailey, S. (2004). Prevention of antisocial personality disorder: Mounting evidence on optimal timing and methods. *Criminal Behaviour and Mental Health, 14*, 75–81.

Harris, A., & Lurigio, A. J. (2007). Mental illness and violence: A brief review of research and assessment strategies. *Aggression and Violent Behavior, 12*, 542–551.

Harris, A. M., Orav, E. J., Bates, D. W., & Barksy, A. J. (2008). Somatization increases disability independent of comorbidity. *Journal of General Internal Medicine, 24*, 155–161.

Harris, T. O. (1989). Disorders of menstruation. In G. W. Brown & T. O. Harris (Eds.), *Life events and illness* (pp. 261–294). New York, NY: Guilford Press.

Hartley, S. L., Barker, E. T., Seltzer, M. M., Floyd, F., Greenberg, J., Orsmond, G., & Bolt, D. (2010). The relative risk and timing of divorce in families of children with an autism spectrum disorder. *Journal of Family Psychology*, *24*, 449–457.

Harvey, A. G. (2008). Insomnia, psychiatric disorders, and the transdiagnostic perspective. *Current Directions in Psychological Science*, *17*, 299–303.

Harvey, A. G. (2011). Sleep and circadian functioning: Critical mechanisms in the mood disorders? *Annual Review of Clinical Psychology, 7*, 8.1–8.23.

Hasin, D. S., Stinson, F. S., Ogburn, E., & Grant, B. F. (2007). Prevalence, correlates, disability, and comorbidity of *DSM-IV* alcohol abuse and dependence in the United States: Results from the National Epidemiologic Survey on Alcohol and Related Concerns. *Archives of General Psychiatry*, *64*, 830–842.

Hay, D. F., Pawlby, S., Waters, C. S., Perra, O., & Sharp, D. (2010). Mothers' antenatal depression and their children's antisocial outcomes. *Child Development*, *81*, 149–165.

Hay, P. J., Sachdev, P. S., Cumming, S. S., & Smith, J. S. (1993). Treatment of obsessive-compulsive disorder by psychosurgery. *Acta Psychiatrica Scandinavica*, *87*, 197–207.

Heaton, P., & Wallace, G. L. (2004). Annotation: The savant syndrome. *Journal of Child Psychology and Psychiatry*, *45*, 899–911.

Heiden, W., & Häfner, H. (2000). The epidemiology of onset and course of schizophrenia. *European Archives of Psychiatry and Clinical Neuroscience*, *250*, 292–303.

Heiman, J. R. (2002). Psychologic treatments for female sexual dysfunction: Are they effective and do we need them? *Archives of Sexual Behavior, 31*, 445–450.

Helmes, E., & Landmark, J. (2003). Subtypes of schizophrenia: A cluster analytic approach. *Canadian Journal of Psychiatry*, *48*, 702–708.

Henker, B., & Whalen, C. K. (1989). Hyperactivity and attention deficits. Special Issue: Children and their development: Knowledge base, research agenda, and social policy application. *American Psychologist*, *44*, 216–223.

Herbenick, D. (2009). *Because it feels good: A woman's guide to sexual pleasure and satisfaction.* Emmaus, PA: Rodale Books.

Herman-Jeglinska, A., Grabowska, A., & Dulko, S. (2002). Masculinity, femininity, and transsexualism. *Archives of Sexual Behavior, 31*, 527–534.

Herpetz, S. C., Werth, U., Lukas, G., Qunaibi, M., Schuerkens, A., Kunert, H. J., . . . Sass, H. (2001). Emotion in criminal offenders with psychopathy and borderline personality disorder. *Archives of General Psychiatry*, *58*, 737–745.

Hettema, J. M., Prescott, C. A., Myers, J. M., Neale, M. C., & Kendler, K. S. (2005). The structure of genetic and environmental risk factors for anxiety disorders in men and women. *Archives of General Psychiatry*, *62*, 182–189.

Hicks, B. M., Krueger, R. F., Iacono, W. G., McGue, M., & Patrick, C. J. (2004). Family transmission and heritability of externalizing disorders. *Archives of General Psychiatry*, *61*, 922–928.

Hill, M. N., Han, H. R., Dennison, C. R., Kim, M. T., Roary, M. C., Blumenthal, R. S., . . . Post, W. S. (2003). Hypertension care and control in underserved urban African American men: Behavioral and physiologic outcomes at 36 months. *American Journal of Hypertension, 16*, 906–913.

Hines, M. (2004). Psychosexual development in individuals who have female pseudohermaphroditism. *Child and Adolescent Psychiatric Clinics of North America*, *13*, 641–656.

Hinshaw, S. P., & Melnick, S. M. (1995). Peer relationship with boys with attention deficit hyperactivity disorder with and without comorbid aggression. *Development and Psychopathy*, *7*, 627–647.

Hirschfeld, R. M. A. (2001). Antidepressants in the United States: Current status and future needs. In M. M. Weissman (Ed.), *Treatment of depression: Bridging the 21st century* (pp. 123–134). Washington, DC: American Psychiatric Press.

Hoek, H. W., & van Hoeken, D. (2003). Review of the prevalence and incidence of eating disorders. *International Journal of Eating Disorders*, *34*, 383–396.

Hogan, B. E., & Linden, W. (2004). Anger response styles and blood pressure: At least don't ruminate about it! *Annals of Behavioral Medicine*, *27*, 38–49.

Hollon, S. D., Thase, M. E., & Markowitz, J. C. (2002). Treatment and prevention of depression. *Psychological Science in the Public Interest, 3,* 39–77.

Hooley, J. M. (2007). Expressed emotion and relapse of psychopathology. *Annual Review of Clinical Psychology, 3,* 329–352.

Hopper, K. Harrison, G., Janca, A., & Sartorius, N. (Eds.). (2007). *Recovery from schizophrenia: An international perspective: A report from the WHO Collaborative Project, the international study of schizophrenia.* New York, NY: Oxford University Press.

Hornstein, N. L., & Putnam, F. W. (1996). Abuse and the development of dissociative symptoms and dissociative identity disorder. In C. R. Pfeffer (Ed.), *Severe stress and mental disturbance in children* (pp. 449–473). Washington, DC: American Psychiatric Press.

Houghton, S., Saxon, D., Bradburn, M., Ricketts, T., & Hardy, G. (2010). The effectiveness of routinely delivered cognitive behavioural therapy for obsessive-compulsive disorder: A benchmarking study. *British Journal of Clinical Psychology, 49,* 473–489.

Houts, A. C. (2005). Behavioral and functional models of OCD. In J. S. Abramowitz & A. C. Houts (Eds.), *Concepts and controversies in obsessive-compulsive disorder* (pp. 73–86). New York, NY: Springer.

Howell, R. T., Kern, M. L., & Lyubomirsky, S. (2007). Health benefits: Meta-analytically determining the impact of well-being on objective health outcomes. *Health Psychology Review, 1,* 83–136.

Hsu, L. K. (1996). Epidemiology of the eating disorders. *Psychiatric Clinics of North America, 19:* 681–700.

Hsu, L. K. G., Crisp, A. H., & Callender, J. S. (1992). Recovery in anorexia nervosa: The patient's perspective. *International Journal of Eating Disorders, 11,* 341–350.

Hudson, J. I., Hiripi, E., Pope, H. G., & Kessler, R. C. (2007). The prevalence and correlates of eating disorders in the national comorbidity survey replication. *Biological Psychiatry, 61,* 348–358.

Hudziak, J. J., van Beijsterveldt, C. E. M., Althoff, R. R., Stanger, C., Rettew, D. C., Nelson, E. C., . . . Boomsma, D. I. (2004). Genetic and environmental contributions to the child behavior checklist obsessive-compulsive scale: A cross-cultural twin study. *Archives of General Psychiatry, 61,* 608–616.

Hurwitz, T. A. (2004). Somatization and conversion disorder. *Canadian Journal of Psychiatry, 49,* 172–178.

Husain, S. S., Kevan, I. M., Linnell, R., & Scott, A. I. F. (2004). Electroconvulsive therapy in depressive illness that has not responded to drug treatment. *Journal of Affective Disorders, 83,* 121–126.

Hussong, A. M., Hicks, R. E., Levy, S. A., & Curran, P. J. (2001). Specifying the relations between affect and heavy alcohol use among young adults. *Journal of Abnormal Psychology, 110,* 449–461.

Iwamasa, G. Y. (1993). Asian Americans and cognitive-behavioral therapy. *The Behavior Therapist, 16,* 233–235.

Jacobi, C., Hayward, C., de Zwaan, M., Kraemer, H. C., & Agras, W. S. (2004). Coming to terms with risk factors for eating disorders: Application of risk terminology and suggestions for a general taxonomy. *Psychological Bulletin, 130,* 19–65.

James, D. (1998). Multiple personality disorder in the courts: A review of the North American experience. *Journal of Forensic Psychiatry, 9,* 339–361.

Janicak, P. G., Keck, P. E., Davis, J. M., Kasckow, J. W., Tugrul, K., Dowd, S. M., . . . Strakowski, S. M. (2001). A double-blind, randomized, prospective evaluation of the efficacy and safety of risperidone versus haloperidol in the treatment of schizoaffective disorder. *Journal of Clinical Psychopharmacology, 21,* 360–368.

Jiménez-Genchi, A., Ávila-Rodríguez, V. M., Sánchez-Rojas, F., Terrez, B. E., & Nenclares-Portocarrero, A. (2009). Sleep paralysis in adolescents: The "a dead body climbed on top of me" phenomenon in Mexico. *Psychiatry and Clinical Neurosciences, 63,* 546–549.

Johns, L. C., Rossell, S., Frith, C., Ahmad, F., Hemsley, D., Kuipers, E., & McGuire, P. K. (2001). Verbal self-monitoring and auditory verbal hallucinations in patients with schizophrenia. *Psychological Medicine, 31,* 705–715.

Johnson, J. G., Cohen, P., Brown, J., Smailes, E. M., & Bernstein, D. P. (1999). Childhood maltreatment increases risk for personality disorders during early childhood. *Archives of General Psychiatry, 56,* 600–606.

Johnson, S. L., & Kizer, A. (2002). Bipolar and unipolar depression: A comparison of clinical phenomenology and psychosocial predictors. In I. H. Gotlib and C. L. Hammen (Eds.), *Handbook of depression* (pp. 141–165). New York, NY: Guilford.

Johnson, S. L., & Roberts, J. E. (1995). Life events and bipolar disorder: Implications from biological theories. *Psychological Bulletin, 117,* 434–449.

Joiner, T., Coyne, J. C., & Blalock, J. (1999). On the interpersonal nature of depression: Overview and synthesis. In T. Joiner & J. C. Coyne (Eds.), *The interactional nature of depression* (pp. 3–20). Washington, DC: American Psychological Association.

Jones, S. (2004). Psychotherapy of bipolar disorder: A review. *Journal of Affective Disorders, 80,* 101–114.

Jordan, J., Joyce, P. R., Carter, F. A., Horn, J., McIntosh, V., Luty, S. E., . . . Bulik, C. M. (2008). Specific and nonspecific comorbidity in anorexia nervosa. *International Journal of Eating Disorders, 41,* 47–56.

Kabot, S. Masi, W., & Segal, M. (2003). Advances in the diagnosis and treatment of autism spectrum disorders. *Professional Psychology: Research and Practice, 34,* 26–33.

Kaehler, L. A., & Freyd, J. J. (2009). Borderline personality characteristics: A betrayal trauma approach. *Psychological Trauma: Theory, Research, Practice, and Policy, 1,* 261–268.

Kafka, M. P., & Hennen, J. (2002). A DSM-IV Axis I comorbidity study of males (n = 120) with paraphilias and paraphilia-related disorders. *Sexual Abuse: A Journal of Research and Treatment, 14,* 349–366.

Kahler, C. W., Read, J. P., Stuart, G. L., Ramsey, S. E., McCrady, B. S., & Brown, R. A. (2004). Motivational enhancement for 12–step involvement among patients undergoing alcohol detoxification. *Journal of Consulting and Clinical Psychology, 72,* 736–741.

Kane, J. M. (1996). Treatment-resistant schizophrenic patients. *Journal of Clinical Psychiatry, 57* (Suppl. 9), 35–40.

Kane, J. M. (2004). Tardive dyskinesia rates with atypical antipsychotics in adults: Prevalence and incidence. *Journal of Clinical Psychiatry, 65,* 16–20.

Kanner, L. (1943). Autistic disturbances of affective contact. *Nervous Child, 2,* 217–250.

Kanner, L. (1973). Follow-up of eleven autistic children originally reported in 1943. In L. Kanner (Ed.), *Childhood psychosis: Initial studies and new insights.* Washington, DC: Winston/ Wiley.

Karvonen, J. T., Veijola, J., Jokelainen, J., Läksy, K., Järvelin, M. R., & Joukamaa, M. (2004). Somatization disorder in young adult population. *General Hospital Psychiatry, 26,* 9–12.

Kasen, S., Cohen, P., Skodol., A. E., Johnson, J. G., Smailes, E., & Brook, J. S. (2001). Childhood depression and adult personality disorder: Alternative pathways of continuity. *Archives of General Psychiatry, 58,* 231–236.

Katzman, D. K. (2005). Medical complications in adolescents with anorexia nervosa: A review of the literature. *International Journal of Eating Disorders, 37,* S52–S59.

Kaye, W. (2008). Neurobiology of anorexia and bulimia nervosa. *Physiology & Behavior, 94,* 121–135.

Kaye, W. H., Strober, M., & Rhodes, L. (2002). Body image disturbance and other core symptoms in anorexia and bulimia nervosa. In D. J. Castle & K. A. Phillips (Eds.), *Disorders of body image* (pp. 67–82). Petersfield, England: Wrightson Biomedical Publishing.

Kazdin, A. E., & Whitley, M. K. (2006a). Pretreatment social relations, therapeutic alliance, and improvements in parenting practices in parent management training. *Journal of Consulting and Clinical Psychology, 74,* 346–355.

Kazdin, A. E., & Whitley, M. K. (2006b). Comorbidity, case complexity, and effects of evidence-based treatment for children referred for disruptive behavior. *Journal of Consulting and Clinical Psychology, 74,* 455–467.

Keane, T. M., Fisher, L. M., Krinsley, K. E., & Niles, B. L. (1994). Posttraumatic stress disorder. In M. Hersen & R. T. Ammerman (Eds.), *Handbook of prescriptive treatments for adults* (pp. 237–260). New York, NY: Plenum.

Keane, T. M., Marshall, A. D., & Taft, C. T. (2006). Posttraumatic stress disorder: Etiology, epidemiology, and treatment outcome. *Annual Review of Clinical Psychology, 2*, 161–197.

Kelly, J. F., Magill, M., & Stout, R. L. (2009). How do people recover from alcohol dependence? A systematic review of the research on mechanisms of behavior change in Alcoholics Anonymous. *Addiction Research and Theory, 17*, 236–259.

Kelly, M. P., Strassberg, D. S., & Turner, C. M. (2004). Communication and associated relationship issues in female anorgasmia. *Journal of Sex & Marital Therapy, 30*, 263–276.

Kent, L. (2004). Recent advances in the genetics of attention deficit hyperactivity disorder. *Current Psychiatry Reports, 6*, 143–148.

Kernberg, O. F. (1985). *Borderline conditions and pathological narcissism*. Northvale, NJ: Jason Aronson.

Kessler, S., & McKenna, W. (2000). Who put the "trans" in transgender? Gender theory and everyday life. *International Journal of Transgenderism, 4*(3). Retrieved from http://www.sypmposium.com/ijt/gilbert/ kessler.htm.

Kessler, R. C., Merikangas, K. R., & Wang, P. S. (2007). Prevalence, comorbidity, and service utilization for mood disorders in the United States at the beginning of the twenty-first century. *Annual Review of Clinical Psychology, 3*, 137–158.

Kessler, R. C., Sonnega, A., Bromet, E., Hughes, M., Nelson, D. B., & Breslau, N. (1999). Epidemiological risk factors for trauma and PTSD. In R. Yehuda (Ed.), *Risk factors for posttraumatic stress disorder* (pp. 23–59). Washington, DC: American Psychiatric Press.

Khan, A. A., Jacobson, K. C., Gardner, C. O., Prescott, C. A., & Kendler, K. S. (2005). Personality and comorbidity of common psychiatric disorders. *British Journal of Psychiatry, 186*, 190–196.

Kiehl, K. A., Bates, A. T., Laurens, K. R., Hare, R. D., & Liddle, P. F. (2006). Brain potentials implicate temporal lobe abnormalities in criminal psychopaths. *Journal of Abnormal Psychology, 115*, 443–453.

Kihlstrom, J. F. (2005). Dissociative disorders. *Annual Review of Clinical Psychology, 1*, 227–253.

Kilpatrick, D. G., & Acierno, R. (2003). Mental health needs of crime victims: Epidemiology and outcomes. *Journal of Traumatic Stress, 16*, 119–132.

Kim, B. S. K. (2007). Adherence to Asian and European American cultural values and attitudes toward seeking professional psychological help among Asian American college students. *Journal of Counseling Psychology, 54*, 474–480.

Kim, C., Koo, M., & Kim, E. (2010). The biological treatment of obsessive compulsive disorder. *Clinical Psychopharmacology and Neuroscience, 8*, 55–62.

Kim, M. T., Han, H. R., Hill, M. N., Rose, L., & Roary, M. (2003). Depression, substance use, adherence behaviors, and blood pressure in urban hypertensive black men. *Annals of Behavioral Medicine, 26*, 24–31.

Kim-Cohen, J., Caspi, A., Taylor, A., Williams, B., Newcombe, R., Craig, I. W., & Moffitt, T. E. (2006). MAOA, maltreatment, and gene-environment interaction predicting children's mental health: New evidence and a meta-analysis. *Molecular Psychiatry, 11*, 903–913.

Kinderman, P. (2001). Changing causal attributions. In P. W. Corrigan & D. L. Penn (Eds.), *Social cognition and schizophrenia* (pp. 195–215). Washington, DC: American Psychological Association.

King, S. M., Keyes, M., Malone, S. M., Elkins, I., Legrand, L. N., Iacono, W. G., & McGue, M. (2009). Parental alcohol dependence and the transmission of adolescent behavioral disinhibition: A study of adoptive and non-adoptive families. *Addiction, 104*, 578–586.

Kingston, D. A., Seto, M. C., Firestone, P., & Bradford, J. M. (2010). Comparing indicators of sexual sadism as predictors of recidivism among adult male sexual offenders. *Journal of Consulting and Clinical Psychology, 78*, 574–584.

Kirmayer, L. J. (2009). Nightmares, neurophenomenology and the cultural logic of trauma. *Culture, Medicine and Psychiatry, 33*, 323–331.

Kirmayer, L. J., Groleau, D., Looper, K. J., & Dao, M. D. (2004). Explaining medically unexplained symptoms. *Canadian Journal of Psychiatry, 49*, 663–672.

Kirmayer, L. J., & Young, A. (1998). Culture and somatization: Clinical, epidemiological, and ethnographic perspectives. *Psychosomatic Medicine, 60*, 420–430.

Kjeldsen, S. E., Knudsen, K., Ekrem, G., Fure, T. O., Movinckel, P., & Erikssen, J. E. (2006). Is there an association between severe job strain, transient rise in blood pressure and increased mortality? *Blood Pressure, 15*, 93–199.

Kleifield, E. I., Wagner, S., & Halmi, K. A. (1996). Cognitive-behavioral treatment of anorexia nervosa. *Psychiatric Clinics of North America, 19*, 715–737.

Klein, D. A., & Walsh, B. T. (2004). Eating disorders: Clinical features and pathophysiology. *Physiology & Behavior, 81*, 359–374.

Kliem, S., Kröger, C., & Kosfelder, J. (2010). Dialectical behavior therapy for borderline personality disorder: A meta-analysis using mixed-effects modeling. *Journal of Consulting and Clinical Psychology, 78*, 936–951.

Klin, A. (2009). Embracing the challenge of bold theories of autism. *British Journal of Psychology, 100*, 29–32.

Klin, A., Lin, D. J., Gorrindo, P., Ramsay, G., & Jones, W. (2009). Two-year-olds with autism orient to non-social contingencies rather than biological motion. *Nature, 459*, 257–263.

Klonsky, E. D., Oltmanns, T. F., Turkheimer, E., & Fiedler, E. R. (2000). Recollections of conflict with parents and family support in the personality disorders. *Journal of Personality Disorders, 14*, 327–338.

Kluft, R. P. (1995). The confirmation and disconfirmation of memories of abuse in DID patients: A naturalistic clinical study. *Dissociation: Progress in the Dissociative Disorders, 8*, 253–258.

Klump, K. L., Suisman, J. L., Burt, S. A., McGue, M., & Iacono, W. G. (2009). Genetic and environmental influences on disordered eating: An adoption study. *Journal of Abnormal Psychology, 118*, 797–805.

Knox, S., Burkard, A. W., Johnson, A. J., Suzuki, L. A., & Ponterotto, J. G. (2003). African American and European American therapists' experiences of addressing race in cross-racial psychotherapy dyads. *Journal of Counseling Psychology, 50*, 466–481.

Kolko, D. J., & Pardini, D. A. (2010). ODD dimensions, ADHD, and callous-unemotional traits as predictors of treatment response in children with disruptive behavior disorders. *Journal of Abnormal Psychology, 119*, 713–725.

Kong, L. L., Allen, J. B., & Glisky, E. L. (2008). Interidentity memory transfer in dissociative identity disorder. *Journal of Abnormal Psychology, 117*, 686–692.

Kopelowicz, A., Liberman, R. P., Mintz, J., & Zarate, R. (1997). Comparison of efficacy of social skills training for deficit and nondeficit negative symptoms in schizophrenia. *American Journal of Psychiatry, 154*, 424–425.

Kraepelin, E. (1971). *Dementia praecox and paraphrenia* (R. M. Barclay, Trans.). Huntington, NY: Krieger. (Originally published 1919.)

Krakow, B., & Zadra, A. (2006). Clinical management of chronic nightmares: Imagery rehearsal therapy. *Behavioral Sleep Medicine, 4*, 45–70.

Kratochvil, C. J., Greenhill, L. L., March, J. S., Burke, W. J., & Vaughan, B. S. (2004). The role of stimulants in the treatment of preschool children with attention deficit/hyperactivity disorder. *CNS Drugs, 18*, 957–966.

Kringlen, E. (1970). Natural history of obsessional neurosis. *Seminars in Psychiatry, 2*, 403–419.

Kroenke, K., Sharpe, M., & Sykes, R. (2007). Revising the classification of somatoform disorders: Key questions and preliminary recommendations. *Psychosomatics, 48*, 277–285.

Kroenke, K., West, S. L., Gilsenan, A., Eckert, G. J., Dolor, R., Stang, P., . . . Weinberger, M. (2001). Similar effectiveness of paroxetine, fluoxetine, and sertraline in primary care: A randomized trial. *Journal of the American Medical Association, 286*, 2947–2955.

Krueger, R. B., & Kaplan, M. S. (1997). Frotteurism: Assessment and treatment. In D. R. Laws & W. O'Donohue (Eds.), *Sexual Deviance*. New York, NY: Guilford.

Krueger, R. F., & Eaton, N. R. (2010). Personality traits and the classification of mental disorders: Toward a more complete integration in DSM-5 and an empirical model of psychopathology. *Personality Disorders: Theory, Research, and Treatment, 1*, 97–118.

Kushner, M. G., Abrams, K., & Borchardt, C. (2000). The relationship between anxiety disorders and alcohol use disorders: A review of major perspectives and findings. *Clinical Psychology Review, 20*, 149–171.

Kuwert, P., Klauer, T., Eichhorn, S., Grundke, E., Dudeck, M., Schomerus, G., & Freyberger, H. J. (2010). Trauma and current posttraumatic stress symptoms in elderly German women who experienced wartime rapes in 1945. *Journal of Nervous and Mental Disease, 198*, 450–451.

Ladwig, K. H., Marten-Mittag, B., Erazo, N., & Gündel, H. (2001). Identifying somatization disorder in a population-based health examination survey: Psychosocial burden and gender differences. *Psychosomatics, 42*, 511–518.

Lahey, B. B., Schwab-Stone, M., Goodman, S. H., Waldman, I. D., Canino, G., Rathouz, P. J., . . . Jensen, P. S. (2000). Age and gender differences in oppositional behavior and conduct problems: A cross-sectional household study of middle childhood and adolescence. *Journal of Abnormal Psychology, 109*, 488–503.

Landhuis, C. E., Poulton, R., Welch, D., & Hancox, R. J. (2007). Does childhood television viewing lead to attention problems in adolescence? Results from a prospective longitudinal study. *Pediatrics, 120*, 532–537.

Långström, N., & Seto, M. C. (2006). Exhibitionistic and voyeuristic behavior in a Swedish national population survey. *Archives of Sexual Behavior, 35*, 427–435.

Larkin, K. T., & Zayfert, C. (2004). Anger expression and essential hypertension: Behavioral response to confrontation. *Journal of Psychosomatic Research, 56*, 113–118.

Laroi, F., & Woodward, T. S. (2007). Hallucinations from a cognitive perspective. *Harvard Review of Psychiatry, 15*, 109–117.

Lau, J. Y. F., & Eley, T. C. (2010). The genetics of mood disorders. *Annual Review of Clinical Psychology, 6*, 313–337.

Laumann, E. O., Gagnon, J. H., Michael, R. T., & Michaels, S. (1994). *The social organization of sexuality: Sexual practices in the United States*. Chicago, IL: University of Chicago Press.

Lavigne, J. V., LeBailly, S. A., Hopkins, J., Gouze, K. R., & Binns, H. J. (2009). The prevalence of ADHD, ODD, depression, and anxiety in a community sample of 4-year-olds. *Journal of Clinical Child and Adolescent Psychology, 38*, 315–328.

Lawler, C. P., Croen, L. A., Grether, J. K., & Van de Water, J. (2004). Identifying environmental contributions to autism: Provocative clues and false leads. *Mental Retardation and Developmental Disabilities Research Reviews, 10*, 292–302.

Lee, J. K. P., Jackson, H. J., Pattison, P., & Ward, T. (2002). Developmental risk factors for sexual offending. *Child Abuse & Neglect, 26*, 73–92.

Leekam, S. R., Prior, M. R., & Uljarevic, M. (2011). Restricted and repetitive behaviors in the autism spectrum disorders: A review of research in the last decade. *Psychological Bulletin*. Advance online publication.

LeFever, G. B., Dawson, K. V., & Morrow, A. L. (1999). The extent of drug therapy for attention deficit-hyperactivity disorder among children in public schools. *American Journal of Public Health, 89*, 1359–1364.

Lehman, B. J., Taylor, S. E., Kiefe, C. I., & Seeman, T. E. (2009). Relationship of early life stress and psychological functioning to blood pressure in the CARDIA study. *Health Psychology, 28*, 338–346.

Le Grange, D., Lock, J., Loeb, K., & Nicholls, D. (2010). Academy for Eating Disorders position paper: The role of the family in eating disorders. *International Journal of Eating Disorders, 43*, 1–5.

Leibbrand, R., Hiller, W., & Fichter, M. M. (2000). Hypochondriasis and somatization: Two distinct aspects of somatoform disorders? *Journal of Clinical Psychology, 56*, 63–72.

Leiknes, K. A., Finset, A., Mourn, T., & Sandanger, I. (2007). Current somatoform disorders in Norway: Prevalence, risk factors and comorbidity with anxiety, depression and musculoskeletal disorders. *Social Psychiatry and Psychiatric Epidemiology, 42*, 698–710.

Lejuez, C. W., Hopko, D. R., Acierno, R., Daughters, S. B., & Pagoto, S. L. (2011). Ten year revision of the brief behavioral activation treatment for depression: Revised treatment manual. *Behavior Modification, 35*, 111–161.

Lenzenweger, M. F. (2008). Epidemiology of personality disorders. *Psychiatric Clinics of North America, 31*, 395–403.

Leonard, L. M., & Follette, V. M. (2002). Sexual functioning in women reporting a history of child sexual abuse: Review of the empirical literature and clinical implications. *Annual Review of Sex Research, 13*, 346–388.

Letourneau, E. J., & O'Donohue, W. (1997). Classical conditioning of female sexual arousal. *Archives of Sexual Behavior, 26*, 63–78.

Leue, A., Borchard, B., & Hoyer, J. (2004). Mental disorders in a forensic sample of sexual offenders. *European Psychiatry, 19*, 123–130.

Lev, A. I. (2005). Disordering gender identity: Gender identity disorder in the DSM-IV-TR. *Journal of Psychology & Human Sexuality, 17*, 35–69.

LeVay, S., & Valente, S. M. (2003). *Human sexuality*. Sunderland, MA: Sinauer Associates.

Levin, R., & Nielsen, T. A. (2007). Disturbed dreaming, posttraumatic stress disorder, and affect distress: A review and neurocognitive model. *Psychological Bulletin, 133*, 482–528.

Levin, R., & Nielsen, T. A. (2009). Nightmares, bad dreams, and emotion dysregulation: A review and new neurocognitive model of dreaming. *Psychological Science, 18*, 84–88.

Levine, S. B. (1999). The newly revised standards of care for gender identity disorders. *Journal of Sex Education and Therapy, 24*, 117–127.

Levinson, D. F., Umapathy, C., & Musthaq, M. (1999). Treatment of schizoaffective disorder and schizophrenia with mood symptoms. *American Journal of Psychiatry, 156*, 1138–1148.

Levy, K. N., Mcchan, K. B., Kelly, K. M., Reynoso, J. S., Weber, M., Clarkin, J. F., & Kernberg, O. F. (2006). Change in attachment patterns and reflective function in a randomized control trial of transference-focused psychotherapy for borderline personality disorder. *Journal of Consulting and Clinical Psychology, 74*, 1027–1040.

Lewins, F. (2002). Explaining stable partnerships among FTMs and MTFs: A significant difference? *Journal of Sociology, 38*, 76–88.

Lewis, C. E. (2002). Impact of substance abuse and dependence on patients with schizophrenia. In J. G. Csernansky (Ed.), *Schizophrenia: A new guide for clinicians* (pp. 267–283). New York, NY: Marcel Dekker.

Li, L. C., Kim, B. S. K., & O'Brien, K. M. (2007). An analogue study of the effects of Asian cultural values and counselor multicultural competence on counseling process. *Psychotherapy: Theory, Research, Practice, Training, 44*, 90–95.

Lidbeck, J. (2003). Group therapy for somatization disorders in primary care: Maintenance of treatment goals of short cognitive-behavioural treatment one-and-a-half year follow-up. *Acta Psychiatrica Scandinavia, 107*, 449–456.

Lieb, K. Zanarini, M. C., Schmahl, C., Linehan, M. M., & Bohus, M. (2004). Borderline personality disorder. *Lancet, 364*, 453–461.

Lilienfeld, S. O., & Lynn, S. J. (2003). Dissociative identity disorder: Multiple personalities, multiple controversies. In S. O. Lilienfeld & S. J. Lynn (Eds), *Science and pseudoscience in clinical psychology* (pp. 109–142). New York, NY: Guilford.

Lilienfeld, S. O., Lynn, S. J., Kirsch, I., Chaves, J. F., Sarbin, T. R., & Powell, R. A. (1999). Dissociative identity disorder and the sociocognitive model: Recalling the lessons of the past. *Psychological Bulletin, 125*, 507–523.

Lindahl, K. M. (1998). Family process variables and children's disruptive behavior problems. *Journal of Family Psychology*, *12*, 420–436.

Lindeman, G., Korlin, D., & Uddenberg, N. (1986). Long-term follow-up of "sex change" in 13 male-to-female transsexuals. *Archives of Sexual Behavior*, *15*, 187–210.

Linden, W. (2003). Psychologic treatment for hypertension can be efficacious. *Preventive Cardiology*, *6*, 48–53.

Linehan, M. M. (1993). *Cognitive behavioral treatment of borderline personality disorder: The dialectics of effective treatment.* New York, NY: Guilford.

Lion, J. R. (1978). Outpatient treatment of psychopaths. In W. H. Reid (Ed.), *The psychopath: A comprehensive study of antisocial disorders and behaviors.* New York, NY: Brunner/ Mazel.

Lis, E., Greenfield, B., Henry, M., Guilé, J. M., & Dougherty, G. (2007). Neuroimaging and genetics of borderline personality disorder: A review. *Journal of Psychiatry and Neruoscience*, *32*, 162–173.

Litt, M. D., Kadden, R. M., Cooney, N. L., & Kabela, E. (2003). Coping skills and treatment outcomes in cognitive-behavioral and interactional group therapy for alcoholism. *Journal of Consulting and Clinical Psychology*, *71*, 118–128.

Littleton, H., & Henderson, C. E. (2009). If she is not a victim, does that mean she was not traumatized?: Evaluation of predictors of PTSD symptomatology among college rape victims. *Violence Against Women*, *15*, 148–167.

Loewenstein, R. J. (2006). DID 101: A hands-on clinical guide to the stabilization phase of dissociative identity disorder treatment. *Psychiatric Clinics of North America*, *29*, 305–332.

Looper, K. J., Kirmayer, & L. J. (2002). Behavioral medicine approaches to somatoform disorders. *Journal of Consulting and Clinical Psychology*, *70*, 810–827.

LoPiccolo, J., & Stock, W. E. (1986). Treatment of sexual dysfunction. *Journal of Consulting and Clinical Psychology*, *54*, 158–167.

Lorber, M. F. (2004). Psychophysiology of aggression, psychopathy, and conduct problems: A meta-analysis. *Psychological Bulletin*, *130*, 531–552.

Lord, C. E. (2010). Autism: From research to practice. *American Psychologist*, *65*, 815–826.

Losh, M., & Capps, L. (2006). Understanding of emotional experience in autism: Insights from the personal accounts of high-functioning children with autism. *Developmental Psychology*, *42*, 809–818.

Lotter, V. (1978). Follow-up studies. In M. Rutter & E. Schopler (Eds.), *Autism: A reappraisal of concepts and treatment.* New York, NY: Plenum.

Lovaas, O. I. (1987). Behavioral treatment and normal educational and intellectual functioning in young autistic children. *Journal of Consulting and Clinical Psychology*, *55*, 3–9.

Lowe, M. R., Thomas, J., Safer, D. L., & Butryn, M. L. (2007). The relationship of weight suppression and dietary restraint to binge eating in bulimia nervosa. *International Journal of Eating Disorders*, *40*, 640–644.

Luczak, S. E., Glatt, S. J., & Wall, T. L. (2006). Meta-analyses of *ALDH2* and *ADH1B* with alcohol dependence in Asians. *Psychological Bulletin*, *132*, 607–621.

Luczak, S. E., Wall, T. L., Cook, T. A. R., Shea, S. H., & Carr, L. G. (2004). *ALDH2* status and conduct disorder mediate the relationship between ethnicity and alcohol dependence in Chinese, Korean, and White American college students. *Journal of Abnormal Psychology*, *113*, 271–278.

Lukoschek, P. (2003). African Americans' beliefs and attitudes regarding hypertension and its treatment: A qualitative study. *Journal of Health Care for the Poor and Underserved*, *14*, 566–585.

Lynam, D. R., Caspi, A., Moffitt, T. E., Loeber, R., & Stouthamer-Loeber, M. (2007). Longitudinal evidence that psychopathy scores in early adolescence predict adult psychopathy. *Journal of Abnormal Psychology*, *116*, 155–165.

Lynn, S. J., Fassler, O., Knox, J. A., & Lilienfeld, S. O. (2006). Dissociative identity disorder. In J. E. Fisher & W. T. O'Donohue (Eds.), *Practitioner's guide to evidence-based psychotherapy.* (pp. 248–257). New York, NY: Springer.

Lyons, M. J., True, W. R., Eisen, S. A., & Goldberg, J. (1995). Differential heritability of adult and juvenile traits. *Archives of General Psychiatry, 52,* 906–915.

Macmillan, R., McMorris, B. J., & Kruttschnitt, C. (2004). Linked lives: Stability and change in maternal circumstances and trajectories of antisocial behavior in children. *Child Development, 75,* 205–220.

Mai F. (2004). Somatization disorder: A practical review. *Canadian Journal of Psychiatry, 49,* 652–662.

Maldonado, J. R., Butler, L. D., & Spiegel, D. (2002). Treatments for dissociative disorders. In P. E. Nathan & J. M. Gorman (Eds.), *A guide to treatments that work* (2nd ed., pp. 463–496). London, England: Oxford University Press.

Maletzky, B. M. (1997). Exhibitionism: Assessment and treatment. In D. R. Laws & W. O'Donohue (Eds.), *Sexual deviance.* New York, NY: Guilford.

Manari, A. P., Preedy, V. R., & Peters, T. J. (2003). Nutritional intake of hazardous drinkers and dependent alcoholics in the UK. *Addiction Biology, 8,* 201–210.

Mann, B. J., & MacKenzie, E. P. (1996). Pathways among marital functioning, parental behaviors, and child behavior problems in school-age boys. *Journal of Clinical Child Psychology, 25,* 183–191.

Mann, K. (2004). Pharmacotherapy of alcohol dependence: A review of the clinical data. *CNS Drugs, 18,* 485–504.

Manschreck, T. C. (1992). Delusional disorders: Clinical concepts and diagnostic strategies. *Psychiatric Annals, 22,* 241–251.

Marlatt, G. A. (1985). Controlled drinking: The controversy rages on. *American Psychologist, 40,* 374–375.

Marshall, W. L., Eccles, A., & Barbaree, H. E. (1991). The treatment of exhibitionism: A focus on sexual deviance versus cognitive and relationship factors. *Behavior Research and Therapy, 29,* 129–135.

Marshall, W. L., Jones, R , Ward, T., Johnston, P., & Barabee, H. E. (1991). Treatment outcomes with sex offenders. *Clinical Psychology Review, 11,* 465–485.

Marshall, W. L., Marshall, L. E., & Serran, G. A. (2006). Strategies in the treatment of paraphilias: A critical review. *Annual Review of Sex Research, 17,* 162–182.

Masters, W. H., & Johnson, V. E. (1970). *Human sexual inadequacy.* Boston, MA: Little, Brown.

Mathews, A., & MacLeod, C. (2005). Cognitive vulnerability to emotional disorders. *Annual Review of Clinical Psychology, 1,* 167–195.

Matthys, W., van Goozen, S. H. M., Snoek, H., & van Engeland, H. (2004). Response perseveration and sensitivity to reward and punishment in boys with oppositional defiant disorder. *European Child and Adolescent Psychiatry, 13,* 362–364.

Maughan, B., Rowe, R., Messer, J., Goodman, R., & Meltzer, H. (2004). Conduct disorder and oppositional defiant disorder in a national sample: Developmental epidemiology. *Journal of Child Psychology and Psychiatry, 45,* 609–621.

Maughan, B., Taylor, A., Caspi, A., & Moffitt, T. E. (2004). Prenatal smoking and early childhood conduct problems. *Archives of General Psychiatry, 61,* 836–843.

Mayes, S. D., & Calhoun, S. L. (2007). Learning, attention, writing, and processing speed in typical children and children with ADHD, autism, anxiety, depression, and oppositional-defiant disorder. *Child Neuropsychology, 13,* 469–493.

Mazzeo, S. E., Mitchell, K. S., Bulik, C. M., Aggen, S. H., Kendler, K. S., & Neale, M. C. (2010). A twin study of specific bulimia nervosa symptoms. *Psychological Medicine, 40,* 1203–1213.

Mazzucchelli, T., Kane, R., & Rees, C. (2009). Behavioral activation treatments for depression in adults: A meta-analysis and review. *Clinical Psychology: Science and Practice, 16,* 383–411.

McBride, P. A., Anderson, G. M., & Shapiro, T. (1996). Autism research: Bringing together approaches to pull apart the disorder. *Archives of General Psychiatry, 53,* 980–983.

McCabe, M. P. (2001). Evaluation of a cognitive behavior therapy program for people with sexual dysfunction. *Journal of Sex and Marital Therapy, 27,* 259–271.

McCann, D., Barrett, A., Cooper, A., Crumpler, D., Dalen, L., Grimshaw, K., . . . Stevenson, J. (2007). Food additives and hyperactive behaviour in 3-year-old and 8/9-year-old children in the community: A randomized, double-blinded, placebo-controlled trial. *The Lancet, 370,* 1560–1567.

McCart, M. R., Priester, P. E., Davies, W. H., & Azen, R. (2006). Differential effectiveness of behavioral parent-training and cognitive-behavioral therapy for antisocial youth: A meta-analysis. *Journal of Abnormal Child Psychology, 34,* 527–543.

McCarthy, B. W. (2004). An integrative cognitive-behavioral approach to understanding, assessing, and treating female sexual dysfunction. *Journal of Family Psychotherapy, 15,* 19–35.

McConaghy, N. (1994). Sexual deviations. In M. Hersen & R. T. Ammerman (Eds.), *Handbook of aggressive and destructive behavior in psychiatric patients.* New York, NY: Plenum Press.

McConaghy, N. (2005). Sexual dysfunctions and disorders. In J. E. Maddux & B. A. Winstead (Eds.), *Psychopathology: Foundations for a contemporary understanding* (pp. 225–280). Mahwah, NJ: Erlbaum.

McEachin, J. J., Smith, T., & Lovaas, O. I. (1993). Long-term outcome for children with autism who receive early intensive behavioral treatment. *American Journal on Mental Retardation, 97,* 359–372.

McEwen, B. S. (1998). Protective and damaging effects of stress mediators. *New England Journal of Medicine, 338,* 171–179.

McGee, R., & Feehan, M. (1991). Are girls with problems of attention underrecognized? *Journal of Psychopathology and Behavioral Assessment, 13,* 187–198.

McGuffin, P., Rijsdijk, F., Andrew, M., Sham, P., Katz, R., & Cardno, A. (2003). The heritability of bipolar affective disorder and the genetic relationship to unipolar depression. *Archives of General Psychiatry, 60,* 497–502.

McLean, P. D., Whittal, J. L., Thordarson, D. S., Taylor, S., Sochting, I., Koch, W. J., . . . Anderson, K. W. (2001). Cognitive versus behavior therapy in the group treatment of obsessive-compulsive disorder. *Journal of Consulting and Clinical Psychology, 69,* 205–214.

McMurran, M., Huband, N., & Overton, E. (2010). Non-completion of personality disorder treatments: A systematic review of correlates, consequences, and interventions. *Clinical Psychology Review, 30,* 277–287.

McNally, R. J. (2003). Progress and controversy in the study of posttraumatic stress disorder. *Annual Review of Psychology, 54,* 229–252.

Meehl, P. E. (1964). *Manual for use with checklist of schizotypic signs.* Unpublished manuscript, University of Minnesota Medical School, Minneapolis.

Mehler, P. S. (2011). Medical complications of bulimia nervosa and their treatments. *International Journal of Eating Disorders, 44,* 95–104.

Menza, M., Lauritano, M., Allen, L., Warman, M., Ostella, F., Hamer, R. M., & Escobar, J. (2001). Treatment of somatization disorder with nefazodone: A prospective, openlabel study. *Annals of Clinical Psychiatry, 13,* 153–158.

Merritt, M. M., Bennett, G. G., Williams, R. B., Edwards, C. L., & Sollers, J. J. (2006). Perceived racism and cardiovascular reactivity and recovery to personally relevant stress. *Health Psychology, 25,* 364–369.

Merskey, H. (2004). Somatization, hysteria, or incompletely explained symptoms? *Canadian Journal of Psychiatry, 49,* 649–651.

Messerli, F. H., Williams, B., & Ritz, E. (2007). Essential hypertension. *The Lancet, 370,* 591–603.

Messias, E. L., Chen, C., & Eaton, W. W. (2007). Epidemiology of schizophrenia: Review of findings and myths. *Psychiatric Clinics of North America, 30,* 323–338.

Meyer, J. K., & Reter, D. J. (1979). Sex reassignment: Follow-up. *Archives of General Psychiatry,* *36,* 1010–1015.

Meyer, W. J., Cole, C., & Emory, E. (1992). Depo provera treatment for sex offending behavior: An evaluation of outcome. *Bulletin of the American Academy of Psychiatry and the Law, 20,* 249–259.

Michel, A., Ansseau, M., Legros, J. J., Pitchot, W., & Mormont, C. (2002). The transsexual: What about the future. *European Psychiatry, 17,* 353–362.

Miklowitz, D. J. (2007). The role of the family in the course and treatment of bipolar disorder. *Current Directions in Psychological Science, 16,* 192–196.

Miklowitz, D. J., & Johnson, S. L. (2006). The psychopathology and treatment of bipolar disorder. *Annual Review of Clinical Psychology, 2,* 199–235.

Miklowitz, D. J., & Johnson, S. L. (2009). Social and familial factors in the course of bipolar disorder: Basic processes and relevant interventions. *Clinical Psychology: Science and Practice, 16,* 281–296.

Millberger, S., Biederman, J., Faraone, S. V., Chen, L., & Jones, J. (1996). Is maternal smoking during pregnancy a risk factor for attention deficit hyperactivity in children? *American Journal of Psychiatry, 153,* 1138–1142.

Miller, M. B., Useda, J. D., Trull, T. J., Burr, R. M., & Minks-Brown, C. (2001). Paranoid, schizoid, and schizotypal personality disorders. In P. B. Sutker & H. E. Adams (Eds.), *Comprehensive handbook of psychopathology* (3rd ed., pp. 535–559.). New York, NY: Kluwer Academic/ Plenum.

Mineka, S., & Zinbarg, R. (1995). Conditioning and ethological models of social phobia. In R. G. Heimberg, M. R. Liebowitz, D. A. Hope, & F. R. Schneier (Eds.), *Social phobia: Diagnosis, assessment, and treatment* (pp. 134–162). New York, NY: Guilford.

Miric, D., Hallet-Mathieu, A. H., & Amar, G. (2005). Etiology of antisocial personality disorder: Benefits for society from an evolutionary standpoint. *Medical Hypotheses, 65,* 665–670.

Miró, E., & Martínez, M. P. (2005). Affective and personality characteristics in function of nightmare prevalence, nightmare distress, and interference due to nightmares. *Dreaming, 15,* 89–105.

Mishra, B. R., Nizamie, S. H., Das, B., & Praharaj, S. K. (2009). Efficacy of repetitive transcranial magnetic stimulation in alcohol dependence: A sham-controlled study. *Addiction, 105,* 49–55.

Misra, M., Aggarwal, A., Miller, K. K., Almazan, C., Worley, M., Soyka, L. A., & Klibanski, A. (2004). Effects of anorexia nervosa on clinical, hematologic, biochemical, and bone density parameters in community-dwelling adolescent girls. *Pediatrics, 114,* 1574–1583.

Mitchell, K. J., & Porteous, D. J. (2010). Rethinking the genetic architecture of schizophrenia. *Psychological Medicine, 41,* 19–32.

Modestin, J. (1992). Multiple personality disorder in Switzerland. *American Journal of Psychiatry, 149,* 88–92.

Moffitt, T. E. (1993). Adolescence-limited and life-course-persistent antisocial behavior: A developmental taxonomy. *Psychological Review, 100,* 674–701.

Moffitt, T. E., Harrington, H., Caspi. A., Kim-Cohen, J., Goldberg, D., Gregory, A. M., & Poulton, R. (2007). Depression and generalized anxiety disorder: Cumulative and sequential comorbidity in a birth cohort followed prospectively to age 32 years. *Archives of General Psychiatry, 64,* 651–660.

Moltó, J., Poy, R., Segarra, P., Pastor, M. C., & Montañés, S. (2007). Response perseveration in psychopaths: Interpersonal/affective or social deviance traits? *Journal of Abnormal Psychology, 116,* 632–637.

Monahan, J. (2001). Major mental disorders and violence: Epidemiology and risk assessment. In G. Pinard & L. Pagani (Eds.), *Clinical assessment of dangerousness: Empirical contributions* (pp. 89–102). New York, NY: Cambridge University Press.

Monroe, S. M., & Harkness, K. L. (2005). Life stress, the "kindling" hypothesis, and the recurrence of depression: Considerations from a life stress perspective. *Psychological Review, 112*, 417–445.

Monuteaux, M. C., Mick, E., Faraone, S. V., & Biederman, J. (2010). The influence of sex on the course and psychiatric correlates of ADHD from childhood to adolescence: A longitudinal study. *Journal of Child Psychology and Psychiatry, 51*, 233–241.

Moore, B. A., & Krakow, B. (2010). Imagery rehearsal therapy: An emerging treatment for posttraumatic nightmares in veterans. *Psychological Trauma: Theory, Research, Practice, and Policy, 2*, 232–238.

Morey, L. C., & Zanarini, M. C. (2000). Borderline personality: Traits and disorder. *Journal of Abnormal Psychology, 109*, 733–737.

Moritz, S., Kempke, S., Luyten, P., Randjbar, S., & Jelinek, L. (2011). Was Freud partly right on obsessive–compulsive disorder (OCD)? Investigation of latent aggression in OCD. *Psychiatry Research, 187*, 180–184.

Moss, A. C., & Albery, I. P. (2009). A dual-process model of the alcohol-behavior link for social drinking. *Psychological Bulletin, 135*, 516–530.

MTA Cooperative Group. (1999). Moderators and mediators of treatment response for children with attention-deficit-hyperactivity disorder. *Archives of General Psychiatry, 56*, 1088–1096.

Mufson, L., Dorta, K. P., Wickramaratne, P., Nomura, Y. I., Olfson, M., & Weissman, M. M. (2004). A randomized effectiveness trial of interpersonal psychotherapy for depressed adolescents. *Archives of General Psychiatry, 61*, 577–584.

Muhle, R., Trentacoste, S. V., & Rapin, I. (2004). The genetics of autism. *Pediatrics, 113*, 472–486.

Murphy, W. D. (1997). Exhibitionism: Psychopathology and theory. In D. R. Laws & W. O'Donohue (Eds.), *Sexual deviance*. New York, NY: Guilford.

Myrick, H., & Anton, R. (2004). Recent advances in the pharmacotherapy of alcoholism. *Current Psychiatry Reports, 6*, 332–338.

Narash-Eisikovits, O., Dierberger, A., & Westen, D. (2002). A multidimensional metaanalysis of pharmacotherapy for bulimia nervosa: Summarizing the range of outcomes in controlled clinical trials. *Harvard Review of Psychiatry, 10*, 193–211.

Nasrallah, H. A., Ketter, T. A., & Kalali, A. H. (2006). Carbamazepine and valproate for the treatment of bipolar disorder: A review of the literature. *Journal of Affective Disorders, 95*, 69–78.

Nestor, P. G. (2002). Mental disorder and violence: Personality dimensions and clinical features. *American Journal of Psychiatry, 159*, 1973–1978.

Newman, J. P., Patterson, C. M., & Kosson, D. S. (1987). Response perseveration in psychopaths. *Journal of Abnormal Psychology, 96*, 145–149.

Newschaffer, C. J., Croen, L. A., Daniels, J., Giarelli, E., Grether, J. K., Levy, S. E., . . . Windham, J. C. (2007). The epidemiology of autism spectrum disorders. *Annual Review of Public Health, 28*, 235–258.

Nezu, A. M. (2010). Cultural influences on the process of conducting psychotherapy: Personal reflections of an ethnic minority psychologist. *Psychotherapy Theory, Research, Practice, and Training, 47*, 169–176.

Nguyen, S. D. (1985). Mental health services for refugees and immigrants in Canada. In T. C. Owen (Ed.), *Southeast Asian mental health: Treatment, prevention, services, training, and research* (pp. 261–282). Washington, DC: National Institute of Mental Health.

Nigg, J. T. (2001). Is ADHD an inhibitory disorder? *Psychological Bulletin, 127*, 571–598.

Nigg, J. T., & Breslau, N. (2007). Prenatal smoking exposure, low birth weight, and disruptive behavior disorders. *Journal of the American Academy of Child and Adolescent Psychiatry, 46*, 362–369.

Nigg, J. T., Lohr, N. E., Westen, D., Gold, L. J., & Silk, K. R. (1992). Malevolent object representations in borderline personality and major depression. *Journal of Abnormal Psychology, 101*, 61–67.

Nigg, J. T., Nikolas, M., Knottnerus, G. M., Cavanagh, K., & Friderici, K. (2010). Confirmation and extension of association of blood lead with attention-deficit/hyperactivity disorder (ADHD) and ADHD symptom domains at population-typical exposure levels. *Journal of Child Psychology and Psychiatry*, *51*, 58–65.

Nixon, R. D. V., Sweeney, L., Erickson, D. B., & Touyz, S. W. (2003). Parent-child interaction therapy: A comparison of standard and abbreviated treatments for oppositional defiant preschoolers. *Journal of Consulting and Clinical Psychology*, *71*, 251–260.

Nock, M. K., Kazdin, A. E., Hiripi, E., & Kessler, R. C. (2007). Lifetime prevalence, correlates, and persistence of oppositional defiant disorder: Results from the National Comorbidity Survey Replication. *Journal of Child Psychology and Psychiatry*, *48*, 703–713.

Nolen-Hoeksema, S. (2002). *Sex differences in depression*. Stanford, CA: Stanford University Press.

Nordin, V., & Gillberg, C. (1998). The long-term course of autistic disorders: Update on follow-up studies. *Acta Psychiatrica Scandinavica*, *97*, 99–108.

North, C. S., Thompson, S. J., Pollio, D. E., & Ricci, D. A. (1997). A diagnostic comparison of homeless and nonhomeless patients in an urban mental health clinic. *Social Psychiatry and Psychiatric Epidemiology*, *32*, 236–240.

Novaco, R. W., & Taylor, J. L. (2006). Anger. In A. Carr & M. McNulty (Eds.), *The handbook of adult clinical psychology: An evidence-based practice approach* (pp. 978–1009). New York, NY: Routledge/Taylor & Francis Group.

Noyes, R., Stuart, S., Watson, D. B., & Langbehn, D. R. (2006). Distinguishing between hypochondriasis and somatization disorder: A review of the existing literature. *Psychotherapy and Psychosomatics*, *75*, 270–281.

Nunes, E. V., & Levin, F. R. (2004). Treatment of depression in patients with alcohol or other drug dependence: A meta-analysis. *Journal of the American Medical Association*, *291*, 1887–1896.

Nurnberger, J. I., Wiegand, R., Bucholz, K., O'Connor, S., Meyer, E. T., Reich, T., . . . Porjesz, B. (2004). A family study of alcohol dependence. *Archives of General Psychiatry*, *61*, 1246–1256.

Obasi, E. M., & Leong, F. T. L. (2009). Psychological distress, acculturation, and mental health-seeking attitudes among people of African descent in the United States: A preliminary investigation. *Journal of Counseling Psychology*, *56*, 227–238.

Oberman, L. M., & Ramachandran, V. S. (2007). The simulating social mind: The role of the mirror neuron system and simulation in the social and communicative deficits of autism spectrum disorders. *Psychological Bulletin*, *133*, 310–327.

O'Brien, K. M., & Vincent, N. K. (2003). Psychiatric comorbidity in anorexia and bulimia nervosa: Nature, prevalence, and causal relationships. *Clinical Psychology Review*, *23*, 57–74.

Ogedegbe, G., Harrison, M., Robbins, L., Mancuso, C. A., & Allegrante, J. P. (2004). Barriers and facilitators of medication adherence in hypertensive African Americans: A qualitative study. *Ethnicity and Disease*, *14*, 3–12.

Ohayon, M. M. (2000). Prevalence of hallucinations and their pathological associations in the general population. *Psychiatry Research*, *97*, 153–164.

O'Leary, D. S., Flaum, M., Kesler, M. L., Flashman, L. A., Arndt, S., & Andreasen, N. C. (2000). Cognitive correlates of the negative, disorganized, and psychotic symptom dimensions of schizophrenia. *Journal of Neuropsychiatry and Clinical Neuroscience*, *12*, 4–14.

Orne, M. T., Dinges, D. F., & Orne, E. C. (1984). On the differential diagnosis of multiple personality in the forensic case. *International Journal of Clinical and Experimental Hypnosis*, *32*, 118–169.

Osborn, I. (1998). *Tormenting thoughts and secret rituals*. New York, NY: Dell Publishing.

Osterman, J. E., Erdos, B. Z., Oldham, M., & Ivkovic, A. (2011). Antidepressant treatments in PTSD. In D. A. Ciraulo & R. Shader (Eds.), *Pharmacotherapy of depression* (2nd ed., pp. 275–307). New York, NY: Springer Science + Business Media.

Ozer, E. J., & Weiss, D. S. (2004). Who develops posttraumatic stress disorder? *Current Directions in Psychological Science*, *4*, 169–172.

Palermo, M. T., & Curatolo, P. (2004). Pharmacologic treatment of autism. *Journal of Child Neurology, 19*, 155–164.

Paradis, C., Friedman, S., & Hatch, M. (1997). Isolated sleep paralysis in African Americans with panic disorder. *Cultural Diversity and Mental Health, 3*, 69–76.

Paradis, C., Friedman, S., Hinton, D. E., McNally, R. J., Solomon, L. Z., & Lyons, K. A. (2009). The assessment of the phenomenology of sleep paralysis: The Unusual Sleep Experiences Questionnaire (USEQ). *CNS Neuroscience and Therapeutics, 15*, 220–226.

Paris, J. (2004). Personality disorders over time: Implications for psychotherapy. *American Journal of Psychotherapy, 58*, 420–429.

Park, A., Sher, K. J., Todorov, A. A., & Heath, A. C. (2011). Interaction between the DRD4 VNTR polymorphism and proximal and distal environments in alcohol dependence during emerging and young adulthood. *Journal of Abnormal Psychology*. Advance online publication.

Parker, S. K., Schwartz, B., Todd, J., & Pickering, L. K. (2004). Thimerosal-containing vaccines and autistic spectrum disorder: A critical review of published original data. *Pediatrics, 114*, 793–804.

Parmet, S., Glass, T. J., & Glass, R. M. (2004). Obsessive-compulsive disorder. *Journal of the American Medical Association, 292*, 2040.

Patrick, C. J., Bradley, M. M., & Lang, P. J. (1993). Emotion in the criminal psychopath: Startle reflex modulation. *Journal of Abnormal Psychology, 102*, 82–92.

Patterson, G. R. (1982). *Coercive family process*. Eugene, OR: Castalia.

Paul, R. (1987). Communication. In D. J. Cohen, A. M. Donellan, & R. Paul (Eds.), *Handbook of autism and pervasive developmental disorders* (pp. 61–84). New York, NY: Wiley.

Pauls, D. L., Alsobrook, J. P., Goodman, W., & Rasmussen, S. (1995). A family study of obsessive-compulsive disorder. *American Journal of Psychiatry, 152*, 76–84.

Pelham, W. E., McBurnett, K., Harper, G. W., Milich, R., Murphy, D. A., Clinton, J., & Thiele, C. (1990). Methylphenidate and baseball playing in ADHD children: Who's on first? *Journal of Consulting and Clinical Psychology, 58*, 130–133.

Perkins, D. O. (2002). Predictors of noncompliance in patients with schizophrenia. *Journal of Clinical Psychiatry, 63*, 1121–1128.

Perkins, P. S., Klump, K. L., Iacono, W. G., & McGue, M. (2005). Personality traits in women with anorexia nervosa: Evidence for a treatment-seeking bias? *International Journal of Eating Disorders, 37*, 32–37.

Pescosolida, B. A., Monahan, J., Link, B., Stueve, A., & Kikuzawa, S. (1999). The public's view of the competence, dangerousness, and need for legal coercion of persons with mental health problems. *American Journal of Public Health, 89*, 1339–1345.

Peters, R. M., Butler, K., Gjini, K., Yeragani, V., & Boutros, N. N. (2011). The role of sensory gating in the racism/blood pressure relationship: A pilot study. *Journal of Psychophysiology, 25*, 40–49.

Peterson, C. B., & Mitchell, J. E. (1999). Psychosocial and pharmacological treatment of eating disorders: A review of research findings. *Journal of Clinical Psychology, 55*, 685–697.

Picchioni, D., & Hicks, R. A. (2009). Differences in the relationship between nightmares and coping with stress for Asians and Caucasians: A brief report. *Dreaming, 19*, 108–112.

Pierce, E. W., Ewing, L. J., & Campbell, S. B. (1999). Diagnostic status and symptomatic behavior of hard-to-manage preschool children in middle childhood and early adolescence. *Journal of Clinical Child Psychology, 28*, 44–57.

Pilling, S., Bebbington, P., Kuipers, E., Garety, P., Geddes, J., Martindale, B., . . . Morgan, C. (2002). Psychological treatments in schizophrenia: II. Metaanalyses of randomized controlled trials of social skills training and cognitive remediation. *Psychological Medicine, 32*, 783–791.

Piper, A., & Merskey, H. (2004). The persistence of folly: A critical examination of dissociative identity disorder. Part 1. The excesses of an improbable concept. *Canadian Journal of Psychiatry, 49*, 592–600.

Piren J., Palmer, P., Jacobi, D., Childress, D., & Arndt, S. (1997). Broader autism phenotype: Evidence from a family history study of multiple-incidence autism families. *American Journal of Psychiatry, 154*, 185–190.

Pogue-Geile, M. F., & Gottesman, I. I. (2007). Schizophrenia: Study of a genetically complex phenotype. In B. C. Jones & P. Mormede (Eds.), *Neurobehavioral genetics: Methods and applications.* (2nd ed.), (pp. 209–226). Boca Raton, FL: CRC Press.

Polivy, J., & Herman, C. P. (2002). Causes of eating disorders. *Annual Review of Psychology, 53*, 187–213.

Polivy, J., Herman, C., & Boivin, M. (2008). Eating disorders. In J. E. Maddux & B. A. Winstead (Eds.), *Psychopathology: Foundations for a contemporary understanding* (2nd ed., pp. 251–279). New York, NY: Routledge/Taylor & Francis Group.

Pollard, T. M., & Schwartz, J. E. (2003). Are changes in blood pressure and total cholesterol related to changes in mood? An 18-month study of men and women. *Health Psychology, 22*, 47–53.

Pope, H. G., Barry, S., Bodkin, A., & Hudson, J. I. (2006). Tracking scientific interest in the dissociative disorders: A study of scientific publication output 1984–2003. *Psychotherapy and Psychosomatics, 75*, 19–24.

Poythress, N. G., Edens, J. F., Skeem, J. L., Lilienfeld, S. O., Douglas, K. S., Frick, P. J., . . . Wang, T. (2010). Identifying subtypes among offenders with antisocial personality disorder: A cluster-analytic study. *Journal of Abnormal Psychology, 119*, 389–400.

Putnam, F. W. (1989). *Diagnosis and treatment of multiple personality disorder.* New York, NY: Guilford.

Putnam, F. W. (2006). Dissociative disorders. In D. Cicchetti & D. J. Cohen (Eds.), *Developmental psychopathology* (Vol. 3; pp. 657–695). Hoboken, NJ: Wiley.

Quay, H. C. (1997). Inhibition and attention deficit hyperactivity disorder. *Journal of Abnormal Child Psychology, 25*, 7–13.

Rabinowitz-Greenberg, S. R., Firestone, P., Bradford, J. M., & Greenberg, D. M. (2002). Prediction of recidivism in exhibitionists: Psychological phallometric, and offense factors. *Sexual Abuse: A Journal of Research and Treatment, 14*, 329–347.

Raj, Y. P. (2004). Psychopharmacology of borderline personality disorder. *Current Psychiatry Reports, 6*, 225–231.

Rasmussen, S. A., & Eisen, J. L. (1992). The epidemiology and clinical features of obsessive compulsive disorder. *Psychiatric Clinics of North America, 15*, 743–758.

Remington, B., Hastings, R. P., Kovshoff, H., Espinosa, F. D., Jahr, E., Brown, T., . . . Ward, N. (2007). Early intensive behavioral intervention: Outcomes for children with autism and their parents after two years. *American Journal on Mental Retardation, 112*, 418–438.

Riccardi, C. J., Timpano, K. R., & Schmidt, N. B. (2010). A case study perspective on the importance of motivation in the treatment of obsessive-compulsive disorder. *Clinical Case Studies, 9*(4), 273–284.

Rice, M. E., Harris, G. T., & Cormier, C. A. (1992). An evaluation of a maximum security therapeutic community for psychopaths and other mentally disordered offenders. *Law and Human Behavior, 16*, 399–412.

Richman, L. S., Kubzansky, L., Maselko, J., Kawachi, I., Choo, P., & Bauer, M. (2005). Positive emotion and health: Going beyond the negative. *Health Psychology, 24*, 422–429.

Rieber, R. (2006). *The bifurcation of the self: The history and theory of dissociation and its disorders.* New York, NY: Springer.

Rief, W., Pilger, F., Ihle, D., Verkerk, R., Scharpe, S., & Maes, M. (2004). Psychobiological aspects of somatoform disorders: Contributions of monoaminergic transmitter systems. *Neuropsychobiology, 49*, 24–29.

Robins, L. N., & Regier, D. A. (Eds.). (1991). *Psychiatric disorders in America: The Epidemiologic Catchment Area Study.* New York, NY: Free Press.

Rodebaugh, T. L., Holaway, R. M., & Heimberg, R. G. (2004). The treatment of social anxiety disorder. *Clinical Psychology Review, 24*, 883–908.

Rodrigo, C., Rajapakse, S., & Jayananda, G. (2010). The "antisocial" person: An insight into biology, classification and current evidence on treatment. *Annals of General Psychiatry*, *9*, 31–43.

Roelofs, K., & Spinhoven, P. (2007). Trauma and medically unexplained symptoms: Towards an integration of cognitive and neuro-biological accounts. *Clinical Psychology Review*, *27*, 798–820.

Rogers, C. R. (1951). *Client-centered therapy*. Boston, MA: Houghton Mifflin.

Rogers, C. R. (2007). The necessary and sufficient conditions of therapeutic personality change. *Psychotherapy: Theory, Research, Practice, Training*, *44*, 240–248.

Room, R., Babor, T., & Rehm, J. (2005). Alcohol and public health. *Lancet*, *365*, 519–530.

Root, R. W., & Resnick, R. J. (2003). An update on the diagnosis and treatment of attention-deficit/hyperactivity disorder in children. *Professional Psychology: Research and Practice*, *34*, 34–41.

Rosenbloom, M., Sullivan. E. V., & Pfefferbaum, A. (2003). Using magnetic resonance imaging and diffusion tensor imaging to assess brain damage in alcoholics. *Alcohol Research and Health*, *27*, 146–152.

Ross, C. A. (1997). *Dissociative identity disorder: Diagnosis, clinical features, and treatment of multiple personality* (2nd ed.). New York, NY: Wiley.

Ross, C. A. (2009). Errors of logic and scholarship concerning dissociative identity disorder. *Journal of Child Sexual Abuse*, *18*, 221–231.

Roth, W. T., Wilhelm, F. H., & Pettit, D. (2005). Are current theories of panic falsifiable? *Psychological Bulletin*, *131*, 171–192.

Rothbard, A. B., Schinnar, A. P., Hadley, T. P., Foley, K. A., & Kuno, E. (1998). Cost comparison of state hospital and community-based care for seriously mentally ill adults. *American Journal of Psychiatry*, *155*, 523–529.

Rowe, R., Maughan, B., & Eley, T. C. (2006). Links between antisocial behavior and depressed mood: The role of life events and attributional style. *Journal of Abnormal Child Psychology*, *34*, 293–302.

Rowe, R., Maughan, B., Pickles, A., Costello, E. J., & Angold, A. (2002). The relationship between DSM-IV oppositional defiant disorder and conduct disorder: Findings from the Great Smoky Mountains Study. *Journal of Child Psychology and Psychiatry*, *43*, 365–373.

Roy-Byrne, P. P., Craske, M. G., Stein, M. B., Sullivan, G., Bystritsky, A., Katon, W., . . . Sherbourne, C. D. (2005). A randomized effectiveness trial of cognitive-behavioral therapy and medication for primary care panic disorder. *Archives of General Psychiatry*, *62*, 290–298.

Rump, K. M., Giovannelli, J. L., Minshew, N. J., & Strauss, M. S. (2009). The development of emotion recognition in individuals with autism. *Child Development*, *80*, 1434–1447.

Russell, J. J., Moskowitz, D. S., Zuroff, D. C., Sookman, D., & Paris, J. (2007). Stability and variability of affective experience and interpersonal behavior in borderline personality disorder. *Journal of Abnormal Psychology*, *116*, 578–588.

Saleh, F. M., & Berlin, F. S. (2003). Sexual deviancy: Diagnostic and neurobiological considerations. *Journal of Child Sexual Abuse*, *12*, 53–76.

Saleh, F. M., Niel, T., & Fishman, M. J. (2004). Treatment of paraphilia in young adults with leuprolide acetate: A preliminary case report series. *Journal of Forensic Sciences*, *49*, 1343–1348.

Salekin, R. T., Worley, C., & Grimes, R. D. (2010). Treatment of psychopathy: A review and brief introduction to the mental model approach for psychopathy. *Behavioral Sciences and the Law*, *28*, 235–266.

Salkovskis, P. M. (1999). Understanding and treating obsessive-compulsive disorder. *Behaviour Research and Therapy*, *37*, S29–S52.

Salmon, P., Peters, S., & Stanley, I. (1999). Patients' perceptions of medical explanations for somatisation disorders: Qualitative analysis. *British Medical Journal*, *318*, 372–376.

Salmon, P., Skaife, K., & Rhodes, J. (2003). Abuse, dissociation, and somatization in irritable bowel syndrome: Towards an explanatory model. *Journal of Behavioral Medicine*, *26*, 1–18.

Sanislow, C. A., Grilo, C. M., & McGlashan, T. H. (2000). Factor analysis of the *DSMIII-R* borderline personality criteria in psychiatric inpatients. *American Journal of Psychiatry, 157,* 1629–1633.

Sansone, R. A., & Levitt, J. L. (2005). Borderline personality and eating disorders. *Eating Disorders, 13,* 71–83.

Sar, V. (2006). The scope of dissociative disorders: An international perspective. *Psychiatric Clinics of North America, 29,* 227–244.

Sar, V., Akyuz, G., & Dogan, O. (2007). Prevalence of dissociative disorders among women in the general population. *Psychiatry Research, 149,* 169–176.

Sartor, C. E., Lynskey, M. T., Bucholz, K. K., Madden, P. A. F., Martin, N. G., & Heath, A. C. (2009). Timing of first alcohol use and alcohol dependence: Evidence of common genetic influences. *Addiction, 104,* 1512–1518.

Saudino, K. J., & Plomin, R. (2007). Why are hyperactivity and academic achievement related? *Child Development, 78,* 972–986.

Scherrer, J. F., Xian, H., Bucholz, K. K., Eisen, S. A., Lyons, M. J., Goldberg, J., . . . True, W. R. (2003). A twin study of depression symptoms, hypertension, and heart disease in middle-aged men. *Psychosomatic Medicine, 65,* 548–557.

Schiffman, J., Abrahamson, A., Cannon, T., LaBrie, J., Parnas, J., Schulsinger, F., & Mednick, S. (2001). Early rearing factors in schizophrenia. *International Journal of Mental Health, 30,* 3–16.

Schlam, T. R., & Wilson, G. (2007). Relapse prevention for eating disorders. In K. A. Witkiewitz & G. Marlatt (Eds.), *Therapist's guide to evidence-based relapse prevention* (pp. 169–190). San Diego, CA: Elsevier Academic Press.

Schneider, K. (1959). *Clinical psychopathology.* New York, NY: Grune and Stratton.

Schreiber, F. (1973). *Sybil.* Chicago, IL: Henry Regnery. (Reprinted by Warner Paperback Library, New York, 1974)

Schuckit, M. A., Smith, T. L., Danko, G. P., Bucholz, K. K., Reich, T., & Bierut, L. (2001). Five-year clinical course associated with *DSM-IV* alcohol abuse or dependence in a large group of men and women. *American Journal of Psychiatry, 158,* 1084–1090.

Schum, J. L., Jorgensen, R. S., Verhaeghen, P., Sauro, M., & Thibodeau, R. (2003). Trait anger, anger expression, and ambulatory blood pressure: A meta-analytic review. *Journal of Behavioral Medicine, 26,* 395–415.

Segal, N. L. (2006). Two monozygotic twin pairs discordant for female-to-male transsexualism. *Archives of Sexual Behavior, 35,* 347–358.

Seivewright, H., Tyrer, P., & Johnson, T. (2002). Change in personality status in neurotic disorders. *Lancet, 359,* 2253–2254.

Selby, E. A., Anestis, M. D. Bender, T. W., & Joiner, T. E. (2009). An exploration of the emotional cascade model in borderline personality disorder. *Journal of Abnormal Psychology, 118,* 375–387.

Selby, E. A., Braithewaite, S. R., Joiner, T. E., & Fincham, F. A. (2008). Features of borderline personality disorder, perceived childhood emotional invalidation, and dysfunction within current romantic relationships. *Journal of Family Psychology, 22,* 885–893.

Seto, M. C., & Kuban, M. (1996). Criterion related validity of phallometric tests for paraphilic rape and sadism. *Behaviour Research and Therapy, 34,* 175–183.

Shaner, R.(2000). Benzodiazepines in psychiatric emergency settings. *Psychiatric Annals, 30,* 268–275.

Shapiro, J. R., Berkman, N. D., Brownley, K. A., Sedway, J. A., Lohr, K. N., & Bulik, C. M. (2007). Bulimia nervosa treatment: A systematic review of randomized controlled trials. *International Journal of Eating Disorders, 40,* 321–336.

Shapiro, L. J., & Stewart, S. (2011). Pathological guilt: A persistent yet overlooked treatment factor in obsessive-compulsive disorder. *Annals of Clinical Psychiatry, 23,* 63–70.

Shattuck, P. T., & Grosse, S. T. (2007). Issues related to the diagnosis and treatment of autism spectrum disorders. *Mental Retardation and Developmental Disabilities Research Reviews, 13,* 129–135.

Shea, V. (2004). A perspective on the research literature related to early intensive behavioral inter-vention (Lovaas) for young children with autism. *Autism, 8*, 349–367.

Sher, K. J., Bartholow, B. D., Peuser, K., Erickson, D. J., & Wood, M. D. (2007). Stress-response-dampening effects of alcohol: Attention as a mediator and moderator. *Journal of Abnormal Psychology, 116*, 362–377.

Shi, L., & Nicol, J. (2007). Into the mind of a juvenile sex offender: A clinical analysis and rec-ommendation from an attachment perspective. *The American Journal of Family Therapy, 35*, 395–402.

Shoebridge, P. J., & Gowers, S. G. (2000). Parental high concern and adolescent-onset anorexia ner-vosa: A case-control study to investigate direction of causality. *British Journal of Psychiatry, 176*, 132–137.

Silberg, J. L., Rutter, M., Tracy, K., Maes, H. H., & Eaves, L. (2007). Etiological heterogeneity in the development of antisocial behavior: the Virginia Twin Study of Adolescent Behavioral Development and the Young Adult Follow-Up. *Psychological Medicine, 37*, 1193–1202.

Simon, G. E., & Gureje, O. (1999). Stability of somatization disorder and somatization symptoms among primary care patients. *Archives of General Psychiatry, 56*, 90–95.

Simon, G. E., VonKorff, M., Piccinelli, M., Fullerton, C., & Ormel, J. (1999). An international study of the relation between somatic symptoms and depression. *New England Journal of Medicine, 341*, 1329–1335.

Simon, N. M., & Pollack, M. H. (2000). The current status of the treatment of panic disorder: phar-macotherapy and cognitive-behavioral therapy. *Psychiatric Annals, 30*, 689–696.

Simpson, G., Tate, R., Ferry, K., Hodgkinson, A., & Blaszczynski, A. (2001). Social, neuroradio-logic, medical, and neuropsychologic correlates of sexually aberrant behavior after traumatic brain injury: A controlled study. *Journal of Head Trauma and Rehabilitation, 16*, 556–572.

Simpson, K. J. (2002). Anorexia nervosa and culture. *Journal of Psychiatric and Mental Health Nursing, 9*, 65–71.

Sing, C. Y., & Wong, W. S. (2010). Prevalence of insomnia and its psychosocial correlates among college students in Hong Kong. *Journal of American College Health, 59*, 174–182.

Skeem, J. L., Edens, J. F., Camp, J., & Colwell, L. H. (2004). Are there ethnic differences in levels of psychopathy? A meta-analysis. *Law and Human Behavior, 28*, 505–527.

Skodol, A. E. (2005). Manifestations, clinical diagnosis, and comorbidity. In J. M. Oldham, A. E. Skodol, & D. S. Bender (Eds.), *Textbook of personality disorders* (pp. 57–88). Washington, DC: American Psychiatric Publishing.

Skodol, A. E., & Bender, D. S. (2003). Why are women diagnosed borderline more than men? *Psychiatric Quarterly, 74*, 349–360.

Skodol, A. E., Clark, L., Bender, D. S., Krueger, R. F., Morey, L. C., Verheul, R., . . . Oldham, J. M. (2011). Proposed changes in personality and personality disorder assessment and diagno-sis for DSM-5 Part I: Description and rationale. *Personality Disorders: Theory, Research, and Treatment, 2*, 4–22.

Skoog, G., & Skoog, I. (1999). A 40-year follow-up of patients with obsessive-compulsive disorder. *Archives of General Psychiatry, 56*(2), 121–127.

Smith, A. (2006). Cognitive empathy and emotional empathy in human behavior and evolution. *The Psychological Record, 56*, 3–21.

Smith, C. A., & Farrington, D. P. (2004). Continuities in antisocial behavior and parenting across three generations. *Journal of Child Psychology and Psychiatry, 45*, 230–247.

Smith, C. J., Lang, C. M., Kryzak, L., Reichenberg, A., Hollander, E., & Silverman, J. M. (2009). Familial associations of intense preoccupations, an empirical factor of the restricted, repetitive behaviors and interests domain of autism. *The Journal of Child Psychology and Psychiatry, 50*, 982–990.

Smith, L. A., Cornelius, V., Warnock, A., Bell, A., & Young, A. H. (2007). Effectiveness of mood stabilizers and antipsychotics in the maintenance phase of bipolar disorder. *Bipolar Disorders. 9*, 394–412.

Smith, L. D., & Peck, P. L. (2004). Dialectical behavior therapy: A review and call to research. *Journal of Mental Health Counseling, 26*, 25–38.

Smith, Y. L. S., van Goozen, S. H. M., Kuiper, A. J., & Cohen-Kettenis, P. T. (2005). Sex reassignment: Outcomes and predictors of treatment for adolescent and adult transsexuals. *Psychological Medicine, 35*, 89–99.

Sobell, M. B., & Sobell, L. C. (1976). Second-year treatment outcome of alcoholics treated by individualized behavior therapy: Results. *Behavior Research and Therapy, 14*, 195–215.

Sohn, M., & Bosinski, H. A. G. (2007). Gender identity disorders: Diagnostic and surgical aspects. *Journal of Sexual Medicine, 4*, 1193–1208.

Somers, J. M., Goldner, E. M., Waraich, P., & Hsu, L. (2004). Prevalence studies of substance-related disorders: A systematic review of the literature. *Canadian Journal of Psychiatry, 49*, 373–384.

South, S. C., Oltmanns, T. F., & Krueger, R. F. (2011). The spectrum of personality disorders. In D.H. Barlow (Ed.), *Oxford handbook of clinical psychology* (pp. 345–389). New York, NY: Oxford University Press.

Spiegel, D. (2001). Deconstructing the dissociative disorders: For whom the Dell tolls. *Journal of Trauma and Dissociation, 2*, 51–57.

Spitzer, C., Barnow, S., Gau, K., Freyberger, H. J., & Grabe, H. J. (2008). Childhood maltreatment in patients with somatization disorder. *Australian and New Zealand Journal of Psychiatry, 42*, 335–341.

Sprague, R. L., Cohen, M., & Werry, J. S. (1974). *Normative data on the Conners Teacher Rating Scale and Abbreviated Scale*. Technical Report. Children's Research Center, University of Illinois, Urbana.

Staiger, P. K., Thomas, A. C., Ricciardelli, L. A., Mccabe, M. P., Cross, W., & Young, G. (2011). Improving services for individuals with a dual diagnosis: A qualitative study reporting on the views of service users. *Addiction Research & Theory, 19*, 47–55.

Steadman, H. J., Mulvey, E. P., Monahan, J., Robbins, P. C., Appelbaum, P. S., Grisso, T., . . . Silver, E. (1998). Violence by people discharged from acute psychiatric inpatient facilities and by others in the same neighborhoods. *Archives of General Psychiatry, 55*, 393–401.

Steiner, H., & Remsing, L. (2007). AACAP Official Action: Practice parameter for the assessment and treatment of children and adolescents with oppositional defiant disorder. *Journal of the American Academy of Child and Adolescent Psychiatry, 46*, 126–141.

Steinhausen, H. (2002). The outcome of anorexia nervosa in the 20th century. *American Journal of Psychiatry, 159*, 1284–1293.

Steinhausen, H. C. (2009). The heterogeneity of causes and courses of attention-deficit/hyperactivity disorder. *Acta Psychiatrica Scandinavica, 120*, 392–399.

Stephan, U., & Roesler, U. (2010). Health of entrepreneurs versus employees in a national representative sample. *Journal of Occupational and Organizational Psychology, 83*, 717–738.

Stephens, J. H., Richard, P., & McHugh, P. R. (2000). Long-term follow-up of patients with a diagnosis of paranoid state and hospitalized, 1913 to 1940. *Journal of Nervous and Mental Disease, 188*, 202–208.

Steptoe, A., & Willemsen, G. (2004). The influence of low job control on ambulatory blood pressure and perceived stress over the working day in men and women from the Whitehall II cohort. *Journal of Hypertension, 22*, 915–920.

Stern, J., Murphy, M., & Bass, C. (1993). Personality disorders in patients with somatisation disorder: A controlled study. *British Journal of Psychiatry, 163*, 785–789.

Stewart, J. C., Janicki, D. L., & Kamarck, T. W. (2006). Cardiovascular reactivity to and recovery from psychological challenge as predictors of 3-year change in blood pressure. *Health Psychology, 25*, 111–118.

Stice, E., Marti, C. N., Shaw, H., & Jaconis, M. (2009). An 8-year longitudinal study of the natural history of threshold, subthreshold, and partial eating disorders from a community sample of adolescents. *Journal of Abnormal Psychology, 118*, 587–597.

Stock, W. (1993). Inhibited female orgasm. In W. O'Donohue, J. H. Geer, W. O'Donohue, J. H. Geer (Eds.), *Handbook of sexual dysfunctions: Assessment and treatment* (pp. 253–277). Needham Heights, MA: Allyn & Bacon.

Stoller, R. J. (1985). *Presentations of gender*. New Haven, CT: Yale University Press.

Stormshak, E. A., Bierman, K. L., McMahon, R. J., & Lengua, L. J. (2000). Parenting practices and child disruptive behavior problems in early elementary school. *Journal of Clinical Child Psychology, 29*, 17–29.

Strober, M. (1997). Consultation and therapeutic engagement in severe anorexia nervosa. In D. M. Garner & P. E. Garfinkel (Eds.), *Handbook of treatment for eating disorders* (2nd ed., pp. 229–247). New York, NY: Guilford.

Stuart, H. L., & Arboleda-Florez, J. E. (2001). A public health perspective on violent offenses among persons with mental illness. *Psychiatric Services, 52*, 654–659.

Sue, D. W., Capodilupo, C. M., Torino, G. C., Bucceri, J. M., Holder, A. M. B., Nadal, K. L., & Esquilin, M. (2007). Racial microaggressions in everyday life: Implications for clinical practice. *American Psychologist, 62*, 271–286.

Sue, D. W., & Sue, D. (1999). *Counselling the culturally different*. New York, NY: Wiley.

Suen, L. K. P., Hon, L. K. E., & Tam, W. W. W. (2008). Association between sleep behavior and sleep-related factors among university students in Hong Kong. *Chronobiology International, 25*, 760–775.

Sugarman, P., Dumughn, C., Saad, K., Hinder, S., & Bluglass, S. (1994). Dangerousness in exhibitionists. *Journal of Forensic Psychiatry, 5*, 287–296.

Sung, M., Fung, D. S. S., Cai, Y., & Ooi, Y. P. (2010). Pharmacological management in children and adolescents with pervasive developmental disorder. *Australian and New Zealand Journal of Psychiatry, 44*, 410–428.

Swanson, J., Estroff, S., Swartz, M., & Borum, R. (1997). Violence and severe mental disorder in clinical and community populations: The effects of psychotic symptoms. *Psychiatry: Interpersonal and Biological Processes, 60*, 1–22.

Swendsen, E. J., King, D. W., King, L. A., Wolfe, J., Erickson, D. J., & Stokes, L. R. (2000). Mood and alcohol consumption: An experience sampling test of the self-medication hypothesis. *Journal of Abnormal Psychology, 109*, 198–204.

Sysko, R. R., Sha, N. N., Wang, Y. Y., Duan, N. N., & Walsh, B. T. (2010). Early response to antidepressant treatment in bulimia nervosa. *Psychological Medicine, 40*, 999–1005.

Szklo-Coxe, M., Young, T., Finn, L., & Mignot, E. (2007). Depression: Relationships to sleep paralysis and other sleep disturbances in a community sample. *Journal of Sleep Research, 16*, 297–312.

Tager-Flusberg, H. (2007). Evaluating the theory-of-mind hypothesis of autism. *Current Directions in Psychological Science, 16*, 311–315.

Tan, Y., & Zhong, Y. (2001). Chinese style psychoanalysis—assessment and treatment of paraphilias: Exhibitionism, frotteurism, voyeurism, and fetishism. *International Journal of Psychotherapy, 6*, 297–314.

Tardiff, K. (2001). Axis II disorders and dangerousness. In G. Pinard & L. Pagani (Eds.), *Clinical assessment of dangerousness: Empirical contributions* (pp. 103–120). New York, NY: Cambridge University Press.

Taylor, E. (2009). Developing ADHD. *Journal of Child Psychology and Psychiatry, 50*, 126–132.

Teplin, L. A., Abram, K. M., & McClelland, G. M. (1996). Prevalence of psychiatric disorders among incarcerated women: Pretrial jail detainees. *Archives of General Psychiatry, 53*, 505–512.

Terao, T., & Nakamura, J. (2000). Exhibitionism and low-dose trazodone treatment. *Human Psychopharmacology: Clinical and Experimental, 15*, 347–349.

Thewissen, V., Bentall, R. P., Lecomte, T., van Os, J., & Myin-Germeys, I. (2008). Fluctuations in self-esteem and paranoia in the context of daily life. *Journal of Abnormal Psychology, 117*, 143–153.

Thigpen, C. H., & Cleckley, H. M. (1957). *The three faces of Eve*. New York, NY: McGraw-Hill.

Thomas, A. (2001). Factitious and malingered dissociative identity disorder: Clinical features observed in 18 cases. *Journal of Trauma & Dissociation, 2*, 59–77.

Thomas, J. T., Vartanian, L. R., & Brownell, K. D. (2009). The relationship between eating disorder not otherwise specified (EDNOS) and officially recognized eating disorders: Meta-analysis and implications for DSM. *Psychological Bulletin, 135*, 407–433.

Thomson, L. D. G., Bogue, J. P., Humphreys, M. S., & Johnstone, E. C. (2001). A survey of female patients in high security psychiatric care in Scotland. *Criminal Behaviour and Mental Health, 11*, 86–93.

Thornton, C., & Russell, J. (1997). Obsessive compulsive comorbidity in the dieting disorders. *International Journal of Eating Disorders, 21*, 83–87.

Tiet, Q. O., & Mausbach, B. (2007). Treatments for patients with dual diagnosis: A review. *Alcoholism: Clinical and experimental research, 31*, 513–536.

Timmer, B., Bleichhardt, G., & Rief, W. (2006). Importance of psychotherapy motivation in patients with somatization syndrome. *Psychotherapy Research, 16*, 348–356.

Toates, F. (2009). An integrative theoretical framework for understanding sexual motivation, arousal, and behavior. *Journal of Sex Research, 46*, 168–193.

Tolin, D. F., Hannan, S., Maltby, N., Diefenbach, G. J., Worhunsky, P., & Brady, R. E. (2007). A randomized controlled trial of self-directed versus therapist-directed cognitive-behavioral therapy for obsessive-compulsive disorder patients with prior medication trials. *Behavior Therapy, 38*, 179–191.

Tolin, D. F., & Steketee, G. (2007). General issues in psychological treatment for obsessive-compulsive disorder. In M. M. Antony, C. Purdon, & L. J. Summerfeldt (Eds.), *Psychological treatment of obsessive-compulsive disorder: Fundamentals and beyond* (pp. 31–59). Washington, DC: American Psychological Association.

Tomasson, K., Kent, D., & Coryell, W. (1991). Somatization and conversion disorders: Comorbidity and demographics at presentation. *Acta Psychiatrica Scandinavia, 84*, 288–293.

Torres, A. R., Prince, M. J., Bebbington, P. E., Bhugra, D., Brugha, T. S., Farrell, M., . . . Singleton, N. (2006). Obsessive-compulsive disorder: Prevalence, comorbidity, impact, and help-seeking in the British National Psychiatric Morbidity survey of 2000. *American Journal of Psychiatry, 163*, 1978–1985.

Treasure, J. L. (2007). Getting beneath the phenotype of anorexia nervosa: The search for viable endophenotypes and genotypes. *Canadian Journal of Psychiatry, 52*, 212–219.

Trull, T. J., Jahng, S., Tomko, R. L., Wood, P. K., & Sher, K. J. (2010). Revised NESARC personality disorder diagnoses: Gender, prevalence, and comorbidity with substance dependence disorders. *Journal of Personality Disorders, 24*(4), 412–426.

Tully, L. A., Arseneault, L., Caspi, A., Moffitt, T. E., & Morgan, J. (2004). Does maternal warmth moderate the effects of birth weight on twins' attention-deficit/hyperactivity disorder (ADHD) symptoms and low IQ? *Journal of Consulting and Clinical Psychology, 72*, 218–226.

Turk, C. L., & Mennin, D. S. (2011). Phenomenology of generalized anxiety disorder. *Psychiatric Annals, 41*, 72–78.

Turner, M. S., & Stewart, D. W. (2006). Review of the evidence for the long-term efficacy of atypical antipsychotic agents in the treatment of patients with schizophrenia and related psychoses. *Journal of Psychopharmacology, 20*, 20–37.

Ullman, S. E., & Filipas, H. H. (2001). Predictors of PTSD symptom severity and social reactions in sexual assault victims. *Journal of Traumatic Stress, 14*, 369–389.

Vaillant, G. E. (1996). A long-term follow-up of male alcohol abuse. *Archives of General Psychiatry, 53*, 243–249.

Vaillant, G. E. (2003). A 60-year follow-up of alcoholic men. *Addiction, 98*, 1043–1051.

Van den Bergh, B. R. H., & Marcoen, A. (2004). High antenatal maternal anxiety is related to ADHD symptoms, externalizing problems, and anxiety in 8- and 9-year olds. *Child Development, 75*, 1085–1097.

van den Oord, E. J., Boomsma, D. I., & Verhulst, F. C. (1994). A study of problem behaviors in 10- to 15-year old biologically related and unrelated international adoptees. *Behavior Genetics, 24*, 193–205.

van der Ham, T. (1997). Empirically based subgrouping of eating disorders in adolescents: A longitudinal perspective. *British Journal of Psychiatry, 170*, 363–368.

van der Voort, T. Y. G., Gossens, P. J. J., & van der Bijl, J. J. (2007). Burden, coping and needs for support of caregivers for patients with a bipolar disorder: A systematic review. *Journal of Psychiatry and Mental Health Nursing, 14*, 679–687.

van Hanswijck, J. P., van Furth, E. F., Lacey, J. H., & Waller, G. (2003). The prevalence of DSM-IV personality pathology among individuals with bulimia nervosa, binge eating disorder and obesity. *Psychological Medicine, 33*, 1311–1317.

Veenstra, E. M., & de Jong, P. J. (2011). Reduced automatic motivational orientation towards food in restricting anorexia nervosa. *Journal of Abnormal Psychology*. Advanced online publication.

Verster, J. C., & Volkerts, E. R. (2004). Clinical pharmacology, clinical efficacy, and behavioral toxicity of alprazolam: A review of the literature. *CNS Drug Reviews, 10*, 45–76.

Voeller, K. K. S. (2004). Attention-deficit hyperactivity disorder (ADHD). *Journal of Child Neurology, 19*, 798–814.

Volkmar, F. R., Chawarska, K., & Klin, A. (2005). Autism in infancy and early childhood. *Annual Review of Psychology, 56*, 315–336.

Volkmar, F. R., Lord, C., Bailey, A., Schultz, R. T., & Klin, A. (2004). Autism and pervasive developmental disorders. *Journal of Child Psychology and Psychiatry, 45*, 135–170.

Wade, T. D., Bergin, J. L., Tiggemann, M., Bulik, C. M., & Fairburn, C. G. (2006). Prevalence and long-term course of lifetime eating disorders in an adult Australian twin cohort. *Australian and New Zealand Journal of Psychiatry, 40*, 121–128.

Wakschlag, L. S., Briggs-Gowan, M. J., Carter, A. S., Hill, C., Danis, B., Keenan, K., . . . Leventhal, B. L. (2007). A developmental framework for distinguishing disruptive behavior from normative misbehavior in preschool children. *Journal of Child Psychology and Psychiatry, 48*, 976–987.

Wakschlag, L. S., Tolan, P. H., & Leventhal, B. L. (2010). "Ain't misbehavin": Towards a developmentally-specified nosology for preschool disruptive behavior. *Journal of Child Psychology and Psychiatry, 51*, 3–22.

Waldinger, M. D., Zwinderman, A. H., & Olivier, B. (2001). Antidepressants and ejaculation: A double-blind, randomized, placebo-controlled, fixed dose study with paroxetine, sertraline, and nefazodone. *Journal of Clinical Psychopharmacology, 21*, 293–297.

Waldinger, R. J., & Gunderson, J. G. (1984). Completed psychotherapies with borderline patients. *American Journal of Psychotherapy, 38*, 190–202.

Walker, E., Kestler, L., Bollini, A., & Hochman, K. M. (2004). Schizophrenia: Etiology and course. *Annual Review of Psychology, 55*, 401–430.

Walsh, E., Gilvarry, C., Samele, C., Harvey, K., Manley, C., Tattan, T., . . . Fahy, T. (2004). Predicting violence in schizophrenia: A prospective study. *Schizophrenia Research, 67*, 247–252.

Wang, J. L., & El-Guebaly, N. (2004). Sociodemographic factors associated with comorbid major depressive episodes and alcohol dependence in the general population. *Canadian Journal of Psychiatry, 49*, 37–44.

Waraich, P., Goldner, E. M., Somers, J. M., & Hsu, L. (2004). Prevalence and incidence studies of mood disorders: A systematic review of the literature. *Canadian Journal of Psychiatry, 49*, 124–138.

Warshaw, R. (1994). *I never called it rape: The Ms. report on recognizing, fighting, and surviving acquaintance rape.* New York, NY: Harper & Row.

Watson, D. (2001). Dissociations of the night: Individual differences in sleep-related experiences and their relation to dissociation and schizotypy. *Journal of Abnormal Psychology, 110*, 526–535.

Wazana, A., Bresnahan, M., & Kline, J. (2007). The autism epidemic: Fact or artifact? *Journal of the American Academy of Child and Adolescent Psychiatry, 46*, 721–730.

Webster-Stratton, C., & Hammond, M. (1997). Treating children with early-onset conduct problems: A comparison of child and parent training interventions. *Journal of Consulting and Clinical Psychology*, *65*, 93–109.

Wegner, D. M. (1994). Ironic processes of mental control. *Psychological Review*, *101*, 34–52.

Wegner, D. M., Wenzlaff, R. M., & Kozak, M. (2004). Dream rebound: The return of suppressed thoughts in dreams. *Psychological Science*, *15*, 232–236.

Weiss, B., Tram, J. M., Weisz, J. R., Rescorla, L., & Achenbach, T. M. (2009). Differential symptom expression and somatization in Thai versus U. S. children. *Journal of Consulting and Clinical Psychology*, *77*, 987–992.

Weiss, M. D., & Salpekar, J. (2010). Sleep problems in the child with attention-deficit hyperactivity disorder: Defining aetiology and appropriate treatments. *CNS Drugs*, *24*, 811–828.

Weissman, M. M. (2007). Recent non-medication trials of interpersonal psychotherapy for depression. *International Journal of Neuropsychopharmacology*, *10*, 117–122.

West, S. L., Vinikoor, L. C., & Zolnoun, D. (2004). A systematic review of the literature on female sexual dysfunction prevalence and predictors. *Annual Review of Sex Research, 15*, 40–172.

Whalen, C. K., Henker, B., Buhrmester, D., Hinshaw, S. P., Huber, A., & Laski, K. (1989). Does stimulant medication improve the peer status of hyperactive children? *Journal of Consulting and Clinical Psychology, 57*, 545–549.

White, C. N., Gunderson, J. G., Zanarini, M. C., & Hudson, J. I. (2003). Family studies of borderline personality disorder: A review. *Harvard Review of Psychiatry*, *11*, 8–19.

Widiger, T. A., & Samuel, D. B. (2005). Evidence-based assessment of personality disorders. *Psychological Assessment, 17*, 278–287.

Wiegel, M., Wincze, J. P., & Barlow, D. H. (2002). Sexual dysfunction. In M. M. Antony & D. H. Barlow (Eds.), *Handbook of assessment and treatment planning for psychological disorders* (pp. 481–522). New York, NY: Guilford.

Wilcox, D. T., & Sosnowski, D. F. (2005). Polygraph examination of British sexual offenders: A pilot study on sexual history disclosure testing. *Journal of Sexual Aggression, 11*, 3–25.

Wilens, T. E., Faraone, S. V., Biederman, J., & Gunawardene, S. (2003). Does stimulant therapy of attention-deficit hyperactivity disorder beget later substance abuse? A meta-analytic review of the literature. *Pediatrics*, *111*, 179–185.

Williams, P. (2010). Psychotherapeutic treatment of Cluster A personality disorders. In J. F. Clarkin, P. Fonagy, & G. O. Gabbard (Eds.), *Psychodynamic psychotherapy for personality disorders: A clinical handbook* (pp. 165–185). Arlington, VA: American Psychiatric Publishing.

Williams, R. B., Barefoot, J. C., & Schneiderman, N. (2003). Psychosocial risk factors for cardiovascular disease: More than one culprit at work. *Journal of the American Medical Association, 290*, 2190–2192.

Williamson, D. A., Cubic, B. A., & Gleaves, D. H. (1993). Equivalence of body image disturbance in anorexia and bulimia nervosa. *Journal of Abnormal Psychology*, *120*, 173–176.

Willoughby, M. T. (2003). Developmental course of ADHD symptomatology during the transition from childhood to adolescence: A review with recommendations. *Journal of Child Psychology and Psychiatry*, *44*, 88–106.

Wills, L., & Garcia, J. (2002). Parasomnias: Epidemiology and management. *CNS Drugs*, *16*, 803–810.

Wilson, G. T., Grilo, C. M., & Vitousek, K. M. (2007). Psychological treatment of eating disorders. *American Psychologist, 62*, 199–216.

Wilson, G. T., & Sysko, R. (2006). Cognitive-behavioural therapy for adolescents with bulimia nervosa. *European Eating Disorders Review*, *14*, 8–16.

Wing, Y. K., Chiu, H., Leung, T., & Ng, J. (1999). Sleep paralysis in the elderly. *Journal of Sleep Research, 8*, 151–155.

Witkiewitz, K., & Marlatt, G. A. (2007). Modeling the complexity of post-treatment drinking: It's a rocky road to relapse. *Clinical Psychology Review, 27*, 724–738.

Wonderlich, S. A., Brewerton, T. D., Jocic, Z., & Dansky, B. S. (1997). Relationship of childhood sexual abuse and eating disorders. *Journal of the American Academy of Child and Adolescent Psychiatry*, *36*, 1107–1115.

Woods, S. (2004). Untreated recovery from eating disorders. *Adolescence, 39*, 361–371.

Woolfolk, R. L., & Allen, L. A. (2010). Affective-cognitive behavioral therapy for somatization disorder. *Journal of Cognitive Psychotherapy: An International Quarterly, 24*, 116–131.

Woolfolk, R. L., Allen, L. A., & Tiu, J. E. (2007). New directions in the treatment of somatization. *Psychiatric Clinics of North America, 30*, 621–644.

World Health Organization. (1990). *International classification of diseases and related health care problems* (10th ed.). Geneva, Switzerland.

Wu, E. O., Birnbaum, H., Hudson, T., & Kessler, R. (2006). Annual prevalence of diagnosed schizophrenia in the USA: A claims data analysis approach. *Psychological Medicine, 36*, 1535–1540.

Yadin, E., & Foa, E. B. (2007). Cognitive behavioral treatments for posttraumatic stress disorder. In L. J. Kirmayer, R. Lemelson, & M. Barad (Eds.), *Understanding trauma: Integrating biological, clinical, and cultural perspectives* (pp. 178–193). New York, NY: Cambridge University Press.

Yan, L. L., Liu, K., Matthews, K. A., Daviglus, M. L., Ferguson, T. F., & Kiefe, C. I. (2003). Psychosocial factors and risk of hypertension: The Coronary Artery Risk Development in Young Adults (CARDIA) Study. *Journal of the American Medical Association, 290*, 2138–2148.

Yeager, C. A., & Lewis, D. O. (1997). False memories of cult abuse. *American Journal of Psychiatry, 154*, 435.

Yoon, E., Langrehr, K., & Ong, L. Z. (2011). Content analysis of acculturation research in counseling and counseling psychology: A 22-year review. *Journal of Counseling Psychology, 58*, 83–96.

Young, A. H., & Newham, J. I. (2006). Lithium in maintenance therapy for bipolar disorder. *Journal of Psychopharmacology, 20*, 17–22.

Young, A. S., Klap, R., Shoai, R., & Wells, K. B. (2008). Persistent depression and anxiety in the United States: Prevalence and quality of care. *Psychiatric Services, 59*, 1391–1398.

Young, S., & Amarasinghe, J. M. (2010). Non-pharmacological treatments for ADHD: A lifespan approach. *Journal of Child Psychology and Psychiatry, 51*, 116–133.

Yung, P. M., & Keltner, A. A. (1996). A controlled comparison of the effects of muscle and cognitive relaxation procedures on blood pressure: Implications for the behavioural treatment of borderline hypertensives. *Behaviour Research and Therapy, 34*, 821–826.

Zadra, A., & Donderi, D. C. (2000). Nightmares and bad dreams: Their prevalence and relationship to well-being. *Journal of Abnormal Psychology, 109*, 273–281.

Zanarini, M. C. (2004). Update on pharmacotherapy of borderline personality disorder. *Current Psychiatry Reports, 6*, 66–70.

Zanarini, M. C. (2009). Psychotherapy of borderline personality disorder. *Acta Psychiatrica Scandinavica, 120*, 373–377.

Zhang, J., Niaura, R., Todaro, J. F., McCaffery, J. M., Shen, B., Spiro, A., & Ward, K. D. (2005). Suppressed hostility predicted hypertension incidence among middle-aged men. *The Normative Aging Study. Journal of Behavioral Medicine, 28*, 443–454.

Zimmerman, F. J., & Christakis, D. A. (2007). Associations between content types of early media exposure and subsequent attentional problems. *Pediatrics, 120*, 986–992.

Zito, J. M., Safer, D. J., dos Reis, S., Gardner, J. F., Boles, M., & Lynch, F. (2000). Trends in the prescribing of psychotropic medication to preschoolers. *Journal of the American Medical Association, 283*, 1025–1030.

Zohar, J., Juven-Wetzler, A., Myers, V., & Fostick, L. (2008). Post-traumatic stress disorder: Facts and fiction. *Current Opinion in Psychiatry, 21*, 74–77.

Zucker, K. J. (2001). Biological differences on psychosexual differentiation. In R. K. Under (Ed.), *Handbook of the psychology of women and gender* (pp. 101–115). New York, NY: Wiley.

Zucker, K. J. (2005). Gender identity disorder in children and adolescents. *Annual Review of Clinical Psychology, 1*, 467–492.

Zucker, K. J., & Bradley, S. J. (2000). Gender identity disorder. In C. H. Zeanah (Ed.), *Handbook of infant mental health* (2nd ed., pp. 412–424). New York, NY: Guilford.

Zucker, K. J., & Lawrence, A. A. (2009). Epidemiology of gender identity disorder: Recommendations for the Standards of Care of the World Professional Association for Transgender Health. *International Journal of Transgenderism, 11*, 8–18.

Zucker, N. L., Losh, M., Bulik, C. M., LaBar, K. S., Piven, J., & Pelphrey, K. A. (2007). Anorexia nervosa and autism spectrum disorders: Guided investigation of social cognitive endophenotypes. *Psychological Bulletin, 133*, 976–1006.

INDEX

A

AA. *See* Alcoholics Anonymous (AA)
Abstinence violation effect, 250
Addiction/Addictive behaviors, 9, 165
ADHD. *See* Attention-deficit/hyperactivity
    disorder (ADHD)
Affect distress, 260
African Americans, 52–107. *See also*
    Hypertension in an African
    American man
Aggression, 343
  proactive aggression, 343
  reactive aggression, 343
Aggressive obsessions, 8
Agoraphobia, 17–34. *See also* Panic
    disorder with agoraphobia
Alcohol abuse, 165
Alcohol dependence, 159–170
  criteria, 164–165
    withdrawal symptoms, 164
  etiological considerations, 166–168
    environmental influence, 166
    genetic influence, 166
    prenatal exposure to alcohol, 167
    social acceptability of
      drinking, 167
  follow-up, 163–164
  lifetime prevalence rates for, 165
  and negative moods, 168
  reducing people's stress response, 167
    altering response to stressful
      stimuli, 167
    muting anxiety, 167
  social history, 160–162
  tension-reducing effects of alcohol,
    167–168
  treatment, 162–163, 168–170
    AA treatment, 169
    abstinence as goal, 162–163
    assertiveness training, 169
    benzodiazepines, 168
    disulfiram, 169
    naltrexone, 169
    outpatient group therapy, 169
    relaxation training, 169
    social skills training, 169
Alexithymia, 124
Alprazolam (Xanax), 22, 29, 33
Alter personalities, 75–76. *See also*
    Multiple personality
Amphetamine (Adderall), 334
Anger, hypertension and, 61–62
Angold, A., 348
Anhedonia, 135
Anorexia nervosa, 221–233
  binge-eating/purging type, 228
  comorbid disorders, 228
  DSM-IV-TR diagnostic criteria, 227
  etiological considerations,
    229–231
    biological factors, 229
    cultural attitudes and standards, 230
    family factors, 230
    genetic factors, 229
    sexual abuse, 231
  gender based prevalence rates, 227
  onset of eating disorder, 224–226
    binge eating, 225
    restricted food intake, 224
    surgery, 224
  physical effects of starvation, 224
  restricting type, 228
  social history, 221

Anorexia nervosa (*Continued*)
  divorce, 223
  overprotective parents, 222
  relationships, 222–223
  treatment, 226–227, 231–233
    behavioral techniques, 232
    CBT, 231
    CBT and psychodynamic techniques
      combination, 231
    family therapy, 232
    hospitalization, 226, 232
Antidepressants
  autistic disorder, 320
  borderline personality disorder (BPD),
    287–289
  female orgasmic disorder, 186
  major depressive disorder, 98–99
  rape trauma, 49–50
  somatization disorder, 127
Antipsychotic drugs, 151
  atypical, 156–157
  autistic disorder, 320
  paranoid personality disorder, 281
  psychotic disorder NOS, 156
  schizophrenia, paranoid type,
    137, 142
Antisocial personality disorder
    (ASPD), 297–308. *See also*
    Psychopathy
  DSM-IV-TR concept of, 301
Anxiety disorders, 1–16. *See also*
    Obsessive-compulsive disorder
    (OCD); Panic disorder with
    agoraphobia
Aphonia, 121
ASPD. *See* Antisocial personality disorder
    (ASPD)
Assertion training
  alcohol dependence, 169
  bulimia nervosa, 243–244
  obsessive compulsive disorder (OCD),
    5–6, 12
Attention-deficit/hyperactivity disorder
    (ADHD), 323–335
  conceptualization and treatment,
    326–330
    expanded school program, 329

    operant-conditioning framework, 326
    time-out procedure, 328
  conduct disorder and, 331
  Conners Rating Scale, 324–325
  DSM-IV-TR criteria for, 330
  etiological considerations,
    331–334
  social history, 323–324
  target behaviors during
    treatment, 327
  television exposure and, 333
  treatment, 334–335
    amphetamine (Adderall), 334
    long-term treatment, 334
    methylphenidate (Ritalin), 334
  types of, 330
Atypical antipsychotic drugs, 142
Auditory hallucinations, 137, 139, 145,
    152–154, 281
Authoritarian parenting, 305
Autistic disorder, 309–322
  conceptualization and treatment,
    310–315
    addressing temper tantrums, 312
    expanding vocabulary, 311
    eye contact, 310–311
    feeding skills, 313
    following commands, 311
    haloperidol (Haldol), 314
    language skills, 311
    punishment system
      implementation, 314
    self-stimulatory behavior,
      addressing, 314
    teaching Sam to dress and
      undress, 312
    toilet training, 312
    training to play, 313
  DSM-III classification, 315
  etiological considerations, 318–320
    cognitive explanations, 319
    environmental factors, 319
    genetic factors, 318–319
    neurobiological factors, 318
  features of, 315–316
    abnormality in social development, 315
    communication deficits, 316

eating problems, 317
hyperresponsiveness, 317
repetitive sensorimotor behavior, 316
restricted or stereotyped
interests, 316
gender based prevalence, 317
treatment, 320–322
antidepressants, 320
antipsychotics, 320
behavior therapy, 320
intensive behavior therapy program,
321
modeling, 321
self-stimulatory behavior, 320
Autoimmune diseases, 59
Autonomic underarousal, 345
Aversion therapy, 199
Avoidance responses, 50

B

Barbiturates, 29
Behavior therapy/Behavioral treatment
methods. *See also* Cognitive-
behavioral therapy (CBT)
for autistic disorder, 320
for OCD, 7, 13–14
Benzodiazepines, 33, 168
Bereavement, 59, 94
Berlin, F. S., 196
Biederman, J., 331–332
Billstedt, E., 316
Binge-eating/purging type anorexia
nervosa, 228
Bipolar disorder, 102–114
conceptualization and treatment,
106–108
cyclothymia, 110
etiological considerations, 110–112
genetic factors in, 111
hypomanic episodes, 109
manic episodes, 108
DSM-IV-TR criteria for, 108
marital adjustment in, 112
prevalence, 110
psychotherapy for, 113
residual symptoms, 107

schizophrenia versus, 109
social history, 106
symptoms, 102–103
depression, 103
periods of unusual ambition and
energy, 103
treatment, 104, 112–113
lithium carbonate, 104,
107–108, 112
unipolar and, 108
Bleuler, E., 139
Bluglass, S., 196
Boardman, A. P., 125
Body dysmorphic disorder, 120
Body image, 231–232, 244
Borchard, B., 196
Borderline personality disorder (BPD),
283–296
antidepressant medication,
287, 289
conceptualization and treatment,
288–291
cognitive therapy, 289
day-treatment program, 291
DSM-IV-TR criteria for, 291
eiological considerations, 292–294
abnormalities in serotonin
activity, 293
childhood family
environments, 293
social history, 285–288
treatment, 294
dialectical behavior therapy (DBT),
295–296
object relations psychotherapy,
294–295
BPD. *See* Borderline personality
disorder (BPD)
Brown, G. W., 96
Bulimia nervosa, 234–250
binge/purge cycle, 235, 238
conceptualization and treatment,
239–246
cognitive-behavioral
approach, 239
controlling appetite, 235
etiological considerations, 247

Bulimia nervosa (*Continued*)
  biological factors, 247–248
  cultural influence, 248
  psychological factors,
    248–249
  serotonin in, 248
  sociocultural influences, 248
  social history, 236–239
    negative emotional responses, 238
    substance-use problems in
      family, 236
  treatment, 10, 249–250
    CBT, 249
    drugs and CBT combination, 249
    medication, 249

C

Cade, J. F. J., 112
Callousness, 345
Cameron, N., 279
Carbamazepine (Tegretol), 113
Carr, L. G., 167
Castellanos, F. X., 332
Catastrophic thinking, 25–26
Catatonic patients, 139–140
CBT. *See* Cognitive-behavioral
    therapy (CBT)
Chen, L., 31, 332
Child abuse
  anorexia nervosa, 231–232
  borderline personality disorder
    (BPD), 293
  multiple personality, 69
  paraphilias, 190, 198
  psychopathy, 304
  somatization disorder, 126
Cleaning and washing rituals, 9
Cleckley, H. E., 306
Cleckley, H. M., 84, 301
Client-centered therapy
  borderline personality disorder, 295
  hypertension, 64
  paranoid personality disorder, 281
Clomipramine (Anafranil), 14
Clozapine (Clozaril), 142, 156
Coercive cycle, 346

Cognitive approach
  anxiety disorders, 31–32
  autistic disorder, 319
  borderline personality disorder
    (BPD), 289
  bulimia nervosa, 239
  female orgasmic disorder, 186
  multiple personality, 83
  oppositional defiant disorder
    (ODD), 349
  panic disorder with agoraphobia,
    31–33
  paranoid personality disorder, 281
  rape trauma, 40–41
  somatization disorder, 128
Cognitive-behavioral therapy (CBT)
  for anorexia nervosa, 231
  for anxiety disorders, 31
  borderline personality disorder, 289
  for bulimia nervosa, 239, 249
  for OCD, 7, 12–14
  for oppositional defiant disorder
    (ODD), 349
  for panic disorder, 31–33
  for paranoid PD, 281
  for PTSD, 49–50
  for rape trauma, 40–43
Cognitive distortions, 25,
    231–232, 281
Cognitive restructuring
  agoraphobia, 23, 25
  borderline personality disorder,
    289–290
  panic control treatment, 32
  posttraumatic stress disorder, 42–43
Colby, K. M., 279–280
Command hallucinations, 155
Community mental-health care,
    145, 286
Compton, S. N., 348
Compulsions. *See also* Obsessive-
    compulsive disorder (OCD)
  addictive behaviors and, 9
  DSM-IV-TR defining, 7–8
  repetitive checking, 9
Conditioning model of panic
    disorder, 31

Conduct disorder and ADHD, 331
Conners Rating Scale, 324–325
Contamination, fear of, 8
Contingency management,
       326–327
Conversion disorder, 120
Cook, T. A. R., 167
Cooney, N. L., 169
Coping mechanisms, 62
Cormier, C. A., 306
Costello, E. J., 348
Counting rituals, 1, 5
Craig, T. K. J., 125–126
Criminal activity, 301
Cross-gender identity, 216. *See also*
       Transsexualism
Cyclothymia, 110

D

Dandescu, A., 200
Danesh, J., 156
Davison, G. C., 200
DBT. *See* Dialectical behavior therapy
       (DBT)
Delusional beliefs, 215
    obsessive thoughts versus, 10
Delusions, 155
Dementia praecox, 109, 139
Depo-testosterone, 210
Depression. *See also* Major depressive
       disorder
    bipolar disorder, 103
    female orgasmic disorder, 182
    hypertension and, 61–62
    in OCD, 10
    versus mourning, 95
Developmental model, dissociative
       identity disorder, 84
Deviant sexual practices, 188–201. *See*
       also Paraphilias
Dialectical behavior therapy (DBT),
       295–296
Diathesis-stress model, 111
Diazepam (Valium), 33
DID. *See* Dissociative identity disorder
       (DID)

Disruptive behavior, 343
Dissociative identity disorder (DID),
       71–86. *See also* Multiple
       personality
Disulfiram, 169
Dizygotic (DZ) twins, 140, 218, 247, 304,
       319, 332, 345
Drake, H., 125
Dual diagnosis, 152
Dumughn, C., 196
Dyspareunia, 180
Dysthymia, 76, 94
Dysthymic disorder, 196

E

Eating disorders, 221–233. *See also*
       Anorexia nervosa; Bulimia
       nervosa
Echolalia, 316
EE. *See* Expressed emotion (EE)
Eisen, J. L., 8
Electroconvulsive therapy (ECT), 100
Emmers-Sommer, T. M., 198
Emotional dysregulation, 291, 294
Environmental factors
    alcohol dependence, 166
    autistic disorder, 319
    borderline personality disorder (BPD),
       293
    oppositional defiant disorder (ODD),
       346
    psychopathy, 304
    transsexualism, 218
ERP. *See* Exposure and response
       prevention (ERP)
Essential hypertension, 60–63
Ethnicity and psychological disorders,
       52–107. *See also* Hypertension in
       an African American man
Excitement phase of sexual response
       cycle, 180
Exhibitionism, 188–201
    conviction for, 196
Exposure and response prevention (ERP),
       for OCD, 7
Expressed emotion (EE), 141–143

F

Fairburn, C.G., 239
Family therapy approaches, oppositional
    defiant disorder (ODD), 349
Faraone, S. V., 332
Fazel, S., 156
Fear of contamination, 8
Female orgasmic disorder,
    171–187
  behavioral model of, 183–184
  conceptualization and treatment,
      175–179
    addressing sexual fantasies, 176–177
    attitudes and beliefs about sexual
        behavior, 176
    communication during intercourse,
        175, 178
    ejaculatory control issue, 178
    sensate focus, 177
    "start-stop" procedure, 178
  DSM-IV-TR definition, 182
  excitement phase, 180
  guilt over frequent
      masturbation, 171
  intercourse, inability to reach orgasm
      during, 171–172
  limited foreplay, 171
  orgasmic phase, 180
  past events influence, 183
  personal distress issue, 182
  premature ejaculation and,
      171–187
  psychoanalytic approach, 182–183
  resolution phase, 180
  response patterns provoking,
      184–185
  social history, 173–175
  social skills approach to, 184
  treatment, 185–187
    antidepressant medication, 186
    cognitive-behavioral
        approach, 186
    prognosis for orgasmic dysfunction
        in women, 186
    sensate focus exercise, 186
    start-stop procedure for treating
        premature ejaculation, 186

Female sexual arousal disorder, 180
Fetishism, 195
Fink, P., 122
Fluoxetine (Prozac), 14, 32, 92, 99–100
Fluvoxamine (Luvox), 14, 32, 99
Freud, S., 11, 95, 278
Frotteurism, 188–201

G

GAD. *See* Generalized anxiety disorder
    (GAD)
Gender differences
  anorexia nervosa, 227
  autistic disorder, 317
  bipolar disorder, 110
  hypertension, 60, 62
  nightmare disorder, 258
  obsessive-compulsive disorder (OCD), 10
  posttraumatic stress disorder
      (PTSD), 47
  schizophrenia, paranoid type, 139
  somatization disorder, 123
Gender identity disorders, 202–220.
    See also Transsexualism
Generalized anxiety disorder (GAD),
    28–29, 47
Genetic factors
  alcohol dependence, 166
  anorexia nervosa, 229
  autistic disorder, 318–319
  bipolar disorder, 111
  psychopathy, 304
  schizophrenia, paranoid type, 140–141
  somatization disorder, 127
  transsexualism, 218
Gillberg, C., 316
Gillberg, I. C., 316
Goodman, R., 332
Green, R., 127
Group cognitive-behavioral therapy
    (CBT), 128
Gunderson, J. G., 295

H

Hallucinations, 134
Haloperidol (Haldol), 106, 314

Hancox, R. J., 333
Harris, G. T., 306
Harris, T. O., 96, 126
Hennen, J., 196
Hinder, S., 196
Homelessness, 145, 149, 152
Homosexuality, transsexualism
    and, relationship
    between, 216
Hopelessness, 98, 150
Hormone therapy, 210–211
Hostility, hypertension and,
    61–62
Hoyer, J., 196
Hyperarousal, 48, 60
Hyperresponsiveness, 317
Hypertension
    biological theories, 59
        body's immune system, 59
        somatic-weakness theory, 59
        specific-reaction theory, 59
        stress effect, 59
    death rates, 60
    in industrialized countries, 60
    prevalence, 60
    psychological theories, 60
    psychosocial factors related to, 61
        anger and hostility, 61–62
        depression, 61–62
        effects of racism, 61
        social isolation, 61
Hypnagogic hallucinations, 260
Hypoactive sexual desire
    disorder, 180
Hypochondriasis, 8
Hypomanic episodes, 109
Hysterectomy, 126–127

I

Iatrogenic harm, 122
ICD. See International Classification of
    Diseases (ICD)
Imagery Rehearsal Therapy (IRT),
    254, 261
    educational component, 261
    imagery training component, 261

Imipramine (Tofranil), 32, 272
Impulse control, 290
    anorexia nervosa, 228
    borderline personality disorder, 287
Individual play therapy, 341–342
International Classification of Diseases
    (ICD), 47
Interpersonal psychotherapy
    (IPT), 99
IRT. See Imagery Rehearsal
    Therapy (IRT)
Isolated Sleep Paralysis (ISP),
    251–264
    cultural name, 259

J

Johnson, V. E., 185
Jones, J., 332

K

Kabela, E., 169
Kadden, R. M., 169
Kafka, M. P., 196
Kanner, L., 318
Kanner, Leo, 315
Keeler, G., 348
Kernberg, O. F., 294
Kraepelin, E. 109, 139
Kringlen, E., 10
Kruttschnitt, C., 305

L

Landhuis, C. E., 333
Learned illness behavior, 125
Leue, A., 196
Lindahl, K. M., 295, 348
Linehan, M. M., 295
Lithium carbonate, 104, 107–108,
    112–113
Litt, M. D., 169
Lotter, V., 318
Lovaas, Ivar, 321
Luczak, S. E., 167

M

Macmillan, R., 305
Major depressive disorder,
    87–101
  clinical depression versus unhappiness
    and disappointment, 94
  conceptualization and treatment, 90–93
  depression versus mourning, 95
  depressive triad, 93
    negative view of the self, the world,
      and the future, 93
  etiological considerations, 94–98
    stressful life events, 96
  social history, 89–90
    divorce, 89–90
  social-learning views of depression, 97
  treatment, 98–100
    antidepressant medication, 99
    deficits in social skills, addressing,
      99
    fluoxetine (Prozac), 92, 99–100
    fluvoxamine (Luvox), 99
    interpersonal communication,
      improving, 99
    monoamine oxidase (MAO)
      inhibitors, 99
    parenting skills, improving, 99
    parent-training group, 90
    paroxetine (Paxil), 99
    problem-solving approach, 91
    psychotherapy and antidepressant
      medication combination, 98
    sertraline (Zoloft), 99
    SSRIs, 99
    tricyclics (TCAs), 99
Male erectile disorder, 180
Male orgasmic disorder, 180
Malingering, 76, 82
Manic episodes, 108–110. See also
    Bipolar disorder
  hypomanic episodes, 109
Marcoen, A., 333
Marlatt, G. A., 170
Masters, W. H., 185
Masturbation
  female, 171
  paraphilias, 188–189, 192, 195–200

  sexual dysfunction, 171, 175–176, 182,
    185–186
  transsexualism, 209, 211
Maturational problems, 229
McMorris, B. J., 305
Medication
  borderline personality disorder (BPD),
    287, 289
  bulimia nervosa, 249
  female orgasmic disorder, 186
  hypertension, 56, 63
  major depressive disorder, 98–99
  obsessive-compulsive disorder
    (OCD), 14–15
  panic disorder with agoraphobia, 32
  paranoid personality disorder, 281
  psychotic disorder NOS, 156
  for PTSD, 49–50
  rape trauma, 49–50
  schizophrenia, paranoid type, 137
Meditation, 65
Meehl, P. E., 135
Menorrhagia, 126–127
Methylphenidate (Ritalin), 334
Millberger, S., 332
Mills, K., 125
Minnesota Multiphasic Personality
    Inventory (MMPI)-2, 253
Moffitt, T. E., 305
Monoamine oxidase (MAO)
    inhibitors, 99
Monoamine oxidase A (MAOA)
    gene, 304
Mood disorders, 109–110. See also
    Bipolar disorder
Motivational interviewing, 14
Multiple personality, 68–86
  conceptualization and treatment, 76–78
  diagnostic signs, 81
  by disruption of consciousness,
    precipitated by stressful
    experiences, 77
  DSM-IV-TR diagnostic criteria for, 80
  etiological considerations, 82–84
    malingering, 76, 82
    sociocognitive model, 83
  follow-up, 78–79
  media attention to, 80

social history, 75–76
treatment, 70
  dissociative episodes, resolving, 77
  hypnosis use in, 70, 74, 83
  integrating the disparate personalities
    into one, 77, 84–85
  interpersonal, problem-solving
    approach, 78
  nondissociative coping skills, 78
  stabilizing the most functional
    personality, 77, 84
  traumatic incident, recalling, 71
  videotape use, 74, 84–85
Mutism, 316

N

NA. *See* Narcotics Anonymous (NA)
Naltrexone, 169
Narcissistic PD, 277
  DSM-IV-TR criteria for, 277
Narcotics Anonymous (NA), 290
National Comorbidity Study
  (NCS), 47
National Health and Social Life Survey,
  44, 181
Neurosurgery, 15
Nightmare disorder, 251–264
  gender-based prevalence, 258
  treatment, 253–256
    imagery, practicing, 254
    relaxation techniques, 254–255
Nolen-Hoeksema, S., 97
Noncompliance, 128–129
  attention-deficit/hyperactivity disorder,
    327–328
  psychotic disorder (NOS),
    152, 157

O

Object relations psychotherapy,
  294–295
Obsessive-compulsive disorder (OCD),
  1–16. *See also* Compulsions
  conceptualization and treatment, 5–7
    addressing religious concerns, 6
    anxiety-reducing rituals, 7

assertion training, systematic
  program of, 5–6, 12
behavioral treatment, 7, 13
interpersonal skills, development,
  5–6
motivational interviewing, 14
neurosurgery, 15
response-prevention procedure, 7
depression in, 10
DSM-IV-TR defining, 7
epidemiological studies, 10
follow-up assessments, 10–11
medication, 14–15
  clomipramine (anafranil), 14
  fluoxetine (Prozac), 14
  fluvoxamine (Luvox), 14
  sertraline (Zoloft), 14
  SSRIs, 14
obsessive-compulsive personality
  disorder (OCPD) versus, 9
obsessive thoughts versus delusional
  beliefs, 10
phobic disorders and, 9
prevalence, 10
self-injury thoughts, 4
social history, 2–5
symptoms, 1, 8
theoretical perspectives, 11–15
treatment implications, 11–15
ODD. *See* Oppositional defiant disorder
  (ODD)
Olanzapine, 156
Oppositional defiant disorder (ODD),
  336–350
  aggression, 343
    proactive aggression, 343
    reactive aggression, 343
  conceptualization and treatment,
    339–342
    family sessions, 341
    individual play therapy, 341–342
    time-out procedure, 340–341
  disruptive behavior, 343
  DSM-IV-TR criteria for, 342
  etiological considerations,
    344–348
    autonomic underarousal, 345
    biological factors, 346

Oppositional defiant disorder
  (ODD) (*Continued*)
    conduct disorder, 344
    environmental causal factors, 346
    marital dissatisfaction, 347
    parenting, 346
    personality traits, 345
    social factors, 346
    temperament, 345
  social and family history, 337–339
    moodiness, 338
  studies using clinical samples, 344
  treatment, 348–350
    cognitive behavioral
      approaches, 349
    family therapy approaches, 349
Orgasmic disorder, 171–187. *See also*
  Female orgasmic disorder

P

Panic control treatment, 32
Panic disorder with agoraphobia, 17–34
  conceptualization and treatment, 22–27
    catastrophic thinking, 25–26
    cognitive restructuring, 23, 25
    probability overestimation, 25
    reducing generalized anxiety, 23
    relaxation training, 23–24
    situational exposure, 23
  DSM-IV-TR definition, 28
  etiological considerations, 30–31
    conditioning model, 31
  medications, 32
  panic control treatment, 32
  social history, 19–22
    family background, 19–20
    relationships, 20–21
  treatment, 31–33
    relaxation and cognitive approach,
      combined use of, 31–33
Paranoid patients, 139–140
Paranoid personality disorder, 265–282
  DSM-IV-TR criteria for, 276
  features of, 275–281
  follow-up, 273–275
  later adjustment, 268–273

  psychological theories, 278–280
  social history, 265–268
  treatment, 280–281
    antipsychotic medication, 281
    cognitive therapy, 281
    difficulties in, 280–281
    social skills development, 281
Paraphilias, 188–201
  conceptualization and treatment,
    192–194
    changing sexual fantasies, 192
    marital therapy, 192–193
  etiological considerations, 197–199
    childhood emotional abuse, 198
    as a disorder of courtship behaviors
      and skills in men, 198
  exhibitionism, 188–201
  frotteurism, 188–201
  masturbatory fantasies, 189
  Paraphilia NOS, 195
  sexual deviance, 188
  social history, 190–191
  treatment, 199–201
    alternative behavioral completion,
      200
    antiandrogen cyproterone acetate
      for, 200
    aversion therapy, 199
    biological interventions, 200
    changing masturbation fantasies, 200
    ethical issues in, 199
    involuntary surgical castration, 199
Parasomnia, 251–264. *See also* Isolated
  Sleep Paralysis (ISP); Nightmare
  disorder
  Asian Americans and psychological
    intervention, 261–263
    cultural background, 262
    ethnic background, 262
    ethnicity, 262
    racial self-hate, 263
  criteria, 257
  cultural issues, 261–263
  etiological cnsiderations, 259–261
    affect distress, 260
    distressing dreams, 260
    hypnagogic hallucinations, 260

reduced sense of self-consciousness,
259
social history, 252–253
abusive father, 252
academic pressure, 252
nightmares, 252
treatment, 253–256, 261
Paroxetine (Paxil), 99, 186
Pathological doubt, OCD and, 8
Patterson, G. R., 346
Pauls, D. L., 278
Pedophilia, 195–196
Personality disorders. *See* Antisocial
personality disorder (ASPD);
Borderline personality disorder
(BPD); Multiple personality;
Paranoid personality disorder;
Violence and mental disorders
Pervasive developmental disorders,
315. *See also* Autistic disorder
Phobias, 29
Phobic disorders, 9
Placebo-controlled outcome studies, for
panic attacks, 33
Play therapy, 341–342
Polygraph (lie detector) testing, 197
Positive reinforcement, 355
Posttraumatic stress disorder
(PTSD), 35–51. *See also*
Rape trauma
as an anxiety disorder, 47
classification, criticisms for, 46
prevalence, 47
Poulton, R., 333
Premature ejaculation, 171–187
Prison inmates, psychopathology among,
302, 306
Probability overestimation, 25
Prodromal phase, 138
Psychopathy, 297–308
autonomic nervous system
role in, 303
etiological considerations, 302–306
arousing negative emotions, 303
child maltreatment, 304
deficits in neurological functions, 305
environmental factors, 304

genetic factors, 304
monoamine oxidase A (MAOA)
gene, 304
physical abuse, 304
social factors, 305
neurobiological investigations, 302
stealing, 298–300
traits, 300–301
treatment, 306–307
Psychotic disorder not otherwise specified
(NOS), 145–158
auditory hallucinations, 154
community treatment, 150–152
detoxification programs, 150
rehabilitation program, 150
dual diagnosis, 152
etiological considerations,
153–154
hostile behaviors, 151
impulsivity, 151
schizoaffective disorder, 153
social history, 146–150
substance dependence, 145–158
treatment, 156–157
antipsychotic medication, 156
Punishment
attention-deficit/hyperactivity disorder,
326
autistic disorder, 313–314
borderline personality disorder,
292–293
major depressive disorder, 95
obsessive-compulsive disorder, 3
oppositional defiant disorder,
345–346
paraphilias, 199
psychopathy, 303
Putnam, F. W., 83–84

R

Race issues and psychotherapy, 65–66.
See also Hypertension in an
African American man
Racism, hypertension and, 61
Rape trauma, 35–51
anxiety symptoms, 38

Rape trauma (*Continued*)
  cognitive-behavioral intervention
      for, 40
    anger-management training, 43
    "reliving" traumatic experience, 40
  conceptualization and treatment,
      38–41
  DSM-IV-TR criteria for, 44
  etiological considerations, 48–49
  impact of rape, 42
    avoiding emotional intimacy, 42
    strained relation with men, 42
  PTSD development following, 47–48
  reexperiencing of trauma, 45
  social history, 37–38
  symptoms, 35
  treating distorted thoughts, 43
  treatment, 49–50
    antidepressant medication, 49–50
    cognitive-behavior therapy, 49–50
Rasmussen, S. A., 8
Relaxation training
  agoraphobia, 23–24
  hypertension, 65
  nightmare disorder, 254–255
  for panic disorders, 23–24
Reliability, interrater, 276–277
Repetitive transcranial magnetic
      stimulation (rTMS), 169
Repression, 77, 121, 279
Resolution phase of sexual response
      cycle, 180
Response patterns, 11, 99, 184, 275
Restricting type anorexia nervosa, 228
Rice, M. E., 306
Risperidone (Risperdal), 137, 142, 156
Ritalin, 334
Rogers, C. R., 281
rTMS. *See* Repetitive transcranial
      magnetic stimulation (rTMS)

S

Saad, K., 196
Saleh, F. M., 196
Schizoaffective disorder, 153
  DSM-IV-TR criteria for, 153

Schizophrenia versus bipolar
      disorder, 109
Schizophrenia, paranoid type,
      130–144
  conceptualization and treatment,
      134–138
    anhedonia, 135
    antipsychotic medication, 137
    delusional thinking, 137
    home-based program, 136
    interpersonal aversiveness, 135
    self-talk, 136
    stimulus-control procedure, 136
  DSM-IV-TR diagnostic criteria, 138
    characteristic symptoms, 138
    duration, 138
    social/occupational
        dysfunction, 138
  etiological considerations, 140–141
  gender differences in prevalence, 139
  genetic factors in, 140–141
    expressed emotion (EE), 141–143
    nutritional deficiencies, 141
    prenatal infections, 141
    viral infections, 141
  social history, 133–134
  subgroups, 139–140
    based on symptom dimensions,
        140
    catatonic, 139–140
    disorganization, 140
    negative symptoms, 140
    paranoid, 139–140
    psychotic symptoms, 140
    symptomatically defined, 140
  symptoms, 130–131
    delusional beliefs, 131–132
    intrusive and repetitive thoughts,
        131
    self-talk, 130, 136
    social isolation, 130
  treatment, 142–143
    antipsychotic drugs, 142
    clozapine (Clozaril), 142
    risperidone (Risperdal), 142
Schneider, K., 135
Segal, N. L., 218

Selective serotonin reuptake inhibitors (SSRIs), 14, 99
  for panic attacks, 32
  major depressive disorder, 99
  obsessive-compulsive disorder (OCD), 14
  panic disorder with agoraphobia, 32
Self-imposed starvation, 224–226
Self-stimulatory behaviors, 309
Sensate focus, 177
Serotonin, 248, 293. *See also* Selective serotonin reuptake inhibitors (SSRIs)
Sertraline (Zoloft), 14, 99
Sexual abuse
  anorexia nervosa, 231
  borderline personality disorder (BPD), 293
  multiple personality, 69
  paraphilias, 190, 198
  psychopathy, 304
  somatization disorder, 126
Sexual aversion disorder, 180
Sexual dysfunctions, 171–187. *See also* Female orgasmic disorder
  dyspareunia, 180
  female orgasmic disorder, 180
  female sexual arousal disorder, 180
  hypoactive sexual desire disorder, 180
  male erectile disorder, 180
  male orgasmic disorder, 180
  premature ejaculation, 180
  sexual aversion disorder, 180
  vaginismus, 180
Sexual masochism, 195
Sexual obsessions, 8
Sexual sadism, 195
Shea, S. H., 167
Shock therapy, 100
Sleep disorders, 256–264. *See also* Parasomnia
Sobell, M. B., 169
Social isolation, hypertension and, 61
Social phobia, 27, 29
Sodium benzoate, 333

Somatic obsessions, 8
Somatic-weakness theory, 59
Somatization disorder, 115–129
  age of onset of, 123
  alexithymia and, 124
  aphonia, 121
  diagnostic criteria, 120
    gastrointestinal symptoms, 120
    pain symptoms, 120
    pseudoneurological symptom, 121
    sexual symptom, 120
  DSM-IV-TR defining, 120
  emotional stress, 121
  emotional upset role in exacerbating pain, 119
  etiological considerations, 124–127
    childhood adversity, 126
    childhood illness, 126
    cultural factors, 124
    psychological distress, 124
  genetic factors in, 127
  group cognitive-behavioral therapy (CBT) for, 128
  histrionic nature, 121
  physical symptoms due to psychological problems, 119–120
  prevalence, 123
  secondary gain, 125
  social history, 117–118
  symptoms, 115–116
    abdominal distention, 116
    anxiety, 116
    frequent headaches, 116
    physical problems, 115–116
    sharp pain, 116
    uncomfortable bloating, 116
  treatment, 118–119
    antidepressants, 127
    tryptophan levels and, 127
    types of surgery for somatizers, 122
Specific-reaction theory, 59
Spiegel, D., 79
SSRIs. *See* Selective serotonin reuptake inhibitors (SSRIs)
'Start-stop' procedure, 178
Stevenson, J., 332

Stoller, R. J., 217
Stormshak, E. A., 347
Stigma, of mental disorders, 154
Stress
  hypertension and, 59, 61
  immune system weakening
    by, 59
Stimulus-control procedures, 136
Stress
  alcohol dependence, 167
  bulimia nervosa, 238
  female orgasmic disorder, 182
  hypertension, 59, 61
  multiple personality, 77
  parasomnia, 260
  somatization disorder, 121
Substance dependence, 145–158. *See also*
    Psychotic disorder not otherwise
    specified (NOS)
Sue, D. W, 262
Sugarman, P., 196
Suicidal ideation/thoughts, 69
Superstition, 5, 9, 232
Symmetry, need for, 8

T

Tardive dyskinesia, 142
Television exposure and attention
    problems, 333
Test anxiety, 20
Thalidomide, 319
Thigpen, C. H., 84
Thimerosal, 320
Theory of mind, 319
Thought insertion, 135
Time-out procedure, 340–341
Transsexualism, 202–220
  conceptualization and treatment,
    209–210
  disturbances in gender identity, 215
  DSM-IV-TR description of, 214
  etiological considerations, 217–218
    environmental events, 218
    genetic factors, 218
    parents and family, importance of, 217
    peer relations role, 217

female transsexuals versus male
    transsexuals, 216
and homosexuality, relationship
    between, 216
intimate relationships, 203,
    205, 207
social history, 204–209
subjective perception, 203
symptoms, 202–203
and transvestic fetishism, comparing,
    215
treatment, 219–220
  surgery for female-to-male
    transsexuals, 219
  surgery for male-to-female
    transsexuals, 219
Transvestic fetishism, 195, 215
Tricyclics (TCAs), 99
Tryptophan, 127
Twin studies, 61
  anorexia nervosa, 229
  attention-deficit/hyperactivity disorder,
    332
  autism, 319
  bulimia nervosa, 247
  oppositional defiant disorder, 345
  psychopathy, 304
  schizophrenia, 140–141
  somatization disorder, 117
  transsexualism, 217–218

U

Unipolar disorder, 108

V

Vaccines, autism and, 320
Vaginismus, 180
Vaillant, G. E., 169
Valproic acid (Depakote), 113
Van den Bergh, B. R. H., 333
Victim versus survivor, 46
Victimization, 348
Violence and mental disorders, 154–156
  command hallucinations, 155
  delusions, 155

  personality disorders, 155
  substance-use disorders, 155
Violence, 145–158
Voyeurism, 195–196

W

Waldinger, R. J., 295
Wall, T. L., 167
Welch, D., 333
Whalen, C. K., 334
Wolfe, R., 200

Women, disorders in. *See* Gender
  differences
World Health Organization International
  Study of Schizophrenia, 139

X

Xanax, 22, 29, 33

Z

Zoloft, 14, 50, 99